# REVELRY, RIVALRY, AND LONGING FOR THE GODDESSES OF BENGAL

# Revelry, Rivalry, and Longing for the Goddesses of Bengal

*The Fortunes of Hindu Festivals*

Rachel Fell McDermott

COLUMBIA UNIVERSITY PRESS NEW YORK

Columbia University Press
*Publishers Since 1893*
New York Chichester, West Sussex



Library of Congress Cataloging-in-Publication Data
McDermott, Rachel Fell.
Revelry, Rivalry, and Longing for the Goddesses of Bengal : the fortunes of Hindu festivals / Rachel Fell McDermott.
p. cm.
Includes bibliographical references and index.
ISBN 978-0-231-12918-3 (cloth ) — ISBN 978-0-231-12919-0 (pbk.) —
ISBN 978-0-231-52787-3 (e-book)
1. Durga-puja (Hindu festival)—India—West Bengal. 2. Jagaddhatri-puja (Hindu festival)—India—West Bengal. 3. Kali-puja (Hindu festival)—India—West Bengal. 4. West Bengal (India)—Religious life and customs. I. Title.
BL1239.82.D87M33 2011
294.5'36095414—dc22
2010020693

*For*
*Keshab Chandra Sarkar*
*and Hena Basu*

# Contents

*List of Illustrations* *ix*
*Preface* *xi*
*Acknowledgments* *xiii*
*Notes on Transliteration* *xvii*

Introduction 1

1. Pūjā Origins and Elite Politics 11

2. The Goddess in Colonial and Postcolonial History 39

3. Durgā the Daughter: Folk and Familial Traditions 76

4. The Artistry of Durgā and Jagaddhātrī 103

5. Durgā on the *Titanic*: Politics and Religion in the Pūjā 130

6. The "Orientalist" Kālī: A Tantric Icon Comes Alive 161

7. Approaches to Kālī Pūjā in Bengal 183

8. Controversies and the Goddess 197

9. Devī in the Diaspora 224

Conclusion 241

*Appendix: An Overview of the Press in Bengal up to 1947* *251*
*Notes* *255*
*Bibliography* *327*
*Index* *351*

# Illustrations


Fig. 0.1. Artisans working on images for the upcoming Durgā Pūjā season. 2
Fig. 1.1. Inside the *ṭhākurdālān* at the Shovabazar Rāj house. 21
Fig. 1.2. Bathing the *kalā bau.* 34
Fig. 1.3. Releasing the *nīlkaṇṭha pākhī.* 35
Fig. 2.1. William Prinsep, "Entertainment during the Durga Puja," 1840. 42–43
Fig. 2.2. "For the Poojahs." 60
Fig. 2.3. "Poojah Holidays." 69
Fig. 3.1. Feeding the Goddess in the shape of a little girl at *kumārī pūjā.* 88
Fig. 3.2. *Sindūr-khelā* at a house in Howrah city. 89
Fig. 3.3. *Āgamanī.* 94
Fig. 4.1. The traditional *ekcāla* image. 104
Fig. 4.2. Durgā holds Kṛṣṇa in her lap. 108
Fig. 4.3. Gopeśvar Pāl. 111
Fig. 4.4. A Gopeśvar Pāl tableau from 1939. 112
Fig. 4.5. Jagaddhātrī. 117
Fig. 5.1. A Durgā Pūjā pandal shaped like Ajanta Caves. 134
Fig. 5.2. A Durgā Pūjā pandal in the shape of a Tata Motors factory. 139

Fig. 5.3. A Durgā Pūjā pandal in the shape of the *Titanic*. 143
Fig. 5.4. Plane crashing into the World Trade Center. 144
Fig. 5.5. Mahiṣa in the shape of Osama bin Laden. 145
Fig. 5.6. A Goan church being dismantled at the conclusion of Jagaddhātrī Pūjā. 157
Fig. 6.1. Two types of Kālī. 162
Fig. 6.2. The Kālī of Kālīghāṭ Temple. 169
Fig. 6.3. Siddheśvarīkālī at the Citpur Temple. 170
Fig. 6.4. N. C. Pāl's new Kālī of the 1930s. 175
Fig. 6.5. A modern Kālī, with Śiva nearly sitting up. 178
Fig. 7.1. Goat heads placed before the image of Kālī at a house Pūjā in Belpukur. 188
Fig. 7.2. Kālī seated on Śiva. 190
Fig. 7.3. A Jurassic Park dinosaur entertaining onlookers at Kālī Pūjā. 194
Fig. 7.4. The Kālī too horrible to worship. 195
Fig. 8.1. The Kālī at Kaliganj. 203
Fig. 8.2. Children protesting against animal sacrifice, Kālīghāṭ Temple. 212
Fig. 9.1. The Durgā image at the Garden State Cultural Association. 226
Fig. 9.2. The ritual of *baraṇ*. 228
Fig. 10.1. Processing Śītalā in her palanquin from her temple to the bathing *ghāṭ*. 245
Fig. 10.2. Women performing the arduous rite of *daṇḍī-kāṭā*. 246

# Preface

My interest in the annual public festivals for the three Hindu goddesses Durgā, Jagaddhātrī, and Kālī began in 1988, when I arrived in October for the commencement of two years of dissertation work on something else. I had come to study the devotional poetry tradition to Kālī and Durgā in her form as Umā, and the festivals, or Pūjās, were a fascinating sideshow, effectively and forcibly stopping all work possibilities for nearly three weeks each autumn. I remember the stern and utterly astonishing advice of my new mentor, Professor Narendra Nath Bhattacharyya, who told me when I first met him in mid-October to get out of Calcutta—no, Bengal—as soon as possible, as the Pūjās were a form of gaudy, pseudo-religious commercialism that had nothing to do with the heartfelt devotion to the Mother that I had come to study. I did not get out, and the experiences I had of Durgā and Kālī Pūjās that year were formative. One, as recounted in chapter 8 below, turned me off the Goddess's temple ritual for nearly eight years; as a whole, however, I realized that I wanted to know more about the ebullient, mesmerizing, carnivalesque festivals that engulfed the entire state. I saw three Pūjā seasons (1988, 1989, 1991) before work on the project began in earnest, in 1995. Thereafter, thanks to the happy chance that the festivals' lunar calendrical schedule coincided with Columbia University's Election Day holiday, as well as to the kindness of various colleagues who taught for me for a week before or after the holiday, I was able to escape to Calcutta for ten days in the fall semesters of 1995, 1996, 1998, 1999, and 2001, thus enabling me to drop in on at least one Pūjā in each of those years. In 2000, by grace of a grant from the American Institute of Indian Studies, I spent an entire semester in Calcutta, and much of the present book stands on interviews and material gathered during that four-month period.

In 2002, with the plan of a book in mind, I realized that I needed to think of the Pūjās in a transnational context, and that no study of Bengali public festivals in our current world could be undertaken without an appreciation of the diasporic forms. So I spent the Pūjā seasons of 2002–2008 in the New York / New Jersey area, attending the celebrations of local Bengali groups and watching how they developed over time. During the years that I was unable to attend the Pūjās in Bengal, I was remarkably fortunate to benefit from the research assistance of Hena Basu and Jayanta Roy, who sent me, respectively, packages of newspaper clippings and professional photographic coverage of the Kolkata Pūjās.

Every year something new happens in the Pūjās—some new form of creativity, some unexpected controversy, some innovative mode of festival aggrandizement. One is tempted to keep gathering information forever. However, I take a lesson from the Goddess, who allows her images to be immersed at the conclusion of each Pūjā, her beauty and form consigned to a disintegrating, watery fate. All good things come to an end. I am blessed to have lived with this project for so long.[1]

# Acknowledgments

This book is dedicated to two extraordinary individuals, without whose help, intellectual curiosity, and long-suffering kindness it would never have come to fruition in its present form. Keshab Chandra Sarkar was my first Bengali teacher in Calcutta. He started teaching me the moment I saw him, at the desk of the Ramakrishna Mission Institute of Culture, where I had come hoping to meet him in 1986. I said, in my best fledgling Bengali, "So you are Keshab Chandra Sarkar! *Āpni bikhyāta*! (You are famous!)." He smiled at me, shook my hand, and immediately corrected my pronunciation of the Bengali conjunct consonant in *bikhyāta*. The friendship was born. I studied with him nearly daily for two years, 1988–1990, and then daily for the four months I was in Calcutta in 2000. He read Bengali newspaper clippings with me, answered my questions about his Pūjā experiences and reminiscences, shared his voluminous learning, and welcomed me into his family. I count myself blessed to have been his student.

Hena Basu, of the Basu Research and Documentation Service, is a scholar's dream. She is able to find documents in inaccessible archives, she locates and makes contact with people whom one needs to meet, and, best of all, she is willing to go on adventures. She accompanied me on all my interviews of the traditional families of Calcutta in 2000, we took train trips together as far as Krishnanagar, and she even conducted interviews in my absence. The faded illustration from the 1930s that appears in chapter 4 (fig. 4.4) was given to me by the renowned Kumartuli artist Siddheśvar Pāl because he trusted Hena. During the years when I was unable to come personally to Bengal, she painstakingly clipped Bengali and English newspaper articles during the Pūjā season and sent them to me in huge wrapped packages. Many a scholar of Bengali culture has been guided by Hena's acumen. She too has been a real gift.

Many other artisans, scholars, Pūjā sponsors, and friends helped me in Kolkata, particularly Mahārājādhirāj Sadaycānd Māhtāb Bāhādur, Abhijit Ghosh, Minati Kar, Aditi Sen, and the late Narendra Nath Bhattacharyya. Others whom I met and interviewed, and whom I thank for their kindness, are the Kumartuli artisans Pārtha Pāl, Pradīp Pāl, the late Siddheśvar Pāl, and the late Alok Sen; Kolkata scholars of Bengali culture Nṛsiṃhaprasād Bhāḍuri and Sanatkumār Mitra; activists Debāśis Cakrabartī, Subhās Datta, Asit Mukherjee, and Purnima Toolsidass; and members of the elite families of the city who shared with me their ancestral Pūjā customs: Śephāli Bose, Bhaskar Chunder, Śubhamay and Amarnāth Dawn, Gītā Datta, Milan Datta, Kalyāṇkumār Deb, Ārati Deb, Alok Kṛṣṇa Deb, Sujay Ganguli, Priya Gopāl Hājrā, Śiśir Mallik, Chāmeli Mitra, and Maṇimohan Rāy Caudhurī. I also thank Pūrbā Mukhopādhyāy for allowing me to use her published poem in chapter 8.

I am also especially grateful to Jayanta Roy, an outstanding photographer in Kolkata who did a superb job, over many years, of documenting the Pūjās for me. Many of his photographs grace this book. For my sake he and his camera were nearly crushed by the crowds in February 2001 at Shalkia, Howrah, where he had gone to cover Śītālā's bathing festival.

I feel grateful also to Kolkata artisan Swaroop Mukerji, whose paintings of the Pūjās so charmed me in 2000 that I bought one for the cover of this book.

I very much miss the late Mohit Roy, historian extraordinaire of the Nadia district, who welcomed me into his Krishnanagar home on several occasions and personally conducted my husband Scott and me on a hair-raising trip into the West Bengal night on Kālī Pūjā of 1999. Future scholars of Nadia are impoverished by his absence.

In London, where I conducted for many summers in a row the backbone of the newspaper archival work for this book, I met, and benefited from the knowledge of, many kind friends and scholars: Laura Bear, T. Richard Blurton, Henrike Donner, Lynn Foulston, Christopher Fuller, Sanjukta Gupta and Richard Gombrich, Jacqueline Suthren Hirst, Dermot Killingly, Anna

King, Julius Lipner, Partha and Swasti Mitter, and John Shepherd. I am also grateful to the staff at the India Office Library, where I spent many happy hours squinting over newspaper microfilms.

In the United States and Canada, I have benefited enormously from the advice and support of numerous colleagues in the fields of Bengal studies and, more generally, religion: Susan Bean, John Carman, David Curly, Richard Davis, Elinor Gaden, Brian Hatcher, Jyotindra Jain, Jeffrey Kripal, Philip Lutendorf, John McLane, Malcolm McLean (when he was visiting from New Zealand), Joseph O'Connell, Kimberley Patton, Laurie Patton, Indira Peterson, Clinton Seely, Hugh Urban, Judith Walsh, and Christian Wedemeyer. To Ralph Nicholas, who amazingly sent me his near completed manuscript, *Night of the Gods: Durga Puja and Authority in Rural Bengal* (Calcutta: Chronicle Books, 2012), just as I was correcting the proofs of this book, I express abundant thanks. *Night of the Gods* makes many insightful arguments about Durga Puja that I had not thought of, and I look forward to our books being read together.

To all the kind people in New York and New Jersey who welcomed my family and me into their Pūjā celebrations over the past seven years—a heartfelt "thank you." Among those to whom I feel a special gratitude are Nirmal Cakrabarty, Ashis Sengupta, and the members of the Adyapeath Temple.

Three institutions contributed to this work financially: the American Institute of Indian Studies, which funded the four months in Calcutta in 2000; the National Endowment for the Humanities, which gave me a writing grant in the spring of 2001; and Barnard College, whose rich collection of wonderful administrators and colleagues has helped my work flourish. Thanks especially, at Barnard and Columbia, to Dwijen Bhattacharjya, Irene Bloom, Elizabeth Boylan, Lucy Bulliet, Karen Dobrusky, Jack Hawley, Mary Missirian, and Gary Tubb.

Wendy Lochner and the staff at Columbia University Press—Leslie Kriesel, Christine Mortlock, Anne Lovering Rounds, Do Mi Stauber, and Kerri Cox Sullivan—have had the patience of Job. They are wonderful to work with, and I thank them all. Two (formerly) anonymous readers, Brian Hatcher and Jeffrey Kripal, pushed me to greater theoretical acumen, for which I am also extremely grateful.

I would also like to thank my husband, Scott, who has made all things possible, and our son, James, whose coming into our lives in 2004 ensured that I would write chapter 9. At the age of two he was beating the drum for Durgā in New Jersey.

New York, New York

# Notes on Transliteration

Accepted Sanskrit conventions for rendering deities' names have been followed throughout in my own prose. In Bengali titles or quotations from Bengali sources, however, I utilize Bengali transliteration (Śiva vs. Śib).

Proper names are rendered with Bengali diacritics if the person in question wrote in Bengali, spoke to me in Bengali, and/or did not have or request an Anglicization. Commonly Anglicized names are retained (Swami Vivekananda, Bankim Chandra Chatterjee, Subhas Chandra Bose). Some names vacillate between conventions, depending on the context: the Bengali saint Rāmakṛṣṇa is spelled Ramakrishna when I am discussing the American branches of the organization founded in his name.

Place names, including those for districts, subdivisions, cities, towns, villages, roads, and the names of neighborhood Pūjā committees, have all been rendered without diacritics. For recognizable names that already have Anglicizations, I utilize them; for names of small towns or villages, I keep as close to the nondiacriticized Bengali originals as possible. Since the great majority of people living in the time period covered in this work (the late eighteenth century up to the present) knew Calcutta as "Calcutta" and not "Kolkata" (the latter coming into legislated usage only in 2001), I retain "Calcutta" for the sake of consistency until 2001, whereafter I use

Kolkata. The only place names that receive diacritics are Bengali temples (Kālīghāṭ Temple).

Many lowercase words with italics and diacritics follow Bengali spoken forms: for instance, *bhadralok*, *darśan*, *ghaṭ*, and *sarbajanīn*.

Months, Pūjā days, and caste names are capitalized with diacritics, spelled as they are pronounced in Bengali (the month of Āśvin; Nabamī, the ninth day of the festival; and Kumārs, or hereditary potters).

Festivals generally retain their Bengali forms with diacritics (Bhāi-phõṭā, Caḍak Pūjā, Dol Yātrā, Gājan, Rās Pūrṇimā), but pan-Indian festivals like Diwali are spelled as such.

Goddess is capitalized when the reference is to "the" Goddess, but written in lower case when the referent is plural or generic.

# REVELRY, RIVALRY, AND LONGING FOR THE GODDESSES OF BENGAL

# Introduction

## *An Introductory Tour: The Mansions, the Streets, and the Progression of Days*

We begin with the Goddess, where she begins, painstakingly and professionally fashioned by artisans in their workshops. Hence we travel to north Kolkata, to Kumartuli, one of the city's several artisans' districts, where temporary images of Durgā and her family, or Jagaddhātrī and her lion, or Kālī and Śiva, are being fashioned out of straw, clay, paint, and decorations (fig. 0.1).

The Bengali Durgā is a combination of the classical Mahiṣamardinī—she who kills the shape-shifting demon Mahiṣa—and the gentle daughter Umā, who returns home to her parents once a year, accompanied by her four children, Gaṇeśa, Kārtikeya, Sarasvatī, and Lakṣmī. In the form sculpted for the ritual worship, she is said to be beautiful, youthful, and plump, with prominent breasts; her left knee, waist, and neck are bent in three places; her ten arms hold (on the right from the top down) a trident, cleaver, discus, arrow, and missile, and (on the left, from the top down) a shield, bow, noose, iron goad, and axe. The hand that holds the noose also has Mahiṣa by the hair. Her left foot touches Mahiṣa's shoulder, and her right foot sits firmly on the back of her lion mount. Tradition has it that Durgā travels to Bengal via one of four modes: by boat, litter, elephant, or horse.[1]

FIGURE 0.1. Artisans working on images for the upcoming Durgā Pūjā season. Kumartuli, September 2008. Photo by Jayanta Roy.

Jagaddhātrī, She who Supports the World, is very similar—she too has a feline mount and is killing a demon, but she usually has no attendants. She has only four arms (she holds a discus and arrow in her right hands and a conch and bow in her left), she sits, not stands, on her lion, and she allows the lion to kill the demon, in this case an elephant. Kālī, the most fierce of the three goddesses, stands astride the prone body of her husband Śiva. Her tongue is outstretched, her body is covered in trophies of death, and her four hands hold (on the left) a cleaver and a severed head and (on the right) gestures of protection and fearlessness. Sculpting these images takes weeks, and the finished products are masterpieces of skill. The day before the Pūjās begin, for Durgā on the sixth day of the pan-Indian ten-day Navarātrī, the images are brought from Kumartuli to localities throughout the city where they are temporarily installed and infused with the Goddess's presence through a ritual involving Sanskrit *mantras*.

When the Goddess leaves the artisans, she travels to one of two types of abodes. The first are the *ṭhākurdālāns*, or "God-buildings": large, often open-aired brick or stone halls especially erected in decades or even centuries past to receive the deities and provide space for their worship. Such *ṭhākurdālāns* are attached to the homes of the wealthy, and most of them are situated in areas of the city that were once, under the British, the residential quarters of the Hindu zamindars, rich landowning families sometimes called "*rājās*."[2] Some of these belong to families who have managed to sustain their wealth; their homes and halls are well maintained, and the large columns outside their *ṭhākurdālāns*, as well as the chandeliers, portraiture, and decorations within, bear the marks of loving care. Other families have performed less well in the economic climate of the twentieth and twenty-first centuries; the descendants of the Sābarṇa Rāy Caudhurī family, who originally deeded to the British the land that became Calcutta, cannot afford to repair the crumbling exterior of their once-proud *ṭhākurdālān*. Yet whatever the state of their mansions and accompanying buildings, these families all have three things in common: their claim to ancient pedigree in the history of the city; the associated prestige such "ancientness" confers; and an effort to reproduce, in their worship of the Goddess each year, the exact model handed down from their forefathers. Thus the deities brought into their houses are all sculpted according to traditional artistic tastes, with large eyes, small mouths, and stolid, stationary body poses. Moreover, the family priests are enjoined to perform the worship with attention to every *śāstric* detail.

The second destination for the goddesses comprises the numerous pandals that are crowded by building specialists into every nook and cranny of the city landscape. They are made of bamboo poles, colored cloth, and decorations, and range from small temple-like structures to huge buildings. Inside there is a platform for the goddess and, in front, a large space for visitors to take *darśan*. Outside, electricians are busily preparing elaborate lighting shows. Once the festivals begin, the goddesses are worshiped according to scriptural injunctions by priests hired to tend to their ritual needs. Most people spend little time bothering about priests, however. This is an occasion for revelry, and people mill about in the thousands, especially at night, when the lighting is visible and the mood electric. Durgā Pūjā, which lasts four to six days and is the longest of the three Pūjās,[3] affords ample time for *darśan*-seekers to roam the city, visiting as many pandals as possible, showing off new clothes, and delighting in the exuberant quality of the religious holiday.

Such Pūjā celebrations are called *sarbajanīn* Pūjās, or public Pūjās for people regardless of background. They are financed by neighborhood associations and civic groups, who band together, collect subscriptions, and arrange for the Goddess, the pandal design, and the lighting displays. One of the biggest motivators in their decisions is the prospect of garnering status and prestige through winning prizes for the best image, best pandal, or best lighting. Such awards provide the impetus for both creativity and rivalry among Pūjā organizers.

At last the festivals conclude. On the tenth day, or Bijayā Daśamī (Victory Tenth, when Durgā slays Mahiṣa, or Rāma slays Rāvaṇa), the priests invite the Goddess to leave her clay casings, and once the life is removed the images must be ceremoniously immersed in a body of water. Goddesses are processed through the streets, whether from mansion or street shrine, and carried (or trucked) to the nearest river. Families clean out their *ṭhākurdālāns*, leaving them empty and waiting for the next festival. Pandals and lighting displays, too, are dismantled, their creators taking with them as much as can be reused for the next festival or the next year. People are sad. The Goddess brings joy, a chance to relax and be merry, an occasion to reunite with loved ones home for the holidays.

Ritually, of course, things are more complex than the above sketch would indicate. For most devotees, Durgā Pūjā actually begins on Mahālāya, the new-moon night of the month of Āśvin, which concludes a fifteen-day period (*pitṛpakṣa*) when the ancestors are venerated and offered water, rice, fruits, and sweets. On the day after Mahālāya, whence begins the bright fortnight of the month, people state their intention to undertake the worship of Durgā and perform preliminary rites for six days, until the Goddess is formally invoked. Originally Mahālāya had nothing to do with Durgā Pūjā, but in the 1930s the directors of All India Radio created a two-hour program heralding Durgā's arrival that entertained with stories, recitation of the "Devī-Māhātmya" (popularly known in Bengal as the *Caṇḍī*), and songs. It was so popular that it became an immediate tradition, continued to this day.

On the evening of the sixth day of the waxing moon of Āśvin, in a rite designed to emulate Rāma's "untimely" (*akāl*) awakening of Durgā from her four-month sleep for help in his battle against Rāvaṇa,[4] the priest rouses the Goddess (*bodhan*) under a *bel* tree. A pot of water (*ghaṭ*), a group of nine plants, and the images brought from the artisans' district are established next to her, although none of these is yet vivified.

The main rites of the seventh day (Saptamī) are the ceremonial bathing of the nine plants, the invitation to the deities to reside for the duration of the festival in the plants, the pot of water, and the images, and then their elaborate worship, with a sixteen-item *pūjā*, blood sacrifice, fire, and the worship of a little girl (*kumārī pūjā*). The most important part of the eighth day (Aṣṭamī), after the usual morning preliminary worship, is the conjunction of the eighth and the ninth days—an auspicious rite known as the *sandhi pūjā*—when the fierce form of the Goddess, Cāmuṇḍā, is worshiped, along with Gaṇeśa and other gods. Then follows the sixteen-item *pūjā*, goat sacrifice, the dedication of 108 lamps, fire sacrifice, and additional *kumārī* worship. The ninth day (Nabamī) is the same as the eighth, except that more animals are sacrificed, and if one chooses to offer an animal only once in the festival, it has to be on this day.

In the rest of India, Victory Tenth, or Duśerā, is a day of triumph, when Rāma returns to Ayodhya, having slain Rāvaṇa. In Bengal, Bijayā is a day of poignant loss, as the priest ritually dismisses the Goddess and her entourage, asking her to return again when her devotees call. Then women crowd around the image to bid goodbye to the Goddess as they would their real daughters, offering her *sindūr*, *pān*, and sweets in a ritual of tearful farewell (*kanakāñjali*). After the images have been immersed, water from the river is brought back to the priest, who then sprinkles it on all assembled.

Jagaddhātrī and Kālī Pūjās share many elements with the foregoing. In the nineteenth century, Jagaddhātrī Pūjā was prescribed in times of distress, when Durgā Pūjā could not be held; Jagaddhātrī Pūjā occurs exactly one month after Durgā Pūjā, beginning on the seventh day of the bright fortnight of Kārtik, and is celebrated in a manner very similar to that of Durgā, except that prescriptions allow for the three days to be amalgamated into one day, the ninth. In addition, her festival is currently more popular in towns outside Kolkata than it is in the capital itself. Kālī's festival is the shortest of the three Pūjās considered here, as it occurs on the dark-moon night of Kārtik, with the prescribed rituals—the statement of intention, initial worship of Gaṇeśa, incantations of *mantras* and hymns, and donation of offerings, including the sixteen-item *pūjā*, wine, and animals—commencing at midnight.

## Approaching the Pūjās

Although ritual is important—some would say, from the Goddess's perspective, preeminent—this book does not delve further into the details of priestly rites. Other scholars have already provided wonderful overviews of such prescriptions,[5] leaving me free to investigate the Pūjās historically and thematically. This book begins chronologically, with two chapters that cover the seventeenth century to the post-Independence period in areas that are now West Bengal and Bangladesh: chapter 1 chronicles the origins of Durgā and Jagaddhātrī Pūjās in the homes of the elite, landowning zamindars, where worship of the goddesses has been integral to the articulation of political and social aspiration; and chapter 2 examines the life of the three Śākta, or goddess-centered, Pūjās under colonial rule, demonstrating what Durgā, Jagaddhātrī, and Kālī meant, both to the British and to Bengali Hindus. The Pūjās, in fact, are an illuminating lens through which to analyze the various types of interaction that occurred between ruler and ruled under the Rāj. These two chapters establish a key ingredient of the Śākta festivals: their link to royal power, wealth, and status. Chapter 3 focuses on Durgā and describes the many ways in which she is identified with a little girl, for she is at once the martial demon-slayer and Umā, the humble wife of Śiva, whose festival resonates with details of the mother–daughter relationship as experienced in Bengali cultural history.

Chapter 4 introduces another key element of Durgā Pūjā: the association with agriculture. Prior to an in-depth look at the iconographic development of the Pūjā images, this chapter discusses the earlier forms into which the Goddess was invoked: water, grains, and plants. That the anthropomorphized Pūjā images were late iconographically proves that the martial aspects of the festival were likely grafted onto an earlier rite connected with the rhythms and products of the autumnal harvest. Chapter 5 continues the focus on Durgā and Jagaddhātrī by examining the evolution of the public, street character of the Pūjās, charting the inception and development of the *sarbajanīn*, or universal, format, with its outlets for revelry and rivalry and its arenas for the expression of social and political commentary.

Chapters 6 and 7 focus exclusively on Kālī, and parallel the topical treatment of chapters 4 and 5: iconography and public festivity. Although it is clear that Kālī Pūjā has been molded and influenced by Durgā Pūjā, there are differences that derive from Kālī's more overt link to Tāntrikas, dacoits (thugs), blood, and fear,[6] and these deserve their own separate treatment.

In chapter 8 we look at three controversial aspects of the Śākta Pūjās: the reaction by prostitutes to the injunction to offer earth from their doorposts to Durgā in her ritual; the impact of Pūjā-inflicted pollution on the environment; and the highly disputed issue of animal sacrifice. Particularly in relation to the theme of blood, we see that however much the goddesses at the center of the Śākta Pūjās have undergone a sweetened makeover for the consumption of popular holidaymakers, they are nevertheless fierce and potentially destructive; *śakti*, or feminine power, is not always neat and tidy.

Chapter 9 takes us away from India, to the Pūjā committees and celebrations of the American diaspora, where I narrate the transformations occurring in the homes of Bengali immigrants. To what extent are rivalry, innovation, longing, and linkage of the goddesses with the land of Bengal to be found in contexts outside India? This chapter derives from material gained in nearly thirty visits to Durgā, Jagaddhātrī, and Kālī Pūjās in New York and New Jersey.

The brief concluding chapter nests the three Śākta Pūjās within the Bengali Hindu festival year, in the process attempting to determine what it is that makes Durgā Pūjā in particular so unique. Why has this festival dominated all others in the construction of a specific Bengali identity?

Along the way I have posed and tackled several interpretive puzzles. Did Durgā Pūjā become easier or harder to sponsor after the advent of the British (chapter 1)? How did the Umā-daughter tradition become integrated with the martial Durgā-Mahiṣamardinī in Bengal (chapters 3 and 4)? How did Kālī's specific image evolve (chapter 6)? What are the chronological steps in the development of the public festivals, from the aristocratic home Pūjās of the eighteenth century to the public "Theme Pūjās" of today (chapters 5 and 7)? Why is blood sacrifice so integral to the Goddess (chapter 8)?

Apart from my own participant observation in Pūjā settings in India and the United States, the sources for this study have been books and newspapers in English and Bengali, the latter from as far back as I was able to find. Altogether I have looked at 678 individual newspapers for the Pūjā season, covering a span from 1781 to 2008, some years obviously with multiple coverage. Methodologically, I have not followed one theory or theorist; *Revelry, Rivalry, and Longing for the Goddesses of Bengal* is not meant to illuminate or prove the veracity of one particular way of looking at public festivals. This is not, in other words, a book about ritual or ritual theory, such as the excellent study by Caroline Humphrey and James Laidlaw, *The Archetypal Actions of Ritual: A Theory of Ritual Illustrated by the Jain Rite of Worship* (Oxford: Clarendon Press, 1994); a book that exemplifies the benefits of a particular sociological lens, such as William Sax's *Mountain Goddess: Gender and Politics in a Himalayan Pilgrimage* (New York: Oxford University Press, 1991); or a monograph that makes a valuable contribution to the field of collective memory studies, such as Elizabeth A. Castelli's *Martyrdom and Memory: Early Christian Culture Making* (New York: Columbia University Press, 2004). The drawback to my multiple toolbox approach is that no one theory is given the depth of coverage that might be expected were it the sole lens for interpretation; the benefit is that—in a modus operandi I feel to be most respectful of the multifaceted material under study—perspectives, theories, and lenses appropriate to each chapter have been pulled in as necessary. For instance, chapter 2, on colonial history, can be read as validating postcolonial scholarly descriptions of colonial stereotypes or tropes concerning Indian peoples and their religions; chapter 3, on Durgā Pūjā and the seventeenth- to early-twentieth-century relationships between mothers and daughters, presents us with a clear case of the social reflectiveness of ritual; chapters 4 and 6 are illuminated by the literature on the history of iconic sexualization and the intersection of goddess portrayals with Indian nationalism; and chapter 8 situates the proclivity for blood in Bengali Śākta contexts within the scholarship on sacrifice. Throughout the process of writing this book, I have been aware of the oscillating nature of my material, with many supposed binaries encompassed in historical, theological, and sociological layerings: royal, elite, and domestic; Durgā and Umā; Vaiṣṇava and Śākta; tribal and Brahmanical; middle class and lower class; the "refined" taste of the gentlefolk (*bhadralok*) and the propensities of the so-called smaller folk (*choṭolok*); agricultural and martial; and British and Indian. The field of the Pūjās is wide.

However, there are three touchstones, leitmotifs, or undertones of my approach to the Pūjās that were presented to me over time by my research itself; they are, as reflected in the title of the book, revelry, rivalry, and longing. First, revelry. Whatever else the Pūjās have become, they are today preeminently an occasion for fun. We see this throughout the book: in chapter 1, in the lavish entertainments that accompanied the Pūjās from their very inception in the homes of the zamindar elites; in chapter 2, through the zealousness with which the festivals were guarded from interference by the British prior to 1947 and the post-1857 enjoyment of the Pūjā season by the British themselves; in chapters 5 and 7, in the raucous, fun-packed public forms of the festivals; and in chapter 9, by noting the attempts of transnational Bengali communities to replicate the gaiety and joie de vivre of the Pūjā experience. It is not easy to gauge or measure the "fun quotient" in a festival whose ostensible object is the religious veneration of a powerful goddess, but especially today, with the endeavors of Kolkata tourist officers to market Durgā Pūjā as the equivalent of Mardi Gras in Rio de Janeiro or Carnival in Spain or Trinidad, the Pūjā has become a spectacle to be displayed or performed, for public pleasure.

Second, as theorists like Johan Huizinga, Roger Caillois, and Tom Driver note, part of the fun of ritual "play," no matter how light or effervescent it may be, is the agonistic, competitive, or "ludic" element contained within it.[7] And here we come to the second of the main themes of the book: rivalry. Throughout the period under study in *Revelry, Rivalry, and Longing for the Goddesses of Bengal* we find continual evidence for the enjoyment that rivals take in broadcasting their talents and feeling the tension that derives from risk-taking in the competition for prizes, status, and recognition. The aristocratic Pūjā patrons from the seventeenth century (chapter 1), the goddess-creating artisans working since the early twentieth century (chapters 4 and 6), the exuberant will-to-win Pūjā committee chairmen in the public festival culture since 1926 (chapters 5 and 7), and even the outstation diasporic Bengalis, in their local American communities since the 1980s (chapter 9), embody the rivalry that is endemic to all Pūjā culture. We consider this phenomenon from several vantage points—the quest for symbolic capital (chapter 1), the desire to be seen engaging in conspicuous consumption (chapter 5), and the utilization of the public sphere for recognition, reward, or lobbying opportunities (chapters 2 and 5).

The third theme of this book is longing, whether this be a personal ache for the past or a cultural nostalgia or both, which permeates seemingly every aspect of the Pūjās. This hearkening back to the remembered or recreated past is exemplified in the craze for "traditionalism" felt by both purveyors and audiences of the Pūjā experience (chapter 1); the poignant desire for the daughter, her welfare, her return home, and her renewed bond with her mother (chapter 3); and the nostalgia-fueled urge on the part of Bengalis settled outside of Bengal to recreate "authentic" Pūjās for their children and grandchildren (chapter 9). This material is a fruitful arena for considering the links between memory, the past, and cultural identity.

Revelry, rivalry, and longing: these three themes are central to my study of the Pūjās in two ways. They "fit" the material for Durgā and Jagaddhātrī in a positive sense, in that Durgā Pūjā and Jagaddhātrī Pūjā are occasions for the unabashed display of pomp, the exercise of competitiveness, and the expression of nostalgic feeling. By contrast, these have become the main elements of Kālī Pūjā only lately, and only by proximity to and influence from the Durgā model. To be sure, Kālī Pūjā has always been enjoyed as an opportunity for various sorts of entertainment, including gambling, fireworks, and rowdy-ism; rival gangs have expressed their influence through their sponsorship of the Pūjā; and Kālī *bhaktas* await the festival with an emotive desire. Yet Kālī's main provenances are power, fear, and secrecy, and chapters 6 and 7 demonstrate the degree to which these underlying characteristics still present challenges to those who would attempt to make this Goddess conform to Durgā's more normative pattern. Revelry, rivalry, and longing, therefore, are borrowed elements for Kālī Pūjā, through a process of conscious ascription still unevenly accomplished.

As might be expected, there are many things that this book does not attempt to do. Readers will not find much on the foods, recipes, or musical releases that appear during the Pūjā season, or on the history of the goddesses' classical art historical evolution. A serious omission—except as occurs in chapter 2, on the colonial period, and in chapter 4, on the potential breadth of Durgā's iconographic meaning—is consideration of Islam or of Bengali Muslims' interactions with the Pūjās. Muharram, arguably the second biggest festival in the state of West Bengal, receives almost no attention. This is a conscious oversight; there is simply no room in this book for the sort of comparative analysis that would be required if Bengali Islamicate culture were to be taken into account in a serious way. Another analytical lens that is rarely found here is caste. Chapter 1 does argue that Durgā Pūjā was built up through the efforts of the middle- to upper-caste nouveaux riches, or those who aspired to such prominence; chapters 2 and 5 show how the *sarbajanīn* Pūjās were established in the 1920s to open the field of festival sponsorship to people of all caste backgrounds; and chapters 7 and 8 reproduce upper-caste claims that blood and raucousness in Śākta worship belong to those of low caste. Nevertheless, there is no sustained caste analysis of the festivals, a task that would have required orienting my interviews and research in a direction I did not wish to go.

What has engaged me instead for the past twenty years is the history of the *experience* of the Pūjās: how the festivals began, developed, took on their characteristic visual and political forms; what has gone into the making of the unique *rasa*, or taste, of the festival, be it extravagance and revelry, rivalry, devotional fervor, or nostalgia; and the polydextrous nature of the festivals, such that they produce, provide the stage for the expression of, and adjudicate any number of controversies. These festivals have been beloved of many Hindus. We find them mentioned in the life stories, letters, or reminiscences of, for instance, Rāmakṛṣṇa, Swami Vivekananda, Keshab Chandra Sen, Subhas and Sarat Chandra Bose, Bipin Chandra Pal, and Surendranath Banerjea. The Pūjās travel with emigrating Bengalis. And they live in the artwork of creative innovators, who willingly sacrifice the fame that might have been theirs by agreeing to abandon their goddesses and their pandals at the conclusion of each festival season. Durgā, Jagaddhātrī, and Kālī give fortune, *are* fortune. And they invite a sustained, astonished gaze at all they have inspired in the public festival culture of Bengal.

# 1 Pūjā Origins and Elite Politics

The extravagance of Durgā Pūjā as it can be experienced today in the cities and towns of Bengal, with elaborately decorated pandals, expensive images, creative entertainments, and audience-catching gimmicks, is not so very different in grandeur and marvel from the Pūjā as it could have been encountered in the late eighteenth and early nineteenth centuries. Consider the very appreciative British description from 1825 of the house of "Baboo Pron Kissen Holdor" in Chinsurah, said to look like a European mansion. Pūjā guests were entertained in a huge salon, with beautiful furniture, a carpet imported from Brussels, sparkling lights, tables spread with meats and wines, excellent singing and dancing girls, and even jesters and jugglers.[1] Aristocracy, real or aspired; opulence; the desire to impress; the use of a festival to demarcate and solidify one's sense of identity and prestige: these are enduring characteristics of the Durgā Pūjā festival that have been true of its various forms nearly since its inception. In this chapter we look at the history of the Pūjā, investigating its contexts, its patrons, the meanings they attached to it, and the legacy they bequeathed to their modern-day heirs.

## Who Gets the Credit for Durgā? Pūjā Polemics, Festival Fortunes

The worship of Durgā has been associated with royalty and success in battle since the *Mahābhārata*: both Yudhiṣṭhīra and Arjuna pray to her before clashing with their enemies (*MBh* IV.6 and VI.23), and much later, in Kṛttibās's Bengali *Rāmāyaṇa*, Rāma entreats her for victory over Rāvaṇa.[2] Textual evidence for an autumnal festival in honor of Durgā or Caṇḍikā is as old as the sixth-century "Devī-Māhātmya" section of the *Mārkaṇḍeya Purāṇa*, where King Suratha and his merchant friend Samādhi are exhorted by the Goddess to worship her for blessings, specifically agricultural prosperity and freedom from troubles (12.1–29). The festival is also described and explained in a number of Śākta Purāṇas, most deriving from regions of eastern India: *Bhaviṣya Purāṇa* 138; *Brahmavaivarta Purāṇa* 1.16.60; *Bṛhaddharma Purāṇa* 22; *Devī Purāṇa* 22.1–24; *Devībhāgavata Purāṇa* 3.24.19–20; *Kālikā Purāṇa* 60.1–44; and *Mahābhāgavata Purāṇa* 36.71–72, 45.33–42, 48.15.[3] These make grandiose claims for the Pūjā, asserting that it is obligatory (*nitya*) but may be performed for the obtaining of desires specific to the sponsor (*kāmya*), that it is open to people of any caste or sex, including mlecchas (outcaste foreigners) and even demons,[4] and that it is the most important of all conceivable forms of worship. The *Devī Purāṇa* 22.23 equates Durgā's Pūjā with a royal *aśvamedha*, and the *Bhaviṣya Purāṇa* avers that "rites like Agnihotra, solemn sacrifices described in the Vedas and completed with dakṣiṇā are not equal even to one hundred-thousandth part of the worship of Caṇḍikā."[5]

The earliest reference to the festival as practiced in Bengal appears to be the twelfth-century *Rāmacarita* by Sandhyākaranandin, which speaks of the festivities in Varendri, present-day northern Bengal.[6] Furthermore, at least since the fourteenth century, Pūjā digests have been written specifically on the Durgā festival—famous examples include the *Kālaviveka* of Jīmūtavāhana (eleventh to twelfth centuries), the *Durgotsavaviveka*, *Vāsantaviveka*, and *Durgotsava Prayoga* of Śūlapāṇi (twelfth century), the *Durgābhaktitaraṅginī* of Vidyāpati (written ca. 1440–1460), and the *Durgotsavatattva* and *Durgāpūjātattva* of Raghunandana (mid-sixteenth to early seventeenth century). The most systematic treatment (by Rāmtoṣaṇ Tarkabāgīś, in his *Prāṇatoṣiṇī*, from 1821) cites the earlier Purāṇas and Vidyāpati as authorities. Modern-day Pūjā manuals advertise themselves as following guidelines derived from the *Devī Purāṇa*, the *Kālikā Purāṇa*, or the *Bṛhannandikeśvara Purāṇa*, the last being the most elaborate.[7] Through a detailed comparison of these medieval Bengali ritual texts with similar ones on Navarātrī from South and North India, R. C. Hazra has identified the beginnings of a specific Durgā Pūjā regional tradition in Bengal: other digests from elsewhere in India do not prescribe the awakening of Durgā under a *bel* tree on the sixth night of the festival, do not include the worship of the nine plants trussed up to Durgā's right on the pandal dias, and do not encourage raucous songs and dances on the tenth day, a custom known as Śabarotsab, after the Śabara tribal peoples who apparently initiated it.

Clues regarding actual Pūjā performances in Bengal can be found in a number of texts, including the late medieval Maṅgalakāvyas, or epic poems in praise of specific, often local, gods and goddesses. According to the *Viṣṇuyamalā* of the fifteenth century, the worship of Durgā is done in "every house" (*gṛhe gṛhe*),[8] and Bṛndāvandās, author of a Caitanyamaṅgal from 1538–1550, writes that "*mṛdanga* drums, cymbals, and conch shells are kept in all houses for playing instrumental music at Durgotsab time" (23.90).[9] In a catalogue of festivals, month by month, as found in Mukundarām Cakrabartī's *Caṇḍīmaṅgal*, Durgā Pūjā features prominently for the month of Aśvin.[10] The ballads discovered by Dineshchandra Sen in eastern Bengal also make mention of the Pūjā: it is said to occur in September–October, to be performed in every house, and to represent a time of intense anticipation for family reunions.[11] But as we shall see, the exact precedent for the Pūjā as we see it today may not predate the late sixteenth or early seventeenth century.

Texts from the *Mahābhārata* and the "Devī-Māhātmya" onward indicate that the worship of Durgā confers strength, rejuvenation, deliverance from evil or trouble, riches, grain, and children.[12] She is also consistently linked with tribal peoples—for instance, Śabaras, Barbaras, and Pulindas—from whom she gains her Sanskritized epithets Śabarī and Parṇaśabarī, and she is said to live among tigers and lions in mountains (Vindhyas or Himalayas), inaccessible forests, and caves. It is a curious feature of goddess worship in eastern India that while scholars are nearly unanimous in claiming that Durgā, Kālī, and other *devī*s probably derive from a non-Brahmanical, indigenous stratum,[13] not only does her worship, from the seventeenth century on, not betray much evidence of this influence,[14] but Durgā's festival in contemporary tribal religious life either has a totally different meaning, as the conclusion to a month-long training session in traditional medicinal arts, or appears to be a non-indigenous, Hindu import.[15] Old Bengali *smṛti* writings, such as Jīmūtavāhana's *Kālaviveka*, Raghunandana's *Aṣṭāviṁśatitattva*, and Śūlapāṇi's *Durgotsavaviveka*, provide evidence that tribal culture was once more intrinsic to the worship of the Goddess; she was described as being angry if there were no engagement with tribal enemies or sexual orgies. Indeed, until recently ribald post-Daśamī dances were common practice in rural Pūjā celebrations,[16] and since the late 1990s it has been fashionable for urban *sarbajanīn* Pūjā committees to invite Santals to perform their hereditary tribal dances in cultural shows aimed at reclaiming lost tradition. One must conclude that the process of Brahmanization, which occurred quite late in Bengal, from the eight to ninth centuries CE, has so assimilated and transformed goddesses like Durgā that, invested with new concerns for royalty and riches, they have lost their once-ubiquitous tribal associations.[17] The same is true of Kālī; if she had ever "originally" been a tribal goddess or a deity of the lower classes, those origins are now quite obscured. Tribal peoples today who celebrate her festival are those who are influenced by Hinduism or who live in close proximity to major Bengali cities—such as the Munda and Murma tribes inhabiting the Ayodhya hill region of Purulia district. They are not seen as indigenous Kālī *bhaktas*.[18]

English and Bengali sources consistently present contradictory explanations for the rising popularity and success of the Pūjā, first in the late sixteenth century, but later and more prominently in the eighteenth century, which witnessed an explosion of interest in the Śākta deities Durgā, Jagaddhātrī, and Kālī. Some authors are specific and attribute the first public Durgā Pūjās to particular figures: candidates include Kaṁsanārāyaṇ, zamindar of Taherpur, Rajshahi district, now in Bangladesh, who sponsored the festivity as a substitute for an *aśvamedha* ceremony upon his succession to the zamindari in 1583;[19] the head of the Sābarṇa Rāy Caudhurī family, which ceded the East India Company the lands that became Calcutta and which has been celebrating the Pūjā since 1610;[20] Gobindarām Mitra (d. 1766?), founder of the Mitra family of Kumartuli and one of the earliest "Bābus" of the city, who celebrated a sumptuous Pūjā in his house from the year he became deputy zamindar in 1720;[21] Rājā Nabakṛṣṇa Deb (1733–1797), founder of the Shovabazar Rāj family, who is said to have presided over an impressive Pūjā in 1757 to felicitate the British in their victory at Plassey; and, perhaps most often cited, Rājā Kṛṣṇacandra Rāy, zamindar of the Nadia district from 1728 to 1782, who instituted the public worship of Durgā on a grand scale, exhorting those tenants in his district who were rich enough to do likewise.[22]

In spite of the early dates of some of these Pūjās, none of my sources disputes the fact that it was during the 1700s that interest in Durgā was greatest.[23] What is unclear from the reports, however, are the reasons behind this great upsurge of attention to the public worship of the Goddess, especially as these reasons relate to shifting power configurations in the region. Some historians argue that the lavish Durgā Pūjās were attributable to a new climate of stability and opportunity under the British, after or in anticipation of 1757, when—in contrast with the earlier period of governorship by local Mughal representatives, or *nawābs*—the zamindars dared show off their wealth and assert their prestige.[24] Others believe that the Pūjās became popular during the period prior to the Battle of Plassey and the transfer of power from the *nawābs* to the East India Company in 1765,[25] when the *nawābs*' lenient rule allowed for the amassing of great wealth among Hindu zamindars. At stake in these competing arguments are reconstructions of the relationships between zamindars, *nawābs*, and the British, as well as judgments concerning the relative values of so-called Muslim and Christian rulership.

According to the first view, conditions in the rural areas under *nawāb* rule were harsh and not conducive to such demonstrations of pomp and prestige as the Pūjās would necessitate. Only when it was clear that the control of the *nawābs* was waning could people like Rājā Kṛṣṇacandra feel free to engage in traditional acts of patronage. I quote from a representative English-language newspaper published in Calcutta in 1820:[26]

> [T]o the bigoted Mussalmans, the worship of the Hindoo gods was ever viewed with feelings of jealousy, if not of extreme hostility . . . [T]he English government . . . has allowed for general diffusion of wealth and security of property. Formerly, such a display of wealth would have subjected the patron to the rapacious exactions of his petty sovereign. Under the present system, the government makes no inquiry into the private wealth of its subjects. In consequence of this security, the natives have given themselves up to unlimited extravagance in all that relates to their public festivals.

This same point was repeatedly noted and written about by English Company servants in Bengal; the soldier-historian Robert Orme, for instance, commented that under the *nawābs* everyone in the property hierarchy, from the ryots, village heads, and zamindars up to the *nawābs* themselves, looked with fear upon the jealousy of their immediate superiors. "The nawab fixes his eye on every portion of wealth which appears in his province," said Orme.[27] Another indication that the zamindars feared to demonstrate to the *nawābs* the true degree of their resources comes from a story about Kṛṣṇacandra's grand-uncle, Rājā Rāmakṛṣṇa (ruled on and off from 1694 to 1715), who impressed the Mughal prince Asim-us-Shāh as being the only zamindar who dared come to court at Murshidabad with a stately retinue. All the rest "came attended with only a few followers, not daring to show their wealth."[28] Some contemporary Bengalis see in the custom of creating disposable images a vestige of the fear that gripped Hindus during Muslim rulership of Bengal: did the practice of immersions derive from people wanting to worship quickly and then destroy the evidence?[29]

According to other sources of this same persuasion, the trouble was not simply fears of Muslim greed, but actual experiences of oppression. Aparna Bhattacharya, a modern-day historian, writes that the worship of the powerful goddess Durgā attracted the Hindu *rājās* as a means of overcoming their inferiority complexes vis-à-vis the *nawābs*; further, they hoped to imbibe some of Durgā's strength, which could be used for political purposes.[30] This sense of subjugation was apparently not entirely fictitious; there are indications that Hindu zamindars were not on the best terms with their *nawāb* rulers, who were displeased with the zamindars' rebelliousness and, later, increasing attachments to the British in the region. Murshid Qūlī Khān (r. 1704–1725) was a notoriously strict revenue collector, punishing those who failed to comply; even under the more tolerant 'Alīvardī Khān (r. 1740–1756), the Bengali economy began to be impoverished, with the *rājās*' assets increasingly squeezed. The Burdwan *rājā*, Tilakcānd, wrote to the Company in 1757, on the eve of Plassey,

> By the rapaciousness of the government nothing is left to me. These three years I have no power left me in my country, and my own servants refused to obey me. But by the blessing of God by your coming the country shall flourish, and all men have their hearts at ease. I hope in God your power will be as great as I could wish it, that you may be good to every one. On this depends my own welfare.[31]

Even after Plassey, the puppet *nawāb*, Mīr Qāsim (r. 1760–1763), had several prominent zamindars jailed, tortured, and killed in the mid-eighteenth century.[32]

This view attributes large-scale celebrations of Durgā Pūjā to British tolerance and governing policies, particularly Cornwallis' Permanent Settlement of 1793, according to which taxes were determined by fixed land holdings, not personal wealth.[33] Indeed, in the rural areas where the landed gentry managed to stay financially viable after 1757 and in the urban streets of Calcutta from the 1790s, we find much evidence of Hindu nouveaux riches sponsoring Pūjās in grand style as a means to confirm, and enhance, their growing social status. The Bengali *Samācār Darpaṇ* newspaper commented in 1829: "Gradually those who became rich under British rule, in order to show off their wealth to those they ruled, cast aside their former fear and spent a lot of money on the Pūjās."[34]

But there is a second explanation for the rise of Durgā Pūjā. Here, it is the Mughal representatives and later the semi-independent *nawābs* who, prior to Plassey, bring sufficient prosperity and stability to the region to allow the flourishing of zamindari interests. There is much to commend this argument.

The rise of several of the zamindari houses in Bengal occurs in the context of the seventeenth-century Mughal need for loyalty and nonthreatening allies in Bengal who could help bring the newly conquered territory under imperial government control. Prior to 1700, the Mughals in Delhi had a very laissez-faire attitude toward Bengal; their rule was conducted through *rājās*, chiefs, and other landowners, leading to autonomy and stability. The Burdwan zamindari, for instance, by 1702 the premier estate west of the Hooghly, grew in fortune and prestige from the beginning of Jahāngīr's reign through that of Muḥammad Shāh. Murshid Qūlī Khān, the first *nawāb* to rule Bengal with some independence from the arm of Mughal control in Delhi, consciously attempted to support and even aggrandize the large zamindaris, such as Burdwan, Birbhum, Bishnupur, Nadia, Dinajpur, and Natore. These increasingly wealthy zamindars modeled themselves after the *nawābs* and their courts, patronizing indigenous crafts, industries, and religious institutions, to indicate social position. Although there are very few references to Durgā Pūjā before the mid-eighteenth century in the rural areas, the patronage by these Hindu landowners in other religious spheres is well documented: from the early eighteenth century they spent lavishly at marriages and funerals, went on pilgrimages, built mosques, temples, and charitable institutions, and supported Brahmans, pandits, and Muslim holy men (*pīrs*) with land and cash donations. Such modeling after *nawābs*, coupled with increasing inter-zamindar rivalries for local prestige, certainly predate the British victory at Plassey.

Moreover, this second perspective on the history of Durgā Pūjā asserts that after the coming of the British the ability of the zamindars to patronize religious functions was severely hampered. Again, there is much merit to this contention. In symbolic terms, the Company reforms of the late eighteenth century curtailed opportunities for Bengalis to establish political and ritual relationships of loyalty and fealty, upon which public events like the Pūjās depended. As noted by historian John R. McLane, the abandonment by the British, and hence perforce by the zamindars, of the court ceremony at which dependents brought their revenues to the landlord and received robes of honor in return "signaled a retreat from symbolic to more purely contractual relations with [their] principal subjects." And this "diminution of the [zamindars'] ability to make gifts and distribute patronage struck at the currency of political bonding."[35] Moreover, it is a well-known fact that after Plassey the British bled Bengal, squeezing the rural landowners, breaking up their estates for arrears of revenue, demilitarizing their lands, and making no allowance for reduced revenue payments during the devastating famine of 1769–1770. Almost all the major houses of Bengal suffered during the last quarter of the eighteenth century, their zamindars struggling—some successfully and others not—to keep a grip on their estates. In 1758 Rājā Kṛṣṇacandra, who had apparently helped the British to victory at Plassey, defaulted on Company payments. Under his grandson and great grandson, Īśvarcandra and Girīścandra, respectively, much of his Nadia property was sold, due to revenue debts. The Burdwan zamindari under Tilakcānd (1744–1770), who as we have seen above had welcomed the British in 1757, sank to its lowest levels ever by the time of his death in 1770 during the Bengal famine, when he and his family were reduced to indigence.

Some British observers were astute and candid in their assignation of blame for the country's ruin. Richard Becker, Resident of Murshidabad from 1769, attributed the degeneration of the economy to overassessments, and specifically compared the British system with that of the *nawābs*, showing how the latter was more favorable to the zamindars.[36] The connection between poverty under the British and the inability to perform Durgā Pūjā is explicitly stated in the case of the Dinajpur Rāj, a family that had risen to success and wealth prior to 1760 under the patronage of Nawāb 'Alīvardī Khān; the zamindari plummeted in fortune during the tenure of Rājā Baidyanāth (1760–1780). I quote below a letter which he sent to the East India Company's Board of Revenue in 1773:[37]

> As I consider the discharge of my debts to Government as prior even to the provision of my food and raiments, I readily submit to this. But since the 'Poojah Dessehra' is near at hand and this festival supersedes amongst those of my caste all religious and worldly affairs, God forbid that the customs which have been kept up of old [should be compromised,] seeing the same would reflect greatly on me in the opinions of men in general. I therefore hope that you will grant me some allowance

to support the charge of the Poojah and that I may in a becoming manner be thereby entitled to keep up my reputation.

Perhaps the most telling argument in favor of this second view of the history of the Pūjās is the change wrought in the Pūjās themselves by the collapse of traditional patronage systems. The Permanent Settlement Act of 1793, while regularizing taxable rates on land divisions, abolished the mechanisms whereby zamindars might exact timely payment from their own tenants, effectively ensuring their powerlessness in meeting their financial commitments.[38] It was in this context that the *bāroiyāri* Pūjā, or Pūjā sponsored by twelve (friends), was first introduced in 1790. Instead of the expenses of the festival being defrayed by one zamindar family alone, the Pūjā was democratized, its costs spread out and shared among people not necessarily of the hereditary aristocracy.[39] The *sarbajanīn* (or public) Pūjā of Kolkata today is heir to this intermediate, *bāroiyāri*, type; now, instead of twelve or so friends, the Pūjās are sponsored by neighborhood groups and civic associations that vie with each other to produce the best, most opulent, and most beautiful displays.

Adjudicating between these two perspectives on the origins of the Pūjās may not require an absolute choice. First, it seems likely that some of the rhetoric on both sides is colored by political considerations. One can detect in the early-nineteenth-century English newspaper reports about the benefits for Durgā Pūjā of British rule a desire to justify the wresting of power from the *nawābs* by the Company. Likewise, quotes about the oppression of Hindu zamindars by British greed often come from sources authored by Muslims.

Second, it is perhaps wiser to combine than to juxtapose the two viewpoints. Following the arguments of the second perspective, it is clear that the zamindar-sponsored worship of Durgā did originate in pre-British times and was to a certain extent facilitated by the *nawābs*' consolidation of large zamindari estates, which made their job of governing easier. For those six or so zamindaris, such as Nadia, Burdwan, Natore, Dinajpur, Birbhum, and Bishnupur, which were consciously patronized by the *nawābs*, conditions prior to the British were, at least to some degree, conducive to the amassing and displaying of wealth; that Durgā Pūjā was already an accepted means to such status is perhaps best indicated by the fact that new claimants to power in the region (such as the Mārāṭhas in 1742 and even the British in 1765) attempted to use the festival as a self-authenticating measure.[40] Likewise, it seems clear that the fifty to sixty years after Plassey were difficult economically for the large landed estates of Bengal; the eroding of their wealth and autonomy rendered traditional acts of patronage burdensome. As a historian of the Rajshahi zamindar in modern-day Bangladesh relates,

> Until 1757, the Rani and her officials operated within a system which they clearly understood. Relations with the Nawabs of Murshidabad seem to have been good; the revenue bargain was made on lines indicated by custom, and made less onerous by a certain flexibility and by the readiness of the great bankers of Murshidabad to lend their assistance in difficult years. . . . Then, from 1757 to 1765 there must have been a difficult period, as Mir Jafar attempted to raise the revenues necessary to liquidate his debts to the Company, and as Mir Qasim pushed up the demand to unheard of heights in his attempt to gather the resources with which to resist the Company's encroachment upon his authority.[41]

Nevertheless, following the first argument, life under the *nawābs* was not entirely easy, and accounts of the harshness of Murshid Qūlī Khān, for instance, even in relation to the zamindaris he was consolidating, must be considered.[42] Brijen Gupta, in a fascinating aside, mentions that such persecution by Murshid Qūlī and his successor, Shujāᶜ-ud-dīn Khān (1725–1739), led directly to revivals of "Hindu feeling" and of "court rivalries which had been dormant for over half a century."[43] If this is true, then, in a surprising twist on the two arguments surveyed above, one might say that the Pūjās were given their impetus during the time of Mughal rule, not because conditions were particularly easy, but as a means to assert zamindari power in politically uncomfortable times. Finally, I am also convinced, again by the first argument, that new opportunities for Pūjā sponsorship did open up under British rule, particularly in the urban context of Calcutta, but also through the innovations introduced by the *bāroiyāri* Pūjās, which were necessitated, ironically, by the demise of zamindari fortunes.

Although there is thus controversy as to when and under what specific conditions Durgā Pūjā was first celebrated in Bengal, no one doubts that it arose among a class of newly affluent landowners who used the festival as a self-authenticating ritual for the conferral of new status, as an opportunity for conspicuous displays of wealth, and as a visible show of strength and power. Commensurate with their wealth and sense of importance, many of the nouveaux riches built themselves large houses—their outside facades in the earlier period imitative of Mughal court architecture and in the growing city of Calcutta replicating Doric, Ionic, Late Renaissance, or

Palladian building styles.[44] Still today in north Kolkata, where most of the old families have their ancestral residences, one can see houses with large courtyards, big pillars and verandahs, wrought iron balconies, imported furniture, prized gifts from foreign trading contacts,[45] chandeliers, mirrors, and a large hall attached to the house, called the *ṭhākurdālān*, built specifically for the annual worship of Durgā and other deities (fig. 1.1).

While "Pūjā" used on its own almost always refers to Durgā Pūjā, it is worth remembering that Jagaddhātrī Pūjā arose under similar circumstances, probably trailing on the sari fabric, so to speak, of Durgā Pūjā, of which it is a multiform. It is likely that Jagaddhātrī as a goddess was once more popular than she is at present, for the very first recorded *bāroiyārī* Pūjā was performed to her, not Durgā, in 1790. Jagaddhātrī has become a particularly regional goddess; that is, she is worshiped especially in the areas around Chandannagar and Krishnanagar, both north of Kolkata and once under the jurisdiction

FIGURE 1.1. Inside the *ṭhākurdālān* at the Shovabazar Rāj house (minor branch); family members prostrating in front of Durgā and her children. Kolkata, October 2001. Photo by Jayanta Roy.

of Rājā Kṛṣṇacandra Rāy, the eighteenth-century Śākta patron of the arts. All three accounts of the inception of Jagaddhātrī's Pūjā involve him. According to the most popular, in 1757 the *rājā* was in Mongir Fort, imprisoned there by Nawāb Mīr Ja'far because of his part in the British victory at Plassey. He was released just too late to be home in time for Durgā Pūjā, which distressed him greatly. On his way, however, he had a dream of an armed goddess sitting on a lion. She told him not to worry that he had been unable to worship her, but to do so exactly one month later in the form that she was now assuming. Other origin stories credit Indranārāyaṇ Caudhurī, Kṛṣṇacandra's friend and the *dewān* of French Chandannagar, with introducing the Pūjā in the Chaulpatti section of the city in 1780–1781. This Pūjā and the one nearby at Tetutala in Bhadreshwar, founded in 1793, remain the most famous of all local Jagaddhātrī Pūjās. A third explanation focuses on a Brahman logician named Candracūḍacintāmaṇi, who under the patronage of Kṛṣṇacandra's grandson, Mahārājā Girīścandra, was the first to do the Pūjā.[46]

Indeed, Jagaddhātrī is not very old, at least in the form we find her in Bengal. Jagaddhātrī does not appear as an epithet of the Goddess until the Purāṇas, where it occurs infrequently and is not accompanied by any specific iconographic description or mention of a separate cult.[47] Several Tantric texts also mention her name tangentially; for example, she occurs in *Kāmākhya Tantra* 10.8, *Kubjikā Tantra* 3.65, and *Kālikā Purāṇa* 37.24–27,[48] but in none of these is there any iconographic description, and the specific festival in the month of Kārtik is not detailed. The first extant reference to an annual public worship occurs in Śūlapāṇi's fifteenth-century *Kālaviveka*, where one is instructed to worship Jagaddhātrī, depicted seated on the back of a lion, three times on the ninth day of the bright half of Kārtik.[49] Similar instructions are provided in fifteenth-century works by Bṛhaspati Rāy and Śrīnātha Ācārya Cuḍāmaṇi, the *Smṛtiratnahāra* and the *Krityatattvārṇava*, respectively.[50]

Given this steady if lightly trickling stream of references to Jagaddhātrī Pūjā since the fifteenth century, it is surprising that neither the Bengali poet Bhāratcandra Rāy (1712–1760), a beneficiary of Kṛṣṇacandra Rāy, who in his *Annadāmaṅgal* lists the yearly religious holidays current in his day, nor Raghunandana, the famed seventeenth-century Bengali author of the law book *Aṣṭāviṁśatitattva*, mentions Jagaddhātrī in his work.[51] Perhaps the most one can infer from the origin stories and the scant textual evidence is that Kṛṣṇacandra Rāy, an avid Śākta patron, incorporated Jagaddhātrī into his larger program of popularizing Śākta traditions. He had already been credited with the spreading of Kālī Pūjā (see chapter 7), and he was also a devotee of the goddess Durgā. It makes sense therefore to assume—even if one does not accept the specifics of the prison story—that this Nadia zamindar used his prestige and financial capital to revive the worship of a goddess whose ritual prescriptions, though evidenced in earlier texts, had by the mid-eighteenth century fallen into disuse.[52] Such a supposition has merit whether the initial popularizer was Kṛṣṇacandra or his friend Indranārāyaṇ Caudhurī, in Chandannagar: no matter who was first, the festival was a renewal of an older rite, and occurred in the context of aggressive Śākta patronage in regions of West Bengal fairly close to Calcutta that were experiencing power struggles under the *nawābs*.[53]

Initiating an annual Durgā Pūjā tradition was not the only way families entered public life or exhibited their wealth and honor. There were lineage associations, or *dals*, formed to lobby for the influence and prestige of particular families,[54] and the monied classes used marriages, funerals, and various forms of philanthropy to curry favor with their peers. Rāmdulāl De, who started his family's Pūjā between 1770 and 1780, apparently donated one-quarter of his total fortune to fund thirteen temples in Varanasi, had his wife weighed and the equivalent in gold donated to Brahmans, and fed eight thousand Brahmans and ten thousand poor people at his funeral.[55]

Durgā Pūjā was especially important to these aspiring families for three reasons. First, while the Pūjā necessitated wealth, it was not at all bound by caste prohibitions; as we have seen above, even Śūdras, mlecchas, and women have been claimed to gain rewards from its sponsorship. Since most of the newly rich were not Brahmans, but Kāyasthas, such ritual leniency was a great boon. Second, it provided occasions for showing off social standing, often amid "preposterous luxury, ostentation, and waste—a nouveau riche adaptation of feudal pomp and arrogance."[56] *Bhaviṣya Purāṇa* 138 indicates that the Pūjā is to be performed in every house, especially royal palaces, and that the worshiper should spend the eighth evening listening to singing and watching theater, offer a large number of animals and wine, and immerse the image at the conclusion of the festival in the presence of the king, with his army. Such directives assume, if not actual royalty, wealth and status. Indeed, Bengali and English sources indicate that once a man rose in social standing or financial worth, one of the first acts he undertook was his own family celebration of the Pūjā. Prominent examples include the famed early-eighteenth-century zamindar Gobindarām Mitra; Akrūr Datta, an East India Company employee who owned the first shipping line in Bengal; Rādhānāth Basumallik, the moving spirit behind the construction of the Hooghly Dockyard in 1842; the family of Gurucaraṇ Prāmāṇik, whose business sheathed the bottoms of ships with brass; and the Kailās Boses of Hatkhola, who pioneered steam communication on the Hooghly.[57]

Third, in spite of the fact that "*rājā*" in Bengal was an honorific title and did not connote true royalty, the rich and powerful appreciated Durgā's long history of involvement with kings. In their essay "Kings, Power, and the Goddess," Sanjukta Gupta and Richard Gombrich detail the association between Durgā and royalty, noting in particular her importance to the Gupta, Pallava, and Vijayanagara dynasties, who used Navarātrī—the equivalent of Durgā Pūjā in the rest of India—as a political occasion to reestablish their power and overlordship vis-à-vis their tributary chiefs.[58] Aspects of the Pūjā make this royal overtone particularly compelling: the *Devī Purāṇa*'s equation of the festival with an *aśvamedha*, mentioned earlier; the expectation, expressed in Manu and Kauṭilya, that right after the harvest, which is the Pūjā season, kings were to take *digvijayas*, or expeditions for gaining and consolidating territory;[59] and the form of Mahiṣamardinī herself. "From early times Durgā in this form is often shown with a lion, emblem of royalty. A king's throne is a 'lion throne' (*siṁhāsana*), its feet being carved with lions; when the king ascends it (first at his consecration) he is joining the Goddess there and making her 'his' *śakti*."[60] C. J. Fuller adds more flesh to this argument, noting that Navarātrī celebrates the victories of both Durgā and Rāma over demonic chaos, activities tied explicitly to the kingly, warrior class.[61] That ordinary zamindars were aware of this link between their temporal authority and the worship of the Goddess is indicated by family stories: in 1863 the widow of a zamindar in Malabar celebrated her victorious court case against another claimant to her land by choosing to be consecrated on the final day of Navarātrī; and the sixteenth-century son of Śaṅkar Caṭṭopādhyāy, the great Bengali general of Mahārājā Pratāpāditya, started celebrating a yearly Pūjā so that his father would beat the armies of the Mughal emperor.[62] Whether or not these up-and-coming lineages really enjoyed the status and power they claimed through their sponsorship of the Pūjās—Gupta and Gombrich speculate that in reality the zamindars had less and less autonomy over time, such that their patronage of magical means to maintain it was just a "substitution of fantasy for reality"[63]—one cannot gainsay the symbolic value of these festivals to those who sought to express their identities and aspirations through them.

In this vein, one might profitably utilize Pierre Bourdieu's notion of "symbolic capital" to interpret the zamindars' thirst for status through their showy patronage of public ritual. Capital, for Bourdieu, does not simply refer to economic wealth but to social prestige and special knowledge, derived—in this case—from occupational privilege, social status, interpersonal networks, and group solidarity. Even the refinement of aesthetic "taste" tends to be determined by one's social class, with the dominant classes jealously guarding their version of culture and the subordinate classes being obliged to define their aesthetic in relation to it. Numerous scholars have found this theoretical lens to be illuminating: to give just three examples, Jun Jing has written about the symbolic capital of Confucius to emerging royal cults in rural China; Sanjay Subrahmanyam argues that the symbolic capital associated with the legend of Vasco da Gama, the Portuguese explorer to India, not only helped Gama's career trajectory in his own lifetime but also facilitated his emergent identity as a Portuguese national treasure; and Hugh B. Urban understands the popularity to the lower social orders of the Kartābhajā sect in Bengal from the perspective of the new prestige and symbolic capital they gained from its community and teachings. While it is not my interest here to present such a Bourdieu-inspired analysis in detail, I think it obvious that in the context of the Pūjā-sponsoring nouveaux riches whom we have been considering, the race for recognition with those above and below reveals that perceptions of taste, cultivation, and social position are every bit as valuable to the ambitious as the harder currencies of bank accounts, land holdings, and actual power.[64]

## "All the Rich Celebrate a Festival of this Kind in their own Houses"[65]

European residents, visitors, and Company personnel of the early nineteenth century all commented on the extravagant displays of wealth among Hindu "Bābus" during the autumnal holiday season. De Grandpre, a French traveler to Calcutta in 1789–90, noted that all the affluent families of the city "are ambitious of displaying the greatest luxury, lighting up their apartments in the most splendid manner."[66] The *Calcutta Journal* of 1819 went further, describing the competitive aspects of the Pūjā: "The approach of the Great Hindoo festival of the Doorgah Poojah has once more called forth into action that feeling of emulative rivalry so conspicuously displayed at the season, by the wealthy Natives in the splendid preparations for the Nautches."[67]

Although the theme of rivalry will be discussed from a more theoretical and comparative perspective in chapter 5, here we look at the many practical ways a family could show off its purse and its social standing. Families constructed and then lavishly decorated large *ṭhākurdālāns* for receiving the Goddess and her nightly guests. They also maintained their reputations at Pūjā time by the novelty and beauty of their entertainments. The most memorable, at the least to British journalists and memoir-writers, appear to have been the dancing girls, or nautch performers, with their musician accompanists, who danced and sang before the host and his assembled company. We hear repeatedly in the second and third decades of the nineteenth century of "Neekhee and Ushoorun," who dazzled by their beauty and bewitching movements.[68] Some entertainments were more traditional, with the introduction of new Bengali musical forms or the staging of traditional theater, or *yātrās*,[69] whereas others were clearly influenced by or attempting to cater to an English audience. One reads, for instance, of foreign bagpipe troupes, English bands, and even renditions of "God Save the King"![70] Other amusements consisted of pantomimes; ventriloquists; masquerades (where sometimes the British were imitated); buffoons (one set of performers dressed as cows and ate grass[71]); and feats of daring, such as "a native chewing and eating bits of glass" (including an English bottle, which he ate in chunks of 3–4 inches), and a man perched "on a wooden horse on two 10'–12' stilts; he preserved his balance and displayed sword maneuvers, while so seated."[72] Even in the 1860s, long after the British had begun officially to frown on these Pūjā extravaganzas, a "native contributor" to the *Bengal Harkaru and India Gazette* noted that at the three favored houses, those of "Radhakanto Deb," "Kali Krishna Bahadur," and "Baboo Heera Lall Seal," the entertainments included European acrobats, a farce entitled "Babes in the Wood" performed by the Amateurs of H. M. S. 54th Regiment, and "native melodies" by the Indian members of the same regiment.[73]

Food and refreshments were another important element of the Pūjās. British guests remarked approvingly of the sweetmeats, fruits, and liquors, laid out on gold and silver dishes, that were offered them in separate refreshment rooms, and in their attempt to woo Company guests, Hindu hosts even prepared meats. Indeed, the number of Englishmen one attracted was considered the seal of prestige, the crowning touch of honor—especially if those who came were of higher standing than those who went to a rival house. Invitations were sent out early in the season, and the newspapers also advertised the events, including what entertainments and foods could be had where.[74] Early governor-generals, from Lord Clive, who arrived on an elephant, to Lord Bentinck, were regular guests,[75] and judging from reports and letters, they and their compatriots looked forward to the Pūjās with anticipation.

However, showy externals serving to attract foreign notice were only one aspect of the three-day event, one avenue through which the monied classes expressed their symbolic status in the festivals. Others were more Hindu, more traditional, more associated with religion, and most of these were never written up in the English press of the period. For example, although one occasionally reads of a British guest viewing "the goddess Doorgah,"[76] little British attention was paid to the temporary clay images prepared and worshiped on the occasion, and one has to consult Bengali sources to learn about the *aṣṭadhātu* figures (permanent images made from eight metals) that wealthy families also commissioned, often at the founding of their first Pūjā.[77] Heads of important lineages also made their mark in society by their lavish giving to Brahmans or to the poor, the latter known as *Daridra-Nārāyaṇ-sebā*, or the service of Viṣṇu in the form of the poor. Rājā Rājkṛṣṇa of the Shovabazar Rāj house in Calcutta gave gold coins to 108 Brahmans, who each recited the "Devī-Māhātmya" (known as *Caṇḍīpāṭh*), and Gobindarām Mitra has gone down in folk history for his lavish patronage of the festival, offering 30–50 mounds of rice to the Goddess, for eventual distribution to the poor, and feeding one thousand Brahmans.[78]

Ritual practice is a further arena for self-expression. From the first days of preparation to the last days of mournful conclusion, the worship of the Goddess provides numerous opportunities for solidifying and articulating the aspiring "royal" status of its sponsors. The first ritual step is the sanctification of the *kāṭhāmo*, or wooden frame handed down through the generations, on which the clay images of the Goddess and her children are to be affixed.[79] This is typically done by most traditional families on the Rath Din or Ulṭo Rath Din, three months before Durgā Pūjā, on the days, respectively, that commemorate Lord Jagannātha's exit on his chariot (*ratha*) from his Puri temple and his return seven days later. The king in Puri, who is the Lord's viceroy or servant, is supposed to clean the road on which the chariot comes with a golden broomstick, and then pull the rope once the chariot arrives. Consecrating the *kāṭhāmo* on these days, therefore, is evocative of wood (Lord Jagannātha), of the "royal idiom" of service to the deity, and of the elaborate canopied processions, especially on the tenth day, that used to characterize the conclusion of the Goddess' festivities.[80]

Associations between ritual practice and the claim to royalty are even more visible in the treatment of the *nabapatrikā*—the nine plants trussed up together, adorned with a sari, placed next to Gaṇeśa on the dias, and referred to affectionately as the *kalā bau*, or banana-plant-wife—which is bathed and consecrated on the morning of Saptamī, the seventh day. Nineteenth-century Bengali newspapers and histories tell us that eminent families like the Shovabazar Debs would escort their *nabapatrikā* to the family *ghāṭ*, or bathing spot, under silver umbrellas, cooling her with silver fans and sometimes even entertaining her with a Scottish highlander bagpipe band. Other rituals are similarly marked: *sandhi pūjā*, or the auspicious conjunction of the eighth and ninth days, was heralded with cannon-firing and rifle shots from the estate house[81]; and the procession to the river at Daśamī, when the Goddess is consigned to the waters, was accompanied by processions, elephants, drummers, bands, the blowing of conch-shells, and foot-soldiers carrying the family flag.[82] Among the Malla *rājās* in Bishnupur it was customary for the *rājā*, after immersing the Goddess, to come home, get dressed in his weaponry, and have a mock battle with his army.[83] It is also noteworthy that the majority of the old family goddess images depict Durgā riding on a horse-faced lion. To some interpreters this is reminiscent of royalty and of British coats of arms, which up-and-coming Bengali families were trying to imitate.

Wealth, royalty, and now devotion: another set of Pūjā customs religiously and proudly followed by the nouveaux riches expressed their *niṣṭhā*, or faith, as well as the specialness and uniqueness of their worship. For instance, those families who could afford it paid to have Brahmans come daily, from Mahālayā through the conclusion of the Pūjā, to chant the "Devī-Māhātmya." Except for Vaiṣṇava families, many of whom sponsored the Pūjā but in a non-Śākta, vegetarian fashion, most of the traditional monied houses also offered numerous blood sacrifices, or *bali*s, typically of goats but also of buffaloes and other unusual animals if desired. As we shall see in greater depth in chapter 8, the more goats offered, the more notoriety the family was perceived to gain. Another ritual, not obligatory in the texts and therefore prized by those who performed it, was *kumārī pūjā*, the worship of a small Brahman girl as the Goddess, which can be done on all three days but is especially common on Saptamī.[84] A third optional custom was called *dhuno* or *dhunā* and involved the women of the family, who sat in the *ṭhākurdālān* facing the Goddess and holding on their palms and on their heads shallow clay dishes filled nine times with burning incense. Particularly endearing customs of this sort—necessitating wealth and expressing care, but not compulsory ritually—concern Daśamī. Affluent families used to buy two blue-throated birds, *nīlkaṇṭha pākhī*s, or Indian Rollers, and set them free—one when Durgā was setting out to the river from the *ṭhākurdālān* and the other when she had been immersed—with instructions to fly to the Himalayas to inform Śiva that his wife was beginning the journey home. Unlike the practices of today, where images are manually immersed by crowds at the riverbank, rich families would hire two boats and balance their image of the Goddess on bamboo stilts between them. When they got to the middle of the river they would pull out the stilts and let her fall. Jagaddhātrī also had her traditional farewell rituals; Chandannagar was known for its night-time *śobhāyātrās*, or processions, in which almost one hundred bearers would carry the biggest images, surrounded by parallel lines of bystanders holding kerosene torches.

Old Bengali Pūjās thus became synonymous with traditionalism, or *banediyānā*, and even among foreigners their reputation was encapsulated in the expression "the three blues": 108 blue lotuses (*nīlpadma*) offered during the worship; blue-throated birds (*nīlkaṇṭha pākhī*) released on the tenth day; and blue blood (*nīlrakta*) of aristocratic families.[85] The saying "The *Caṇḍī* [reciting the 'Devī-Māhātmya' at the Pūjā], *piṇḍi* [elaborate funeral arrangements], and *kuśaṇḍī* [sacrifices to be performed at a wedding]: these three make up a Brahman"[86] also hints at the class of religious acts into which most people placed Durgā's festival.

It is important however not to homogenize or stereotype the group of people for whom Pūjā sponsorship was an important status marker. Nearly all were *bhadralok*, to be sure, either hereditary gentry or newly wealthy businessmen who came from the middle to upper classes. The majority were also in contact with the British, through employment, trade, or inherited status. Many endeared themselves to the British by their civic-minded behavior, especially when they built English schools, repaired roads in their districts, or distributed food and clothing to the poor.[87] The Shovabazar Debs, the Tagores of Pathuriaghata, and the *rājās* of Burdwan all held powerful positions in the managing committees of Hindu College from the time of its inception. In 1844 Rājā Kālīkṛṣṇa of Shovabazar even wrote an ode to Queen Victoria, which she formally acknowledged.[88] But not all of the gentry liked or benefited from the British, and many of them were strident opponents of British meddling in Hindu custom. Nandakumār Rāy, the goddess-devotee *dewān* of Bengal, Orissa, and Bihar, was hanged in 1775 by Lord Hastings for his alleged part in a conspiracy against the Company, and Prāṇkṛṣṇa Hāldār, the man whose entertainments were described in the first paragraph of this chapter, was transported for forgery in 1829.

Rādhākānta Deb (1783–1867), son of Gopīmohan Deb and grandson of Nabakṛṣṇa Deb of the Shovabazar estates, is perhaps the best example of this combination of modern and conservative traits that characterized most of the influential members of Hindu society in the early to mid nineteenth century. He knew English no less well than Ram Mohan Roy, sat on the Executive Committee of Hindu College, helped establish the Calcutta School Society to spread education, was a special friend of David Hare, acted as president for sixteen years of the pro-zamindar British Indian Association, and encouraged his women to loosen purdah restrictions. However, he was a staunch supporter of the Dharma Sabhā,[89] which opposed the Widow Remarriage Act, and he attacked the abolition of *sati*, petitioned against the anti-polygamy bill, persuaded the Chief Magistrate to lift the ban on religious processions in the Calcutta streets, and tried to abrogate the Lex Loci bill, which gave Christian converts the right of inheritance. Although he was decorated by the British with a Knight Commander of the Star of India medal, in the obituary that appeared in the *Calcutta Review*, his religious "shortcomings" were noted: the "superstitious element which had been mild in his father, Rajah Gopeemohan, and torpid in his uncle, Rajah Rajkissen, assumed in him an aggressive development."[90] One is reminded of the complex and sometimes uneasy relationship between the British and the native elite in the song still sung by members of the prestigious Hatkhola Datta family as they return to the house from the immersion of the Goddess on the tenth day: "*Banga āmār jananī āmār*" ("My Bengal is my mother"), probably a nationalist holdover from the colonial period.[91]

But what about the vast majority of Bengali Hindus, those not wealthy enough to worship the Goddess in this flashy manner? In the seventeenth and eighteenth centuries such people could "go to their neighbors' houses; there are at least one of these celebrations in every quarter of town, so that everyone can pay their devotions."[92] Balthazar Solvyns' painting of Durgā Pūjā from 1808–1812 reflects this passive, almost voyeuristic posture of the poor, who stand meekly to one side of the picture, watching the scene. Scope for Bengalis of few means to participate actively, as sponsors, in the Pūjā did not widen until the early twentieth century, with the *sarbajanīn* Pūjās; the earlier *bāroiyārī* Pūjā from 1790, while enlarging the base of festival patronage, did so only among friends already from the middle to upper classes. Throughout all such changes—one might say especially because of such changes—however, the monied families continued to maintain and champion their traditional customs. The nationalist politician Bipin Chandra Pal recalled proudly of his childhood in the 1860s that only five families in his village had the means to conduct the Pūjā in its full form—although he added that his family always fed Muslims and Untouchables, in addition to Brahmans.[93] Haimabatī Sen, a child widow who rose to become a doctor, wrote of her marriage at the age of ten to a forty-five-year-old man in 1876 that her family chose the groom because he was a deputy magistrate, two of his brothers were police officers, they had a brick house, and they were wealthy enough to celebrate the worship of Durgā at home.[94] For an elderly gentleman reminiscing about his youth in the 1880s, Pūjās were "primarily individualistic and proprietary. No Bengali family acquired respectability even in its own eyes until it had its private Puja. Going to the Barwari or collective function was decidedly plebeian,"[95] and certainly not in conformity with the scriptures.[96] In spite of this dominance of the monied classes, one can glean a hint of the way in which the not-so-well-off may have tried to manipulate the wealthy to their own advantage: one finds, in the early- and mid-nineteenth-century sources, references to people thrusting goddess images into each others' houses, to force them to perform a Pūjā.[97]

That Durgā was not primarily a deity of the common people—at least not in her form as the demon-slayer during Pūjā time—is further demonstrated by popular rhymes, songs, and sayings, in most of which Durgā and her festival are ciphers for pretension. Bikāśkānti Midyā has made a study of these sayings, and all of the examples he provides poke sarcastic fun at people who, by aspiring to the performance of the Pūjā, show a misguided judgment of their social station: "At their birth they didn't even have a small *pūjā,* and now they're worshipping the ten-armed Goddess?!" (they are overstepping their bounds; they are conceited); "There's no corn or hemp in the house, but the name of the boy is Durgārām" (he has a highfalutin' name, but not the wealth to match); "At Durgā Pūjā you are only ringing the bell, and at Ṣaṣṭī Pūjā you are playing the drums" (you are doing too little when you should be doing more, and too much when you should be doing less); "Durgā's festival should not wait for betel nut and betel leaf" (do not be concerned with inessentials); and he has done everything "from sewing shoes to reading the *Caṇḍī*" (all kinds of jobs, from the lowest to the highest). Even the Goddess herself in these rhymes and aphorisms is symbolic of arrogance or selfishness: "The girl is extravagant, like Durgā" (someone who throws what she has to the winds); and "O Gopāl's grandson! You have brought home a girl as beautiful as Durgā, but she'll *act* like Durgā too" (i.e., as a belligerent daughter-in-law). "A popular story explains why Gaṇeśa never married. It is said that he once planned to marry, but came home one day and found that his two-armed mother had sprouted ten arms. 'Why, mother?' he asked. 'If your wife [*bau*] doesn't feed me, I am going to store up food for myself with my ten hands.' What son could hear that and still want to marry?"[98]

These sayings help to confirm the point of this chapter: Durgā Pūjā was initiated, built up, and enthusiastically promulgated by upper-class families who used the festivities as occasions to express and if possible to raise their social status.

## Still the Three Blues: Old Family Pūjās Today

Almost no one can maintain the same standards as in the bygone days, although most old families have a common bond in their desperate clinging to a nostalgic past.[99] They are a "generation of caretakers" who "exalt [sic] in being the privileged custodians of a legacy that has seen the city through all its heights and lows, since the transient 19th century."[100] *Rājās* are gone, their processions and royal elephants have disappeared, and the fabulous wealth that enabled such opulent displays is part of a lamented past. Nevertheless, as far as possible aristocratic families keep up the old traditions, jealously guarding their reputations for affluence, their figurative status of royalty, and their devotion to the Goddess, who is typically Durgā but sometimes also Jagaddhātrī.[101] Nowadays Pūjās celebrated in the homes of the wealthy (or once wealthy) are called *banedi bāḍīr* Pūjās, or traditional family Pūjās; this differentiates them from the community, or *sarbajanīn,* Pūjās.[102] Bāsantī Mitra, born into the Hatkhola Datta family but married into the Darjipara Mitra family, says—proudly—that in all her sixty years of doing the family Pūjā, she has never once been outside the house to see the street festivities.[103]

One can see the concern to project an image of prosperity in the renovations and repaintings or redecoratings of family *ṭhākurdālāns*; in the gold jewelry, precious stones, and silk clothes that adorn their images of Durgā or Jagaddhātrī; and in the many types of traditional food offered to the Goddess and her devotees during the three main days of the festival. Families whom I interviewed during the course of my research were always eager to explain their traditions regarding *naibedya* (uncooked rice, fruits, ghee, and sweets placed on large platters before the Goddess), *bhog* (cooked food, including vegetables, luchis (deep fried bread), fish, and even meat, depending on the family, but not generally rice, all of which is offered to the Goddess and then consumed by the family), and other foods prepared for the public. All such cooking is done either by the women of the household, if they are Brahmans, or by hired male Brahmans.[104] This ensures the purity of the food and the ability of all, from low-caste family host to high-caste outside guest, to partake of it.[105]

These celebrations are costly, even for those families whose ancestors had the foresight to establish a trust for the defraying of expenses or who divide up the costs among lines or branches of the family by turns (*pālās*). I interviewed all the famed Pūjā-sponsoring houses in Kolkata in 2000, and their annual festival costs ranged from Rs. 5,000 to Rs. 1 lakh. The Thanthania Dattas, Shovabazar Debs, Rāmdulāl Des, and Janbazar Hājrās appear to spend the most, although, interestingly, some lesser-known families, such as the Malliks of Darpanarayan Tagore Street and the Dawns in Darjipara, also expend Rs. 60,000–80,000 per year. Several of the senior family members with whom I spoke evinced pride in the financial burdens they and their relatives shoulder; they are not, they said, like the organizers of the big-budget *sarbajanīn* Pūjā committees, whose purses are filled through public subscription or corporate advertising.[106]

Most families told me that although they have had to dispense with many customs, like theatrical or dance entertainments, they still try to maintain, even in diminished form, the important—and I would add, symbolically significant—rites or *niyams*. The *kāṭhāmo* is still consecrated on Rath or Ulṭo Rath Din; those who can, make the bathing of the *kalā bau* as elaborate as possible at the river steps (fig. 1.2); some families still fire rifles at *sandhi pūjā*;[107] almost all interviewees said that their priests adhere to the ritual prescriptions of the *Bṛhannandikeśvara Purāṇa*, which are more complicated than those used by priests hired for the community Pūjās; as a whole these families are much more scrupulous in engaging priests for ritualized readings of texts such as the "Devī-Māhātmya," the *Rāmāyaṇa*, and the Vedas, after which there is occasionally a formal Paṇḍit Bidāy, or Felicitation of the Scholars, in which Brahmans are given cash gifts; many families continue to sacrifice animals in their house courtyards; a number do *kumārī pūjā*;[108] a smaller number perform *dhuno pūjā*; and still fewer release blue-throated birds (fig. 1.3). Because of strict environmental protection laws, it is now illegal to buy or sell wild birds, so those families who want to alert Śiva in the traditional way that his wife is on her way home must buy the birds from the black market, at Rs. 800–1,000 per bird.[109]

FIGURE 1.2. Bathing the *kalā bau*. Kolkata, October 2000. Photo by Jayanta Roy.

Almost none of these *niyams* can be practiced by the leaders of the community Pūjās, a fact of which the scions of the old family Pūjās are proudly aware. When I asked them how their worship of the Goddess differed from that done in the public arena, they mentioned other juxtapositions as well: the image of Durgā in the *sarbajanīn* Pūjā pandals looks like a film star, whereas "ours inspires reverence and even awe"[110] (see chapter 4); there is always noise, microphones blaring film songs in the streets, whereas "our celebrations are more somber and conservative";[111] and while the community Pūjā organizers are influenced by a desire for prizes (see chapter 5), the *banedi bāḍīr* Pūjās are not.[112] Indeed, *utsāha*, or ardor, and *niṣṭhā*, or devotion to the ritual and its true religious meaning, were consistent themes in the self-descriptions of the people with whom I spoke. Two of the women in the major line of the Shovabazar Rāj family said that they consider their *ṭhākurdālān* a *pīṭhasthān*, or a holy seat of the Goddess, and told me quite clearly, "We have more *niṣṭhā* than anyone else."[113] There is a further expression of satisfaction in the careful adherence to ritual purity laws, even if they are exclusionary. Mr. Alok Kṛṣṇa Deb, of the Shovabazar Rāj estate, said, referring to the Goddess, "We don't touch her; we're not Brahmans."[114]

Looking back over the four hundred years for which we have definite evidence of Durgā Pūjā sponsorship in Bengal, the number of home Pūjās

FIGURE 1.3.
Releasing the *nīlkaṇṭha pākhī*. Kolkata, Daśamī day, October 1999.
Photo by Jayanta Roy.

of the *banedi* variety is undoubtedly decreasing, relative to the total number of celebrations.[115] This has been due both to the break-up of joint families and to a steady decline in zamindari fortunes since 1793, up through and including the zamindari abolition acts of the 1950s and 1960s[116] and the Communist attempts to redistribute land since the mid-1960s. The traditional family Pūjās once acted as adhesives for the community; local artisans and various dependents would work for the zamindar's Pūjā in return for payment taken from the Goddess's *naibedya*,[117] and neighborhood folk would come to watch and participate in some of the rituals. Now these are more private, and it is the community Pūjās that generally cater to public demands.[118]

But there is a role for the old family Pūjās in Bengal today, a role clearly visible to everyone, zamindari descendant and "average" Bengali alike. There is tremendous public nostalgia for and pride in these once-illustrious houses, for they are envisaged to perpetuate the past and to embody the essence of traditional values. Moreover, they function as cultural mascots, markers of national Bengali identity, and reminders of a special heritage. The West Bengal Tourist Office recognizes these cultural valences and organizes a very popular seasonal *banedi bāḍīr* bus tour, which takes *darśan*-seekers through eight to ten of the most prestigious Pūjās houses on each of the main days of the festival. One of these is the residence of the venerable Sābarṇa Rāy Caudhurīs.[119] They have so little money that their *ṭhākurdālān* is in a completely dilapidated state (*bhagnadaśā*), with only the outside columns still standing. Nevertheless, people flock to this site. Families so honored enjoy the status this affords, with newcomers to the bus tour list especially pleased by their inclusion. For instance, Mr. Bhaskar Chunder, whose house has been included on the itinerary since 1999, has prepared a special leaflet for tourists that explains the venerable history of his lineage. In fact, the more people wandering through one's premises at Pūjā time, the better. Mr. Priya Gopāl Hājrā told me proudly that two to three thousand people visit the Rāṇī Rasmaṇī house every day during Durgā Pūjā.[120] In the office of the Rāmdulāl De estate, which boasts by far the most impressive of the *ṭhākurdālāns* I saw in Kolkata, in terms of upkeep and grandeur, the senior member of the family, Mr. Kalyāṇkumār Deb, enunciated the reasons for the popularity of his and other traditional celebrations: "There's a craze now to see these old family Pūjās—a sentimental desire."[121] A BBC television documentary on Lord Robert Clive was filmed in 2001 in the Shovabazar Rāj estate, with Mr. Alok Kṛṣṇa Deb playing the part of his illustrious forebear and Clive's contemporary, Nabakṛṣṇa Deb; pride in this heritage overshadows censure of the unprincipled British adventurer who extorted so much from Bengal.[122]

For it is not just the families themselves who gain from their traditions. The public yearns for them, feels pride in them, and rewards their sponsors with conferred status. Newspapers always feature numerous stories about the *banedi bāḍīr* Pūjās, complete with photographs and interviews, and the reporters inevitably compose paeans about their significance and importance to community history. These traditional Pūjās are "not only ancient, but also Bengal's heritage (*aitihya*) and the fountain of our glory (*gauraber dhārāk*)." They "are now very elite, and a matter of pride, especially if they stick to their inherited traditions."[123] A few years ago the newspapers even reported public attempts by the citizens of Bishnupur to resuscitate, via subscription, the Durgā Pūjā to Devī Mṛnmayī that the Malla *rājas* once so lavishly celebrated. Why? The traditional Pūjā is Bishnupur's "pride and glory (*garimā*)."[124] As David Lowenthal argues in *The Past Is a Foreign Country*, reviving—or manufacturing—events from our past and putting our own stamp on them makes us feel more at home with our heritage and is integral to our sense of identity.[125]

Another expression of this craze for the past is evident in the pandal themes chosen by the leaders of the community Pūjās. Since the mid-1990s one can see a burgeoning of interest in zamindari-house look-alikes, with traditional images of the Goddess and her children displayed inside. Some Pūjā organizers even hire artisans to recreate homes that are dilapidated and falling apart, mimicking the feel of the fading aristocratic glory most Bengalis see around them.[126] If ordinary people cannot be zamindars themselves, then they can, with their neighborhood, imaginatively reconstruct that lifestyle for the five days of the Pūjā season.

As chapter 3 will argue more fully, one can interpret the Bengali feeling for Pūjā traditionalism through the lens of cultural nostalgia. If nostalgia is defined as a romanticized "orientation toward the past as a time of value and meaning," where "what is authentic . . . is what is past,"[127] then the present mania among the Bengali public for honoring and finding pride in the aristocratic family Pūjās of their cities and towns, as well as their efforts to recreate zamindari homes in their own community pandals, can be understood as a nostalgic longing. Durgā becomes synonymous with cultural identity, an icon from the past that can come to stand for one's entire lost self.[128] Just as in Britain, where the heritage preservation movement began in the 1970s with the wealthy upper classes, whose country houses and estate lands were threatened by Labor government laws and heavy taxation, but was supported by the middle-class, country-house-visiting public for whom the allure of a fading national grandeur was worth paying money to preserve,[129] so also in Bengal: the vast majority of the people being ferried around by the West Bengal Tourist buses to the opened *ṭhākurdālāns* of this or that renowned Pūjā-sponsoring family have no link to the lifestyle of those whose traditions they admire. One could even say that they have no personal "memories" of such grandeur in their family backgrounds. And yet, as the work of Christian Novetzke, following Jan Assmann and others, has shown, memories, whether historically viable or not, are socially bonding and constitutive of community identity. Memory "gives back; it restores the connection severed by the lapse of time and returns the observer to the immediacy of an event. Memory is the site of continuity."[130] In the words of Svetlana Boym, this is a "restorative nostalgia," which "proposes to rebuild the lost home and patch up the memory gaps, . . . [manifesting] itself in total reconstructions of monuments of the past."[131] Hence even though very few members of the middle class in Bengal would want to return to a world of overt feudalism, what is admired as a part of aristocratic zamindari culture is the sense of family cohesiveness, leisure, devotion, and community caring that their Pūjās supposedly engendered, and to which the middle class also aspires. Even fifty years ago, people were ruing the passing of these old customs. Nirad C. Chaudhuri, writing in 1953 about his young days, reminisced that the old-style Pūjās were more social, were more expressive of their links to agricultural cycles, and, because of their slower pace, drew out human sentiments more.[132] "Sanjay," in the *Sunday Statesman Magazine* for September 1954, agreed: because the Pūjās are now community efforts, they are shorn of human emotion; entertainment becomes the chief motive. These elements represent "symptoms of a coarsening of sensibility and an acceptance of vulgarity."[133] Whether or not these memories represent true experiences, their currency today guarantees health for the aristocratic-prestige market, the tourism business, and artisans who excel in constructing pandals in the shape of old mansions. For nostalgia is profitable, and reflects vested interests.

There is therefore a self-perpetuating feedback loop between elite families and the public. The *niṣṭhā* that is reportedly characteristic of the *banedi bāḍīr* Pūjās may certainly be genuine; I have met some extremely earnest devotees of the Goddess among the families whom I interviewed. But such faith is also, if visible and recognized by a public that longs to be made proud by means of the traditionalism of its cultural guardians, a symbolic asset to be protected and aggrandized. In this, *niṣṭhā* also constrains. Community Pūjās may be as novel and as modern as the imaginations of their organizers can manage, but the public demands, as an anchor amid the frenzied changes of the streets, traditional homes in which the Goddess still represents their own desired pasts.

# 2 The Goddess in Colonial and Postcolonial History

The celebration of the Śākta Pūjās to Durgā, Jagaddhātrī, and Kālī certainly predates the arrival of European merchant-traders and colonialists in Bengal, but not by a great deal. One could in fact argue that it was the presence of the British that provided the initial impetus for the festivals' development into the characteristic forms we see today, with goddesses worshiped in temporary temples, or pandals, placed to the side of public urban thoroughfares. This chapter covers the entire period of British rule in Bengal—from the mid-eighteenth century until 1947 and beyond—illustrating the history of English–Indian relations in miniature, through the lens of the Pūjās. How did the various, and changing, British attitudes toward Indians, Bengalis, Hindus, Muslims, festivals, rulership, and intercommunity mixing affect their perspectives on the Pūjās? And how did Bengali choices regarding Pūjā sponsorship and organization reflect their views of British suzerainty in Bengal? As is indicated in the wealth of information to be found in old newspapers, English and Bengali, from the 1780s until Independence and after, attitudes to the Pūjās, whether by Europeans or Bengalis, varied considerably, not only over time but also across constituency.[1] Newspapers reflecting the opinions of East India Company officials tended to differ from those of the mercantile, banking, and "pro-native" Englishmen, all of whom differed from each other and from Christian missionary publications. Likewise, Indian-owned and -run papers, printed sometimes in Bengali and sometimes in English, expressed a multitude of opinions: those of the Brāhmo Samāj; the orthodox, anti-reforming pandits; and nationalists, whether "Moderate" or "Extreme." That there never was one monolithic "British" perspective on India, or one "Hindu" response to it, is amply demonstrated by a glance at the developmental history of the Pūjās. There is one constant, however, and that is the Janus-faced nature of the Pūjā symbol, which always looks both ways, reflecting to its British and Indian interpreters what is occurring in the public, political, and interethnic spheres.

## Early Interactions: The Late Eighteenth Century to 1858

### *Uncontested Patronage, Unabashed Delight*

On tables heaped, reveal their varied charms,
Porcelain from France and England glittering o'er . . .
And from the ceilings droop stupendous lustres,
And girandoles and chandeliers, that vie
With wall shades stuck around in sparkling clusters,
Which Doorga, often, for her annual nautches musters. [2]

A survey of Calcutta newspaper reports on Durgā Pūjā confirms the rough periodizations regarding the shifting relations between Indians and Europeans given by scholars such as David Kopf and Sumanta Banerjee[3]: in general, from the time of Plassey in 1757 until the coming of Lord William Bentinck (1828–1835) as the East India Company's governor-general, British policy toward Indian religious and social customs was fairly relaxed. This period also coincided with the liberal, acculturative intellectual programs of Warren Hastings (1772–1784) and Marquess Richard Wellesley (1798–1805), who tried to encourage British civil servants to form friendships with Bengalis and to learn their languages and culture. Indeed, early Europeans were primarily military and mercantile in orientation, and were not themselves terribly religious; in fact, it was crucial to their trading and ruling concerns that matters of religion *not* jeopardize their relationships with the Hindus and Muslims in their territories. Accordingly, they resorted to various means to conciliate those with whom they traded and whom they ruled, among which was a readiness to patronize Hindu and

Muslim religions. For instance, they took over the organization of Hindu temples, collected pilgrim taxes for their running, visited Hindu places of pilgrimage, and occasionally even worshiped Hindu deities. Such policies of appeasement are reflected in generally positive attitudes toward the Pūjās, characterized in an 1831 news item describing the visit at Durgā Pūjā of the vice president of the Company to the house of Nabakṛṣṇa Deb and his two grandsons at Shovabazar. "From these marks of favor conferred on the Rajas year after year by the Rulers . . . nothing is more clear than that the Government endears itself to his Britannic Majesty's Hindoo Subjects."[4]

As we have seen in chapter 1, the zamindars of this period welcomed—even fought with each other over—British visitations to their houses during the festivals. Pūjā hosts whose open invitations to their homes recur repeatedly in the British newspapers in these early decades include Gobindarām Mitra of Kumartuli; Shovabazar's Nabakṛṣṇa Deb (as well as his sons Gopimohan and Rājkṛṣṇa and grandsons Rādhākānta and Kālīkṛṣṇa); Pathuriaghata's Nīlmaṇi and Baiṣṇabdās Mallik; Borobazar's Nimāicānd Mallik; Āśutoṣ De of Simla; Sukhamay Rāy and his son Rāmcandra of Shukhbazar; Darpanārāyaṇ Ṭhākur; Rūplāl Mallik of Chitpore Road; Bābu Benoylāl Tagore; and Prāṇkṛṣṇa Hāldār of Chinsurah. Interestingly, newspapers of the time never contain invitations from the Sābarṇa Rāy Caudhurī family, who apparently even in the early nineteenth century resented the British presence in Bengal.[5]

Up until the 1830s, Europeans enjoyed themselves thoroughly—and unabashedly—at the Pūjā celebrations in honor of Durgā and, to a lesser extent, Jagaddhātrī.[6] As early as 1766, J. Z. Holwell described Durgā Pūjā as "the grand general feast of the *Gentoos*, usually visited by all *Europeans* (by invitation) who are treated by the proprietor of the feast with fruits and flowers in season, and are entertained every evening whilst the feast lasts, with bands of singers and dancers."[7] English papers such as the *Calcutta Gazette*, the *Calcutta Journal*, and the *Bengal Hurkaru* did not simply print invitations from the Hindu aristocracy; British reporters themselves announced the festivities and urged their compatriots to attend. "In a word, if the reader be one who has never witnessed the magnificent spectacle of a Doorgah Poojah in Calcutta, we can only assure him that he will find the splendid fiction of the Arabian Nights completely realized in the Fairy Palace of Rajah Ramchunder Roy, on the evenings of the 26th, 27th, and 28th instant."[8]

Indeed, the British commented favorably, even enthusiastically, on the "pomp and magnificence," the "splendid arrangements and well regulated expenses," the food, drink, and dancing, and the "wonder mixed with delight" they felt upon seeing scenes "grand beyond description" in the

FIGURE 2.1. William Prinsep, "Entertainment during the Durga Puja," 1840. Pl. 25 in J. P. Losty,

*Calcutta, City of Palaces: A Survey of the City in the Days of the East India Company, 1690–1858* (London: Arnold Publishers, 1990).

"native" houses[9] (fig. 2.1). They also appreciated the reverence and hospitality shown them by their Bengali hosts. Said Mary Graham about her visit to the "fine house" of Rājā Rājkṛṣṇa Deb in 1810, "I was pleased with the attention the Rajah paid to his guests, whether Hindoos, Christians, or Mussalmans; there was no one to whom he did not speak kindly or pay some compliment on their entrance; and he walked around the assembly repeatedly, to see that all were properly accommodated. I was sorry I could not go the nautch the next night."[10] In 1825 the *Bengal Hurkaru* printed an editorial in which a British gentleman commented, "I went the first night and assure you I was much gratified," and then urged everyone else to go as well.[11] This unselfconscious British pleasure in the Pūjās, in which opulence, grandeur, and occasions for excess were provided and enjoyed, extended late into the nineteenth century.

Although one can find occasional reference to Durgā herself in European newspapers or travel diaries—L. de Grandpre from 1789–1790 and Maria Graham from 1810 both note that the clay statues of "Madam Doorgah" and her children were placed on a stage or a raised verandah inside the mansions[12]—she was rarely the focus of attention and was treated as a quaint sideshow vis-à-vis the main entertainments. This was not, of course, true for the Hindu hosts who opened their homes to the British. In addition to garnering prestige among their peers for the lavishness of their festival arrangements and the number of European guests whose praise they earned, Pūjā-sponsoring zamindars, even if working for the British, also tended to be religiously traditional. Their British guests simply did not understand what Durgā meant.

## *The Impact of Missionary, Reforming, and Anglicizing Critiques*

*. . . Offering incense to a God*
*Nothing but a painted clod.*[13]

Durgā and her sister goddesses, as well as a host of Hindu deities especially including Jagannātha at Puri, were very much at the center of the social and political changes evident in Bengal in the third decade of the nineteenth century. The Company's early policy of noninterference, encapsulated by Gov.-Gen. Charles Cornwallis's Regulations of 1793, in which he had promised to "preserve the laws of the Shaster and the Koran, and to protect the natives of India in the free exercise of their religion"[14]—in effect implying that the British could know the society they ruled without sharing in it or revolutionizing it—came under Christian critique almost immediately. Some Christians, like Charles Grant, were in the Company's Court of Directors, but most were missionaries, like Baptists William Carey and John Marshman, who strove after 1793 to overturn the Company's ban on missionary presence and to gain unrestricted entry into India.[15] Carey and his fellow missionaries at Serampore near Calcutta used their English and Bengali papers, *The Friend of India* and *Samācār Darpaṇ*, to claim that the Cornwallis Code should not be taken literally. After 1805, when the Company imposed the pilgrim tax at Puri, supposedly for the upkeep of the Jagannātha temple, Christian missionaries, company chaplains, and former officials began to take their cause back to England, where public opinion was formed, nursed, and inflamed by letters, travelogues, exposés of returning military men, and even the circulation of public petitions. By 1813 Evangelical petitions to Parliament had resulted in a clause in the Company's Charter Renewal Act that admitted the principle of missionary activity in India. But since this was not mandated, and was left up to the local government, missionaries continued to be liable to cold-shouldering in or deportation from India.[16]

By the 1830s Europeans associated with the British reform movement began to arrive in India, people like Thomas Macaulay (arrived in 1834), the Scottish missionary Alexander Duff (arrived in 1830), and Governor-General Bentinck, all of whom believed that what was progressive for the West should be exported to the East. However, change did not occur immediately. Even Bentinck, famous for his criminalizing of sati in 1829, attempted suppression of the Thugs, diminishment of Wellesley's College of Fort William, and replacement of Persian with English as the language of the courts in 1835, decreed in 1831 that his duty was to protect, not interfere with, Indian custom; he refused to bend to missionary pressure to abolish either slavery or the pilgrim tax (the latter being quite lucrative for the Company), and he would not force Hindus and Muslims to work on their religious holidays. Declaring that the government ought to show "a friendly feeling and . . . afford every protection and aid toward the exercise of . . . harmless rites . . . not contrary to the dictates of humanity and of every religious creed,"[17] Bentinck regularly attended the Pūjā celebrations at the Shovabazar Rāj estates.[18]

But at the end of the 1830s utilitarian and evangelical criticisms in London combined to mandate change in Company policy. After the famous Dispatch in 1838, spearheaded by the two sons of Charles Grant, who claimed that intervention in Indian religious custom implied tacit approval of those customs that was unseemly and hypocritical for Christians, Parliament insisted that the Company dissociate itself from religious festivals, temples, and endowments. Full separation of the British from "idolatrous" rites, however, was effected only in 1863, when the government, now the British Crown, passed an act that could be enforced.[19]

This gradually evolving sea change in British attitudes toward Indian religion is reflected as if by script in the Pūjā festivities. While one looks hard to find even one or two criticisms of the festivals in the period before 1820, after this an increasing crescendo of critique leads eventually to the problematization of European attendance at the nautches. New values, characteristic of Protestant sobriety and utilitarian moderation and simplicity, caused Britons in Calcutta to begin viewing the Pūjā extravagances in a different light. Now judged to be decadent, immoderate, without taste, and obsessed with the pursuit of name and fame through the wasteful squandering of wealth, Pūjā sponsors were challenged instead to spend their money on something socially useful, like philanthropic charity. Some British commentators remarked wryly that they themselves might be responsible for the "natives"' gaudy opulence, since "the more general diffusion of wealth and security for property introduced by the English government has contributed greatly to this change."[20] But, they continue, there is fault on the Indian side as well, since the showy pretenses of the Pūjā belie the degradation of the Hindu religion: Hindus have forgotten "the monotheistic spirit of the Vedas" and have favored immoral ostentation over sincere devotion, ritual over scripture;[21] moreover, in allowing "Moosulman singing women" (later called prostitutes) into their mansions, and in serving meat and liquor, which goes against their own creed, they had ruined their faith.[22] One can immediately recognize these early British tropes, as discussed historically and theoretically by Bernard Cohn, Richard King, David Lorenzen, Arvind-Pal Mandair, Thomas Metcalf, Brian Pennington, and Sharada Sugirtharajah: the assumption that Hindus and Muslims have, or should maintain, separate and non-intersecting spheres, governed by "creeds"; the degeneration of religion; the nostalgia for the perceived Golden Age of Hinduism, partly constructed by the British through their selective search for the "classical" in Hindu history; and the valuation of the rational, ethical, and private over the ritualistic, effervescent, and public forms of religion.[23]

In addition to financial and moral profligacy and the departure from tradition, Hindus were accused of idolatry, their worship compared to outmoded "Old Testament" practices. Missionaries tried to impress upon the minds of their British readers that mixing with Hindus at the nautches was in effect doing Durgā honor.[24] "We must not forget that the disbursement of money from the funds of Government to perform the worship of the 'Belly God,' however insignificant it may appear[,] produces an equally false and pernicious impression on the minds of the Natives. For the preservation of our national honor and our Christian dignity, the system of affording public patronage to idolatry must be entirely demolished."[25] This theme of dignity is ubiquitous in the late 1820s and 1830s, and accounts in large part for the strenuous attempts of missionary and other sober-minded Britons to stop their compatriots from shaming the entire foreign community in front of the "natives" by their bad behavior at the Pūjās. "We regret that these hospitable 'spectacles' given by the native gentlemen are so frequently abused. We are sorry to state that four Europeans carried off a buggy, which was yesterday morning found broken in pieces, and the horse discovered in a street tied to a post!"[26] Although sometimes the scandalous behavior was exhibited by people who ought to know better—the *Friend of India* reported disapprovingly of a Mrs. Atkinson dancing publicly in the house of Gopimohan Deb of Shovabazar[27]—often English-newspaper editorials betray European class schisms, with "polite" society frowning upon the raucous and unmannered deportment of the lower orders.[28]

In a splendid poem from 1829, a British writer describes Britons who attend the festivals as idolaters, hypocrites, and low-class sops:

Infidels to England's God, —
Doorgah's mysteries may applaud —
Or, bowing, may before her stand, —
Lords of a holy Christian land. —
And others who would fairly go —
To Latin for a *quid pro quo* —
Religion, with such men as these
You may rely on is — Rupees . . .

Petty fops, with spurs and boots —
Uniform that any suits —
Pert un-civil clerks who then
Put aside for once their pen
Youngsters of all sorts and hues,
Indians, English, French and Jews
Saturated with champaign —

May *we* never meet again.[29]

Missionaries endeavored to suggest new ways of intercommunity mixing that did not lend themselves to shameful antics—"conversation parties," for instance, in order that the "Natives be brought under the full power of the courtesy and intelligence of superior minds"[30]—and the anti-Indian, anti-missionary, pro-military *Englishman* tried to provoke its readers into eschewing the Pūjā festivities by printing a fabricated letter demonstrating the horrifying results of interracial mixing. Writes Ramchunder Chingree: "Then in few time no difference in country. Black people white people—black dancer, white dancer, all same. Glory to Bramah and Gopee Mohun Deb. Now all same equal people and Free Press is the great commission."[31] That even by the late 1830s there were varied British responses to the issue of Pūjā attendance is illustrated by a flurry of letter and counter-letter writing in 1839: a writer for the *Englishman* proffered the opinion that attending the nautches was an opportunity to reform the Hindu aristocracy, while the *Bengal Hurkaru*, often pro-Indian, urged the propriety of supporting the idolatry of the country through the resources of the state as a restitution for the murder and spoliation inflicted upon them by British governance. To both of these the *Friend of India* replied that "the best way to make up for wrongs, if there be any, is by giving India the blessing of a Christian Government."[32]

Britons were not the only critics of the Pūjās. Indian Christian converts, Brāhmos, Vedāntins, Derozians, and members of the Hindu Theophilanthropic Society also joined in the attacks. Dakṣiṇrañjan Mukherjee (1814–1898), a Derozian reformer, led a crusade against Pūjā "vulgarities" in his paper, the *Jñānānveṣan*, and Ram Mohan Roy is said to have refused a Pūjā invitation by Dwaraknath Tagore. Dwaraknath's son Debendranath (1817–1905) also later condemned idol worship. Representative of the Brāhmo viewpoint is an editorial in Debendranath's journal, the *Tattvabodhinī Patrikā*, for 1846. Image worship is stated to be mere play-acting by childish people who wish to gain fame by their sponsorship.[33] Point 2 of the Brāhmo Covenant, as formulated by Debendranath, avers, "I will never worship any created object as representing that Supreme Being."[34]

Starting in mid-1820s, several Calcutta papers began congratulating their readers for the diminution in European attendance at the yearly nautches, resulting, they asserted, in a decrease in wasteful spending on the part of wealthy Hindus, purification of their religion, and safe-guarding of British respectability.[35] However, other evidence undercuts their claims;

indeed, one finds continuous reports of Britons enjoying themselves at Pūjā festivities all the way up to and even beyond the 1857 revolt. From 1846: "If the sermon, last Sunday, at the Scotch Kirk, has had any effect in deterring parties from attending the nautches given by the rajahs during the present native festival, it has been of an extremely partial nature. For the last two nights, the house of the Rajahs Radhakant and Shiva Krishna—but especially of the former—have been thronged by Christians, many of them men of rank and standing in Society. . . . The visitors, on both occasions, were equally numerous and respectable, members of the Military Service and the Legal Profession forming a large portion of the whole."[36] In an unsuspected twist, some British attendees even mourned the lavishness of the "old days," the beauty and sensuousness of the former dancing girls—"Niku is lost, and lies in the cold grave without a successor . . . Where are [her] rich tones, [her] unequaled music?"[37]—while others, as late as 1855, are clamoring for invitations, so that they do not miss the Pūjā fun: "[P]eople of all classes are being responded to in the [Shovabazar] Rajahs' usual kind and liberal spirit. We hear that the services of the 'Wizard of the North' have been engaged for both nights."[38]

In spite of the continued enthusiasm into the mid-nineteenth century of much of British society for the most famed Pūjās, it does appear that Hindus whose celebrations were smaller or less noted did begin, from the 1830s, to close their doors to British guests.[39] Some Indians appear to have been persuaded by British and Brāhmo arguments condemning opulence, religious degeneration, and debauchery; others, squeezed by British mercantile and business interference, and affected by the collapse of traditional patronage systems after the Permanent Settlement of 1793, simply became too poor to throw parties. Such impoverishment of the "natives" rarely finds acknowledgment in the British press, and when it does it is attributed not to the imperialist economy but to Indians' "injudicious spending."[40] Hence the Pūjās were symbolic of the relations between Indians and Britons in several ways: they provided the means for intercommunity prestige and muscle-flexing; they represented, to both Hindu and Briton, the essence of Hindu tradition, either to be reformed, transformed, dissociated from, or protected; and they fell victim to ideological and economic changes wrought throughout the colonial state in Bengal.[41]

To illustrate just how central the Pūjās were to the continuing negotiations over Hindu–British relations in the early decades of the nineteenth century, we should briefly examine the controversy over vacation days that erupted in 1834. In 1793, when the judiciary courts were first introduced in

Bengal, Cornwallis apparently consulted the relevant pandits and chose, in his Regulation III, section 1, of that same year, to "frame the list of holidays in the public offices according to the religious prejudices and customs of the inhabitants."[42] In July of 1834, however, the Bank of Bengal—allowing itself to be swayed by business and merchant petitions—announced that bank holidays would be reduced from 34 to 16, effectively cutting out, among other holidays, Kālī Pūjā.[43] The Hindu reaction was swift: an outpouring of letters to the government, claiming that (a) the bank was bending to the wishes of a few merchants, (b) the government, in turn, was being swayed by the city's financial institutions, and (c) since the bank had not consulted any pandits, how could it know which Hindu holidays were to be kept holy? "Is the religion of the Hindoos to be guided by the bank directors?" Further, the letter-writers countered that (d) such bowing to a Christian lobby was a violation of the impartiality to which the British government had pledged itself; it is barbaric, they stated, to think that "Might constitutes Right."[44] A slew of replies and counter-replies ensued: Englishmen claimed that Hindus too transacted business on holidays when the banks were open; Hindus retorted that their compatriots had been bribed to do so and thanked English merchants who had refrained from using the bank on the Hindu holiday; other merchants came forward to say that they and their agents had indeed been inconvenienced by there being so many bank holidays; Hindus accused the Hindu dewan of the Bank of Bengal, Rām Komal Sen, of pandering to his own Vaiṣṇava leanings by cutting out Kālī Pūjā but retaining Kārtik Pūjā; and Englishmen responded that "Kaly Poojah is *not* incumbent upon Hindoos."[45]

The principles upon which the matter was contested were, for the British, Hindu authenticity and, for the Hindu protesters, British commitment to the ideal of neutrality. Both tried to hold the other to what they believed to be the other's stated precepts, often founded on precedent. For instance, the vice president of the bank announced that the Kālī Pūjā order would be rescinded if it could be shown that to do business on the holiday was a violation of religion. Ultimately, in reply to a petition signed by four hundred Hindu inhabitants and merchants of Calcutta, the government replied that while it could not mandate the closing of all offices on all Hindu holidays, it could allow Hindus to take holidays on those days, provided they understood that in some cases they might have to work. And "we know that the transaction of business does not contradict Hindoo holiday law."[46]

The tussle between productivity and the policy of noninterference in religious custom—between merchants and banks, on the one hand, and government officials (who tended to support "native" sentiment in this period) and Hindus, on the other—was never fully resolved. Although the 1834 proposals were defeated, a perusal of newspapers during the Pūjā season from the 1830s through the end of the nineteenth century indicates just how volatile the issue of holidays continued to be. Until 1861 the total number of Hindu holidays for the year remained at thirty-five days, with the usual twelve for Durgā Pūjā.[47] Even in 1879, when the holidays were reduced to twenty-two days per year, or in 1900, when the Government of India issued orders that Christian holidays and Sundays were necessarily to be observed in all offices, but that Hindu holidays, such as Durgā Pūjā, were up to the discretion of employers, Durgā Pūjā stayed at its full length of twelve days—although some Hindus were required to work part or all of this time.[48] Twice, in the October months of 1840 and 1860, Britons proposed that the Pūjās be moved to Christmastime, when the weather would be better, Christians would be more inclined to support the idea of long holidays, and "Madam Doorgah" would be pleased, as the increased coolness would help invigorate her worshipers.[49] Interestingly, while missionaries occasionally sided with the mercantile position, they appeared to take very little interest in the length of the Pūjā festivities, preferring to concentrate their efforts on dissociating Europeans from attending such idolatrous functions.

The thirty-year period, then, prior to the uprising of 1857, was a time of testing, challenge, and debate, as Anglicizing, Utilitarian, Christianizing attitudes met and sparred *both* with more tolerant, pro-Indian British commitments *and* with Hindu conservatives, who themselves were working to defeat the anti-idolatry programs of the Brāhmo Samāj. The Pūjās were the nexus of these ideological and social fights, accommodations, and dissonances.

## After the Transfer of Power: Evolutions of the Pūjās from 1858 to 1918

### *A Good Excuse for a Holiday: British Experiences up to the Close of the Great War*

*"We have won India, but we have not yet beaten Doorga."*[50]

After the government of India had passed from the East India Company to the British crown in 1858, a clearer, more explicit policy of noninterference in Indian religious and customary law was articulated and followed by Britain. And it appears that almost immediately the Pūjās reflect the new sociopolitical currents. While one can still observe British critiques of Hindu idolatry, irrationality, and the lack of social usefulness as demonstrated in the festivals,[51] overall there is an astonishing change in British attitudes toward the holidays. One writer for the *Bengal Hurkaru* articulated the new rule in 1865: "Our friends would persuade us that absence from business for the period of ten days at the time of the Pooja is to them a necessity of the faith. It is thus that we, the ruling power of the country, have come to look upon the Pooja as a domestic institution, and arrange our own yearly holiday so as to accord with it."[52] Even more poetically, from 1870: "Doorga is supreme, high above all powers and potentates, banks, and custom houses—everything! . . . The holiday is of most importance to us Westerns, or to such of us as can make a holiday; and Doorga is strong enough to secure the holiday as if with a band of iron."[53]

After 1860 evidence abounds that Britons, having accepted the policy of noninterference in the Pūjās, made them a welcome excuse to get away from Calcutta. Newspaper editors bemoaned the fact that they were marooned in the dull, "empty" city that has "gone to sleep for a fortnight in honor of the Doorga poojah festival; at least that portion of Calcutta society which has been unable to transfer itself from the ditch to the heights of Simla or Nynee Tal, or to go down to the Bay, braving a prophesied cyclone in the desire to inhale ozone."[54] Moreover, the English-language papers, such as the *Bengal Hurkaru*, the *Englishman*, and the *Friend of India*, sponsored aggressive advertising campaigns for travel and holiday goods, such as skates, insecticides, pruning knives, sparkling champagne, hats, rugs, picnic baskets, and English boots. There are fewer outcries from the nonmercantile community for the curtailment of the holidays;[55] to the contrary, in 1861 one European inhabitant of Calcutta wrote to say that the fourteen-day office closing that had been granted by the Viceroy to Hindus should be granted to everyone, since even Christians looked forward anxiously to a chance to escape the killing climate.[56]

For those Britons who stayed in the city, interestingly, entertainments proffered especially by the Shovabazar *rājās* continued to be an attraction. The *Englishman*, the *Friend of India*, and the *Statesman and Friend of India* newspapers publicized invitations year after year from the early 1860s until the 1880s. As in the halcyon Pūjā years, writers praise their hosts' music, dancing girls, acrobats, magicians, theater performances, and hospitality. By 1890, however, the mixing seems to have fallen off completely, with the Pūjā connoting vacations and law-and-order problems for the

British, and something both more private and more publicly defended for the Hindu.

## *Hindu Defense and Reconstruction*

*"Who is she?"*
*"The Mother."*
*"Who is this Mother?" asked Mahendra.*
*The monk answered, "She whose Children we are."*
*"Who is she?"*
*"You will know her in time," was the answer. "Now sing Bande Mataram, and follow me."*[57]

The post-1858 half-century was troubled for Britain's Indian subjects. British suspicion of Indians as a result of the "mutiny" only deepened the lines of separation between the two communities, spatially and ideologically; the result was increasing racism and imperialism, coupled with a desire to order, control, and categorize, on the part of the British, and the generation of incipient nationalist feelings, on the part of Indians. For instance, by the 1880s public controversies raged over the 1883 Ilbert Bill, concerning the right of Indian judges to try European cases; the Bengal Tenancy Act, which attempted to redress some of the grievances felt by peasants as a result of the Permanent Settlement of 1793 (zamindars, represented by the British Indian Association, strongly opposed this act); and the growing feeling of political impotence, in spite of apparent advances in local self-government as embodied in the Bengal Municipal Act of 1884 and the Bengal District Board Act of 1885.

Indeed, many Indians were not persuaded by the rhetoric of neutrality and secularity as promulgated by the colonial state, and perceived the government to be Christian, biased, and patently dishonest in its rule. However, we do not get a full-blown nationalism in this period; post-1858 Bengali leaders tended to be *bhadralok*—elite, high-caste, and interested in cultural and religious revivalism. There was no Pūjā news coverage, in English or Bengali, of the years immediately following 1857 that made recourse to politicized Śākta imagery. With very few exceptions, newly formed political organizations, such as the Hindu Sabhā, founded in 1869 by men drawn from the Ādī Brāhmo Samāj and several aristocratic families of Calcutta for the glorification, unity, and improvement of Hinduism, could not yet conceive of complete independence and did not resort to the language of religion to whip up fervor or explain their platforms. The Hindu *melās*, or national festivals, established in 1867 to provide a space for the display of indigenous identity and virility, offered lectures, songs, agricultural produce, animals, birds, machinery, handicrafts, athletic competitions, and plays. But they claimed no overlap with the Pūjās, and did not utilize the language of *śakti*.[58] Satyendranath Tagore's famous song, "Mile sabe Bhāratsantān" ("All together, children of Bhārat"), which he composed for the first *melā*, evoked national pride, but did not yet express hostility toward British rule.

Even the Indian National Congress, founded in 1885 as a loyalist, moderate political institution, was not yet a vehicle for politicized religion. The closest connection I have been able to find between the Congress and the Pūjās is a metaphor from 1887 in which the Congress is a Pūjā to the Motherland, whose ten hands are the ten classes of Indians. She is fighting two anti-Congress demons, the orthodox and reformist Hindus. The English too must be beaten, but by the employment of their own methods and weapons, in a battle on English principles.[59]

That "for the most part, politics and religion were not yet intermingled"[60] can also be seen by examining the overtly religious voluntary organizations that tried to influence the British for social change: the Ādī Brāhmo Samāj and the Sādharan Brāhmo Samāj of Debendranath Tagore and Sivanath Sastri (1847–1919), respectively, which eschewed image worship and, by extension, the Pūjās[61]; and the highly devotional and emotional practices of Keshab Chandra Sen (1839–1884) in his "New Dispensation," where the veneration of the "Mother Divine" as a guiding inspiration was a personal outpouring, not the recourse to an image of a colonized Motherland.[62] The same interiorized perspective on religion is evident in the life of Rāmakṛṣṇa (1836–1886), the Bengali saint of Calcutta; as a temple priest of the goddess Kālī, he performed the Śākta Pūjās yearly and encouraged his disciples to do so as well, all in a nonpoliticized arena of spiritual development.

Bankim Chandra Chatterjee (1838–1894), now considered one of the forerunners of early Indian nationalism for his 1882 novel *Ānandamaṭh*, its theme song, "Bande Mātāram," and its likening of India to a goddess, may come closest to the sort of religious nationalist that we later find in the early twentieth century.[63] The novel depicts a group of citizens-turned-renouncers in the 1770s who are fighting the *nawāb*'s men, and the British, for control of Bengal. They revere both the martial figure of Kṛṣṇa from the *Mahābhārata* and the powerful Goddess, and in their leader's cave they have erected three statues, representing India past (Jagaddhātrī), India present (Kālī), and India future (Durgā). "Victory to the Mother" ("Bande Mātāram") is thus a conflation of the Mother and the Land.

Powerless? How so, Mother
With the strength of voices fell,
Seventy million in their swell!
And with sharpened swords
By twice as many hands upheld!

To the Mother I bow low,
To her who wields so great a force,
To her who saves,
And drives away the hostile hordes![64]

*Bhakti*, image worship, and the ideal of active participation in society were essential to Chatterjee, and he was also a fervent advocate of Indian rights over British arrogance, as can be seen in his excoriating public letters published in the *Statesman* to one W. Hastie, who had critiqued the extravagant funeral ceremony performed at the Shovabazar Rāj estates in September 1882. Writing first under a pseudonym, Chatterjee defended the rituals and then challenged Hastie to learn something about India, not from Europeans but from a "believing Native."[65] Nevertheless, as scholar S. N. Mukherjee points out, Chatterjee was only constructed as the hero of "Extremist" nationalists thirty years after the publication of *Ānandamaṭh*[66]; the mood in the forty years after 1857 was defensive as concerned religion and still hopeful as concerned Moderate politics.

The wealthy Hindu doyen apart, most average Hindus had always, when possible, used the holidays as a time to visit their ancestral villages, but with the introduction of public train travel in 1853 and the birth in the 1850s and 1860s of various Bengali newspapers dedicated to chronicling the public sphere—the *Bengalee*, the *Amrita Bazar Patrika*, and the *Hindoo Patriot*—we get reports of such journeys. Now Calcutta is characterized as "empty" from a non-British perspective as well. The idea of the Pūjās as an opportunity to relax on holiday, an import from the British, also slowly began to catch on among the Hindu public. Noted the great Moderate politician Surendranath Banerjea (1848–1925) about his trip to England in 1868, where he watched Britons going south for the summer to seaside towns: "[O]ur people during the great *Durga Puja* vacation stayed at home, celebrating the Pujas and enjoying the festivities, but neglecting the golden opportunity that the holidays presented for rest and change. Later on a change to Madhupur and Baidhyanath, and sometimes to Darjeeling, grew to be popular, and I had the proud satisfaction of strengthening the popular feelings and the popular movement by helping to make Simultolla a health-resort for the middle classes."[67]

In the post-1858 era, Pūjā coverage written about or from an Indian perspective was focused almost entirely on a vigorous defense of the holidays, on their own grounds. Some of this polemic was written to justify Hindu rituals in the face of British critiques, and indicates the self-identification of the colonized with the perspective of the colonizers, even as the former struggled to validate a separate self.

Answering the charge that they were socially irresponsible, several of the old aristocrats began to use their wealth for public welfare projects, educational endeavors, and the founding of hospitals. After the Rebellion, in 1860, the *Bengal Hurkaru* reported that the scion of the Shovabazar Rāj house, Rādhākānta Deb, issued invitations to a pyrotechnic display, "not in honor of Durgah, but to celebrate peace in India."[68] But even those who continued to celebrate the festival began to argue for its significance in a new way: as a social institution with a "benign and wholesome influence," inculcating in Hindus what Christmas does in Christians: joy, charity, love of home, forgetfulness of toil, and the chance to reunite with loved ones.[69] Bankim Chandra Chatterjee, in his essay "On the Origin of Hindu Festivals," tried to trace the original impetus behind Durgā Pūjā to ancient Indian astronomical observations, separating the proto-scientific from the present superstitious elements of the festivals.[70]

Further explanation, justification, and implicit or explicit argumentation for the importance of the Pūjās as a national religious festival occur in a spate of mostly Bengali pamphlets that appeared in the 1870s. Several of them presented their material in an objective, descriptive manner, narrating what happens when and why during the four days of the celebrations, and omitting all references to nautches or secular entertainment; others were plays or poetry collections in which stories of the Pūjās were preserved for posterity; and still others presented satirical sketches of Bābu culture at the Pūjā season.[71] One early play by Kirancandra Bandyopādhyāy, from 1873, *Bhārat Mātā*, is similar to Bankim's *Ānandamaṭh* in that it foreshadowed a later explicit use of the Goddess-Motherland equation: Bhārat Mātā is a widow, with hardly a trace of her former beauty and auspiciousness.[72]

This defensive, apologetic, even proud attitude was certainly intended as a foil to British stereotypes and judgments. The other important interlocutors continued to be the Brāhmos, who in their various split branches maintained their critique of the festivities for idolatry, irreverence, and animal sacrifice. The *Indian Mirror*, in a very judgmental article about

Durgā Pūjā from 1889, claims that people clamor for Western luxuries as basic necessities. "The Durga Pujah then, would seem to be the festival of English-fashioned shoes, the Chinese shoe-makers officiating as high priests of the ceremony! . . . The festival has become a shameful travesty of religion, a season for the selfish enjoyment of the rich, and a period for the lamentation of the poor. And nature herself resents the approach of the time, and famine and flood scourge the land. All round there is nothing but misery, and Durga deserts her votaries in disgust!"[73]

The Brāhmo position was influential but not triumphant; voiced alongside it were the opinions of Hindus who included the Pūjās within an emerging program of cultural revivalism, pride, and self-expression. By contrast, British Pūjā experiences, now zealously guarded and enjoyed in the hill stations, clubs, and mini-English enclaves of the country, showed the increasing separation between Indian and British during the half-century after 1857.

## *1905–1918: Partition, Pūjā, and the Rigors of War*

*The Mother's worship can no longer be performed with fruit and flowers.*
*The Mother's hunger can no longer be appeased with words only.*
*Blood is wanted!*
*Heads are wanted!*
*Workers are wanted!*
*Warriors and heroes are wanted!*
*Labor is wanted, and firm vows and bands of followers;*
*The Mother can no longer be worshipped with fruits and flowers.*[74]

From the Bengali point of view, British insensitivity, arrogance, and imperialistic ambition reached intolerable heights at the turn of the twentieth century. Under Lord George Curzon's administration (1899–1905), during which there was severe inflation and a steady rise in English-educated Indian unemployment, the British continued to disregard local sentiment by passing the Calcutta Municipal Bill and the Universities Act, in essence tightening control over the Calcutta Council and university education, even though Indians had strenuously protested. One sees in the Indian press evidence of a new emphasis on strength and manliness, associated now with the Goddess. In its lead article on Durgā Pūjā for 1903, the *Bengalee* stated that the Durgā image was "the emblem of our Indian nationality, not as it is but as it should be." "Save thy suffering children, for life to them is an eternal anguish, save them from famine, from . . . pestilence, from . . . misery . . . , and teach them, O

Dread Mother, above all things, teach them to be MEN."[75] This desire to prove wrong the British stereotype of the effeminate Bengali by infusing youth with physical pride found expression in the efforts of Śaralādebī Caudhurāṇi (Ghoṣāl) (1872–1945), a niece of Rabindranath, who in 1902 established the practice of celebrating heroes (*bīras*) on what she called Bīrāṣṭamī Utsab, on the eighth (Aṣṭamī) day of the Pūjās. She also founded an academy for martial arts in south Calcutta. These initiatives are evidence of all-India linkages and influences, as Śaralādebī had spent her young years in Western India with her uncle Satyendranath, where she witnessed B. G. Tilak's revival of the Gaṇapati and Shivaji coronation festivals in the mid-1890s, as well as the organization of societies for physical and military training.[76]

The shock came on July 20, 1905, with the announcement of the partition of Bengal into two manageable administrative divisions, as a result of which Muslims would be in a majority to the east and Hindus to the west. Protest meetings were held at over three hundred cities, towns, and villages in Bengal. The tactic decided upon was a swadeshi boycott, where Bengalis would refuse to buy or use anything not made in India.

Sumit Sarkar has thoroughly summarized and analyzed the various Moderate, Constructive Swadeshi, Political Extremist, and Terrorist reactions to the partition[77]; for our purposes here it is sufficient to note that the increasingly aggressive Extremist factions made use of religious symbols for explicitly political and anti-British purposes. Moderate "beggars" like Surendranath Banerjea were mercilessly pilloried by new leaders such as Aurobindo Ghosh and Bipin Chandra Pal and in nationalist newspapers like the *Amrita Bazar Patrika*, *Baṅgabāsī*, *Yugāntar*, and Ghosh and Pal's paper, *Bande Mataram*, begun in 1906. Revolutionary societies, such as the Anuśīlan Samiti, a countrywide organization for an armed revolution, often preached violence, and many gymnasia teaching wrestling, lathi play, and martial arts, following upon the example of Śaralādebī Caudhurāṇi's academy, were formed for the purposes of armed resistance. In Mymensingh, she and Bipin Chandra Pal also founded a festival modeled on that for Shivaji; in searching for a Bengali hero, they settled upon Rājā Pratāpāditya of Jessore, who had headed an unsuccessful rebellion against Aurangzeb.[78] They also celebrated Kālī, Pratāpāditya's tutelary deity, consciously creating a parallel between Kālī and Bhavānī, Shivaji's goddess. Wrote Pal, crediting his colleague for her inventiveness, "As necessity is the Mother of Invention, Sarala Devi is the mother of Pratapaditya to meet the necessity of a Hero for Bengal."[79] Another "first" associated with her name is the employment of "Bande Mātāram" as a national slogan: this occurred in 1905 under the auspices of the Mymensingh Suhrid Samiti, of which she was a member.[80]

Overall, as Barbara Southard has argued, Bengali militants in the 1905 partition upheavals used a Śākta idiom to rouse passion and support for their cause.[81] Two images of the Goddess-Motherland equation alternated in public discourse: one drew upon the Goddess's martial, all-conquering strength, or *śakti*; and the other focused on her frailty, weakness, and need for protection. Bankim's *Ānandamaṭh* also contributed to this oscillating, complex construction of the Mother; her renouncer-children had to be strong both with her and for her.[82]

Aurobindo drew self-consciously from *Ānandamaṭh*, in his "Bhawani Mandir" of 1905, utilizing the trope of the Goddess-Motherland to awaken her sons to self-sacrificing obedience. "For what is a nation? What is our mother-country? It is not a piece of earth, nor a figure of speech, nor a fiction of the mind. It is a mighty Shakti, composed of the Shaktis of all the millions of units that make up the nation, just as Bhawani Mahisha Mardini sprang into being from the Shakti of all the millions of gods assembled in one mass of force and welded into unity."[83] Or, in a letter home on 30 August 1905: our country "is not merely a division of land, but it is a living thing. It is the Mother in whom you move and have your being."[84]

Practical applications of this championing of Śakti-worship were many in partition years, and the uses to which the Pūjās were put changed considerably from those of the previous period. The Durgā Pūjā, which had symbolized harmony, mending of broken relationships, and joy, tended still to be the provenance of the Moderates[85]; more politicized valences were added by swadeshi politicians who wanted to fuse in the popular mind the identification of the Mother Goddess with the Motherland. Revolutionary Jogesh Chandra Chatterji recounts that when he was nine or ten in 1904–1905 a group of nationalists arrived in his village in Dacca district, clad only in *khādi* and singing, "[B]ow to the coarse cloth[,] as our poverty-stricken unhappy Mother India cannot afford to give us anything better." Most of the children that year, he wrote, did not get Manchester-made clothes for the Pūjā season.[86] The Bengali-owned papers of the period were full of gift advertisements "For the Poojahs. Nothing Bideshi, Everything Swadeshi"[87]: indigenous oils, silks, dhutis, saris, shoes, tea, sugar, and cigarettes with brands named like Vidyasagar, Sri Durga, and Durbar (fig. 2.2). Many people came to Kālī temples to take swadeshi oaths, and Bankim Chandra's "Bande Mātāram" became the political slogan of the time throughout Bengal.

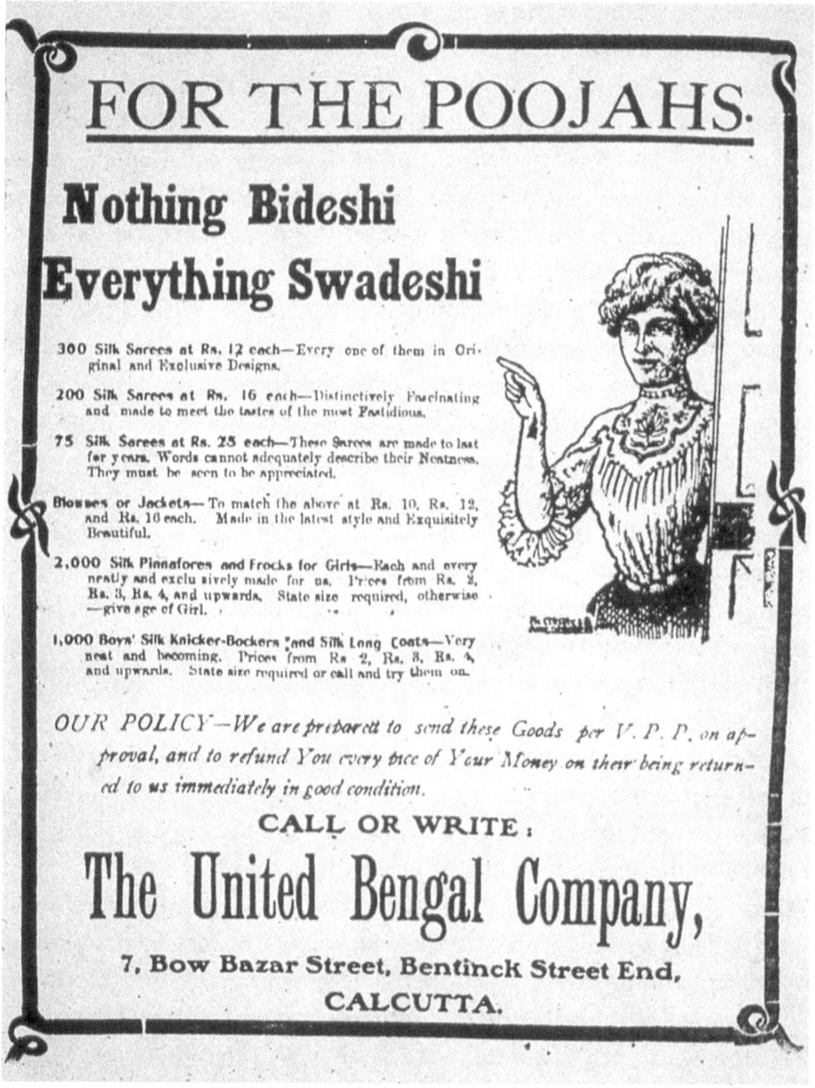


FIGURE 2.2. "For the Poojahs." *Bengalee*, 3 Oct. 1909, p. 10.

Although all Bengali political groups participated in and supported the national Durgā Pūjā festival, organizations that condoned violence tended to emphasize Kālī over her sister goddess. Bipin Chandra Pal explained this preference in a lecture given at the Shovabazar Rāj estate on 25 May 1907. As a tribal war deity, he stated, Kālī is a symbol of race-consciousness; besides, Bankim Chandra had already established her as the symbol of India, the ravaged and hungry "Mother as She is," and hence revolutionaries of his time should build upon Bankim's image. Pal urged the establishment of Kālī Pūjās in every village every month, but counseled that she be given the heads of white goats, not the typical black ones. This, he felt, would energize Bengali spirits and demoralize British ones.[88]

Revolutionary societies such as the Anuśīlan Samiti in Dacca created small hand-held bombs called "Kālī Māi's boma"s and made reverence for Kālī a signal part of their induction rituals: a person could become a full member only if he took a vow in front of a Kālī image that he would, in a manner parallel to that of the renouncers of *Ānandamaṭh*, sacrifice everything for the cause.[89] The Samiti's paper, *Yugāntar*, advocated this same self-sacrifice in prose; according to the 2 May 1908 issue: "The Mother is thirsty and is pointing out to her sons the only thing that can quench that thirst. Nothing less than human blood and decapitated human heads will satisfy her . . . On the day on which the Mother is worshiped in this way in every village, on that day will the people of India be inspired with a divine spirit and the crown of independence will fall into their hands."[90] Again, "Without bloodshed the worship of the goddess will not be accomplished . . . And what is the number of English officials in each district? With a firm resolve you can bring English rule to an end on a single day."[91]

The British were certainly one object of Śākta-colored political aggression. The other "other" of the partition years was the Muslim community. After the announcement of partition on 16 October 1905, Muslims were taken by surprise at the virulence of Hindu opposition to the British fiat. The swadeshi boycott also hurt poor rural Muslim shopkeepers, who could ill afford to exchange their goods for swadeshi products and who resented being forced to join the movement.[92] By October 1906, Muslims all over Bengal were celebrating the anniversary of the partition, and two months later the Muslim League was founded in Dacca, for the protection of Muslim interests. The communal antagonisms continued to worsen; in Mymensingh in eastern Bengal in 1906–1907, Muslim peasants, newly emboldened because they thought they had the British government's backing, rose up against their Hindu landlords. Encouraged by religious leaders, they refused to render traditional acts of service and declined to participate in Hindu festival processions. In some areas there was vandalism of temples, in response to "Bande Mātāram"–chanting Hindu provocateurs.

It is important to realize that communal disturbances had been relatively rare in Bengal up until this point. From the 1880s on, political leaders among Hindus and Muslims would regularly meet in advance of their mutual festivals to discuss precautionary measures; very little occurred in

Bengal that resembled the riots over cow-killing at Bak'r-Id in Bihar, the United Provinces (U.P.), or the North West Frontier Provinces in 1893. In what may seem to be an exception, Dipesh Chakrabarty, in a study of riots in Calcutta jute mills in the 1890s, demonstrates that communal tensions did arise in parts of the city in which large numbers of immigrant merchants and laborers had settled; agitations were sparked over the government's proscription of cow-killing (*korbāni*) during Muslim festivals, and jute workers, Hindu and Muslim, began to assert their rights to observe their religious festivals without interference either from the other community or from the government. Nevertheless, Chakrabarty also argues that this communal culture was essentially imported, with the majority of the rioters hailing from precisely those districts of Bihar and U.P. that had seen cow-killing riots from 1889 to 1893. Most of the Muslims who petitioned the government to allow cow-sacrifice were Urdu-speaking, and the majority of the Hindu leaflets protesting the same were remarkably similar to those distributed in Bihar and U.P. a few months earlier.[93]

Why did controversies over language, cow slaughter, religious and social festivals, representation on consultative and legislative bodies, education, and government jobs not assume the same communally explosive proportions in Bengal as elsewhere? John R. McLane, in his analysis of the partition era in Bengal, notes that prior to 1900 and unlike in north and central India, there was no large-scale sense of a "Hindu community" in Bengal, nor a "Muslim community" defined in relation to pan-world Islam and against the influences of local Hindu culture.[94] Indeed, in Bengali rural areas in the late nineteenth century Hindus and Muslims had more in common with each other than either did with their mainly Hindu *bhadralok* landlords. Moreover, the circumstances that gave rise to communal unrest in towns in U.P. in the 1890s, for instance, did not arise in Calcutta or in rural Bengal: what Nandini Gooptu calls "bazaar industrialization" among rapidly developing towns like Allahabad, Banaras, Kanpur, and Lucknow, with great influxes of migrant poor, a competitive labor market, especially between Śūdras, Untouchables, and poor Muslims, and the proliferation of unskilled work, did not arise in the more stable port towns of Calcutta, Bombay, and Madras.[95]

Another reason for the relative communal quiet in Bengal, before and even during the anti-partition struggles, is the position of the Moderate politicians. Sensitive to the need to keep Muslims and Hindus together, Moderates urged both communities to forget their political differences, blaming the British for their attempt to divide and rule. "The enemies of our race, the birds of prey and passage, are interested in fostering and promoting [dissension]. Let us not play into their hands . . . let us profit by the legend of the Bijoya Dasami ceremony, and once again let the voice of amity and good-will be heard among all [Hindu, Muslim, and Christian] sections of our great community."[96] In 1905 Rabindranath Tagore extended the symbolism of Brother's Second, a ritual of bonding between brothers and sisters that is celebrated right after the Pūjās have concluded, to evoke friendship between Hindus and Muslims: members of both communities would tie red threads of brotherhood on each others' wrists. All throughout the partition period, these *rākhi-bandhan* ceremonies were regularly announced in the Bengali and English papers. In addition, some landlords, even the British Indian Association, saw that the boycott and emphasis upon swadeshi items were disturbing peace with rural Muslims in their areas, and withdrew their support. Liberal Hindus also continued to offer a countervailing interpretation of the Pūjās: the *Hindoo Patriot* maintained its critique of idolatry and urged that the festivities be viewed as a time of social harmony and happiness that unites Hindus, Muslims, and Christians.[97]

Hence, while militant Hindus did draw upon Śākta imagery to whip up anti-British fervor, when it came to relations with Muslims, the Pūjās were sites of conflict, but not cited as symbolic of the dominance of a Hindu *śakti* over a Muslim demon. Instead, it is the festivities' potential for social cohesion that is frequently employed in the effort to rein in communal tension.

The fervor of the partition period could not sustain itself. There are many reasons for this—the withdrawal of support by the landed classes and the British Indian Association in 1908; the split of Congress in 1907; the weakening of the Extremist lobby through the departure of Bipin Chandra Pal for England in 1908 (when he returned to India he sided with the Moderates) and the imprisonment of Aurobindo in connection with the Alipore bomb case of 1908 and then his departure for Pondicherry in 1910; British repressions of the press, illegalizing of many Samitis, and deportations of the movement's leaders; and British attempts at conciliation through the Morley-Minto Reforms of 1909 and the 1912 reunification of Bengal. However, many of the tactics tried in Bengal at that time were later used to greater effect by Gandhi, and the politicizing of the Śākta tradition, particularly Durgā, Kālī and their Pūjās, now became a historical resource that could be drawn upon again, when the time came.

After the removal of the capital from Calcutta to Delhi in 1912, the next six to seven years were taken up principally with preparations for involvement in the First World War. During the war itself, there is little attention to the Pūjās, in either English or Bengali, mostly due to wartime restrictions, the bridling of newspapers, and the need for print space to provide maximal coverage of the war. Some Hindu sentiments carried on, seemingly unchanged: the anti-idolatry campaign voiced in the *Tattvabodhinī Patrikā*, and the concern to protect Hindu holidays from reductions and Hindu employees from being deprived of their chance to join their families. That even in the war years the British were still attached to the Pūjā is indicated by a complaint from one "Indian assistant" in the *Amrita Bazar Patrika* on 18 October 1917. He claims that Pūjās appear to cater to the Europeans, who cannot wait to get away to the hill stations and who leave their Indian workers in charge of their offices during the festival. "So it seems that the festival is for the Europeans!"[98] The most belligerent the papers get in the war years is to moralize to the British about peace. "Jesus Christ preached the Kingdom of Heaven. His white followers, generally speaking, however, hunger for a different kind of kingdom. The result is, that they fly at and cut one another's throats."[99] At the outbreak of war, the *Amrita Bazar Patrika* had this to say to its readers about the Pūjā: "The main object of Christmas, we believe, is also the same. But the Christian nations have clean forgotten it, and they are now behaving in a manner which makes every good man shed tears of bitter sorrow. How we wish that the Bijoya or Christmas spirit prevailed among the belligerents in Europe, so that they might lay down their blood-stained arms and embrace one another in brotherly love. The spirit of the Bijoya means the spirit of peace and goodwill, and nothing but this spirit can kill the demon which is carrying destruction and demolition among the so-called civilized nations of Europe."[100]

## The First World War to Independence

*How can a person agitated by bombs, famine, and disease do the puja?*[101]
*The way to conquer fear is to worship Power.*[102]

Much has been written about the decade after World War I in India: the Montagu-Chelsmford Reforms, which held out dyarchy as an intermediate step to self-governance, the repressive postwar measures of the Rowlatt Bills, and the massacre at Jallianwala Bagh in Amritsar, all in 1919; the growing politicization of Indian Muslims, demonstrated in the early 1920s by the Khilafat movement to restore the Ottoman caliph; the rise of Gandhi as an all-India political leader and his recourse to *satyāgraha* as a political technique of nonviolent resistance, first tried in the Non-Cooperation movement of 1920–1922; Gandhi's temple-opening movement for Untouchables; the popularity of C. R. Das (1870–1925), Bengal's foremost nationalist spokesman, who led his Swaraj Party from 1922 and who spearheaded the Bengal Pact of 1923, which tried to forge links between Hindus and Muslims; and the growth of Hindu nationalism, with the founding of the Hindu Mahāsabhā in 1915, the leadership of V. D. Savarkar (1883–1966), and the creation of the Rashtriya Swayamsevak Sangh (RSS) in 1925. Common themes in the political arena include increased urgency regarding the quest for independence from Britain and increased alarm on the part of certain Hindus and Muslims about each others' political aspirations; this led both to conciliation and to the creation of strong protective communal boundaries. In the 1920s, then, one can speak of the first efforts to produce a "Hindu nation," "an all-encompassing catholic national Hinduism overriding divisions of sect and caste."[103]

In the Bengali papers in the early 1920s Durgā was importuned for her compassion in difficult times. Wrote the editor of the *Ānanda Bājār Patrikā* for 4 October 1922: "In the Pūjās we forget that we cannot speak, we have no land, no authority, no power, no royal glory. We forget that we are a race of servants, that the country has become a prison. We forget all this, but not the Mother's love. That is why we see her smiling face piercing all our fears."[104] By 1923, the same paper was identifying broken Bengal as the Pūjā temple to which Durgā was invited. Then, employing an image from the first of the three stories from the "Devī-Māhātmya," the author goes on to equate Bengal with Nārāyaṇa, lying asleep on the black shadow of suffering, the ocean of hopelessness, the serpent bed of domination. "Today please awaken Bengalis in order that they might save themselves from the pair of demons, Madhu and Kaitabha, which are domination and sycophancy."[105] This same theme is illustrated in a number of clever cartoons from the 1920s onward; Durgā is said to leave her temple for the streets, her weapons for compassionately open arms, and her elite patrons for her disconsolate children.[106]

The 1920s were momentous not only for the symbolic resonances of the Goddess but also for her Pūjās. Reacting both to a perceived need for Hindu solidarity in face of potential Muslim threat and to Gandhi's exhortation to abolish Untouchability—ironically, a similar thrust toward unity but for opposite reasons—several Bengali Hindu leaders called for religious celebrations embracing everyone, from whatever caste or class background. Thus the birth in 1926 of the *sarbajanīn*, or "universal," Pūjā, organized by locality rather than by clique, and open to all, regardless of birth or residence. For the first time, pandals, or temporary temples made out of bamboo or cloth, were constructed in public thoroughfares, alleyways, and cul-de-sacs and used as centers for people to come for *darśan* of the Goddess and her four children. The first such "universal Pūjā" was dubbed the "Congress Pūjā," and was organized in Maniktola, in north Calcutta. The image of the Goddess was uncharacteristically unornamented and entirely militant.[107] In 1927 one newspaper article explained to the public that these new festivals "will be celebrated in order to give facilities to Hindus of all classes and denominations without the least distinction of caste" "to bring about solidarity in the caste-ridden Hindu community."[108]

Nationalists of the period who were jailed by the British often expressed their patriotism, even while incarcerated, by demanding the right to perform Durgā Pūjā. The most famous example of this is the Śākta-leaning Subhas Chandra Bose, who, after celebrating the Pūjā in Mandalay jail in September 1925, wrote to C. R. Das's wife, Bāsantīdebī, "The Divine Mother is being worshipped today in many a Bengali home. We are fortunate enough to have Her in this prison also. The Mother probably did not forget us, and so it has been possible to arrange for Her worship even though we are away. She will depart day after tomorrow, leaving us in tears. . . . If the Divine Mother will make Her appearance once a year, I expect prison life will not be so unbearable."[109] Several months later he went on a two-week hunger strike in order to be compensated by the prison authorities for the expenses he had incurred in the worship.

After the Communal Award in 1932, the Untouchability Abolition Bill of 1933, and the Depressed Classes Status Bill of 1934, none of which pleased the Bengali *bhadralok*, the obsession with trying to forge a common identity, across caste lines, became imperative for Hindu leaders. "From the mid-thirties onwards, Bengal witnessed a flurry of caste consolidation programmes, initiated chiefly under the Hindu Sabha and Mahasabha auspices." These included reconversion, or *śudhhi*, efforts; lobbying Nāmaśūdras and other very low castes to stop working for Muslims; enlightening Hindu zamindars about the necessity of separating Hindu from Muslim workers; constructing Hindu temples in villages; and introducing *sarbajanīn* Pūjā festivals.[110]

As might be expected, such communalization of politics, and of the Pūjās, led to tensions and even riots between Hindus and Muslims. "Festivals were a benchmark against which the changes in the local balance of power between competing communal groups could be measured," writes Joya Chatterjee, who convincingly shows the degree to which Bengali Hindu and Muslim festivals in the 1930s and 1940s were public sites for the antagonistic display of community wealth, solidarity, and power.[111] In his writings, Gandhi lamented that Hindus were playing music in front of mosques,[112] and during the Pūjā season of 1926, in areas both west and east of the Hooghly River, the papers reported desecration of Durgā images and harassment of Hindu processions by brick- and bat-wielding Muslims from local mosques.[113] Typically the quarrels broke out over street rituals—either Muslims celebrating Bak'r-Id by sacrificing a cow or Hindus playing drums as they processed their image of Durgā or Kālī either in front of a mosque at prayer time or during Muharram or Ramadan processions.[114] The British responded by declaring that no one could be seen in public with a weapon, but it took some days for calm to return to the affected areas. The editors of the *Ānanda Bājār Patrikā* commented sadly on 19 October 1926, "[F]or the last five to six hundred years, Muslims have been joining in the Pūjā celebrations. In fact, Durgā Pūjā was not just a Hindu festival, but a Muslim one as well. But [now] such friendship has gone far away, and the country's peace has been destroyed." The writer assigned blame in all directions: to those whom he called the "new pirs," responsible for stirring up communal hatred among Muslims; to the British, who did not exert themselves to keep the peace; and to Hindus themselves, whose cowardice in the face of the bricks and stones proved their weakness.

Hence by the late 1930s and early 1940s the Pūjās had shifted the focus of their reflective abilities: no longer perceived as a possible symbol to galvanize support in the struggle against the British (by this time Britain had lost the political will to hold onto India much longer), the festivities were now images, indications, signs of the times: mostly of the communal violence that would erupt at Partition in 1946–1947; but also of current events. In 1943, in the midst of the Bengal famine, a journalist in an article entitled *Āgamanī* invited, called, pleaded with the Mother to come home to save her children in their terrible distress.[115]

The communalization of politics in the 1920s and 1930s should be seen in a larger context. Indian towns during this period saw the growth of public arena activities through Britain's gradual postwar devolution of power; as Nandini Gooptu phrases it, "the consequent expansion of representative politics and its flip-side, the need for popular political mobilisation, changed the entire nature of Indian politics."[116] Agitations, protests, political rituals, and the forging of alliances emerged as Indians sought to maneuver against imperial institutions on behalf of their own group interests. Such attempted strengthening of "the Hindu community" often led to anti-Muslim actions or rhetoric. Moreover, the phenomenon of the *nagarkīrtan*, or street procession, with large numbers of people marching through the streets parading their images or performing their vows and rites, was an innovation only of the 1920s, and resulted directly from the expansion and democratization of public arena rituals throughout India.[117] Such public ostentation was also true of Muslim festivals, particularly Muharram.

This increased public-sphere activity also inflamed British fear of unruly crowds; police forces were enlarged to quell or deter communal violence at demonstrations, meetings, processions, and festivals, and preemptive curfews or arrests of suspected rowdies added to the perception of a dangerous, politicized street culture. Other regions outside Bengal also witnessed *sarbajanīn*-like festivals with widened access and scope: in 1924, the Allahabad Rāmlīlā processions included a live Brahman and sweeper sitting together, illustrating the putative integration of lower- and upper-caste groups.[118] It is doubtful whether one should credit the "universal" Pūjās with true integration, however; in this vein I take Gooptu's warning seriously, that we not presuppose actual social cohesion between elites and popular classes or think that communal conflict necessitates a completely shared sense of community identity.[119] Indeed, as Anne Hardgrove also warns, "community" is "constituted by a set of practices, a series of 'performances' through which claims are made about collective and intersubjective identities." Yet "these claims may be contradictory, produced through relationships of power, and are open to resistance and contest. . . . The community, in other words, represents no consensus."[120] This is true in Bengal, from top to bottom, even among Hindus: neither the subordinate classes, whose presence was co-opted and necessitated by the new exigencies of political inclusiveness, nor the Hindi-speaking non-Bengali population, such as the wealthy and influential Marwaris, felt the Bengali Pūjās to be their own.[121]

Turning now to the British perspective on the period after World War I, British newspapers reported on the rise of the *sarbajanīn* Pūjās and on the communal disturbances that accompanied them; the British investigative police were wary of Bengali nationalists' uses of seditious language and their ability to whip up anti-state fervor through recourse to religious, especially Śākta, imagery.[122] However, the majority of Bengal's British residents continued to think of the Pūjās in rather less political and, surprisingly, increasingly catholic terms.

Just like the "average Hindu" who enjoyed returning to his village or, after the 1920s, decided to come from the village to Calcutta to sample the city's entertainments,[123] the "average Briton" still anticipated the Pūjās as

FIGURE 2.3. "Poojah Holidays." *Statesman*, 1 Oct. 1929, p. 6.

a time of relaxation and travel (fig. 2.3). Indeed, the Pūjās were by this time an established industry. English newspapers introduced "Special Puja Holiday Pages" or "Puja Supplements" detailing holiday train schedules and fares to hill stations, seaside towns, and resorts; announcing seasonal concerts, theater shows, garden parties, and sport events; and publishing overviews of which stores were selling what for the festivities. After 1920 the English papers also began to include descriptive essays and human-interest stories about the holidays, the majority authored by Indian writers. Even the *Englishman*, that bastion of pro-British sentiment, began to show a more accepting attitude toward the Hindu festivals for Durgā and Jagaddhātrī, arguing that the Pūjās are like Christmas for the Bengalis, "offering hearty Pujah greetings to all our Indian readers," lamenting the close of the Pūjā season, and complaining of "Puja-itis."[124]

In the late 1930s and 1940s, the British were taken up with World War II, the terrible famine in Bengal in 1943, and the last throes of planning for the transfer of power; the Pūjās command very little newsprint in papers of either community, except the stray comment on how the festivals have been curtailed by rain, blacked-out streets, economic problems, war, and famine. One Bengali monthly, *Māsik Basumatī*, includes in 1943 an essay modeled on a famous song to Kālī, "Śmaśān bhālobāsis bale" ("because you love cremation grounds [I have made my heart one]"). The author of the 1943 essay identifies the cremation ground not with his heart but with Bengal and asks his readers to shed their blood for independence and self-government from the *bideśīs* (foreigners).[125] But the British, it appears, had ceased to fear such Śākta-derived nationalist symbols of anti-empire antagonism. What perturbed them more was the threat of communal riots. The Pūjā season after the Great Calcutta Killings, or Direct Action Day (August 16, 1946), was perceived as a potential stabilizer, if the British could police it properly. By September 30, 1946, in announcing a relaxation of curfew for the holiday season, the headlines were clear: "Government determined to see Pujahs pass off peacefully."[126]

## Pūjās in Post-Independence West Bengal

*Peaceful Puja, Id Assured.*[127]

Since 1947 the political situation in eastern India has changed dramatically. With no more British imperialists to oust, and a Communist-led government in West Bengal that has been virulent in its efforts to curb or even suppress communalism, how have the Pūjās fared? Is there any way in which they can still be said to mirror political events or express political aspirations?

The answer of course is yes, although in a changed fashion. The festivities still provide the impetus for nationalist sentiment, and the Goddess is still perceived by many as the foundation of the country's strength (*deś-śakti*[128]).

In the years immediately after Independence, when violence had subsided, communal tensions somewhat abated, and prosperity partly returned, Pūjā organizers again gloried in the emancipation of the Mother; in patriotic zeal they decorated their pandals in the colors of the flag, hung pictures and created clay models of Vivekananda, Gandhi, Nehru, and Subhas Bose on the walls, and played "Bande Mātāram" in the background. One journalist in 1948 saw Gaṇeśa and Kārtik wearing Nehru caps.[129] Such nationalism in the context of the Pūjās is, one might say, celebratory, self-congratulatory, and nostalgic, rather than exhortatory or revolutionary. It also builds upon a Śākta valuation of might, not a self-sacrificing exhortation to nonviolence. Said one Dr. Rameścandra Majumdār when inaugurating a Pūjā in 1951, "After Independence people are saying that our culture will be built up. But what is our culture? Not Vedic or Vedantic, but that built on Śakti-sādhanā; this is our uniqueness."[130] That the Pūjās are at heart a vehicle for the expression of muscle, prestige, and honor is shown through their patronage by soldiers and rulers: almost every year the Calcutta newspapers report on the traditional worship of Durgā by the Gurkha Rifles and the Assam Rifles, who vivify the Goddess with blood sacrifice and apply oil and vermilion to their weapons. And in spite of the outwardly anti-religious stance of the CPI(M) cadres, they too patronize the Pūjās, utilizing the occasion for the selling of literature and the disbursement of political favors.[131]

Of course, the British and local government aside, there are plenty of "others" for India to worry about, chief among whom are China and Pakistan. The Pūjā season in 1962 was full of patriotic fervor and lamentation; the same was true in October 1964, when China conducted its first atomic test: "China's atomic explosion on this year's Vijaya Dasami day—though coincidental—underlines, by a tremendous shock, the growing ascendency of the forces of evil and the retreat, as it were, of the forces of goodness and peace symbolized by the Divine Mother. . . . [W]e fervently hope that she will bring back those competitors in total destruction to sobriety and good sense before they have proceeded too far along the road to Calvary."[132] In 1965, during the Pakistani intrusion into Kashmir at the end of September, politicians asked people to pray to Durgā for national strength in the face of the "naked and wanton aggression by Pakistan." "Pakistan and China are threatening to attack us . . . However formidable the aggressors might be, the people's unflagging mood is that they will withstand and crush the enemies with the Mother's blessings."[133] In 1971, during the birth pangs of Bangladesh, feelings of tremendous solidarity with East Pakistan caused pandal organizers to broadcast Sheikh Mujib's speeches and sell his writings at their Pūjā stalls. In addition, East Pakistani refugees, living in camps in West Bengal, were given money to enable them to perform Durgā Pūjā in their traditional manner.

One of the chief elements that differentiates these types of politicized Pūjās from those in the colonial period is that the "others" or enemies are not in one's midst and hence do not interfere with one's processions or provide impetus for street fights, or worse. As mentioned above, the CPI(M) has been vigilant in policing the Pūjās, not only as a routine matter when they coincide with Id or Muharram but also when special national or world events occur that might lend themselves to communal, Hindu–Muslim unrest. Common compromises include assurances that Muslims will herd sacrificial cattle through specified routes only, and then quickly clean the refuse, and that Hindus will avoid blaring loudspeakers or planning procession routes near mosques. The police routinely mandate the cessations of Pūjā immersion rituals during Id or Muharram.

The West Bengal political atmosphere during L. K. Advani's *rath-yātrā* for the "liberation" of the Babri Masjid in 1989 was tense, but although there were places in the city where bricks for the construction of the new temple to Lord Rāma were blessed, the local police reported with satisfaction that such *rāmśila pūjā*s never occurred in the context of a Durgā Pūjā.[134] In Pūjā season 2001, one might have expected the pandals or lighting exhibits to have reflected or represented the World Trade Center disaster. But CPI(M) workers prohibited artisans from sculpting the demon whom Durgā slays in the likeness of Osama bin Laden, and the bombing of the Twin Towers was almost nowhere depicted (but see p. 145 and figs. 5.4 and 5.5 below).

This does not mean that the Pūjās are always peaceful. One reads periodic reports of rival Pūjā committees attempting to deface each other's images or to prevent each other from having pride of place in processions to the local river. Often such conflicts result in injuries, stabbings, and even death. Nevertheless, under the watchful eye of an avowedly secular state government, religious festivals are prevented from acting as the framework for social upheaval.

## Conclusion

> *[Durgā Pūjā is] the only national festival [Hindus] have clung to more tenaciously than even to the most highly prized political rights and privileges.*[135]

If one places in parallel British and Hindu attitudes toward the Śākta Pūjās from the late eighteenth century up to Independence, one sees interesting convergences and mutual influences. In the earliest period of interaction, when social roles were fluid, the festivities were a site for intercommunity interaction. In the thirty or so years after the missionary impact was felt and before the revolt, both Britons and Hindus struggled to cope with an exhorted separation of their communities. After 1860 and the British Crown's stated policy of non-interference, the British seem to have adopted the Pūjās as a secular holiday, acquiescing more or less to its season and schedule, as dictated by the Hindu calendar. They understood the Pūjās thus all the way up to 1947, except that they were perforce involved in the surveillance and even policing of the festivities, both when Hindus used them as anti-British sites of protest during the 1905 anti-partition agitations and when they became central to Hindu–Muslim communal unrest in the 1920s. The modern, post-Independence period has seen a retreat of the communally politicized Pūjā, with communally sensitive subjects simply omitted.

A study of the Śākta Pūjās during the colonial period in Bengal also provides corroboration for many postcolonial claims about British attitudes toward the people they ruled and the customs they encountered. Once the missionaries and the Anglicizing Liberalist policies of Bentinck were in place in the 1830s, Hindu festivals were party to familiar critiques: the Pūjās were said to betray decadence, decay, and a departure from the timeless truths of Hindu textual learning; the exuberant focus on a ten-handed Goddess was denounced as idolatrous; and Hindus and Muslims, as well as Hindu and Muslim festivals, were to be kept separate, not only for reasons intrinsic to their essential natures, but also to prevent trouble. Other British attitudes find expression not so much in the writings of Britons themselves about the Pūjās as in the way Hindus felt constrained to defend them: Durgā is begged to make her votaries "MEN"; her worship is described as enhancing interior feelings of brotherhood and spiritual unity rather than "simply" exciting public forms of evanescent (and potentially dangerous) fervor; and the Pūjās are celebrated in terms that accentuate their moral resonance and depth. Even the early, pre-1830s period of relative British openness to Indian religious custom cannot be seen outside the framework of increasing imperial ambition; as Bernard Cohn has argued, pluralism is rarely equitable. It is tolerated and even encouraged to further goals of empire, for showing respect to institutions and people who define the traditions of the conquered is perceived as bestowing legitimacy.[136]

I take three main morals from this overview. First, there was no consistent response to the Pūjās, either by the British or by the Hindus. Missionaries, bank managers, merchants, Company and Government officials, not to mention normal British citizens living in Bengal—they each had their own attitudes toward the holidays, attitudes that differed depending on the decades in which they lived. Class snobbery and British anxieties about their own compatriots shaming their dignity in India also played a role in evolving views. Hindus too argued among themselves about the meaning of the public worship of Durgā, Jagaddhātrī, and Kālī: were the festivals an opportunity to impress the British and assert prestige? a chance to rest with one's family from the grind of work in the colonial state? a reminder of the Mother Goddess and Motherland, who should be lauded and protected? a symbol of the value of friendship and brotherly affection? a site for subversive anti-British or anti-Muslim hatred? Or a "chimera" and "an idle tale" to be disregarded in favor of a more rational religion?[137]

Second, one of the most surprising discoveries to come out of this material is just how *un*affected the Pūjās were by communal violence the majority of the time. This is in stark contrast to North India, where communalism was far more problematic and where festivals were often marred by tension and violence. There are really only two periods of Pūjā-related politicized religion in Bengal: 1905–1908, and the mid-1920s. In the first, the anti-partition years, Śākta symbolism was used by swadeshi revolutionaries, sometimes but not always in connection with the festivals themselves. Between 1907 and 1926, Bengal saw little communal unrest. There are two main reasons for this, political and sociological. Politically, this twenty-year period saw the shifting of British administrative power from Calcutta to Delhi in 1911; the prominence in local Bengali politics of men like C. R. Das, Rabindranath Tagore, and Subhas and Sarat Bose, all of whom were trusted by both Hindus and Muslims; and the North India–based leadership of the Indian National Congress.

Indeed, one could argue that the Gandhian nationalistic program was not well suited to the Bengali temperament. Durgā, Jagaddhātrī, and Kālī connote *śakti*, or strength, and even, according to several scriptural injunctions, require blood sacrifice. They are also intimately bound up with the display of human power, whether royal or social, and hence of worldly wealth. These values do not, in the main, mesh well with a Gandhian ethos built on simplicity or spartan living, and although many Hindus did take to the swadeshi program, many others did not. Opined the author of an article in the *Statesman*, for 9 October 1921, "Picturesque costumes, in spite of Mr. Gandhi's boycott, are much in evidence, dealers reporting record sales. The spirit of boycott, in fact, is altogether out of keeping with the occasion."[138] This perspective was shared by Bengali Moderate politicians, for whom the festival symbolized harmony, mending of broken relationships, and joy.

In social terms, the period prior to 1926 was not wracked with public expressions of communalism during the Pūjā season, because prior to 1926 the festivities were largely paid for, organized, and hosted by the local elites in their own homes, who used their celebrations to claim respect, curry favor with the British, and assert political muscle. Even while partition agitations were raging, wealthy Hindus continued to use the Pūjā season as an opportunity to impress rather than to rebel against their European overlords.[139] One can appreciate, therefore, why there was little use of the Pūjās to express anti-British feeling during pre-1920s political crises such as the revolt of 1857: there were few public pandals, and hence few venues for the expression of a community-based nationalism.

After the mid-1920s, of course, Bengal, like elsewhere in the subcontinent, descended into a maelstrom of politicized communalism, but as far as they were able, the British used the lessons learned in 1926 to police the autumnal festivals so that Durgā Pūjā and Muharram would not be occasions for communal confrontation.

The final lesson I take from this historical overview is that what can pass for the cultural or artistic in one context can turn to the communal or politicized in another. What transforms the artistic into the politicized is the rhetoric of nationalism or of a bounded community that views itself as living under threat. The moral, as Gyanendra Pandey says in his book, *Remembering Partition*, is that violence is frequently associated with community formation and othering; violence and community, in fact, constitute one another, he claims.[140] Although there is much that one can criticize about the CPI(M) in West Bengal, the fact that they seem intent upon preventing such "othering" is cause for celebration. One wonders what would happen to the Pūjās if the Bharatiya Janata Party or a like-minded political body gained sway in the state; would Durgā again be employed as a vehicle for stirring up violent communal unrest in the name of a putative community's aggrandizement?

That Durgā and her sister goddesses Jagaddhātrī and Kālī are indeed so malleable proves the durability, flexibility, and complexity of their festivals. In their centuries-long histories the Pūjās have meant many things to many people. Those who care about Bengal and about communal harmony should be happy that the communal problems of the mid-1920s are such relative anomalies.

# 3 Durgā the Daughter: Folk and Familial Traditions

In chapters 1 and 2 we focused on the grandeur of Durgā Pūjā: the martial goddess with her power to confer strength, status, and riches; the opulence of the displays, entertainments, and feasts hosted in her honor; and the political multivalence of her festival as a cipher for the colonial relationship between Britons and Bengalis. But Durgā Mahiṣamardinī is just one of the three important personalities, or threads, expressed in the rich tapestry of this festival. A second—just as prominent and, in fact, more vital to the emotional center of the Pūjā—is the daughter, Umā. Durgā is the protectress, the mother who slays demons and rids the world of obstacles. But she is not close to the heart. It is Umā, Śiva's gentle wife and the daughter of Menakā and Himālaya, who, standing in for the missed daughters of youth, evokes real longing. In this chapter we review literary, ritual, and iconographic evidence for the importance of Umā to the Pūjā, attempt to account for her role in the history of the festival, and return to the theme of nostalgia to interpret her significance.

## The Daughter's Centrality to the Pūjā: Umā's Life, Women's Lives

Almost everyone who knows anything about the Hindu religious tradition has heard of Śiva and Pārvatī—the divine couple who live with their two sons on Mount Kailasa, and who are celebrated in myth and art as the embodiments of the male and female principles (*puruṣa* and *prakṛti*), on the one hand, and of the tension between the renouncer and householder lifestyles, on the other. This association between Śiva, the "Benevolent," the erotic ascetic, the dancing lord of destruction, and Pārvatī, the daughter of the mountain, has a long history in Sanskrit literature, dating back at least as far as the epic period, in the centuries immediately preceding and following our Common Era.[1] It is in Kālidāsa's *Kumārasambhava* and in the range of Purāṇic literature spanning the fourth to the sixteenth centuries, however, where we see the real flowering of stories about Śiva and Pārvatī: here we get detailed accounts of Pārvatī's former existence as Satī; Satī's suicide in mortification over her father's insult to her new husband, Śiva; Satī's rebirth as Pārvatī in the home of the mountain Himālaya and his wife, Menā; her marriage, once again, to Śiva; and the descriptions of their wedded life on Mount Kailasa. It is not only the Sanskrit tradition which has delighted in the myths and personalities of this divine pair; Śiva and Pārvatī have also found a place in vernacular literatures, folktales, and folksongs all over India, where their stories gain regional flavors and meanings.

The Bengali regionalization of the Śiva–Pārvatī story has taken expression in a variety of narrative, poetic, ritual, iconographic, and political registers from the fifteenth century to the present. Here I mention five chief ways in which Umā can be seen to occupy center stage in the Pūjā experience.

First, the literary genre most germane to our study of Durgā Pūjā is a devotional poetry tradition that began to be composed at the end of the eighteenth century and that takes the relationship between Śiva and Pārvatī as a principal theme. Indeed, one of the most endearing characteristics of Durgā Pūjā in Bengal is the belief that during the three main days of the festival the goddess Umā, or Gaurī—the name Pārvatī is rarely used in this genre—returns home from her life with Śiva on Kailasa to visit her parents. *Āgamanī* songs celebrate her coming and *bijayā* songs, sung at the end of the three-days festival, lament her imminent departure.[2] Together, these *āgamanī* and *bijayā* songs are referred to as Umā-*saṅgīt*, or songs on Umā.

*Āgamanī* and *bijayā* poems are essentially much-shortened versions of the stories about Umā and Śiva as narrated in the Bengali Maṅgalakāvyas of the fifteenth to the eighteenth centuries. As their generic titles, *maṅgala-kāvya* or *vijaya-kāvya*, indicate, these long narrative poems celebrate the auspicious character or victory of a particular god or goddess. The divine heroes and heroines of such poems are manifold, but are principally female, and Umā figures prominently in the literature.

As a general matter, the deities of the Maṅgalakāvyas come close to humans. They do this through the medium of the vernacular Bengali, in poems whose scenes incorporate regional scenery and whose stories describe normal people in intense interaction with divine figures. Several of these poems include tellings of the Śiva and Umā story, but from a Bengali perspective. Here Śiva is a rustic figure who tills the soil, and he leads a vagabond, drug-addicted, irresponsible life. Moreover, he is old. In Bhāratcandra's *Annadāmaṅgal*, Umā's mother, Menakā, says, "Ai, ai, ai, is *this old man* Gaurī's bridegroom?" Umā's life with him is hard and unhappy—so much so that in one Maṅgalakāvya a human woman takes pity on the Goddess and offers to help her.[3] Depictions more favorable to Śiva can be seen in voluminous and popular Śiva-centered Maṅgalakāvyas, the *Śivāyanas*. One, written by Rāmeśvara Bhaṭṭācārya in about 1750, shows fully Bengali-ized domestic scenes between Śiva, Umā, and their two sons in Kailasa. Here, in a family meal, Umā serves Bengali dishes.[4]

This humanization and regionalization of Umā and Śiva is also evident in the *āgamanī* and *bijayā* songs. The earliest poets to compose in this new genre were Rāmprasād Sen (ca. 1718–1775) and a few of his late-eighteenth-century contemporaries.[5] In form, the poems are short, lyrical, rhymed vignettes, sung to a specified tune and meter. At the end of each is a *bhaṇitā*, or signature line, when the composer inserts his name into the action of the story. Probably since their inception these *āgamanī* and *bijayā* songs have been strung together to form a coherent story in several parts, similar in format to the Maṅgalakāvyas.

Though the Umā-*saṅgīt* style began in the last decades of the eighteenth century, it was composers of the nineteenth century who developed the story line and wrote poems of lasting artistic value. Kamalākānta Bhaṭṭācārya (ca. 1769–1820), Rāmprasād's most famous follower, was a prime mover in this regard; he is the first Śākta poet to devote a substantial portion of his corpus to this theme, establishing patterns that were copied and elaborated upon by subsequent poets.

These poems tell the story of Umā's return home to her parents, Menakā and Girirāj. Girirāj *is* actually the mountain Himālaya, although his abode in "the Mountain City" is usually understood to be somewhere in Bengal.[6] Umā spends the entire year in Kailasa with Śiva, the dubious husband found for her by the unscrupulous matchmaker Nārada, and her parents miss her terribly, worrying over her welfare. Reports they hear abut Śiva are not reassuring: he is said to live in the cremation grounds, wear nothing except a tiger's skin, be addicted to hemp and other intoxicants, and keep a second wife, the Ganges, who dwells in his matted hair. Umā's once-yearly homecoming to Bengal, therefore, is anticipated with mingled concern and excitement: Menakā, Girirāj, and their friends will have her all to themselves again from the evening of the sixth day of the Durgā Pūjā festival until the morning of the dreaded tenth day, which robs them of their daughter and their joy for another year.

The story usually opens in the weeks before the autumnal Pūjā season, with Menakā pining for and dreaming of Umā. She hears the worst possible news through Nārada—namely, that her daughter is unhappy and blames her mother for her situation:

> Hey, Mountain King, Gaurī is sulking.
> Listen to what she told Nārada in anguish —
>
> "Mother handed me over to the Naked Lord
> and now I see that she has forgotten me.
> Hara's robe is a tiger's skin,
> his ornaments a necklace of bones,
> and a serpent is dangling in his matted hair.
> The only thing he possesses is the *dhuturā* fruit!
> Mother, only you would forget such things.
> What's worse, there's the vexation of a co-wife
> which I can't tolerate.
> How much agony I've endured!
> Suradhunī, adored by my husband,
> is always lying on my Śaṅkara's head."
>
> Take Kamalākānta's advice.
> What she says is absolutely true.
> Jewel of the Mountain Peaks,

your daughter has become a beggar,
just like her husband.[7]

Horrified, Menakā nags lazy Girirāj to go to Kailasa to fetch their daughter home, but he procrastinates, or says that he has gone when he really has not. Bemoans his wife, constrained by social convention to depend upon a man for the permission and means to travel:

Tell me,
what can I do?
Unkind fate made me
a woman controlled and ruled by others.
Can anyone understand my mental pain?
Only the sufferer knows.
Day and night
again and again
how much more can I plead?
The Mountain, Jewel of the Hilly Peaks,
hears but does not listen.
Whom can I tell
the way I feel for Umā?
Who will be sad
with my sadness?
Let the Mountain King be happy;
he has no heart.
Friend, I've decided to forget my shame.
I'll take Kamalākānta and go to Kailasa.
She's my very own daughter —
I'll fetch her myself.[8]

Meanwhile the same argument is going on in Kailasa, with Umā begging Śiva for the permission to go see her parents.

Hey, Hara, Ganges-Holder,
promise I can go to my father's place.

What are You brooding about?
The worlds are contained in Your fingernail,

but no one would know it,
looking at Your face.

My father, the Lord of the Mountain,
has arrived to visit You
and to take me away.
It has been so many days since I went home
and saw my mother face to face.
Ceaselessly, day and night,
how she weeps for me!
Like a thirsty *cātaki* bird, the queen stares
at the road that will bring me home.
Can't I make You understand
my mental agony at not seeing her face?
But how can I go without Your consent?

My husband, don't crack jokes;
just satisfy my desire.
Hara, let me say good-bye,
Your mind at ease.
And give me Kamalākānta as an attendant.
I assure You
we'll be back in three days.[9]

Eventually Śiva is persuaded, and Umā returns with her father to the Himalayan kingdom. Menakā, ecstatic, rushes out to greet her daughter.

The Queen takes Gaurī on her lap
and says sweet words to her.
"My Umī, golden creeper,
Mṛtyuñjaya lives in the cremation grounds.
I die in grief over him, and also over you
and me, being separated.

"My heart laments day and night,
but since I'm a mountain woman
unable to move
I can't go see you.

Thinking over my life,
I stare in hope at the road;
I weep when I don't see you.

"Shame, shame, shame!
Is this a matter for debate?
I'm mortified every time I hear about it:
the Mountain gave you away
to a man who doesn't fear snakes
and who smears his body with ashes.

"You are all-auspiciousness,
a raft over the sea, able to ferry us
to the other side.
But when I see this suffering of yours
my grieving chest bursts;
for even you can't destroy *this* suffering."[10]

In some of the poems, Umā tries to calm her mother's worries. In others, it is obvious that she is unhappy, but is attempting to spare her mother the truth of her condition.

After a joyful three days, it is time once again for Umā to leave her parents' home. Menakā vows not to let Śiva take her away, and pleads with the day of her departure, asking it not to dawn. But the inevitable must occur. Umā leaves, and her mother is plunged into darkness. The following is a *bijayā* poem, sung as the Goddess is bid farewell.

What happened?
The ninth night is over.
I hear the beat beat beat
of the large *ḍamaru* drums
and the sound shatters my heart.
How can I express my agony?
Look at Gaurī;
her moon-face has become so pale.
I would give that beggar Trident-Bearer
anything He asked for.
Even if He wanted my life

I'd give it up.
Who can fathom Him?
He doesn't know right from wrong.
The more I think of Bhava's manners
the more stony I become.
As long as I live,
how can I send Gaurī?
Why does the Three-Eyed One crave Her so needlessly?

Take Kamalākānta along
and make Hara understand:
if You don't behave honorably,
you can't expect others to treat you with honor,
either.[11]

Viewed from a Sanskrit, Purāṇa-inspired perspective, there are many ways in which the portrayal of Umā and Śiva in these Bengali poems is strange and distinctly regional. While it can be argued that the cycle of Sanskrit myths that includes Pārvatī—the necessity for the birth of Skanda in order to slay the demon Tāraka, Pārvatī's former birth as Satī, daughter of Dakṣa, and Pārvatī's life with her erotic-ascetic lord[12]—focuses primarily on Śiva, and does so in context of Kailasa, the *āgamanī* and *bijayā* poems place Umā center stage and concentrate on her relationship with her parents, in the *Bengali* Himalayan city.[13] Several important themes from the Sanskrit myth cycle are mentioned either only obliquely in the Umā-*saṅgīt*, or not at all. In particular, the action of these Bengali poems occurs *after* Śiva's marriage to Umā, and derives its emotional force from the motif of waiting. There is no retelling of the Satī story, Umā is never depicted doing ascetic practices to gain Śiva's hand, the wedding is never described, and Kailasa as a setting for the poems is rare. Śiva the erotic lover is nowhere to be found; there are no bed scenes.[14] While Umā often returns home with her two children, Pot-Belly and Six-Face, the latter, Skanda, who is the whole reason for her marriage to Śiva in the Purāṇas—so as to kill the demon Tāraka—is never singled out for mention at all. The reason for Umā's birth in the *āgamanī* and *bijayā* songs is to reward Menakā for her great devotion.

In other words, Umā is in the foreground. She is her parents' only daughter, and they bitterly regret having been forced to give her in marriage to Śiva.[15] Unlike the Sanskrit myths, in which the seven sages and Arundhatī negotiate on Śiva's behalf with Umā's father for her hand in marriage (note that it is Śiva who initiates in the Sanskrit Purāṇas), here it is Himālaya and Menakā, who because of their poverty seek out the services of Nārada, who finds them a match commensurable with their means.[16] You pay for what you get—Śiva.

Indeed, in the Umā-*saṅgīt* Śiva is given almost no respect. This can be seen in the lack of details one receives about his heroic, godlike personality; though there are allusions to his Sanskrit alter ego in his Bengali epithets, there is no narration of his burning of Kāma, his defeat of the Triple City, or his various other exploits.[17] Instead, his nakedness, homelessness, oddball ornaments, drug addiction, and the bad company he keeps (namely, his troupes of ghosts and ghouls) are primarily the results of his poverty; he has no money to buy clothes or pay rent, and he ate poison because he was hungry.[18] Moreover, his keeping of a co-wife does not endear him to Umā's parents, who resent him and never invite him home to spend the Pūjā holidays with them.

Bengali scholars have argued that the Umā-*saṅgīt* is built upon, mirrors even, the experiences of real Bengali families in the late medieval period. The circumstances of Umā's family appear similar to a mild form of Brahman Kulīnism—that is, two to three wives living in the husband's house, where the wives are considerably younger than their husband, their fathers having been constrained, often through the matchmaking services of people whom they did not trust, to give them away as children.[19] According to the census of 1881 Kulīnism was widely practiced by one of the two largest groups of Brahmans in Bengal, the Rāḍhī Brahmans. "Of aristocratic or noble descent," Kulīns practiced strict hypergamy: Kulīn women could only marry Kulīn men. The consequent surfeit of Kulīn women resulted in multiple marriages for Kulīn men, many of whom left their brides with their natal families and visited them only rarely, to collect the obligatory gifts from their fathers.[20] The poetry about Menakā's concern over Umā's co-wife, the Ganges River, reflects the agony of such polygamous situations.

In addition, expectations that a father would give his daughter away (*kanyādān*) well before puberty led to increasingly tender marriageable ages; it was normative in early medieval Bengal for little girls to be married off at age eight, and for their husbands to be three times their age.[21] One of the meanings of Umā's name Gaurī is "eight-year-old girl"; hence the poignancy of the link between the Umā-*saṅgīt* and the lives of real women. Margaret Urquhart put it well in 1925: "From childhood a woman's view is directed away from her own patriarchal group, in which she has little part to play, to the possible family tree on which she will be grafted. This is what makes the story of the marriage of Gaurī, the girl wife of the god Śiva, so popular and full of poignant meaning to the zenana women. The period of a girl's connection with her father's house is made as brief as possible. . . . A special traditional sanctity attaches to the age of eight as a suitable one for marriage, Gaurī, Śiva's wife, according to general belief, having been married at that age."[22] From this vantage point, reading the descriptions of Śiva in the *āgamanī* and *bijayā* songs is like being introduced to a Kulīn mother's worst fear: her little daughter married perforce to an old, totally unsuitable man.

Women's lives in general were highly restricted in late medieval Bengal, with clearly delineated divisions between the male public world and the female domestic one. The only women who bridged that divide—those who danced in the "nautches" in the homes of the wealthy—were not considered "respectable" role models for daughters to emulate, and many of them, in any case, were Muslim dancers.[23] Daughters-in-law in particular were largely confined: when inside, to the *antaḥpur*, zenana, or women's quarters, and when outside, to the palanquin or covered bullock cart or boat. Education was not typically available for women, even for the wives of the traditional elite. Menakā's laments that she cannot visit her daughter by herself, must rely on men for information from the outside world, and is hampered by her simple nature all reflect this cultural environment of eighteenth- to nineteenth-century Bengal.

Wherever the North Indian custom of marriage prevails—that is, between families whose members are not related by blood, as counted back to seven generations on the male sides—one finds rhymes, folksongs, and proverbs expressing the pain of losing a daughter to a family of strangers, away from the safety of her father's village.[24] The following Bengali rhyme poignantly conveys the anticipation of unbearable loss:

> Granny, why are you crying, holding the basket full of *sindūr*?
> Only yesterday you rubbed my hair parting with heaps of it!
> Mā, why are you crying, holding that jug of milk?
> Only yesterday you fed me heaps of milk.
> Sister-in-law, why are you crying, holding a basket of rice?
> Only yesterday you fed me heaps of rice.
> Daddy, why are you crying, holding the beams of the thatched
>     roof house?
> Only yesterday you used that stick to beat me![25]

Some Bengali aphorisms do not bewail the pain of customary child marriage, but attack it for its cruelty. For instance, the following decries those who would cover up the heinousness of the Kulīn match—or the injustice meted out to any innocent: "You gave Gaurī into the hands of a forty-two-year-old. Saying mantras won't lessen the fact that you have sacrificed her."[26]

Given such conditions, daughters-in-law looked forward with anticipation to the Pūjā holidays, when they might be allowed to return home to their parents. At stake was both the joy of reunion with family and the pampered leisure time with fewer restrictions, and also the reliving of Pūjā holidays, remembered for their magic. For those who did not or could not go home to their fathers' houses, Pūjās in their in-laws' residences—as also marriages—gave women "a chance to participate in activities that had meaning beyond the immediate surroundings," even if, in wealthy families, this meant no more than watching the festivities through screens. By the end of the nineteenth century, Pūjā vacations, affected by British attitudes to travel, leisure, and holiday, were "no longer only used as an opportunity to visit the ancestral village, but as a time to go away for a holiday. Sarasibala Ray described her excitement at the prospect of a trip to Murshidabad in the *pūjā* holidays of 1900, which she looked forward to as an escape from the normal conventions of the antahpur."[27]

Through its reflection of contemporary Brahmanical customs of polygamy, child marriage, and the experience of mother–daughter bonding, the Umā-*saṅgīt* renders Durgā Pūjā meaningful on a whole host of levels not apparent merely from a glance at the image of Mahiṣamardinī. *Āgamanī* and *bijayā* songs are clear in their message: the goddess who comes is the daughter, not the demon-slayer. Moreover, she is the universal Bengali daughter of every house, and her coming transforms the life of Bengali Menakās everywhere.

A second indicator that the daughter-goddess is integral to the meaning of Durgā Pūjā is her inclusion, or that of references to little girls, in the festival itself. To begin with, the origin stories of many *banedi bāḍīr Pūjā*s are centered around girls. Either a daughter asks her father to start celebrating the Pūjā at their home,[28] or a founding father dreams of a *devī* in the form of a girl, who expresses her wish to be worshiped not as the martial Durgā but as the daughter Umā with her two children,[29] or the Pūjā is founded by parents mourning the loss of their own daughter, for whom the goddess Umā substitutes. Sometimes this loss is due to marriage, as in the case of Gaṇeścandra Chunder, who married off his daughter in 1876, but missed her so much that he started a Pūjā, not only to remind him of her but also so that he could have an excuse to bring her home for the holidays.[30] At other times the loss is more final; the historic Dawn family Pūjā was begun in 1760 by Rāmnārāyaṇ Dawn after his young daughter came home from her parents-in-laws' house and, while there, died of cholera.[31]

The presence of Umā is also evidenced in rituals associated with the Pūjā. Mahālayā, the holy day that falls six days before the Pūjā on the new-moon *tithi* of *devī pakṣa* and whose primary function is to honor the ancestors (*tarpaṇa*), has been hijacked, so to speak, by Durgā Pūjā. For most Bengalis, Mahālayā is the day on which Umā sets out for Bengal from her home on Mount Kailasa; since the 1930s, generations of Bengalis have awoken at dawn to the voice of Bīrendrakṛṣṇa Bhadra singing the *Caṇḍīpāth,* or "Devī-Māhātmya," story on All India Radio. That this new layer on the older Mahālayā festival is truly the undisputed harbinger of the Pūjās is demonstrated by what happened in 2001, when the almanac called for Mahālayā to occur one month and six days before the start of Durgā Pūjā: All India Radio decided to postpone the broadcast of its traditional radio show by a month.[32]

Apart from the singing of the *āgamanī* and *bijayā* songs, other rituals pointing to the importance of girls and daughters to the Pūjā include the *kumārī pūjā*, described in chapter 1, by which the majestic goddess is rendered irresistibly lovable and pure (fig. 3.1); homey customs particular to certain families, such as at the Bagbazar Sānyāl house at Kasi Bose Lane, Kolkata, where they feed the Goddess morning tea;[33] and, most suggestive of all, the farewell rites for the Goddess on the tenth day, or Daśamī. The image of Durgā is treated exactly like the married daughter who, after spending time at home in her father's house, is sent back to her husband's place: she is adorned with vermillion, fed sweets (these are daubed onto the image's mouth), and given betel nuts into her hands. After this, all the women of the locality daub each other with red powder, in a jovial ritual called *sindūr-khelā*, or playing with vermillion (fig. 3.2). Even the rite in which blue-throated birds are released at the moment of Durgā's immersion in the river, and hence departure for Kailasa, expresses the belief that the goddess who has just left Bengal is Śiva's gentle wife, not the martial demon-slayer. According to historian Mohit Rāy, the real purpose of these *nīlkaṇṭha pākhī*s was actually quite plebeian and woman-centered: in the Krishnanagar Rāj family these were pet birds set free at the waterside who flew back to their mistresses in the zenana, who otherwise would not have known when the immersion had occurred, since they were not allowed to go out.[34]

FIGURE 3.1. Feeding the Goddess in the shape of a little girl at *kumārī pūjā*. Kolkata, October 2008. Photo by Jayanta Roy.

A third gauge of Umā's importance to the Pūjā is iconographic, and can be seen in the fact that she brings her four children home with her to her parents' house. Indeed, the clay image of Durgā Mahiṣamardinī is typically flanked, on her right, by smaller images (*mūrtis*) of Gaṇeśa and Lakṣmī, and on her left, by Kārtik and Sarasvatī. I am not aware of any other Indian regional tradition in which Pārvatī/Umā is said to be the mother of Lakṣmī and Sarasvatī, but in Bengal this has been claimed—iconographically, at least—since the late seventeenth century. A few old family Pūjās substitute Umā's friends, Jayā and Bijayā, for the four children, and others omit the demon-slayer entirely from their Pūjā tableaux, showcasing instead: a two-handed Durgā, with her lion but without the buffalo demon; Hara-Gaurī, the husband-and-wife team, where Gaurī is diminutive beside or on top of her lord[35]; or even Gaṇeśa-Jananī, where the only image displayed is a seated Umā with the chubby elephant-god in her lap.[36] In general, those families who sponsor a Pūjā without explicit representation of the martial Durgā have something in their backgrounds that militates against sacrifice, blood, or fear. Sometimes they are Vaiṣṇava or Vaiṣṇava-leaning, and sometimes they simply do not wish to emphasize the Goddess's death-dealing aspect. According to traditional stories of the Tripura Rāj family, for example, which claims to have been worshiping a

FIGURE 3.2. *Sindūr-khelā* at a house in Howrah city. October 2000. Photo by Jayanta Roy.

two-armed goddess for five hundred years, she appeared to an ancestress, Mahārāṇī Sulakṣaṇādebī, and said, "I'm not going to harm you. There's no cause for fear, so you don't need all those hands."[37] At the other end of the spectrum in terms of elitism and the longevity of its Pūjā, but with the same proclivity to sideline Durgā for Umā, is the very recent tradition of sculpting Durgā at a remote tribal village near Santiniketan. Here Durgā arrives with lotuses rather than weapons in her hands. "Ma Uma is coming to her father's house. Why will she come with arms in her ten hands?"[38] No matter how the Goddess is represented—with or without children, with or without a buffalo-demon—the face of Śiva is almost always painted on the backdrop above and behind her, as if to remind her and the viewer that this is his wife, and that he expects her to return to him from her father's house quite soon.

Fourth, Umā's salience in the context of the Pūjās is demonstrated by her use by Bengali nationalists in the late nineteenth and twentieth centuries, when, as we have seen in chapter 2, the Goddess herself became a lithe, needy, human figure, needing to be saved, like a daughter. R. K. Dasgupta, in an essay in 1980, describes this idea of the Divine Mother in bondage as a theologically ambiguous and essentially Bengali idea, for the Supreme Mother is also Umā in distress: "The Mother who will wipe your tears is herself in tears."[39] Hence the presence of the daughter within the Bengali goddess tradition has humanized the Divine, making her uniquely tender and affectionate, even weak.

Fifth, the importance of the daughter tradition is further indicated by the centrality of children to the Pūjā hoopla and excitement. All the major newspapers, in English and Bengali, run special inserts at the season for children, not only featuring articles on clothes, music, and food, but offering Pūjā quizzes and requesting children to send in their Durgā-centered pictures, poems, and experiences for publication. In 1999 the *Statesman*'s themes in such children's sections were "When Durga was a Little Girl" and "When Durga was Young." In 2006 a Behala Pūjā committee took children's depictions of the Goddess (holding water guns or lightsabers from Star Wars) and employed an artist to patch them together to create murals to decorate the inside of their pandal; in 2008 the Santoshpur Lake Pally Committee made children's fantasy the theme of its pandal, and asked the artist to sculpt her as he would have visualized her as a child.[40]

When the literary, ritual, iconographic, political, and contemporary evidence presented thus far is reviewed, it is abundantly clear that Umā is integral to Durgā Pūjā. The song cycle celebrating her return home to Menakā and Girirāj, the various ways in which the women's rituals of the festival mirror or express the importance of daughters and the sadness of their departure at marriage, the visual impact of the images as worshiped in *ṭhākurdālāns* and pandals, and the theologically intriguing resonance in political discourse of the vulnerable Invincible—all these elements point to a strongly emotive attachment to the Goddess-as-daughter, and a longing to bring her home.[41] One is reminded in this context of the work of William Sax, whose research on the goddess Nandā-devī in Uttarkhand demonstrates how a literary and ritual tradition of reenacting the Goddess's return to her husband's home helps women to enunciate, but not necessarily to change or escape from, the pain they experience through the Gahrwal system of out-marriage. Sax's work also underscores the importance to women, despite the male emphasis on the husband's house, of the father's home and all that it represents: love, acceptance, leisure, and true belonging.[42]

## Durgā the Daughter? The Interpretive Puzzle

It is not intuitively obvious why one would find Umā so prominently displayed in an agricultural festival used by the elite to aggrandize their wealth and position. When did Durgā Mahiṣamardinī gain four children? And when did Mahiṣamardinī/Umā become the universal Bengali daughter who returns exactly once a year, at the Pūjā holiday?

There are no easy answers. The Sanskrit Purāṇas and Tantras, and even Tantric digests such as Āgamavāgīśa's *Tantrasāra*, say nothing about Gaṇeśa, Lakṣmī, Kārtik, or Sarasvatī, mentioning only the Goddess, her lion, and the buffalo-demon.[43] The first allusions to Durgā's children occur in ritual and narrative texts of the medieval period: Vidyāpati's *Durgābhaktitaraṅginī* of the fourteenth to fifteenth century, Mukundarām Cakrabartī's *Caṇḍīmaṅgalakāvya* of the sixteenth century, and Raghunandana's *Durgāpūjātattva* of the late sixteenth to early seventeenth century.[44] But it is not until the Umā-*saṅgīt* of the late eighteenth century that the explicit link is made between Umā, Durgā, daughters, and the Pūjā season. The same evidential lacuna is true of the iconographic evidence. Bengali sculptures of the Buffalo-Slayer, from the earliest discovered samples in the seventh century[45] up to late Pāla period art in the twelfth century, mirror their famed predecessors from places such as Mahabalipuram, Aihole, and Udayagiri: they depict Durgā killing Mahiṣa. Indeed, prior to the Mughal period, no sculptures of Durgā Mahiṣamardinī anywhere in Bengal, whether free-standing or on temple walls, include the four children.[46] When Gaṇeśa and Kārtik, or Lakṣmī and Sarasvatī, do appear in conjunction with a goddess in Bengali sculptures, the goddess in question is in her peaceful, gentle aspect as Pārvatī, or Pārvatī and Śiva, not in her manifestation as the battle queen. This of course makes sense, considering the popularity from the early Gupta period of Umā-Maheśvara statues of the husband-and-wife team, together with Kārtik or Gaṇeśa.[47]

By the late seventeenth century, however, terracotta temples were displaying Gaṇeśa, Lakṣmī, Kārtik, and Sarasvatī on engraved slabs together with Mahiṣamardinī, although their positioning was not always at Durgā's side, but above and below her. In a few cases, the inclusion of children heralded the loss of Durgā's martial aspect entirely: the Goddess was accompanied by her husband instead of her lion and buffalo enemy.[48] In other cases, the children softened the Goddess; in 1910, members of the Jalpaiguri Rāj family added Gaṇeśa, Kārtik, Lakṣmī, and Sarasvatī to the previously lone image of Mahiṣamardinī, and her skin color became paler.[49]

Causes of this eventual iconographic change can only be surmised; as far as I am aware, no scholar in English or Bengali has attempted to construct a connected narrative that makes sense of all known evidence. With the rise of Sultanate power in the region after the thirteenth century, Brahmanical influence and culture were challenged and eclipsed, leading to the proliferation of folk forms of religion.[50] Some of these were expressed in literature such as the Maṅgalakāvyas, discussed earlier, where local deities were humanized, their desires and powers portrayed through stories based in the Bengali environment. Maṅgalakāvyas eventually gave way to the *āgamanī* and *bijayā* songs on Umā, as well as to a genre of street entertainment known as *kabigān*, in which popular culture, including the marriage of little girls to aged husbands and their return once-yearly to the natal homes, was satirized by groups of musicians who vied with each other in extemporaneous versifying. The same regionalization and adoption into folk culture is also true of art, evidence of which becomes especially plentiful in the form of brick temples from the sixteenth century. Such temples to Brahmanical deities began to appear in western Bengal concurrently with the rise of Mughal power; their façades were covered with panoramic battle scenes; mythological friezes, on the life of Kṛṣṇa, Rāma, or Durgā's battle with Śumbha and Niśusmbha; depictions of social life (hunters, soldiers, kings, etc.); divine or lay figures in rows; and floral and geometric patterns.[51] Especially by the eighteenth century secular life makes its way onto these friezes: bearded priests and servers attend to Durgā, violinists serenade her, and her devotees are even dressed in European clothing. On other slabs, Gaṇeśa can be seen feeding from a bottle, zamindars are strutting about in Western dress, and European boats sail into Bengali ports.[52]

After the late seventeenth century some of the engraved slabs on the walls of terracotta temples displayed tableaux of Durgā that bear striking resemblances to other contemporaneous popular artforms, painted *paṭs* and clay *lakṣmīsarāis*. *Paṭs* were watercolor paintings done on scrolls or thick paper, and were used either for decoration purposes or in Pūjā contexts, sometimes prior to the adoption of clay images. *Lakṣmīsarāis* originally derived from the painted bottoms of clay pots but eventually attained their own freestanding autonomy as decorated clay dishes used during Pūjā time.[53] Among the many examples of Durgā-centric *paṭs* and *lakṣmīsarāis* that I have seen, if the children are included at all they are stationed above each other, or above and below the Goddess. Sometimes even Śiva appears over her head. This spatial arrangement of the figures may reflect space considerations, but it also conforms with the pattern established for the clay image tableaux on display at Pūjā time in homes of zamindar families.

The temple slabs also closely resemble the ways in which the earliest-known clay images were being produced for the families of the wealthy from the early seventeenth century (see chapter 4): those slabs that included the four children arranged them in two groups of two, with Lakṣmī placed above Gaṇeśa and Sarasvatī above Kārtik, they often added sculpted copies of the painted backdrops, or *cālcitras*, used behind the clay images of the Goddess and her family, and the lion mounts upon which the Goddess sat frequently sported horses' heads. Some scholars infer from these similarities that the temple slabs of Durgā with children were sculpted in imitation of what was visible already in the homes of the rich, Pūjā-sponsoring landowners—i.e., that elite ritual was influencing local popular art.[54] Says Malavika Karlekar, "It is possible . . . that as Durga Puja became increasingly popular in the zamindari homes of Bengal of the eighteenth and nineteenth centuries, the goddess was 'domesticated.' She symbolised the supreme mother who would destroy so as to protect her children and the children of forthcoming generations."[55]

It is extremely difficult to know which of these artforms arose first or can be considered primary in influence, although, as we shall see in chapter 4, it is likely that the worship of Durgā with the two-dimensional *paṭ* preceded that with the clay image. Perhaps the best one can do is to postulate some sort of folk tradition reaching back into the fifteenth century through which, as Durgā Mahiṣamardinī's festival was increasingly popularized and as her link with Śiva's wife became more explicit, she inherited the deities iconographically (but not textually) portrayed as accompanying Pārvatī: her two sons, Gaṇeśa and Kārtik, and her two "sister goddesses," Lakṣmī and Sarasvatī, who together provided the auspiciousness, learning, and fortune necessary for householder life. The next step in the process, however, the association between Mahiṣamardinī/Umā (and children) with the myth of her homecoming at the Pūjā season, may owe more to the influence of the zamindars than to popular custom.

It is possible to conjecture that it was the *rājas*' aggrandizement of the festival that led to the specific conjunction of (a) Durgā, (b) Umā the daughter of Menakā, (c) a festival during which daughters return home, and (d) the conception of Umā as the universal daughter of the land. Because there have never been many permanent Durgā temples in Bengal—still an interpretive mystery[56]—her festival represents a once-yearly chance to welcome and worship her. And since the Pūjās were originally organized under the jurisdiction of the elite, it was they who set the trends and built up the holiday during the annual event. So the tradition of bringing daughters to their natal villages would have occurred with the growth of the harvest festival, which was being lavishly patronized as Durgā Pūjā by the elite.[57] Additional considerations include the following: nineteenth-century oils of Menakā and Girirāj depict Umā's parents as affluent zamindars (fig. 3.3)[58];

FIGURE 3.3. *Āgamanī* ([Home]coming). Traditional iconography with a European landscape and distant horizon. Oil painting, ca. 1890. British Museum 1990.10–31.01.

it was the wealthy who patronized the composers and singers who made the Umā theme popular at the Pūjā season; these elite scions sometimes composed such songs themselves;[59] and their estates were the site for the performance of all daughter–centered songs and rituals. In an English article from 1952 by noted historian Jadunath Sarkar, he says of the Pūjās of his youth seventy-five years earlier, "There was an artistic rivalry between village and village [in terms of boat immersions]. The zamindar's pansay proudly rowed up and down (music playing on its foredeck) for some time." As the boats went back, the rowers sang in chorus, " 'I have sent away my golden Gauri with the vagabond Shiva. The fair is broken up and Darkness has descended.' . . . I can still feel this tragedy of the Dusserah day."[60] Many of the rituals emphasizing the daughter-goddess also bespeak confinement and prosperity; the poor probably could not have afforded pet birds, could not have presented their departing daughters with such gifts, and did not have the leisure time to listen to the *āgamanī* and *bijayā* song cycles.

Whether one traces the origin of the Pūjā's daughter aspect to a folk or women's stratum or to a set of practices fanning out from zamindari custom, the fact remains that the first explicit evidence we have for the Mahiṣamardinī-Umā-daughter-Pūjā confluence is the Umā-*saṅgīt* literary genre, which does not predate the mid-eighteenth century and was largely the product of poets writing under the patronage of zamindari courts.

From where the original impetus for such a layering of ideas came, therefore, it is hard to tell. But once established, such multifaceted conceptions of the Goddess, social meanings of her festival, and domestic rituals connected with it were adopted and patronized by elite culture as its champions strove to publicize and popularize Durgā Pūjā.

## *Vātsalya*, Even *Viraha*: Longing and the Pūjās

Although one can claim historically, visually, and textually that the primary meaning of the Pūjās relates to the conferral of strength, or *śakti*, the destruction of obstacles, and the consequent enjoyment of blessing, it is arguable that the real underlying feeling, or *rasa*, of the festival is one of tenderness for the returning beloved. Heads of old family Pūjās are proud to continue their traditions in part because, unlike the community pandals, erected yearly and then dismantled, *their* Durgā, the daughter, still has a home to return to.[61] Artisans who create the clay images feel similarly: for months they have lovingly modeled, painted, and adorned their Durgās, and when the goddesses leave for the homes and pandals of the city, their makers feel bereft. Said the president of the Kumartuli Artisans Association, "For how long we have been decorating and dressing the girl. And at the start of the puja we feel as if our house's daughter has gone. Believe me, when everyone else is rejoicing, we here are in the darkness of the cremation ground." Mohan Bhanshi Rudra Pal agreed: "It's a feeling of a pain that's almost like bidding goodbye to your daughter when she leaves for her in-laws' home."[62]

For some Bengalis, the desire for the daughter completely overshadows the importance of the martial Mahiṣamardinī. This is reflected playfully and poignantly in certain nineteenth-century *āgamanī* songs, many of which refuse to accept that the darling daughter is really the slayer of demons. For the sake of comparison, recall that in the Sanskrit Purāṇas the primary mode of identifying Pārvatī with Durgā and Kālī is through battle scenes, when Pārvatī assumes the form of a warrior goddess to help the male gods slay demons. Moreover, the Sanskrit myths evince no distaste with such transformations of Śiva's demure wife; in fact, her darker sides add to her glory.[63] Here, in the Umā-*saṅgīt*, however, the opposite could not be more in evidence, for the Bengali poets portray Menakā accepting only reluctantly the equation of her daughter with Kālī and Durgā.

For instance, Menakā dreams that Umā has become black—i.e., Kālī—and this terrifies her.

Giri,
what a nightmare!
I dreamed I saw Umā in the cremation grounds.
She was black,
roaring with laughter.
Her hair was a mess,
and she was naked,
sitting on a corpse.
There were three eyes
on her terrible face;
a half-moon shone on her forehead.
She wandered about on a lion
with a group of *yoginīs*.
I got so scared
looking at her.
Get up! Get up, lazy Mountain!
I'm consumed with worry;
hurry to Kailasa,
and bring my ambrosial Umā home.[64]

In other poems, Menakā hears rumors from Kailasa:

I got some news from Kailasa!
Oh, my God!
What are you doing, Mountain Lord?
Go, go,
go see if it's true.

Śiva has put on Umā
the burden of their household life,
while he does yoga on the cremation grounds!
Seeing him thus engaged,
people seize the chance, seize his wealth
and scatter to the winds.

Look what happened! His moon ended up
in the dome of the sky, the Ganges now

courses the earth, his snakes
live in the underworld, and his fire
endangers forests!

Umā thought so hard
about Śiva's habits
that she turned into black Kālī!
My daughter, a king's daughter,
deranged from hurt feelings?!
Now she wears strange ornaments —
completely shameless.
And this is the worst of it:
I hear she's drunk![65]

In these and other similar poems, Umā becomes black Kālī, or skin-and-bones Cāmuṇḍā, because of her poverty, misery, and indifferent husband. It is only the mixed tears of mother and daughter that once a year wash away her darkness, at home.

Another poem of this variety depicts Menakā actually receiving her daughter at the Pūjā time but being unable to recognize her.

Mountain,
whose woman have you brought home to our mountain city?
This isn't my Umā;
this woman is frightening —
and she has ten arms!
Umā never fights demons
with a trident!
Why would my spotless, peaceful girl
come home dressed to kill?
My moon-faced Umā
smiles sweetly, showering nectar.
But this one causes earthquakes
with her shouts and the clattering of her weapons.
Who can recognize her?
Her hair's disheveled, and she's dressed in armor!
Rasikcandra says,
If you recognize her,
your worries will vanish.

But it's in this form
that the Mother destroys my fear of death.[66]

This ambivalence toward the Sanskritic Durgā and Kālī spills over into the Bengali presentations of the Sanskrit "Devī-Māhātmya," or *Caṇḍī*, sung daily by Brahman priests during the Durgā Pūjā festivities. Menakā wants nothing of this dry, Sanskrit ritual text, when Umā, or the *real* Caṇḍī, is coming home.

Get up, Giri, get up!
Here, hold your daughter!
You see the *Caṇḍī* and teach the *Caṇḍī*,
but your own Caṇḍī has come home![67]

Giri,
where is my Ānandamayī?
When is She coming?
How all the Brahmans bustle about,
installing pots at their posts!
I guess my Caṇḍī has gotten stuck somewhere,
listening to the *Caṇḍī*.[68]

Dāśarathi Rāy (1806–1857), a famous poet in this literary genre from the mid-nineteenth century, describes Menakā looking everywhere for Umā. She searches in the ritual *ghaṭ*, or water pot, and she also inspects the Sanskrit *Caṇḍī*, but cannot find her daughter anywhere.[69] This is symbolic of how the Śākta poets prize the Bengali daughter goddess over the Sanskritic martial goddess. To the extent that it is Durgā Mahiṣamardinī who arrives on the sixth evening, Menakā's fears have come true.

One way of describing or understanding the feelings expressed for Umā is to use language derived from the Vaiṣṇava context—a context extremely germane to Śākta religiosity, given the proximity and mutual influence of these two major groups in Bengal. Many of those who wrote poems on Śākta themes also wrote poems about Kṛṣṇa and Rādhā, and the six-century literary tradition associated with the latter deities colored Umā as well. For instance, Menakā's motherly love for and attachment to her daughter Umā (*vātsalya bhāva*) can be compared to Yaśodā's emotions for Kṛṣṇa, and Sucī's for Caitanya. The myth cycles of all three include scenes of the mothers staring at the roads by which their children must return home, and having nightmares about danger to their loved ones. Just as Yaśodā occasionally glimpses the true nature of her son, but quickly retreats behind the veil of adoring motherhood, so also Menakā is frequently told about Umā's real identity as the Mother of the World, but can rarely hold the knowledge. Moreover, when these children eventually leave their mothers—Umā for Kailasa, Kṛṣṇa for Mathura, and Caitanya for Puri—the plants and animals in their natal homes droop and faint. Some Śākta poets even copy Kṛṣṇa's penchant for butter and cream, creating scenes in which Menakā feeds Umā hand-churned milk products.[70] The most astonishing example of these Vaiṣṇavizing tendencies comes from Rāmprasād Sen, in an early composition called the *Kālīkīrtan*. Here his Umā is a cow-girl who takes her cows to pasture and plays to them on her flute. She and Śiva sport together in flower groves reminiscent of those belonging to Rādhā and Kṛṣṇa, and she even has a Rāsalīlā dance.[71] Therefore, the sweetening and humanizing of Umā, as well as the desire to concentrate on her as a daughter, may well owe much to the influence of Vaiṣṇavism and its articulation of *vātsalya bhāva*. Although there is nothing overtly erotic in the Umā-centered story of Menakā's longing, one could perhaps see a touch of *viraha* here as well—that is, the pain of love-in-separation that the mother endures for her distant girl.

The significance of this attachment to the daughter Umā, especially as rendered through the *āgamanī* and *bijayā* songs, is underscored by the degree of emotion expressed by those who sense its disappearance in modern Pūjā contexts. It is true, in fact, that the Umā-*saṅgīt* is far less noticeable in Pūjā festivities than it apparently once was. One can hardly find occasion to listen to the songs anywhere, in homes or in Pūjā pandals, the only exception being at public concerts or on cassettes and DVDs. In other words, the very songs that once heralded the coming of the Pūjā festivities are now strangely absent from their intended context. Bengali interviewees indicated several types of reason for this absence: the increasingly fast pace of community and even home Pūjās, where there is no time to stop for the lugubrious tunes of a mother's heartache; the slow disappearance of singing troupes who would travel house to house, performing; the impact of urban culture, not only in cities but also in rural settings; the easing conditions of marital life, such that Menakā's grief is no longer relevant to present-day women; and the lack of complementarity between the *āgamanī* and *bijayā* songs and the Sanskrit, "Devī-Māhātmya"–inspired ritual context of the Pūjā, which does not reinforce the presence of Umā.[72]

People looking back nostalgically on the Pūjā celebrations of their youths often cite the decline of interest in the Umā-*saṅgīt* as a major cultural loss.

Even in the 1940s and 1950s their demise was being lamented: "The raucous gramophone blaring the latest cinema tunes brings a heartache for the Agamani songs, our counterparts of the carols and the Nativity songs." Their haunting quality seems to "have gone with the mellow lamp-light, the street-singer and the unbought grace of life. . . . It is sad to think that these songs are no longer sung."[73] The Pūjā, now shorn of the Umā-*saṅgīt*, is a "lifeless, soulless, mechanical affair, . . . the logical conclusion to the process of urbanization" and loss of pride in [our] heritage. Nevertheless, because the *āgamanī* and *bijayā* songs are in [our] background, "we still find them moving."[74]

When one hears Bengalis reminiscing or planning on how to bring back the true spirit of the Pūjās, it is this domestic, feeling, daughter aspect that is most often singled out for urgent attention. One can find notices of revival movements going back to the mid-twentieth century: village women are said to be coming to Calcutta to restore the emotional heart of the Pūjās by singing the songs of Gaurī's return to her father's place;[75] various famed folk and devotional singers such as Rāmkumār Caṭṭopādhyāy and Amar Pāl always bring out Umā-*saṅgīt* cassettes at the festival season, hoping that they will catch on; and in 2001 a Delhi-based Bengali named Āśis Ghoṣ made it his mission to revive the art of *kathakatā*, narration interspersed with *āgamanī* and *bijayā* songs, in which one person acts all the different roles. In a number of newspaper interviews, he explains that the stories he has heard of women's hardships creep into his telling of the tales. "The 80-minute stage show speaks almost entirely on behalf of the female folk," he says. "Menaka and Uma's story is still the story of contemporary India."[76]

At its broadest level, one can interpret the sense of longing for the daughter Umā in terms of cultural nostalgia. Though first used in 1688 to refer to a medical condition of homesickness (*nostos* + *algia*) noticed in Swiss mercenaries, "nostalgia" is now considerably widened in semantic scope.[77] It typically refers to a desire to return to a romanticized past conceived less in terms of place than of time—a time in one's early life when certain experiences, feelings, places, or people are recalled with heartfelt longing. Nostalgia is not a simple memory of the past, for it carries with it a painful awareness of lack and a desire for (impossible) restoration. Roberta Rubenstein, in her work on the yearning for specific visions of "home," calls nostalgia a "haunted longing" and describes its "painful awareness, the expression of grief for something lost, the absence of which continues to produce significant emotional distress."[78]

Causes for nostalgia vary; at its most general, nostalgia is set in motion by present fears, anxieties, or uncertainties that would appear to be calmed by a memory of or a return to the past.[79] In chapter 1 we saw a nostalgic craving among the middle classes for an aristocratic zamindari culture that connotes, in addition to family cohesion, leisure, and true faith, pride in a uniquely Bengali past. Place (or recreated place) and a displayed material artifact, the Durgā image, serve as the trigger for or site of the nostalgic sensibility. Here, in this chapter, the nostalgia is oriented less at architecture, custom, or artifact than at lost time, lost youth: one rues one's own aging and that of one's family and friends; one longs for childhood, whether one's own, one's children's, or one's culture's. Indeed, the "universal exile from childhood" is what Jean Starobinski calls nostalgia.[80] Rubenstein mirrors this in her discussion of mothers who mourn younger versions of themselves when they had not yet lost centrality in their children's lives; they are pained by time's passing and their own stagnation in it.[81] Mr. Umazume, the man responsible for starting the revival of the nearly lost Awaji puppet tradition in Japan in the 1940s, commented to Jane Marie Law about his motivations: "A terrible sense of loss . . . Something slipping away. My childhood. The sounds . . . It was painful to feel something so meaningful sliding through your fingers, and yet do nothing but talk about the good old days."[82] Often related to the yearning for childhood is the identification of urbanization as the underlying cause of deplored change. Law found this as the operative reason for the dying puppetry in Awaji, and identified in her informants a bias toward the rural as the ultimate source of authenticity.[83] Grief at the passing of an entire cultural tradition was therefore linked to a championing of "the old ways" as envisioned before industrialization rendered them seemingly obsolete.

If cultural mourning is "an individual's response to the loss of something with collective or communal associations, a way of life, a cult, a homeland, a place with significance for a larger group, a history from which one feels exiled," then the healing afforded by nostalgic thinking or artforms is—to borrow Rubenstein's thoughtful phrasing—an imaginative fixing of the past by revising its meanings in and for the present.[84] One can never return home or recapture one's childhood, but a certain pleasure is derived by remembering it or even attempting physically to reproduce it. This is so even if—whether one is aware of it or not—the relived or recreated will always be censored, a false version of a once-complex experience.[85]

Theorists also note the degree to which the nostalgic sentiment can be used to generate lucrative rewards for the tourist and entertainment industries, can be co-opted by big businesses for advertising, and can even aid the candidacy of particular political parties. Nostalgia has made the past, says David Lowenthal, "the foreign country with the healthiest tourist trade of all."[86] Nevertheless, those committed to encouraging nostalgic renewal feel that the gains are worth these potentially undercutting side-effects. Mr. Umazume, for instance, believed strongly that reviving the Awaji Nongyō tradition for theatrical rather than ritual performances was far better than having it lost forever. Even in theater the puppets might transform people.[87]

Much of this elucidation of cultural nostalgia applies also to the case of Bengal. As the biggest yearly Hindu festival, no matter what one's sectarian leanings, Durgā Pūjā evokes the same sort of passionate anticipation in children that Christmas does; if one is removed from those memories by increasing age, or by a forced emigration from one's home, as in the case of refugees from Bangladeshi villages after 1947 and 1971, or by choosing to live in the diaspora, the Pūjā takes on a rosy hue and symbolizes the essence of what has been lost through the passage of time. Many urban Bengalis still speak of "home" as the village of their forebears, even if they have never visited it, and many of them who were brought up in the village recall with wistfulness the Pūjās as they occurred there. No matter how much one enjoys the hoopla of the urban Pūjās, one aches for the rural, truly "authentic" festivals in remembered villages. In new environments, joining in or even initiating the Pūjā celebrations is one way of adjusting. "Nostalgic memory, creatively reconfigured, [becomes] one source through which [refugees can build] a new communal culture and construct a new collective identity to serve their changed needs."[88] Refugees or immigrants also aim to engender in the second generation a nostalgia for their parents' past through clubs, associations, cultural events, and educative programs. Hence the significance to Bengalis, wherever they live, of cultural soirees in which the Umā-*saṅgīt* is performed by professional singers: retrieved ritual, even in an entertainment milieu, is still important, still heartwarming and stirring.

Thus even if Durgā Pūjā had no association with Umā, as the national Hindu festival par excellence it would still provoke feelings of bittersweet nostalgic craving. As Benedict Anderson and many others after him have shown us, the nation is often conceived in the vocabulary of kinship or of home;[89] the expectation that wherever one finds Bengali Hindus one will encounter Durgā Pūjā celebrations and Kālī temples implies that "home"—or Bengal or India—is intimately tied to the Mother, to Bhārat Mātā, as a means of self-expression. The fact that this festival, in addition, honors a mother–daughter bond built on feelings of loss and longing accentuates the love-in-separation, or *viraha*, at the heart of the event. Bengalis join Menakā in yearning for Umā as they yearn as well for their own daughters, for their own childhoods, pasts, homes, and Durgā Pūjās of old.

# 4 The Artistry of Durgā and Jagaddhātrī

This chapter surveys Durgā, and to a much lesser extent Jagaddhātrī, from the perspective of her "looks": how and why has the Bengali Goddess changed iconographically over time, and what are the current trends and controversies in terms of her depiction? Two larger themes contextualize and illuminate the evolution under survey: the history of the sexualized Indian female icon, and the intersection of goddess portrayals with Indian nationalism.[1]

## Corporal Transformations in a Beloved Deity

### *Before She Had a Face*

It is hard for a modern participant in Bengali Pūjā celebrations to imagine that there was ever a time when beautifully sculpted images of the Goddess and her divine companions were not central to Pūjā festivities. And yet this was so. The many aspects of contemporary Durgā and Jagaddhātrī Pūjā stand on an agricultural base, for before the popularity of the festivals in the late medieval period, with their deities, myths, and rituals, autumn was the occasion for harvest festivals among local farming communities.

FIGURE 4.1. The traditional *ekcāla* image, with the *nabapatrikā*, or *kalā bau*, to Gaṇeśa's right, at the Shovabazar Rāj house (main branch). Kolkata, October 2000. Photo by Rachel Fell McDermott.

Durgā came late to this celebration, and Jagaddhātrī even later, and both were enfolded into it, enveloping as they gained ascendancy its prior symbols and resonances.[2] Vestiges of this older, agricultural stratum are still evident today in Pūjā contexts: the *ghaṭ*, or pot of water, established in front of the Goddess's image[3]; the plates of dried grains and fruit offered to the Goddess during the several days of her worship; and the *nabapatrikā*, or nine plants,[4] that are trussed up together and ritually bathed at the commencement of the festivities before being dressed in a sari and placed on the shrine dias next to Gaṇeśa, as though it were his bride (see fig. 4.1).[5] These vegetal elements of the ritual lead Bengali scholars to believe that the Goddess was once conceived as "a personification of the vegetation spirit."[6] Of the two—*ghaṭ* and *nabapatrikā*—the former is probably older, as the *nabapatrikā* is not mentioned in the "Devī-Māhātmya," the *Kālikā Purāṇa*, or other early Pūjā digests.[7]

The centrality of the *nabapatrikā* and the *ghaṭ*, even today, is indicated by the ritual unimportance of the Goddess's image, which is not essential to the efficacy of the worship. It is the *nabapatrikā* that must be present for the validity of the ritual, and the *ghaṭ*, not the image, into which the Goddess's presence is invoked. Old Bengali families who have been worshiping Durgā for generations, and who use their own permanent metal images of the

Goddess, not the temporary bazaar-bought clay ones, bring their figures to the special halls set aside for her yearly festival, but ritually establish a *ghaṭ* and *nabapatrikā* in order to perform the worship. Tantric *sādhakas* claimed as the progenitors of particular temples are often said to have initiated the worship of the Goddess with a *ghaṭ*; it was later devotees who added the anthropomorphized *mūrti* (image).[8]

Intermediate between the agricultural symbols and the three-dimensional *mūrtis* are two genres of pictorial depiction, both popular from the mid-nineteenth century: the *paṭs*, or two-dimensional watercolor drawings of the Goddess, sold in bazaars near Kālī temples for the pilgrim souvenir market, and the *kāṭhkodāis*, or woodcut prints, which were colored by hand.[9] Relatively cheap and popular in the market, both *paṭs* and woodcut prints soon began to be employed in Pūjā contexts as well; this usage derived from a mutual desire among both potters and Pūjā-sponsors to "see" the Mother in increasing detail.[10] Indeed, in textual sources prior to the early seventeenth century, worship of the Goddess was done at home according to what was called a *ghaṭe-paṭe pūjā*.[11]

Although they are rarely used nowadays, due to the popularity and standardization of the clay images, one can still see *paṭs* and *kāṭhkodāis* of Durgā and various other goddesses in museums, as well as in families and villages that insist on keeping up the older traditions. The Gurusaday Museum in Kolkata, for instance, in its displays of Bengali snake worship, exhibits *ghaṭs* with snake hoods drawn on them, later paper drawings of the same, and then even more recent *mūrtis* of Manasā. Vishnupur still predominantly uses *paṭs* in its Durgā Pūjā, as do the members of the Hetampur Rāj, in the Dubrajpur district of Birbhum, and Hatserandi village, near Bolpur, also in Birbhum.[12] Even local names of the Goddess can give hints as to her origins: Mallabhum's Durgā, whose worship is attested from the fourteenth century, the Burdwan Rāj's Durgā, and Shantipur's Kālī, from the early eighteenth century, are all called Paṭeśvarī, or the Queen of the Paṭ.[13] Some Pūjā committees, wishing to claim authenticity and the recovery of ancient custom, even choose to go against the trend and commission *paṭs* instead of *mūrtis* for their pandals.

The transition to clay images is hard to date with precision, particularly since artistic styles may have changed at different tempos depending on locale. Tradition has it that Rājā Kṛṣṇacandra Rāy of Nadia was the first to introduce the practice of anthropomorphized deity worship in the mid-eighteenth century; certainly by 1766, when the British were ensconced in Calcutta, enjoying the invitations of wealthy Bengalis to their lavish

Durgā Pūjā "nautches," the Goddess was visible in her humanized form—fashioned from straw and clay, decorated with ornaments and flowers, and depicted in the act of slaying Mahiṣa with her lion mount and ten arms. She was usually placed on a stage in front of the guests in the opulent mansion setting, surrounded by the additional images of her children. By at least the mid-eighteenth century, therefore, and probably much before, *ghaṭe-paṭe pūjā* had given way to *mūrti pūjā*.

## *The Aristocratic Durgā of Old*

In present-day Kolkata there are several artisans' districts; the most famous, Kumartuli, in the northern part of the city, is home to around 150 artisans, who together employ approximately one thousand workers.[14] In preparing for a Pūjā celebration today, most committee organizers go to one of these districts, commission an image, and make arrangements for it to be brought to their locale at the beginning of the festival. However, such was not always the case, and in some elite contexts still is not. "In the old days," say Bengali interviewees—I take this to mean up until the early 1920s, when the celebrations were still principally home affairs, sponsored by affluent zamindar families—there were no prefabricated goddess images. Artisans came directly to the house and did their modeling there, in front of family onlookers. They had no studios.[15] Pratapchandra Ghosha, author of the most authoritative English manual on Durgā Pūjā from the nineteenth century, opined, "No respectable family purchases a ready-made idol from the bazaar."[16]

Judging from old newspaper accounts, interviews with artisans, and families who still design their Pūjā decorations in the precise fashion of their eighteenth-century ancestors, until the early twentieth century Durgā was sculpted and decorated by teams of *kumārs* (potters), *sūtradhars* (carpenter/builders), and *paṭuyās/citrakārs* (painters) in conformance with certain iconographic conventions, characterized today as *sābekī*, or old-fashioned, traditional.[17] She strikes the buffalo demon with a spear held in two of her ten arms; the other eight arms bear weapons. Her face ought to resemble the roundness of a betel leaf (*pān-pānā mukh*). Her eyes are to be elongated, stretched up to the ears (*ṭānāṭānā ākarṇa bistṛta*); her mouth tiny, relative to the rest of her face; her chin square; her nose hooked, like the beak of a parrot; and her body heavy (*bhārī deha*), with overly long arms and large hands (*moṭā hāt*).[18] Her blank gaze (*śūnyadṛṣṭi*), without a fixed object of sight, enables her to return the glance of the devotee from any angle.

Such iconic figures with their unearthly faces are further enhanced by the bold lines and primary colors of their bodies, which instantly distinguish them from mortal models. According to orthodox prescriptions, Durgā, Lakṣmī, and Kārtik should be a golden yellow washed with orange, Sarasvatī white, Gaṇeśa red, and the buffalo demon a loud green. Gaṇeśa and Lakṣmī, and Kārtik and Sarasvatī, stand to the right and left of the Goddess, respectively, and she places her left foot on the demon and her right on her equine mount, which is slim, white colored, and engaged in biting Mahiṣa. It is likely—given the evidence of old temple images, terracotta temple slabs, and the customs of families who have been sponsoring Durgā Pūjā since at least the eighteenth century—that Durgā's original vehicular animal was either a horse or a stylized lion with a horse's head.[19] The move to a muscular lion represents a desire to simulate the descriptions of the "Devī-Māhātmya" and famous sculptures such as those at Ellora Caves—but may also have been reinforced by attempts to imitate lions in the coats of arms of the British royal family.[20]

As far as one can ascertain, the earliest Durgā images were decorated with clothes and jewelry—a crown, necklaces, rings, armlets, toe-rings, bangles, and earrings—sculpted from the painted clay itself or carved from the *solā* plant. Of course, wealthy families wanting to outdo one another in the adornment of the Goddess had recourse to finer materials: in the mid-eighteenth century, when there was such rivalry between Nabakṛṣṇa Deb and Gobindarām Mitra, the latter gentleman ordered gold and silver leaf to cover Durgā's entire body, instead of paint.[21] By the mid-nineteenth century, clay decorations had given way to cloth ones, and what is now known as *ḍāker sāj* (intricately cut tinsel decorations, whether of *solā* or other material; lit. "decorations by post") derived from silver foil imported from Germany. This recourse to the foreign market functioned both to garb the Goddess in proper regal fashion and to provide impressive ammunition in the houses of Calcutta's Pūjā rivals.

Another element of the traditional Durgā image is the backdrop, or painted *cāl*, of which there were two principal types prior to the early twentieth century: the *ekcāl*, or single wooden frame, which extended from the floor behind the images of Durgā and her children to form a halo-like half moon slightly above their heads (see fig. 4.1); and the *cupḍicāl*, in which a single wooden base rose to gave way, behind the images, to three backdrops shaped like upside-down wicker baskets, or truncated steeples.[22] On the cloth or paper stretched across the wooden frames of both types, artisans paint figures—a varied potpourri of gods and goddesses, such as Kālī, Viṣṇu's ten *avatāras* and the ten *mahāvidyās*, Indra and other Vedic gods, Rāma and his family, Śiva and the sixty-four *yoginīs*, Durgā in her battle with Śumbha and Niśumbha, and Rādhā and Kṛṣṇa. In most such *cālcitras*, or decorative paintings, a tiny depiction of Śiva's head can be seen, looming over and behind the clay images. This is a reminder that Durgā's husband watches the scene and awaits her return to him in the Himalayas at the conclusion of the Pūjā.

Most of the prominent, historic families of Kolkata who have the means to do so strive to keep up the traditions of their progenitors, especially with respect to the *cāl* style, and the coloring, decoration, and placement of their divine images. In the words of a slightly smiling Mr. Kalyāṇkumār Deb, scion of the Chātu-Bābu Lātu-Bābu family, whose Pūjā was started by

FIGURE 4.2. Durgā holds Kṛṣṇa in her lap, Pañcānan Pāl's house. Nathbagan, Kolkata, October 2000. Photo by Jayanta Roy.

Rāmdulāl Sarkār Deb between 1770 and 1780, "Every year the image is the same, no change, at least to my knowledge."[23] The only occasional concessions to modernity consist in allowing the artisans to do some of the sculpting work at their studios; reducing the quantity of each offering made to the Goddess; and choosing to keep her valuable gold or jeweled ornaments off her body and under lock and key (or hiring security guards to keep watch). The two most notable permanent variations from the norm—that is, adaptations that are as old as the families who sponsor them—are indications that not everyone prefers the martial Durgā over the daughter Umā. As we have seen in chapter 3, in several prominent Vaiṣṇava or Vaiṣṇava-leaning households, Durgā is flanked not by Lakṣmī and Sarasvatī but by Umā's childhood friends, Jayā and Bijayā. Some families go further, and remove the image of Durgā Mahiṣamardinī entirely from center stage, placing in its stead images of a diminutive Umā sitting on Śiva's lap or standing by his side—or even Durgā holding Kṛṣṇa in her lap (see fig. 4.2).

In sum, the typical old-fashioned tableaux of Durgā and her children functioned rather in the manner of a Western icon: through their static poses, somewhat disproportional body sizes, loud colors, and faces dwarfed by huge eyes, they invited *darśan*, a seeing and being seen by the awe-inspiring, majestic deity, effortlessly quelling evil.

## *From Icon to Drama: The Innovations of the 1920s*

Iconographically, the biggest transformation in Durgā's face, body, and accompanying figures—away from the traditional style and toward something more akin to what we see today—occurred in the 1920s, although the various impetuses that led to it had long been brewing.

Indian art styles, especially in the colonial city of Calcutta, were greatly affected by the British and their tastes. By the mid-nineteenth century, the city's artists were already being influenced by the naturalistic style taught and patronized by Europeans. Although in general sculptors lagged behind painters in the acquisition of this new training, the emphasis on realism did touch many of the city's traditional clay potters, several of whom began to create models of animals and humans. An early example of this facility are the clay figures acquired by one Captain Briggs, who brought seven naturalized images to America in 1823, where they now reside in the Peabody Essex Museum in Salem, Massachusetts.[24] By 1851 Indian potters' work was being showcased in the great world exhibitions of London, Paris,

Melbourne, Amsterdam, Boston, and Glasgow. Potters were also conscripted when the scientific classification of India's native peoples was being undertaken as part of the colonial anthropological project.[25]

Some artisans were even sent to the world's fairs as representatives of their art. One such was Gopeśvar Pāl (1894–1944), who traveled in 1924, when he was twenty-nine years old, as a representative of the famed Krishnanagar clay-sculpting tradition to the Empire Exhibition at Wembley in London.[26] Pāl was stationed at the India Exhibition, where, with a basket of earth and clay, he spent his day making figures of the people he saw. When they moved on, he squashed the figures and started anew. On July 6, Arthur, Duke of Connaught, and his daughter, Lady Patricia Ramsey, entered the tent. Reported the *Daily Telegraph* the next day, "His Royal Highness was one of the first English subjects to have his head modelled by Gopfor Pal, the Indian sculptor who has just arrived at Wembley, and who fashioned a remarkable likeness of the Duke in less than five minutes."[27] According to Pāl's family—though I cannot find record of this in the British papers—Pāl was introduced to the royal family, who rewarded him by offering to send him on a tour of Europe. But Pāl responded that he would prefer to study Italian sculpture; he stayed in Europe for seven and a half months doing so, and then returned to India in the spring of 1925.[28]

It is tempting to try to infer what Pāl might have seen and learned in such a brief sojourn. According to his son, the late Siddheśvar Pāl, an elderly gentleman when I met him in 1988, Gopeśvar did not get any formal training in Italy, but visited several stone sculptors' studios and "soaked up like a sponge" the styles and techniques they used. His son cannot remember any specific Italian pieces that his father loved, and he did not bring home any souvenirs or photographs, but if his tastes were similar to those of most Indians of the late nineteenth and early twentieth centuries, the Italian sculptural tradition he probably most admired was that embodied by the voluptuous Venuses and Apollos of the classical Greek and Roman styles. In any case, his return to India coincided with a new revolution in Pūjā presentations, for in 1926 we find the first evidence of the *sarbajanīn* Pūjās. By 1928 or 1929, Pāl had been asked to take charge of sculpting the Goddess image for the local Kumartuli Sarbajanin Puja club; he assented, somewhat reluctantly, but after his initial success continued as chief artisan there until 1939, a few years before his death.

Influenced significantly by the conventions of European realism, and probably by several decades of prior artistry in which naturalism had come to influence the depiction of deities,[29] Pāl started experimenting

FIGURE 4.3. Gopeśvar Pāl in front of one of his images in his studio. Jayanta Dās, "Kumorṭulir Cārśo Bacharer Bibartan," *Deś* 64, no. 24 (19 Sept. 1998): 68.

with Durgā Pūjā images. Within a couple of years of his first attempts, he had removed the space-constraining single *cāl* backdrops from behind the images, which freed him to enlarge the deities and model them in ways expressive of movement (see figs. 4.3–4.4). Thus instead of standing placidly, staring straight ahead at the viewer, with one foot on her lion mount and the other on Mahiṣa, Pāl's Durgā rides her lion into battle or energetically spears the demon, realistically. In his hands her visage changed as well. He rounded her face (*golpānā mukh*), decreased the size of her eyes, painted them with eyelashes, gave them a more naturalistic stare (*svabhābikdṛṣṭi*), enlarged her lips, so that they were proportionate to the rest of the face, and began to color her skin with tones of pink. The whole effect was of a humanized Goddess, in an image in which the Mahiṣamardinī scene was depicted according to the exact descriptions of the "Devī-Māhātmya," the Pūjā manuals, and the Tantric *dhyānas*, or meditational images—"according to Sastric conception" and "in right Oriental fashion," to quote a contemporary newspaper.[30] Due to this location of iconographic authority in scripture as opposed to tradition, Pāl diminished, or often even removed entirely, the customary figures of Dugā's four "children."

Pāl was keen to represent the Goddess as realistically as possible, and was particular about every anatomical detail. Before making the Durgā

FIGURE 4.4. A Gopeśvar Pāl tableau from 1939. Photo gifted by Siddheśvar Pāl.

image he would take his sister up to the rooftop of their house and ask her to pose for him. The same naturalism touched Pāl's lion and demon, as well. "It is said that he would go to the zoo and pay money to have the lions fed meat. Then he would sit and copy them chewing. At that time a Muslim bearer lived at Kumartuli. He had a daredevil look, and . . . Pāl used him as a model for the demon. This was the beginning of the muscular Mahiṣa"[31]—whose neck muscles stand out and whose hands go taut as he leans back to brace himself against the onslaught of the Goddess. Pāl would invite a medical surgeon to check that the disemboweled stomach of the demon was physically accurate, and he consulted a wrestler to make sure that the demon's biceps and triceps were lifelike.[32]

Another of Gopeśvar's sculptor contemporaries at Kumartuli, N. C. Pāl, also contributed to the transformation of the Goddess's image. He developed a school of "Oriental Art," according to which Durgā was crafted in imitation of actual artifacts from periods of Indian history. He created goddesses in the style of Ajanta and Ellora Caves, Gupta art, or Orissa temples, and sculptors in his school even looked to renowned painters such as Nandalal Bose, Jamini Roy, or Ravi Varma for inspiration. In the sense that they were plumbing Indian history for goddess prototypes, these Orientalists were also sometimes dubbed "traditionalists."[33]

As a whole, the goddesses spearheaded by the two Pāls came to be labeled "art" *ṭhākurs*—i.e., *mūrtis* with separate backdrops or none at all, and a realistic naturalism in the presentation of facial and bodily features. They were tremendously popular, and were repeatedly written up, with photos, in the newspapers of the 1920s and especially 1930s. Some of the new *sarbajanīn* community Pūjās, such as those at Kumartuli and Bagbazar, became associated with Gopeśvar and N. C. Pāl's names, respectively, as they were commissioned to sculpt their images each year, and people came from far and wide to view their creations.[34] What attracted onlookers was the combination of novelty, striking realism, and a beauty that imparted religious feeling. Said a newspaper reporter in 1932 about the Bagbazar image: it is "quite in consonance with the conception of the Mother in the Hindu Shastras. The pose is Oriental, the painting is devoid of superficial arthobby. The image is, in fine, simple and beautiful, splendid and awe inspiring and at the same time devotion creating."[35] This same evaluation is made today by Gopeśvar and N. C.'s iconographic heirs. Said sculptor Rameścandra Pāl, one of N. C.'s pupils who graduated from a Calcutta art college in 1947: "I want to give humanness to the devī. I don't deny tradition, but the large-eyed, round-faced, stationary-bodied image—this I want to change. This is why I experiment . . . Mā Durgā who has big hands, a heavy body, and is burdened by age: when does this occur? The *śāstras* say that the goddesses are ever-youthful; one must realize the conception of the *dhyānas*."[36]

The priests responsible for the proper worship of Durgā during the Pūjā season were not, apparently, happy with the changes occurring in the late 1920s and 1930s, for their definitions of "traditional" and "devotional" were different. Whether it was Gopeśvar Pāl's or N. C. Pāl's brand of "realism," the former harkening back to the "Devī-Māhātmya" text and the latter to cave or temple sculptures, the priests resented the loss of the *cāls*, the diminution or removal of Gaṇeśa, Lakṣmī, Kārtik, and Sarasvatī; and the softened, Memsahib-like aspect of the Goddess's demeanor.[37] Initially, in fact, they boycotted the Kumartuli images. After 1947, immigrant and refugee artisans from East Bengal, who took enthusiastically to the new, humanized image styles but were aware of the dangers presented by too much departure from custom, kept the emphasis on realism but added individual backdrops to their images and returned the Goddess's children to her side. This evolving style, which by this time had been termed the "Bāṅgāl Durgā" because of its patronage by East Bengalis, modeled the Goddess after real women, especially movie stars like Narges from "Mother India" or stars from 1960s hits like "Saptapadi," "Bipāśā," "Dīp Jvele Yāi," and "Sānt Pāke Bādhā."[38] Some Durgās were even Madhubala or Suchitra Sen lookalikes. Such *devī*s were draped realistically in women's saris, painted with human tints, and made as curvaceous as possible. The old, *sābekī* style of portraying Durgā, with the flaming eyes, large, heavy body, and static pose—though increasingly dwarfed in the *sarbajanīn* market by the naturalistic *mūrti*s—continued to be in demand for the home Pūjā celebrations; the production of such "Ghaṭi Durgās" was mostly taken over by West Bengali artisans.

## *The Dual Legacy: Competing Goddesses*

Since the 1960s, when the art *ṭhākur*s exploded in imaginative design, there have been scores of examples of creative experimentation, as artists have vied with each other for novelty and acclaim. As one observer noted in 1957, "The style of image-making has suffered in recent years. The typical 'Bengal' face, which gave a sense of [the] power and majesty of the goddess, has now practically disappeared. In this particular type, Bengal's craftsmen reached a high level of artistic abstraction. With long eyes, an oval face and dilated nostrils, the goddesses inspired awe among devotees. Such images are rarely made and are only worshipped in some orthodox families."[39] Truly, since the 1960s Durgā has been made to fit almost every whim of fashion. She has been clothed with shells, paper, grass, coins, and wax. Even more radically, her entire body has been fashioned from paddy, gold, oyster shells, fish scales, nuts, mirrors, sawdust, tea leaves, sugarcane husks, coconut, biscuits, toffy, rubber pipes, recyclables like rusty forks, matchsticks, empty toothpaste tubes, biscuits, peacock feathers, snake-skins, metro tickets, and lozenges. Durgā comes seated on an elephant or dressed in tiger skins, with matted hair. She sheds her demon-killing form and looks like a real Bengali women, in traditional attire,[40] or she is a real woman; at the Prajapita Brahma Kumari Vishvavidyalaya, at the Elgin Road–Chowringhee crossing in Kolkata, the images are actual people who hold their poses for four hours a night.

Although such creativity has been in evidence from at least the 1960s, since about 2000 a new fillip has been given to the attraction for art deities: the entrance into the Pūjā field of students from accredited art colleges. Graduates of institutions like Rabindra Bharati, having been taught to emphasize novelty and being unused to the restraints of texts and traditions, create unusual images that are much in demand by Pūjā committees hoping to win prizes for the distinctiveness of their displays.[41] Art students apparently enjoy being commissioned to create Pūjā *pratimās*, too, as it gives their work a mass appeal, "unlike our exhibition works which are for a select few."[42] The presence in the Pūjā market of art college work, however, presents its own new challenges. Traditionally, images are immersed in water at the conclusion of the festivities. Many art college graduates, viewing their work less as religious worship than as artistic product, are hesitant to consign their Durgās to a watery grave, selling or donating them to hotels, restaurants, and museums. The evanescent, fleeting Durgā is hence becoming a little more permanent as a result of trends in the image market.

Whoever the artist, the result for the Goddess is more-or-less the same: as scholar-commentator Bimalcandra Datta wrote in the late 1980s, "Durgā used to be *raṇaranginī* (delighting in war), but now she has become *rangaranginī* (delighting in dramatic flirtation)! She gets younger every day—more like a child. She looks at the demon, no longer with wrath or sternness, but with a smile!"[43] This humanization—indeed, sexualization—of the Goddess is underscored by the many film stars who continue to play her part on screen. Following the success of famed beauties like Hema Malini playing Durgā in the TV series, "Jāi Mātā Di," and Mallika Sarabhai enacting the Goddess in her road show, "Devi: The Mother Goddess," in 2000 director Ravi Chopra chose Indrani Haldar to play Durgā in his movie, "Mā Śakti," because, he said, she has a pious, round face, is shapely, and looks very pure. She seems to have the look of "*debī bhāb*."[44]

Such realism extends as well to the Goddess's companions. Her son Kārtik is often made to look like a Bābu, complete with *dhoti* and pump shoes, and every year Mahiṣa either looks like some film "baddie," such as famed Hindi stars Amjad Khan and Sadashiv Amrapurkar, or appears with the likeness of real-life villains such as the late Saddam Hussein or Veerappan.

It is only natural in a competitive environment, with the public, *sarbajanīn* image market skyrocketing decade by decade, and innovation and originality the tickets to fame, that artisans would choose predominantly to sculpt art images. Not only are they more amenable of change and adaptation, but they are also more pleasing to the eye. If the Goddess is the mother, may she look like one—beautiful, tender, and compassionate. One of the hybrid forms that I have noticed in the past several years is the growth of images sporting the traditional body—that is, a static, stolid torso—with the new, humanized doll-face. Year after year, from the 1950s into the first decade of the twenty-first century, if one consults the Bengali and English newspapers one will find photo spreads in which about 90 percent of the Durgās made in Kumartuli and similar districts are either of the Gopeśvar and N. C. Pāl types (that is, with natural movement and humanized proportions throughout) or of the hybrid types, with sweet faces on stationary bodies. One also sees a continuous stream of images modeled on some famed Indian sculpture or painting tradition, such as the images at Mahabalipuram or the paintings of Nandalal Bose or Jamini Roy. Only 10 percent are *sābekī* Durgās, with the flaming eyes, tiny mouths, and iconic poses.[45] In the 1968 Pūjā season, one reporter wrote that there were hardly three images in the whole city where the artists had followed the scriptures. The demon in one pandal, for example, was hanging on a trapeze rope, making it hard for Durgā to kill him.[46] The only time where one invariably sees printed photos of the old-style image is on Bijayā Daśamī, where there appears to be a tradition of photographing the *ekcāl* image as it is immersed in the river.

This same process of gradual humanization and naturalization has also affected Jagaddhātrī, Durgā's "sister" goddess, who is worshiped exactly one month after Durgā Pūjā has concluded and whose iconography is strikingly similar to that of Mahiṣamardinī. She is beautiful, holds weapons in her hands, sits on a lion, and is in the process of subduing a demon.[47] However, a closer look reveals important differences. Durgā's ten arms are replaced by Jagaddhātrī's four; the latter holds a discus and arrow in her right hands and a conch and bow in her left. Durgā is usually standing with one leg on the back of her lion; Jagaddhātrī sits on hers in a half-lotus, with one leg hanging down, in the fashion of a South Indian goddess. Durgā is actively spearing the buffalo-demon Mahiṣa; Jagaddhātrī leaves the goring of the elephant-demon to the ferocity of her lion, who squashes the

FIGURE 4.5. Jagaddhātrī, Hatkhola pandal. Chandannagar, November 2000. Photo by Rachel Fell McDermott.

elephant's head with one of his paws.[48] Absent are Durgā's four children; Jagaddhātrī, if flanked at all, is accompanied by Jayā and Bijayā, two friend-attendants. The Goddess herself is typically yellowish in color and arrayed in white—often the white *solā* decorations that are characteristic of her adornment (see fig. 4.5).

Like Durgā, Jagaddhātrī too can be classed according to types of facial depiction. The oldest Jagaddhātrī faces are fairly stylized, with wide faces, elongated eyes stretching up to the ears, relatively tiny mouths, and a serious, even fierce expression. Newer facial varieties, introduced in Calcutta in the 1930s and 1940s, humanize the Goddess's visage; her face is rounded, her features are normalized relative to one another, in imitation of a young woman, and her mouth is sculpted into a charming smile. In present-day Chandannagar, Jagaddhātrī's eyes are decorated with mascara, and her dimpled chin is adorned with a beauty mark. The overwhelming number of Jagaddhātrīs I have seen, either in person in Chandannagar or Kolkata or in newspaper photographs, are of the sweetened, girlish type. Even the famed and fairly old, late nineteenth-century *sarbajanīn* Pūjā celebration in Bagbajar, Kolkata, which is frequently photographed, never departs from its beauteous goddess.

It is a peculiarity of Durgā, and even to a greater extent Jagaddhātrī—but not Kālī—that their manifestation at the Pūjā season is practically the only time in the year when their devotees get to see and worship them; this is because there are very few permanent temples to either goddess in the state. Although there are a lot of Jagaddhātrīs depicted on the walls of brick temples after the time of Caitanya, there is only one temple dedicated to her: in the village of Somra, Balagar subdivision, in Hooghly district. Built in 1755 by Dewān Rāmcandra Rāy, the temple is home to a deity made of eight stones, common for the expensive tastes of zamindar patrons of the time.[49] This lack of architectural attestation to her popularity prior to the mid-eighteenth century serves to confirm what one gleans from her festival history: Jagaddhātrī did not become popular much before the time of Kṛṣṇacandra Rāy,[50] and if one wants to worship her, one must participate in her yearly Pūjā.

Chandannagar, about one hour north of Kolkata by train, is the town most famed for its yearly worship of Jagaddhātrī. In the entire Chandannagar environs, I could find only two "old-style" images of the Goddess, with the big eyes and static torsos, and both of these, unlike all the myriad other images in the region, receive blood sacrifice. In fact, wherever Jagaddhātrī is still depicted in the traditional, *sābekī* manner, whether in Chandannagar, Krishnanagar, Kolkata, or Murshidabad, she is likely to demand blood offerings.[51]

Before leaving the subject of modern-day iconographic images and trends, it is important to note that the priests of the 1930s have not been alone in disliking the "shocking ingenuity in the making of images"[52] and the move toward a more humanized, sexualized Goddess. This is especially true of the artisans, many of whom feel loyal to the traditional icon. In a 1953 interview, Nirad Chaudhuri told the story of some young men who asked a potter to make the Sarasvatī in the image of one of their girlfriends. The artisan went into a rage.[53] In 1961, one potter "admitted that to keep in business he had to strike a compromise between the tastes of his customers and religious convention. Of course, he disclosed, some requests were so preposterous that they could not be complied with. He recalled that on one occasion it was suggested that the Goddess Durga be dressed in *kurta* and *salvar* in the North India style. He had obliged one customer, however, by adorning the Goddess's face with a beauty spot, though orthodox opinion would certainly frown at this. After all, by refusing to put that one black dot he might have lost Rs. 250, he argued."[54] In 2006 artisan Sanātan Rudra Pāl was asked by his Pūjā committee clients to create a dark, African Durgā to blend with the theme of their pandal, which was modeled on a temple in Ghana. "How can we worship someone who does not look like Durga?" He compromised by giving her only a hint of African features, and not coloring her completely brown.[55]

Pradīp Pāl, a senior Kumartuli artisan, told me in 1998 that he does not like modernisms in the Goddess's face and body, because they detract from her godliness; she is no longer a *ṭhākur*, or God.[56] Senior Kumartuli artisan Mohanbāśi Rudra Pāl agrees; remembering the old days, before and right after his family had moved from East Pakistan to Kolkata, he described the Goddess as properly looking angry, showing "fuming shakti in all her valour": "We did not digress from the way mahisasuramardini is depicted in our shashtras and hence her eyes were round and bulging, her nostrils flamed up and her mouth taut. The image was supposed to inspire awe in humans, not familiarity—that most of the Puja organizers want today."[57] Even the noted modern Bengali artist Paritosh Sen prefers the traditionalism of the old Durgā images: "The propensity for naturalism," he avers, is "inimical to our traditional values."[58] For those who choose or are constrained to adopt the new naturalism, however, there is the additional challenge of maintaining authenticity; in 2004 the organizers of Ajeya Sanghati in the Haridevpur area of Tollygunge, who were trying to make a splash with their Nagamese Durgā, were forced to change the Goddess's attire, after the Students Union of Nagaland complained that it was not correct.[59]

Departures from tradition that seem to arouse less ire from artisans or the public are those that contribute to some form of universally acknowledged public good, such as *ahimsā*, peace, and environmental protection. The late Alok Sen was preeminent in this regard; his Durgās, always showcased at the pandal at Muhammad Ali Park, were famed for their social messages. In 2001 his Durgā stood in front of two defaced Bamiyan Buddhas; in 2000 she was organically connected to a weeping tree.

The public is fickle, and goes through fads. Even though I would maintain that the sexualized, contextually-relevant Goddess is here to stay, and will keep her competitive edge, in some years one finds enunciated a real appreciation for the older, pre-1920s type of visage. This occurs particularly in cases where there is an overall sense of nostalgia for the "old days" of the zamindars and their Bābu-culture. Announced a confident (and, I would add, ultimately incorrect) newspaper reporter in 1988: "The search for novelty is over. . . . Durga is once again iconic looking like what she used to in the thakur dalans of zemindars or well-to-do households. . . . Time was when the wind was in favor of goddesses resembling humans, which earlier was unthinkable. . . . Then Durga started looking like screen goddesses of the day. But once again, she is back, made up as of old, with bold lines, primary colors which at once distinguish her from mortals, and simplicity."[60] While most committees flip-flop back and forth, from one type of image one year to another the next, several *sarbajanīn* Pūjā organizers proudly proclaim that even from the 1920s they have never gone in for the humanized Durgā. A famous example is an image at Bagbazar in north Kolkata, which has always been traditional. Its large eyes, seemingly looking in opposite directions, "give relief from all of life's pain."[61] People flock to this image, and almost every year it wins a prize. Apparently, beauty is not only in the imitation of a woman's charms.

If, then, one views the image-making at Kumartuli as a popular artform, in line with the woodcuts, Kalighat *paṭs*, and mass-produced lithography, the artistic pedigree of its humanized, sexualized *mūrtis* becomes clear: under the impact of the expanding urban economy, print culture, mechanical replication, photography, European-style theater, and British art schools, Bengali artisans used the technologies available to them to imbue their folk iconography with an earthy realism. The fact that clay images of Durgā and her family lagged behind in their adoption of this humanism can be accounted for by the timing of their own entrance into the popular market. It was not until the rise of the *sarbajanīn* Pūjā in the late 1920s that the demand for images skyrocketed, creating the same prerequisites for transformation as occurred with the earlier artforms: mass consumption and public dissemination. One suspects that even without a Gopeśvar Pāl, someone would have revolutionized the Goddess's visage.

As seen above, however, for those who hold on to a vision of the Goddess formulated before the mechanics of mass production had spread her to a wide public, her popularity has come at a loss. To such devotees the Goddess should not be a movie star, not because such a representation smacks of Western degradation or because it is gaudy and unrefined, but simply because it fails to move the heart. What Gopeśvar Pāl thought he was doing with his new style of goddess image—restoring the authentic meaning of the scriptures and the beauty of the divine—destroys that meaning and beauty for a select few. One man's voluptuous woman is not always another man's goddess. And herein lies the creative tension of the Durgā Pūjā season. How will the Mother look, this year?

## A History of Artistic Sexualization

This brief overview of the development of Durgā's iconography is interesting in itself as a case study of evolving artistic styles. However, as indicated at the beginning of this chapter, I would like to place Durgā's beautification in two larger contexts. We will first look at attitudes toward and perspectives on women in nineteenth- to twentieth-century Bengal.

The desire of Gopeśvar Pāl and his contemporaries and followers to humanize the Goddess and her family is heir to several social, literary, and artistic trends. Although I shall concentrate here on the art world, let me preface this by mentioning concomitant developments in society and literature.

As Meredith Borthwick, Partha Chatterjee, Rajat Kanta Ray, and Judith Walsh have shown, the expected roles of women were fast changing in the mid-nineteenth century.[62] Prior to 1800, the accepted norms for women included child marriage, lack of choice regarding sexual partners, constant scrutiny by the elders, prohibition against divorce, enforced widowhood, and outcasting; in such a milieu a woman had little freedom, and a man's only outlet for romantic love was with a courtesan. By the midcentury, however, elite male Bengalis, among them many Brāhmos, were inspired by the ethos of chivalry and romantic love available to them through English education—and were attracted to the ideal of companionate marriage with a mature woman who had a personality and mind of her own.[63]

These sea changes in the roles and expectations of women correspond to, and are reflected in, the conditions necessary for the inception of the novel as a new literary expression. Anchored in a new appreciation for individualism and realism, and enabled by a new stress on education and the success of the printing press, the novel "arose in Bengal in the nineteenth century because there was a new middle class, a substantial number of literate women with leisure[,] and a group of English-educated young men who craved for a new genre in literature reflecting their problems."[64] Indeed, nineteenth-century novels are preoccupied with moral questions related to domestic issues in the new modernity—love, passion, and illicit affairs. The most famous of these early writers, of course, is Bankim Chandra Chatterjee (1838–1894), whose novels focus on strong, romantic, pathos-filled heroines.[65] The unique character of the Bengali novel, writes Rajat Kanta Ray, is its blending of indigenous concepts, such as the expression of *viraha,* or pain-in-separation, from the love story of Rādhā and Kṛṣṇa, with Western notions of romanticism.[66] Although social reality lagged several decades behind the possibilities fleetingly entertained in such novels, the space was nevertheless created for a new conception of woman, one which emphasized her adult feelings and individualism. When modern-day Kumartuli sculptor Rameścandra Pāl says that he wants his image of the Goddess to be an individual, a learned woman, one can hear the resonance of past literary history.

The same revolution in female portraiture was also occurring in the art world, and here one can see the clearest evidence of influence upon the Kumartuli artisans. As charted and illustrated by Partha Mitter in his book *Art and Nationalism in Colonial India*, from the early nineteenth century Western artistic conventions began to impact the taste of aristocratic Indian collectors and the techniques of Indian artists. Perhaps the earliest indications of such effects can be seen in the hybrid genres of "company drawings" and "company paintings" from the early to mid-century, where Indian artists were commissioned to paint for Europeans, but according to Western canons of naturalism, shading, and proportion.[67] With the establishment of European art schools in Calcutta from the 1850s, in order "to inculcate good taste in the natives," we find the rise of elite Indian artists who vied for patronage, no longer from a wealthy sponsor, but from an increasingly art-conscious public. The taste for naturalism, realized through techniques such as modeling in the round, the effects of light, shading, proportion, and perspective, was reflected in the enthusiastic reception not only of Indian art students but also of novelists like Bankim Chandra, who liked academic naturalism and used it in his descriptions of Bengali homes.[68] In addition, Western naturalism permeated the art collections of the monied classes in Calcutta, who, to signify their wealth and status, filled their mansions with duplicates of Greek and Roman classical art—Venuses, Apollos, and Minervas, with their sensuous realism and silken drapery—and copies of the European masters, such as Leonardo da Vinci, Raphael, and Rubens. When they could, fortunate art students would travel to Italy, to see this art at firsthand, or even to study the techniques of classical art in art schools established for the purpose in Rome. It is in this context that Gopeśvar Pāl's eagerness to study Italian sculpture makes eminent sense.

Hence the impact of the Western art canon was certainly felt in what one might call the elite world of the individual artist and collector. But it was also palpable in the folk, and soon popular, art worlds of the street. From the early nineteenth century, with Bengalis quickly joining the revolution spearheaded by the printing press,[69] a genre of mass produced, cheap books and periodicals appeared on the market, most of which were illustrated by woodcut block printing. Called Bat-tala publications, after the area in north Calcutta where they were first produced, their favorite themes were Hindu deities, episodes from the epics and Purāṇas, and scenes from contemporary social life, which they satirized and dramatized.[70] At roughly the same time, in the 1830s, appeared the Kalighat *paṭs*, a genre of watercolor paintings on cheap paper, with bold lines, simplicity of style, and figures in frontal or three-quarters profile.[71] These too depicted gods and goddesses, mythological scenes, and caricatures of city life. Both of these genres were galvanized by the new technology of mechanical reproduction; the rise of secular literature; and the opening up of Calcutta, via the railway, to the national pilgrim market.

One can see little trace, in these illustrations, of Western artistic conventions, such as shading, lighting, or proportion. However, European stimuli can be seen in their mass-produced nature, as well as their reflection of the colonial environment—woodcuts and *paṭs* depicting the top-hatted Sahib, the Westernized Bābu, European furniture, Gothic arches and pillars, hanging glass lanterns, gatekeepers wearing coats and trousers, winged angels around deities' heads, and gods clothed in pump shoes and dresses.[72] Women, particularly new female types such as stage heroines, fashionable ladies, and courtesans, make up a substantial percentage of the figures portrayed in these woodcuts and *paṭs*, for from the 1850s and 1870s, respectively, photography and theater had introduced new, public roles for the display of the female figure, and much street art was influenced by memories of photographic tableaux or staged productions. As Jyotindra Jain notes in his excellent study of the Kalighat paintings, there is no difference between the depictions of these Bengali women and goddesses like Lakṣmī, Sarasvatī, and Durgā: all have the same postures, gestures, figures, composition, sari drapery, limb exposure, and ornamentation.[73] He even goes so far as to postulate that some of the women in these nineteenth- and early-twentieth-century engravings and paintings may have been likenesses of renowned theater actresses of the day.[74]

While all of this is suggestive, for our purposes the links between street art and the conventions of temporary Pūjā image iconography can be made even stronger. In general, the potters, or image makers, could not afford to enter the academic art schools of Calcutta, where they might receive formal European training,[75] and Indian sculpture was not encouraged by English art teachers, as it was considered "decorative" and hence inferior. However, the same artisans who were producing the Kalighat *paṭs* were also engaged in painting the clay images and the *cālcitras*, or decorated backdrops behind them. This means, says Jyotindra Jain, who juxtaposes *paṭs* of goddesses with *mūrtis* of goddesses to show their striking similarities, that the same conventions—secularization and the homologization of divine figures to human ones—color both painted and sculpted genres.[76] This affinity between two-dimensional street art and three-dimensional Pūjā image is also seen in the case of the woodcut blocks, which were "known to have been used for depicting deities and mythological stories on independent sheets of paper probably meant for use like a type of pat as objects of worship or of display" at Pūjā time.[77] In other words, the world of the goddess image market was closely associated with the worlds of print-making and watercolor painting, and as such inherited their close mirroring of contemporary secular life in the colonial city. Such cross-cutting artistic influences ensured that the *kumārs*, who were once confined to replication and stasis, adapted: from the early twentieth century they enthusiastically joined the craze for the sort of innovation and creativity that is necessitated by a sensitivity to social and political events.

The impact of the painting world upon that of the Kumartuli artisans is even clearer when we move to lithography, the success of which eventually drove the woodcuts and *paṭs* out of business at the end of the nineteenth century. Lithography was invented in 1798, reached India in 1822, and became big business in the hands of Bengali artists after 1876 at the Government School of Art in Calcutta. The lithographs specialized in Hindu "mytho-pictures," churned out for a mass market. The style was realistic, with flesh and muscles showing, volume, depth, and perspective emphasized, costumes made to look like velvet or silk, and captivating backgrounds. Female figures were depicted with fair skin; buxom torsos; long, open hair; sugary, naturalized faces; and flowing robes adorned with gold or gems. Many of these gods and goddesses were inspired, says Partha Mitter, by "the art school casts of Apollo, Artemis, and Aphrodite, and above all by Renaissance painting.[78]

The biggest name associated with this lithographic revolution in mass-produced art is Ravi Varma (1848–1906), the South Indian–born master who captured the attention of the British with his talents for naturalism, European shading, and dramatic lighting techniques in oil. The melodrama and sentimentalism associated with his opulent beauties derived in part from the influence of Renaissance and post-Renaissance European art,[79] but he was also trying to communicate an "emotion," or *bhāva*, as derived from the Sanskrit classics. At his hand, female figures were palpable, alluring, real women (he often used live models)—and his goddesses, cast in the same mold, were domesticated as mothers, daughters, or wives. The modern genre of calendar art, which can be traced to Varma's high-speed olegraphic presses brought to India from Germany in 1894, with its blurring of the categories of the religious and the domestic, derives squarely from his legacy.[80] To be sure, one has only to compare the humanized types of Durgā Pūjā image with calendar art depicting Durgā to see their stylistic intersections.

During and after the Swadeshi and antipartition period from 1905, the naturalism of Ravi Varma's style came under fire from a new breed of "Orientalist" artists like the famed Amrita Sher-Gil, Balendranath Tagore, and Jamini Roy, who decried naturalism as a Western colonial import and who championed as more authentically Indian the local, the "simple," or the "primitive" art of the village; in their eyes, one did not need naturalism to evoke *bhāva*.[81] Although this modernist critique and its important artistic output are still cherished in Bengal—consider how consistently Durgās are fashioned in a Jamini-esque style, for instance—it was countered in the 1920s by a new wave of committed academic naturalists who denied that the pursuit of naturalism was equivalent to a betrayal of national ideals. The voluptuous paintings of semi-clad but respectable middle-class women that issued from the brush of Hemendranāth Majumdār in the 1920s and 30s, for example, were not so dissimilar in genre from the paintings of the Varma brothers, and it is this type of female depiction that continues, from the 1920s to the present, to influence the deity market.[82] Indeed, the nationalist critics who argued that Varma's beauties were too sensual, sexy, and healthy, and without sufficient dignity or divinity, and who preferred instead thinner, ethereal, spiritual heroines, have not found common cause with public taste. "For the Hindu critics and the mass of consumers, it is the Ravi Varma–influenced goddesses who have come to represent today's acceptable worshiped image of the goddess."[83] As long as goddess-centered calendar art remains within the bounds of acceptability, suggesting eroticism but not showing too much female flesh, then "forces that operate at one level as alien Western influences [can be] made to serve very different ends within the framework of popular pictures. The new realism, far from being perceived as a Western intrusion, [can be] seen as an essential ingredient of the 'art' of . . . Indian iconography."[84] This is even true for modern forms of popular nationalist art, where the woman, conceived as the chaste, virtuous protector of the home and guarantor of the nation, is portrayed in calendar-art pin-ups in sensuous poses: holding a child, threshing rice, cooking in the kitchen, or riding astride her lion as Bhārat Mātā. An exhibition curated by Patricia Uberoi and Pooja Sood called "From Goddess to Pin-up: Icons of Femininity in Indian Calendar Art" graphically details the uniformity of this genre. In many ways in parallel, the *Amar Chitra Katha* comic book series, founded in 1967, has also experimented with the same idealization of gender roles and racial cues, where fairness, handsomeness, and voluptuousness typify heroes and heroines, gods and goddesses.

A sensuous iconism, then, that straddles and unites the religious and the domestic spheres: this is what the blending of colonial art influences and indigenous values has produced in popular art.[85]

## Bhārat Durgā? Banga Mātā? The National Iconocity of the Pūjās

The second frame for the iconographic material of this chapter is nationalist. In the context of this sexualized, humanized artistic ethos, what can we conclude about the sculpted, clay, festal Durgā as a visual icon of Bengal, or of the Indian nation? To put it another way, to what extent does a study of Durgā's iconographic development help illuminate what was argued in chapters 2 and 3—that Durgā has historically been utilized as an ambidextrous symbol of both strength for resistance and poverty-stricken weakness in need of protection and sacrifice? As Richard Davis and Christopher Pinney have separately shown, even if popular visual forms do not have as their explicit raison-d'être the cultivation of specific ideas of nationhood, they do influence people's ideas, and "visual iconography plays a fundamental role in the imagining of nationhood."[86]

To answer this question we need to consider the intersection of the Durgā Pūjā image with that of Bhārat Mātā, or Mother India. Indeed, the visual form of Bhārat Mātā can to some degree claim a Bengali pedigree. Bankim Chandra Chatterjee's visual rendition in *Ānandamaṭh* of Durgā as the resplendent India of the future and his equation of the Goddess with the land in the "Bande Mātāram" slogan, as well as Abanindranath Tagore's famous antipartition Banga Mātā painting from 1905,[87] provide a Bengali base for subsequent developments. But two sets of circumstances seem to make Bhārat Mātā's subsequent trajectory veer away from a Bengali mooring. The first concerns Bhārat Mātā's cartographic depiction. What Sumathi Ramaswamy calls "bodyscapes," where the figure of a woman occupies the map of a nation, exuberantly spilling over actual boundaries,[88] is something I have only rarely seen in a Bengali iteration—that is, either an icon of Mahiṣāsuramardinī and her children covering a map of India or a stand-alone goddess in a map of Bengal. There are exceptions, to be sure: a Bengali newspaper in 1952 published a photo of a Pūjā pandal where Durgā was standing in a map of India,[89] and in the post-Kargil patriotic days after 1999 I saw pandals in the shape of huge globes, with India placed toward the viewer and Durgā housed inside. One Pūjā committee had dispensed entirely with the lion, the demon, and the children, presenting Durgā as Bhārat Mātā with an Indian flag in her hand.[90]

Second, several elements of Durgā's iconographic tradition may militate to some extent against her ready accommodation to a visually explicit Bhārat Mātā symbology. First, the Pūjā tableau as it has developed, with its five deities, lion, and demon, is rather more complex than the lone Simhavāhinī or lithe standing maiden with her sari billowing out over the Indian map. When Durgā does appear without her lion and demon, it is often in a Vaiṣṇava milieu that eschews the violence associated with the Goddess's stance on Mahiṣa and prefers to pair her with a dominant Śiva. The Bengali Durgā, then, is a more complicated figure than Bhārat Mātā, with resonances unfamiliar to those outside the region. What non-Bengali would naturally conceive of Lakṣmī and Sarasvatī as Durgā's daughters? The only Bengali hero consistently incorporated into the Bhārat Mātā calendar-art tradition is Subhas Chandra Bose, and even he is portrayed with the North Indian icon of Bhārat Mātā rather than Bengal's regional Mahiṣamardinī. Second, Bhārat Mātā evokes compassion and a willingness to sacrifice herself, due to her portrayal as vulnerable mother. In Bengal, it is certainly true that Durgā has been utilized as a symbol for the suffering of the land and its people. Nevertheless, in iconographic terms it is not generally Mahiṣamardinī but Umā who is vulnerable, and Umā is rarely physically depicted at the Pūjā. Third, although one finds word-pictures of the linkage between Durgā and the nation—for instance, Aurobindo's reference to Mahiṣāsuramardinī springing into being from the combined *śakti*s of the assembled gods, just as the Goddess-Motherland draws upon the energies of her sons[91]—even when employed for nationalist causes Śākta symbolism is not usually drawn from the iconographic specifics of the Pūjā festivals. Instead, she is perceived in more abstract terms, as the ground of the country's strength *(deś-śakti)*.[92] Fourth, the calendar-art genre, where most of the most creative Bhārat

Mātā depictions are to be found,[93] is much more decontextualized, portable, and artistically unrestricted than the Pūjā images that are used, in spite of their position in the midst of a carnivalesque spectacle, for worship. In 1985 R. P. Gupta referred to this dual focus on art and worship as the "bilingual" character of the Bengali Goddess.[94]

In other words, what keeps the specific Durgā Pūjā image out of the realm of an aggressive Hindutva politics are the complex regional meanings of the Bengali Durgā, in contrast with the universal, pan-Indian register of Bhārat Mātā; the fact that the vulnerability of the Bengali goddess does not call for arms but for a mother's love and a ticket home; the emphasis by Bengali nationalists on the Goddess's *śakti* rather than on any particular visual item on her person; and her intertwined significance both to the art world and to religious sensibilities. In the mid-1970s, Indira Gandhi earned the ire, not the approbation, of Bengali voters when she was pictured as the Bengali Durgā in a Congress campaign poster. Of course, these compromising iconographic elements are only one perspective from which to see the disqualifying regionalism of the Durgā symbol. Also linked is the linguistic character of the Goddess's persona: unlike Hindi, as Francesca Orsini has shown in her study of the links between language, literature, and emergent nationalism,[95] Bengali was never a candidate for the national language, never a metaphor for the nation, never the key to a common cultural identity.

If there is no simple visual equation between Bhārat Mātā and the Bengali Durgā, what about Durgā as a pictorial self-representation of Bengal? Certainly, as we have seen throughout this chapter, the beautiful visages and postures of Durgā and Bengali women are increasingly coming to influence and resemble one another: the Goddess's modern bone structure and ornaments are those of a Bengali woman, and companies looking to sell their wares at Pūjā time publish advertisements of ten-armed women, each holding something the public should be convinced to buy. In 1922, a writer for the *Statesman* opined that real immersion scenes on Bijayā Daśamī, with "processions of women carrying offerings for the goddess[,] reminded one of scenes made familiar by the paintings of Ravi Varma."[96]

But of course this conflation of the Bengali woman with Durgā, and vice versa, is only partially successful. There are many Bengali women, or women living in Bengal, likely to be left out by this idealization of Durgā. According to the 2001 census, approximately 25 percent of West Bengal is Muslim. Traditionally Muslims have participated in the Pūjā to some degree, typically in ancillary jobs, such as making wigs for the images or playing the drums during the worship. It is hard to know how many Muslims are in the crowds thronging the streets at Pūjā time, but one suspects that in non-communally divisive times they enjoy sharing the electric atmosphere along with everyone else. Very occasionally, pandals include some Islamicate theme or detail on their exteriors; in 1991, for instance, the Vivekananda Sporting Club established Durgā in a structure that was part temple, part mosque, and part church; in 2001, two pandals were decorated inside with Mughal motifs. A few Pūjā committees proudly advertise the "secular" nature of their celebrations by naming Christians and Muslims who are prominent committee members, and apparently a few Muslims do choose to be involved in the festival in its Hindu forms, viewing it as an icon of traditional culture or a means of preserving social harmony.

These examples aside, however, and even without the history of occasional communal tension over Pūjā, Id, and Muharram, it is hard to imagine that the Durgā wearing traditional Hindu symbols of marriage and auspiciousness, flanked by four additional deities, and worshiped by Brahman priests, could be a truly "national" Bengali icon. Moreover, the doll-faced Durgā is only the most recent phase in a long developmental history; in addition to the stylized *sābekī mūrti* there are many other local variations in her depiction, like the Goddess with cat's paws, or with a fox's face, or with a starving, skeletal frame.[97] Given such a profusion of iconographic types, some of them strange and even somewhat off-putting, her ability to be "translated" to a non-Hindu, national, or even secular context becomes compromised.

Durgā's visage, then, may be too Bengali to resonate entirely with the needs and political agendas of those who champion Bhārat Mātā, and too Hindu for her festival to become a unifying symbol for all of Bengal. Still, she does unite most Bengali Hindus, of Śākta, Śaiva, atheist, and even Vaiṣṇava persuasions, and in her more humanized form she represents a general Indian ideal of feminine beauty, strength, vulnerability, and pride that stretches from Bengal to Bhārat and that mirrors to a large degree the pictorial images of female icons found in films, calendar art, and even comic books. Durgā's face, experienced since the time of the "Devī-Māhātmya" "as pleasing as the lustre of the finest gold," continues to enchant.[98]

# 5 Durgā on the *Titanic*

## *Politics and Religion in the Pūjā*

### Prologue: Jesus in a Hospital

Imagine that it is midnight, December 23, and you and your friends are strolling around your neighborhood.[1] You have a map in your hand, prepared by the police, to guide you. You are looking for crèche scenes. Everywhere—on rooftops and building facades—neon lights brighten the sky with their colored designs. One depicts Santa sailing through the sky on his reindeer chariot. In another, candidates in recent election battles are heatedly arguing. Down the street you see a lighted display of a melting glacier forming a torrential river that sweeps away mountain villages. Your first crèche scene is in a school playground under a stunning thatch-roofed stable. Outside, the benign face of your city mayor welcomes you to the festivities on behalf of St. Paul's Catholic Church. Three days ago the neighborhood was abuzz because he had inaugurated the nativity scene by placing Jesus in the manger. You approach. The holy family seems traditional enough, but the three kings look remarkably like the U.S. president, vice president, and secretary of state. This St. Paul's crèche is apparently in fierce competition with that of the Methodist church, a few blocks away, whose sponsors support the opposition political party. There, instead of a stable, you see a replica of a makeshift U.S. military hospital in Iraq. In order to see the baby Jesus and his parents, you enter the building and pass by lifelike images of wounded men lying prostrate in beds. Fastened to the walls of the rooms are anti-war slogans and pictures of grieving parents. Back outside, you are handed an ad by a representative from AOL: Use the Internet to vote on your favorite crèche scenes, and win a sport utility vehicle!

This is of course preposterous, in a United States setting. Public crèche scenes, decorated to reflect contemporary events, with the hope of attracting viewers and prizes, is not a part of American Christmas traditions. However, this is precisely what one finds in Bengali celebrations of Durgā, Jagaddhātrī, and Kālī. In what follows I describe these festivals and their fusion of religious, social, and political themes, and then try to account for why, and how, they have taken such a form. Keeping the chapter title in mind, is Durgā really on the *Titanic*? What does that mean? And why is it acceptable?

## The Growth of the Public Pūjās from the 1920s to the Early Twenty-first Century

Anyone who has had the good fortune to experience recently (since 2004) the public Pūjās in Kolkata can probably not imagine that they were not always this way: extravagantly creative houses for the Goddess that exquisitely replicate actual buildings or structures, sometimes in mammoth proportions. And yet when I sought to determine through interviews when such pandals arose ("What were pandals like in the 1970s, for example?"), no one could quite remember. The overview of the developmental evolution of the pandals as presented below has thus been made possible only by archival work amid more than eighty years of Calcutta newspaper reporting and photography.

Apart from the continuation of private, elite home Pūjās, the nineteenth century was the era of *bāroiyāri* Pūjās. In 1820 the *Calcutta Journal* explained the mechanism of such celebrations—five to six Brahmans get together, form a committee, collect subscriptions, set up a "temporary shed," construct an idol, and engage singers[2]—and the Rev. Alexander Duff, in 1838, attested to the prevalence of temporary images being made for ordinary people's homes. But as yet there were no street festivities.[3] All of this changed in the 1920s, when public festivals of the *sarbajanīn* variety, with their illuminations, temporary houses for the Goddess, processions and gatherings, and free musical entertainments, were initiated and celebrated with great enthusiasm. The newspapers of the time, however, seem to evince little interest in anything apart from the new iconographic styles of Goddess depiction, as discussed in chapter 4, and the illuminations in the streets.[4] Indeed, not until the 1950s do the papers comment at all on pandals or their shapes, and even then the coverage is minimal; when pandals are photographed they are not labeled, which indicates that there was not yet any competition between named clubs.

What seems to attract most attention are the people chosen to organize and inaugurate the festivities, the outside illuminations, athletic performances, like lathi duels and boxing, and the associated displays inside or near the pandal. Prior to the late 1970s, if a group wanted to make a political or social statement, its members would typically decorate the inside of the pandal with hanging pictures or have an adjoining tableau of images reenacting a particular event. In 1952, for example, the Simla Byayam Samiti exhibition used clay figures and posters to illustrate the one hundred years from Plassey to the Mutiny; Indian Independence; the speech by Swami Vivekananda at the 1893 World's Parliament of Religions in Chicago; Gandhi's death; and starvation.[5] Clues to future direction are the film studio backdrops—temple scenes, mountains, lakes, and maps of India—placed behind certain images *inside* the pandal.[6] The only descriptions or photos of pandals I have seen for the entire 1950s decade reference decorated gateways and columns.[7]

Looking at the Pūjā dates in the news of the 1960s and 1970s reminds one that the festivals are vying for coverage in an increasingly troubled world: in newspapers for the Pūjā dates in 1962, for example, reporters discussed Kennedy and a possible war with Cuba; bloody riots in Mississippi over the admission of the first "Negro" to the University of Mississippi; Nehru and India's relation with China; and anti-Hindi riots in the South. In 1965, the Pūjās coincided with the Pakistani intrusion into Kashmir; fighting in Vietnam; and the Beatles. Early 1970s Pūjā reporting occurred on the same pages as news articles about Naxalites in West Bengal, the war between East and West Pakistan, and the continuing U.S. bombing of Hanoi. In 1976 Muhammad Ali beat Ken Norton on the eve of Durgā Pūjā, and Jimmy Carter defeated Gerald Ford at Kālī Pūjā. But even during such momentous events, the Pūjās continued their trajectory forward, for the 1960s saw several innovations: the police begin to publish "road maps," showing where traffic was being diverted during the congestion of the Pūjās; the papers record crowds in the act of "pandal-hopping" to prominent named clubs (but give no description of the pandals' shapes[8]); "information stalls" are set up adjacent to pandals by the Communist Party of India (Marxist) [the CPI(M)], the Jan Sangh, and even Maoist Naxalites[9]; and in 1966 some large structures introduce the custom of separate entrances for men and women.[10] The first time one finds the effort to simulate a real-life structure is in 1969, when the pandal at 27 Palli, designed like the Mīṇākṣī Temple, is said to draw large crowds.[11] But in the festivals throughout the 1960s and 1970s, even such modeled pandals appear quite crude in comparison with what one is used to in the twenty-first century.

Suddenly in the 1980s several new, and long-lasting, components enter the festivities: open competition between neighborhood committees; the mention of "big budget" pandals that are now dependent upon sponsorships by commercial companies; the replacement of mercury lights with neon lights in the outside illuminations; the open worship of the Goddess by military units such as the Assam Rifles and the Gurkhas[12]; and the increasing number of pandals now shaped as copies (*ādalṭis*) of real buildings or structures—Belur Maṭh at Calcutta, Paśupatināth Temple in Kathmandu, the Sun Temple at Konark, and the crash of Air India's Kanishka jet, which broke up in mid-air in 1985. I can only find one example of a site replicated from outside India: the Olympic Coliseum in Los Angeles, from 1984. Though not expressed in external pandal construction, during this decade some Pūjās reflected political events; in 1984, Jagaddhātrī Pūjā coincided with the assassination of Mrs. Gandhi; several committee organizers, in all parts of the state where the Pūjā was celebrated, affixed photographs of her on their *pāṇḍāl* walls or positioned Mrs. Gandhi next to the Goddess herself.[13] However, as stated in chapter 2, it is noteworthy that although Calcutta was host in 1989 to many blessing ceremonies (*rāmśila pūjās*) of bricks to be used in the building of the proposed new Rāma temple at Ayodhya, not a single one occurred in the context of a Durgā, Jagaddhātrī, or Kālī Pūjā.

All of these aspects and characteristics of the Pūjās burgeon in the 1990s and early 2000s. Almost every committee that could afford it employed builders to create a pandal in the shape of something beautiful, innovative, and reflective of Indian social or political life. By 2000 the creativity was dazzling: we find pandals representing recent events such as new Indo-Bangladesh train connections, the Amarnath pilgrimage attacks, the Bhuj earthquake, and the Nepal palace murders. At yet another site Durgā resides in a flooded village, complete with real stream and (not real) dead carcasses of animals; she is also welcomed into the Leaning Tower of Pisa,

FIGURE 5.1. A Durgā Pūjā pandal shaped like Ajanta Caves. Muhammad Ali Park, Kolkata, September 1998. Photo by Rachel Fell McDermott.

the Golconda Fort, a tree stump with an entrance portal, an Egyptian pyramid complete with scattered sand, Ajanta Caves (fig. 5.1), and Alibaba's Cave, where the door opens to a spoken mantra.[14] In 2006 one could visit Durgā in St. Isaac's Cathedral in Leningrad, in one of Khajuraho's temples, inside Lord Jagannātha's temple chariot at Puri, in Vatican City, in the ruins of Harappa, and next to Swami Vivekananda at Vivekananda Rock in Kanyakumari.[15] That the scope is as large as the world is indicated by a cartoon from 2001, in which a man says to his wife, in the Pūjā crowds: "I have seen all of India, now let's go to America. Let's start with the White House."[16]

The most recent innovation in pandal construction occurred in 2004, with the "Theme Pūjā"—that is, a total package where the lighting displays, the pandal shape, and the Goddess's attire or physiognomy cohere in the representation of a single theme, whether artistic, social, media-derived, or crisis-related. This development carries forward the desire for accolade and crowd-dazzling that had been steadily growing since the 1980s: already pressured by the need to introduce novelty (*abhinabatva*)—"If we don't think up something new every year, people won't take it. And sponsorships won't come, either," said an exasperated chair of one Pūjā committee in 2006—the move toward overall coherence is meant to bag prizes, wow competitors, and charm the *darśan*-seekers, who are now called *rasiks*, or those who are expert in aesthetic taste.[17] Examples abound: a pandal designed like Berlin's Olympiastadion, where Mahiṣa is sculpted in the likeness of Zinedine Zidane, the French soccer star, head-butting the lion, while Gaṇeśa acts as the referee[18]; a pandal made of more than ten lakh pencils, in the interior of which are panels portraying people committed to education and the development of writing[19]; a spacey-looking ethereal Durgā arriving from above into a spaceship pandal and blessing the illiterate *asura* with the light of knowledge[20]; an Egyptian theme, with Durgā in the form of Isis, Mahiṣa as the god of death, and her four children as other Egyptian gods, all inside a pandal shaped as the Luxor temple, decorated with ancient Egyptian art[21]; and a host of pandals where the coherence is achieved through the raw materials chosen to construct the pandal and the Goddess: special wood brought from Manipur; silkworms, silk, and cocoons; even postage stamps. In 2008 the Suruchi Sangha in New Alipore decided to focus its pandal on Assam. Five artists toured Assam for over a month and came back ready to make copies of various temples, including Kamakhya, decorated with Assamese handicrafts. Durgā was placed on a platform in the mountains. Outside the pandal, stalls sold Assamese food and musicians played Assamese music.[22] Other pandals from 2008 include the theme of the Goddess's third eye (the pandal was constructed in the shape of a huge eyeball, and *darśan*-seekers, once inside the ocular structure, could pledge to donate their eyes after death to the blind[23]); and the dense forests of the Sundarbans, from which fallen wood was brought both to create and decorate the pandal and to carve the image of Bonbibi, the local forest goddess.[24] In 2006 two pandal committees made a splash when they hosted press conferences, where each screened a short film to explain their focus and their creative process.[25]

Along with the increased complexity and size of the community Pūjās, the scope and cost of the displays have also increased. Although comparative statistics are hard to assess with accuracy, it seems that in Kolkata alone the number of street pandals has grown from about six to seven hundred in the 1950s to about 1,300 in 2008 (the number of permitted street pandals has remained constant at least since 2000). In 1953 a typical *sarbajanīn* Pūjā cost anywhere from Rs. 4,000 to Rs.14,000, where the lion's share of the expense went to the outside illuminations and lighting shows. In 1976 artisans charged Rs. 3,000 for a good-sized image; in 2008 the price was Rs. 20,000. The six top-notch committees in 2004 spent Rs. 5 million each, for their total packages. Hence the Pūjās are big business, and connect major cities, especially Kolkata, to areas throughout the state; local industries that the festivities support are legion, from the growers and conveyers of lotus flowers, and traditional Muslim wig-makers and drummers, to the coolies who travel into the cities to carry images from the artisans' districts to pandals or homes, and then from there to the immersion sites at the conclusion of the festival.

The same growth is true for Jagaddhātrī, especially in her home territory of Hooghly and Nadia districts. The number of Central Committee–approved Pūjās in Chandannagar has risen steadily every year since 1956: in 1968 there were 44, in 1977 89, in 2002 132, and in 2008 142.[26] Only 64 of these 142, collectively taking 240 trucks from four zones of the city, are permitted to join the *śobhāyātrā* to the river. Krishnanagar has its own procession traditions; first, each of its 126 Pūjā committees takes the *ghaṭ*, or pot of water that officially houses the spirit of the Goddess, to the Jalangi River for immersion, and then, later in the evening, the committees return to the river with their images. All processions must pass by the Nadia Rāj estate, where at one time the *rājā* and his wife viewed the images and awarded prizes.[27]

Hence, as commercial ventures that capitalize on human enterprise and creativity, the Śākta Pūjās as a unit have burgeoned since the 1920s into a festival period that dwarfs all others in allotted vacation time, hoopla, cost, grandeur, and Bengali pride.

## Prestige and Politics in Pūjā Contexts

### *Mine Is Better than Yours*

Two interrelated aspects of the Pūjās deserve closer scrutiny: the craze for competition, common to both old family and street pandal settings; and the intersection, particularly in the pandals, of religion, social concerns, and political commentary.

Rivalries come in many forms. As we have seen in chapter 1, for the monied classes of Pūjā organizers, this is a muted, rather polite battle. I interviewed the heads of about fifteen such aristocratic families in Calcutta in 2000, and most were very aware of the other traditional Pūjās in the city, ranking their own celebration against them in terms of age, adherence to custom, expenditure, and inherited prestige. Although there seem to have been rivalries between such families and the organizers of the "new" *bāroiyāri* Pūjās in the nineteenth century, the former disdaining the latter as "low and common beggars,"[28] by now the community festivities are so accepted and beloved that the chief rivals of the aristocratic classes are each other. Some interviewees told me that they scour the newspapers at festival time, seeing how often their family celebration is written about, in comparison with those of their peers.

Matters are more urgent and more extreme for the soldiers in the public contests, where the language of war pervades all aspects of the festivities. *Sarbajanīn* Pūjā organizers freely admit that they want to fight, beat, and trounce their competitors, and many of them employ "think-tanks" to come up with new ideas and succeed in the "ṭāg ab oyār" (tug of war) between pandals. Novelty, size, the ability to confer notoriety: these are the coveted values. Organizers approach artisans and lighting experts who have won prizes in the past. They invite celebrities—politicians, authors, sportsmen, movie stars, and even national figures such as the now-late Phoolan Devi and Mother Teresa—to inaugurate their Pūjās. Multinationals such as Bata, Coke, Goodrich, Heinz, Hindustan Lever, Maruti, Pepsi, Phillips, Proctor and Gamble, and Whirlpool donate money to particular pandals with the stipulation that their products be advertised near the gates or in recorded songs played on loudspeaker. In the struggle to garner such company sponsorships, Pūjā committees defame one another, and during the celebrations they anxiously watch the papers. Who is drawing the biggest crowds? Who is giving most to charity? Who pays the bigger electric bills? How do we stop spies from rival committees stealing our ideas? In 2006 certain Pūjā clubs began handing over the construction and running of their pandals to event management companies, in the hopes of further professionalism, and hence notoriety. There has even been physical violence and death associated with inter-Pūjā rivalries.[29]

Prizes—which bestow funds but, more importantly, prestige—form the coveted material core of the Pūjā industry. Begun in 1969 by the West Bengal State Tourist Bureau, originally the conferral of prizes was designed to increase Pūjā development for the sake of tourism; in the same year the bureau also announced its first tourist launch to watch the immersions in the river.[30] By 1975 the Public Relations and Information Department of the Government of West Bengal was awarding a total of eight prizes: three for the best overall *sarbajanīn* Pūjās, and one each for the best traditional image, best solemnity and atmosphere, best decoration, best new forceful image, and best traditional rituals.[31] By 2008 so many different prize-awarders had come forward, ranging from companies to newspapers to charities, that it has become difficult to keep count. The newest prize categories include the best apartment building Pūjā (Bāḍīr Serā Pūjā), since 2001; the best priest (to be judged on his correct pronunciation and ritual precision), from 2002[32]; the most child-friendly in safety and accessibility, since 2002[33]; the most "green," from 2004;[34] and the most caring. In 2006 the *Telegraph* newspaper offered the distinction of a "True Spirit" Pūjā badge to pandals that provide a caring, clean, and fire-proof atmosphere, together with safe drinking water, toilets, and a special gate for the handicapped.[35] In general, the mania for prizes, together with increasingly stringent police regulations, in order to manage the crowds and ensure safety, have encouraged an upscaling of the festivities, as no committee wants to have its permit rescinded or to receive negative publicity.[36]

There are as yet no major prizes for social outreach, but many committees band together to raise money for worthy causes, like flood relief, life-saving operations for poor children, and gifts of food or new clothes for the city's marginalized. Such generosity underlines one of the fault lines of the Pūjās: although ostensibly created in their public form in the 1920s to appeal to both rich and poor, the festivities are not truly universal. The newspapers publish photos of street families or people living inside abandoned drainage pipes, unable to join the festivities or being fed once a year by a Pūjā committee. "Puja is another world to us," said one such person to a *Hindustan Times* reporter in 2001.[37] The pandals themselves might decorate their interiors with displays exhorting kindness to the poor, ill, or outcaste, but in spite of some integrative success stories there are as many reports of prejudice, fear, and refused inclusion in Pūjā committees or pandals.[38] Those who do minister to the needy, however, use their altruism as yet another weapon in their arsenal of victory over their rivals.

Not simply neighborhoods, but even towns vie with one another for recognition. Krishnanagar and Rishra have both attempted to supercede Chandannagar, the traditional star of Jagaddhātrī Pūjā, Krishnanagar through the financing of a Mumbai business, which has started a Jagaddhātrī Web site and announced the awarding of prizes, and Rishra, which extends its Jagaddhātrī festival three days after the conclusion of its rival's. Even Pūjās appear to do battle. Naihati, an hour by train upriver from Kolkata, tries to prove, by its gigantic Kālī images over 50 feet high, that its Kālī Pūjā is superior to Kolkata's Durgā Pūjā.

To me one of the interesting types of local sparring—some of it deadly—is political. The Communist Party of India (Marxist) has been in power in the state of West Bengal uninterruptedly since 1967, for thirty years without significant political rival. In 1997, however, a woman named Mamatā Banerjee founded the Trinamul Congress, or Grassroots Congress, in order

FIGURE 5.2. A Durgā Pūjā pandal in the shape of a Tata Motors factory, after it was stopped from producing Nano cars. Kolkata, October 2008. Photo by Jayanta Roy.

to overthrow the Communist stranglehold. To this end she has been willing to ally herself with anyone powerful; until April 2001, for instance, she was a minister in the Bharatiya Janata Party (BJP)–led government, responsible for railways and transportation. After the embarrassment over the Centre's bribery scam in March 2001, Mamatā quit the BJP government and formed an alliance with the West Bengal State Congress Party. In 2008, as a result of her anti-industrialization protests, Tata Motors withdrew its proposed Nano car factory from the state, exacerbating the already acrimonious relations between Mamatā and Buddhadeb Bhaṭṭācārya, the state's CIP(M) chief minister (see fig. 5.2). Mamatā's alliance with the Congress in the 2009 elections caused the Left Front to suffer its worst setback in years; in fact, it did not retain a single parliamentary seat in Kolkata. Moreover, in summer 2010 the Trinamool Congress inflicted a crushing blow to the ruling Left Front Party in the Kolkata civic elections, as a result of which Mamatā predicted that she would sweep West Bengal in the 2011 Assembly elections. In general, then, Mamatā's party threatens Communist hegemony in Bengal, and since the year 2000 the state has witnessed politically motivated mutual violence, property destruction, and evictions; in such contexts, the ability to hold Pūjās is a symbol of peace and normalcy that is coveted by both parties in the districts under their jurisdiction.[39]

In Kolkata, where there has been posturing but less violence between Communists and Trinamul workers, pandals organized by Trinamul members sport pictures of their leader, sell her literature, and festoon their displays with political slogans. Some of the big-budget Pūjās are backed by politicians close to Mamatā. They not only rival one another, but in particular enjoy attempting to humiliate the "Congress Pūjās"—even though after 2009 the Congress Party is the third, and weakest, claimant for power in the state.

It is noteworthy that there is no Communist Pūjā, no pandal allied with a name in the state government. This is because, strictly speaking, the Communist ideology does not permit an acknowledgment of religion, devotion, or grandiose spectacles of piety funded by the elite.[40] Even now, Communist Party members are publicly admonished against taking part in the Pūjās. But there is also a countervailing trend. After the mid-1990s, perhaps because Jyoti Basu was nearing retirement, valued pragmatism, or desired to combat Mamatā Banerjee on her own turf, he began practicing lenience and even indulgence toward the Goddess. "As I grew up, party ideologies alienated me from the simple fun of Durga Puja. For a very long time, I did not actively take part in celebrations. Things are different now. I have grown old and the memories come rushing back."[41] Since 1995 I have seen newspaper articles and even photos of CPI(M) chiefs inaugurating pandals, offering flowers to the Goddess, and wandering the streets of their neighborhoods, enjoying the season's delights. This is in addition to the over 4,500 seasonal bookstalls, strategically placed throughout the city, for the spread of Marxist teachings. One CPI(M) minister explains that the political costs of turning down requests to cut ribbons at the festivals can be very high. "Don't forget these are the people who vote for us and stay with us year round as many of the puja organizers are our workers," he told a newspaper reporter bluntly.[42] While the new breed of liberal Communist justifies his behavior by claiming that the Goddess is the *śakti* of Communist rule, that Durgā Pūjā is a secular, national, artistic festival, not a religious one, that Durgā Pūjā is a form of "social communism,"[43] or even that "theme pandals" can convey the truths of communism (one committee in 2006 illustrated the CPI(M) slogan, "agriculture is our base, industry our future," by erecting a factory and a farm in the same pandal structure[44]), many others censure what they perceive to be a sellout of the Party to hypocrisy, opportunism, and social pressure.[45]

The urge to best rivals through the creative use of the festivities extends beyond West Bengali contexts. The West Bengal State Tourist Bureau, continuing its efforts to project Durgā Pūjā as a national and even international visual event, has put together a Kolkata Mahotsava five-star, five-day package of fun and excitement that is aimed at placing the festival in the same league as the Mardi Gras of Rio and the Carnival of Goa.[46] We return to this theme below.

Before leaving the topic of rivalry and challenge (even Bengali newspapers utilize the transliterated word "cyālenj"), it is important to note that competition based on the quest for novelty inspires nostalgia for the simplicity of old, which is often replicated in an "authentic" manner that ironically feeds the revival of traditional artisanry. Starting in 2006, I have noted the use of the word "Bāngāliyāna" in characterizations of the craze to go back to one's cultural roots in the creations of pandals and their designs. Committees search out and bring to Kolkata folk or tribal artists, who weave their traditional bamboo or shape pots with special Krishnanagar clay, in situ, on the pandal site. Other committees hire art college graduates or even professional filmmakers in order to create their pandal sets; they also secure cinematographers to design their outside illuminations. Such realistic, professional efforts toward inculcating nostalgia, even if nostalgia for a way of life never experienced by the onlooker, Arjun Appadurai reminds us, is a central theme of modern merchandizing: "The much-vaunted feature of modern consumption—namely, the search for novelty—is only a symptom of a deeper discipline of consumption in which desire is organized around the aesthetics of ephemerality."[47] The more outlandishly gorgeous and, to some, garish the pandals become, the more the newspapers are filled with poignant, longing reminiscences of "the Pūjā Days of Old," when simplicity and faith supposedly reigned.

And yet very few Bengalis, I infer, would want actually to go back to the simple pandal structures of the 1950s or lose the carnivalesque enjoyment of the total event that grips the state during the festival days. And nor, as we shall see below, was there probably ever a time when competition was absent from the atmosphere of the Pūjās. Indeed, I would claim that Bengali Goddess worship is inextricably bound up with competition, be it artistic, social, or political. A few years after Independence, in the midst of the Nehruvian five-year plans, one newspaper commentator, worried about what would happen to the Pūjās in the face of increasing industrialization, suggested that the state government should take over their sponsorship. He obviously need not have worried about the drive of private enterprise.[48] Said an astute observer thirty years earlier, in 1924, noting that even Indian Christians and Brāhmo Samāj reformers were moved by the festivities, "You cannot underestimate the power of Durgā Pūjā on a Bengali!"[49] One is practically compelled to join the fray.

## *Durgā on the* Titanic

The second striking element of the Bengali Śākta Pūjās is the manner in which the street festivities act as barometers of social and political events and controversies. To be sure, Durgā, Jagaddhātrī, and Kālī are often installed inside pandals that look like temples or shrines, and the associated lighting displays frequently depict scenes from religious texts. One can see woodcuts, paintings, or lighting shows depicting Durgā's *akāl bodhan*, or untimely awakening, when Rāma entreated her help in autumn before his war with Rāvaṇa; her war with Mahiṣa; and the dream in which Jagaddhātrī appears to Rājā Kṛṣṇacandra Rāy in the mid-eighteenth century and orders him to establish her worship. Religious scenes are not confined solely to the Śākta *sampradāya*, however. Equally popular are illustrations from the *Rāmāyaṇa* and depictions of Kṛṣṇa's play with Rādhā.

Most temple-pandals are what is called "*kālpanik*," or imaginary, but some, as seen above, are copies of actual temples—all magically transported to the streets and alleyways of Bengali towns. Other sorts of pandals are those which simulate some natural environment, such as a Bengali village or a Rajasthani desert (with two camels shipped in especially for the occasion); those which replicate civic buildings, locally important sites like Kolkata's Victoria Memorial, distinguished buildings in other parts of South Asia, like the parliament building in New Delhi, and eminent places in Europe or America, like Buckingham Palace, the Eiffel Tower, and Harvard University; and those which parrot some theme or image from the popular media. I have seen goddesses housed in a huge mailbox, a computer, a house of cards, and, of course, the *Titanic* (fig. 5.3). This was all the rage in 1998, after the release of the blockbuster movie, and every Bengali city of any size could boast at least one ocean liner in its precincts.[50] The same was true of Jurassic Park dinosaurs, soccer and cricket stars, and even Harry Potter's castle.[51] The subjects of the neon lighting vary with the whims of the time. For children there is Humpty Dumpty, Mickey Mouse, Godzilla, and vampires. For larger children and adults, the Hindi version of "Who Wants to Be a Millionaire?," and the Olympics.

FIGURE 5.3. A Durgā Pūjā pandal in the shape of the *Titanic*. Salt Lake, Kolkata, September 1998. Photo by Rachel Fell McDermott.

Disasters, accidents, and social problems are also popular themes for pandal designers and electricians. A group in Calcutta made the floods of 2000 in West Bengal the center of their pandal, depicting homelessness, lack of clean water, and the threat of flood-borne poisonous snakes. Too, the hijacked Indian Airlines plane at Kandahar in 2000 became a shelter for Durgā and her family, who were—like the actual trapped passengers—unable to see outside during the course of their confinement. Other themes of this ilk are the 1999 sinking of the Russian submarine Kursk and the crash of the Concorde in Paris in 2000. Mother Teresa and Princess Diana died all over again in the lighting shows of 1998, and several organizations have used the festivities as an occasion to raise consciousness about women—in particular, dowry abuses, child marriages, and bride-burning.[52] Other pandals advertise the necessity of wildlife preservation (one 2000 pandal depicted Durgā as a tree, crying), the problem of political corruption, and the fight against disease.[53] Two of my favorite reflections of popular culture are lighting shows, one from 1995 in which a fat Gaṇeśa drinks milk, and another from 1999 in which Bill and Monica carry on. I have even heard of, but never seen, a Durgā whose face was Monica's.[54]

And then there are the nationalistic and patriotic pandals and lighted scenes. Although politics was reflected inside Pūjā pandals in the early to midcentury—in 1939 Gopeśvar Pāl apparently placed Durgā against backdrop that resembled a World War II battlefield[55]—whole pandals reflective of political themes made a splash only really in the 1990s. In 1991 such structures depicted the Gulf War and the assassination of Rajiv Gandhi, in 1995 the skirmishes between India and Pakistan in the Siachen heights, and in 1999, Kargil. For those wanting to experience the battles on Tiger Hill, one only had to go to Shealdah Athletic Club in Calcutta, where Bofors guns sounded in the background and Indian soldiers resisted Pakistani shelling, or visit Santosh Mitra Square to see a replica—160' high, 140' long, and 80' wide—of the INS Vikrant, India's aircraft carrier, equipped with an MiG fighter plane and a Chetak helicopter. In 2001 Durgā was still in Kargil, seated on a Bofors cannon in a mountain cave and surrounded by army personnel and dead bodies. She can also be depicted more symbolically—as Bhārat Mātā, as a map of India, or as residing *in* a map, with India at its center. In these exhibitions, the best way to indicate one's "enemy" is to give Mahiṣa, the demon killed by Durgā, his likeness. Demons of recent years have been Nawaz Sharif, the LTTE chief Veerappan, Fiji's George Speight, and even Bill Clinton and Tony Blair. Although not everyone approves of such patriotic and congratulatory propaganda at Pūjā time, I have seen or heard of very few groups choosing to criticize the prevailing sense of national pride through the medium of such pandals.[56]

Interestingly, although one might have suspected that the bombing of the World Trade Center and the Pentagon in the United States would

FIGURE 5.4. Plane crashing into the World Trade Center. Illuminations at the College Square pandal. Kolkata. *Hindustan Times*, Kolkata, 22 Oct. 2001, p. 3.

FIGURE 5.5. Mahiṣa in the shape of Osama bin Laden, before he was smashed. *Hindustan Times*, Kolkata, 26 Sept. 2001, p. 3.

have provided ample scope for both lighting displays and creative transformations of Mahiṣa into bin Laden during the 2001 Pūjā season, such was not tolerated by the CPI(M), whose cadres expressly prohibited Pūjā committees and artisans from creating any human representation of the disaster that might stir up communal discord in the state. Lighting shows and even an occasional pandal structure were permitted to depict the crash of the planes into the World Trade Center (fig. 5.4), but artists who began to sculpt Mahiṣa in the likeness of bin Laden (fig. 5.5) were ordered to destroy their work because of its sensitive nature (*sparśakātar biṣay*). Even with such preventative measures, however, Hindu–Muslim tensions were palpable in the closing months of 2001. The implication of such proscriptions appears to be that Pūjās may reflect delights, concerns, or problems common to all, but that Muslim feelings (*manomālinya / manakaṣākaṣi*) must be protected from perceived slight.[57] Post-2001 nationalist pandals have concerned themselves with terrorism, not only by depicting Mahiṣa, for example, as a would-be suicide bomber, with a gas cylinder strapped to his body,[58] but also by strengthening police surveillance squads in the streets.

The association of Durgā Pūjā with social, national, and patriotic concerns is reinforced in the public sphere by seasonal newspaper cartoons that depict Durgā in battle with various evils. In 1962 she is being chased by five bull-Mahiṣas, bearing the titles Casteism, Corruption, Communalism, Linguism, and Disintegration; in 1984 Mahiṣa is inflation; in 1987 the demon swims ahead of Durgā and her children in the midst of a flood to reach the relief supplies first; and in 2001 someone approaches the Goddess, sitting at a desk, and informs her that there are two new demons for her to combat: the Twin Towers tragedy and the threat of anthrax.[59]

## Making Sense of the Melee

To recapitulate: the two aspects of this public religious festival season that appear to be most prominent are competition and the exuberant embracing of sociopolitical themes. Certainly there are a few analogues in the history of Western holiday celebrations—for example, department store rivalries at Christmas time in late-nineteenth-century Britain and America—but there is something distinctly surprising about these Pūjās, especially if one does the mental exercise I suggested at the outset. How then to explain, or trace the lineage of, these aspects of the Śākta Pūjās?

### *The Fate of Aristocratic Competitiveness*

The first component—the Goddess as an occasion for battle over prestige—is not hard to understand, given the context of the festivals' inception. None of them, as we have seen in chapter 1, is very old. We have evidence for their performance only as far back as the late sixteenth century, and from the very beginning they were sponsored by the wealthy—landowners and rent collectors under the jurisdiction of the Mughals and then the British—who resorted to them as signs of status and power. Ever since the Gupta period, Durgā Mahiṣamardinī has been associated with royalty, and the early Bengali landowners adopted her public worship as a substitute for an *aśvamedha*, as prescribed in the medieval *Devī Purāṇa*.[60] By the early nineteenth century Britons were commenting on the bellicose nature of Pūjā sponsorship. "The natives have given themselves up to unlimited extravagance in all that relates to their public festivals, vying with each other. . . . Calcutta is the arena in which the various combatants for fame, assemble to adjust their claims; and it is astonishing to behold the immense sums which are annually squandered in order to acquire a name, and to attract ephemeral popularity."[61]

Competitive feelings carried over even into the newly democratized forms of the festival, the *bāroiyāri* and *sarbajanīn*. A Bengali spoof from 1852 describes the Pūjā frenzy and then concludes poignantly: "[A]fter it's all over, people discuss, 'whose image was best?' or 'who had the best clothes?' or 'who had the best arrangements?,' but no one asks, 'whose bhakti was best?' "[62] The famed historian Jadunath Sarkar, thinking back to his childhood in the 1870s, described the rivalry within villages over their boat immersions, each family trying to outdo the others, even in terms of the music played as the Goddess was being lowered overboard.[63] The new *sarbajanīn* format also gave tremendous new scope for creativity and rivalry. For the constituents of the *sarbajanīn* Pūjā were now "Everyman," whose pockets could be plumbed for subscription money and whose entertainment tastes had to be satisfied. What we see, then, is a widening of sponsorship and audience, but the same opportunities for prestige, and hence the same scope for inter-Pūjā competition.

Such rivalry, and its changes in outward expression as the Pūjās devolved from the hands of the zamindars to those of the middle class, can also be placed in a larger comparative framework. Scholarship during the past three decades on the emergence of the consumer market in Europe—particularly France and England—indicates that similar paths were traveled in societies where an aristocratic ethic of taste and consumption gave way, though revolutions of swords or industry, to bourgeois values. The nobility, who were close to the monarch and wanted to remain that way, vied with each other in the acquisition of furniture and tapestries for their stately mansions and in the display of courtly politeness, taste, and restraint. Imitation of the king or queen and the maintenance of traditionalism were the keys to honor and social standing, and noblemen outspent themselves, often to financial ruin, in their pursuit.[64] Holiday festivities, such as masques and Christmas celebrations, were encouraged by both monarch and nobility as occasions not only to show off their own wealth and prestige but also, by allowing the "public" a time of feasting, revelry, and even antinomianism, to undergird social order and royal authority.[65]

After the French Revolution in France and the victory of Puritanism in England, when the aristocracy lost its financial and feudal privileges, abandoned its control over public rituals, and even suffered exile or execution, the focus of economic activity switched to the cities and to the bourgeoisie, who in the eighteenth century in both France and England were the prime beneficiaries of the Industrial Revolution and the increased prosperity and mass-produced goods it generated. For our comparative purposes here, the two chief characteristics of this democratization of culture, in France and in England, were, first, the fact that the upper middle classes continued, like the aristocracy before them, to vie with others in their peer groups. To use the words of Rosalind Williams in her study of eighteenth-century France: "The social terrain was leveling out. Instead of looking upward to imitate a prestigious group, people were more inclined to look at each other. Idolatry decreased; rivalry increased."[66] People consumed conspicuously, using goods as symbolic markers to new status and power, but not—and this is the second useful comparative point—in the manner of the nobility before them, whom, after all, they had swept away. No, the new middle classes did not emulate the *specific* lifestyle patterns of the old nobility—patterns in which a closed, traditional set of prized goods and codes of conduct, patterned on those of the monarch, were the basis for social competitiveness. However, certain *general* characteristics of the noble lifestyle—luxury goods, leisure activities, and a "culture of refinement"—were desirable, even the object of middle-class nostalgia, and all of these were undergirded by an insatiable need for newness. Colin Campbell, in his brilliant study of the roots of modern consumerism and in particular of its unquenchable thirst for novelty, sees in the very foundations of Puritanism itself an assertion of the individual, a romantic longing for unfulfilled ambition, which lends itself to mobility, initiative, and the quest for innovation. This sensibility, he says, combined with new opportunities for variety through mass production, created the conditions for modern forms of mass consumer appetites.[67]

Studies of medieval to modern urban Indian economies reveal similar trends. The transition from courtly rule to societies governed more by mercantile elites occurred at different times in different Indian states, depending on the impact in their regions of Mughal and then British power, but one can trace a common pattern of assimilation by the nouveaux riches to courtly expectations of consumption. C. A. Bayly discusses such lavish expenditures by North Indian trading communities in the late eighteenth to late nineteenth centuries, noting that these often theologically ascetical (and Vaiṣṇava) merchants justified their opulent displays of wealth because they were occurring in overtly religious contexts.[68] Sandria Freitag, also writing about North India, finds the same devolution of power from the courtier classes in the eighteenth century to the Hindu merchants and their allies in the nineteenth, but notes that because the Raj restricted free access to state institutions, these new leaders frequently resorted to the only domain left to them—what she calls "public arena activities," such as public festivals and charitable functions—to demonstrate their status and prestige.[69] The public arena, then, "the realm in which status had come to be defined," "provided a structure through which . . . social and religious competitions could be expressed." "The style of Hinduism most characteristic of revivalist and merchant-dominated cities quite consciously aimed at public time and public space."[70] For Rajasthan, Lawrence Babb analyzes the ways in which Rajasthani merchants overcame the disjunction they felt between the courtly Rājput norms of ostentatious spending, which in some sense they were attempting to emulate, and their own ethic of resource "husbanding";[71] and for south India, Joanne Waghorne notes that the mercantile period there began with a new round of temple building—not by the royal houses, but as a result of new merchant wealth and control, "fully part of a global interchange of goods and people."[72]

Bringing the discussion back to Bengal, one can see some parallels. Before the Permanent Settlement Act of 1793, the mostly Hindu zamindars under the *nawābs* and then under the British imitated and fought with one another to gain the favor of their Mughal and East India Company overlords. They had more freedom of cultural expression than did the nobles under Louis XIV or Queen Elizabeth I, since they had no Hindu king providing them with a behavioral model, but it is arguable that they had much less political and social maneuverability. In any case, as argued in chapter 1, they sponsored religious festivals with great pomp, establishing a uniform model that is still today followed by their financially diminished heirs. In Bengal the aristocracy was not killed or forced out of power, but squeezed into financial bankruptcy. As soon as the sponsorship of the Pūjās was taken over by larger groups of successful merchants, banyans, and urban landlords after 1793, its character changed. Still the site for intense rivalry between Bengalis of more-or-less equal status, such rivalry now began increasingly to rest on the endless search for originality and novelty. After the revolution of the "universal" Pūjās in the 1920s, the base of sponsorship widened still further, opening out from the control of elite families to the shared, more democratic, and more politicized patronage of the middle class. While it is beyond the scope of my project here to delineate in a Campbellesque fashion the historical foundations of such an openness to novelty, one can say, generally, following Walter Benjamin and others, that mass production releases art from ritual into politics, from elite contexts into a display culture, where the exhibition of novelty is valued over the repetition of cultic rites.[73]

What one sees, then, in the streets of Kolkata and other Bengali towns today are modern forms of competition that stand squarely upon those derived from the eighteenth-century zamindars. And all such rivalries, whether zamindar or middle class, bespeak a more global phenomenon: the use of goods, behaviors, and special occasions to mark and claim status.[74]

## *Accounting for the Political, Looking for Analogues*

Here we turn to the second phenomenon, the use of the Pūjās as arenas for the voicing of sociopolitical concerns. How is one to interpret this? Here I look at six different vantage points: Śākta theology; the history of the festivals themselves; the tradition of satire in Bengal; the impact of economic liberalization; the family resemblance between the Bengali Pūjās and other, similar festivals in India; and the parallels between the Pūjās and festivals outside the subcontinent, such as carnival.

Theologically speaking, the mixing of the sociopolitical and the religious is not a problem at all, for we know that from as far back as the sixth-century "Devī-Māhātmya," Durgā is the Goddess of both *bhukti* and *mukti*, enjoyment and liberation.[75] Śāktism values the world and looks for the divine within it; as such, the centrality of Durgā, Jagaddhātrī, and Kālī to rituals of opulence and sociopolitical relevance seems appropriate. We also know, to put it very generally, that the mixing of religion and politics has always been characteristic of Indian history; moreover, "the very idea of Indian secularism is 'equal respect for all religions,' thus encouraging religion in the public sphere as a repository of cultural legitimacy."[76] Americans might not be able to countenance their president as one of the three kings in a neighborhood nativity scene, but this speaks mostly about their monotheistic upbringing, separation of church and state, and sense of the inappropriateness or even blasphemy in combining sacred and secular in iconic depiction.

A second method of approaching the cosmopolitanism of the Śākta Pūjās, this turning outside to other parts of India and the world for ideas to enhance the Goddess's worship, is to look, once again, at the history of the festivals. The original sponsors of the festivities, the landowning zamindars who curried favor with the British, filled their opulent houses with foreign objects and entertained their British guests at Pūjā time with English songs, even bagpipes and "God Save the King." In other words, the importation of the exotic and different was a sign of prestige and "culture." The situation is no different now: "Since the colonial era, the upper levels of metropolitan Indian society have been conscious of the importance of operating on an international scale as a means of preserving their impermeability to the classes below."[77] Newspapers in Kolkata carry stories of artists reading up on the exact dimensions of the Royal Albert Hall in London, or of a Bofors gun in Kargil. If, as was argued in the last section, one is in search of novelty in order to trounce a rival pandal, then one needs a field as wide as the world for thematic inspiration.

The public artistic tradition of satire provides a third parallel. Durgā and Kālī, especially, have always lent themselves to appropriation by Bengalis wishing to reflect, lament, or censure current events. This use of the Goddess has its roots in the medieval Bengali Maṅgalakāvyas, long narrative poems in honor of local, humanized deities, but it explodes in popular culture in the eighteenth and nineteenth centuries, with watercolor paintings, ribald poetry contests, and a whole host of dramatic farces and satires. One could marshal literally scores of examples, but three may be taken as representative here. First is a Kālīghāṭ *paṭ* from the mid-nineteenth century, in which Kālī is shown trouncing Śiva—except that the scene is really poking fun at the Memsahib-influenced woman who dominates her foppish, weak, Bābu husband.[78] The second is a cartoon from 1875, lampooning Īśvarcandra Bidyāsāgar's Society for the Prevention of Obscenity; Kālī is demurely covered in Victorian clothes.[79] The third is a satire called *Bodhan Bisarjan* by Ahibhūṣaṇ Bhaṭṭācārya, from 1895. The scene is the Himalayas, where Durgā and her children are getting ready to come to Bengal for the Pūjā holidays. Śiva has the "flu," and Durgā, who appears in a Memsahib's dress with a nurse's cap on her head, tells him that the best doctors are in Calcutta. Sarasvatī wants to go to Calcutta to get her veena, or lyre, repaired and flyers printed for her agitation on behalf of women's rights in heavenly Vaikuntha. Kārtik, the perfect Bābu, is keen to sample Calcutta's selection of towels, toiletries, silk handkerchiefs, cigars, and British pump shoes. Gaṇeśa, on the other hand, is afraid to go, lest he be deposited in the new zoo![80] In this light, dressing Durgā like a movie star or even like Monica Lewinsky is perfectly in keeping with former trends.

Indeed, visual art intended for a popular public audience—whether cartoon, painting, sculpture, drama, or poetry—has never been aimed simply at illustration; it acts as a forum for pressing concerns, making arguments, and debating about culture. Sandria Freitag has proposed that it was the religious and political procession (an obvious and purposeful public mixing of politics and religion) that allowed for the creation of the public sphere in colonial India; following the lead of Christopher Pinney, Ajay Sinha, and Joanne Waghorne, we could also claim the same for mass-produced visual arts that, despite their ephemerality, respond to a demand for relevant commentary on the part of the enjoying or purchasing audience and represent not kitsch but a process of democratization.[81]

Frank Korom, in his recent study of Bengali scroll painters and performers (*paṭuās*), notes this exact same showcasing of current events in their two-dimensional art: Osama bin Laden fleeing to Tora Bora, the crashing of the planes into the World Trade Center, the threat and decimation of AIDS, the *Titanic*, the funeral of Mother Teresa, George Bush ordering the American invasion of Afghanistan, and famines, birth control, floods, and the 2006 tsunami. According to Korom, while the *paṭuās* have always been innovators and indigenizers, their recent spate of political scrolls may be viewed in the context of audience requests for what Susan S. Bean might call "edutainment."[82] In one *paṭuā*'s depiction of the World Trade Center disaster, the couple at the center of the tragedy was a Bengali husband and wife.[83]

Fourth, even though the Pūjās have always been politicized, as argued above, one can situate the rise of the newly opulent, outlandishly creative pandal decorations of the last twenty years in India's relatively recent liberalization policies. In answer to my request of my Bengali interviewees that they try to pinpoint when the goddesses' temporary shrines began to take on thematic coherence, and why this change was effected, one astute woman observed that the austerities and uncertainties of the post-Partition period, coupled with the rise of the Naxalites in Bengal in the late 1960s and early 1970s, probably account for the relatively reserved Pūjā decorations of the 1950s, 60s, and 70s.[84]

Nehru's five-year plans had assumed a virtually closed economy, the prioritizing of heavy industry over consumer goods, and the massive involvement of an overbureaucratized government in trade and industry; by contrast, the consumer goods revolution, started by Rajiv Gandhi in the early 1980s but pushed ahead by Narasimha Rao after 1991, spurred at least the upper echelons of Indian society to new growth. The spread of satellite television and the entry of India into the global market "transformed the face of many Indian cities, as advertising, fancy shops, new cars, televised soap operas, luxury goods, and still more visible youth culture proliferated."[85] Ravi Srivastava sees such liberalization as partly responsible for the increasing regionalization of India's politics, as communities press for favor from the Union government or compete for foreign investment.[86] One could make a related point for the Pūjās: the more universal and democratic they become, the more local, neighborhood-centered, and political their focus.[87] In this sense the post-1980s market openness has not only served to provide Pūjā committees with access to global influences and products; it has also enlarged the arena, scope, and terms of their local rivalries. A small but pertinent example of this is the impact on the 2006 Pūjās of the World Cup Soccer games. Some pandal organizers, in protest against the near-monopoly of Italy's colors, players, and stadia in Kolkata's pandals, decided to showcase local football players instead. For instance, the Kasba Kheyali Sangha made their theme "Bānglār Football." "Everyone is ready to stay up late for matches abroad but no one thinks of local football any more," lamented a club organizer." Commented the newspaper reporter rhetorically, "Which side will you roll, local or global?"[88]

A fifth way to gain insight into the particular melding of sociopolitical themes in the Bengali Śākta Pūjās is to compare them with similar festivals in India, to see whether there are any unifying features. In India, three regions immediately come to mind: the area around Varanasi, especially Ramnagar; Maharasthra, particularly the urban center of Mumbai; and Tamilnadu, especially Chennai.

The first example coincides, in fact, with Durgā Pūjā: the Rāmlīlās, or reenactments of the life of Rāma, performed during Navarātrī in North India, the most famous site being Ramnagar, across the river from Varanasi. Although the *līlās* employ live actors to replay the adventures of Rāma and Sītā, and not sculpted images, and while the action moves from site to site, not being situated in a stationary pandal, like Durgā Pūjā the Rāma festival has been built up by virtue of its royal or elite character. Environmental theater and performative theory expert Richard Schechner explains the enormous popularity of Ramnagar's theatrical spectacle. "The most direct answer is that since the early nineteenth century, the Ramlila has been the defining project of the Maharajahs of Benares. The current line was established in the mid-eighteenth century and, caught between a failing Mughal power and an emergent British presence, was not secure on the throne. Sponsoring a large Ramlila was the way for the Maharajahs of Benares to shore up their religious and cultural authority at a time when they were losing both military power and economic autonomy."[89] Festivals that legitimate and provide scope for the advancement of elite aspirations have a certain family resemblance in India.

Two examples that come closer to the external form of Durgā Pūjā are connected to each other in their celebration of Gaṇeśa Pūjā, also called, in Mumbai, Gaṇapati Utsav and, in Chennai, Vināyaka Caturthī. Both festivals have forms very similar to what one sees in Bengal: urban epicenters, with Mumbai influencing trends in Maharasthrian towns and villages, and Chennai, Madurai, and Coimbatore doing the same for the Tamil countryside; hundreds or even thousands of images displayed in temporary neighborhood pandals; group sponsorship, financing, and advertising of such pandals; competition for prizes; public processions; controversies over the polluting of the environment by the dumping of the images and their paraphernalia into rivers and seas; and the borrowing of cultural themes for the decoration of images and their temporary homes (although neither region appears to approach Bengal's exuberant reflection of social and national events in their festival displays). Researchers doing work in Maharashtra, for instance, report a wide range of innovations in the depiction of Gaṇapati: photographer Stephen Huyler saw the elephant-headed deity as the lead singer in a band of pop stars, accompanied by Elvis and Madonna;[90] and in a more political twist, Thomas Blom Hansen reports a 1992 pandal in which Gaṇapati is surrounded by a tableau of the freedom struggle featuring the hero B. G. Tilak—whose unfinished work is being carried on by the Sangh Parivar and the BJP.[91] Christopher Fuller, who is working on the Tamil Vināyaka festivals,[92] found the Vināyaka of 1999 often worshiped amid replicas of Kargil scenes and accompanied not by his traditional rat vehicle but by an Indian army tank. Although, like the Bengali case, "unconventional innovations are particularly common in Chennai, where novelty is at a premium,"[93] Fuller thinks that there is, as yet, nothing comparable in Tamilnadu to the lavish and creative pandal arrangements one finds in Kolkata.[94]

The histories of both Gaṇeśa festivals have also been embedded in political nationalism. Prior to the 1890s, when B. G. Tilak and others propagated the public form of the Maharashtrian Pūjā, the festival had been confined primarily to the temple and the house.[95] But Tilak intended for it to encourage Hindu revivalism and mobilize culture for a political purpose. Like Durgā's festival, Gaṇapati's also underwent a change in the 1920s, when Pūjā associations emerged to link classes and neighborhoods. According to Gérard Heuzé, such mass Pūjās—with their street culture and their elite management—have become a "powerful but ambivalent medium for expressing popular opinion," and "constitute one of the strongest sources of melting-pot effects."[96] Although it was regulated and de-politicized during certain periods under the British and again after Independence, since the 1980s the Shiv Sena / BJP combine has employed it for nationalistic, anti-Muslim purposes[97]; after 1995, when the BJP came into power in the Centre in alliance with the Shiv Sena, about 60 percent of the images of Gaṇapati had as a backdrop something to do with Shivaji's martial exploits.[98] Partly in imitation of this, since 1983 the VHP equivalent in South India, the Hindu Munnani ("Hindu Front"), has consciously popularized and sponsored the Vināyaka festival, using it to promote nationalism and assert Hindu muscle. In this they have been phenomenally successful; what started with a few images in 1983 had expanded in 1999 to 6,500 in Chennai alone.

In both Maharashtrian and Tamil cases, however, what gained impetus fifteen or twenty years ago under right-wing groups for political purposes has also caught on among independent groups (businessmen and professionals, particularly the proliferating middle classes), who are either non- or less politicized but who nevertheless join in to finance and enjoy the festivals as expressions of regional identity. Fuller refers to this expansive quality of the Caturthī as the "normalization of Hindu nationalism,"[99] and claims that it is largely (though not entirely) a middle class, urban phenomenon. Even in Right-dominated Maharasthra, where it seems that representations of the (Muslim) "Other" are more allowable in the Pūjā context, in 1999 the Mumbai police requested one organization to take down the Pakistani flag from a dragon-like beast whom Gaṇapati was fighting, for fear that it might disturb the "sensitive fabric of the multi-religious demography of south Mumbai."[100]

Joanne Waghorne, a scholar of Tamil urban space, comes to similar conclusions in her ongoing studies of modern-day temple construction in Chennai. She describes the impulse to build lavish temples with humanized deities on the *śikharas*—deities whose features often model contemporary political or theatrical icons—as deriving from what she calls "middle-class religion." For her, such gentrified religion seeks to soften, humanize, and dignify; to forge links between religious and consumer realms; and to offer strong statements of national identity in religious ritual contexts. Although Waghorne does not discuss public festivals per se, her work nicely dovetails with that of Fuller and his research team: when religion enters an urban, middle-class–dominated public space, social and political concerns get reflected in its manifested forms.

Perhaps one can see in the Kolkata, Mumbai, and Chennai cases something of a similar history: in each, a festival is consciously aggrandized, universalized, and politicized by leaders tuned in to national politics and ideological thinking, for an initial purpose of religious solidarity and definition.[101] However, although in all three instances the initiators had nationalistic, political motivations, subsequent history has shown the festivals to have been taken over in large part by a wider spectrum of the non- or differently politicized public, which, over time and in a global environment, has used the festivals for their own purposes. The fact that Durgā Pūjā is the least politicized and most ostentatiously and creatively celebrated of the three may be explained by the facts (1) that Durgā Pūjā was *the* public cultural icon of Bengali Hindus long before 1926, and hence was woven in myriad ways—some satirical and even playful—into the public and private lives of ordinary people, and (2) that the CPI(M) has consciously striven to downplay communalism in the public arena. One does not see the sort of explicit propagandizing of the Durgā Pūjā by the CPI(M) in Bengal, for instance, that we do of Gaṇapati Utsav by the Shiv Sena in Maharashtra. Although Vināyaka Caturthī is too new in Tamilnadu to offer any lasting comparisons as yet, it is interesting to note that the Munnani has not gravitated toward Murugan, the indigenous mascot of Tamil identity, but toward a deity linked with pan-Indian nationalism. And one suspects that the more tightly controlled a festival is, by a nationalist state or political agenda, the more wary individual organizers become in choosing to communicate countervailing platforms through their pandals. One wonders, for instance, whether Munnani-sponsored Vināyaka Caturthī celebrations could occur in pandals depicting churches from Europe or Goa (fig. 5.6), the Taj Mahal, or the proposed Ayodhya temple, surrounded by a mosque, a church, and other places of worship[102]—all of which have been created in Kolkata over the past two decades.

Still looking within India for parallels, we find another striking similarity in the cohesive national iconism of the Republic Day Parades. Jyotindra Jain writes, "[In] India's post-Independence . . . systematic structuring of the Republic Day Parade, the pageant and performances comprise . . . cultural tableaux depicting highly romanticized versions of landmarks in Indian history, essentialized representations of tribal and village communities, [and] traditional handicrafts." For instance, Mysore's palace goes by on a float, as do Meghalaya's tribal peoples, Gujarat's artistry and ethnic culture, Sravanabelgola's giant Jain statue, and Orissan Pipli applique craft. Such a "performed archive" presents "authentic" tribal peoples and their dances and culture as living examples of India's ancient roots.[103]

Lest one get the mistaken impression that all public festivals in India conform to a style similar to that of Durgā and her sister goddesses in Bengal and Gaṇeśa in Maharashtra and perhaps Tamilnadu, it is worthwhile

FIGURE 5.6. A Goan church model being dismantled at the conclusion of Jagaddhātrī Pūjā, Circus Math Sarbajanin. Chandannagar, November 2000. Photo by Rachel Fell McDermott.

briefly to consider the additional examples of festival culture given by Paul Younger in his book, *Playing Host to Deity: Festival Religion in the South Indian Tradition.* While his survey of several South Indian festivals, Hindu and Christian, mentions the festivals' independence from official political and clerical authorities, their warm, playful type of religion, their inclusion of social castes and communities, and their creative genius—all of which could be said of the Pūjās—several of the deities studied by Younger also inspire trance, possession, exorcism, and bodily mortification, none of which appears to obtain in the Bengali cases.[104] Why this is, I surmise, has to do with the middle-class sponsorship of the Bengali festivals, which brings with it a middle-class concern for respectability, self-control, and emotional tidiness.

Let us, lastly, briefly take the discussion even further afield, from India to the carnival societies of Europe, South America, and the Caribbean. Carnival celebrations in Spain, Mexico, and Trinidad are strikingly similar to the Bengali Śākta Pūjās—and to the Gaṇapati Caturthīs of Mumbai and Chennai. First, they are public, galvanize almost all of society, and act as markers of national identity. Second, the characteristic features of Durgā, Jagaddhātrī, and Kālī Pūjās are replicated here as well: the democratization of masquerade, calypso, and music costs over wide sections of the population, who compete with each other in fierce rivalries for coveted prizes; an emphasis on thematic novelty as the chief element of a successful bid for recognition; and the incorporation of contemporary life in the artforms created for the celebrations each year. Peter Mason, in his book on carnival in Trinidad, notes the following themes in the costumes, floats, and lyrics composed for the occasion in the mid-1990s: fantasy, outer space, insects, ghosts, vampires, government ineptitude, male/female relationships, West Indian unity, problems with the national highway, the lottery, and even haircut trends.[105]

Moreover, all scholars of carnival note that, in whatever society it is celebrated, it goes through periods of greater or lesser distanciation from politics. For example, although the Trinidadian festival began in the 1800s during the planter days, it became highly politicized from 1940 to 1962, when it functioned as an outlet for anti-British sentiment. Nowadays, increasingly patronized by the middle class and by women, it has become more mainstream and socially acceptable.[106] To quote Peter Stallybrass and Allon White, theorists of carnival culture, "for long periods carnival may be a stable and cyclical ritual with no noticeable politically transformative effects but . . . given the presence of sharpened political antagonism, it may often act as catalyst and site of actual and symbolic struggle."[107]

To bring all of this back to the Bengali Pūjās: It appears that what we are seeing right now in Bengal is a politicized but not communal stage in a national holiday season that has, many times in the last two hundred and fifty years, been used for communal purposes—first, by the zamindars in their articulation of political strength against the Mughal representatives and then against the British, and second, by Hindu nationalists of the pre-Independence era who resorted to the public festivals as occasions to educate and whip up Hindu sentiment, often against the minority communities. In a fairly prosperous modern Bengal, where middle-class wealth and consumerism have built up Kolkata, the urban center of all Pūjā trends, the Pūjās reflect a *pan-Indian* glorying in national pride, but do not, as do the Shiv Sena or the Hindu Munnani, pick on "enemies" (read: Muslims) within the state. In this sense, the goddesses can be seen as mascots of national, not narrowly religious, honor; and what Svetlana Boym calls the "danger of nostalgia"—namely, that we confuse the actual past with the imaginary one, being ready to die or kill to protect it—is averted for the present.[108] One wonders to what use Durgā, Jagaddhātrī, and Kālī Pūjās would be put, were a Hindu nationalist party to gain ascendancy in West Bengal.[109] Note, however, that neither Jyoti Basu and nor Buddhadeb Bhaṭṭācārya has been immune to seeking the Goddess when she could advance his own agenda.

As an example, the pandal that demonized Bill Clinton and Tony Blair was organized by a neighborhood of CPI(M) supporters. Although too much *bhakti* may be discomfiting, these multivalent Pūjās can also be useful to—and stabilizing of—the status quo.

The claim that the Pūjās are at base "secular" serves not just the Communists; it is also integral to a common lament by the older generation, who rue the passing of a faith-based age (and note that this grievance can be found as far back as the early nineteenth century, and probably earlier[110]), as well as to a spirited defense of Pūjā hoopla by those who read history differently and who celebrate the festival's effervescence. Reminding their readers that the zamindars exulted in "pomp and wildness" and that the nineteenth-century *bāroiyāri* Pūjās met the entertainment needs of the masses as well as of the "Fast Bābus" (people who enjoyed amusements),[111] such writers exhort the shedding of "nasṭyāljik" feelings: "Durgā Pūjā is far more than a ritual to us; it is a people's festival . . . [it is] secular. Durgā Pūjā is much greater in dimension, and its appeal will increase manifold if it can shed its ritualistic strictness and inhibitions."[112]

In sum, to link both halves of this chapter: The modern Bengali Śākta Pūjās represent the transformation of an aristocratic mode of self-promoting self-expression by goddess worship, in which, though democratized through the influence of urbanization, the consumer market, and expanding middle-class participation, the same rivalries and opportunities for self-definition still exist today, if on a widened scale. At the moment, in the early decades of the twenty-first century, the festivals are relatively locally integrative, their sponsors aspiring to a national and even international arena of public, visually dazzling notoriety.

## Why Pūjā Isn't Christmas

Every holiday the world over has a history, a sort of flavor or *rasa*—one might even say a dominant tone, or a *bīja mantra*—that gives it distinctiveness. I do not mean to imply that festivals such as Durgā, Jagaddhātrī, or Kālī Pūjā are unchanging or static. However, I do believe that both of the characteristics I have mentioned—the entwining of religious rituals with (1) a competitive search for prestige and (2) a mirroring of social and political themes—have a common origin and make sense given their developmental history and their status as urban, largely middle-class festivals expressive of cultural identity. In 1906, during the furor over the first partition of Bengal, one Bengali author tried to differentiate between Christmas and the Pūjās. Christmas, he said, values individual humility and repentance, whereas Durgā Pūjā is a national sacrament, and "self-assertion is the essential method."[113] Although this author may have been too kind to Christmas (after all, like Durgā Pūjā, Christmas partly owes its success as a state tradition to its perceived secularism and its unabashed engagement in commercial extravagance[114]), and although, as we have seen, Christmas may be less appropriate as a measuring rod for the Pūjās than carnival, I think the 1906 description of the Śākta festivals is apt. From their beginning, status and reputation have been the prizes of these celebrations. And at their center is a Goddess whose humanization and symbolic malleability allow her to stand for and against, inside and outside, the social contexts of her votaries. Hence she appears aboard both the *Titanic* and an aircraft carrier, tacitly blessing those who, whether in the fields of artistry or arms, assert themselves for honor.

# 6 The "Orientalist" Kālī

## *A Tantric Icon Comes Alive*

### Seeing and Not Seeing

I first encountered the Bengali Goddess Kālī in her dressing room—the workshops where she is prepared from straw and clay for her annual Pūjā—in November of 1989.[1] I was making my first visit to Kumartuli, the section of northern Calcutta where many of the city's professional image makers (Kumārs) have their studios. This was also my first adventure with Jeffrey Kripal, a new friend and colleague in the study of Bengali Śāktism. We were guided by Aditi Sen, of the American Institute of Indian Studies, a friend and mentor to us both.

Jeff, Aditi, and I meandered through the alleyways of the artisans' district, gazing at the many images (*pratimās*) of Kālī that awaited completion by their creators. Some were no bigger than a foot high, while others were so tall that painters had to perch atop ladders to design their faces. Some showed evidence of the straw innards underneath their drying clay molding, whereas more finished Kālīs glistened with the sheen of fresh paint and tinsel decorations. But as Jeff and I stared delightedly at these evolving figures, we noticed that there were two different types of Kālī images under production (fig. 6.1). The types had similar bodies, with shapely women's curves, large round breasts, the right foot firmly planted on the chest of

FIGURE 6.1. Two types of Kālī. Kumartuli, Kolkata, November 1989. Photo by Rachel Fell McDermott.

prostrate Śiva, and her four arms holding the traditional items (a cleaver [*khaḍga*] and severed head in her two left hands, and fearlessness- and boon-conferring hand positions [*abhayā* and *varadā mudrās*, respectively] displayed by her two right hands). The two types were also decorated in a comparable fashion, with paint, long black hair, ornaments, and clothes. The main differences concerned their colors and faces. To be sure, the black Kālī's face was anthropomorphized, but the eyes were much larger than a human's, and the requisite lolling tongue was distended below the chin to the point where the neck meets the torso. Her smile was hard to discern, and the overall effect, before clothes and decorations had somewhat modified it, was formidable. The visage of the blue Kālī, on the other hand, was modeled on a human woman's face; the features were normal in size, the tongue was short, extending to slightly above the chin, and the upturned corners of the mouth formed an obvious smile.

Jeff and I were puzzled by the disparity in these two depictions, but we had no time to inquire about their origins, meaning, or comparative popularity. Nonetheless, this initial glimpse alerted me to the multifacetedness of the Goddess's iconographic traditions, and set me on a quest for further understanding. I stayed in Calcutta over eight Kālī Pūjā celebrations (1989, 1991, 1995, 1996, 1998, 1999, 2000, and 2001), during which time I saw and photographed hundreds of Kālīs, and interviewed many artisans and scholars knowledgeable about their iconographic development. In the years since that first trip to Kumartuli, I have also become fascinated by other aspects of Kālī's history in Bengal: the upsurge of interest in Tantric rites and texts after the fifteenth century; the place of Kālī worship in the political and social consciousness of the landed gentry in the medieval and early modern periods; their avid patronage from the eighteenth century of new Śākta vernacular literatures; Kālī temple construction; and Kālī Pūjā festivities. It is now clear to me that all such features of Kālī's involvement in the Bengali environment are pertinent to the understanding of her iconic portrayal.

It is my aim here to relate, I believe for the first time,[2] a connected narrative about the evolution of Kālī's iconography, tying together artistic, literary, religious, social, and political history—with a special emphasis on the relationship between the festival *pratimās* and the Goddess's Tantric roots. This is a story unique to Bengal and—of late—to its West Bengali geographic locales; it describes Tantra on Bengali ground. Furthermore, it tells of revelations and concealments, meanings explicit and implicit, and the ironies of human motivation. To return to Kumartuli and our visit there in 1989, I now realize that Jeff and I had eyes discerning enough to identify fewer than half of the differences between the two types of Kālī figure. However, to have been so long unseeing only adds to present delight.

## The Tantric Goddess Comes Forth

### *"Equipped with Tantric Paraphernalia:" Kālī in the Eleventh to Fourteenth Centuries*

Although Kālī as a goddess has been known at least since the Epics and early Purāṇas,[3] she begins to gain her characteristic Bengali iconic form[4] and association with Tantric rituals beginning from around the eleventh century. Popular opinion assigns the creation of the modern Kālī image to the seventeenth century, with Kṛṣṇānanda Āgambāgīś and his famed vision of a servant girl slapping dung on a wall, which he saw as the promised revelation of Kālī's form. However, Kālī's iconography certainly predates Āgambāgīś; not only did he himself quote earlier Tantric descriptions of the Goddess's appearance in his Tantric digest, the *Tantrasāra*, but we have independent corroboration from other texts and relics that at least from the eleventh century Kālī had been envisioned in terms very similar to what one sees today. To give just a few examples, the tenth- or eleventh-century *Mahābhāgavata Purāṇa*, the eleventh-century *Devībhāgavata Purāṇa*, and the thirteenth-century *Bṛhaddharma Purāṇa* (all written in Bengal or by Bengalis) describe Kālī in several places as a naked goddess with big teeth, a lolling tongue, a garland of cut heads, four arms, a corpse seat, and a covering of blood;[5] and both the twelfth-century *Kulacūḍāmaṇi Tantra* and fifteenth-century *Kālī Tantra* are sources for some of Kālī's *dhyānas* (descriptions used for Tantric meditation on the deity in the heart).[6]

Kālī's early origins in eastern India can also be proven by her incorporation into Tantric ritual. Teun Goudriaan claims the early-thirteenth-century *Yonigahvara* as the oldest text on Kālī worship; its instructions on Tantric meditation, heroic rites, and heterodox practices all involve Kālī.[7] By the time of Brahmānanda Giri and his pupil, Pūrṇānanda Giri, from the Dhaka region in the early and late sixteenth century, respectively, their rival Kṛṣṇānanda Āgambāgīś, also from the late sixteenth century, Raghunāth Tarkabāgīś Bhaṭṭācārya, in the late seventeenth century, and Rāmtoṣaṇ Tarkabāgīś, of the early nineteenth century, Kālī had become an important component of Śākta religious practice (*sādhanā*) and praise verse (*stuti*).[8]

Thus one must agree with Pratapaditya Pal, who argues that it was between the eleventh and fourteenth centuries that Kālī came to be worshiped with "all sorts of [T]antric paraphernalia," such as skulls, corpses, and instruments of death, and who sat or stood on a corpse identified as Śiva.[9] Evolving, therefore, from a fairly minor deity in the world of the Epics and earlier Purāṇas, Kālī makes her splash in Sanskrit literature in the first half of the second millennium as a deity of life, death, transformation, and ritual. While still shared by both Purāṇas and Tantras, she is primarily a Tantric deity, for she develops few myths or stories, except by association with Pārvatī, and her primary appearances occur in the context of instructions to spiritual adepts, or *sādhakas*.

An additional difference in these Purāṇic and Tantric portrayals of Kālī appears in a detailed examination of the Goddess's *dhyānas*. Of the nine *dhyānas* reviewed here—six from Tantric and three from Purāṇic texts[10]—all refer to Dakṣiṇākālī as: terrible or frightening (*karālā, bhayaṅkarī*); toothy; naked; endowed with four arms holding the usual items; and adorned with a necklace of freshly severed, blood-dripping heads (*muṇḍamālā*) and a skirt of amputated arms, sewn together at the elbows. Other features of her iconographic portrayal include black skin color, disheveled hair, three eyes, a lolling tongue, a mouth that is both drinking and dripping blood, babies' corpses dangling from her ears, a proclivity for quaffing liquor and bellowing horrid shrieks, and a preference for cremation grounds, where she wanders with her jackal and *yoginī* friends. Most of these *dhyānas* attempt to attenuate the off-putting nature of this Goddess by stressing her boon- and fearlessness-conferring hand gestures, her gorgeous smile, the crown and/or half-moon perched upon her head, the serpentine sacred thread draped around her torso, and her heavy, uplifted breasts.

What is intriguing to me about these *dhyānas* is their uneven references to Kālī's activities with Śiva. Prior to the fourteenth or fifteenth century, Kālī may have been seated on Mahādeva in the form of a corpse, but there was nothing sexual about their interaction; he was just a seat. This Purāṇic and even early Tantric vision of the pair changes with the most famous of Kālī's meditational images, from the *Kālī Tantra*, where the word *viparītaratā* is introduced to indicate that Kālī and Śiva are "engaged [in intercourse] in the reversed position," with the female on top in a seated pose. This emphasis is repeated in later Tantric *dhyānas* from the *Svatantra Tantra*, the *Mantramahodadhiḥ* and the *Āgamatattvavilāsa*—an indication of Kālī's growing importance to the sexualized philosophical and ritual Tantric context.

It is important to remember that these *dhyānas* were for meditational purposes only. The Tantric adept was to worship the Goddess in his heart; the construction of an actual image out of stone or clay was not the ideal. It is true that he was to invite her to step out from his heart into the specially prepared *yantra*, or mystic diagram, which he had created in front of him in order that he might make offerings to her, but her origin and form were always of the heart.[11]

Thus, Kālī's presence in the world of Sanskrit ritual as practiced in eastern India began in the early centuries of the second millennium C.E., and she gained increasing attention over time in Tantric manuals, digests, and compendia. But she was principally a deity of the tutored elite, and the details of her appearance derived from and were germane to the largely esoteric arena of Tantric ritual and power. It is not until the seventeenth century that this Goddess of meditation and heterodox rite took her first steps out into the vernacular, popular world.

## *Looming Larger: Kālī's Vernacularization and Popularization in the Seventeenth to Eighteenth Centuries*

Much has been written about conditions in Bengal in the late medieval period: the revival from the time of Caitanya in the fifteenth century of Vaiṣṇava religiosity, which led the older Śākta and Tantric lineages into creative strategies of accommodation and rebuttal; the opportunities for expansion and frontier building under the Mughals; the rise of landed estates headed mainly by Hindus of a Śākta persuasion, who used Śākta symbols in the service of their own aspirations to power; after the arrival of the British in the seventeenth century, the new occasions for political and social jockeying among Bengalis, Mughal rulers, and British adventurers; and finally, in the eighteenth century, tremendous social upheavals emanating from famines, Mārāṭhā raids, and the burden of increased taxation. Such religious, social, and political contexts provide the backdrop for how the Goddess Kālī emerged from her narrow Tantric enclave and became accessible to a wider audience in this period: (1) the spate of Tantric texts, sometimes with Bengali translations, available from the sixteenth century; (2) Kālī's entrance into two new vernacular literary genres, that of the Maṅgalakāvyas from the seventeenth century and the Śākta *padas* from the eighteenth; (3) the construction of many new goddess temples, also from the eighteenth century; and (4) the development, again in the eighteenth century, of the yearly Kālī Pūjā.

Why the sudden flowering of these literary and religious venues for the worship of the Tantric deity? Why the urge to make Kālī more publicly recognizable and accessible? Two answers suggest themselves again and again in the literature: the influence of, or threat from, the increasingly prominent Vaiṣṇava community; and the obvious "fit" between the martial imagery of the Goddess of power and the royal ambitions of the elite class of Hindu zamindars, who sought to legitimate their expanding social and religious status through Śākta symbolism.

THE PROLIFERATION OF TANTRIC TEXTS Take, as an example, the outpouring of Tantric texts and digests from the seventeenth century onward, many of which are repositories of thought on Kālī's significance, ritual worship, and iconography. While scholars disagree as to the positive or negative valence of the interaction between Śāktas and Vaiṣṇavas after the time of Caitanya—some arguing that the relations were friendly and others that they were antagonistic[12]—it cannot be denied that the popularity of Vaiṣṇava literature spurred many Śākta writers into action. A new genre of Tantric texts was created to marry Vaiṣṇava and Śākta interests, stories, and rituals,[13] and Kṛṣṇa found a favored place even in the Śākta Tantric compositions. Pratapaditya Pal notes that Āgambāgīś's real reason for writing the *Tantrasāra* was to make more public those goddess traditions which were under threat of being lost in the wave of enthusiasm for Kṛṣṇa.[14]

Moreover, many of these Tantric ritual texts were written either by members of the landed gentry or by retainers and scholars under their patronage. Appendix I of S. C. Banerji's *Tantra in Bengal* lists 97 unpublished Bengali Tantras. All of these for which there are dates derive from 1605 to 1843, and all of the writers are landlords or their proteges.[15] One can make the same argument by glancing at the history of the Śākta poetry, which gains prominence with Rāmprasād Sen in the middle of the eighteenth century: everyone who composes in the genre, until well into the late nineteenth century, is associated with the largely Śākta-leaning aristocracy.[16]

KĀLĪ IN MEDIEVAL MAṄGALAKĀVYAS AND EIGHTEENTH-CENTURY ŚĀKTA POETRY The second indicator that Kālī was becoming more noticeable in Bengali contexts is her inclusion in the genre of medieval Bengali Maṅgalakāvya poetry. This forms the bulk of middle Bengali epic poetry, probably derived from an earlier, oral tradition used as part of ritual worship,[17] and represents popular, non-Brahmanical religiosity during the Sultanate period in Bengal.

The *Kālikāmaṅgalakāvyas*, which glorify Kālī, are noteworthy on several counts. First, unlike the case for Durgā, Caṇḍī, and Manasā, there is nothing at all written on Kālī in the vernacular until the seventeenth and eighteenth centuries, when Bengalis started incorporating her into the Maṅgalakāvya genre. Second, one can see the growth of Kālī in Bengali devotion by looking at her increasingly prominent role in the poem's main love-story about Vidyā and Sundara. Carol Salomon compared the Vidyā-Sundara sections in the twenty-three extant *Kālikāmaṅgalakāvyas* and discovered that whereas in the early versions Kālī has a minor, almost cosmetic role, in the later renditions, from the late seventeenth and eighteenth centuries, she directly intervenes in the story, moving the plot through her appearances and boons.[18] Third, the *Kālikāmaṅgala* authors tend to sweeten and decorate the fierce Goddess, in a fashion similar to the earlier Sanskrit Tantras. While being described as grotesque, with a distended tongue, a garland made of severed heads, matted hair, and a tiger's skin around her waist, deafening the atmosphere with her stamping thuds and raucous laughter, she is also painted with endearing language: her corpse earrings are decorated with jewels; she wears ankle bracelets with tinkling bells; gold and jewels cover her entire body; the crescent moon adorns her hair; and she stands in the charming three-bends *tribhaṅga* pose, like Kṛṣṇa.[19] Here we have evidence, therefore, that the iconography of the slowly vernacularizing Kālī is in direct continuity with her Tantric past.

The Kālī of the *Kālikāmaṅgala* gives way, by the eighteenth century, to the Kālī of the Śākta *padas*, short lyrical poems of praise, petition, and complaint set to music and sung to the Goddess, now addressed as Mā, or Mother. This Kālī is still the cremation-ground wanderer of the Tantric *dhyānas*—many of the poems are Bengali transcriptions of the Tantric portraits of the deity, with a few petitionary lines added at the end—but she is also the one who can be teased, berated, pouted at, and threatened by her poet, who approaches her in a spirit of devotion (*bhakti*).[20] Rāmprasād Sen, who may be considered the earliest exponent of the new Śākta poetry tradition, also wrote a *Kālikāmaṅgalakāvya*—proof of the literary transition from one genre to another.[21] It is likely that the biggest impetus for the switch from the narrative Maṅgalakāvya style to that of the short, distinct *padas* was the influence of Vaiṣṇava Padāvalī and its pathos-filled descriptions of the love between Kṛṣṇa and Rādhā. Śākta poetry mirrors the rhythm patterns, refrains, and signature lines (*bhaṇitās*) of its Vaiṣṇava counterpart, as well as its imagery. Ways of describing Rādhā's beauty are borrowed for Kālī, who, say some Bengali literary critics, is touched by the Vaiṣṇava sentiment (*rasa*) of sweetness (*mādhurya*); it is thus that she becomes the loving, compassionate, and attractive mother.[22] From the Vaiṣṇava literary world, therefore, the Śākta poets inherit both a style and a set of familiar formulae for indicating the divine–human relationship in all its emotional timbres.

While it is easy to detect the Vaiṣṇava influence upon the composition of Śākta Padāvalī, it is harder to determine who sponsored the inclusion of Kālī in the Maṅgalakāvya literature, and why. Nonetheless, it is clear why the Tantric Goddess sat so lightly in the medieval poetry but endured in her association with the *padas*: as a deity chiefly associated in her former Sanskrit life with rituals and meditation prescriptions rather than with a stock of stories, she was less amenable of enfoldment into the Maṅgalakāvya genre, which depended upon tales of gods and goddesses to popularize their worship. The *padas*, by contrast, inherited the rich tradition of Tantric images and praises, composed for personal devotion and spiritual enrichment.

ERECTING TEMPLES FOR KĀLĪ What the new Tantric compendia, Maṅgalakāvya stories, and Śākta poems were doing for Kālī in the literary sphere in the seventeenth and eighteenth centuries, the construction of new temples was doing in the realm of ritual. It is hard to know just when external *mūrtis* for worship replaced or were added to less anthropomorphic representations of the *devī*, such as the pot of water. There is a tradition that this innovation originated with Rājā Kṛṣṇacandra Rāy, head of the Nadia zamindari from 1728 until 1782,[23] but it is likely that the practice of creating goddess figures began several decades previously; the oldest Kālī temples date from at least the beginning of the eighteenth century.[24] Moreover, the mention of Rājā Kṛṣṇacandra Rāy brings us back to a familiar point: the dedication stones of almost all surviving temples vouch for the involvement of zamindar patronage in the construction of goddess sanctuaries. The same *rājās* and *rāṇīs* who were sponsoring the writing of Tantric digests and Śākta poetry were also paying for the erection of temples in their lands. The zamindars of Nadia, Burdwan, Natore, and Dinajpur were especially prominent in this regard, but temple dedication was enthusiastically pursued by all men and women of means to authenticate their claims to piety and social concern.

FIGURE 6.2. The Kālī of Kālīghāṭ Temple. Kolkata, October 2002. Photo by Jayanta Roy.

The images in these old temples maintain something of the spirit of the Tantric *dhyānas* by portraying a goddess of fierce demeanor. Their stern faces are not very anthropomorphized, for they contain large, flaming eyes, huge teeth, and extended, long tongues. The Kālī of Kālīghāṭ, the most famous of all Kolkata's Kālī temples, is a good example; she is shaped like a huge egg, with four tiny arms on the side, and her face assumes gigantic proportions relative to the rest of her. She has three eyes of equal size, shaped like elongated ovals, a small nose, a row of teeth, and a large golden tongue that hangs down her front (fig. 6.2).[25]

Other famed Kolkata Kālī temples house images that, though more anthropomorphized than the *mūrti* of Kālīghāṭ, nevertheless look quite formidable.[26] Examples include the large-eyed Kālī at Phiringi Kālī Temple, which claims to date from 1498; Ṭhanṭhanīya Kālī Temple on College Street, built in 1704, where the image is very tall, with a large golden

FIGURE 6.3. Siddheśvarīkālī at the Citpur Temple. Kolkata, September 1998. Photo by Rachel Fell McDermott.

tongue, teeth, and big eyes; Siddheśvarīkālī Temple in Citpur (fig. 6.3), built in 1730–1731, in the back room of which is preserved the sword used for human sacrifice by the dacoits who first worshiped her; Dakṣiṇeśvar Kālī Temple, made famous by Rāmakṛṣṇa, who became a priest after the temple was opened in 1855 and who was intensely devoted to the black image with its big eyes and long red tongue;[27] the Kālī at Nimtala Burning Ghat, called Śmaśānakālī or Ānandamayī, whose staring, large eyes and long, pointed tongue engulf the face; and the image at the Ādyāpīṭh Temple in north Kolkata, from 1926, which is naked and somewhat masculine in its features.[28]

Though it is not impossible that additional research might uncover some older, less fearsome Kālīs from the eighteenth and nineteenth centuries, such would not counter the generalized portrait of Kālī seen above. Indeed, Dīptimay Rāy, who traveled quite extensively throughout Bengal in order to prepare his 1984 book on sites associated with Kālī, says of a shapely, graceful image he found at the temple at Uluberiya, Howrah: "This type of charming, affectionate, and blissful image is very rarely seen in West Bengal. There is no sternness on the Goddess's face; rather, it is as if she were suffused with pure bliss."[29] In addition to the iconographic prescriptions in Kālī-centered *dhyānas*, another reason for the fierce visages of many of these images is their associated lore; dacoits, temples amid dark woods, Tantric *sādhakas*' five-headed meditation seats,[30] and activities involving corpses on the cremation grounds are recurrent themes in the stories linked with numerous Kālī temples.

It is clear from the form taken by these early Kālī *mūrtis* that they are modeled directly on guidelines given in the Tantric *dhyānas*. Temple worship, then, is a concession to popular religiosity for those not sufficiently serious, well trained, or spiritually advanced for the internal techniques of mental visualization. The Tantras state unequivocally that offering food, water, and flowers to an image is the lowest form of *pūjā*; *mantra* repetition and meditation in the heart are higher stages along the path. An early-nineteenth-century Tantric compendium, the *Prāṇatoṣiṇī*, actively prescribes the worship of small images for householders, who are not ready to see the Goddess in less obvious forms, such as a woman's genitals (*yoni*), a mystic diagram (*maṇḍala*), a sword, or a stone; these are the provenance solely of the adept.[31]

Thus, although the exact path from the internally conceived Kālī of Tantric ritual to the externally adored Kālī of temple worship is not easy to reconstruct in terms of motivations and dates, it is clear that the emergence of Kālī temples in the early eighteenth century was a third arena in which the Tantric Devī was issuing forth from her specialized, esoteric environment.

FÊTING THE GODDESS But there is a fourth route along which Kālī was invited to travel into the larger world: her annual Pūjā in the month of Kārtik (October–November), which began to be celebrated in the mid-eighteenth century. Although we will investigate Kālī Pūjā more thoroughly in chapter 7, it is appropriate to say a few words about it here, in terms of what we can glean about its influence on Kālī's iconography.

Since all such Pūjā images were created expressly to be immersed after the cessation of the two-day festival, there are very few still extant from which to gauge what the Goddess looked like in the eighteenth and early nineteenth centuries. One must rely on paintings, newspaper and travelogue descriptions, and even cartoons. An additional source is the Kalighat *paṭs*, or watercolors on paper, depicting gods and goddesses, animals and birds, and contemporary social events, which were popular in Calcutta from about 1800 until the 1930s.

All such clues, scanty though they may be, indicate that both temporary images and painted renditions of the Goddess were being created very much in the style of the then-permanent images—in other words, according to the pattern of the Tantric *dhyānas*. In a depiction of the immersion of a Kālī image, dating from 1808 and painted by Balthazar Solvyns, one can see that the image is naked, except for her flowing hair and necklace of cut heads, and that her face is fierce, with an upturned and distended tongue.[32] Though not necessarily intended to portray temporary Pūjā images, *paṭs* also hint at what the nineteenth-century Goddess might have looked like; in one famous example, from 1875, Kālī is black, naked, adorned with her usual getup, and fierce, with a very long, pointed tongue.[33]

Nationalism also had democratizing effects on the Goddess. Although, as we have seen in chapter 2, it was generally not Kālī, but Durgā or Bhārāta Mātā, who galvanized the Bengali anti-British effort in the early twentieth century, Kālī's bloodlust was occasionally used to stir up revolutionary fervor.[34] One excellent iconographic example is an early-twentieth-century painting of the black Kālī standing on a white Śiva in the battlefield amid fleeing human demons.[35] This irked the British, who saw it as anti-English revolutionary propaganda. However, as historians Partha Chatterjee and Lata Mani, among others, have ably demonstrated, the nationalist deployment of goddesses did not only draw upon their capacities for blood-letting and destruction. In seeking to protect and defend their besieged culture from the colonialist onslaught, Bengali nationalists essentialized "woman"—and, by association, deities like Durgā, Bhārat Mātā, and Kālī—as the feminine, maternal representation of the nation and its authentic cultural traditions.[36] In the process, as I have argued in chapter 4, Hindu goddesses gained increasingly voluptuous, motherly personas, for they came to stand for the weak, weeping Motherland, ready to pour out their milk in gratitude for their heroic sons' protection. One can see hints of these increasingly feminine, motherly iconic characteristics in the afore-mentioned painting. Kālī may kill demons, but her face is round and comely, and her body shapely.

Just how far Kālī had come by the early twentieth century is shown by these popular artforms: she is now a familiar vehicle for social and political commentary. Like the deity of the Śākta *padas* and established temple images, this Kālī of the public Pūjās, the cheap watercolor *paṭs*, the political spoofs, and the nationalist construction was a newly externalized representation of the Sanskrit deity of ritual practice, who had emerged into a more specifically Bengali, nonelite milieu in answer to theological and sociopolitical need.

## *"When Religion Is Joined to Beauty": The New Realism of the 1920s and 1930s*

After the breakthroughs of the seventeenth and eighteenth centuries, the next major development in Kālī's iconography occurs in the early twentieth century, with the transition from *bāroiyāri* to *sarbajanīn* Pūjās. In 1926, in the Bagbazar area of Calcutta, the ever-popular Durgā Pūjā entered its third phase. Kālī Pūjā followed suit in 1928,[37] and within six years Kālī's iconographical presentation had changed to meet the new demand for a publicly accessible goddess.

This is how it happened.[38] For the 7 November 1934 Kālī Pūjā, N. C. Pāl, the same Kumartuli artisan who was so instrumental in altering Durgā's image in a genuinely "Indian" or "Orientalist" fashion, also experimented with the conventions of Kālī's traditional *pratimā*. He produced an image that was more realistic, human, and beautiful than ever before. As explained in more detail in chapter 4, Pāl was heir to the late-nineteenth-century Calcutta style of realism popularized in the mythological paintings of elite artists like Ravi Varma, M. V. Dhurandhar, and Bāmapada Banerjee.

In her study *The Making of a New "Indian" Art: Artists, Aesthetics, and Nationalism in Bengal, c. 1850–1920,*[39] Tapati Guha-Thakurta describes the evolution in Indian aesthetic taste during the course of the nineteenth century, when the evocation of volume and perspective and the lifelike appearances of people and scenes made a clean break from the earlier conventions of the Kalighat *paṭs*. Influenced by the colonizers' distaste for native forms and divinities, Bengali artists refined their depictions of Hindu deities, so as to dignify their status and meet the standards of a new artistic ideal. Though Guha-Thakurta does not directly relate the changes she describes for painting to those in the Kumartuli Pūjā workshops, it is certain that the general move toward realism and beauty affected N. C. Pāl, a self-avowed admirer of Abanindranath Tagore (1871–1951) and his student Nandalal Bose (1883–1966), of the Bengal School of Painting.

N. C. Pāl's Kālī first appeared in the Thanthania area of northern Calcutta. Newspapers went wild with excitement, printing photos of and encomia about the new style. Still portrayed with her typical ornaments, stance on Śiva, lolling tongue, and disheveled hair, Pāl's image departed from past models chiefly in the face and in the more realistic conveying of motion. First, her skin got lighter, from black to blue. Then, instead of the large, flaming eyes with their fixed gaze, and the long, distended tongue, the new Kālī looked like a normal woman; Pāl gave her realistic eyes, which made the image less formidable, and an average-sized tongue. Whereas in the older images the Goddess stood in a static pose, with the front of her body facing directly ahead and standing on Śiva, lying lengthwise underneath her feet, Pāl tilted the image forty-five degrees to the right, such that the entirety of Śiva's body was visible. Kālī does not just stand on him; she walks over him, as if heading off to the right, but turns her body to face the viewer (fig. 6.4).[40]

Newspaper reporters in 1934, 1935, and 1936, when Pāl's innovation was still very new and called for commentary, described his image as "a brilliant combination of the artist's versatility and inspiration and the modeler's mastery of craft. It sufficiently demonstrates how the creation of beauty is made practicable if the oriental method of art is vitalized by a sense of reality and an understanding of the rhythm of motion."[41] Again, the "Kali image of Thanthania Sarbajanin offers a new aesthetic interpretation on a time-worn superstructure. A thing of beauty is a joy forever and when religion is joined to beauty, the delight is all the more brightened. No wonder therefore that the city of Calcutta jostled their [*sic*] way to the College Row to pay their tribute of homage and reverence to the Magna Mater."[42]

FIGURE 6.4. N. C. Pāl's new Kālī of the 1930s. Amrita Bazar Patrika, 2 Nov. 1937, p. 6.

From my perspective, the most interesting remarks on the new Kālī are those that relate her beautified appearance directly to the Tantric *dhyānas*. In a 1936 article by Ashokanath Shastri, the older images are critiqued for their *departure* from the spirit of the *dhyānas*, since their stiff postures and stylized faces fail to capture the spirit of motion and energy communicated in the Tantric descriptions, where "the whole atmosphere is surcharged with the mingled expression of fierceness, divine beauty, and sacredness." He ends by referring to N. C. Pāl's sweetened image at Thanthania as a true example of the mood and intent of the *dhyānas*.[43] For this author, then, the move to increased realism is also a fulfillment of the Tantras.

Eventually called the "Orientalist," "Artistic," or "Modern" (*Ādhunika*) school, as opposed to the "Bengali" (*Bāṅglā*) or "Ancient" (*Puraṇa*) school, the conventions initiated by N. C. Pāl were instantly popular, and have remained so up until this day. Pāl's sons and grandsons have continued the tradition at Thanthania, which is still one of the premier attractions in the city at Kālī Pūjā time. If one follows the Calcutta newspapers from 1934 up to the present, with an eye to which type of images are photographed and published, one finds that for many years in a row it was only the new, Orientalist type that was noted and commented upon by the staff reporters.[44] It is not until 1963 that I find a single published photograph of the older, fiercer type of Kālī—and this was offset by another, humanized Kālī on the same page.[45]

More recently, along with the resurgence of interest in old Bengali songs, the traditional Kālīs, who never lost their popularity among established families sponsoring Kālī Pūjā in their homes, have made a comeback in the *sarbajanīn* contexts as well; over a three-year period, 1998–2000, Abhijit Ghosh did a survey of one hundred Kālī images each year in the same Pūjā pandals of southern Kolkata, taking note of various iconic cues: face design (fierce or sweet?), color (black, light blue, gray?), torso depiction (static, in motion?), the position of Śiva relative to the Goddess (lying parallel or perpendicular?), and so on. He found that fully one third of the Kālīs in all three years represented the fierce, old-style tradition.[46] As one Bengali writer phrased it in 1993, "of all the images made according to custom, the ones from the seventeenth to eighteenth centuries are the most important."[47]

## *Which Face Do You Want? The Modern Inheritance*

Which kind of Kālī, indeed, is the more important? Why, and to whom? Certainly the blue, sweet, realistic Kālīs are in greater demand and generate more money on the open market. This is not only because they appeal to the heart, reminding one of the loveliness of one's mother,[48] or because they conform more to the vision of the buxom, near-naked woman promulgated by Hindi films—although these are probably influential connotations. Indeed, the explosion of the modern media—portrayals of film actresses and the use of goddesses in advertising—has affected popular ideas of how the Goddess should look. As Satish Bahadur observed sagely in the mid-1970s,

> Popular art in any society serves the functions of myth creation and social catharsis. In India, the film is the primary vehicle for the spread of popular culture; the other media tend to model themselves after the style of the film. . . . Even the traditional iconography of statues and pictures for religious worship has accepted the visual values of the film; the

conventional Durga image for the Bengali puja festival is looking more and more like Suchitra Sen![49]

In 1995 film star Hema Malini came to Calcutta at Kālī Pūjā time and expressed her hope one day to play Mā Kālī in a film. In the same year, the leaders of the Thanthania Pūjā invited Madhu, "proudly proclaim[ing] how they have been leading the competition in the city to rope in silver screen idols to inaugurate their puja."[50] Idols and idols. Both beautiful.

The newer Kālīs are also, it must be noted, less expensive to make and therefore to buy. Pārtha Pāl and Pradīp Pāl, Kumartuli artisans from different families whom I interviewed in October of 1995, both stated without hesitation that they make more of the modern type of Kālī, and that their numbers are increasing every year.[51] These softer Kālīs also sell postcards and inspire calendar art, nine tenths of which depict the newer Kālīs. Comments Kajri Jain, a scholar of Indian mass culture, Kālī in her more terrifying aspects has gradually receded from depiction in calendar art, and is being replaced by a sensuous treatment that can "sometimes verge on soft-focus eroticism."[52]

The artisans themselves prefer the older style. According to Pradīp Pāl, they are more "godly" (*Bhagavāner mata*) and more demure, with their attractive decorations covering the entire front of the Goddess's body. It is only the modern Kālīs whose upper torso, including her breasts, are regularly exposed (fig. 6.5). The modern goddesses, catering to whim and the vagaries of innovation, also appear more outlandish to the pious. Should Kālī be dressed as Mother Teresa, with a blue-bordered white sari, as occurred in 1997, or as Hanumān, her skin replaced with the furry black hair of a monkey, as found in 2004?[53]

There are a number of transitional varieties, the most popular being the traditional body (Kālī standing on Śiva lengthwise, her torso lavishly decorated) with the new, smiling, humanized, blue or gray face. This type of intermediate Kālī is at least as old as 1970, where I found it in a newspaper photograph,[54] but from the mid- to late 1990s it has become quite the fashion for people who want to maintain something of the older feel without losing the more attractive face. As an indication of its importance, both Pārtha Pāl and Pradīp Pāl informed me that when people want to found a permanent Kālī temple, they most often commission an image with a traditional body and a modern face. Perhaps it is not appropriate to worship, year round, a naked Kālī; indeed, even the permanent Kālī images that are decades or even centuries old are all so draped in saris, flower garlands, and adornments that their bodies are lost to sight. The attempts of the priests

FIGURE 6.5.
A modern Kālī, with Śiva nearly sitting up. Kolkata, October 1998.
Photo by Rachel Fell McDermott.

in these Kālī temples to emphasize the Goddess's decency and sanctity (or to preserve those of her viewers) are enhanced by her ornaments, signs of a married woman: bangles, earrings, and red powder on the hair parting.

Let me return to the comment made in 1936 by Ashokanath Shastri, on the relation between these new images and the Tantric *dhyānas*. Is it true that N. C. Pāl and his followers have brought us closer to the spirit of the Tantras? Has Kālī's popularization enriched the appreciation of her Sanskrit, ritual past? A comparison between the iconographic prescriptions of the Tantras and the "Artistic" Pūjā images of today yields interesting results. Certainly, the nakedness (from the waist up) of the modern Kālīs, which enables one to get a clear view of the skirt of cut arms and her *muṇḍamālā*, is more in keeping with what the *dhyānas* designate. Furthermore, most artists add jackals poised hungrily underneath the dripping head in her hand, and even, occasionally, *yoginī* companions—all part of the

Tantric description. Kālī's alluring smile can also be said to derive from the *dhyānas*, which praise her face for its beauty.

On the other hand, the traditional Kālīs outdo their newer counterparts in their faces. Through their large eyes outlined in red, barred teeth, and longer tongue, they preserve the spirit of what nearly all the *dhyānas* state about this deity—that she is *ghorā* (horrible) and has a frightening face (*karālavadanā*). Also, although the realistic portrayal of motion and activity in the modern Kālīs undoubtedly brings the scene alive in a way that the older images do not, it is questionable whether the Tantric *sādhaka*, sitting alone meditating on the Goddess in his heart, was endeavoring to watch a simulated battle, complete with movement. What modern craftsmen have done is to turn an icon meant for contemplation into an imitation of life.

But there are aspects of Kālī as depicted in the *dhyānas* that neither old nor new Kālīs display at Pūjā time. Where, for instance, is the depiction of her open-mouthed horrid laughter (*aṭṭahāsa*), her drunkenness, her corpse earrings, or the blood dripping from the corners of her mouth and from the recently cut necks of her necklace onto her breasts and torso? Most especially, why is she standing and not seated on Śiva? And why is there no hint of the *viparīta rati*, or reversed sexual intercourse, which the two are enjoying? What does one make of the fact that most of these missing items are prescribed in Kālī's most famous *dhyāna* from the *Kālī Tantra*, which is printed in all of her ritual manuals (*pūjā paddhatis*)?

Although there are a few old-style images that do retain some of these more forbidding elements,[55] they are obviously a minor tradition, and both old and new Pūjā images appear to leave out significant details of Kālī's Tantric demeanor. It is my contention, however, that the new ones leave out more. For what seems quite far from the vision of the Tantric *dhyānas* is not so much the lack of iconographic details—in some senses the more realistic, modern goddesses include more of these—but the *intent behind* those details; there is very little that frightens in most modern renditions. Kālī's beautiful face and shapely, graceful body make her bloody accoutrements seem incidental or even comic by comparison. In this same vein, the position of Śiva, relative to that of the Goddess, has now been transformed even more radically than what was conceived under N. C. Pāl: Kālī sometimes stands atop her Lord, legs akimbo, so that the two are completely perpendicular to one another; and sometimes he nearly sits up, his head resting on his hand, to watch her (fig. 6.5). The overall inherited form of Kālī is still more or less present, therefore, but the implied meaning appears to have changed. Of the nine *dhyānas* surveyed for this chapter, the realistic Kālīs of the Kumartuli workshops conform most closely to that of the *Bṛhaddharma Purāṇa*, which contains little blood and gore and includes plenty of references to her smiling face and shapely breasts. The Purāṇic, nonsexual Kālī, once overshadowed by her Tantric counterpart, has regained market share.

The Kumartuli artisans admit their departure from the Tantric models. Pārtha Pāl told me that he had never seen a Pūjā image with blood dribbling out of Kālī's open mouth or with corpses dangling at her ears. "That's too dreadful (*bhayaṅkara*)," he told me. His older colleague, Pradīp Pāl, later agreed: "If we follow the Śāstric injunctions, no one will buy our images." Professor Nṛsimhaprasād Bhāḍuri, a specialist on Śāktism, had perhaps the most intriguing comments to make about Kālī's new form. The traditional Kālī, standing lengthwise over Śiva, is closer to the purport of the *dhyāna*s, since it is possible to conceive of engaging in amorous activity from that position. In other words, while not actually depicted, *viparīta rati* is suggested. But this suggestion is masked when Kālī is turned to the right, as in the modern versions. Bhāḍuri claimed that this was the conscious decision of the artisans, who, with a "gentle touch" (*bhadrāyana*), altered the image for the sake of humanization (*mānabāyana*) and—I might add—propriety.[56]

Looking over Kālī's iconographic history as a whole, it appears that certain aspects of the Tantric meditational prescriptions have always been overlooked in the externalization of her image: hints of sexuality, her peculiar earrings, her drunken bellowing, and the glistening blood on her body. With N. C. Pāl's innovation and the attempt to create more realistic images, some parts of the *dhyāna*s not often depicted in the older Kālīs—such as her nakedness and smile—were retrieved. As a result, the frightening effect of the fierce-faced Kālī with the bloodshot eyes and thirsty, extended tongue was attenuated. Sweetness and humanization are now preferred to the static icon of awe.

But must one choose? Pradīp Pāl informed me that, although it is rarely commissioned, there is a form of Kālī that holds together the suppleness of the new Kālī body and the "godly" look of the old Kālī face. Apparently, Belur Mah, the monastic headquarters of the Rāmakṛṣṇa Mission, requests this every year. Not everyone wants to see a movie star or one's mother in the Goddess's face.

## Gains and Losses in the Travels of an Icon

Now when I visit Kumartuli and pass by an artisan's godown, where Kālīs-in-waiting are drying or having their bodies painted and bedecked, I see a lot more than I did in 1989. Especially when the studio is home to old and new styles of image, standing next to one another, Kālī's processional history seems to stand in front of me. I am reminded of the glossy pictures produced by the International Society for Krishna Consciousness, in which the stages of a man's life are depicted by several images in succession: first the baby, then the adolescent, then the mature adult, and then the wrinkled man bent over his stick. At Kumartuli we do not see either the Kālī of the Tantric *dhyānas*, meant to be visualized inside the adept's heart, or the Goddess as her seventeenth- to eighteenth-century sculptors first externalized her for temple worship, though the *Bāṅglā* or *Puraṇa* Kālī, with her formidable, fearsome mien, is a close approximation. It is the blue Kālī—looking younger and younger under the craftsmanship of N. C. Pāl's inheritors—who is furthest away from her Tantric birth. And it is she who epitomizes and embodies the average devotee's disquiet over the bloody, sexualized, power-conferring properties of Tantric ritual.

However, there continue to be people for whom the worship of Kālī is not genuine if the Tantric elements are omitted. One wonders what Swami Vivekananda (1863–1902), who died before the innovations of the 1930s, would say about this avoidance of Kālī's dread nature. For while alive he castigated in biting language those who smoothed away her awesome side:[57]

> Lo! how all are scared by the Terrific,
> None seek Elokeshi whose form is Death.
> The deadly frightful sword, reeking with blood,
> They take from Her hand, and put a lute instead! . . .
> True, they garland thee with skulls, but shrink back
> In fright and call Thee, "O All-merciful!"

But Vivekānanda's is a minority voice. As I have tried to demonstrate in this chapter, Kālī's emergence into the popular world, with its consequent humanization and animation, was encouraged by many, in different decades and walks of life, who benefited from making her symbolism, might, and allure more accessible. For some the publicizing of her Tantric ritual in digests and manuals represented a means of countering, or subsuming, the threat of Vaiṣṇava popularity. For others, the patronage of her vernacular literature, her temples, and her annual festival offered legitimation for social and political ambition. Still others, fighting British imperialism, either emphasized her puissance in the name of political subversion, quoting Tantric ritual *mantras* to justify killing in her name,[58] or folded her into a generic symbol of Motherland, to be cherished and protected. In the more recent past, in response to public taste and the exigencies of economic demand, her artisans have softened her yet more, creating with their "gentle touch" a Goddess who not only acts but also looks like one's beautiful mother. In other words, Kālī's path—remarkably similar to that traveled by Durgā and Jagaddhātrī, as we have seen in chapter 4—is the outcome of the intersection between historical, social, and political circumstance, and the active choices of her Bengali mediators.

But the end result has been the transformation of an icon, an image that—like those in the Eastern Orthodox churches of Byzantium and Russia—was meant for installation in the heart, an adoring inner gaze, and not the reproduction of reality. Through their frontal depictions, immobile bodies, often distorted facial proportions, and dignified colors, icons evoke feeling, express metaphysical profundity, and encourage absorption. The Jesus of the icons, to continue with the Christian parallel, is not the "friend" of modern Protestant posters, for there is nothing sentimental about iconic portraits, which guard against overfamiliarity with the divine. The same can be said for the older Kālī, who, with her stationary stance, exaggerated eyes with their fixed stare, severe visage, and bold colors of red, white, and black, invites a return gaze, a contemplative touching of eye and heart. But Russian icon painters of the late seventeenth century, influenced by Western Renaissance reforms, began to value naturalism, perspective, beauty, gentleness, and motion, which detracted eventually from the intense, spiritual effect of their former art. The same has happened in the modern Bengali milieu. Kālī is pretty, pleasing to behold, but to many Bengali devotees she is in danger of losing her "godly" side.

It is ironic indeed that in spite of their being claimed to communicate best the specifics of the *dhyānas*, the newest Kālīs conceal as much as they reveal about her Tantric origins. How many Bengalis know, or admit to knowing, that the primary reason Kālī stands on Śiva is not because she mistakenly stepped on him but because she is about to sit for conjugal bliss?[59] Or what about the outstretched tongue, which in the newer images is so short that it lends credence to the popular story of Kālī sticking it out in embarrassment, rather than extending it thirstily for blood? Finally, many a blue Kālī has a red lotus painted around her mouth; what is this but a creative maneuver to mask her blood-smeared lips? In sum, while her artisans may have altered Kālī's stance, literally and figuratively, to reflect changes in public taste, at least one of her feet remains firmly planted on Tantric ground—and this in a manner befitting Tantric esotericism, whether her votaries acknowledge and approve of it or not.

# 7 Approaches to Kālī Pūjā in Bengal

This chapter[1]continues our focus on Kālī but moves from an emphasis on iconography to a discussion of the festival proper—chapters 6 and 7, then, mirror chapters 4 and 5, which covered the same two large topics, for Durgā and, to a lesser extent, Jagaddhātrī. Kālī's festival follows Durgā's by three weeks, on the dark-moon night of the month of Kārtik, coincidentally also Diwali.[2] In many ways their pairing makes sense, as from at least the sixth century C.E., Kālī has been claimed as a multiform of Durgā who issued like a daughter, younger sister, or helper from Durgā's angry forehead to help her battle demons.

Not surprisingly, the two Pūjās have developed in tandem: as we have seen in chapter 2, Kālī, like Durgā, was utilized in the expression of anti-colonial and communal political rhetoric; chapter 5's discussion about Durgā's debut from elite origins and her evolution through to the public, popular form of her festival is equally true for Kālī, even up to the modern craze for the "Theme Pūjā"[3]; and chapters 4 and 6 illustrate how the iconographic depictions of both goddesses have changed in the direction of softer, more humanized portrayals. The two festivals are even linked in the artisans' studios, for Durgā faces salvaged from the river after immersions are turned into the *ḍākinī* and *yoginī* figures that accompany Kālī at the next Pūjā. Notwithstanding these significant areas of overlap, there are also important differences between the two festivals, and these will concern us for the remainder of the chapter.

## Not Twins: Different Births, Different Lives

### *Kālī's Spotlight Is Smaller*

Even the staunchest devotee of Kālī must admit that her pedigree cannot match Durgā's. While we have evidence for the performance of Durgā Pūjā as far back as the sixteenth century, and perhaps even earlier, we cannot date Kālī Pūjā much before the mid-eighteenth century. The most well known story of its rise in Bengal concerns Rājā Kṛṣṇacandra Rāy, Nadia zamindar and Śākta patron of the mid-eighteenth century. William Ward, writing in the second decade of the nineteenth century, states that Kṛṣṇacandra ordered all his subjects to perform Kālī Pūjā on pain of penalty; apparently more than ten thousand people in the Krishnanagar area complied. Kṛṣṇacandra's grandson, Īśāncandra (who would presumably have been alive during Ward's day), also patronized Kālī Pūjā on a grand scale, offering eighty thousand pounds of sweets, one thousand goats, sheep, and buffalos, and one thousand saris to the Goddess. Finally, Ward notes that Rājā Rāmakṛṣṇa Rāy of Natore expended one lakh rupees on a Kālī Pūjā image.[4]

There are indications that Ward's claim for the late date may be correct. Many of the sixteenth-century ballads from eastern Bengal retrieved by Dīneshchandra Sen contain *bāromāsī* ("twelve month") sections, with stylized descriptions of what festivals occur each month of the year; while Durgā Pūjā is almost always referred to in September/October, Kālī Pūjā is rarely included for October/November. Again, mentions of Kālī Pūjā are completely missing from Tantric texts that are otherwise devoted to the specifics of her worship.[5] Chintaharan Chakravarti suggests Kāśīnāth's *Śyāmāsaparyāvidhi* of 1777 as the oldest reference to Kālī Pūjā, since Kāśīnāth quotes Tantric passages in a manner calculated to prove Kālī's importance.[6]

Moreover, of the two, Durgā Pūjā has always been the more popular and has always received more news coverage, in both English and Bengali; indeed, Kālī Pūjā is virtually absent from the papers into the early twentieth century. When there is a story it focuses on Diwali, and mentions street illuminations, firecrackers, foods, new account books, Lakṣmī, day trips for Europeans, and gambling. Kālī does not appear at all, except in the context of the Kālīghāṭ Temple, where people go *on Diwali* for sacrifice and the starting of the new year.[7] Published interest in Kālī Pūjā per se begins to grow slowly, and only from the late 1920s with the new *sarbajanīn* festivals, and the 1930s with the new humanized goddess depictions. Diwali always tops the Pūjā in terms of photos and news coverage, however, and this remains true into the 1980s. Striking as an example of the imbalance of attention to Kālī vis-à-vis Durgā is the Pūjā season coverage for 1964 of the Bengali newspaper *Ānanda Bājār Patrikā*: there are three photos, total, of Kālī images, compared with 143 of Durgā.[8]

Kālī Pūjā pandals also tend to be smaller, less often thematically decorated, and less gorgeous than Durgā's counterparts,[9] although, interestingly, since the mid-1970s Kālī Pūjā pandals have totaled more than twice the number of Durgā Pūjā pandals. The reason for this, explained Subhas Ray, personal assistant to the deputy commissioner of police at Lal Bazaar, is that Durgā Pūjā pandals are larger, are more expensive, cause more traffic congestion, and hence are more strictly regulated.[10] Kālī, I have also been told, does not need splendid temporary shrines in which to take residence, as Bengal is dotted with thousands of Kālī temples, which become the nexus of activity at the Pūjās. This is not true for Durgā, however, who, due to some peculiarity of fate in Bengal, has almost no permanent temples.

## *Her Reputation Is More Formidable*

A second major difference between Durgā and Kālī Pūjās is Kālī's association with fear and power. Rarely identified with the girl or daughter of the house, as is Durgā,[11] Kālī's iconography *is* more forbidding, and she is more prone to punish for ritual infractions. Even twenty-five years after the *sarbajanīn* Pūjā format had become popular, certain people were still hesitant to take it on. Stated Śākta expert Narendra Nath Bhattacharyya when commenting about his college days in the late 1950s, "Kālī *bāroiyāri* was rare, because one was afraid."[12] In an article for the *Statesman*'s Puja supplement for 1957, Tapanmohan Chatterji writes that Kālī's tongue is out "for a taste of the warm blood of her victims" and that people worship her out of fear of her curses.[13] Sudhīr Kumār Cakrabartī, writing a Bengali article specifically aimed at explaining the various aspects of Kālī, omits discussion of the three eyes, bloody tongue, and cremation-ground dwelling, "for fear."[14] This sense that Kālī's power is not to be disregarded is exemplified in a news story from 2003 about a father who dreamed that if he did not marry off his two minor sons immediately, the Goddess would kill them.[15]

As we saw in chapter 2, Kālī's fearsome demeanor and connoted potency were particularly efficacious in galvanizing public support for nationalist causes. During the early 1920s, an author writing for the *Ānanda Bājār Patrikā* during Kālī Pūjā season used her cremation-ground imagery to challenge Bengalis to act: "Are the great *bhairavas* awake, those who will sit doing *śakti-sādhanā* on the corpses of this race? Are the priests of the new era ready, those who have prepared the offerings for the worship of the Mother who dwells on the great charnel grounds of Bengal, flooded with skeletons of our past glory? Will they be able to satisfy the Destroyer by their *pūjā*, offering bestial things such as the fear, shame, dirt, and the unending sorrow of Bengalis? If not, then there is only darkness, and the fear of ghosts. . . . In order to receive without fear her boons of fearlessness and aid, call on the Mother without fear in the midst of the famine and hardship pervading our country."[16] One of the forms of Kālī, in fact, is specifically called Cremation-Ground Kālī, or Śmaśānakālī, and there are both permanent temple images and sporadic temporary images of this type erected during the Pūjās.[17]

Kālī is not only potentially frightening herself; she also has strong links to fearful people. Antisocials and goondas, for instance, are frequently central to her temple foundation stories. Indeed, there is a whole genre of Kālī images called Ḍākāt Kālīs, for their association with the robbers or dacoits who founded or patronized them. The town of Shantipur, in Nadia, a Śākta heartland, specializes in Ḍākāt Kālīs.[18] Modern-day goondas are often involved in the sponsorship of Kālī Pūjā pandals: "Criminals in Bengal have always been attracted to the rituals associated with Kali Puja. . . . Community Kali pujas are basically by the goondas, of the goondas, for the goondas."[19] As Nazrul Islam, deputy police commissioner, further explains, rowdies are attracted to Kālī because people are afraid of her and her devotees and hence are more likely to give money to support pandals; because intoxicants are considered her *prasād*; and because it is widely believed that if you commit a crime on Kālī Pūjā and evade capture, you will be protected the whole year.[20] Anyone who has spent any time in West Bengal will have heard stories of harassment and forced subscription payments by local toughs at Kālī Pūjā time, and of rowdy behavior, drunkenness, and gambling.

Corruption or bad behavior exhibited by people responsible for Kālī's numerous temples also lends her a dubious reputation, by association—

something that does not happen with Durgā because of her lack of permanent temples. In Kolkata, the most famous temple is Kālīghāṭ, widely critiqued as a dirty, unkept zone where pilgrims are harassed by greedy ritual specialists. In 2004 the Government of West Bengal announced that it would pay to have the temple renovated, but the Temple Trust did not cooperate, fearing interference in the running of the site, and in 2006 the courts banned the pilgrim guides (*pāṇḍas*), widely experienced as rapacious, from entering the inner sanctum of the temple. In responding to accusations that the temple authorities were misappropriating devotees' offerings, the courts also mandated that offerings would have to be dropped into sealed boxes, and that a representative from the district magistrate would have to be present when they were opened. Kālī temple functionaries are not necessarily, it appears, a trustworthy lot.

Another type of person associated with and attracted to Kālī's worship is the Tāntrika, or practitioner of ritual derived from the Tantras. Almost every Kālī temple of any repute, especially if established in the eighteenth century or earlier, is said to have had a Tāntrika in its history or to have been established by a Tāntrika on a human corpse.[21] In Kolkata this is true of Ānandamayīkālī of Nimtala, Siddheśvarīkālī on Citpur Road, Siddheśvarīkālī of Thanthania, Jaykālī of Shyambazar, and even the fairly new Lake Kālī Temple, from 1948; one can find numerous similar stories from all over the state. Moreover, all Bengali towns and cities have their resident Tantric astrologers and *siddhi*-wielders, men who offer to help you with love, marriage, business, children, education, family troubles, and even enemies. One fervent Kālī devotee, Tāntrika, and Ph.D. student whom I met at the University of Calcutta told me that he could arrange to have anyone who was troubling me killed. The dacoit or lawbreaker and the Tāntrika are sometimes conjoined in Kālī contexts. Two of the biggest Kālī Pūjās today are organized by clubs in Chetla and Kalighat that have rather dubious reputations. They worship the Chinnamastā and Cāmuṇḍā forms of Kālī, complete with blood sacrifices performed by red-robed Tāntrikas.

In addition, old families with traditions of worshiping Kālī often do so according to Tantric rites. Belpukur, a village in Nadia district north of Krishnanagar, for example, is famed for its Tantric Kālī Pūjās: animal sacrifice is important (fig. 7.1), alcohol (*kāraṇabāri*) replaces Ganges water for ritual sanctification, and alcohol is also offered to the deity.[22] It goes without saying that iconographically all of these temple and home images are of the old, traditional, fierce variety.

In spite of the fact that Durgā, too, came into prominence through the active patronage of elite families, her history does not include dacoits or Tantric *sādhakas*. Although Durgā Pūjā is described in Sanskrit and Bengali Tantric texts at least since the tenth century, Durgā's worship has been linked with royalty and with householders, not with heterodox rituals.[23] Nor does she have the same fearful reputation. She is, to be sure, dread-inspiring to Mahiṣa and other demons whom she kills, but her iconography includes a plethora of weapons *for war*, not heads, severed limbs, or other dismembered trophies *of war*. Because of her closer mythological ties to Śiva, her identification with the Bengali daughter and daughter-in-law, and her more benign visage, Durgā appears to have been less heavily Tantricized.

In this context, the fact that Kālī Pūjā and Diwali, the pan-Indian festival of lights that celebrates the pacific deities Lakṣmī and Gaṇeśa, occur on the same night results in a rather peculiar conjunction of ideas, rituals, and ideological associations—more so than occur as a result of the parallel conjunction of Bijayā Daśamī with the slaying of Rāvaṇa by Rāma.[24] Diwali is a home-based festival, and it communicates auspiciousness, new beginnings, and a sense of well-being—not the awe associated with blood sacrifice and midnight ritual. Wrote Abhī Dās, in "Sekāle Bāṅgālīr Kālīpūjā," in 1985: the

FIGURE 7.1. Goat heads placed before the image of Kālī at a house Pūjā in Belpukur, a village in Nadia district north of Krishnanagar. November 1999. Photo by Rachel Fell McDermott.

conjunction of Diwali and Kālī Pūjā is ironic, as they are exact opposites. Diwali represents fortune and victory, Lakṣmī's face is yellow and smiling, and she is worshiped with lamps and white flowers. Kālī, on the other hand, represents famine, war, rebellion, and fear; her face is black and fearsome, and she is worshiped with red flowers and darkness.[25] Another Bengali author noted with chagrin how much Kālī Pūjā is being affected, Indianized, and genericized by its conjunction with Diwali.[26] Local stories abound as to the reason for the simultaneity of the festivals: Lakṣmī and Kālī came together, as opposites, from the churning of the milk ocean; Kālī needs light to fight demons; and light helps establish the boundary between the living and the dead, since the dead visit the earth at Kālī Pūjā, and one needs to keep the evil spirits at bay.[27] Clearly there is a perceived disjunction between the festival cultures that occur on the dark-moon night of the month of Kārtik.

### *She Is Raw, Sexualized, Immodest*

In spite of the normative iconographic tradition of Kālī *standing* upon the chest of her husband Śiva, since the fifteenth century the Tantric *dhyānas* that describe her meditational form actually indicate that she is supposed to be *seated* on him, since they are engaged in *viparīta rati*, or the pleasure of reversed sexual intercourse.[28] A few old images and paintings from the nineteenth century mirror this prescription: Śiva's penis, testicles, and pubic hair are prominently depicted in a late-nineteenth-century Kalighat *paṭ* in Kolkata's Asutosh Museum;[29] the British Museum houses a fierce black clay Kālī, with red-ringed breasts, children's corpses adorning her ears, a girdle of hands that fails to cover her pubic area, and an ithyphallic Śiva;[30] the same museum retains a large watercolor painting (ca. eighteenth–nineteenth century) depicting a three-cornered yantra, inside of which is a seated light-colored Kālī engaged in intercourse with a three-eyed, ugly, dark blue demon whose erect penis is clearly visible (they are seated on Śiva, who is seated on a corpse);[31] in Krishnanagar at the Ānandamayī Kālī Temple, Kālī sits on Śiva, who is acting as her Tantric meditation seat (fig. 7.2);[32] and in Hooghly district one can visit the home of Abadhūt, a Tantric *sādhaka* from the early twentieth century who painted a picture of Kālī nude from the waist up, seated in intercourse with Śiva, blood trickling from her open mouth onto her exposed breasts.[33]

FIGURE 7.2. Kālī seated on Śiva, Ānandamayī Temple. Krishnanagar, October 1998. Photo by Rachel Fell McDermott.

Seeing all these images reminds one that this goddess derives from an esoteric, Tantric world that is neatly disguised by today's pretty Pūjā images, where Śiva is either asleep, amused, or focused on something else. The sexual element is not however completely missing, even if intercourse is not indicated, for many of the post-1926 images of Kālī (but not Durgā) leave the breasts uncovered. Some contemporary Bengali women find this immodesty unbecoming and embarrassing; Kālī's sexuality is uncomfortable.[34] When I was in Kolkata in 2000, a local controversy raged over a seventy-five-year-old Tantric priest who for the prior fifty years had been worshiping a series of ten-year-old girls over a wooden pyre in the Kasi Mitra Burning Ghat in northern Kolkata on Kālī Pūjā night. The Tāntrika removed all his clothes for the event, and he and his assistants went into trances, cut themselves with knives, collected their blood, and offered it to the Goddess. He then washed the little girl's feet with alcohol and licked them clean. Neither the police nor the health department nor the current little girl's mother was happy about the practice, but, citing "tradition," they were all reluctant to stop it.[35] Tantra, sexuality, blood, and fear: these are unavoidable aspects of Kālī's inheritance.

Durgā's persona is not nearly as sexualized as this; in one Oriya version of the Mahiṣa myth, she is said to be enraged that Mahiṣa is granted a boon of being able to be killed only if she shows him her privates,[36] but such is never depicted or exhorted for meditation in Bengal, and sexual rites are not a part of her worship. There is an aspect to Kālī Pūjā that is, or has the potential to be, both more fearful *and* more immoderate than anything one finds in its more popular sister festival.

## *Differently Empowered: Comparative Conceptions of Śakti*

The various contrasts we have been enumerating can perhaps best be summed up by recourse to notions of *śakti*. I asked several scions of the old families who still carry on the tradition of celebrating Durgā Pūjā and/or Kālī Pūjā how they would compare the two goddesses. Two themes predominated in their comparative responses. First, they said, Durgā is either the daughter of the house (*bāḍīr meye*) or the universal mother (*sabāier mā*), whereas Kālī is a symbol of power (*śaktir pratīk*), whose wrath, in case of a ritual mistake, is a cause for fear (*bhay*).[37] Second, Durgā fights for us in battle, as would a mother, whereas Kālī is angry (or has *rāg*) in general, and could turn against us with her uplifted *khaḍga*.[38] Keeping these contrasts in mind, it is easy to see why some interviewees asserted that "Kālī is only for Śāktas; Durgā is for everyone."[39]

Although one would not want to draw these distinctions too tautly, especially given the *bhakti* perspective on Kālī, one might characterize Durgā's power as protective, maternal, and distributive, and Kālī's as contractual, won by or offered to the deserving, and associated with aggrandizement and personal power. As a result, it is easy to understand how Kālī became associated with revolutionaries' power quests, whether during the colonial period or during the 1970s reign of terror by the Naxalites, for whom, "like the red flag of the Communists, Kālī is a symbol of revolution."[40] Even today, the trail to the Kālīghāṭ Temple of aspirants to would-be regal power continues this connection between Kālī and political *śakti*; for instance, in 2002, erstwhile King Gyanendra of Nepal, following the custom begun by his father and brother, came all the way to Kālīghāṭ from Kathmandu to offer two goats and several gold pieces to the Goddess.

## Held Back, Pulled Forward: Analyzing Kālī's Pūjā

Given Kālī's Tantric origins, it is perhaps not surprising that her persona maintains something of its esoteric, fearsome, sexualized character. While it is true that since the eighteenth century Kālī has been softened and maternalized by her incorporation into a *bhakti* tradition, the preceding layers of her history—her bloodlust for demons, her utilization by Tāntrikas in meditation for the acquisition of *siddhi*s, and her reputation for wrath—have been neither superceded nor entirely hidden. And one would not *expect* them to be, for a goddess's past, and a community's past, are defining for their present. As Peter Berger and Thomas Luckmann stated in their landmark study, *The Social Construction of Reality*, remembering the past is very significant in the socialization of individuals and contributes decisively to the formation of their identities.[41] Even if they are somewhat afraid of the Goddess, Śāktas who consider themselves Kālī-devotees value her historical associations with *siddhi*s, power, and particular *sādhaka*s such as Rāmakṛṣṇa and Rāmprasād. These are part of a "pastness" that contributes to her authenticity and that creates a context for popular memory and nostalgia.

This estimation of her heritage becomes all the more important when one considers that Kālī Pūjā is not in fact old at all, since, as indicated earlier, we have no evidence that it predates the eighteenth century. In the language of Eric Hobsbawm, what Rājā Kṛṣṇacandra Rāy of Nadia and his contemporaries did for Kālī Pūjā was to create an "invented tradition," establishing within a fairly brief period a public celebration that was legitimized by the simultaneous sponsorship of newly translated Tantras and the construction of goddess temples.[42] Not only was Kṛṣṇacandra thus encompassing his newly ritualized Pūjā within supporting structures; he was also following the injunctions of the Goddess herself, to whom the maintenance of her "traditions" is said to be extremely important. Thus the zamindars' innovations were presented as continuous with a valued past. The same impulse to legitimize by reference to antiquity can be seen in the admiring reactions of journalists to the innovations of the 1920s; they were careful to point out that the *sarbajanīn* festival format was no more boisterous or ostentatious than were the celebrations of the monied classes in the eighteenth and nineteenth centuries. And one art critic defended the new realism of the N. C. Pāl school as conforming *more* accurately to the spirit of the medieval *dhyānas* than did the traditional *Bāṅglā* style. In other words, newness is acceptable only as a more authentic return to or recapitulation of an esteemed perceived past model. One can perhaps understand the modest revival of the traditional, fierce Kālī images in many contemporary Bengali pandals as an effort to reclaim the power of, as well as even to market, that past.

If this heritage that differentiates Kālī from Durgā is thus so important, what accounts for the near parallelism between the two goddess festivals? How can we understand the pull, the draw, of the Durgā pattern for Kālī? Here I find three models helpful. The first is the work of Milton Singer, who was a pioneer in theorizing the effect of urbanization on traditional religion.[43] Drawing upon his work in what was then Madras, he showed that the cultivation of *bhakti* allowed for the relaxation of strict ritual rules, allowing devotees to adapt to situations where traditional practice was either impossible or undesirable. In our Bengali context, the influence of *bhakti* upon the cult of Kālī over the last two hundred and fifty years has meant that, for some, Kālī the mother pushes aside Kālī the Tantric power, and hence that her softened features can be celebrated without fear and in novel ways, including in an effervescent public festival (fig. 7.3).

A second model derives from the work of Gananath Obeyesekere, who, in his work on the Sri Lankan Buddhist goddess Pattini, describes what happens to the personality of a deity when she becomes more universally popular and hence must appeal to a wider audience: her rough edges are smoothed over, and her purity and benevolence are emphasized.[44] To the extent that the Bengali Kālī is, in some quarters, becoming less interested in blood sacrifice and is looking more like a shapely sixteen-year-old or a young version of one's mother than a skeletal hag, she is following the rubric suggested by Obeyesekere. The greater a deity's claim to devotee numbers, the more accommodative she must become to their varied tastes.

The final lens through which to view the emergent parallels between Durgā and Kālī Pūjās since the 1920s is that of the leveling effects of middle-class urban religion. To turn again to the work of Joanne Waghorne, who has written about what she calls this middle-class "sensibility," she argues that all public rituals have been transformed by new contemporary idioms of public culture, where public festivals, of whatever religion,[45] take on characteristics of political rallies, movie theater enactments, and mass

FIGURE 7.3. A Jurassic Park dinosaur entertaining onlookers at Kālī Pūjā. Kolkata, October 1998. Photo by Rachel Fell McDermott.

media entertainment. The middle-class urge to compete in the display of wealth and status, as well as its desire for respectability and its tendency toward gentrification, find expression in temple building and renovation, festival patronage, and the founding of charitable institutions. Writes Waghorne about Mariyamman's new popularization in Chennai: "As willing as the middle classes are to appropriate the power of the goddess, they do this by cleaning her house and purifying or isolating her coarser elements."[46] From this perspective, Kālī's Pūjā looks increasingly like Durgā's because both share in a common urban style of Hindu public religiosity, a globalized local form. Although this is a story for another day, this common idiom is now affecting other deities in Bengal as well, such as Śītalā, Viśvakarmā, and even Lakṣmī.[47]

So which is it? Does Kālī Pūjā contain reminders of her fierce past that provide devotees cause for pride—and discomfort—regarding her Tantric origins and distinctiveness? I have certainly argued for this. Or is Kālī Pūjā so much like Durgā Pūjā that both have become examples of a form of urban religion characterized by revelry, rivalry, and even nostalgic longing that has developed fairly uniformly since the 1920s? I have provided evidence for this point as well.

In the end I am forced to conclude—like Kālī herself, holding Tantric reminders in one set of hands and devotional reassurances in the other—that both interpretations are true. One cannot judge as anything other than a desire to control and enhance the experience of Kālī Pūjā, the spate of police-initiated directives forbidding rowdy-ism, dangerous firecrackers, noise level above a certain decibel, and Kālī images too tall to pass under electric wires on their way to river immersions. The 2004 announcement that Kālīghāṭ and Dakṣiṇeśvar were being scheduled by the Government of West Bengal for massive renovations—to be directed by the Kolkata Municipal Development Authority, overseen by the State Tourism Department, and paid for by a Boston-based NRI group called the Boston Pledge—was welcomed by most pilgrims, since the plans included guesthouses of international standards and even carparks.[48] Such a move was intended to

FIGURE 7.4. The Kālī too horrible to worship. *Bartamān*, 27 Oct. 1995, p. 3.

commodify, market, and upgrade the Goddess. That, as of 2009, the temple renovations were still blocked by the temple authorities themselves shows that not everyone values the middle-class ideals of cleanliness, order, and public accountability.

Other reminders of the older, fiercer, less controlled Kālī also lurk underneath the surface. In Kālī Pūjā 1995, the Bengali newspaper *Bartamān* ran a story about a *sarbajanīn* image of a Cāmuṇḍā-esque Kālī, copied from a real image supposedly found in a cave in Himachal Pradesh and set up in a Kolkata pandal. It was so ugly and horrifying that no Bengali Brahman priest was willing to perform her *pūjā* (fig. 7.4).[49] Two Tāntrikas appeared and informed the pandal organizers that if one wanted to worship this type of image, human sacrifice would be necessary. At the conclusion of the Pūjā, it was immersed without ever having had the Goddess's life invited to vivify it. Thus even an expansive *bhakti* perspective and an inviting street-festival context were powerless to transform the ugliness and dread of such an image.

It is not surprising that in the worship of a deity there are limits to how much the past can be watered down or smoothed over. One would not expect Kālī to become dissociated from her moorings and transmuted into a copy of Durgā, for the two goddesses are quite distinct—textually, philosophically, and in the context of private devotion and ritual. And yet the fact that, *even if only on the surface*, Kālī's festival has become so like Durgā's, with its sexy goddess images, its jocular, competitive, public nature, and its incorporation into a yearly round of familiar rituals for the divine Mother, testifies to the democratizing and leveling effects of *bhakti*, popularity, and urban religion. The street festival forms it own homogenizing world.

# 8 Controversies and the Goddess

Like any festivals the world over that claim wide popularity and practice, Durgā, Jagaddhātrī, and Kālī Pūjās are multifaceted and symbolically capacious.[1] This also makes them controversial or prone to debate, as people approach them from widely disparate angles and find them suitable arenas for the promotion of local causes. In this chapter we discuss three such controversies: debates over the place of the "prostitute's earth," an essential ingredient according to the ritual texts in the worship of Durgā; arguments over the harm caused the environment by erection of Pūjā pandals and their associated hoopla; and critiques of the practice of animal sacrifice, which in West Bengal is integral to the worship of all three goddesses. We spend most time on the last case study, as sacrifice and its critique permeate all levels of all three Pūjās. As a whole, the identities of the three sets of complainants, the justifications for their arguments, and the modes in which they choose to lobby represent a wide spectrum in West Bengali Hindu sensibility.

## The Prostitutes' Critique

Although centered on a goddess who is conceived alternately as a daughter and a mother, the Pūjā festivals have traditionally been male-dominated affairs. Certainly, as wives—of zamindars, community Pūjā organizers, artisans, engineers, and priests—women have played a supporting role, and the crowds milling about on the streets at the Pūjā season attest to the fact that the celebrations appeal to all, whether male or female. Exceptional women have been central to selected Pūjās; for instance, Girish Chandra Ghosh, Rāmakṛṣṇa's disciple, would not do the *sandhi pūjā* unless Śāradādebī came to his house personally to receive his worship.[2] But the marginality of women to leadership roles is borne out by the fact that women's initiative in a Pūjā context is still cause for news reporting: I have seen stories on women founding, organizing, or decorating individual pandals; on the artistry of Chinā Pāl, the only woman chief sculptor of Kumartuli; and even on the difficulty of newly trained women priests being hired by pandal committees, due to stereotypes, prejudice, and the convention that women cannot touch the Nārāyaṇśil (the stone representing Viṣṇu), which is an intrinsic part of Durgā and Kālī Pūjās.[3]

The general absence of mainly middle-class women from the organizational aspects of the festivals may be juxtaposed with the mandated symbolic presence of prostitutes (*beśyās*), a handful of earth from the doorposts of whose houses is said to be integral to the worship of Durgā. On Saptamī, the ritual texts prescribe that the *nabapatrikā* is to be bathed by an assortment of oils, waters and liquids, and earths. The ten types of earth are taken from a crossroads, an anthill, a riverbank, the bank of the Ganges, an ocean shore, the doors outside a prostitute's house, a temple, and a palace, and the dirt remaining on the horns of a wild boar and a bull after they have dug up the ground.[4] Some explanations for the use of the prostitute's earth honor the profession of prostitution and the women involved: all women are said to be worshiped as part of the fertility of the Goddess; prostitutes are models of dispassion, as they make no distinction of caste, religion, beauty, or language; and they selflessly take upon themselves the sins of the community.[5] In general, however, prostitutes are not looked upon with approval by much of today's "polite" *bhadralok* society,[6] and the most typical reason given for the inclusion of the prostitute's earth in the Pūjā context denigrates them: the earth from their lintel is holy not because of their own virtue but because honorable people leave their merit at the prostitute's door when they enter.[7] When I asked about this practice, most Pūjā organizers looked vaguely embarrassed. Many said that their hired priest "took care" of procuring the necessary worship items, and that Pūjā supply stores sold the requisite types of earth, the authenticity of which could not be verified, in little plastic bags. One informant told me in hushed whispers, so his daughters did not hear, a story he had just read about a priest who discovers that his daughter is a *beśyā*. Obviously the prostitute's earth is not something widely advertised in Pūjā contexts.

Sex workers are aware of this, and in 2002 they formed a committee to try to prevent outsiders from coming to their homes to collect dirt from their front doors. News commentators generally did not take their side on the issue, claiming that they were misunderstanding the catholic nature of the scriptures, which prescribed the inclusion of all strata of society. Nor did the practice stop of selling the ten types of earth. But obviously prostitutes do not feel that Durgā's festival is, in any significant way, "for" them. The romanticized scene in the 2005 remake of the popular film "Devdas"—in which a chaste wife obtains the essential earth from the harlot's house, invites the harlot to the Pūjā celebration at the zamindari house, and then dances together with her, the two women becoming one under the powerful gaze of the Mother—is not an experience of acceptance that most ordinary sex workers can identify with.[8] But as a highly marginalized group that is arguing about a relatively minor point, their voices remain muted. Just like the very poor, whose inclusion matters symbolically to the mainly middle-class sponsors and enjoyers of the festival but whose actual participation is minimal, except as objects of charity (see chapter 5), so also here: the Pūjā can be perceived as demeaning and exclusionary, and this community of women at least would like to refuse compliance with the supposedly national festival.

## "The Goddess Herself Is in Danger": Pūjās and Pollution

In tune with worldwide concern over the environment, many Pūjā-watchers (both participants and not) in West Bengal challenge the organizers of the festivities to become more "green" in their operations. Sometimes environmental consciousness is conveyed in the pandals themselves, with the Goddess demonstrating care for the earth; a pandal in 2000, for example, depicted a weeping Durgā arising from a mute, cut banyan tree.[9] The police, directed by the Union Ministry of Environment and Forests, are also fairly stringent in their regulation of the public festivals: in 2000 the Calcutta High Court gave the sensational order, effective from Kālī Pūjā night, that from then on all the wooden frames for the images (*kāṭhāmos*) would have to be retrieved from the river after the immersions; in 2001 conch-shell fishing was banned, effectively ensuring that there would be fewer conch shells heard during the Pūjās; and in 2002, in an effort to curb the felling of tree branches during the processions on Bijaya Daśamī day, the police issued an order that no image could be higher than ten feet.

Behind all such prohibitions and regulations lie years of advocacy work by committed individuals. Perhaps the most vocal environmentalist in the Kolkata area is Mr. Subhās Datta, by profession a chartered accountant.[10] In 1977 he founded the Citizens' Democratic Association (Gaṇatāntrik Nāgarik Samiti) in the city of Howrah to bring civic failures to the attention of the government. Issues he has spotlighted to date include damage to city parks and trees, atrocities against women, unhygienic hospitals, poor telephone service, rampant load-shedding, auto emission pollution, judicial failures, garbage overflows, decomposing bodies in morgues, clinical waste, arsenic poisoning, gas leakage, river pollution, and politicians' abuse of taxpayers' money. It was he who shocked the Supreme Court in 1995 into forming a Green Bench, after he filed a five hundred–page report on the city of Howrah, proving it to be a municipal disaster.

Datta asserts unequivocally that "public Pūjā means public nuisance," for *sarbajanīn* Pūjās begin with organizers extorting money from ordinary citizens, are celebrated with pilfered electricity, road blockages, animal sacrifices, noise pollution, and tree felling, and conclude with extreme river pollution. In 1997 he conducted his own survey of the Hooghly River after Durgā Pūjā, taking photos of the decomposing images and their hazards to river life. In spite of several petitions submitted to the High Court in 1998, nothing was done, for fear of hurting religious sensibilities. Datta retorted that the state of West Bengal should not, for religious sentiments, sacrifice the greater public interest,[11] and in 2000 he filed another petition, asking the court to mandate Pūjā committees to clean up images after immersion. For this he was threatened by the BJP; the *kāṭhāmo*-removal order mentioned above was a compromise.[12] Datta remarked to me ruefully in 2000 that few people bothered to comply with this ruling.

His efforts spurred others to act, however. News articles in the Pūjā season of 2000 described citizens demanding that the river be cleaned up. One pandal showed a disgusted Durgā and her family holding signs saying, "Goddess Durga and family on Hunger-Strike," and a news reporter for the Bengali daily *Pratidin* remarked about the floods of the season, because of which corpses were being washed ashore, intertwined with bits and pieces of the *kāṭhāmos*, straw, and lions' heads, "sometimes a sinking person tries to catch hold of one of these to save himself from drowning. But the

Goddess herself is in danger."[13] Even the *New York Times* caught the environmental fervor, though focused on the parallel problems occurring in Mumbai at Gaṇeś Cāturthi. "Within 24 hours you get massive fish deaths from the toxins in the paint," said Bittu Sahgal, editor of *Sanctuary Asia*, an environmental magazine. "The sentiment is pure but the reality is polluted. All that plaster forms an impermeable layer on the water's bottom so that organisms can't breathe."[14]

The trimming or felling of trees perceived to interfere with a committee's desired pandal location has been another issue taken up by Datta and his cohorts. In 2000, in a peaceful act of Gandhian *satyāgraha*, Datta and his organization went to specific sites where trees were to be cut down and performed the ceremony of *bhai-phõṭā*, where they dabbed the trees with vermilion and honored them as brothers. People for Animals, a parallel organization, rescued two half-starved camels imported from Rajasthan for a Pūjā pandal that was being constructed to replicate a desert scene (see chapter 5).[15] Wildlife advocates are also lobbying for Pūjā organizers to refuse to hire traditional drummers (*ḍhākis*) who use the plumes of rare birds to adorn their drums.[16]

That "green" consciousness is trickling down from the arena of activists to that of people with a stake in the festivals themselves is indicated by strictures adopted even by the priests. In 2007, priests who were members of the Vaidik Pandit o Purohit Mahamilan Kendra refused to accept food offerings for the Goddess donated in plastic bags; moreover, they distributed tree saplings to be planted locally by the committees for which they worked, and stated that no priests would be sent to a pandal that had been built by cutting off parts of a tree.

Unlike the controversy over the prostitute's earth, where there are few supporters of the complainants outside the red light district itself and where the issue is easily covered up and/or finessed by clever Pūjā supply stores, the various dangers to the environment posed by the Pūjās are enunciated by a series of organizations and individuals who speak out loudly on behalf of mute, seemingly defenseless nature. And their cause appears, to an outsider, to be self-evident and rather worrying. Those who seem not to care for the trees, rivers, and wildlife affected by the Goddess's festivals can be critiqued as shortsighted, greedy, or even politically motivated. In 2008 a Pūjā committee and some local youth tussled over whether or not pandal construction should encroach on a recently restored park, the youth vowing to protect the park. Amazingly, the CPI(M) took the part of the committee, vowing to protect the religious views of its members. The local Trinamul

Congress MLA (member of the Legislative Assembly) stood with the "rebel" youth.[17] This resort to "religious sensitivities" as a justification for opinions taken on the Pūjās is a theme we shall encounter in the last and most complex of the Pūjā controversies of the chapter, animal sacrifice.

## Does the Goddess Require Blood?

My own introduction to animal sacrifice occurred in the late 1980s, and it was not a pleasant experience. I vividly remember standing at the back of a surging crowd at the third-largest Kālī temple in Calcutta, watching thirty goats be ritually washed, blessed, garlanded, bound, and then coerced into placing their necks between the two forks of a stake in front of the Goddess's image, where they were decapitated to deafening drum rolls and shouting devotees. This was the midnight climax of the Kālī Pūjā celebration in November 1988, just one month after I had arrived in Calcutta for two years of dissertation research, and I recall struggling to hold back my tears. I identified with those goats—powerless, bleating, watching each other die, looking for escape. As I watched I wrote mental letters to my dissertation advisor, telling him that I had made a big mistake in my choice of field research.

Luckily, I had not come to study goat sacrifice, but rather *bhakti* poetry centered on Kālī the compassionate mother; so I did not need to send that letter, or even to visit another Kālī temple. Indeed, although I spent many hours talking with Śākta devotees during my months of research, I actively avoided the bloody, ritual side of the Goddess's worship. Besides, my devotionally oriented informants assured me that *bali* (lit. "gift"; but usually understood as a shortened form of *paśubali*, or animal sacrifice) was on the decline.

But my attitude changed in the mid-1990s, when I felt that I would never understand Bengali Śāktism if I did not turn from devotion centered in song to that occurring in temples. I began to force myself to attend animal sacrifices. The most memorable such event occurred on 7 November 1999—again, at Kālī Pūjā, this time at Kaliganj, a village in Nadia district, an eight hours' drive from Calcutta. My husband, Scott, and I had gone with Mohit Roy, our local guide, and we were driving north in the dead of night on the West Bengal national highway (full of potholes, with no lights except for the glare from oncoming trucks, and no rest stops or telephone booths). I was frankly terrified. Eventually we reached our destination: a well-to-do family house with a huge, frightening Kālī image in an open-air building, in front of which hundreds of people were pushing forward for *darśan* (fig. 8.1). Then I noticed the 108 goats, tethered around the walls of the compound, and the nearby stake. Women and children were camping out, picnic-like, to safeguard their places near it, and we were told that the *bali* would begin two hours later, at 3 A.M. We did not stay. I had seen other killings earlier that evening, and I could stand no more. Later I realized that, in a sense, I had met the Goddess that night in my fear of her bloodlust, for the Tantras say that she is supposed to inspire dread. I also decided that I ought to revise my ideas about the prevalence of *bali;* certainly there was no lack of enthusiasm for it in Kaliganj.

But how to gauge whether a goddess is or is not losing her taste for sacrifice? Temples keep no statistics, and no local field studies have been done with this question in mind. So, while in Bengal during the fall of 2000 I decided to consult people who approach the issue from the other side:

FIGURE 8.1. The Kālī at Kaliganj. Nadia, November 1999. Photo by Rachel Fell McDermott.

anti-*bali* advocates, NGOs like Beauty Without Cruelty, Compassionate Crusaders, and People for Animals.[18] These groups tackle a wide variety of injustices against animals, and the abolition of *bali* is a significant part of their agendas. They aim to get West Bengal to follow six other states and one union territory, which have outlawed the sacrifice of animals and birds within all temple precincts—Andhra Pradesh, Gujarat, Karnataka, Kerala, Pondicherry, Rajasthan, and Tamilnadu.[19] However, such NGOs admit that they are having little success in Bengal. By posing as a journalist, I got close enough to Menaka Gandhi, on one of her brief visits to Calcutta, to ask her why West Bengal was so different from these other states in the battle against *bali*. She fobbed me off, saying that the subject was too big to handle just then, but she did say that the issue was complicated by a host of interlocking vested interests.[20]

This discussion is an attempt to answer the question I posed to Menaka Gandhi. What are the special historical, social, and religious factors unique to West Bengal that make animal sacrifice so embedded in Śākta contexts? In the following survey I briefly outline seven reasons why blood continues to pour, and then look at the opposition, and why it fails to catch on.

## *Reasons for Bali's Popularity and Survival in West Bengal*

"BECAUSE THE TANTRAS TELL ME SO" There are two types of *bali*: that done to give thanks for a boon or in anticipation of one (*mānasik*) and that done yearly, as an ongoing ritual commitment regardless of individual circumstance (*bātsarik*). In both, but especially the latter, *bali* of some sort is obligatory at least on the ninth day of Durgā Pūjā and during Kālī Pūjā—the Śākta Tantras, Purāṇas, and their derivative ritual manuals are unanimous in claiming that the Goddess enjoys and demands blood. Exhortations to donate blood offerings to Kālī and Durgā can be found in "Devī-Māhātmya" 12:19, where the recitation of the Māhātmya is said by the Devī to delight her as much as "the finest animals"; chapter 57, or "the blood chapter," of the *Kālikā Purāṇa*; chapter 6 of the *Mahānirvāṇa Tantra*; and chapter 4 vv. 1–35 of the *Muṇḍamālā Tantra*. These texts, and more, are summarized and quoted in the two most famous Tantric ritual digests from eastern India, Kṛṣṇānanda Āgambāgīś's *Tantrasāra* and Raghunāth Tarkabāgīś Bhaṭṭācārya's *Āgamatattvavilāsa*,[21] which are, in turn, synthesized and condensed in the Pūjā manuals used by Bengali priests.[22]

In general, all of these materials describe the types of vegetables, sweets, fish, and animals that are appropriate for slaughter, how much pleasure the Goddess gets from each type of offering, and the precise methods for preparing for and executing the immolation. In a well-known passage from the *Kālikā Purāṇa*, Kālī is said to be best satisfied by the blood of a human, but to be willing also to receive animal and even vegetable offerings. The list of acceptable offerings includes male birds, tortoises, alligators, fish, buffalos, iguanas, bulls, goats, rams, antelopes, wild boars, rhinoceroses, *śarabha* (an eight-footed mythological animal), lions, tigers, and humans. Whether the offering is blood or flesh, that of a man is most highly valued. Vegetal offerings—such as pumpkins, bananas, sugarcane, cucumber, shaddock, flour, betel-nut, and bilva fruit—are consecrated in the same manner as live animals.[23]

The decapitating sword is homologized to Kālī's thirsting tongue, which benefits the victims by slaying them, for the cleaving stroke of knowledge releases them from their bestial (*paśu*) nature to true consciousness. When the sacrifice is a goat, buffalo, or sheep, the priest whispers into its ear that through its death it will obtain the place of Śiva and be released from future birth. According to the *Mahānirvāṇa Tantra* (6:107–111), the officiating priest selects a beast with good signs and ritually sprinkles it with water. Then he worships it and whispers the Gayatrī *mantra* into its ear, which severs the animal from its bestial karma: "Let us bring to mind the bonds of the life of a beast. Let us meditate upon the Creator of the Universe. May he liberate us out of this life (of a beast)." P. V. Kane cites verses from the *Ṛg Veda* and the *Laws of Manu* to claim that since even the Vedic period the sacrificial victim has been thought to go straight to heaven.[24] Indeed, said a Rāmakṛṣṇa Mission swami to me in Burdwan, 17 March 1990, "we believe that the goats attain heaven." For those donating animals, the sacrificed can be seen to represent their human passions, and the Tantras even specify which passions are symbolized by which animals: the goat stands for lust, the ram greed, the buffalo anger, the boar egotism, the swan delusion, and the chicken envy. *Bali*, then yields spiritual emancipation for the sponsor. "Śankara said, 'O Dear One, . . . even one *bali* brings the four aims of human life. If one give many *bali*s, one attains the state of the highest Brahman.' "[25] The head-cleaving sword is addressed in *Manu* 5.39 as "the tongue of Caṇḍikā"; "you accomplish heaven (for the worshiper)." Devotees are aware of these scriptural promises and injunctions. Said a Calcutta homeowner to me in October 2000, a man who proudly sponsors the yearly Durgā Pūjā, with *bali*: "Goat sacrifice is *śāstric*, so we must do it."[26]

Śākta legends and iconography also underscore the martial aspects of goddesses who willingly kill to protect their devotees. Durgā's most famous exploits in the "Devī-Māhātmya" involve the slaughtering of the buffalo-demon Mahiṣa and of the twin generals, Śumbha and Niśumbha, and according to the fifteenth-century Bengali version of the *Rāmāyaṇa* by Kṛttibās, Rāma worshiped Durgā, with animal sacrifice, on the eve of his battle with Rāvaṇa, at what is now the autumnal Durgā Pūjā season, in order to ensure his victory. Pūjā manuals enjoin the recitation of a *mantra* to this effect when the Goddess is roused under the bilva tree on the evening of the sixth day of the festival—"In order to kill Rāvaṇa and to bestow grace upon Rāma, you were roused at an unusual time. Hence I also awaken you on the evening of the sixth *tithi* of the month of Ashvin"[27]—and in commemoration of Rāma's own offering, *bali* is to be given to Durgā during her festival.

Kālī is even more graphically associated with decapitation. During her brief appearance in the "Devī-Māhātmya," she slices off the heads of two troublesome demons, Caṇḍa and Muṇḍa, and uses her tongue-sword to lick up all the blood from a third, Raktabīja. Although she is rarely depicted artistically in such acts, her static iconic image bears reminders of her proclivity for chopped body parts: her skirt of arms cut at the elbows, her garland of heads cloven at the neck, and the severed head held in her left hand, by its hair. Even if the scriptures did not enjoin blood sacrifice, therefore, its prominence in story and art would be hard to avoid.

BALI, KĀLĪ TEMPLES, AND TĀNTRIKAS The next three points are all historical, and seek the prevalence of animal sacrifice today in customs rooted in the Bengali past.

As we have seen in chapter 7, the legends associated with nearly all old (seventeenth to the early nineteenth century) Kālī temples in Bengal display the same group of nested themes: jungle settings; gangs of dacoits or Tāntrikas who gain *siddhi*s through the practice of *narabali*, or human sacrifice; and an aura of great power. Three temples in present-day northern Kolkata are famed as having been the site of numerous *narabali*s before and even during the time of the British: Citeśvarī Devī in Citpur, a Kālī temple named after Cite, a noted dacoit who apparently had five hundred members in his gang; Siddheśvarīkālī in Bagbazar; and Kālīghāṭ, where there were accusations of human sacrifices as late as 1836.[28] Reflecting such associations between outlaws and Kālī, several temples throughout Bengal are called the Ḍākātī Kālī Temple.

Indeed, one finds records from the early nineteenth century of individuals offering *narabali* at Kālī temples. Said Rev. James Long, "Human sacrifices were also frequent even as late as 1822. A Hindu at Kalighat sent for a Musalman barber to shave him. He asked him afterward to hold a goat while he cut off its head as an offering to Kali. The barber did so but the Hindu cut off the barber's head and offered it to Kali. He was sentenced by the Nizamut to be hung."[29] The British eventually decided to interfere—"To our great shame it is remembered, that we allowed more than half a century quietly to elapse before we thought that this duty [of stopping such practices] was attached to the advent of a civilized power in India"[30]—but even after 1850, when they claimed to have succeeded, contemporary newspapers continued to report incidents.

Indeed, I have collected quite an arsenal of chilling accounts from the nineteenth into the twenty-first centuries. They describe sword decapitations, slayings, or even suicides by devotees of Kālī. A sampling from the beginning and end of my collection: in 1924, at an abandoned Kālī temple, a man kills a woman whom he had fooled into thinking that if she did a *pūjā* there, alone, she would get a child; a man named Kshetri, "said to be a religious maniac [who had] been fasting for a week in preparation for his sacrifice before the goddess," attempts to slit his throat before Kālī at Kālīghāṭ in 1927; in 1999 a man in the West Singhbhum district cuts off the head of a seven-year-old boy and offers it to Durgā, hoping that she will return his own dead son to life in exchange; in 2000, near Sirajganj, a mother kills her two children in the name of Kālī with a crescent-shaped knife; in 2001 a Dhaka woman kills her five-year-old son and seven-year-old daughter to please the goddess Kālī, who had appeared to her in a dream and asked for the sacrifices; in 2006 a little boy was mutilated and dismembered by a woman who was advised by a local Tāntrika that her nightmares would vanish if she offered blood to the Hindu goddess of destruction; and in 2010, the BBC reports, the severed head and torso of a man were found at a Kālī temple in Birbhum district in what the local police interpreted as a human sacrifice to "propitiate the gods."[31] These tortures and beheadings appear to have been undertaken to ensure fertility, health or wealth, power, and, most frequently, the grace of the Goddess.[32] In our postcolonial world, it is, of course, extremely risky to present as true claims of sacrifice by British sources, and for the modern period to give too hasty credence to reports of sacrifice-cum-murder in religious contexts. Even Felix Padel, in his book *The Sacrifice of Human Being* (1995)—where he maintains that British arguments against human sacrifice among tribal peoples in Orissa were motivated by colonial and missionary projects—does not deny that real human sacrifice occurred.[33] It is indisputable that locals themselves tend to see the murder of religious persons, especially children, as having some link to Tantric or goddess-centered motivations. That people are willing to associate killing with Tāntrikas and Śāktism, even without proof, is indicated by a story from 2001 about the discovery of 500 skulls and bones in a Kolkata building, only a few months after a similar find at a Siliguri bus stand. All the skulls, in both sites, had been carefully sawn off, leading police to assume that they might have been collected for use in Tantric rites, for the acquisition of *siddhis*.[34]

Even where actual *narabali* is no longer performed, its importance is indicated by continuing rituals utilizing its symbolism. For example, according to popular accounts, four hundred and fifty years ago Rājā Naranārāyaṇ of Kuch Bihar used to sacrifice up to one hundred and fifty humans at a time. After the practice was discontinued in his family, as late as the mid-nineteenth century, the ritual was carried on by the substitution of a "sacrificed" human effigy and the offering of blood from a human finger. Today, the famed Kāmākhyā Temple in Assam, a center of Tantric history and practice, follows this same substitutionary practice. Note that a Brahman is not entitled to offer blood from his own body, as this would be equivalent to the slaying of a Brahman, so in Brahman families where such is the custom, non-Brahmans are hired to have their fingers pricked.[35] The rice-flour doll is also integral to rites observed by several old families in the Kolkata area; the effigy represents the passions, and hence its "slaying" is termed *śatrubali*, or the sacrifice of the enemy.[36] If human offerings—real or symbolic—are this integral to the theological, ritual, and historical strands of the Śākta tradition, how much more so its divinely ordained substitute, animal sacrifice?[37]

Almost all Kālī temples established prior to the early nineteenth century offer facilities for goat or buffalo sacrifice. Numbers of *balis* vary, from temples that do only ten or twelve per festival night, to Kālīghāṭ, where an estimated seven hundred goats are slain at Kālī Pūjā,[38] to a famed temple in Maldah district, where the blood of over five thousand goats floods the temple courtyard.[39] Some of these are paid for by the temple authorities, but most are given by people who have taken vows to feed the Goddess a goat for something she has done or hopefully will do. Chandannagar, famous for its annual celebration of Jagaddhātrī Pūjā, contains one public Pūjā known for its extravagant *bali* offerings. People are proud of it. When I was there in November 2000 I was urged by a posse of policemen to visit the Tetutola pandal, where 902 goats were scheduled to lose their lives on a single day. This was aggressively advertised, probably in open defiance of Menaka Gandhi, who had written a stern letter to the organizers threatening them with consequences if they did not desist.

The three states in India where temple sacrifices are most prevalent are West Bengal, Assam, and Orissa, and every year Bengali news articles at the Pūjā season catalogue this or that excess of blood in these three states, sometimes highlighting what seem to be unusual or very cruel practices.[40] In July 2008, after the United Progressive Alliance (UPA) government headed by Prime Minister Manmohan Singh had passed a national vote of confidence, a grateful MLA from the allied Samajwadi Party, Kishore Samrite, offered 265 goats and buffalos at the Kāmākhyā Temple.[41] The association between the shedding of blood and the maintenance of political power is not, apparently, outdated.

The point is that sacrifice of a living being, whether human or animal, is not only sanctioned by scripture—it is also ingrained in the history of Śākta temple worship. To repudiate it is to challenge founding fathers, popular custom, and several centuries of symbolic resonance.

BALI AND STATUS Tāntrikas, human sacrifice, and Kālī temples are one end of the *bali* spectrum. Another is the sacrificial practices of Durgā Pūjā, the older, more "respectable" annual festival, long associated, like Durgā herself, with royalty. From the Gupta period, when Durgā symbolized royal prowess, through the medieval Purāṇic claim that Durgā Pūjā was equivalent to an *aśvamedha*, to the eighteenth-century sponsorship of the Pūjā by Bengali zamindars for the display of wealth and position, this festival has been synonymous with prestige. One of the best ways that a Hindu family today can claim status is through the age of its Durgā Pūjā, which, one is sure to be told, is done "just as in the old days," with traditional images of the Goddess, scrupulous attention to *śāstric* detail, and liberal food offerings, often including meat.

Although some families have discontinued animal sacrifice, 90 percent of those who still follow the custom are initiated Śāktas. There are traditionally four auspicious moments for the offering of *bali* within the four-day Durgā Pūjā festival—once on the seventh day (Saptamī), once on the eighth (Aṣṭamī), once on the cusp between the eighth and the ninth at the *sandhi pūjā*, and once on the ninth day (Nabamī)—although the ideal total number of goats is said to be 108, a figure several families continue to realize. Those who can afford it also immolate buffalos, sheep, or even pigs. One of the two most famous Pūjā-sponsoring families in Kolkata, the *Sobhabajar Rāj* family, offers a total of four goats, sugarcane (*ākh*), white gourd (*cālkumḍo*), and two catfish (*māgur māch*). The second, the Sābarṇa Rāy Caudhurīs, offers thirteen goats and one buffalo, in addition to the usual vegetarian offerings of sugarcane and white gourd. The meat is typically eaten by the family and shared with neighbors, as *prasād*. One Basu family in Kolkata justifies their continuation of animal sacrifice by telling of the Goddess's aid in providing for its occurrence. In the early 1980s, when the custom of *bali* was under threat in the family, a mysterious stranger turned up at their doorstep, offering to do the butchering. He was still doing so in 2004.[42]

The heads of almost all of the families whom I interviewed in the fall of 2000 oversaw their performance with great care, and were eager to maintain their traditions. Said Subhās Rāy Caudhurī, of the thirty-third generation in the Sābarṇa Rāy Caudhurī family, "We are extremely meticulous about the rites, and changes have come about only by way of quantity."[43] "After all, how can you change a two-hundred-year-old custom?," asked another, referring to *bali*.[44] The most eloquent statement came from Mr. Sujay Ganguli. He admitted that the tradition in his house, according to which the male members of the family must hold the animal's front and back legs while it is being decapitated, can be "off-putting." "But no one questions that it should be done. It is important not to break the tradition."[45] The state government has a stake in these rituals as well. Not only does the West Bengal Tourist Office run a popular bus tour during the holidays—in some cases it even awards grants to enable venerable houses to continue their rites, goats and buffalos and all.

SACRIFICING WHITE GOATS Scripture, temples, families, and now politics: my fourth reason for the continuing salience of *bali* in Bengal is memory of the British period. Whether it was political agitators exhorting people to slake the Mother's thirst with the blood of white goats,[46] or families actually choosing albino goats for their Pūjā axes,[47] goats were used as a cipher of the oppressor. Swami Vivekananda provides a rationale, though in his case the goat is not the enemy but a symbol of patriotism. He remarked in 1901 that the Bengali race had become so enfeebled that it needed to see blood. "This year I want a flood of blood. People will see this and be filled with strength, for one must give blood for the country."[48] At the time of the Non-Cooperation movement in 1922, in a very un-Gandhian tone, one writer for the *Ānanda Bājār Patrikā* challenged his readers to forget themselves, place their heads in the Y-shaped yoke as an offering to the Mother, and become her true sons and *sādhakas*.[49] Twenty years later this same imagery was utilized at the height of the Independence movement. The writer of an editorial in 1945 calls his countrymen to offer themselves—he uses the term *bali*—in the battle to save the Motherland.[50] Such sacrifice is especially valued if the Mother seeks it: an interesting, if admittedly rare, calendar art print found by Sumathi Ramaswamy depicts a line of Indian heroes in front of Bhārat Mātā, who is hacking their heads off, one by one.[51] *Bali*, then, is a metaphor for sacrificial death that is deeply embedded in and highly valued by the culture.

BRAHMAN PATRONAGE: BALI AND CASTE Moving from historical to social factors, one can also see the resiliency of *bali* through the lens of caste. In spite of persistent stereotypes to the contrary,[52] goddess worship appears to be no lower-caste phenomenon, but one sponsored in temples run by Brahman priests, in the wealthy homes of the upper classes, and by a population—and this is terribly significant—that is meat-eating. Bengali Brahmans are often sneered at precisely because they eat fish and meat. Some eat goat meat only at Pūjā time, so the occasion is special, and to be enjoyed.[53] Outlawing animal sacrifice among those who revere vegetarianism or *ahiṁsā* to begin with is one thing; doing so among meat-eaters is quite another.[54]

*BALI* IS GOOD FOR BUSINESS Another big obstacle for the anti-*bali* lobby is the fact that animal sacrifice is nested amid a host of economic and political interests. Said Debāśis Cakrabartī, director of Compassionate Crusaders: "People don't understand the real meaning of *bali*, which is 'sacrifice.' Does the Goddess need a goat? No. The offering of self is what is meant. Goat sacrifice comes for economic reasons. Religion is used to justify what we want."[55] In March 2002, India's prestigious literary prize, the Jnanpith Award, went to Indira Goswami, an Assamese Vaiṣṇava woman whose novel, translated as *The Man from Chinnamasta* (2001), included a polemic against the blood sacrifice of the Kāmākhyā Temple.[56] The priests of the temple apparently threatened her physically for her writing, which was perceived to undercut their livelihood.

*Bali* earns temples catering to it large sums of money, it employs animal sellers, butchers, and temple *pāṇḍās*, and it provides a source of police bribes. Policemen generally collude with sacrificial rites, either standing around to watch or turning a deaf ear to pleas to stop the practice. In places or occasions where goat sacrifice is forbidden, often a well-placed tip can clear the way. Some policemen even join in on the sponsorship of the Pūjās. In anticipation of People for Animals' pre-announced protest vigil against *bali* at Kālīghāṭ during Kālī Pūjā 2000 (see fig. 8.2), the *sevāits* of Kālīghāṭ Temple, of whom there are 365, threatened a massive protest uproar if goat sacrifices were banned. Another agitated staff member retorted that if animal sacrifice were stopped at Hindu temples, then all Muslim "Qurbani" sacrifices, especially at Bak'r-Id, should also be banned. An animal rights lawyer to whom I spoke made the same point more forcefully. The CPI(M), he said, is eager not to alienate the Muslim vote. Since Muslims control most of the meat-slaughtering businesses in the city, putting animal sacrifice under some sort of thorough investigation—whether in the slaughter houses or in the context of religious festivals—would not only anger constituents but would also lead to Hindu–Muslim acrimony.[57] The worry about votes is worth underlining; no political party in West Bengal, Orissa,

FIGURE 8.2. Children protesting against animal sacrifice, Kālīghāṭ Temple, Kālī Pūjā Day. Kolkata, October 2000. *Times of India*, 27 Sept. 2000, p. 1.

Assam, or Bihar is willing to take up the issue of blood sacrifice for fear of losing political support.[58]

"NO ONE CAN ENFORCE A BAN ON THE CUSTOM AS IT IS DONE AS PER APPROVED DESIRE OF [THE] GODDESS"[59] I began this section of the chapter with scripture: the Tantric and Purāṇic justifications for animal immolation. I now return to this theme, and the belief statements it implies, as a way of closing this list of reasons for the continuing relevance of *bali* in West Bengali Śākta contexts.

All of the theological, historical, and even social factors I have enumerated above underscore the strongly held belief that the power inherent in Durgā, Jagaddhātrī, and Kālī has something fundamental to do with blood. This is the Goddess's nature: to give if we give, and to punish if we do not.

A little story about Durgā illustrates the point. An image in a village temple in Murshidabad is known locally as Peṭ Kāṭa Durgā, or Durgā with the Slashed Stomach (her image is the same as the typical Durgā, except that the stomach is always cut). Once, the legend goes, there was a famine, and people were dying on all sides, so no offerings could be given to the Goddess. She was so hungry that on the last day of Durgā Pūjā she caught a young girl and ate her up. That night she appeared to the temple priest in a dream and explained what had happened. The next day he went to the image, cut open her stomach, and released the girl.[60] The Goddess needs food, and is willing to kill to get it; now people come from far and wide to offer goats.

This belief permeates many of the interviews I conducted with Śākta devotees. People trust in the Goddess's power to give boons; goats, chickens, and even pigeons are offered by the average supplicant at times of individual crisis and for the fulfillment of desires—a child, good business, prosperity, and success in battle, armed or political. Devotees are also afraid to stop animal sacrifice lest something bad happen. Mr. Ālok Kṛṣṇa Deb, in the seventh generation from Nabakṛṣṇa Deb's natural son, at the Shovabazar Rāj estate, told me that he would prefer to discontinue *bali* at Durgā Pūjā, but fears to do so lest he be blamed for subsequent familial misfortune. Said another informant, Asīmkumār Datta, about the fact that his family has not been able to stop animal sacrifice because of the insistence of an uncle's wife, "*Bali* is so primitive, and doesn't fit with a loving mother's worship." But the woman is superstitious, and fears Kālī's punishment if an improper act is done.[61] Those who do maintain the custom take great care to ensure that the animal's head is severed with one stroke, as prescribed by the texts. More than one attempt means bad luck, and the senior male of the house must undergo severe purificatory measures: one thousand fire sacrifices (*homas*) and repetitions of Durgā's name. In an article called "Recollections of Durga Puja Fifty Years Ago," the famed nationalist Bipin Chandra Pal states that when he was a boy goats used to be sacrificed in his house. He had no thought of pity, but only of fear lest the goat not be decapitated in one stroke and thus incur the wrath of the Goddess.[62] Even those who would prefer to see the practice fall into disuse are hesitant to intervene actively—for fear of upsetting the Goddess and her followers. In response to the vigil at Kālīghāṭ in October 2000, the Calcutta mayor, Subrata Mukhopādhyāy, said, "It is indeed a very sensitive issue, and we must tread with utmost caution so as not to hurt sentiments. I do agree it is a cruel custom, but ritual animal sacrifice . . . has been prevalent for years, and it is practically impossible to weed it out overnight." The head priest of the temple, Śāntipada Bhaṭṭācārya, concurred: "All I can say is that this is a ritual which has deep and complicated connotations in religion and demands a debate on a larger scale."[63]

Even given the Goddess's acknowledged penchant for blood, however, there are limits. *Bali* is prohibited by city ordinance in all *sarbajanīn* Pūjā precincts. The fierceness of a bloody goddess can be tolerated in an isolated cave or a private home or temple, but it is not appropriate for mass consumption.

## *The Anti-Bali Lobby: Stopping the Flood of Blood*

The debate has been going on for a long time. People for Animals and Compassionate Crusaders are only the most modern versions of nay-saying groups that for years have decried *bali* and attempted to stop it. I have found periodic newspaper reports of protest marches at Kālīghāṭ since 1915; even the poet laureate Rabindranath Tagore signed an anti-*bali* petition—an action in keeping with the critique of the practice in his 1917 play *Bisarjan* about animal and human sacrifice. Such voices were undoubtedly strengthened by the Western colonial critique, with its characterization of Śākta ritual as primitive and barbaric, but there are many other cultural stimuli supporting the denigrations of nonvegetarian offerings, all of which are disseminated through the communication networks of urban life: the ideal of not harming life (*ahiṁsā*); the critique of blood sacrifice by Vaiṣṇavas, Bāuls, and Brāhmos; and the competing interpretations of the

Goddess by the Rāmakṛṣṇa Mission and by the *bhakti* poets, whose songs are sung and played on loudspeakers at the Pūjā season. Many of the people involved in the contemporary anti-*bali* lobby are Vaiṣṇava, and some are even Vaiṣṇavas from other parts of India who have settled in Bengal. Some are simply embarrassed at what they perceive to be a savage practice; in reaction to Kishore Samrite's slaughter of 265 animals at Kāmākhyā in summer 2008, the Samajwadi Party national secretary, Dr. Suneelam, retorted, "People who sacrifice animals are mentally disturbed. The party does not believe in it."[64]

Of course, to some degree even Śākta practitioners feel uncomfortable with the killing of animals in the name of religion. Many goddess shrines around the country have discontinued the practice, converting the bloodlust of their deities into appetites for vegetal fare.[65] And in Bengal, a certain level of discomfort is evidenced in the facts that the slaughter is done by a low-caste person, is often performed out of sight of the main crowds, and is denied in the very *mantras* whispered into the animals' ears.[66] And people are almost too clear that religious sacrifice legitimizes killing. As the mother in November 2000 who killed her two children as an offering to Kālī put it in self-defense to the police: "I didn't murder; I did *bali*."

Opponents of *bali* seek to make this concealment explicit, and to shame practitioners into stopping the carnage. "*Bali* is inhuman, and it is a sin to smear religion with blood."[67] "In my opinion, no god who is worshipped with blood can be holy. . . . I appeal to all thinking persons to stop this practice and be released from the sin of *bali*."[68] "If you want to kill . . . kill the animal inside you."[69] Others, such as the priests at Kālīghāṭ, claim that the Goddess herself is Vaiṣṇavī, or vegetarian, and that it is the *ḍākinīs* and *yoginīs* who eat the blood. From such a perspective, blood sacrifice is for the benefit of the devotees who have made vows, not for her. Said a Kālīghāṭ priest to me in an interview in October 1998, "Mā is *sattvaguṇ* or *nirguṇ*; bloodlust is characteristic of *tamoguṇ*." Such assertions belie the scriptures, which—while they do admit for the substitution of vegetable offerings and do allow for the possibility of consecrating and then letting the animal loose—are, as we have seen, anything but unenthusiastic about blood sacrifice. Still other polemicists argue that a real mother would not ask for the death of other mothers' sons,[70] assert that the goat itself is a form of the Goddess, or claim that the real meaning of the animals dictated for slaughter in the Tantras is figurative; what is intended are the six enemies, or *ripus*: the goat represents lust (*kāma*), the buffalo anger (*krodha*), the cat greed (*lobha*), the sheep delusion (*moha*), the camel envy (*mātsarya*), and the man pride (*mada*).[71] Sometimes a *bhakti* poem is also marshaled for support—like the following excerpt from a poem by Rāmprasād Sen:

> If you really knew the Mother who
> protects the world with such care,
> would you sacrifice
> sheep, buffalos, and young goats?[72]

Anti-*bali* activists are at a legal disadvantage in West Bengal, as there are no laws condemning the practice to which they can turn; the Prevention of Cruelty to Animals Act, from 1960, is not applicable if the killing is done for religious reasons. So People for Animals and other like-minded lobbying groups attempt to enforce existing laws friendly to their purposes—for example, acts legislating that *bali* be done out of public view, that victims be certified suitable for slaughter, and that animal carcasses not violate environmental sanitation regulations.[73] Even the Indian Constitution is brought to bear in their argument, namely, article 51A(g), which states that it is the duty of city dwellers to show kindness to living beings; and article 48, which describes the stoppage of the killing of beasts and other things as falling within the duty of the state. In 2006 these groups achieved a major victory when the High Court ruled that animal sacrifice could no longer be performed within public view in the Kālīghāṭ temple.

To be sure, not all Bengalis who participate in Śākta festivals endorse live sacrifice. Remember, for starters, that Durgā Pūjā is often sponsored by Vaiṣṇavas, who view the festival as a marker of Bengali identity, or of the divine daughter Umā come home to her family, rather than as an occasion to champion *śakti*. Śephāli Bose and Āratī Deb, of the Shovabazar Rāj house, told me with pride in September 2000 that the man who stopped *bali* in their house was a "parama Vaiṣṇava," and the Vaiṣṇava-leaning Khelat Ghoṣ family "sacrifices" brown sugar with a knife on which red powder has been sprinkled, in a symbolic substitution for blood. The family of Milan Datta, of the Thanthania area, goes further. Even though they perform Durgā Pūjā, "we are Vaiṣṇavas with a Gosvāmī guru; we don't believe in Śāktism!" They are so insistent on this point that they do not even make the pretense of cleaving their gourd and sugarcane.[74] Intriguingly, several families—the Dawns, Guhas, and Nāns—have a form of Kṛṣṇa as their a family deity (*kūladevatā*), although their "chosen deity" (*iṣṭadevatā*) is Durgā or Kālī. In such cases, the vegetarianism of the family deity seems to take precedence over the meat preferences of the Goddess. The same is true of priestly lineages in Śākta temples. Sanjukta Gupta has shown how the Hāldār family at the Kālīghāṭ Temple is slowly Vaiṣṇavizing Kālī; the same is true of the Gosvāmī priest in charge of fierce Mātā Āgameśvarī, in Shantipur, Nadia district, who places a Vaiṣṇava *tilak* on her forehead and has stopped the practice of offering her *bali*.[75]

To me, however, the most intriguing rejections of *bali* derive from Śākta-identifying individuals and groups. For instance, some Kālī temples have stopped the practice, forcing those who would worship with *bali* to go elsewhere, and some "old families" cite a time when a forefather ceased bloody offerings. Reasons vary. Certain interviewees speak of valuing *ahiṁsā* or feeling pity for innocent animals, sensing that the Goddess herself no longer wants this type of gift. Often the pity comes from children. One Bengali gentleman interviewed by the *Ānanda Bājār Patrikā* in 2006 recalled the defining incident: in 1982, when his one-and-a-half-year-old son started screaming as he watched the immolation. From that point on, *bali* was forbidden in the house.[76] Other interviewees mention practical inconvenience. Mrs. Cameli Mitra, of the famed Durgācaraṇ Mitra house, told me that *bali* used to occur but was stopped in the early 1990s because it was hard to keep the goats alive in the small family courtyard for the requisite waiting period prior to the sacrifice. Likewise, Mr. Tapan Mukhopādhyāy, one of the *sevāits* of the Siddeśvarī Kālī Temple in northern Kolkata, explained that the last buffalo sacrifice had occurred around the time of Independence. The man who used to do the decapitating died, and they could not find anyone else with sufficient strength to do the job in one blow.[77]

Perhaps the most striking reason proffered for decreases in animal sacrifices is economic hardship. I have heard frequently that lean times prevent people from offering goats, but that as soon as prosperity returns, immolations in temples skyrocket. According to Dr. Jayrāmān Sureś, director of the Hoffmann Institute of Linguistics, Culture, and Education, who is preparing a nine-volume encyclopedia of West Bengali folk culture, in the areas with which he is most familiar—southern Bengal near the Sundarbans—*bali* numbers rise as people's economic conditions improve. Lemons are only a mean substitution for goats, to which devotees return as soon as possible.

There is a striking regularity to the stories I was told, or read, about families who no longer give goats. Either at some point in the past the designated goat ran to the Goddess or to the zamindar head of family and fell down in supplication, or the Mother appeared in a dream, warning the zamindar against the practice, or she physically caused the butcher's hand to miss the neck of the intended victim. Note too that extended families do not always agree on the merits of *bali*. The two most venerable "old families" at Pūjā time in Kolkata, the Sābarṇa Rāy Caudhurīs and the Shovabazar Debs, have split up over time into several lines, some immolating animals and others not. The senior gentleman at one of the three minor lines of the Sābarṇa Rāy Caudhurī family told me that he had stopped *bali* in 1990. "They'd have to kill me first!," he exclaimed proudly.[78] But the main house, where the West Bengal Tourist Office Bus Tour drops people, decapitates goats and buffalos, and it is this house that is always written up in the papers. One suspects that the discontinuation of *bali*, like its championing, plays into status wars.

## *Theorizing the Bengali Data*

When I finished my dissertation work in the early 1990s, I was fairly sure that animal sacrifice was decreasing in modern Bengal. The perspective on the Goddess promulgated by the saintly Rāmakṛṣṇa (1836–1886), as well as the maternalizing, domesticating, and sweetening influence of the *bhakti* poetry tradition, seemed to indicate that the mother, even if she once liked blood, was gradually losing her taste for it. This impression was bolstered by the work I did in the mid-1990s on Kālī's temporary Pūjā images, which since the 1930s have been increasingly humanized and beautified.

However, as my recent research has forced me to see, West Bengali goddess worship has regional characteristics that differentiate it from those, say, in Andhra Pradesh or Rajasthan, and that militate against an easy transition to bloodless worship.[79] Kālī and Durgā are not limited to the "village," and their cult is patronized by both poor and wealthy classes, lower and upper castes.[80] Thus their devotees span the spectrums of urban/rural, rich/poor, and Brahman/Śūdra. And among goddess-worshiping communities, *bali* is normalized, even naturalized. Recall the Kaliganj figure that so unnerved me in northern Bengal in November 1999. In spite of the fact that the actual Pūjā image is very fierce, consonant with the bloody meat dinner she is about to receive, her origin story states that she revealed herself to the Pūjā-sponsoring family as an ordinary, very modest daughter-in-law, and it was the housewives of the community who were jostling and queuing up that night to be near the *bali* stake.

Even the critique of *bali* itself has been folded back into the social matrix, rather the way the anti-caste Lingāyats in Karnataka became their own caste. In other words, *bali* as an image has been generalized and diffused in popular culture, severed, one might say, from the actual contexts of blood.[81] Mechanical goat-chopping models amuse children at public fairs. Cartoons depict goats, oblivious to the fate awaiting them, as comments on human behavior,[82] and spoofs on political corruption often employ the cipher of the wrongly killed animal. One cartoon from 1999 illustrates the decline of the state under Left Rule; Mother Bengal has her head in a stake and is about to be sacrificed by Communist oppressors.[83] Another portrays Mamata Banerjee willingly sacrificing the local Congress Party so that she can align with the BJP against the CPI(M). As an aside to L. K. Advani, she comments that the victim won't suffer or be much inconvenienced.[84] Feminists also draw parallels between goats and women. In a poem by Pūrbā Mukhopādhyāy, women are like goats offered at Kālī temples; they are innocent but raped and killed, their aggressors getting off without punishment.[85] Such uses of *bali* indicate that the act of ritual killing has been expanded and democratized into a multivalent symbol for sacrifice in general.

Given this pervasiveness of *bali*, whether in actual practice or in cultural symbol, what can we say, more generally and theoretically, about sacrifice in the Bengali case? Since Hubert and Mauss's classic study at the end of the nineteenth century,[86] sacrifice as a category has received much attention from anthropologists, psychologists, structuralists, and scholars of comparative religion, who have tested and promulgated theories based on work ranging from India, Greece, Mesoamerica, and Africa to Hawaii. How does Bengali Śāktism fit, reflect, or challenge such views?[87]

In all Bengali cases, the sacrifice of animals is not an isolated event. It is grounded in a larger system of rites, beliefs, and presuppositions that govern the worship of complex, female deities. As we have seen, offerings—whether vegetal or animal—occur in two general circumstances: as a result of vows, individual or collective, undertaken either in supplication for a desired end or in thanksgiving for having received it; or in the framework of prescribed rites in periodic festivals. In all cases, the goddess in question is believed to desire, even command, the offering; as such, ritual sacrifice is a means of communication and transaction between deity and devotee, the former being expected to deliver what the latter hopes to receive. Underlying such transactions is a strong sense of human debt and duty. Since the Goddess gives, so must we; not to do so, when she commands our offerings and gives us what we desire, would merit punishment and be the height of ingratitude.[88]

Almost all theorists of ritual claim that animals are stand-ins for humans in the payment of such debts.[89] Rather than offering oneself in exchange for fertility, health, wealth, or success, one chooses an unblemished animal—or, if this is not to one's taste, a vegetable—as a surrogate. States Luc de Heusch,

> The animal victim is only a substitute. This phenomenon of "displacement" is problematic. If animal sacrifice has received little attention from anthropologists it is because, more often than not, they perceived it as a banal phenomenon, a form of offering, a mere gift. Yet the "thing" given must be put to death in order to affect the invisible forces so that life may be perpetuated. This is surely the crux of the matter of sacrifice.[90]

Although I have not encountered anything quite like René Girard's idea of sacrifice as a way to end or catharcize rivalries and violence, which are put onto a scapegoat victim,[91] the symbolism of substitution is evident in Bengali sacrificial rites, from the Tantric scriptural tradition favoring human over animal and vegetal sacrifice and the equation of particular animals with specific human sins, to the smearing of the slain animal's blood on one's own forehead, marking oneself as the victim and partaking in the power of its death. Sometimes the realization that debts need to be paid to the Goddess is prompted by a personal or social crisis; at other times it is brought to mind by routine ritual prescriptions at an annual festival. In both cases, death resolves tension, for by offering himself, as it were, the devotee can fulfill a sense of responsibility, pay a debt of guilt, or relate positively to the Goddess, while yet garnering prestige and power through the letting of blood in a public arena of potential rivals. Because my own naive, Western identification with the goats at the 1988 Kālī Pūjā was not knitted into a lived Śākta religious framework, this death could not be transformative for me; it could not resolve tension.

But even for committed votaries of tradition, sacrifice can create tension. And here I must agree, at least in part, with theorists like Catherine Bell, Clifford Geertz, and, most germane to my work, Isabelle Nabokov, who in their several ways argue that it is misguided to attempt to view ritual as a mechanism for resolving or disguising conflicts fundamental to sociocultural life.[92] In her work on Tamil ritual, Nabokov identifies a coercive, deeply self-abnegating element to sacrifice.[93] Insofar as the victim is raised in the house as a pet, is said to stand in for the sacrificer, and is killed on behalf of the entire lineage or community, its death is a symbolic erasure of the sacrificer. "We must never forget that the vitality [the sacrifice] confers depends on throwing out constitutive elements of nature (sexuality, biological procreativity) and culture (alliance, reciprocity, and difference). It also requires the exclusion of women, the death of animals and sons, and above all the destruction of individuality."[94]

While I have not done work in Bengal equivalent to that Nabokov has done in Tamil villages, and while the several political, religious, and social contexts of Tamilnadu and Bengal are quite different, my field research does yield a similar sense of angst even among those who are staunch supporters and practitioners of *bali*. The Śākta tradition itself, as a framework of rites, beliefs about the Goddess, and inherited institutions, thus acts to encase the devotee in a set of behavioral expectations, some of which may cause him personal anguish. Indeed, many interviewees voiced deep inner tension about their continuing sacrificial practices, representing themselves as being caught between revulsion of the blood-letting and fear of its suspension. However, Bengal as a ritual arena also provides ample scope for the down-playing of such personal anxieties: the society at large is largely meat-eating; sacrifices are part of the public, commercial meat-selling business; the cooking and eating of the meat ties people together;[95] and justifications that exonerate the sacrificer from the "killing" are built into the rites themselves.[96] Since the Bengali Śākta "self" is therefore not constituted by cultural values of vegetarianism, a recent legislative history against sacrifice, or an embarrassment of low-caste signature rites, it is less likely to experience its ritual as coercive. Nevertheless, the fact that reasons given for the abandonment of blood sacrifice typically involve commands from the Goddess herself (whether through dreams or devotional inspiration) points to the type of heavy arsenal necessary for a redirecting of the typical sacrificial mandate.

Hindu goddess specialist Hugh Urban has recently proposed another way of understanding blood sacrifice. Drawing upon Foucault's and Deleuze's ideas of power as a "capillary system" or "flow," he characterizes the Goddess's penchant for blood as the complementary back-flow of life-energy she had given out in creation. Blood sacrifice therefore returns blood to her, energizing her, the soil, which she represents, and the kings or patrons who offer it to her—but in a specifically transgressive, Tantric, un-Vedic way. Certainly this analysis of blood and power rings true also in Bengal.[97]

From one angle, we can see that the devotional perspective, according to which the Mother wants the sacrifice of our shortcomings and the offering of our love rather than the blood and severed heads of living beings, is ranged in opposition to Tantric injunctions. In this sense the devotional critique is rather like that leveled against early Vedic *yajñas* by later philosophers:

ritual action that aims to coerce the divine for the sake of personal power and aggrandizement—in essence, putting the Goddess in our debt—is hardly praiseworthy. *Bhakti* can thus function to enable people uncomfortable with *bali* to attenuate or stop it, allowing them to repay their indebtedness to the Goddess through other, more interior means. However, goat sacrifice should not be divorced from devotion; to put it in reverse, *bhakti*, at least in Bengal, must not be reduced to something extra-ritual. For what are we to do with the fact that, as far as we know, Kālī's most famous devotional poets, Rāmprasād Sen (ca. 1718–1775) and Kamalākānta Bhaṭṭācārya (ca. 1769–1820), as well as her devotee Śrī Rāmakṛṣṇa, offered goats in their worship? Can we discount the devotion and fervor with which people bring goats to Kālīghāṭ for sacrifice, even if they hope to gain something material from their offerings?

Almost a century ago Henry Whitehead postulated that propitiation of village goddesses in South India had nothing to do with "praise and thanksgiving, . . . gratitude or love, . . . [or] desire for any spiritual or moral blessings."[98] I believe this opposition to be too stark, for Bengal. Devotionalism in the Bengali Śākta context has grown out of a soil heavily enriched with Tantric ideology, iconography, and ritual prescriptions. As such, it is stern, and imbued with a Tantric, nonvegetarian veneer that matches the goddesses on which it focuses. Whether Walter Burkert is correct for all religious traditions when he says that "blood and violence lurk fascinatingly at the very heart of religion,"[99] he is certainly right for the goddesses at the center of this book. If someone of the iconic stature of Rabindranath Tagore could not stop sacrifice in the very temple of the zamindar family about whom he write his famous play *Bisarjan*—still in 2001 the priests of the Tripura Rāj estate were claiming that stopping *bali* would be a mutilation of religion (*dharmer angahāni*)[100]—what can one think of the future? No matter what my personal feelings are regarding the bleating of frightened goats, I am not sanguine about the prospects for success of those who, arguing as devotees of a soft, vegetarian Mother, would save them from the stake.

## A Goddess for Our Times

The three controversies highlighted in this chapter—the critique by prostitutes of their co-option by Brahmanical ritual, the protests by environmentalists over the harm done to nature by the Pūjās, and the ambivalence in the culture over animal sacrifice—are not the only debates we have seen thus far in our study of the Pūjās. From the festivals' very inception,

Bengalis have debated the appropriateness of using them as fodder for status wars, nationalist revolutions, and social critiques, some claiming that such politicizing of the Goddess demonstrates a lack of respect and reverence. The Goddess herself, a cartoon spoof from 1999 reveals, laments that she does not know what the priest is doing or saying, cannot hear the devotees' prayers for the cacophony of film songs blaring outside her pandals, and judges that *bhakti* has fled long ago if this is how the gods are treated.[101] And yet festivals elastic and capacious enough to provide the cause as well as the arena for statewide debate among a wide spectrum of people about important social, political, and religious issues are also festivals that endure. When Durgā, Jagaddhātrī, and Kālī cease to inspire or provide the cultural space for controversy, one will stand witness to their decline.

# 9 Devī in the Diaspora

In 2002, after having spent part of almost every Pūjā season for the prior ten years in Kolkata and other areas of West Bengal, I decided I needed to look further afield, to places outside Bengal where Bengalis had imported their goddesses and their Pūjās.[1] Making a virtue of the fact that the New York / New Jersey area is home to more than a quarter of all South Asians in the United States, I spent the next seven fall seasons "Pūjā-hopping" to celebrations near my own home. How do the West Bengali festivals compare with those managed and sponsored by Bengali-Americans? How, in general, does context color expressions of devotion? And what do the goddesses mean outside "home" to *probāsī* ("out-station") Bengalis? In what follows I present my American data, supplement it with information gathered on Bengali Pūjās in other parts of the world, and then comment on the implications of the transnational Goddess.

## The South Asian Durgā's American Face: Comparative Themes

Durgā follows her Bengali immigrants. She is now everywhere they are: in London, Glasgow, Lagos, Oman, Frankfurt, Lusaka, to name just a few, plus a host of cities in North America. As a writer for the *Amrita Bazar Patrika* commented as early as 1985, "Durga Puja is no longer a puja of the Hindus only in India. It is now a puja of the human race, as it were."[2]

In North America, Durgā Pūjā celebrations have grown steadily in number since the mid-1960s, when the first groups of Bengalis who had come under the new immigration laws moved, settled down, and decided to do something to commemorate their religious heritage. While graduate students may have been the first Bengalis to arrive, from the late 1950s, historians enumerate two chief stages in post-1960s South Asian migration: first arrived the professionals, mainly men admitted under the "special skills" aspect of the new Immigration Act, and then from the early 1970s their relatives, under the "family reunification" aspect of the act.[3] While the seeds of later Pūjā associations were sown in the pre-1970s period—for example, Toronto's first Sarasvatī Pūjā was celebrated in 1957, with only ten Bengalis present (the Goddess of Learning would be especially important to graduate students), and the first Durgā Pūjā in 1965, with only thirty Bengalis[4]—one must wait until the 1970s for the growth of regional-linguistic, sectarian, and caste groups. Early examples of American Pūjā associations include the East Coast Durga Puja Association, which started in 1970, and the Bengali Association of Southern California, which was the first West Coast Pūjā tradition, from 1979.[5] Today there must be at least one hundred groups around the country who, whether humbly or extravagantly, perform the worship of the Goddess in autumn. Some of these groups are mixed Bangladeshi and West Bengali; others stick fairly closely to the communities of their home country. I will return to this issue—Bangladesh vs. India—below.

In general, diaspora Pūjā committees try to stay as close as possible to the traditions of home, duplicating an "authentic" experience of Pūjā as it had been experienced in Kolkata, Dhaka, or the ancestral village. The images or *pratimā*s tend to be made by artisans from Kumartuli in Kolkata, who specialize in the foreign export market and develop images of lightweight materials such as *śolā*, plaster of paris, fiberglass, or thermocol.[6] The images I have seen tend to be of the older, more traditional or semi-traditional variety: Durgās with large eyes, static bodies, and stylized green *asura*s, or Durgās with traditional bodies but sweetened faces (fig. 9.1). Indeed, said the president of the Antorik Bengali Association of Greater Dallas, one of two Pūjā associations in that city, "old is best."[7] Kālīs, by contrast, tend to veer away from the fierce, large-eyed black images one sees in traditional pandals in Kolkata; American organizers prefer instead the sweeter, bluer,

FIGURE 9.1. A close-up of the Durgā image at the Garden State Cultural Association at the Plainfield High School auditorium in New Jersey on Daśamī. October 2003. Photo by Rachel Fell McDermott.

more humanized depictions.[8] As a general rule, images are kept for seven or eight years, stored in a devotee's home or a rented hall, until new ones are commissioned again from India.[9]

Other ritual items also come from India, where possible: for instance, Ganges water, *bel* leaves, the *nabapatrikā* or *kalā bau*, and the almanac, or *pañjikā*, which tells the priest exactly when the auspicious times, or *lagnas*, are for conducting each ritual act. Even when a Pūjā committee cannot accommodate all five days of the traditional Durgā Pūjā into the weekend in which its members have time to attend the function,[10] they nevertheless try to squeeze in as many of the prescribed and customary rites as possible: chanting the "Devī-Māhātmya"; doing the *kalā bau snān*, or bathing the nine plants; feeding the Goddess with food, or *bhog*; offering *bhajans* (songs), *ārati* (worship with prescribed items), and *añjali* (worship); marking special points in the ritual with drum beats, conch shells, and "*ulu ulu*!" sounds; and playing the *sindūr-khelā*, when women decorate the Goddess and then themselves with vermillion in a farewell act on the tenth day, before the festivities come to a close (fig. 9.2).[11] Brahman priests, usually local men hired for the occasion, though sometimes flown in from India,[12] oversee the rituals, and special Bengali foods—rice preparations, curries, and sweets—are made by local families or, if the anticipated crowd is too large, are ordered from a catering firm. Although most associations I studied were strict vegetarians, even at Kālī Pūjā time some organizers were insistent that because Kālī demands blood in the scriptures, she must be fed mutton in their celebrations.[13]

The Pūjās also conform to the models established in Kolkata and elsewhere in Bengal through their use of the prestige market: getting private or business sponsors to underwrite the costs of the hall rental, cultural program, and food;[14] encouraging companies to take out advertisements in their souvenir pamphlets; paying for TV, movie, or music stars to come from India for the evening cultural programs;[15] and getting important people to inaugurate the festivities or to write letters of felicitation to be published in the souvenir booklets.[16] In 2002 New York's Bangladesh Puja Samiti outdid its rival, the Bangladesh Puja Samity, by getting letters and photos from President Bush, Governor Pataki, Mayor Bloomberg, and two Pūjā committee presidents in Dhaka. The atmosphere of the bigger American Pūjā celebrations has a *melā*, or fair-like, quality to it, what with the hundreds or even thousands of milling people, blaring music, and stalls selling books, cassettes, imported clothes, and snacks.

FIGURE 9.2. The ritual of *baraṇ*, or bidding farewell to the Goddess, performed by women of the Garden State Cultural Association at the Plainfield High School auditorium in New Jersey on Daśamī. October 2003. Photo by Rachel Fell McDermott.

Another familiar carry-over in American Pūjā contexts is rivalry. There is a saying that whenever three Bengalis get together disputation, or *jhagḍā*, is inevitable,[17] and this is certainly reflected in the history of Pūjā associations in this country. Rival groups typically spring up when one association splits into two, due to quarrels over leadership, finances, organization, or perceived non-inclusiveness on the part of the parent body. For instance, in both Dallas and Houston, a single Pūjā association, founded typically in the 1970s or 1980s, divided into two in the 1990s, over ideology, personal animosities, and perceived "power mongering." Or, as happened in New York in the 1980s, a new immigrant group of Bangladeshis arrived in the city and, encountering established West Bengali–run Pūjā associations that they experienced as too cliquish and dependent upon high subscription rates, decided, "Let's do a Pūjā of our own."[18] In this particular case, the irony was that within a year the Bangladeshi Hindu community itself was deeply divided along leadership lines; now there are two Bangladeshi factions, two major Pūjās, and considerable acrimony between the organizers.[19] Indeed, in Pūjā season 2002, one prominent member of the splinter group came to a West Bengali Pūjā celebration and handed out protest leaflets against the leadership of the other group, claiming fraudulent financial practices. Rivalries do perform a useful function, however, as in cities where the Bengali population has grown past the point where one association can accommodate the Pūjā crowds, having several to choose from is actually beneficial. Nevertheless, many of the older Pūjā organizations look back nostalgically to the time in the 1970s and early 1980s when the community was small enough to be served by a single Pūjā, where people of all backgrounds came together in joy and without competition. Those celebrations that do not command the big crowds make a virtue of their intimacy; Surajit Mitra, president of the Garden State Puja Committee, wrote in his 2006 letter of welcome in their souvenir booklet that their festival was *gharoyā*—informal and intimate, like a family.

In spite of all the many aspects of American Pūjās that are designed to remind one of home, much is different, and reflects the exigencies of living in diaspora contexts. Many—though not all[20]—associations shorten the Pūjā celebrations from five days to two or three, often in the process moving the dates to the nearest weekend, so that working families with children in school can attend. In what Diana L. Eck calls the new "gala festival," such rearrangement of time is made an occasion for opportunity: the New Jersey Navarātrī celebrations at the Raritan Convention Center in Edison occur for nine weekends in a row, attracting around 10,000 people every weekend.[21] Furthermore, because Pūjā committees cannot build temporary pandals for their deities at all local street corners, and because they cannot decorate the outside facades of the halls, community centers, and churches that they hire for the festivities, diaspora Pūjās are perforce *inside* affairs, with sit-down dinners[22] and entertainments that substitute for the more mobile experience of Pūjā revelry in the subcontinent. Although the after-dinner featured artists may be excellent—for instance, in 2003 I heard a concert by famed Bengali singer Anup Ghoṣāl and a lecture by renowned novelist Sunil Gangopādhyāy[23]—these must perforce substitute for the fuller, more sensuous array of entertainments displayed in India. Absent, for example, are the gorgeous temples, palaces, or even movie sets that one sees in Kolkata. Only once have I seen a committee attempt to replicate, even in small measure, the type of social commentary that one sees in India: in 2001, after September 11, the Bangladesh Puja Samiti placed a huge cutout depiction of the New York skyline, including the twin towers, behind their image of Durgā in the local Catholic church.

Further departures from tradition include the tendency to ask for donations at the door rather than soliciting subscriptions from the neighborhood; the inclusion of local children's and adults' talent shows in the entertainment sections of the festivities; and the curtailment of *bisarjan*, or immersion practices, due to strict American laws against river pollution. Most associations keep their *pratimās* for several years, donating them before buying new ones to a community member, a local temple, or a civic building; at the time of *bisarjan* on Daśamī day, some Bengalis immerse the *ghaṭ* in a bucket, or immerse flower petals—something symbolic that attempts to compensate for the restrictions imposed by the diasporic ritual arena. In September 2006, the British Museum got closer than any committee I have ever heard of, outside India, to an actual immersion. At the conclusion of that year's Durgā Pūjā celebration, co-sponsored by the Museum and the local Hindus of Camden Town, the image was secured to the low-tide floor of the Thames River, and the sea washed over it for twenty-four hours before it was removed.[24] Lesser acts of replication are also frequently "compromised," from the perspective of the Indian pattern. During the traditional rites of farewell, or *baraṇ*, when married women feed the Goddess sweets, sweet-defacement can be a cause for worry in an American context, since the deities must be stored and reused. In October 2006, the women of the Garden State Puja Committee gave the Goddess her sweets, but smeared them under the folds of her clothes, so that they would not be noticeable.

I conclude this brief description of Śākta Pūjās in the New York / New Jersey area by mentioning two additional intriguing characteristics. The first is the differences between the Pūjā associations organized by West Bengalis and those organized by Bangladeshis. In general, mostly because of immigration patterns, West Bengali groups tend to be older, more well established, and wealthier; this reflects the community's reputation for being professional and elite. Often such associations are managed by people who came to the West in the 1970s and 1980s; their children are in college or beyond, and their links back to India, while strong, may not be very recent. Their children, too, may be not very conversant in the Bengali language. In addition, while one can discuss the political melodramas of the CPI(M), the Congress, and Mamatā Banerjee's Trinamul Congress, and while there is always much to complain about in terms of the economic decline of the state over the last thirty to forty years, in general West Bengal is not in a state of crisis. Americans from West Bengal are not looking back to India with fear or a sense of political activism. Bangladeshi immigrants, by contrast, have come more recently to the United States, at least in the New York area tend to be employed in less well paying jobs, and are much more connected to the goings on at home in Bangladesh. Due to the political backlashes against Hindus that have occurred since the early 1990s, and especially since 2001, they are very much aware of what they perceive to be injustices, depredations, and even community cleansings.

Hindu citizens of Bangladesh, even in Bangladesh, celebrate their Pūjās with a wary eye to communal tensions. As far as I can tell from newspapers from 1971 to the present, after the initial euphoria of separation from Pakistan and under the banner of a universal Bengali identity, the Pūjās were celebrated enthusiastically and without a hitch into the early 1980s, and even with Muslim participation. The destruction of the Babri Mosque at Ayodhya, India, in 1992, however, had painful consequences in Bangladesh, for many Hindu temples were looted or destroyed in vengeful rampages, and in 1993 Bangladeshi Hindus refused to celebrate Durgā Pūjā in protest against the nonfulfillment of their demands for government compensation to temples damaged during the 1992 riots. Since 2001, but especially 2004, human rights watchdogs in Bangladesh have reported several incidents of vandalism and violence to Hindu persons, Hindu temples, and images of Hindu deities—some occurring during the Pūjā season. Whether for security reasons or simply as a nod to custom, the main Pūjā pandals in Bangladesh tend to be erected within goddess temple compounds: in Dhaka, for instance, at the Ḍhākeśvarī Durgā Mandir; the Jagannath Hall in Dhaka University; the Rāmakṛṣṇa Mission; the Rāmnā Kālī Mandir; and the Siddheśvarīkālī Mandir. Another feature of Bangladeshi Pūjās is a lack of novelty and innovation in external pandal construction. The focus is on the image, not the gorgeousness of the Goddess's "house"; in the present-day climate of Bangladesh, where it is best to avoid too much public attention, this makes eminent sense.

All of these national differences are reflected in the Pūjā souvenir booklets distributed at Durgā Pūjā time in the New York area. The published essays and poetry in Bangladeshi publications are almost all in Bengali rather than English, and they are overwhelmingly political in nature, discussing Islamic fundamentalism, the current government, the rapes, temple demolitions, and forced evacuations of Hindu Bangladeshis, and the declining percentages of Hindus in Bangladesh since 1947[25]—some of the souvenirs even printing centerfolds of photos of devastated Hindus. Said the opening statement in *Prācī*, the booklet produced by the Bangladesh Hindu Mandir in New York in 2002, "Here in our temple we follow the *śāstras* and the *tithis*. But our bliss is cut by the hellish things going on in Bangladesh right now. Due to political changes the minorities are experiencing a terrible new chapter in their lives. . . . And yet we must worship Durgā." In October 2003, the souvenir booklet began by reminding readers that although they are free and liberated (*svādhīn*) in New York, people in Bangladesh are not. In fact, they experience so many hardships—destruction of images, burning of temples, subscription obstructions, personal harassment—that many cannot perform the Pūjās. "Just staying alive is their chief hope."[26] Even the creation of the Bangladesh temple was said to be for the purpose not of providing pleasure to diaspora Bengalis but of showing solidarity with Hindu sisters and brothers in the home country.[27]

By contrast, the Pūjā souvenir booklets published for older, West Bengali associations have much more English[28]—the publications by the Jersey City Durga Puja group, which is one of the oldest in the area, is 95 percent English—and the subjects discussed are much less likely to reflect political concerns. Instead, rather like *Deś* or some of the other Pūjā magazines in Kolkata, they feature poetry, religious articles, short stories, other cultural essays, and even poems and editorials expressing pride in being American.[29] Instead of printing grisly photographs showing the victimization of Hindus in Bangladesh, West Bengali Pūjā numbers are just as likely to showcase photos from the prior year's Pūjā season, or advertise for property in Kolkata, or solicit help for charitable foundations doing work among the poor.

This juxtaposition between West Bengal and Bangladesh yields some interesting stereotypes, with Bangladeshi Hindus crediting their West Bengali counterparts for having better-funded, more gorgeous images and entertainments, while simultaneously criticizing them for their lack of genuine *niṣṭhā*, or faith.[30] West Bengali groups also rival one another for authenticity and devotion, with each group asserting that its Pūjā is more in accordance with the scriptures than the next.[31] In general, I note that the attendees of the Pūjās, whether Bangladeshi or West Bengali, go back and forth to and from each other's celebration quite freely. The leadership of each organization, however, remains strictly in the hands of Hindus divided along national lines. Ashis Sengupta, one of the founding members of the East Coast Durga Puja Association in 1970, admitted to me that even today not many Bangladeshis are interested in joining their organization.[32] The same is true of the newly inaugurated Kālī Temple in Washington, D.C.; out of the four hundred and fifty or so Bengali families that are loosely affiliated with the temple in the Washington/Baltimore area, almost none are from Bangladesh.[33]

A second observation about diaspora Pūjās in general is that, as events organized principally by lay people, they tend to favor Durgā over Kālī. The popular saying that wherever three Bengalis get together they put up a Kālī Bāḍī[34] may perhaps be true, in terms of temples; one thinks of the beautiful permanent Kālī temples in Toronto, Washington, D.C., and Laguna Beach, or of the ashramas founded by Hindu spiritual teachers or gurus. All Ramakrishna Mission swamis, for instance, perform Kālī Pūjā, whether publicly in their temples or privately in an uncommercialized, personal manner,[35] as do the monks and devotees associated with the Dakshineswar Ramkrishna Sangha Adyapeath, founded in the lineage of the Bengali saint and devotee Annadā Ṭhākur (d. 1928), whose main temple image of Kālī in north Kolkata is replicated and worshiped lovingly in Franklin Township, New Jersey.[36] Kali Mandir, established in Laguna Beach, California, in 1993 by Rāmakṛṣṇa devotee Usha Harding and supported by priests from the Dakṣiṇeśvar Temple in Kolkata, has perhaps the greatest blend of Eastern and Western devotees of any Kālī temple in the United States; the stone image of Ma Dakshineshvari is built in imitation of that at Kolkata's famous shrine, and, as in all of India's Kālī temples, Durgā Pūjā is also celebrated there with traditional images.[37] In none of these settings are there associated public, "secular" song and dance entertainments, as one finds in the diaspora Pūjā setting.

But among the lay Bengali communities who mainly sponsor the yearly Pūjās, it is Durgā who has proven more durable and exportable than Kālī, for although there are some Pūjā associations that include Kālī in their festival schedules, most do not, perhaps preferring to celebrate the pan-Indian Diwali with other, non-Bengali friends. And even when they do organize Durgā and Kālī Pūjās, the expenditures for the former far outweigh those for the latter—reflecting similar trends in Kolkata.[38] Perhaps this preference for Durgā reflects her perceived identity as a unifying religious emblem, a national symbol helpful not only in establishing a Bengali identity in an essentially alien culture but also in bridging the sectarian differences between Vaiṣṇava, Śaiva, and Śākta. I find it striking, for example, that the Bangladesh Hindu Mandir, clearly Vaiṣṇava in religious orientation,[39] chose to make the central, permanent images those of Durgā and her four children. So also is the West Bengali New York Puja Association trying to raise money to build a temple not to Kālī but to Durgā. The same applies to the Houston Tagore Society, which built a Durgā Bāḍī, and the Bengalis resident in Virginia, who erected a Durgā temple in Fairfax Station at a street they lobbied to rename Durga Place!

## What Lies Ahead for the Deśī Durgā?

Let me now analyze these Durgā celebrations of the American East Coast. How can the Bengali Durgā Pūjā be seen as a case study of the more general phenomenon of adaptive strategies and ethnic identity formation among transnational peoples?

Hindus in the diaspora, like deterritorialized peoples everywhere, have certain things in common. Here let me mention three: a mental and emotional yearning for "home"; a desire to strengthen bonds of social cohesion; and pride in ethnic identity. First, many feel strong ties to the motherland, to India or to Bangladesh, and hence live with a type of multilocal consciousness in which memory, nostalgia, yearning, and the maintenance of an idealized, often static, and unchanging view of tradition are important.[40] Indeed, Gurharpal Singh, a modern diaspora theorist, sees the "core feature" of Indian overseas communities to be this "collective imagining of India—of emotions, links, traditions, feelings, and attachments that together continue to nourish a psychological appeal among successive generations of emigrants for the 'mother' country."[41] Such emotions generate a desire for authenticity, the resolve that if home traditions are to be transplanted to the United States—and since South Asians cannot take Hinduism for granted here they must take conscious steps to package, present, and market it[42]—these rituals must be done "properly." The immigrant thus faces the challenge of recalling, renewing, and passing along a treasured, if often imperfectly remembered heritage. Much of the impetus for such an emphasis upon transmission derives from a concern to educate the second generation in the traditions of "home."[43] This is concurrent with an equal drive to communicate to increasingly Americanized youth a version of the home tradition that is not too weird, alien, or off-putting. In this regard I find it charming and perhaps significant that the explanation for Kālī's outstretched tongue that most departs from the bloodlust of her Tantric heritage derived from a devotee at the Kālī Temple in Washington, D.C., who told me that the Goddess stuck out her tongue in embarrassment, not because Śiva lay down to stop her rampage on the battlefield but because she accidentally tripped over him in the dark.[44]

Examples of nostalgia also occur within India itself. The most famous home away from home for Bengali Śāktas in India is Delhi, where the local Kālī temples—in particular, the main one founded in 1938, on Mandir Marg, near the Birla Temple—are the hub of activity at the Pūjā season. Started modestly in 1910, with the shifting of the British capital from Calcutta to Delhi, the city's Durgā, Jagaddhātrī, and Kālī Pūjās do not begin to be covered regularly in the Calcutta newspapers until after Independence, when the numbers of pandals, cultural programs, outreach efforts, and even the sporadic visits of the prime minister are featured yearly, with an accompanying photo. Although the spirit of the Delhi Pūjās is claimed by Delhi locals as unique and hence to be cherished in its own right,[45] the backward glance eastward is clearly noticeable: donations are gathered for flood victims in West Bengal; artisans are invited from Kolkata to perform at Delhi's Pūjā cultural programs; ritual paraphernalia, such as fresh lotuses, are brought from West Bengal; and the celebrations are opportunities for Delhi-ites to affirm their Bengali identity. A reporter for the *Statesman* remarked in 1987 that the Delhi Kālī temple was the "expatriate's life-line," adding that "in preserving the cultural milieu of Bengal with programmes and competitions of Rabindra sangit, Nazrulgeeti, Shyamasangeet, folk songs and poetry recitation, Kali Bari has built up a sense of identity and community-feeling and provided a soothing balm for the pangs of homesickness."[46] Such was also the impetus for the founding in 1974 of the Chittaranjan Park Kali Mandir, established by immigrant refugees from East Pakistan.

This same sentiment is expressed in North America as well. The souvenir booklet from the Garden State Cultural Association in 2008, for example, featured an essay by an older member of the community on what the festivities were like in the village of his remembered youth in the 1950s. There is an equally plaintive tone to the Bengali poem included in the Garden State Puja Association's booklet for 2006:

> If you stay far from home at Pūjā time
> Thoughts of home repeatedly flood into your mind.
> Here no drums sound, no conch shells blow.
> Here one does not hear the call of thousands of busy people.
> On Pūjā days your face floats before my eyes,
> And in my heart arises such distress.
> If I had two very large wings I would take off into the sky;
>   there would be no stopping me.
> But when Mā comes, I forget all my cares.
> Come Mā, come again and again.
> Come, remembering all of us
>   mixed in with other countries.[47]

Such a hankering after home is not felt in the private isolation of a faraway land. Another feature of the diaspora Pūjās is the feedback loop that they and their organizers enable to Bengal. Bengali newspapers send reporters to cover diaspora Pūjās, whose unique characteristics are explained for the home reader. In 2004 a woman from Toronto said that although she missed the crowds and glitter of West Bengal, Canadian Pūjās still afforded her the chance to socialize, mix with other Bengalis, eat good Bengali food, and feel pride in her culture and heritage—elements she valued.[48] Some nonresident Indians express their commitment to home by helping to secure sponsors for the Pūjās in Bengal, giving financial donations, and sometimes aiding their favorite committees with the development of their Web sites. Www.calcuttaweb.com, a site maintained in India, includes a schedule of overseas Pūjās as part of its menu, and various Indian Web sites offer out-station Bengalis the opportunity to make offerings at Pūjā time and to receive sweets and flowers in the mail in return. One of the items available through the store at www.banglalive.com is an "e-Jagaddhatri Pujo," or priestly services at Chandannagar; all you have to do is to send your name, address, and *gotra,* plus $12.74 (price as of December 2008).[49] On www.bangalinet.com one can click onto Bengali Pūjā recipes, music releases, mantras, and Kolkata photo galleries; one can also buy Durgā desktop wallpaper, a Durga screensaver, and Pūjā greeting cards.

Enterprising Indian artisans from the Kumartuli and Kalighat artists' districts in Kolkata, and even as far afield as Krishnanagar, make names for themselves by catering to the overseas image market. Pradyut Pāl launched the www.kumartuli.com Web site in 2005,[50] intending it to be a commercial portal for overseas customers that would bypass the need for middlemen, who take 4–5 percent of every sale's profit. Each year the Kolkata newspapers feature artisans whose work is being sent overseas; their notoriety leads to jealousy and rivalry, innovation, coveted economic advantage, and a new avenue for the commodification of the Goddess. The same is true for singers and entertainers, who seek the accreditation, fame, and financial windfall that an overseas engagement can bring. Nostalgia for Bengal, then, creates transnational markets.

A second way of looking at diaspora communities is to understand them as a cohesive social form, which implies special kinds of social relationships, ways of life, economic strategies, and political orientations. Rituals, then, such as prayers, readings, rites, and festivals, renew the community of worshipers not only by providing opportunities for common activity but also by representing Indian-ness or Bangladeshi-ness to the performers themselves, a phenomenon Milton Singer long ago termed the acting out of "cultural performances."[51] The social aspect of diaspora groups further explains both the social networking function of the West Bengali associations, which includes linguistic ties, the marriage market, and Hindu life-cycle rites, and the politicized lobbying of the Bangladeshi ones, which act as powerful pressure groups in the domestic politics of their host countries.

Intimately tied to the social cohesion of diaspora communities is a third function of diaspora Pūjās: the generation of pride in a common ethnicity. As we saw earlier, starting in the 1970s with the burgeoning of new associations based on regional affiliations,[52] Tamils, Gujaratis, Bengalis, and many other linguistically and ethnically identified groups began gathering to promote their own regional festivals and traditions. During the last forty years, such groups have prospered enormously through increasing immigration, through heightened sophistication in patterns of advertisement and managed organization, and even through the Internet, which has aided Hindus in the diaspora to articulate their traditions and create communities.[53] Some Durgā Pūjā associations are now so large that they serve as pilgrimage centers; the one run by the Garden State Cultural Association and held at the Plainfield High School over three days draws four thousand people, some of whom travel from out of state for the festivities and stay in local hotels.[54]

The ethnic, Bengali, regional flavor of the events leads to a certain exclusivity. Non-Bengalis are certainly not unwelcome, but boundaries are created through the use of the vernacular, the regional style of celebrating Navarātrī (note that Rāma, so central to the North Indian versions of Navarātrī, is nowhere in evidence), and the showcasing of regional dress, cuisine, and arts. Indeed, in all of the Durgā, Jagaddhātrī, and Kālī Pūjās that I have attended (about 28, from 2002 through 2008), I have never seen another non-Indian present who was not obviously married to a Bengali—with the exception of those Pūjās sponsored by the guru-led groups, such as the Ramakrishna Mission.

The bonds of ethnicity and shared culture, it seems, often override those of religion. While white folks and non-Bengalis tend to be absent, Muslim Bengalis or Bangladeshis often join in and are welcomed in these diaspora festivals. They participate in the local talent shows and, if famous artists, are occasionally paid to fly to the U.S. to grace cultural programs. In October 2008, at Our Lady of Mercy Parish, Jersey City, a Bangladeshi singer now resident in Princeton, New Jersey, sang a beautiful program of Rabindra-*saṅgīt*. Such involvement in a "Hindu" festival is not seen to impinge upon Muslim religious sensibilities, since Rabindranath is felt to be a common inheritance and since, in the schools and rented halls of New Jersey, the entertainment stages are foremost, the Goddesses sitting meekly off to one side (fig. 9.2 above). In New York and New Jersey, Pūjā souvenir booklets even accept ads from Bangladeshi fish markets and Halal meat stores.

Ritual, in diaspora communities, thus provides outlets for nostalgic reenactment, functions as a vehicle for social bonding, and helps foster ethnic identity and pride. However, the desire for replicative authenticity, the glue and expression of such identity, is complicated. As many commentators have noted, and as we have seen in the examples I gave earlier, much is compromised in the New World setting. Fred Clothey calls this adaptive strategy "pragmatic ritualism," a willingness to allow license for departures from tradition.[55] And yet, as Paul Younger reminds us in his study of festival religion in the South Indian tradition, "the zeal for a faithful performance of the festival as remembered by the participants becomes a much more central factor [here in the United States or Canada] than it would be in South India or Sri Lanka, and innovation for its own sake is clearly discouraged."[56] This is certainly true in the Bengali ritual sphere of the Pūjās I have witnessed: the Goddess must be worshiped precisely and according to the sacred texts, as far as possible; hence the effort to bring traditional images, ritual aids, and even specialist personnel from India. If a priest, especially one from the subcontinent, tinkers with the ritual, that is probably acceptable—and I think here of ritual elements simply omitted from the performance or the moving of the sacred *tithi*s to a nearby weekend[57]—but the lay organizers of the festivities would likely not take this responsibility knowingly.[58]

Of course, the great opportunity open to Kolkata organizers of Pūjā events—the creation of imaginative, novel, and prize-garnering pandals in which to house the Goddess—is not feasible for American Pūjā associations, and so the urge to express individualism and creativity through decorative novelty, so central to Durgā Pūjā in South Asian contexts, is severely curtailed. Where innovation does appear to be acceptable is inside, in the ritual space of the rented church or hall, and sometimes in the unusual piling up of traditional ritual. At Kālī Pūjā in October 2006, at the East Coast Durga Puja Association in Queens, New York, I noted that the women were performing the *dhuno* ritual of dancing with pots of burning incense balanced on their heads. I asked the priest, Mr. Nirmal Cakrabarty, about this, and he said that the ritual had been added to Kālī Pūjā for the first time that year, in imitation of Durgā Pūjā.

I have been speaking mostly of the American Pūjā association as an ethnic group. What is the future of such groups? Raymond Brady Williams, one of the first and most respected scholars to focus on the South Asian diaspora, has formulated what he calls five ideal types of adaptive strategies, and the formation of an ethnically defined organization is one.[59] A second comprises individual or personal traditions, usually carried out by families where there is not a large Indian community (the fledgling Pūjās of the 1950s and 1960s are examples of this strategy, which is now generally outmoded due to the influx of new immigrants). A third adaptive strategy is adherence to a guru and the involvement in a hierarchical organization based on reverence for his or her leadership and saintliness. While there are Bengali gurus here in the United States—the monks of the Ramakrishna Mission and until 2007 Shri Chinmoy are examples in the New York area—most of the Pūjā associations are lay-led, and I do not see much overlap between the Bengali "congregations" that attend the Ramakrishna Vedanta centers and those that frequent the more cultural, secular, and boisterous Pūjās. While the percentage of Indian attendees, vis-à-vis Western ones, at the Ramakrishna centers throughout the United States has radically risen over the last twenty years, these neo-Hindu, guru groups are still not the focal point of most Bengali attention. Perhaps they are considered too foreign, too willing to adopt Christian worship patterns, and too eclectic. A fourth strategy as enumerated by Williams is participation in "ecumenical" or Westernized organizations, where corporate worship, piano playing, and the adoption of American-style administrative bureaucracy are utilized in worship contexts. Again, it is the guru-led groups that tend toward this approach, and they do not have the membership or the appeal of the more culturally and ethnically identified associations.

The final adaptive strategy proffered by Williams is, it seems to me, the only serious competitor to the ethnic group, and that is association with a national organization focusing on Indian pride and the spread and correct interpretation of Hinduism. The most visible such group is the network of local chapters of the Vishwa Hindu Parishad, a right-wing organization that, in India, has been the source of much Hindu–Muslim strife. As Prema Kurien warns, ethnic organizations can provide receptive soil for the growth of nationalist Hinduism in India,[60] as pride in Bengal, say, can lead naturally to pride in India and a desire to preserve its integrity and purity. Such groups have made little headway in West Bengal, largely due to the vigilance of the Communist-led political party there, and the fact that I note little evidence of communal tension in Pūjā contexts here may reflect the fact that there is little, as well, in India.

But the fate of the ethnic organization is still a point of debate. The current number of Hindus in the United States (.04 percent of the population in 2008) is expected to triple by 2020. What will second- and third-generation South Asians come to value as markers and enablers of their hybrid identities? Many scholars argue that as the new generations gradually lose their fluency in the regional language, Bengali, and as their primary emotional ties are no longer bound up with people and institutions in India or the subcontinent, ethnic groups may become less and less attractive.[61] One can see this, to a certain extent, in the lukewarm participation of teenagers in these New York / New Jersey Pūjā associations—an experience characterized by Jhumpa Lahiri in *The Namesake* as being "dragged off to a high school or a Knights of Columbus hall overtaken by Bengalis."[62] In addition, although there are Club Bangla equivalents at many colleges and universities, it is the multiethnic organizations catering to a pan-Indian or pan–South Asian sensibility that are the most popular clubs to join. How will this tension between the regional groups students grow up in and the broad Indianization to which they are exposed in college be resolved?[63]

Certainly the ethnically defined organizations are trying not to lose the new generations. They print flyers in English about the Pūjās, explaining their meaning and traditions, sell and distribute items of interest to young people (like "Desi Match"), and encourage participation in numerous after-school arts, language, and religious studies programs.[64] Moreover, as long as American immigration policies continue to be fairly liberal, with new waves of Bengali Hindus arriving from India and Bangladesh, there will always be new blood, with fresh ties to the subcontinent, to keep these associations meaningful, vibrant, and, to a certain extent, traditional. This is particularly true for the Bangladeshi community, whose emotional links to the motherland are, at present, not merely born of nostalgia but also fueled by active concern about the persecution and devastation of the minority community left behind.

In sum, Durgā and Kālī—and to a lesser extent Jagaddhātrī—appear to be flourishing in their new diasporic contexts in North America. As in India and Bangladesh, so here: the Goddess is a national symbol of what it means to be a Hindu Bengali, and in celebrating her, Bengali devotees proclaim and nourish their own sense of identity. I do not see Pūjā associations melting away in favor of some sort of pan-Indian homogenization of tradition. And given what we know about the dangerous effects of such Hindu nationalist homogenization, a championing of the local, presided over by a demon-slaying deity who expressly vaunts her partiality for Bengal as a region, can only be lauded.

*But all said and done, as long as the Bengali community will retain its separate identity, Durga Puja will go on, come Marx, come Gandhi.*

*—Syamalendu Banerjee, October 1985*

# Conclusion

The chapters of this book have shown—I hope beyond a doubt—that Durgā Pūjā and its sister festivals for Jagaddhātrī and Kālī are extremely significant to the religious history, past and present, of West Bengal. We have surveyed the Pūjās' growth and development, their symbolic malleability and capaciousness to a variety of Bengali and non-Bengali actors over a three-hundred-year history, their potential for political utilization, their emotional and familial resonances, their commercialization and commodification, their public, performative, even contentious quality, their intersection with the art world, and their import value to Bengalis resident in towns and cities outside Bengal.

To claim, however, as do most Bengalis, scholars, and promoters of West Bengali culture,[1] that Durgā Pūjā is the *most* important festival of West Bengal requires that we compare our three Śākta Pūjās with other festivals, holy days, and holidays of the state, hardly any of which have been mentioned in this book so far. What is the Bengali festival calendar like, and why has Durgā Pūjā, in particular, grown to hold pride of place?

Ralph Nicholas, who has written a most illuminating survey of the Bengali calendar, states that one can divide the religious year in various ways, via several types of categorization.[2] Some festivals, by their placement in spring, summer, the monsoon season, autumn, or winter, coincide with seasonal production and reflect a concern with agriculture; some festivals occur when danger to humans from the environment seems most acute and hence involve protective rituals; and other festivals focus on particular deities—their lives or feats or perceived personalities—for the purpose of honor and worship. In Bengal, the two main groups of deities so revered are Vaiṣṇava and Śākta, the Śaiva *sampradāya* trailing third in terms of popularity. All important Śākta festivals occur during the four-month period when Viṣṇu is asleep, from the end of Āṣāḍh to the end of Kārtik (roughly mid-July to mid-November), a dangerous time that also coincides with the conclusion of the rainy season and the onset of autumn. Following the work of Stanley A. Freed and Ruth S. Freed, we can also add a fourth way of categorizing festivals: those that focus on cementing familial relationships, including the links between the living and the dead.[3]

The New Year in Bengal is the first of the month of Baiśākh, in mid-April. For the next twelve months the calendar is full of festivals, fasts, and holy days (Nicholas estimated over one hundred for an average Hindu villager), some of which are foreign imports, like Christmas, some of which are Bengali regional forms of pan-Indian festivals, and some of which are unique. Certain Indian festivals find no place in Bengal, unless they are celebrated by Indians from other states who bring their festivals with them; examples include Hanumān Jayantī, Gaṇeś Caturthī, the sun-honoring Chāt Pūjā, and the North Indian ending to Navarātrī on Bijayā Daśamī, when effigies of Rāvaṇa are burned to signal Rāma's victory; none of these finds a place in the typical Bengali *pañjikā*.[4] Some annual rituals well known in Bengal, such as the Gangāsāgar bathing ritual at the confluence of the Ganges with the Bay of Bengal at the winter solstice, or Ambubācī, the three-day observance of the earth's menstruation in early Āṣāḍh, which derives from traditions associated with the Kāmākhyā Temple at Gauhati in Assam, are more a site-specific pilgrimage and a site-specific import than pan-Bengali festivals. The most important rites associated with human social networks are Rākhīpūrṇimā, at the end of the month of Śrābaṇ (in mid-August), when people tie strings of brotherhood to each other's wrists; Mahālayā, in the middle of Āśvin, when people venerate their ancestors; and Bhāi-phõṭā, in mid-Kārtik, when sisters honor their brothers by applying vermillion marks to their foreheads, feeding them fruits and sweets, and offering them presents. None of these festivals involves publicly fêted images of deities.

Apart from Durgā, Jagaddhātrī, and Kālī, then, what other Bengali deities are treated to a public street festival, complete with temporary images, pandals, and associated revelry? Interestingly, festivals of this ilk that are "next in line" in terms of popularity are focused on goddesses as well: Sarasvatī and Lakṣmī.

Sarasvatī Pūjā in mid-Māgh (mid-February) is a government holiday aimed at students and those in the arts, and every year more and more Sarasvatīs are made in the style of Durgā and her sister goddesses. The festival is celebrated in homes, in schools, and even in a few pandals, with a slow evolution toward the Durgā Pūjā pattern in evidence. The *Telegraph* paper in 2005 published a spread of the season's most interesting Sarasvatī images; one was depicted like the Virgin Mary, but she held a veena instead of a staff and *rudrākṣa* beads instead of Jesus, and she was arrayed in a pandal shaped like a Gregorian church.[5] Sarasvatī as a figure is fairly bloodless, however, compared to other goddesses, without a fully developed mythology or theological message, and her main clientele is the student population. These factors militate against her festival ever gaining the complexity or popularity of those at the core of this study.

Lakṣmī has a deeper embeddedness in Bengal and is in many ways the goddess most intimately connected to the region's Hindu homes. She is worshiped more frequently than Durgā, Jagaddhātrī, Kālī, or Sarasvatī; every Thursday, in fact, is sacred to her, and another name for Thursday is Lakṣmībār.[6] She is also worshiped on two separate annual dates: on Diwali, when Alakṣmī, or Inauspicious Poverty, is driven out with a broom and Lakṣmī is invoked in paddy grains kept in wooden or silver holders for the year; and on Lakṣmī Pūjā, five days after the conclusion of Durgā Pūjā on the full-moon day of Āśvin. At this time the markets are full of Lakṣmī images (three-dimensional, anthropomorphized *pratimās* or two-dimensional drawings done on earthen plates) made by the Kumartuli artisans.[7] Most of the images are sold to nuclear families, who bring priests into their homes for the occasion, but in some cases the images are worshiped publicly, and it is this occasion for the worship of Lakṣmī that comes closest to the pattern established by Durgā Pūjā. Some Pūjā committees even keep a section of their grandiose Durgā pandals from being torn down and place a small image of Lakṣmī in it for the one-day Lakṣmī festival. Newspapers usually print one photo of a Lakṣmī on this date, although as far as I can tell from my nearly two-hundred-year newspaper survey, this practice began only in the 1970s.

Like Durgā, Lakṣmī also has no permanent temples in Bengal, but unlike her sister, Lakṣmī lives in every house and is worshiped weekly.[8] In a sense, therefore, she is more taken for granted, and her external festivals do not need to match Durgā's in grandeur. However, it is arguable that she is more integral to the daily hopes and fears of the average Bengali Hindu; even her name has entered the language as a cipher for the abstract quality of inner grace and outward prosperity.[9]

Two other deities whose festivals have grown since Independence, in a manner akin to that of Durgā Pūjā, are Viśvakarmā and Kārtik, although neither deity will likely ever equal the popularity of the martial goddesses. Viśvakarmā Pūjā occurs at the end of Bhadra, in mid-September, and is mainly performed by people working in factories or with tools. Keshab Chandra Sarkar, now in his eighties, told me that until the early 1960s, there were no images of Viśvakarmā; only tools were honored. This tallies with my newspaper survey; I have seen single photos of images printed, with announcements of the festivity, only from the 1980s. Kārtik Pūjā, at the end of the month of Kārtik, is the second time that one sees this deity, the first being at Durgā Pūjā, when he arrives as one of Durgā's four children. This bachelor god appeals mainly to prostitutes, who do not celebrate any other Pūjā. Said Shimarani Das of Sonagacchi to a *Times of India* reporter in 2000, "We satisfy many men. But unfortunately, our lives are devoid of love. We do not develop permanent relationships. So we dream of getting a permanent babu like Kartik, and hence the Puja."[10] One sees temporary images of Kārtik in the artisans' districts, but these are brought into people's homes, not placed in pandals. Because of the limited appeal of his festival, Kārtik is unlikely ever to parallel the Durgā model.

But there are other goddesses in Bengal; in fact, the propitiation of Manasā, the goddess of snakes, Ṣaṣṭī, the goddess of children, and Śītalā, the goddess of fevers and erstwhile smallpox, is widespread throughout the state.[11] When temporary images are made, and this is not the rule, they are not immersed at the conclusion of their festivals but left at the roots of trees. Jhāpan, the snake festival held at the end of Śrābaṇ, provides an occasion for snake charmers to showcase their prowess publicly, in acts of bravado on village stages. The Goddess's exploits and powers are sung and celebrated, but images of the Goddess are not necessary. A festival that might seem to come closer to the Durgā Pūjā model is Śītalā's bathing festival, in the month of Caitra (February–March). This is celebrated in an extravagant fashion in Shalkia, Howrah district, every year, when the town's several permanent temple images are taken out of their temple precincts, processed in palanquins around the town, and bathed at the river *ghāṭ*, to the accompaniment of dancing, intoxication, possession, bodily mortification, blood sacrifice, creative floats on wheels, and a mix of Bengali and non-Bengali devotees (figs. 10.1 and 10.2).[12] But Śītalā does not have an upper-class following in urban

FIGURE 10.1. Processing Śītalā in her palanquin from her temple to the bathing *ghāṭ*. Shalkia, Howrah, February 2002. Photo by Jayanta Roy.

Bengal, she is associated historically with a disfiguring, dreaded illness, and her Yātrā is more akin to a chariot festival than to a Durgā-like carnival.

This brings us to the Vaiṣṇava festivals. Is anything here akin to the Śākta Pūjās? The Vaiṣṇava tradition in Bengal is strong, some would argue stronger than the Śākta, and its major festivals are derived textually from the *Bhāgavata Purāṇa* and heavily influenced by the rituals of Puri, where Lord Caitanya lived the last years of his life. Jagannātha's Snān Yātrā and Rath Yātrā, in the month of Āṣāḍh, are miniature Bengali renditions of the bathing and chariot festivals that occur in Puri: members of Vaiṣṇava temples, or individuals in their homes, will process a small chariot with Jagannāth and his siblings on it, around their neighborhood or within their own premises. Other festivals commemorate the life and past-times of Kṛṣṇa and Rādhā: Jhulan, on the full moon of the month of Śrābaṇ, when the lovers are placed on a swing and swung back and forth; Janmāṣṭamī, in early Bhadra, a home festival that marks the birth of Kṛṣṇa and initiates a period of dramas on his life; Rās Pūrṇimā, on the full-moon day of Kārtik, which is mostly observed in temples and marketplaces with singing and clay figures of the dancing of Rādhā and Kṛṣṇa; and Dol Yātrā, known in North India as Holi, on the full-moon day of Phālgun (mid-February), when people soak each other in colored water to reenact Kṛṣṇa and Rādhā's springtime games.

Because of the emphasis on Kṛṣṇa's boyhood in a pastoral, romantic setting, these Vaiṣṇava festivals do not lend themselves to martial imagery, to the pursuit of power, or to grandiose festivity. This perhaps accounts for the number of upwardly mobile Vaiṣṇava families in Calcutta who chose to sponsor Durgā Pūjās in the nineteenth century, and their influence upon the festival is marked, especially in the discontinuation of *bali* or in the muting of the aggressive nature of the Goddess's image. Even Śākta families who have taken Śākta initiation and who practice *bali* in their Śākta Pūjās usually have a Vaiṣṇava *kūladevatā*, or family deity—such as Madhusūdana, Gopāla, Śrīdhara, Lakṣmī-Nārāyaṇa, Śrī Rādhākṛṣṇa, Raghunāthji, Rādhā-Govinda, and Gopīnāth Jiu—which probably means that Vaiṣṇavism is older than Śāktism in such elite contexts. Another indication of the importance of Viṣṇu or Kṛṣṇa to Śākta traditions is the mandatory presence of the *śālgrāmśila*, or small stone representing Viṣṇu, that is involved in all Śākta

FIGURE 10.2. Women performing the arduous rite of *daṇḍī-kāṭā*, or measuring out with their bodies the distance from the Goddess's temple to the bathing *ghāṭ* and back again. Shalkia, Howrah, February 2002. Photo by Jayanta Roy.

*pūjās*, and the fact that every Hindu ceremony begins by invoking Viṣṇu and concludes by repeating his name ten times for the expiation of any defects that might have occurred in the ritual.[13] Kunal Chakrabarti postulates that Bengali Vaiṣṇavas never developed a defining public ritual such as their own version of the Jagannāth chariot festival at Puri because Bengal lacked both a strong temple base and a recognized pilgrimage tradition.[14]

For reasons scholars have not yet come to understand clearly the Śaiva tradition in Bengal runs a distant third in popularity behind the Śākta and the Vaiṣṇava, although Śiva *liṅgas* are present at all Śākta temples, Śivarātrī is widely celebrated on the dark-moon night of the month of Phālgun, especially by unmarried women, and there are many local varieties of the five-day Śiva-centered Gājan or Caḍak Pūjā festival that brings the Bengali year to a close at the end of Caitra. In a book-length study of Gājan, Ralph Nicholas identifies three chief elements that distinguish it from all other Bengali rituals: (1) the temporary asceticism undertaken by those vowing to perform difficult bodily mortifications; (2) the mortifications themselves (body piercing with spikes and hooks, walking on hot embers, rolling bodily across thorns, and swinging head down over a fire); and (3) the worship of the sun at the beginning of the New Year. In a specific comparison with Durgā Pūjā, Nicholas draws attention to the fact that Gājan has no hierarchical committee organization, no history of zamindari sponsorship, and no textual authority.[15] Perhaps of all festivals in the Bengali context that I have seen or read about, Gājan is the most potentially severe. In April 2008 the *Times of India* ran a news article, with grisly photos, about a village in Burdwan where temporary "sannyasis" were dancing with severed heads taken from the morgue, and with the bodies of dead newborns. The festival is called *māthā khelā*, or "play with heads," and is associated with Gājan.[16]

In sum, no other festival or holy day in the Bengali Hindu calendar can match the pan-state magnitude of Durgā's Pūjā—whether because of the caste, class, occupation, or age-specific clientele of the deity; the mainly home or temple base of the ritual; the regional provenance of the festival; the purpose of the festival, which is narrowly defined as propitiatory or commemorative and not theologically and culturally capacious; the lack of associated metaphors of royalty or worldly guardianship; the presence of decidedly un–middle-class uses of the body, such as possession or self-inflicted acts of mortification; or the perceived non-exportability of the festivities (note that Sarasvatī Pūjā, Lakṣmī Pūjā, Rath Yātrā, Janmāṣṭamī, Dol Yātrā, and Śivarātrī have "made it" to the West, along with our Śākta Pūjās, but not the festivals of Śītalā, Manasā, Gājan, or Viśvakarmā, etc.).

This does not mean that everyone celebrates Durgā. Her Pūjā is a non-event in Shantiniketan, as Rabindranath Tagore was a Brāhmo, did not believe in image worship, and started a festival called Śārodotsab (Autumnal Festival) in early October, as a rival. Durgā Pūjā inspires disgust in rationalists, atheists, and some Communists, like M. N. Roy, who refused to carry on the priestly duties of his father, in spite of the pleading of Midnapur locals who felt they were being "blasted by the wrath of the hungry goddess," and "by doing so put an end to a hoary succession of traditionally authorized imposters."[17] And the fear of angering Durgā, Jagaddhātrī, or Kālī can create lifelong anxiety. The noted Moderate politician Surendranath Banerjea (1848–1925) wrote a newspaper article near the end of his life that he called "The Vengeance of Durga," wherein he tells of a boyhood experience of Durgā that left him terrified. One day at the Pūjā season he made a young friend of his touch the Pūjā image, even though the boys were not supposed to do so. The friend died soon thereafter. Banerjee writes, "Has Durga forgotten, or does she merely tarry? Without doubt, of faith I have none, of belief I am empty. Have I not the wisdom of the West? Yet I wait, and as for Durga, she also . . . waits."[18]

Nevertheless, such holdouts, naysayers, and fearful souls are a minority among Bengali Hindus, most of whom welcome the widened opportunity provided by the *sarbajanīn* Pūjās, such that the entire community can take the place of the solitary ritual beneficiary (*yajamāna*)[19] in worship of a multifaceted goddess who, if sometimes fear-inspiring, is also and more importantly a champion demon-killer, a beloved daughter, an agricultural nourisher, a motherland, and hence a cultural unifier. In 1995, in a lead article called "Bāṅglār Durgāpūjā" for *Bartamān*, Atul Sar very cleverly linked the "Devī-Māhātmya," the Ur-text for all goddess worship in India, to the land of Bengal; King Suratha, he claimed, was a king of Birbhum in the first golden age, the *satyayuga*.[20]

Indeed, today in West Bengal Durgā and her sister goddesses fulfill the promise of the *Bhaviṣya Purāṇa*, which avers that the gifts of the festival are "the assurance of happiness, . . . the destruction of spirits, goblins and ghosts, and also . . . festivity."[21] These goddesses provide the occasion for a blessedly good time, an occasion for the flexing of creative and competitive muscle, and, for many, the hope of salvation, for Durgā embodies not wrath or punishment but superhuman power, compassion, inwardness, and bliss.[22] Hence the poignant longing for the return of the Goddess and the dread of her departure. Said Jadunath Sarkar in 1952, reminiscing about his boyhood days in the 1870s when the boatman sang their farewells to the images in the river, "I can still feel this tragedy of the Dusserah day."[23]

I too experience this sense of incipient loss. Like the artisans of chapter 3 who bewail the departure of their images at the start of the festival, as they deliver them into others' hands, I conclude this project about a set of festivals that have engaged me for nearly twenty years and that are now a part of the fabric of my autumnal expectations, with a feeling of personal poignancy and nostalgia. "After all, it's just like the attitude of a poor father towards his daughter. As long as she is with him, she is like a burden. And it is he who takes the initiative to give her in marriage. But then, even as reality strikes, that feeling of void engulfs him; . . . the story's same for us."[24]

And then, of course, I rally, hoping, with a throb of excitement and anticipation, to spend the next Pūjā season in Kolkata.

# Appendix

## *An Overview of the Press in Bengal up to 1947*

A word on the news industry in Calcutta is in order here, since so much of my material derives from news publications.[1]

Initially the East India Company was not favorably disposed to the press, as the Company was fearful of exposure, intolerant of criticism, and suspicious of journalists, whom it saw as representing the interests of those outside the privileged, official side of the administration. Indeed, the first English newspaper in India, the *Bengal Gazette / Calcutta General Advertiser* (1780–1782), was launched by James Augustus Hicky, who savagely satirized Warren Hastings and the Company. Even Parliamentary proceedings in England could not be printed in India, as the Company considered them "seditious literature." The restrictions of the press and the deportations of unwanted journalists did not go without protest from certain conscientious Englishmen, some of whom were even Company men, and one can observe the uneasy balance of power between official government ideals and the mercantile community by the founding of the *Calcutta Chronicle* (1787–1797) and the *Calcutta Journal* (1816–1823), which represented Calcutta merchants. Ultimately the government officials were the losers, as after 1825 they were debarred from having any interest in newspaper production.

Within six years of Hicky's venture, there were four weeklies and a monthly in Calcutta. But most papers were short-lived; only seven of those founded between 1780 and 1800 survived for twenty years or more: the *India Gazette/Calcutta Public Advertiser* (1780–1834), *Calcutta Gazette or Oriental Advertiser* (1784–1818), *Asiatic Mirror* (1788–1820), *Oriental Star* (1793–1820), *Calcutta Monthly Journal* (1794–1841), *Bengal Hircarrah* (1795–1866), and *Calcutta Morning Post* (1797–1818). Why this turnover? Mrinal Kanti Chanda speculates that an English press could hardly flourish if it depended only on a handful of colonial subscribers; in the 1830s only fifty thousand British-born subjects lived in India. Moreover, the English papers had practically no "native" subscribers; in 1843 the Rev. James Long could find only 125 for the leading papers of the time.[2]

Three English-language British papers established in the 1820s and 1830s had better survival rates: the pro-Government and pro-native *Bengal Hurkaru*, which took over from the *Bengal Hircarrah* in 1828; its formidable rival, the *Englishman* (1834–1934), which by the early 1850s was pro-British, bitterly anti-Indian, and supportive of the military and the indigo planters; and the Christian, pro-Western *Friend of India* (1818–present, in various iterations), which began as a missionary organ. Of these three papers, the *Hurkaru* was the most and the *Englishman* the least pro-Indian; and after 1875 the *Friend of India*, newly merged with the *Statesman*, strove to bring Europeans and Indians together.

The first Indian-owned English papers, the short-lived *Bengal Gazette* (1816; no copies survive) and the *Bengal Herald* (1829–1843), were reformist papers influenced by the teachings of Ram Mohan Roy. The same is partly true for the early Bengali press: the *Samācār Darpaṇ* (1818–1852) and *Digdarśan* (1818–?), missionary publications brought out by the Baptists at Serampore, spoke out against social evils and for social reform; initially the Brāhmos wrote for them. But then Bengalis felt the need to have an organ to counteract missionary teaching. Hence was born in December 1821 the *Sambād Kaumudī* (the voice of Roy and the liberals) and in March 1822 the *Samācār Candrikā* (the paper of the conservatives). The supporters of the latter included Rādhākānta Deb from the Shovabazar estate, who also helped established the Dharma Sabhā in 1830. As a mouthpiece of conservative Hindu society, the *Samācār Candrikā* also publicized the Pūjās, festivals, and ceremonies of the Hindu community while simultaneously arguing against the spread of Western education and the movement to abolish *sati*.

Between 1818 and 1839, 38 Bengali and 33 English papers were founded by Indians; between 1838 and 1857, 104 papers and periodicals came out. Again, most were short-lived; only the *Tattvabodhinī Patrikā* (1839–1932) had any longevity, because of its loyal Brāhmo supporters. These papers in general were concerned with political, economic, socio-religious, and educational issues. Some were literary or scientific journals. Political issues addressed included the Indianization of higher branches of the administration, racial discrimination, economic exploitation, poverty, and administrative failures and abuses. During this time the Indian press may have been anti-government, but not anti-British, and there was no suggestion that British rule be ended.

In general, until 1857 the proprietors and editors of the English papers under European management were generally sympathetic toward the Indian press. The *Calcutta Journal* quoted from the *Samācār Candrikā*, the *Sambād Kaumudī*, and the *Mirāt-ul-Ākhbar*, Roy's Persian paper. In fact, the presses of both communities worked together to pass through Act XI of 1835, by which Sir Charles Metcalfe freed the press. Indian-run papers were not quite as conciliatory toward the Anglo-Indian press. The *Hindoo Patriot* (1854–1922), begun by friends of the playwright Girish Chandra Ghosh, was the voice of the zamindars' Indian British Association in their critique of the Company and the indigo planters; it also castigated the *Englishman* for its anti-native tone. However, it looked to Parliament and the British public for justice.

It was the Rebellion of 1857 that drove a wedge between English- and Indian-owned newspapers, as the former—particularly the *Friend of India*, the *Englishman*, and even the pro-native *Bengal Hurkaru*—indulged in post-Rebellion bloodthirsty racial invectives, ferocious tirades, and a chorus of cries for blood and revenge. The *Hurkaru* ceased publication in 1866, but its pre-1857 pro-Indian stance was taken up in 1875 with the merging of the *Friend of India* and *Statesman* by British journalist Robert Knight, who was extremely critical of the government. Alone among the British press, Knight vigorously protested when Surendranath Banerjea was charged with and convicted for contempt of court for an article published in the *Bengalee*, and it was the *Statesman*, again alone, that welcomed the formation of the Indian National Congress in 1885. This liberal perspective was followed all the way up to Independence, with famous editors Arthur Moore (up to 1942) and Ian Stephens (1942–1951) sympathetic to Indian political grievances.

By the early 1880s, several Indian-owned English papers founded in the years soon after 1857 were strong and influential: the *Bengalee* (1858–1932), established by Surendranath Banerjea; *Amrita Bazar Patrika* (1867–present), born as a Bengali weekly in the village of Amrita Bazar in Jessore district to fight the cause of peasants exploited by their indigo planter-landlords; the

*Hindoo Patriot*; and the *Indian Mirror* (1861–1889), run from 1871 by the Brāhmo Keshab Chandra Sen. All of these papers were dominated by Moderate politics, then current in the thirty to forty years after the Rebellion, although the *Amrita Bazar Patrika* began to move in a more overtly nationalist direction after it was forced, in 1878, to escape Lord Edward Lytton's strictures against the vernacular press by becoming, overnight, an English weekly.

The furor over the first partition of Bengal threw up a number of short-lived anti-British, "Extremist" Bengali and English papers: *Bande Mataram* (1906–1908), founded by Bipin Chandra Pal and Aurobindo Ghose, the latter of whom was sarcastically critical of Moderate Indian papers such as the *Bengalee* and the *Indian Mirror*; Brahmobandhab Upādhyāya's *Sandhyā* (1904–1907), *Nabaśakti* (1907–1908), and the most resolutely violent of all, *Yugāntar* (1906–1908). Most of these were suppressed. Interestingly, the partition controversy split the British residents of Calcutta: the Anglo-Indian press, chiefly the *Englishman*, vilified Lord Curzon for departing from the traditions of British rule, while he tried, unsuccessfully, to curb their editors' blatant racial prejudice.

After World War I and the new political leadership of Mohandas Gandhi, several changes occurred in the press. The two most influential papers were, in English, the *Statesman* and *Amrita Bazar Patrika*, both widely read by nationalists. From 1922 and 1937, respectively, the Bengali *Ānanda Bājār Patrikā* and a rejuvenated *Yugāntar* joined the market; these two remain today the largest circulated Bengali dailies. In the early 1930s, however, two English-language papers died deaths of political irrelevancy: the *Bengalee*, which lost support in the Gandhian era for its Moderate stance; and the *Englishman*, whose pro-British policies (in 1919, for example, the *Englishman* contributed for a fund to aid General Reginald Dyer) were deemed, even by the British, to be too extreme.

# Notes

## Preface

1. Along the way I have published two other essays that derive from this same material: "A Festival for Jagaddhātrī and the Power of Localized Religion in West Bengal," in *Breaking Boundaries with the Goddess: New Directions in the Study of Śāktism. Essays in Honor of Narendra Nath Bhatacharyya*, ed. Cynthia Ann Humes and Rachel Fell McDermott (New Delhi: Manohar, 2009), pp. 201–222; and "Playing with Durgā: Ritual Levity in Bengal," in *Sacred Play: Ritual Levity and Humor in South Asian Religions*, ed. Selva J. Raj and Corinne G. Dempsey (Albany: State University of New York Press, 2010), pp. 143–159.

## Introduction

1. Each year Bengali almanacs predict by what conveyance Umā will return home from Kailasa: if she chooses either a boat or an elephant, the following year will enjoy plentiful rain and harvest; but if it is a palanquin (*dolā*) or a horse, there will be pestilence, disorder, and anarchy. Nowadays, of course, she also comes on a lorry! See Bimalcandra Datta, *Durgā Pūjā: Sekāl theke Ekāl* (Calcutta: Ramakrishna Vivekananda Institute of Research and Culture, 1986), p. 140.

2. *Rājās* were titled landowners, not literally "kings," but wealthy estate landowners, or zamindars, who were granted by the Mughals and later by the British hereditary jurisdiction over revenue collection in their properties.

3. Some years, due to the variations of the lunar calendar, Durgā Pūjā extends over five solar days.

4. The springtime worship of Durgā, Bāsantī Pūjā, probably predates the autumn festival, as the latter is always called "untimely" and as there is nothing about the autumn in the "Devī-Māhātmya" 's instructions for the worship of the Goddess. For references to the Rāma tradition, see Datta, *Durgā Pūjā: Sekāl theke Ekāl*, chapter 2, "Pūjā Prasanga." Some Bengali families still celebrate Durgā Pūjā in spring, without the *akāl bodhan*; *Telegraph*, 13 April 2008, Metro section, p. 1.

5. Refer to Joguth Chunder Gangooly, *Life and Religion of the Hindoos, with a Sketch of My Life and Experience* (Boston: Crosby, Nichols, Lee, and Co., 1860); S. C. Bose, *The Hindoos as They Are (A Description of the Manners, Customs, and Inner life of Hindoo Society in Bengal* (Calcutta: Thacker, Spink, and Co., 1883); Pratap Chandra Ghosha, *Durga Puja, with Note and Illustrations* (Calcutta: Hindoo Patriot Press, 1871); Pandurang Vaman Kane, *History of Dharmasastra*, 6 vols., 2nd ed., vol. V, pt. 1 (Poona: Bhandarkar Research Institute, 1974); Shiṅgo Einoo, "The Autumn Goddess Festival: Described in the Purāṇas," in *Living with Śakti: Gender, Sexuality, and Religion in South Asia*, ed. Masakazu Tanaka and Musashi Tachikawa (Osaka: National Museum of Ethnology, 1999), pp. 33–70; Hillary Peter Rodrigues, *Ritual Worship of the Great Goddess: The Liturgy of the Durgā Pūjā with Interpretations* (Albany: State University of New York Press, 2003); Madhu Khanna, "The Ritual Capsule of Durgā Pūjā: An Ecological Perspective," in *Hinduism and Ecology: The Intersection of Earth, Sky, and Water*, ed. Christopher Key Chapple and Mary Evelyn Tucker (Cambridge: Harvard University Press, 2006), pp. 479–485; and Ralph W. Nicholas, *Night of the Gods: Durga Puja and Authority in Rural Bengal* (Calcutta: Chronicle Books, 2012).

6. Durgā Pūjā is not generally Tantric, although there are old family traditions that do incorporate Tantric elements—for instance, the Mallas of Biṣṇupur, as discussed in Nancy Auer Falk, "Mata, Land, and Line: Female Divinity and the Forging of Community in India," in *Invoking Goddesses: Gender Politics in Indian Religion*, ed. Nilima Chitgopekar (Delhi: Shakti Books, 2002), pp. 161–162.

7. See Roger Caillois, *Men, Play, and Games*, trans. Meyer Barash (1958; Urbana: University of Illinois Press, 2001); Tom E. Driver, *The Magic of Ritual: Our Need for Liberating Rites That Transform Our Lives and Our Communities* (San Francisco: Harper San Francisco, 1991); and Johan Huizinga, *Homo Ludens: A Study of the Play Element in Culture* (1938; Boston: Beacon Press, 1955). See also my "Playing with Durgā: Ritual Levity in Bengal," in *Sacred Play: Ritual Levity and Humor in South Asian Religions*, ed. Selva J. Raj and Corinne G. Dempsey (Albany: State University of New York Press, 2010), pp. 143–159.

## 1. Pūjā Origins and Elite Politics

1. *Bengal Hurkaru*, 10 Oct. 1825, p. 2.

2. On the two hymns to Durgā in the *Mahābhārata*, see Kunal Chakrabarti, *Religious Process: The Purāṇas and the Making of a Regional Tradition* (New Delhi: Oxford University Press, 2001), p. 216 n. 27. For Kṛttibās's Bengali text, see *Rāmāyaṇ Kṛttibās Biracita*, ed. Harakṛṣṇa Mukhopādhyāy (Calcutta: Sāhitya Saṁsad, 1957), pp. 384–385.

3. For many of these references, see Chakrabarti, *Religious Process*, p. 334 n. 72, and vol. 2 of Rajendra Chandra Hazra, *Studies in the Upapurāṇas*, 2 vols. (Calcutta: Sanskrit College, 1963).

4. See the *Devī* and *Bhaviṣya Purāṇas*, as discussed in Pratap Chandra Ghosha, *Durga Puja, With Notes and Illustrations* (Calcutta: Hindoo Patriot Press, 1871), pp. 15–16, and Pandurang Vaman Kane, *History of Dharmaśāstra*, 6 vols., 2nd ed. (Poona: Bhandarkar Research Institute, 1974), vol. V, pt. 1, p. 157.

5. Kane, *History of Dharmaśāstra*, vol. V, pt. 1, p. 157 n. 401.

6. *Rāmacarita* III.25; see *Rāmacaritam of Sandhyākaranandin*, ed. Haraprasad Sastri, revised with an English translation and notes by Radhagovinda Basak (Calcutta: Asiatic Society, 1969), p. 70.

7. For discussion of these digests and their contents, see Bimalcandra Datta, *Durgā Pūjā: Sekāl theke Ekāl* (Calcutta: Ramakrishna Vivekananda Institute of Research and Culture, 1986), pp. 43–46; and Hazra, *Studies in the Upapurāṇas*. Note that Śūlapāṇi, Vidyāpati, and Raghunandana mention various earlier exponents of Durgā Pūjā, some from as far back as the eleventh or twelfth centuries during the Pāla period, but none of their texts have come down to us. In spite of the veneration accorded the *Bṛhannandikeśvara Purāṇa*, the text itself is not extant, but is inferred from various quotations preserved in the Pūjā digests of Vidyāpati, Raghunandana, and others. See ibid., pp. 466–469.

8. Pratapaditya Pal, *Hindu Religion and Iconology According to the Tantrasāra* (Los Angeles: Vichitra Press, 1981), p. 11.

9. Vṛndāvanadāsa, *Śrīśrīcaitanyabhāgavata*, Bengali text in Devanagari script, 3 vols. (Vṛndāvana: Śrīcaitanya Gauḍīya Maṭha, 1997–2003), 2:608.

10. See *Kabikaṅkaṇ Caṇḍī* (Calcutta: Basumatī-Sāhitya-Saṁsad, 1963), section called "Phullanār Bilāp," p. 114.

11. From the nineteenth-century ballad entitled "Santi": "In every house the divine mother Durga is worshipped." "The merchant brought from his treasures the best jewels, precious stones, and gold ornaments and with great taste, adorned the girls, just as people adorn the figure of the goddess Durga during the month of October" (Dineshchandra Sen, *Eastern Bengal Ballads, Mymensing*, 4 vols. [Calcutta: University of Calcutta, 1923–1932], vol. 2 [1926], pp. 127 and 175). See also "Malua" and "Kamala" in vol. 1 (1923), pp. 67 and 134.

12. See B. N. Mukherjee, "Foreign Elements in Iconography of Mahishāsuramardinī—The War Goddess of India," in *Zeitschrift der Deutschen Morgenländischen Gesellschaft* (Stuttgart: Franz Steiner, 1985), suppl. 6, pp. 402–414.

13. Hazra, *Studies in the Upapurāṇas*, pp. 17–26, has an excellent discussion of the evidence for Devī's association with tribal peoples and customs. Kunal Chakrabarti, in his *Religious Process*, pp. 173–185, examines Risley's nineteenth-century overview of Bengali tribes and castes and finds the overwhelming presence of goddesses in their worship. He also demonstrates that the Purāṇas acknowledged Bengal's association with such goddesses before the process of Brahmanization began.

14. Studies of Santals (Sāotāls in Bengali) living in West Bengal (these comprise half of the tribal people in the state) indicate that Hindu deities such as Kālī, Dibi (Durgā), Mahādeva (Śiva), and Gaṅgā find a place among household spirits (*orak bon-*

*gas* in Santali), *ojhas*' tutelary spirits (*saket bongas*), and the Santal pantheon of deities (*deku bongas*). See A. B. Chaudhuri, *Witch-Killings Amongst Santals* (New Delhi: Ashish Publishing House, 1984), pp. 107 and 141; M. K. Raha, "Religious Beliefs and Practices Among the Santals," in *To Be with Santals*, ed. Ujjwal Kanti Ray, Amal Kumar Das, and Sunil Kumar Basu (Calcutta: Government of West Bengal: Cultural Research Institute, Scheduled Castes and Tribes Welfare Department, 1982), pp. 49–58; and J. Troisi, *Tribal Religion: Religious Beliefs and Practices Among the Santals* (New Delhi: Manohar, 1978), pp. 79 and 91. But these are widely held to be nontribal additions to the spiritual realm; some scholars see the sponsorship of Durgā Pūjā in particular to be a direct result of the movement into tribal areas of Bengali and Oriya officials after 1857; they celebrated the festivals to "ingratiate themselves with the locals." See Gauri Charan Banerjee, "Durga Puja in the Aboriginal Tracts," in *Amrita Bazar Patrika*, 3 Oct. 1926, p. 30.

15. Called the Dasae Festival, this three-day ritual culminates in a special dance for village men who have passed the training to become *ojhas*, or medicine men. The interface between this tribal celebration and Durgā Pūjā is visible both in the fact that men dance from village to village, stopping at any house or pandal where caste Hindus are worshiping Durgā, and in the legends told to explain the origin of the dance: a great Santal warrior named Hodor-Durga was killed under a *bel* tree by a white-complexioned woman from another tribe, who took the name of her vanquished foe. Then she started attacking Santal villages, and the men dressed as women to avoid being killed by her. Tribal peoples who worship Dibi as their household deity may also go visit Durgā pandals for *darśan*. See S. K. Basu, "Santal Festivals," in *To Be with Santals*, pp. 73–80; S. Chakraborti, "The Dansaey Festival of the Santals," in *To Be with Santals*, pp. 81–89; and Troisi, *Tribal Religion*, pp. 214–216.

16. Amita Ray, "The Cult and Ritual of Durgā Pūjā in Bengal," in *Shastric Traditions in Indian Arts*, ed. Anna Libera Dallapiccola in collaboration with Christine Walter-Mendy and Stephanie Zingel-Avé Lallemant (Stuttgart: Steiner Verlag Wiesbaden GMBH, 1989), p. 140; and Śyāmalkānti Cakrabartī, "Durgā: Anya o Banya," in *Lok Saṁskṛti Gabeṣaṇā*, ed. Sanatkumār Mitra, vol. 13, no. 2 (July–Aug. 2000): 308–313.

17. Traditionally the advent of Brahmanism is traced in Bengal to the post-Gupta period with the invitation by King Ādisura to five Brahmans from Kanauj between 732 and 1017. For further discussion, see Ray, "The Cult and Ritual of Durgā Pūjā in Bengal," p. 133. For an excellent survey of the way in which local goddesses were appropriated for the purpose of achieving Brahmanical social dominance in Bengal, consult Chakrabarti, *Religious Process*, pp. 165–233. A possible hint of Durgā's older, mountainous, and potentially tribal origins may be found in the earlier presence of the tiger in two venerable zamindar families of north Bengal: the bloodred Kuch Bihar goddess has both a lion and a tiger mount, and the Jalpaiguri Durgā sat on a tiger, although over time the lion replaced it; Mohit Roy, *Rūpe Rūpe Durgā* (Calcutta: Adhīr Pāl, 1985), pp. 30–34 and 59–63.

18. See Sumita Mukherjee and Dr. Robin D. Tribhuwan, "Influences of Kali Puja Festival on Tribals of West Bengal," in *Fairs and Festivals of Indian Tribes*, ed. Robin David Tribhuwan (New Delhi: Discovery Publishing House, 2003), p. 119.

19. John R. McLane, *Land and Local Kingship in Eighteenth-Century Bengal* (Cambridge: Cambridge University Press, 1993), p. 109, and Kāliprasanna Sinha, *Hutom*

*Pyāncār Nakśa*, 2nd ed., with commentary (1868; Calcutta: Subarṇarekhā, 1991), p. 235 n. 549.

20. Datta, *Durgā Pūjā: Sekāl theke Ekāl*, p. 111.

21. Sudhīndranāth Bhaṭṭācārya, "Bāṅgālīr Durgotsab," *Śāradīya Utsab* (1406), p. 38, quoted in Ābdur Rauph, "Durgā: Bāṅgāli Musulmān," in *Lok Saṁskṛti Gabeṣaṇā*, ed. Sanatkumār Mitra, vol. 13, no. 2 (July–Aug. 2000): 284–285. "Bābu" is both an honorific title attached to a gentleman's first name and a satirical label for a foppish dandy who—as he was caricatured in the nineteenth century—spent his time and money attempting to imitate the English.

22. This claim for Rājā Kṛṣṇacandra Rāy is made by the *Calcutta Journal*, 7 Oct. 1820, pp. 366–367; the *Samācār Darpaṇ* newspaper of 17 Oct. 1829; and Sinha, *Hutom Pyāncār Nakśa*, p. 235 n. 1. It is possible that Kṛṣṇacandra saw himself in continuity with Kaṁsanārāyaṇ, as he had his own court pandits make the Durgā Pūjā ritual prescriptions, as originally devised by Rameś Śāstrī, the court pandit of Udaynārāyaṇ, the grandson of Kaṁsanārāyaṇ, easier to follow. Bhāratcandra, Kṛṣṇacandra's famous court poet, says of his patron in the introductory section to the first part of his *Annadāmaṅgal* poem, written in 1752–53, that "all the people call Kṛṣṇacandra 'devīputra,' or 'the son of the Goddess' "; Bhāratcandra's editor notes that this is because he used to celebrate the Pūjās with such pomp. See *Bhāratcandrer Annadāmaṅgal*, ed. Nirmalendu Mukhopādhyāy (Calcutta: Modern Book Agency, 1986), p. 15 n. 2. William Ward, while not asserting that Kṛṣṇacandra was the first to initiate this Pūjā, notes that his grandson, Rājā Īśvarcandra, offered 65,535 goats during the course of one three-day festival during the late eighteenth century; William Ward, *A View of the the History, Literature, and Mythology of the Hindoos*, 4 vols., 3rd ed. (1817; Delhi: Low Price Publications, 1990) 3:116 n.

23. One can find numerous references to the celebration of Durgā Pūjā in the eighteenth century. Bimalcandra Datta, for example, devotes a whole chapter of his *Durgā Pūjā: Sekāl theke Ekāl* to early Pūjās in Calcutta (pp. 109–137), and quotes a travel report from James Mitchell, a British clerk, to a sea captain, who describes the Pūjās as he saw them in 1748 (pp. 261–262). J. Z. Holwell's travel account also testifies to the popularity of the festival in the 1760s; see *Événemens historique interéssans, relatifs aux provinces de Bengale, & à l'empire de l'Indostan*, trans. from the English (Amsterdam: Arkstée & Merkus, 1768), pp. 151–154.

24. A *nawāb* was a viceroy or governor of a province who was responsible for law and order.

25. It was the Treaty of Allahabad, concluded in 1765 between Clive and Emperor Shāh 'Ālām II, that gave the British the power to introduce truly drastic changes in the administration of Bengal. Under this agreement the Emperor made the Company the *dewān* of Bengal, Orissa, and Bihar, in exchange for 2,600,000 rupees a year in tribute. The Muslim *nawābs* were to retain the responsibility for defense and law, but in actual fact they were chosen by the Company and were stripped of revenue and military power.

26. *Calcutta Journal*, 7 Oct. 1820, pp. 366–367. A different twist on this argument is presented by other nineteenth-century newspapers, which blame Muslim religious feeling less than the conditions of lawlessness that pertained under their rule.

For example, "[I]n days when spoilation and plunder were practiced with impunity, when robbery and theft were committed in the broad daylight of the sun, or in other words, when the security of property was unprovided by any form of government, it was generally unsafe for the people to make a show of their wealth either by adopting a pleasant and comfortable mode of living, or laying it out in some commercial speculation" (from "An Account of the Denajpoor Raj Family," 2 April 1857, from the *Hindoo Patriot*, cited in Benoy Ghosh, *Selections from English Periodicals of Nineteenth-Century Bengal*, vol. 4: 1857 [Calcutta: Papyrus, 1979], p. 28).

27. Robert Orme, *Historical Fragments of Mogul Empire* (1781; London: F. Wingrave, 1805), pp. 450–451, quoted by Shirin Akhtar in *The Role of the Zamindars in Bengal, 1707–1772* (Dacca: Asiatic Society of Bangladesh, 1982), p. 33. Luke Scrafton also described the "Mahometan governors" looking upon the riches of their subjects "as a boy does on a bird's nest; he eyes their progress with impatience, then comes with a spoiler's hand, and ravishes the fruit of their labour. To counter-act this, the Gentoos bury their money under ground" (Luke Scrafton, *Reflections on the Government of Indostan, with a Short Sketch of the History of Bengal, from 1739 to 1756, and An Account of the English Affairs to 1758* [London, 1763; reprinted London: W. Strahan Ivb., 1770], letter 1, p. 16).

28. "The Territorial Aristocracy of Bengal—The Nadiya Raj," in *Calcutta Review* 55, no. 109 (1872), pp. 93–94.

29. Kesab Chandra Sarkar, interview, 2 Oct. 2000.

30. Aparna Bhattacharya, *Religious Movements of Bengal (1800–1850)* (Patna: Aparna Bhattacharya, 1981), pp. 98–99.

31. *Records of Government*, June 27, 1757, H.H.S. 193, 170–171, quoted in Akhtar, *The Role of the Zamindars*, p. 107.

32. Mīr Qāsim imprisoned Rājā Baidyanāth, Rājā Rāmnārāyaṇ, Rājā Rājballabh, and the Hindu financier Jagat Seṭh in Mongir Fort, Bihar. He had Rāmnārāyaṇ drowned with a sack tied around his neck, Jagat Seṭh was rolled into the river from the ramparts of the fort, and Rājballabh was flayed alive. Baidyanāth bribed the prison guard, however, and escaped. See *Hindoo Patriot*, 9 April 1857, cited in Ghosh, *Selections from English Periodicals*, p. 31.

33. Nirad C. Chaudhuri makes this point about the benefits of the Permanent Settlement in the *Statesman*, 4 Oct. 1953, Puja Supplement, p. 1. For more information on the Permanent Settlement, see: Sirajul Islam, *Permanent Settlement in Bengal: A Study of Its Operation, 1790–1819* (Dacca: Bangla Academy, 1979); J. R. McLane, "Revenue Farming and the Zamindari System in Eighteenth Century Bengal," in *Land Tenure and Peasant in South Asia*, ed. R. E. Frykenberg (New Delhi: Orient Longman, 1979); Ratnalekha Roy, *Change in Bengal Agrarian Society, c. 1760–1850* (Delhi: Manohar, 1979), pp. 73–88; N. K. Sinha, *Economic History of Bengal*, 2 vols. (Calcutta: Firma K. L. Mukhopadhyay, 1962), 2:147–182; and N. K. Sinha, "Administrative, Economic, and Social History, 1757–1793," in his *History of Bengal (1757–1905)* (Calcutta: University of Calcutta, 1967), pp. 96–105.

34. 17 Oct. 1829, quoted in Datta, *Durgā Pūjā: Sekāl theke Ekāl*, p. 192 n. 1.

35. McLane, *Land and Local Kingship*, p. 119. In the second quotation he is citing a statement by C. A. Bayly.

36. See A. B. Mahmood, *The Revenue Administration of Northern Bengal, 1765–1793* (Dacca: National Institute of Public Administration, 1970), p. 36.

37. Rājā Baidyanāth of Dinajpur [Board of Revenue Consultations, 17 Sept. 1773, R49/41, 3088–3089], in Akhtar, *The Role of the Zamindars*, p. 188 n. 6. Baidyanāth's adopted son, Rādhānāth, died at age 24, a virtual prisoner in his own house. The British at the time claimed that he was so profligate a spender that they had to sell off half his estates to meet his revenue arrears, but a later commentator writes that "it is probable that the increase of strictness with which the collections were made [after 1772] was the true cause of the decline in which the family had lived under its Mahomedan masters." See E. V. Westmacott, "The Territorial Aristocracy of Bengal—The Dinagepoor Raj," in *Calcutta Review* 55, no. 109 (1872): 217. A similar letter of protest to the Company was received from the Rājā of Jessore, who asked for an advance on his allowance to defray the expenses of Durgā Pūjā and expressed anxiety for the preservation of the dignity of his family; S. Charter to Bengal Revenue Consultation [13 Sept. 1773, BRC Sept. 17, 1773, R49/41, 3087], in Akhtar, *The Role of the Zamindars*, p. 189 n. 1.

38. Tejascānd, zamindar of Burdwan from 1770 to 1832, wrote to the collector of Burdwan, S. Davis, whom he succeeded in winning over to his cause, the following: "It must have proceeded from the oversight, rather than from any just and avowed principle, that there should be established two methods of judicial process under the same government, the one summary and efficient for the satisfaction of its own claims, the other tardy and uncertain in regard to the satisfaction of claims due to its subjects, more especially in a case like the present, where ability to discharge the one demand necessarily depends on the other demand being previously realized" (quoted by S. Islam, *Permanent Settlement in Bengal*, p. 52). The *rājās* of Nadia and Bishnupur made similar objections.

39. This change had to be vetted by the British. In Bankura in 1793, after the Malla *rājās* could no longer afford to keep up the Pūjās, people belonging to all castes and strata of society apparently applied to the East India Company bosses to allow then to collect money and do a Pūjā. See Pradīpkumār Ghoṣ, "Durgā: Mallabhūmer," in *Lok Saṁskṛti Gabeṣaṇā*, ed. Sanatkumār Mitra, vol. 13, no. 2 (July–Aug. 2000): 347–355.

40. Bhāskara, the leader of the Mārāṭhas, attempted to celebrate the festival with the help of the local zamindars. He was routed by the *nawāb*'s army after the eighth day of the Pūjā, however. See Edward C. Dimock Jr., and Pratul Chandra Gupta, trans., *The Mahārāshṭa Purāṇa: An Eighteenth-Century Historical Text* (Chicago: University of Chicago Press, 1967), p. 40. Regarding the British, "the most amazing act of worship was performed by the East India Company itself: in 1765 it offered a thanksgiving *pūjā*, no doubt as a politic act to appease its Hindu subjects, on obtaining the Diwani of Bengal (including Bihar and Orissa). The sum spent is cited variously as having been between Rs. 5,000 and Rs. 30,000" (see Kalyani Dutta, "Kalighat," in *Calcutta, the Living City*, ed. Sukanta Chaudhuri, vol. 1: *The Past* [Calcutta: Oxford University Press, 1990], p. 25).

41. Mahmood, *Revenue Administration*, p. 219.

42. As an example of the changing styles of leadership under the *nawābs*, consider the case of the Dinajpur Rāj. As Westmacott tells it (in the late nineteenth century), in the initial stages of the Mughal reign over Bengal (i.e., until the end of Akbar's reign in 1657), and even until the beginning of Dinajpur Rājā Prāṇnāth's

reign in 1682, the Hindus had plenty of opportunity to make themselves wealthy and powerful, because no one was watching very carefully. As long as the zamindar paid a certain portion of his rents, he was left alone. But it was in the reign of Prāṇnāth in 1702 that things changed, with the coming of Mīr Ja'far, who "bestowed great attention on the affairs of the province of which he was governor" (see E. V. Westmacott, "The Dinagepoor Raj," p. 214).

43. Brijen K. Gupta, *Sirajuddaullah and the East India Company, 1756–1757: Background to the Foundation of British Power in India* (Leiden: Brill, 1966), p. 30.

44. Note that no matter what the outside structures, the insides of these homes were typically modeled after an Indian palace as influenced by the Mughal court, with separate living quarters for men and women, offices, drawing rooms, servants' quarters, and stables.

45. American silk traders were so pleased with the products furnished them by the trader Rāmdulāl De that they presented his family with a full-sized portrait of George Washington, which was in the house for eighty-five years before being purchased by Warner Brothers. At present it hangs at Washington and Lee University. See Manish Chakraborti, "Beadon Ballads," *Times of India*, "Calcutta Times" section, 6 March 2001, p. 4.

46. See Apūrba Caṭṭopādhyāy, "Ālor Banyāy Bhāsbe Jagaddhātrīr Candannagar," and Premtoṣ De, "Candanagarer Jagaddhātrī Pujo," both in *Sāptahik Bartamān* 12, no. 25 (13 Nov. 1999), pp. 11–12 and 8–10; and *Yugāntar*, 1 Nov. 1995, p. 7.

47. In the "Devī-Māhātmya" section of the *Mārkaṇḍeya Purāṇa*, the Goddess is called Jagaddhātrī twice (1.53, 13.10), Jagatam Dhātrī once (4.27), and Dhātrī once (5.8). See Thomas B. Coburn, *The Devī-Māhātmya: Crystallization of the Goddess Tradition* (New Delhi: Motilal Banarsidass, 1985), pp. 205–206. In *Devī-Bhāgavata Purāṇa* 6.6, Jagaddhātrī is one of several epithets used for the deluding goddess to whom the gods go in supplication for help against the demon Vṛtra. See *The Srimad Devi Bhagawatam*, ed. and trans. Swami Vijñanananda, 2 pts., 2nd ed. (New Delhi: Oriental Books Reprint, 1977), pp. 495–499.

48. See *Kāmākhyā Tantram*, Sanskrit text edited with a Bengali translation by Jyotirlāl Dās (Calcutta: Nababhārat, 1978), p. 78; *Kubjikā Tantram*, Sanskrit text edited with a Bengali translation by Jyotirlāl Dās (Calcutta: Nababhārat, 1978), p. 33; and *Kālikā Purāṇam*, Sanskrit text edited with an English translation by Biswanarayan Shastri, 3 vols. (Delhi: Nag Publishers, 1991), 2:466–467.

49. For the original Sanskrit, see Hamsanārāyaṇ Bhaṭṭācārya, *Hinduder Debadebī: Udbhav o Kramabikāś* (Calcutta: Firma KLM, 1986), 3:308, and Pal, *Hindu Religion and Iconology*, p. 42.

50. Narendra Nath Bhattacharyya, *History of Śākta Religion* (New Delhi: Munshiram Manoharlal, 1973), p. 135; and Ajit Kumar Mukhopadhay and Kalyan Chakrabortty, *Discover Chandernagore* (Chandannagar, Hooghly: Kumar Printers, 1999), accessed online 11/01/03.

51. Bhaṭṭācārya, *Hinduder Debadebī: Udbhav o Kramabikāś*, pp. 308–311.

52. For corroborating opinions, see Mahendranāth Datta, *Kalikātār Purātan Kāhinī o Prarthā*, 2nd ed. (1973; Kalikata: Mahendra Publishing Committee, 1975), pp. 130–131, and *Yugāntar*, 1 Nov. 1995, p. 7.

53. For a more detailed discussion of Jagaddhātrī Pūjā, see my "A Festival for Jagaddhātrī and the Power of Localized Religion in West Bengal," in *Breaking Boundaries with the Goddess: New Directions in the Study of Śāktism. Essays in Honor of Narendra Nath Bhattacharyya*, ed. Cynthia Ann Humes and Rachel Fell McDermott (New Delhi: Manohar, 2009), pp. 201–222.

54. Rajat Sanyal, *Voluntary Associations and the Urban Public Life in Bengal (1815-1876): An Aspect of Social History* (Calcutta: Riddhi-India, 1980), pp. 42–65.

55. Chitra Deb, "The 'Great Houses' of Old Calcutta," in *Calcutta, the Living City*, vol. I: *The Past*, ed. Sukanta Chaudhuri (Calcutta: Oxford University Press, 1990), p. 61.

56. Ibid., p. 58.

57. See Soumitra Das, "Memories of Our Past Splendour," *Statesman*, 15 Oct. 1983, p. 13.

58. *South Asia Research* 6, no. 2 (Nov. 1986): 123–138. See also Mukherjee, "Foreign Elements in Iconography of Mahishāsuramardinī," pp. 404–415.

59. Sanjukta Gupta, pers. comm., August 2001.

60. Gupta and Gombrich, "Kings, Power, and the Goddess," p. 132.

61. C. J. Fuller, *The Camphour Flame: Popular Hinduism and Society in India* (Princeton: Princeton University Press, 1992), pp. 108–127.

62. See Gupta and Gombrich, "Kings, Power, and the Goddess," p. 134; and *Bartamān*, 22 Oct. 2001, p. 11.

63. Gupta and Gombrich, "Kings, Power, and the Goddess," pp. 134–135.

64. See Pierre Bourdieu's classic *La distinction: Critique sociale du jugement* (1979), translated by Richard Nice as *Distinction: A Social Critique of the Judgement of Taste* (Cambridge, MA: Harvard University Press, 1984); Jun Jing, "Knowledge, Organization, and Symbolic Capital: Two Temples to Confucius in Gansu," in *On Sacred Grounds: Culture, Society, Politics, and the Formation of the Cult of Confucius*, ed. Thomas A. Wilson (Harvard East Asian Monographs 217) (Cambridge, MA: Harvard University Press, 2002), pp. 335–375; Sanjay Subrahmanyam, *The Career and Legend of Vasco da Gama* (New York: Oxford University Press, 1997); and Hugh B. Urban, *The Economics of Ecstasy: Tantra, Secrecy, and Power in Colonial Bengal* (New York: Oxford University Press, 2001).

65. L. de Grandpre, *A Voyage in the Indian Ocean and to Bengal Undertaken in the Years 1789 and 1790*, 2 vols. (Paris, 1801, and London, 1803), cited in P. T. Nair, ed., *Calcutta in the Eighteenth Century: Impressions of Travelers* (Calcutta: Firma KLM, 1984), p. 254.

66. Ibid.

67. *Calcutta Journal*, 22 Sept. 1819, p. 183.

68. Lady Maria Nugent reports on a nautch performance in 1812 at the home of "Rajah Raj Kissen," where "Neekhee and Ushoorun" surpassed her expectations; *A Journal from the Year 1811 til the Year 1815, including a Voyage to and Residence in India*, 2 vols. (London, 1839), cited in P. T. Nair, ed., *Calcutta in the Nineteenth Century: Company's Days* (Calcutta: Firma KLM, 1989), pp. 191–192. This love for nautch girls was not confined to the British in Calcutta; as William Dalrymple shows for late-eighteenth to early-nineteenth-century Lucknow, monied European gentlemen would spend their leisure time lying on carpets, smoking hubble-bubbles, and delightedly watching nautch girls; *White Mughals: Love and Betrayal in Eighteenth-Century India* (New

York: Penguin, 2004), p. 211. Dalrymple calls this period the age of the great courtesans and dancing girls (p. 135), citing it as "a libertarian moment in the country's recent history" (p. 173).

69. Some of the nouveaux riches wanted to display their cultured tastes through the patronage of new musical forms. Rājā Nabakṛṣṇa Deb, for example, was one of the first to showcase the *kabioyālās*, or traveling stand-up singers, in his home. See Rachel Fell McDermott, *Mother of My Heart, Daughter of My Dreams: Kālī and Umā in the Devotional Poetry of Bengal* (New York: Oxford University Press, 2001), p. 133; and Rāmratna Pāṭhak, *Durgotsab* (Calcutta: Nūtan Bhārata Yantre, 1281/1874), pp. 20–22. For a *yātrā* performed in 1821 in Chinsurah, see *Sambādpatre Sekāler Kathā*, ed. Brajendranāth Bandyopādhyāy, 3 vols. (Calcutta: Baṅgīya Sāhitya Pariṣad), vol. 1 (1818–1830), 2nd ed. (1339/1932; 1344/1937), p. 138.

70. For references to the early nineteenth century, see *Statesman*, 19 Oct. 1991, p. 3; *Statesman*, 29 Sept. 1995, p. 7; and *The Good Old Days of Honorable John Company*, compiled by William H. Carey (1882; Calcutta: Quins Book Co., 1964), p. 76.

71. This was one of the amusements provided on 11 Dec. 1820 in the home of Dwaraknath Tagore; Bandyopādhyāy, *Sambādpatre Sekāler Kathā*, vol. 1, pp. 138–139.

72. These were reported from "Baboo Gopee Mohun Deb's mansion"; *Bengal Hurkaru*, 11 Oct. 1826, p. 2.

73. *Bengal Harkaru and India Gazette*, 3 Oct. 1865, p. 3.

74. For descriptions of "Natives" trying to tempt Europeans with nautches, suppers, wine, and bands of music, see Carey, ed., *The Good Old Days of Honorable John Company*, pp. 258 and 418–419.

75. Soumitra Das, "Puja Arcades of Calcutta," *Statesman*, 26 Oct. 1982, p. 3.

76. See *Bengal Hurkaru*, 12 Oct. 1829, p. 2, and *Bengal Hurkaru*, 28 Sept. 1830, p. 2.

77. These *aṣṭadhātu* images were made of gold, silver, brass, copper, crystal, stone, and other types of mixed metals. Famed families from the late eighteenth and early nineteenth centuries who were reputed to have had them include Mahārājā Bāhādur Jaynārāyaṇ Ghoṣāl, an important official under Hastings who established a Pūjā to an *aṣṭadhātu* image in 1782; the Gobindarām Mitra family; and the Lāhās of Cornwallis Street. See Śibśaṅkar Bhāratī, "Kalkātār Durgā Pūjā, 1586–1951," in *Bartamān Rabibār*, 10 Oct. 1999, p. 10.

78. Bhattacharya, *Religious Movements of Bengal*, pp. 107–114; and Deb, "The 'Great Houses' of Old Calcutta," pp. 58–59.

79. For a clear description of this sanctification process, see Ghosha, *Durga Puja*, pp. 1–2.

80. I am indebted for this explanation to Minati Kar, pers. comm., 24 July 2001; see also Herman Kulke, "Rathas and Rajas: The Car Festival at Puri," in *Car Festival of Lord Jagannath, Puri*, ed. Sarat Chandra Mahapatra (Puri: Sri Jagannath Research Centre, 1994), p. 87.

81. *Sandhi pūjā* lasts from the last 24 minutes of Aṣṭamī to the first 24 minutes of Nabamī. During this period Durgā is worshiped in her Cāmuṇḍā form. In old families, a special bronze bowl with a tiny hole in it was placed in a bucket full of water. It took 24 minutes for the bowl to be totally submerged. The moment it sank, the cannon balls were fired.

82. For a description of these practices by the Nadia Rāj family in Krishnanagar, see Mohit Rāy, *Rūpe Rūpe Durgā* (Calcutta: Adhīr Pāl, 1985), pp. 1–7.

83. Ibid., p. 49.

84. She must be younger than nine years old, and is placed on a carpet, where she is offered lights, water, oil and turmeric, incense, cosmetics, sweetmeats, ornaments, and clothes. See Ghosha, *Durga Puja*, p. 74.

85. Indralāl Bandyopādhyāy, "Bibarṇa Kyānbhāse Sābarṇa Śāradā," *Sāptahik Bartamān*, 16 Oct. 1999, p. 31.

86. "*Caṇḍī, sapiṇḍī, kuśaṇḍī, tine niye bāmunḍi*"; from Bikāśkānti Midyā, "Durgā: Bāṅglā Lokasāhitye," in *Lok Saṁskṛti Gabeṣaṇā*, ed. Sanatkumār Mitra, vol. 13, no. 2 (July–Aug. 2000): 340.

87. The *Calcutta Review*, for example, devoted three entire articles in 1900–1901 to the "Religious and Charitable Endowments of Bengal Zemindars": vol. 111, nos. 221 and 222 (July and Oct. 1900): 79–100, 223–249, and vol. 112, no. 223 (Jan. 1901): 50–77. A cursory glance at the papers throughout the nineteenth century reveals the extent to which the British praised the elite for their charity. See, for example, *Englishman and Military Chronicle*, 17 Oct. 1844, p. 5; *Statesman and Friend of India*, 15 Sept. 1880, p. 3; and *Statesman and Friend of India*, 14 Oct. 1885, p. 3.

88. See *The Monthly Overland Englishman and Military Chronicle of Calcutta*, 17 Sept. 1844, p. 2.

89. Other members of the Dharma Sabhā include Kālīkṛṣṇa Deb (1808–1874), the second son of Rājkṛṣṇa Deb, son of Nabakṛṣṇa; the Sābarṇabānik Mallik families of Barabajar and Pathuriaghata; the Dattas of Hatkhola (social rivals of the Shovabazar Debs); and Rāmdulāl De's family—all of whom were avid Pūjā patrons. See Sanyal, *Voluntary Associations and the Urban Public Life in Bengal (1815–1876)*. Note that the Brāhmo Samāj and the Dharma Sabhā had the same social base, and both were equally politically loyal to British rule.

90. Anon., "Article III.—Radhakant Deb," *Calcutta Review* 44, no. 90 (Aug. 1867): 323.

91. Reported by Samrāṭ Basu for *Bartamān*, 21 Sept. 2002, p. 5.

92. Grandpre, *A Voyage in the Indian Ocean*, pp. 254–255.

93. Bipin Chandra Pal, *Memories of My Life and Times* (Calcutta: Bipinchandra Pal Institute, 1973), pp. 101, 104–105. The book covers Pal's life from 1857 to 1900.

94. *The Memoirs of Dr. Haimabati Sen: From Child Widow to Lady Doctor*, trans. Tapan Raychaudhuri, ed. Geraldine Forbes and Tapan Raychaudhuri (New Delhi: Lotus Collection, 2000), p. 70.

95. *Statesman*, 4 Oct. 1953, Puja Supplement, p. 1.

96. As early as 1820, a writer in the *Calcutta Journal* noted that the new *bāroiyārī* celebrations were not sanctioned by the *śāstras*; 7 Oct. 1820, pp. 366–367.

97. These were called *cāpāno* Pūjās, or those that were "loaded upon" their sponsors. See the *Bengal Spectator* for Oct. 15, quoted in *The Englishman and Military Chronicle*, 18 Oct. 1842, p. 2, and Nirmal Kar, "Cāpāno Pūjā," in *Ānanda Bājār Patrikā*, 27 Sept. 1998, p. 16. Mr. Maṇimohan Rāy Caudhurī, the senior member of one of the minor lines of the Sābarṇa Rāy Caudhurī family in Kolkata, told me that his grandfather had sponsored Jagaddhātrī Pūjā for four years following such an incident, but had afterward discontinued it. Interview, 14 Sept. 2000.

98. The Bengali originals for these sayings are: "*Janme hayni ghẽṭupūjo, ekebāre daśbhujo*"; "*Ghare nei bhujā bhāṅg, chõḍār nām Durgārām*"; "*Durgāpūjāy śākh bāje nā, Ṣaṣṭi Pūjāy ḍhāk*"; "*Guyāpāner janye Durgotsab bāki thāke nā*"; "*juṭā selāi theke caṇḍī-pāṭh*"; "*meye yeno āupātāli Duggā*"; and "*Āre O Gopāler nāti! Enechile Durgāmūrti, karbei to ei kīrti!.*" For the story about Gaṇeśa, see Midyā, "Durgā: Bāṅglā Lokasāhitye," p. 345.

99. Families whom I interviewed, always accompanied by Hena Basu, were Mr. Bhaskar Chunder, of Bowbazar, descendant of Pratap Chandra Chunder, whose family has been sponsoring the Pūjā since 1877; Mr. Śubhamay Dawn (Dã) and Mr. Amarnāth Dawn, both of Darjipara, spice merchants by caste (Gandhibaṇiks), one of whose ancestors initiated the Pūjā in 1760; Mrs. Gītā Datta, from one of the junior lines in the Hatkhola Datta family, which has worshiped Durgā since 1794; Mr. Milan Datta of the Thanthania Datta family, whose Pūjā was started in 1855 by Dvāraknāth Datta, a banian (merchant) of the export-import company Jardine, Skinner, and Co.; Mr. Kalyāṇkumār Deb, senior member of the family of Rāmdulāl De (alias Deb, alias Sarkār; also known as the Chātu-Bābu Lātu-Bābu family, after the Rāmdulāl's two famous sons), who started the Pūjā some time in the decade 1770–1780; Mrs. Ārati Deb and Mrs. Śephāli Bose, of the major line of the Shovabazar Rāj family, descended from Gopīmohan Deb, adopted son of Nabakṛṣṇa Deb (1733–1797), the tutor and secretary to Warren Hastings, who started his Pūjā in 1757 to celebrate Clive's victory at Plassey; Mr. Alok Kṛṣṇa Deb, senior member of the minor Shovabazar line, descended from Nabakṛṣṇa's natural son, Rājkṛṣṇa Deb, whose Pūjā has been celebrated yearly since 1790; Mr. Sujay Ganguli and his family, rice merchants settled in Chetla, who have been doing Durgā Pūjā since 1899; the office managers of the Pathuriaghata Street estate belonging to the family descended from Khelātcandra Ghoṣ, a noted zamindar and honorary justice of the peace, who founded the Pūjā in about 1840; Mr. Priya Gopāl Hājrā, of Janbazar, descendent of Śrī Rāmakṛṣṇa's patron, Rāṇī Rāsmaṇī, who continued the village Pūjā of her parents-in-law when she and her husband moved to Calcutta; Mr. Śiśir Mallik of Darpanarayan Tagore Street, whose Pūjā was started by a gold jeweler in the family approximately two hundred years ago; Mrs. Chāmeli Mitra, of the Nilmaṇi Mitras of Beadon Street, whose Pūjā was started by the successful businessman Durgācaraṇ Mitra more than two hundred years ago; and Mr. Maṇimohan Rāy Caudhurī, senior member of one of the junior lines of the famed Sābarṇa Rāy Caudhurī family, which claims to have been celebrating the Pūjā since 1610.

100. Swagata Bhattacharya, "Pride and Prejudice," *Statesman*, 25 Sept. 1998, Downtown section, p. 1.

101. Many elite families perform Jagaddhātrī Pūjā. Of the twelve representatives from the "old families" whom I interviewed in Kolkata, six (Mr. Priya Gopāl Hājrā, Mrs. Chāmeli Mitra, Mr. Kalyāṇkumār Deb, managers of the Khelātcandra Ghoṣ estate, Mr. Śubhamay Dawn, and Mr. Amarnāth Dawn), said that they worship Jagaddhātrī, but no one considered her a replacement for Durgā. The same is not true in Chandannagar and Krishnanagar, where many families esteem Jagaddhātrī Pūjā as the premier holiday of the year, and bypass Durgā Pūjā altogether.

102. *Banedi* (*baniyādi*, traditional, aristocratic) Pūjās were also referred to as *ekak* Pūjās, or those performed alone, without external financial help.

103. Reported by Samrāṭ Basu for *Bartamān*, 21 Sept. 2002, p. 5.

104. The Chetla Gangulis and Behala Sābarṇa Rāy Caudhurīs, Brahman families, told me that initiated women of their households do the cooking. By contrast, both houses of the Shovabazar Rāj, some would say the premier Pūjās of the city, hire up to fifty Brahman cooks each for the festival season. For a culinary overview, see Trina Mukherjee, "Eating Religiously," *Telegraph*, 28 Sept. 1998, section 3, p. 1.

105. See Ghosha, *Durgā Pūjā*, appendix, p. xxxix n. 25, on prescriptive leniency for Śūdras.

106. Interviews with Mr. Śiśir Mallik, 30 Sept. 2000, and Mr. Śubhamay Dawn, 5 Oct. 2000.

107. The Pataldanga Basumalliks are reputed to do so; see *Bartamān*, 22 Oct. 2001, p. 9.

108. *Kumārī pūjā* is a hallowed tradition in some quarters. The monks at Belur Maṭh, the headquarters of the Rāmakṛṣṇa Maṭh, have been doing it since 1901; the *kumārī* of the year is invariably photographed for the Kolkata newspapers in the act of being worshiped. Some families take pride in the fact that a Brahman girl is worshiped in their non-Brahman houses, and others differentiate themselves from their peers by performing the rite on all three days of the festival.

109. *Ānandabājār Patrikā*, Kolkata section, 26 Oct. 2001, p. 1.

110. Mrs. Chāmeli Mitra, of the Durgācaraṇ Mitra house (interview, 22 Sept. 2000).

111. The same point was expressed by three interviewees: Mr. Bhaskar Chunder (13 Dec. 2000), Mr. Śubhamay Dawn (5 Oct. 2000), and Mr. Milan Datta (30 Sept. 2000).

112. Mr. Kalyāṇkumār Deb (interview, 22 Sept. 2000). But the very next year, in 2001, the *Times of India* gave a prize for the best home Pūjā.

113. Mrs. Śephāli Bose and Mrs. Ārati Deb (interview, 29 Sept. 2000).

114. Interview, 20 Sept. 2000.

115. A survey in 1995 and 1996 demonstrated the decline through the seventeen districts of West Bengal. In 1995 there were 5,698 home Pūjās, whereas in 1996 there were only 4,605. This was in contrast to the increase in *sarbajanīn* Pūjās, which were 14,809 in 1995 and 14,888 in 1996. See *Ājkāl*, 16 Oct. 1996, pp. 1 and 5.

116. On the West Bengal Estates Acquisition Act for the Abolition of Zamindars, passed in 1954 and subsequently amended, see Nirmal Kumar Roy, *The West Bengal Estates Acquisition Act, 1953 (West Bengal Act 1 of 1954)*, 2nd rev. ed. (Calcutta: Eastern Law House, 1965), and A. N. Saha, *The West Bengal Land Reforms Act (West Bengal Act 10 of 1956)* (Calcutta: S. C. Sarkar and Sons, 1966).

117. For discussion of the traditional relationship between craftsman and zamindar at the festival season, see "The Lie of the Land," *Telegraph*, 30 Sept. 1995, section III, p. 1.

118. Sometimes, in lean economic times, the family Pūjās can still step in to provide public cohesiveness and solace for the poor. For instance, in 2001 in the town of Uluberia, in Howrah, a cash crunch, closed mills, and a depressed farmers' market prevented many from being able to sponsor their customary *sarbajanīn* Pūjās. However, the seventy-two renowned family Pūjās still carried on, and were visited by the public. *Hindustan Times*, Kolkata edition, 24 Oct. 2001, p. 4.

119. In a landmark decision by the Calcutta High Court in May 2003, the Sābarṇa Rāy Caudhurī family won their public interest litigation, with the effect that government textbooks are to be rewritten to indicate that the Rāy Caudhurīs, and not Job Charnock, were the actual founders of the city. See *Hindusthan Times*, Kolkata edition, 17 May 2003, p. 1. But Kolkata historian P. T. Nair avers it was not the Sābarṇa Rāy Caudhurī family but Charnock who made the city what it became. All the local zamindars did was to allow the English to settle there, in order to get more rent from them; see *Times of India*, "Calcutta Times" section, 24 Aug. 2001, p. 4, and *Pratidin*, 17 Sept. 2001, p. 3.

120. Interview, 16 Sept. 2000.

121. Interview, 22 Sept. 2000.

122. See *Times of India*, "Calcutta Times" section, 24 May 2001, p. 6.

123. *Bartamān*, 11 Oct. 2001, p. 5, and *Pratidin*, 28 Sept. 1995, p. 6, respectively.

124. *Ājkāl*, 28 Sept. 1998, p. 6.

125. David Lowenthal, *The Past Is a Foreign Country* (Cambridge: Cambridge University Press, 1985).

126. Debashish Bose, in a lecture at the Baṅgīya Sāhitya Pariṣad, said that he has counted 154 *ṭhākurdālāns* in Kolkata. But now many are being walled off, because their owners cannot afford to keep them up, or are being turned into godowns (warehouses). *Telegraph*, Calcutta section, 16 July 2003, p. 1.

127. Jane Marie Law, *Puppets of Nostalgia: The Life, Death, and Rebirth of the Japanese Awaji Nongyō Tradition* (Princeton: Princeton University Press, 1997), p. 207.

128. Ibid., p. 219.

129. See Howard L. Malchow, "Nostalgia, 'Heritage,' and the London Antiques Trade: Selling the Past in Thatcher's Britain," in *Singular Continuities: Tradition, Nostalgia, and Identity in Modern British Culture*, ed. George K. Behler and Fred M. Leventhal (Stanford: Stanford University Press, 2000), pp. 196–214.

130. Christian Lee Novetzke, *Religion and Public Memory: A Cultural History of Saint Namdev in India* (New York: Columbia University Press, 2008), p. 73; see also pp. 23–31 and 35–41. The reference is to Jan Assman, *Religion and Cultural Memory: Ten Studies*, trans. Rodney Livingstone (Stanford: Stanford University Press, 2006).

131. Svetlana Boym, *The Future of Nostalgia* (New York: Basic Books, 2001), p. 41.

132. *Statesman*, 4 Oct. 1953, Puja supplement, p. 1.

133. "The Puja Festival: A Transformation," in *Sunday Statesman Magazine*, 26 Sept. 1954, pp. 1 and 3.

## 2. The Goddess in Colonial and Postcolonial History

1. For an overview of the newspapers that were consulted for this project, see the bibliography.

2. An ad from the early 1920s for the auction house Taylor & Company, cited without original reference in J. P. Losty, *Calcutta: City of Palaces: A Survey of the City in the Days of the East India Company, 1690–1858* (London: Arnold Publishers, 1990), pp. 86–87.

3. David Kopf, *British Orientalism and the Bengal Renaissance: The Dynamics of Indian Modernization* (Berkeley: University of California Press, 1969); and Sumanta Banerjee, *The Parlour and the Streets: Elite and Popular Culture in Nineteenth-Century Calcutta* (Calcutta: Seagull Books, 1989).

4. *India Gazette*, 22 Oct. 1831, from Benoy Ghose, *Selections from English Periodicals of Nineteenth-Century Bengal*, vol. 1: *1815–1833* (Calcutta: Papyrus, 1978), pp. 67–68.

5. *Bartamān*, 11 Oct. 2001, p. 5.

6. Jagaddhātrī Pūjā was apparently much more popular in the late seventeenth and early eighteenth centuries in Calcutta and outlying areas than it is today. William Ward, for instance, in his *History, Literature, and Mythology of the Hindoos* from 1817–1820, describes "Juguddhatree"'s iconography and the large sums spent on illuminations, songs, dances, the entertainment of Brahmans, and priests employed to read the *Caṇḍī*; Ward, *The History, Literature, and Mythology of the Hindoos*, 4 vols. (1817–1820: Delhi: Low Price Publications, 1990), 3:130. In the early Calcutta newspapers one finds invitations to and descriptions of this festival in a manner parallel to that for Durgā. See, for example, *Calcutta Gazette*, 17 Nov. 1825, in *The Days of John Company: Selections from the Calcutta Gazette, 1824–1832*, compiled and edited by Anil Chandra Das Gupta (Calcutta: Government Printing, 1959), p. 107; *Bengal Hurkaru*, 14 Nov. 1833, p. 2; *Bengal Hurkaru*, 30 Oct. 1838, p. 422; and *Bengal Hurkaru*, 5 Nov. 1849, p. 507. Up to the last decade of the eighteenth century, Jagaddhātrī Pūjā used to be performed for three days, although "Jugutdhatree Poojah" officially got only one day's holiday; *Bengal Hurkaru*, 17 Sept. 1847, p. 54.

7. J. Z. Holwell, *Interesting Historical Events, Relative to the Provinces of Bengal, and the Empire of Indostan*, 3 parts (London: T. Becket and P. A. De Hondt, 1767), 3:128.

8. *Calcutta Journal*, 22 Sept. 1819, p. 183.

9. The mansion being described here belonged to Bābu Prāṇkṛṣṇa Hāldār of Chinsurah. See *Bengal Hurkaru*, 9 Oct. 1826, p. 2.

10. See her *Journal of a Residence in India* (Edinburgh: Archibald Constable & Co., 1812), excerpted in *Calcutta in the Nineteenth Century: Company's Days*, ed. P. T. Nair (Calcutta: Firma KLM, 1989), pp. 88–90.

11. *Bengal Hurkaru*, 10 Oct. 1825, p. 2.

12. L. de Grandpre, *A Voyage in the Indian Ocean and to Bengal Undertaken in the Years 1789 and 1790*, 2 vols. (Paris 1801 and London 1803), excerpted in *Calcutta in the Eighteenth Century: Impressions of Travelers*, ed. P. T. Nair (Calcutta: Firma KLM, 1984), pp. 254–255; and Maria Graham's journal (1812), cited without reference in Losty, *Calcutta: City of Palaces*, pp. 111–112. For other early mentions of Durgā, see Lady Maria Nugent, *A Journal from the Year 1811 til the Year 1815, Including a Voyage to and Residence in India*, 2 vols. (London, 1839), in Nair, *Calcutta in the Nineteenth Century*, p. 159; and *Calcutta Gazette*, 5 Oct. 1829, in Das Gupta, ed., *The Days of John Company*, p. 420; and the *Calcutta Review* 18, no. 35 (July–Dec. 1852), article 5, pp. 49–71.

13. Excerpted from "Doorgah Poojah," a poem printed in the *Bengal Hurkaru*, 12 Oct. 1829, p. 3.

14. All rituals, customs, and endowments were not to be tampered with. See Sir H. Verney Lovett, "Social Policy to 1858," in *The Cambridge History of India*, vol. VI: *The*

*Indian Empire, 1858–1918, with Chapters on the Development of Administration, 1818–1858,* ed. H. H. Dodwell (Cambridge: Cambridge University Press, 1932), pp. 124–127.

15. The Baptists came to India one year after the founding of their world missionary society. Congregationalist missionaries, mostly sponsored by the London Missionary Society, only sent appreciable numbers to Bengal after 1812. Likewise, the Anglican Church Missionary Society sent people to India only in 1814, with the founding of the Calcutta diocese. As for the Presbyterian Church of Scotland, Alexander Duff was their first missionary, from 1830. See Kenneth Ingham, *Reformers in India, 1793–1833: An Account of the Work of Christian Missionaries on Behalf of Social Reform* (Cambridge: Cambridge University Press, 1956).

16. On the pilgrim tax controversy, consult Ingham, "Idolatrous Festivals and the Practice of 'Sati,'" in *Reformers in India*, pp. 33–43.

17. John Rosselli, *Lord William Bentinck: The Making of a Liberal Imperialist, 1774–1839* (Berkeley: University of California Press, 1974), pp. 211–212.

18. See the *Bengal Hurkaru*, 12 Oct. 1829, p. 2, and 28 Sept. 1830, p. 2.

19. On the Dispatch of 1838 [C.R.O.Mss. "Bengal Despatches," vol. 121, fol. 1135], see *Calcutta Review* 17, no. 33, article 5 (Jan.–June, 1852): 114–177; and Lovett, "Social Policy to 1858," pp. 121–143.

20. *Calcutta Journal*, 7 Oct. 1820, pp. 366–367.

21. The *Bengal Spectator* for 15 Oct. 1842, quoted in the *Englishman and Military Chronicle*, 19 Oct. 1842, p. 2.

22. *Englishman*, 25 Sept. 1835, pp. 1828–1829, and *Friend of India*, 4 Oct. 1838, p. 565.

23. See Bernard S. Cohn, *Colonialism and Its Forms of Knowledge: The British in India* (Princeton: Princeton University Press, 1996); Richard King, *Orientalism and Religion: Postcolonial Theory, India, and "The Mystics East"* (London: Routledge, 1999); David N. Lorenzen, *Who Invented Hinduism? Essays on Religion in History* (New Delhi: Yoda Press, 2006); Arvind-Pal Mandair, *Religion and the Spectre of the West: Sikhism, India, Postcoloniality, and the Politics of Translation* (New York: Columbia University Press, 2009); Thomas R. Metcalf, *Ideologies of the Raj* (*The New Cambridge History of India* III.4) (Cambridge: Cambridge University Press, 1995); Brian K. Pennington, *Was Hinduism Invented? Britons, Indians, and the Colonial Reconstruction of Religion* (New York: Oxford University Press, 2005); and a wonderful overview essay on the issues, Sharada Sugirtharajah, "Colonialism," in *Studying Hinduism: Key Concepts and Methods*, ed. Sushil Mittal and Gene Thursby (London: Routledge, 2008), pp. 75–83.

24. For a number of excellent quotations on this point, see *Friend of India*, 6 Oct. 1836, p. 314; and *Englishman*, 7 Oct. 1836, p. 1927.

25. *Friend of India*, 14 April 1836, p. 115.

26. *Bengal Hurkaru*, 7 Feb. 1831, cited in Das Gupta, ed., *The Days of John Company*, p. 626.

27. *Friend of India*, 8 Oct. 1835, p. 322.

28. For an example of such critiques, see the *Calcutta Gazette* for 5 Oct. 1829, in Das Gupta, ed., *The Days of John Company*, pp. 418–420; and *Bengal Hurkaru*, 7 Oct. 1840, p. 355.

29. Excerpted from "Doorgah Poojah," in *Bengal Hurkaru*, 12 Oct. 1829, p. 3.

30. *Friend of India*, 8 Oct. 1835, p. 322.

31. *Englishman*, 1 Oct. 1835, p. 1869.

32. All arguments are summarized in *Friend of India*, 21 Nov. 1839, pp. 739–740.

33. *Tattvabodhinī Patrikā*, 4, no. 38 (1846): 344.

34. Sivanath Sastri, in his *History of the Brahmo Samaj* (1911–1912; Calcutta: Sadharan Brahmo Samaj, 1974), appendix B, p. 558.

35. See various editorials from the mid to late 1920s in Mukul Gupta, "Early Editorials on the Puja," in *Statesman Sunday Magazine*, Oct. 11, 1964, p. 10. Other examples may be found in *Bengal Hurkaru*, 13 Oct. 1826, p. 2; 10 Oct. 1829, p. 337; 28 Oct. 1836, p. 419; 20 Oct. 1837, p. 383; and 1 Oct. 1838, p. 322.

36. *Bengal Hurkaru*, 1 Oct. 1846, p. 371.

37. *Bengal Hurkaru*, 17 Oct. 1850, p. 485.

38. *Bengal Hurkaru*, 15 Oct.1855, supplementary sheet, p. 365. For other notices of British guests at Pūjā entertainments, see *Bengal Hurkaru*, 20 Oct. 1847, p. 447; 27 Sept. 1849, p. 350; 20 Nov. 1850, p. 571; and 17 Oct. 1853, p. 371.

39. *Friend of India*, 19 Oct. 1837, p. 330; and *Bengal Hurkaru*, 1 Oct. 1838, p. 322.

40. See Brajendranāth Bandyopādhyāy, ed., *Sambādpatre Sekāler Kathā*, vol. 1: *1818–1830*, 2nd ed., 2 vols. (1932; Calcutta: Bangīya Sāhitya Pariṣad, 1937), pp. 137–138.

41. To read about Pūjās dependent upon British patronage that were forced to close down, consult Nirmal Kar, "Cāpāno Pūjo," *Ānanda Bājār Patrikā*, 27 Sept. 1998, p. 6, and Ṣibśaṅkar Bhāratī, "Kalkātār Durgā Pūjā, 1586–1951," in *Bartamān Rabibār*, 10 Oct. 1999, p. 10.

42. As reported in the *Bengal Hurkaru*, 30 Oct. 1833, p. 2. Such liberality on the part of Cornwallis is frequently quoted in the debates of 1834 and after.

43. The proposal from the Bank of Bengal is repeated in *Bengal Hurkaru*, 18 Sept. 1834, p. 2.

44. *Bengal Hurkaru*, 15 Aug. 1834, p. 158; 15 Sept. 1834, p. 2; 18 Sept. 1834, p. 2; 1 Oct. 1834, p. 2; and 20 Oct. 1834, p. 2.

45. For these arguments, respectively, see *Bengal Hurkaru*, 25 Aug. 1834, p. 190; 26 Aug. 1834, p. 194; 6 Sept. 1834, p. 2; and 31 Oct. 1834, p. 2.

46. As enunciated, for the government, by H. T. Prinsep. See *Englishman*, 14 Nov. 1834, p. 517.

47. This included the ten days of the Durgā Pūjā, and extended two days further, to include Lakṣmī Pūjā.

48. *Bengalee*, 15 Nov. 1879, p. 524, and *Bengalee Supplement*, Sept. 26, 1900.

49. Reported in the *Bengal Hurkaru*, 6 Oct. 1840, p. 350, and 23 Oct. 1860, p. 3.

50. *Friend of India*, 6 Oct. 1870, p. 7B.

51. See, respectively, n.a., *Durgā Debīr Bṛttānta* (Midnapur Mission Press, 1867), a sixteen-page missionary description of Durgā Pūjā, with exhortations to turn instead to Jesus; and *Bengal Hurkaru*, 14 Oct. 1861, p. 3, and 3 Oct. 1865, p. 2.

52. *Bengal Hurkaru*, 23 Sept. 1865, p. 2.

53. *Friend of India*, 6 Oct. 1870, p. 7B.

54. *Friend of India*, 9 Oct. 1875, p. 920.

55. This is not to say that banks and businesses did not still agitate for fewer holidays. Proposals to shorten them surfaced in the news in 1879, 1889, 1890, and

1900, and were repeatedly resisted by leaders in the Indian community, who were eventually backed by the government.

56. *Bengal Hurkaru*, 3 Oct. 1861, p. 2.

57. Bankimcandra Chatterji, *Ānandamaṭh; or, The Sacred Brotherhood*, translated with an introduction and critical apparatus by Julius J. Lipner (Oxford: Oxford University Press, 2005), p. 149.

58. The idea for the *melās* was apparently taken from Rajnarain Basu's *Prospects for the Promotion of National Feeling Among the Educated Natives of Bengal* (1866), but it was organized by Nabagopāl Mitra, the Tagore family, and Manmohan Basu. See Rosinka Chaudhuri, "Hemchandra's Bharata Sangeet (1870) and the Politics of Poetry: A Pre-history of Hindu Nationalism in Bengal?" in *Indian Economic and Social History Review* 42 (2005): 213–247; Indira Chowdhury, *The Frail Hero and Virile History: Gender and the Politics of Cultures in Colonial Bengal* (Delhi: Oxford University Press, 1998); and Rajat Sanyal, *Voluntary Associations and the Urban Public Life in Bengal (1815–1876): An Aspect of Social History* (Calcutta: Riddhi-India, 1980).

59. *Indian Mirror*, 25 Sept. 1887, p. 2.

60. Leonard Gordon, *Bengal: The Nationalist Movement, 1876–1940* (New York: Columbia University Press, 1974), p. 22.

61. The Brāhmo Samāj, which can be traced back to Ram Mohan Roy in 1828, split twice: first, in 1866, with the Brāhmo Samāj of India breaking off from the parent body; and second, in 1878, when the latter split to form the New Dispensation and the Sādharan Brāhmo Samāj. Sastri himself has this to complain about Durgā Pūjā: "[T]he Hindus of this province throw themselves body and soul into the national celebration, and say and do many things that are, in many cases, morally objectionable. Such practices, for instance, as the slaying of kids and buffaloes, the dancing of public women, the open indulgence in *bhang* and wine, have made the name of Durga Puja or the worship of the ten-handed goddesses of Bengal, otherwise so solemn and sacred in the popular mind, a thing to be dreaded by all lovers of true religion. So long the Brahmos had been decrying, in their speeches and their writings, the worship of the idol deity with its attendant abuses" (Sastri, *History of the Brahmo Samaj*, p. 197). Note, however, that even the famed Bengali nationalist Bipin Chandra Pal, when coming under the sway of Debendranath Tagore and the Brāhmo Samāj, still prayed to Kālī and Durgā and enjoyed the Pūjā festivities; see Bipin Chandra Pal, *Memories of My Life and Times* (Calcutta: Bipinchandra Pal Institute, 1973), p. 113.

62. For some of Sen's comments on the Mother, see Keshub Chunder Sen, *Jeevan Veda: Being Sixteen Discourses in Bengali on Life—Its Divine Dispensation*, trans. Jamini Kanta Koar, 3rd ed. (Calcutta: Nababidhan Trust, 1969), pp. 22, 65. Sen does champion independence, but as a lack of dependence upon sin, not a political freedom from the British; see pp. 35–44. Refer also to David Kopf, *The Brahmo Samaj and the Shaping of the Modern Indian Mind* (Princeton: Princeton University Press, 1979), pp. 249–286.

63. For literary and thematic antecedents to Chatterjee's glorification of the patriotic sannyasi, see Chaudhuri, "Hemchandra's Bharata Sangeet," pp. 213–247.

64. Two stanzas from "Bande Mātāram," as translated by Lipner in *Ānandamaṭh, or The Sacred Brotherhood*, p. 145.

65. *Bankim Rachanavali*, ed. Jogesh Chandra Bagal (Calcutta: Sahitya Samsad, 1969), pp. 200–201.

66. In its obituary of Chatterjee the *Statesman* did not even mention "Bande Mātāram." The first Muslims to critique *Ānandamaṭh* did not express themselves until 1912; nothing was voiced when the novel was published, or even during the partition agitations. See S. N. Mukherjee, "Introduction," *Bankimchandra Chatterjee: Sociological Essays: Utilitarianism and Positivism in Bengal*, trans. and ed. S. N. Mukherjee and Marian Maddern (Calcutta: Rddhi-India, 1986), pp. 1–3, 9–12.

67. Sir Surendranath Banerjea, *A Nation in Making: Being the Reminiscences of Fifty Years of Public Life* (Bombay: Oxford University Press, 1925), pp. 147–148.

68. *Bengal Hurkaru*, 23 Oct. 1860, p. 3.

69. *Bengal Hurkaru*, 7 Oct. 1862, p. 2; and *Bengalee*, 18 Oct. 1879, pp. 498–499; *Bengalee*, 6 Oct. 1883, p. 474; *Bengalee*, 13 Oct. 1888, p. 485; and Pal, *Memories of My Life and Times*, pp. 104–105.

70. This was first read before the Bengal Social Science Association in January 1869. See Bagal, *Bankim Rachanavali*, pp. 91–96.

71. See, in chronological order: Kāliprasanna Sinha, *Hutom Pyāncār Nakśa*, with commentary, 2nd ed. (1862; Calcutta: Subarṇarekhā, 1991); Pratap Chandra Ghosha, *Durga Puja, with Notes and Illustrations* (Calcutta: Hindoo Patriot Press, 1871); Rāmratna Pāṭhak, *Durgotsab* (Calcutta: Nūtan Bhārat Yantre, 1874); Gangādhar Kabirāj, *Durgotsab Bidhi Bijñānam* (Murshidabad: Nabīncandra Caudhurī, 1875); Airābat Candra Pakhirāj, *Durgā Pūjā* (Calcutta: n.p., 1876); Haricaran Bandyopādhyāy, *Durgā Pūjā* (Calcutta: Bānārji & Co., 1877); and Kṛṣṇacandra Pāl, *Durgā Pujā Mahādhūm* (Calcutta: K. C. Pāl, 1882). Bankim Chandra also wrote a satirical piece called "Bābu." "He who in appearance is *Karttik*'s younger brother, in virtue is worthless, in action, inert, and in speech *Saraswati*, he is a Babu. He who performs *Durga-puja* for the sake of a festival, *Lakshmi-puja* at the request of his wife, *Saraswati-puja* at the request of his mistress, and *Ganga-puja* in the lust for goat-meat, he is a Babu" (see Mukherjee and Maddern, *Bankimchandra Chatterjee: Sociological Essays*, p. 28).

72. Discussed in Chowdhury, *The Frail Hero and Virile History*, pp. 102–107.

73. *Indian Mirror*, 5 Oct. 1889, p. 2.

74. Excerpted from a poem called "The Auspicious Time for Worship," which appeared in the second issue of *Suprabhat Magazine*, in 1907. Quoted in James Campbell Ker, *Political Trouble in India, 1907–1917* (1917; Delhi: Oriental Publishers, 1973), pp. 88–89.

75. *Bengalee*, 28 Sept. 1903, p. 3. See also Mrinilanini Sinha's classic *Colonial Masculinity: The "Manly Englishman" and the "Effeminate Bengali" in the Late Nineteenth Century* (Manchester: Manchester University Press, 1995).

76. Bharati Roy, *Early Feminists of Colonial India: Sarala Devi Chaudharani and Rokeya Sakhawat Hossain* (New Delhi: Oxford University Press, 2002), pp. 10–12. In addition to Śaralādebī's Bengali transcreations of Tilak's Maharashtrian festivals, actual enactments of the Shivaji Utsav were organized in Calcutta as well, from 1902. Rabindranath Tagore wrote a famous poem for the occasion in 1904 called "Shivaji Utsav." See Chaudhuri, "Hemchandra's Bharata Sangeet," p. 224.

77. Sumit Sarkar, *The Swadeshi Movement in Bengal, 1903–1908* (Delhi: People's Publishing House, 1973).

78. See Clinton B. Seely, "Raja Pratapaditya: Problematic Hero," in *Barisal and Beyond: Essays on Bangla Literature* (New Delhi: Chronicle Books, 2008), pp. 208–230; Ker, *Political Trouble in India*, pp. 7–8, 10–11; and Sarkar, *The Swadeshi Movement*, pp. 304–305. The recourse to Pratāpāditya did not endear Śaralādebī to her uncle Rabindranath, who countered that the Rājā had not been a man of exemplary moral character.

79. Quoted by Jogesh C. Bagal in "Women in India's Freedom Movement," *Modern Review* 93, no. 6 (June 1953): 469.

80. Radha Kumar, *The History of Doing: An Illustrated Account of Movements for Women's Rights and Feminism in India, 1800–1990* (London: Verso, 1993), p. 39.

81. She claims that this recourse to Śāktism indicated their mainly upper-class backgrounds, as lower-class Bengalis tended to be Vaiṣṇavas or Muslims. See Barbara Southard, "The Political Strategy of Aurobindo Ghosh: The Utilization of Hindu Religious Symbolism and the Problem of Political Mobilization in Bengal," *Modern Asian Studies* 14, no. 3 (1980): 353–376.

82. For further discussion of his theme of the victimized Motherland, see Chowdhury, *The Frail Hero and Virile History*, pp. 86–97, 102–107, 154–159.

83. Sri Aurobindo, "Bhawani Mandir," in *Bande Mataram: Early Political Writings* (Pondicherry: Sri Aurobindo Ashram, 1973), p. 65.

84. *The Speeches of Aurobindo*, pp. 33–34, quoted in Hari Hara Das, *Subhas Chandra Bose and the Indian National Movement* (Delhi: Sterling Publishers, 1983), p. 38.

85. Articles and editorials from the *Bengalee* from 1909–1911 do not criticize the British as much as they seek to reconstruct Bengal; Durgā Pūjā, when mentioned, is seen as a foretaste of brotherhood. See 15 Oct. 1910, p. 5; 29 Sept. 1911, p. 4; and 5 Oct. 1911, p. 4.

86. Jogesh Chandra Chatterji, *In Search of Freedom* (Calcutta: Firma KLM, 1967), pp. 7–8.

87. It is ironic that the illustration accompanying this ad is of an English lady in a high lacy blouse, with her hair done up in a bun! *Bengalee*, 3 Oct. 1909, p. 10.

88. The speech is quoted in Ker, *Political Trouble in India*, pp. 43–48.

89. Ibid., p. 162. The young Samiti cadres were also encouraged to make offerings to Kālī to gain strength; Chatterji, *In Search of Freedom*, pp. 26–27.

90. Ker, *Political Trouble in India*, p. 78.

91. *Yugāntar*, 3 March 1907, p. 383, quoted in Chaudhuri, "Hemchandra's Bharata Sangeet," p. 231.

92. For reports of forced participation in the swadeshi movement, see the *Englishman*, 26 Sept. 1906, p. 8.

93. Dipesh Chakrabarty, "Communal Riots and Labour: Bengal's Jute Mill-Hands in the 1890s," in *Mirrors of Violence: Communities, Riots, and Survivors in South Asia*, ed. Veena Das (Delhi: Oxford University Press, 1992), pp. 146–184. Christopher Pinney provides a fascinating detail about cow protection outside Bengal and its intersection with iconography in his *"Photos of the Gods": The Printed Image and Political Struggle in India* (London: Reaktion Books, 2004). In December 1911 the Bombay Govern-

ment invoked section 12(1) of the Indian Press Act of 1910 to proscribe a Ravi Varma Press image titled "Ashtabhuja Devi," as she was depicted decapitating two Muslim butchers who had just killed a cow. The Press was eventually persuaded to take the blood of the cow's neck off the butchers' knives and to change the cow to a buffalo (pp. 110–112, including fig. 80).

94. See John R. McLane, "Partition of Bengal, 1905: A Political Analysis," in *The History of Bangladesh, 1704–1971*, ed. Sirajul Islam, 2nd ed., vol. 1: *Political History* (Dhaka: Asiatic Society of Bangladesh, 1997): 304–348.

95. Nandini Gooptu, *The Politics of the Urban Poor in Early Twentieth-Century India* (Cambridge: Cambridge University Press, 2001), pp. 6, 35–36, 41.

96. Lead editorial in the *Bengalee*, 29 Sept. 1906, p. 3.

97. See the *Hindoo Patriot* for 15 Oct. 1904, p. 2; and 15 Oct. 1905, p. 2, right on the eve of partition.

98. *Amrita Bazar Patrika*, 18 Oct. 1917, p. 8.

99. *Amrita Bazar Patrika*, 13 Oct. 1913, p. 6.

100. *Amrita Bazar Patrika*, 22 Oct. 1915, p. 6.

101. From the cover of *Māsik Basumatī* 23, no. 6 (Aśvin 1944).

102. Subhas Chandra Bose, from a letter to Haricharan Bagchi from Mandalay jail, in *Netaji: Collected Works*, ed. Sisir K. Bose, 11 vols. (Calcutta: Netaji Research Bureau, 1982), vol. 4: *Correspondence, January 1926–January 1932*, p. 140.

103. Thomas Blom Hansen, *The Saffron Wave: Democracy and Hindu Nationalism in Modern India* (Princeton: Princeton University Press, 1999), p. 56.

104. From the lead editorial called "Bijayā," *Ānanda Bājār Patrikā*, 4 Oct. 1922, p. 2.

105. "Eso Mā Ānandamayi!" in *Ānanda Bājār Patrikā*, 14 Oct. 1923, p. 2.

106. For an excellent illustration, see *Ānanda Bājār Patrikā*, 5 Oct. 1924, p. 7.

107. See *Amrita Bazar Patrika*, 19 Oct. 1926, p. 4; and *Bengalee*, 20 Oct. 1926, pp. 4 and 6.

108. *Bengalee*, 30 Sept. 1927, p. 3.

109. From a letter written on 25 Sept. 1925; *Netaji: Collected Works*, vol. III: *Correspondence, May 1923–July 1926*, ed. Sisir K. Bose (Calcutta: Netaji Research Bureau, 1981), p. 127. For another example of a jailed nationalist petitioning for the right to celebrate the Pūjās, see the memoirs of Jogesh Chandra Chatterji, who did so in Rajshahi jail in 1919. He and his comrades sacrificed a white goat, "symbolic of the white man with whom the Indians identified the British" (Chatterji, *In Search of Freedom*, p. 118).

110. Joya Chatterji, *Bengal Divided: Hindu Communalism and Partition, 1932–1947* (Cambridge: Cambridge University Press, 1994), pp. 191–199; quoted sentence from p. 194.

111. Ibid., p. 210.

112. Mahatma Gandhi, *The Collected Works*, vol. 24: *May–August 1924* (New Delhi: Government of India: Ministry of Information and Broadcasting, 1967), pp. 138–141, 150–151.

113. *Ānanda Bājār Patrikā*, 18 Oct. 1926, p. 9, and 19 Oct. 1926, p. 3. See also *Amrita Bazar Patrika*, 9 Oct. 1926, p. 6; and *Statesman*, 16 Oct. 1926, p. 8. The 9 Oct. paper describes a resolution from the Baṅgīya Brāhman Sabhā to the chief secretary to

the Government of Bengal, quoting scriptural evidence for the necessity of drum-playing during processions and asking for protection for the same. Recall how uncommunalized the Pūjās had been at their inception; Muslim dancing girls were all the rage, and when the Pūjās happened to coincide with Muharram, the result was simply that there were fewer nautches. Even in 1849 one reads of the government's refusal of the "natives"' request to have sepoys attend their nautches, since there is no need to protect the peace; *Friend of India*, 4 Oct. 1849, p. 628.

114. Joya Chatterjee gives many examples of such communal fracases in her *Bengal Divided*, pp. 191–219. So does Dipesh Chakrabarty, in *Rethinking Working-Class History: Bengal, 1890–1940* (Princeton: Princeton University Press, 1989), esp. chapter 6, "Class and Commmunity," pp. 186–218.

115. *Amrita Bazar Patrika*, 5 Oct. 1943. p. 2.

116. Gooptu, *The Politics of the Urban Poor*, p. 8.

117. Ibid., pp. 230–234.

118. Ibid., p. 221.

119. Ibid., pp. 189–191, 236–243.

120. Anne Hardgrove, *Community and Public Culture: The Marwaris in Calcutta* (New York: Columbia University Press, 2004), pp. 20–21.

121. Marwari industrialists, whether Vaiṣṇava or Jain, are influenced by the values of nonviolence, thrift, asceticism, animal protection, and vegetarianism. Diwali, not Kālī Pūjā, is of prime importance to them, as it is the occasion for the opening of new account books. Their aesthetic taste tends toward the type of temple established in Calcutta in 1996 by the Birlas, not toward the Śākta temples already in existence in the city. See Hardgrove, *Community and Public Culture*, pp. 66–67.

122. Bengali newspapers were monitored and their editors sometimes arrested; from 1905 until 1947 the Sedition Committee appointed to investigate revolutionary conspiracies in India was acutely aware of the dangers of Śākta ideology. For collections, in English, from anti-government Indian papers, see, for example, Ker, *Political Trouble in India*, and Sir Valentine Chirol, *Indian Unrest* (London: Macmillan, 1910).

123. From 1924 one sees newspaper advertisements aimed at Indians who want to spend their holidays in Calcutta: recommended sites include cinemas, the Alipore zoo, the Indian Museum, the Victoria Memorial, Eden Gardens, and the Kālīghāṭ Temple.

124. *Englishman*, 20 Oct. 1920, p. 6. For Jagaddhātrī, see a special "Jagadhatri Poojah" announcement of a holiday return fare on the Bengal–Nagpur Railway to visit Sinhachalam, which has one of the oldest hill temples in India; *Statesman*, 26 Oct. 1930, p. 1.

125. *Māsik Basumatī* 22, no. 6 (Asvin number, 1943): 469–472.

126. *Amrita Bazar Patrika*, 30 Sept. 1946, p. 1.

127. *Amrita Bazar Patrika*, 14 Oct. 1980, p. 1.

128. *Ānanda Bājār Patrikā*, 22 Oct. 1950, p. 4.

129. *Amrita Bazar Patrika*, 11 Oct. 1948, p. 9.

130. *Ānanda Bājār Patrikā*, 1 Nov. 1951, p. 4.

131. Early in his tenure as chief minister (1977–2000), Jyoti Basu (1914–2010) used the Pūjās to announce a one-month Pūjā parole for political prisoners. Mention of

Communists and even Naxalites organizing and patronizing Pūjā pandals may be found from the early 1950s onward. Newspaper editors enjoy ridiculing such behavior. Concluded Tārāśankar Bandyopādhyāy in 1952, although "Indian Communists travel a crooked path, . . . no matter what philosophy one adheres to—Buddhist, Marxist, or materialist—one can't disregard the Puja's attraction" (*Ānanda Bājār Patrikā*, 27 Sept. 1952, pp. 1 and 5).

132. *Amrita Bazar Patrika*, 18 Oct. 1964, p. 6.

133. See *Amrita Bazar Patrika* for 30 Sept. 1965, pp. 1 and 12; 2 Oct. 1965, p. 1; and 4 Oct. 1965, p. 1.

134. *Amrita Bazar Patrika*, 12 Oct. 1989, p. 1.

135. "The Doomed Holidays," *Indian Mirror*, 18 Oct. 1879, p. 2.

136. "In the pre-modern state, in Europe as elsewhere, power was made visible though theatrical displays, in the form of processions, progresses, royal entries, coronations, funerals, and other rituals that guaranteed the well-being and continued power of the rulers over the ruled" (Cohn, *Colonialism and Its Forms of Knowledge*, p. 3).

137. Letter to the editor on "The Doorga Vacation," written 16 Oct. 1844 by B. D. and published in *Englishman and Military Chronicle*, 17 Oct. 1844, p. 2.

138. *Statesman*, 9 Oct. 1921, p. 7.

139. During the height of the Partition unrest, the Shovabazar *rājā*s opened their houses to European guests, who, if the *Englishman*'s accounts are accurate, enjoyed themselves thoroughly.

140. See Gyanendra Pandey, *Remembering Partition: Violence, Nationalism, and the History of India* (Cambridge: Cambridge University Press, 2001).

## 3. Durgā the Daughter: Folk and Familial Traditions

1. There is textual and archaeological evidence for the existence of Pārvatī as the wife of Śiva by the time of the *Mahābhārata* and *Rāmāyaṇa*. For discussion and specific references, see Thomas B. Coburn, *Devī Māhātmya: The Crystallization of the Goddess Tradition* (Delhi: Motilal Banarsidass, 1985), p. 179 and notes, and Rachel Fell McDermott, *Mother of My Heart, Daughter of My Dreams: Kālī and Umā in the Devotional Poetry of Bengal* (New York: Oxford University Press, 2001), pp. 164–165.

2. *Āgamanī* literally means "coming," and refers to the goddess Umā on her way home to Bengal from her married life in Kailasa. *Bijayā*, which means "victory," is less easily correlated than *āgamanī* to the content of the poems that bear its name. Most likely *bijayā* refers to the day on which these songs are sung—the last day of the festival, called Bijayā Daśamī, or Victory Tenth, which celebrates both the victory of Durgā over the buffalo demon, Mahiṣa, and the victory of Rāma over Rāvaṇa.

3. See the second part of the *Caṇḍīmaṅgalakāvya*, the best versions of which date from the late sixteenth century.

4. For a short overview of the contents of the *Śivāyana*, see Dīneścandra Sen, *Bangabhāṣā o Sāhitya*, ed. Asit Kumār Bandyopādhyāy, 2 vols. (Calcutta: West Bengal State Book Board, 1986), 2:465–467. More details on the agriculturalist Śiva of the

rice-growing regions of eastern India may be found in William L. Smith, "Śiva, Lord of the Plough," in *Essays on Middle Bengali Literature: Studies by David L. Curley, Rahul Peter Das, Mazharul Isam, Amzad Hossain Mian, Asim Roy, and William L. Smith*, ed. Rahul Peter Das (Calcutta: Firma KLM, 1999), pp. 208–228.

5. Apart from Rāmprasād, the principal composers of *āgamanī* and *bijayā* songs appear to have been *kabioyālās*, or stand-up musicians who performed extemporaneously in urban contexts for entertainment. Of the most famous early *kabioyālās* of the late eighteenth century, anthologists have preserved the Umā-*saṅgīt* of Rām Basu (1786–1828) and Haru Ṭhākur (1738–1824).

6. This is reminiscent of Rajasthani retellings of the Pārvatī–Śiva story cycle in which the divine couple are said to reside on Mount Abu.

7. Kamalākānta Bhaṭṭācārya, "*O he Girirāj, Gaurī abhimān kareche*," in *Śyāmā Saṅgīt* (Calcutta: Barddhamān Mahārājādhirāj Māhtāb Bāhādur, 1857), poem 216. The *dhuturā* fruit is the white thorn apple, which yields a powerful narcotic. Suradhunī, or Divine River, is an epithet for the Ganges. This translation appeared previously in Rachel Fell McDermott, *Singing to the Goddess: Poems to Kālī and Umā from Bengal* (New York: Oxford University Press, 2001), pp. 126–127.

8. Kamalākānta Bhaṭṭācārya, "*Balo āmi ki karibo*," in *Śyāmā Saṅgīt*, poem 219. See McDermott, *Singing to the Goddess*, pp. 129–130.

9. Kamalākānta Bhaṭṭācarya, "*O he Hara Gaṅgaādhar*," in *Śyāmā Saṅgīt*, poem 225. The female *cātakī* bird, a type of cuckoo, is said in poetic literature to subsist on raindrops. Hence it stares at the clouds, hoping for rain. See McDermott, *Singing to the Goddess*, pp. 132–133.

10. Excerpt from Rām Basu, "*Kao dekhi Umā, keman chile Mā*," in *Saṅgīt-Sār-Saṅgraha*, ed. Harimohan Mukhopādhyāy, 2 vols. (Calcutta: Aruṇoday Rāy, 1899), 2:247. Mṛtyuñjaya, or Conqueror of Death, is an epithet for Śiva.

11. Kamalākānta Bhaṭṭācārya, "*Ki halo nabamī niśi hailo abasān go*," in *Śyāmā Saṅgīt*, poem 241. See McDermott, *Singing to the Goddess*, pp. 146–147.

12. In the Purāṇas, the story of Śiva and Pārvatī typically starts with the Satī, the daughter of Dakṣa, who marries Śiva. Dakṣa, not being pleased with his new son-in-law, does not invite him to a sacrifice he is sponsoring, and Satī is so humiliated on her husband's behalf that she throws herself into the sacrificial flames and dies. Śiva grieves for a long time, but eventually returns to his premarital lifestyle of ascetic meditation. Meanwhile, a demon named Tāraka has unseated the gods, and Brahmā promises them that Tāraka will be slain by a son of Śiva. Satī is then born again, as the daughter of the mountain Himālaya and his wife, Menā; as a little girl, Pārvatī undertakes terrible austerities in order to win Śiva's notice, and his hand in marriage. Although her parents are slightly dubious about accepting this ascetic, skull-carrying, snake-ornamented, naked god into their family, the wedding occurs, and eventually a son, Skanda, is born who kills the demon Tāraka. For more on the dual nature of Śiva, see Wendy Doniger O'Flaherty, *Śiva, the Erotic Ascetic* (Oxford: Oxford University Press, 1973).

13. In many poems Menakā and Girirāj do not live in a wealthy city, but in a poor rural home. This is a clear departure from the Sanskrit heritage, in which Girirāj is always rich.

14. Compare with the Purāṇic stories, where Śiva is an eccentric, with antisocial behavior and bizarre looks, or an enjoyer of erotic delights with Pārvatī, or a sedate family man with his wife and two sons. As Wendy Doniger has shown, however, the tradition seems to delight in censuring Śiva; his penchant for mendicancy disrupts normal married life, and Pārvatī, as well as her parents, complains (see *Skanda Purāṇa* 7.7.9.24 and *Bhāgavata Purāṇa* 4.2.11–16). In some Purāṇic accounts Menā threatens to take poison or to drown herself if the marriage goes through (*Śiva Purāṇa* 2.3.44.1–102), faints at Śiva's outlandish appearance at the wedding ceremony (*Śiva Purāṇa* 2.3.43.1–65; for opposite reactions by Menā see *Vāmana Purāṇa* 27.1–62 and *Kumārasambhava*, sarga 7), and after she sees how he acts as a husband, criticizes him for not providing her daughter with a proper place to live (*Skanda Purāṇa* 2.2.12.22–43; *Vāyu Purāṇa* 2.30.29–58; and *Brahmāṇḍa Purāṇa* 3.67.32–36), and for making love to her constantly (*Vāyu Purāṇa* 2.30.38; *Kūrma Purāṇa* 1.14.4–97; *Vāmana Purāṇa* 26.52–53; *Śiva Purāṇa* 2.2.16.41–42, 2.3.27.32, 2.3.36.12; and *Skanda Purāṇa* 1.1.22.67–81, 1.1.35.27–34, 2.25.59–66). Though Pārvatī herself often joins in the complaints (*Brahmavaivarta Purāṇa* 3.2.19–24; *Matsya Purāṇa* 155.5–9; *Padma Purāṇa* 5.41.5–9; and *Skanda Purāṇa* 1.2.27.63–68), in many myths she defends her husband, and it is obvious that they are happy.

15. The poetry mentions an older brother, also a mountain like his father, whose death by drowning in the sea is a source of continuing grief for Menakā. The *Harivaṁśa* (18.13) calls Maināka the son of Himālaya and the father of Krauṭca. The typical Sanskrit myth told about him is that when Indra decided to lop off the wings of all mountains, to prevent them from moving about and landing wherever they chose, disrupting settled human life, Maināka took refuge with his friend, the sea, who has hidden him ever since (*Kumārasambhava*, sarga 1, v. 20). Though the Umā-*saṅgīt* never mentions any other siblings, some Sanskrit stories give Umā two older sisters, Kuṭilā and Rāgiṇī, as well as another brother, Sunābha (see *Vāmana Purāṇa* 25.1–75). Yet another tradition makes Gaṅgā her older sister (*Bṛhaddharma Purāṇa* 2.12–22).

16. In the Sanskrit stories (see *Kumārasambhava*, sarga 6, and *Vāmana Purāṇa* 26.1–71), Nārada never performs the function of matchmaker, though he does predict when Pārvatī is a baby that she will marry Śiva (*Kumārasambhava*, sarga 1, v. 50; *Śiva Purāṇa* 2.3.8.8–11, 2.3.9.5; and *Skanda Purāṇa* 1.2.23.1–59). One can see a foreshadowing of the function Nārada plays in the Umā-*saṅgīt* in the medieval Bengali *Manasāmaṅgalakāvya* of Manakar; see O'Flaherty, *Śiva, the Erotic Ascetic*, p. 363 n. 97.

17. This story of Kāma developed late, reaching its final form only in *Matsya Purāṇa* 154.227–255. Its most beautiful rendition is in Kālidāsa's *Kumārasambhava*, sarga 3. Another favorite Śaiva myth is that of the Triple City. The *Ṛg Veda* knows of a demonic triple city, destroyed by the gods, but it is not until the *Mahābhārata* that Śiva plays a part in its destruction (8.24.1–124).

18. See Mahendranāth Bhaṭṭācārya, in *Śākta Padābalī*, ed. Amarendranāth Rāy (Calcutta: University of Calcutta, 1942), poem 172.

19. Dagmar Engels calls this "truncated legacy of the Kulinist extreme" in *Beyond Purdah? Women in Bengal, 1890–1939* (Delhi: Oxford University Press, 1996), p. 81; see also p. 116 n. 51.

20. The best parallelism between Umā's life and that of a Kulīn bride is that elucidated by Śaśibhūṣaṇ Dāśgupta in *Bhārater Śakti-sādhanā o Śākta Sāhitya* (Calcutta: Sāhitya Saṁsad, 1960), pp. 235–247. On Kulīnism generally, see Meredith Borthwick, *The Changing Role of Women in Bengal, 1849–1905* (Princeton: Princeton University Press, 1984); Engels, *Beyond Purdah?*; and Malavika Karlekar, *Reflections on Kulin Polygamy: Nistarini Debi's* Sekeley Katha, Occasional Paper no. 23 (New Delhi: Centre for Women's Development Studies, 1995).

21. See Shahanara Husain, *The Social Life of Women in Early Medieval Bengal* (Dhaka: Asiatic Society of Bangladesh, 1985), p. 44. The Kulīn system even allowed prepubescent girls to be married to sixty-year-old men. Rāmcandra Mukhopādhyāy received Rs. 250 from the father of his thirty-third wife. The marriage was arranged by one of his sons to pay for Rāmcandra's incipient funeral expenses. Engels, *Beyond Purdah?*, pp. 44, 49, 67 n. 14.

22. Margaret M. Urquhart, *Women of Bengal* (1925; Delhi: Gian Publishing House, 1987), pp. 38–39.

23. By the mid-nineteenth century, even these "nautch girls" were in decline, due to Western critiques, Indian alienation from their own art traditions, and the association of female singers with prostitutes, or *devadāsīs*, considered to be of low repute. See Pran Nevile, "Echoes of a Lost Tradition," *India Today* (15 Aug. 1996): 106–111.

24. Wendy Doniger O'Flaherty, in her *Śiva, the Erotic Ascetic*, often mentions tribal variations on the Śiva-Pārvatī myths, which she takes from Verrier Elwin, *Myths of Middle India* (Bombay: Oxford University Press, 1949) and *Tribal Myths of Orissa* (Bombay: Oxford University Press, 1954); P. Thomas, *Epics, Myths, and Legends of India* (Bombay: D. B. Taraporevala Sons, 1942); and W. J. Wilkins, *Hindu Mythology, Vedic and Puranic* (Calcutta: Thacker, Spink, 1882). For additional examples from outside Bengal, see William Archer, *Songs for the Bride: Wedding Rites of Rural India*, ed. Barbara Stoler Miller and Mildred Archer (New York: Columbia University Press, 1985), pp. 63–69; Lynn Bennett, *Dangerous Wives and Sacred Sisters: Social and Symbolic Roles of High-Caste Women in Nepal* (New York: Columbia University Press, 1983), pp. 281–286; and Brigitte Luchesi, " 'It Should Last a Hundred Thousand Years': Rali Worship and Brother–Sister Bond in Kangra," *Manushi*, no. 130 (May–June 2002): 20–25. For a general discussion of the sadness of the bride's leave-taking, see Gloria Goodwin Raheja, " 'Crying When She's Born, and Crying When She Goes Away': Marriage and the Idiom of the Gift in Pahansu Song Performance," in *From the Margins of Hindu Marriage: Essays on Gender, Religion, and Culture*, ed. Lindsey Harlan and Paul B. Courtright (New York: Oxford University Press, 1995), pp. 19–59.

25. Bikāśkānti Midyā, "Durgā: Bāṅglā Lokasāhitye," in *Lok Saṁskṛti Gabeṣaṇā*, ed. Sanatkumār Mitra, vol. 13, no. 2 (July–Aug. 2000): 341. The wedding rituals referred to here are the rubbing of the newly married girl's hair parting with vermillion, or *sindūr*, and the feeding of rice and milk.

26. "*Biyālliśer hāte Gaurīdān, Ṭhākur mantra paḍe balidān*," quoted in ibid., p. 339.

27. Borthwick, *The Changing Role of Women in Bengal*, p. 238.

28. The Bhūtbāḍīr Pūjā, off Creek Road in Kolkata, is said to have been started a century ago by a nine-year-old girl, a daughter-in-law of the house; Sohini Sarkar,

"Keeping the Faith," in the "Downtown" section of the *Statesman*, 15 Oct. 1999, pp. 1–2. The same is claimed of the golden image of Durgā on display at the Durgābāḍī, Behala, south Kolkata, which was commissioned in response to a daughter's request of her father around 1770; Mohit Rāy, *Rūpe Rūpe Durgā* (Calcutta: Adhīr Pāl, 1985), pp. 84–85.

29. Biśvasingha, one of the progenitors of the Kuchbihar Rāj family in northern Bengal, had a dream of Umā flanked by her two childhood friends, Jayā and Bijayā, so this is how the family has depicted the Goddess ever since; *Pratidin*, 28 Sept. 1995, p. 6. Similarly, Dvāraknāth Datta (1829–1889), the founder of Kolkata's famed Thanthania Datta family, dreamed of Hara-Gaurī—Śiva and Gaurī seated together, without any sign of the buffalo-slayer—which remains to this day as the image worshiped at the Pūjās; pamphlet on the family history given to me by Mr. Milan Datta, 30 Sept. 2000.

30. Interview, Mr. Bhāskar Chunder, 13 Dec. 2000.

31. The image is Abhayā (She who Offers Fearlessness), with only two hands; she is supposed to be five years old. Interview, Mr. Subhamay Dawn, 5 Oct. 2000.

32. See Tanmay Ghosh, "Meaningless Mahalaya," *Times of India*, "Calcutta Times" section, 17 Sept. 2001, p. 1.

33. The originator of this tradition, Baikuṇṭhanāth Sānyāl, a disciple of Śrī Rāmakṛṣṇa, thought that Mā would like what the average person does; *Bartamān*, 22 Oct. 2001, p. 12.

34. Rāy, *Rūpe Rūpe Durgā*, p. 2.

35. Most Hara-Gaurī images in Kolkata depict Umā sitting on Śiva's lap: see those at the Chunders of Bechu Chatterjee Street; the Dattas of Thanthania (see the image on the cover of this book); the Lāhās of Cornwallis Street; the Malliks of Shyambazar; and the Malliks of Darpanarayan Tagore Street. Note that at the mansion of the Pathuriaghata Malliks, in addition to the Goddess on Śiva's lap, her four children are all seated on Nandī's back. In the Baranagar Datta family, Durgā sits at the feet of Śiva, who is astride an ox, and the goddess of the Pañcānan Pāl family in Nather Bagan is depicted as Kātyāyanī, mother of the infant Krishna (see fig. 4.2 below).

36. The most famous private image of this type occurs in the various West Bengali families descended from Kāśīnāth Dhar, originally from Dhaka, whose Pūjā is approximately 250 years old. Dhar had a dream in which the Goddess appeared to him and forbade animal sacrifice; ever after, his image has been Gaṇeśa-Jananī. The Goddess has two hands only, one held up in blessing and the other cradling her baby on her lap, and there is no buffalo or any other signs of battle. For a photo, see *Asian Age*, 20 Oct. 2001, p. 9. Some community Pūjās have taken to this type of image as well; at the Hatibagan Sarbajanīn Pūjā in 1998, Durgā was seated cross-legged with Gaṇeśa on her lap, she was dressed in a Bengali sari, and Mahiṣa was depicted kneeling in front of her in supplication. *Asian Age*, 27 Sept. 1998, p. 11.

37. *Ājkāl*, 6 Oct. 2000, p. 7.

38. This is the Pūjā at Bonerpukur Danga, Bolpur, which has been organized only since 2002. *Hindustan Times*, Kolkata, 7 Oct. 2004, Puja Parikrama section, p. 1.

39. R. K. Dasgupta, "Durga—the Mother and the Motherland," in *Amrita Bazar Patrika*, 17 Oct. 1980, p. 5.

40. See *Times of India*, Kolkata, 29 Aug. 2006, p. 2; and *Hindustan Times Live*, Kolkata, 13 Sept. 2008, p. 2, respectively.

41. For another example of a daughter-Goddess tradition, this one popular among tribal and village folk in the southwest frontier of Bengal, eastern Bihar, and Orissa, consider the goddess Tuṣu, who is believed to return only once a year to visit her parents. Her songs share many features with the *āgamanī* and *bijayā* songs for Umā: apart from the longing of her family for her return, we see emphasized the conditions of women, such as their economic and caste situations, political problems, and unrequited love. See June McDaniel, *Making Virtuous Daughters and Wives: An Introduction to Women's Brata Rituals in Bengali Folk Religion* (Albany: State University of New York Press, 2003), pp. 11–28.

42. William Sax, *Mountain Goddess: Gender and Politics in a Himalayan Pilgrimage* (New York: Oxford University Press, 1991).

43. See discussion of this point in Bimalcandra Datta, *Durgā Pūjā: Sekāl theke Ekāl* (Calcutta: Ramakrishna Vivekananda Institute of Research and Culture, 1986), pp. 63–64, and Pratapchandra Ghosha, *Durga Puja, with Notes and Illustrations* (Calcutta: Hindoo Patriot Press, 1871), appendix, pp. ix–x n. 3.

44. References to Durgā's children are at least as old as Mukundarām's *Caṇḍīmaṅgal*; see the section called "*Gaurīr Khed*," lines 14–16, in *Kabikaṅkaṇ Caṇḍī* (Calcutta: Basumatī-Sāhitya-Mandir, 1963), p. 24. Other scholars claim a longer pedigree for the tradition: Amita Ray, in "The Cult and Ritual of Durgā Pūjā in Bengal," from *Shastric Traditions in Indian Arts*, ed. Anna Libera Dallapicolla (Stuttgart: Steiner Verlag Wiesbaden GMBH, 1989), p. 138, and Haṁsanārāyaṇ Bhaṭṭācārya, in *Hinduder Debadebī: Udbhab o Kramabikāś*, 3 vols. (Calcutta: Firma K. L. Mukhopādhyāy, 1986), 3:246, all assert that Vidyāpati's *Durgābhaktitaraṅginī* is the first to mention Durgā's children in the fourteenth to fifteenth centuries. Pratapaditya Pal makes the astute point that if these texts were familiar with a daughter tradition, then Āgamavāgīśa's decision not to include this element in his Tantric digest, the *Tantrasāra*, may have derived from his desire to emphasize the martial and not householder side of the Goddess. See Pratapaditya Pal, *Hindu Religion and Iconology According to the Tantrasāra* (Los Angeles: Vichitra Press, 1981), p. 11. For a reference to Raghunandana, see Bimalcandra Datta, who quotes his *Durgāpūjātattva* to show that by this time rituals for consecrating the four children were in vogue; *Durgā Pūjā: Sekāl theke Ekāl*, p. 46. On the other hand, the ritual manuals described by Pratapchandra Ghosha in *Durga Puja*, p. xi n. 3, mention nothing about the children.

45. The earliest Bengali Mahiṣamardinī image is from Murshidabad, in the seventh century. She is so early that she is not even associated with the lion mount, but stands on the demon and spears him herself. For this and other, later samples, see Ray, "The Cult and Ritual of Durgā Pūjā in Bengal," pp. 131–141.

46. None of the image slabs of Mahiṣamardinī on the surface of West Bengali temples from the sixteenth century and few thereafter depict her with her sons or daughters. For examples, see the Narasiṁha Temple in Gokarna village in Murshidabad (1580), the Raghunāth Temple in Gurisa in Birbhum (1633), the Joḍbāṅglā Kṛṣṇarāy Temple in Bishnupur (1655), the five-steepled (*pañca-ratna*) temple in Bhattbati village in Murshidabad (mid-eighteenth century), the Rādhāgovinda

Temple in Gopalpur in Midnapur (1744), the Jhaḍeśvarnāth Temple in Kanasol in Midnapur (1837), the five-steepled temple in Khorda in Midnapur (1849), the Rādhādāmodar Temple in Midnapur (1856), the Śītalā Temple in Kalmijor, also in Midnapur (1879), and the Dāmodar Tample in Kalyanpur village in Howrah (1883).

47. A fine representative copper Śiva and Pārvatī with a small Gaṇeśa, from Pāla-period Chittagong in the ninth century, may be seen at the Victoria and Albert Museum (854 [IS]). For two additional examples, see B. N. Mukherjee, "Foreign Elements in Iconographiy of Mahishāsuramardinī—The War Goddess of India," in *Zeitschrift der Deutschen Morgenländischen Gesellschaft* (Stuttgart: Franz Steiner, 1985), supplement VI, p. 405 n. 8. Consult also Pratapaditya Pal, *Durga: Avenging Goddess* (Pasadena, CA: Norton Simon Museum, 2005), pp. 22–24; and Ray, "The Cult and Ritual of Durgā Pūjā in Bengal," pp. 134–136.

48. Examples may be seen at the Byām Rāy Temple in Bishnupur (1643), the Dakṣiṇākālī Temple at Malanca village in Midnapur (1712), the Gaganeśvar Temple at Gopalpur (1795), the Śiva Temple at Jotmudi (1828), and the Śiva temple at Surul (1831). See Tārāpad Sāntrā, "Durgā: On Terracotta/Clay Temple Slabs," in *Lok Saṁskṛti Gabeṣaṇā*, ed. Sanatkumār Mitra, vol. 13, no. 2 (July–Aug. 2000): 221–227; and Kalyan Kumar Sarkar, "Terra-cotta Art of Some Temples of Birbhum: Iconographic Observations," in *Calcutta, Bangladesh, and Bengal Studies*, South Asia Series Occasional Paper No. 40, 1990 Bengal Studies Conference Proceedings, ed. Clinton B. Seely (East Lansing: Michigan State University Press, 1991), pp. 259–262.

49. See Mohit Roy, *Rūpe Rūpe Durgā* (Calcutta: Adhīr Pāl, 1985), p. 61.

50. Richard M. Eaton points out that the Sultans in Bengal did not favor upper-caste Brahmans and Kāyasthas, most of whom were Śaiva or Śākta, but patronized instead the largely Vaiṣṇava middle castes of cultivators and artisans; *The Rise of Islam and the Bengal Frontier, 1204–1760* (Berkeley: University of California Press, 1993), p. 67.

51. David J. McCutchion, *Late Medieval Temples of Bengal* (Calcutta: The Asiatic Society, 1972), p. 14.

52. Many such examples may be seen in the collections of the Asutosh Museum at the University of Calcutta.

53. See Binaybhūṣaṇ Rāy, "Durgā in Lakṣmīsarāis," in *Lok Saṁskṛti Gabeṣaṇā*, ed. Sanatkumār Mitra, vol. 13, no. 2 (July–Aug. 2000): 228–237.

54. Sāntrā, "Durgā: On Terracotta/Clay Temple Slabs," pp. 221–227.

55. Malavika Karlekar, "Woman's Nature and the Access in Education," in *Socialisation, Education, and Women: Explorations in Gender Identity*, ed. Karuna Channa (New Delhi: Orient Longman, 1988), p. 131. I am indebted to Judith Walsh for directing me to this essay.

56. "It remains an unsolved question as to why the temples to [Durgā] as mentioned in these records are so limited in number while the number of Durgā images available in stone from the early Pāla periods down to the late medieval ages are so numerous" (A. K. Bhattacharyya, *A Corpus of Dedicatory Inscriptions from Temples of West Bengal [c. 1500 A.D. to c. 1800 A.D.]* [Calcutta: Shri K. K. Roy, 1982], p. 30).

57. I am grateful to Dr. Sanatkumār Mitra, who helped me think through some of these links in an interview on 6 Dec. 2000.

58. Figure 3.3 is an excellent example from the nineteenth or early twentieth century in which Himālaya, dressed like a *rāja*, is portrayed joyously receiving Umā, who is arriving on her lion and holding Gaṇeśa on her lap. Behind Girirāj, rushing out of a Westernized house with green shutters, come Menakā and other ladies. The whole scene is set in the mountains, and the three other children are visible in the distance, flying toward the house on their bird mounts. Śiva, very ugly, dark, and almost naked, follows behind Umā. I am grateful to T. Richard Blurton for showing me this painting.

59. Rāja Mahendralāl Khān, zamindar of Narajole, Midnapur, wrote a play in six acts on the Menakā/Umā theme: *Śāradotsab (Gītināṭya)* (Calcutta: Īśvarcandra Basu, 1288/1881).

60. "Durga Puja in the Villages of Old," *Statesman Puja Supplement*, 16 Sept. 1952, pp. 1 and 4.

61. This sentiment was expressed concerning the Shovabazar Rāj family, but can be extended to other traditional celebrations; *Statesman*, 29 Sept. 1995, p. 7.

62. See *Ānanda Bājār Patrikā*, 23 Oct. 2001, pp. 1 and 5. Some artisans express less the nostalgia for the daughter than the relief of having given her away, as a father who has been freed of responsibility (*bhārmukta*) for the future of his *kanyā*; *Bartamān*, 28 Sept. 2006, p. 4.

63. A number of Purāṇic accounts state that in order to disguise the Goddess's real identity from the demon Tāraka, Brahmā causes the embryo inside Menā's womb to become black. After the dark Pārvatī grows up and marries Śiva, he teases her about her color so much that she vows to do austerities until Brahmā lightens her complexion. When her wish is granted, her dark skin peels off and becomes a separate goddess, who is worshiped in the Vindhya mountains (*Matsya Purāṇa* 154). In another version, Pārvatī is turned black, into Kālī, so as to provoke a quarrel between Pārvatī and Śiva, which will necessitate her doing more austerities, so as to induce Śiva to produce Skanda (*Kumārasambhava* 8.9.18, 87). Other examples occur in the specific context of battle. In the *Liṅga Purāṇa* (2.100), Śiva asks Pārvatī for help in defeating a demon named Dāruka. She enters the blue, poisoned throat of her husband, emerges as Kālī, and slays the demon. In the *Skanda Purāṇa* (2.83), Śiva again requests Pārvatī's aid in killing a male demon, Durga. After assuming the form of a warrior goddess and dispatching him, she gains the name Durgā. Certainly the most famous account of such transformation occurs in the "Devī Māhātmya" section of the *Mārkaṇḍeya Purāṇa*. At the beginning of the third episode (5.38), the gods pray to Pārvatī for aid against two new demons, Śumbha and Niśumbha. Stepping out of her bath, Pārvatī asks why the gods are praising her. A light-colored goddess named Ambikā emerges from Pārvatī's body in order to answer the question and fight the demons. The dark side of Pārvatī, on the other hand, departs for the Himalayas. Soon after, Ambikā emits the fierce and ugly Kālī from the concentrated wrath in her forehead, and directs Kālī to join the Goddess's dread team against the demon armies (7.4ff; see also *Vāmana Purāṇa* 28.6–25).

64. Girīścandra Ghoṣ, "*Kusvapan dekhechi Giri*," in *Śākta Padābalī*, ed. Rāy, poem 13. A similar poem by Hariścandra Mitra may be found in ibid., poem 12.

65. Īśvarcandra Gupta, "*Kailās-sambād śune*," in ibid., poem 17. See McDermott, *Singing to the Goddess*, p. 128.

66. Rasikcandra Rāy, "*Giri, kār kaṇṭhahār ānile Giri-pure?*" in *Śākta Padābalī*, ed. Rāy, poem 41. See McDermott, *Singing to the Goddess*, pp. 142–143. For more examples, see poems by Dāśarathi Rāy (*Śākta Padābalī*, ed. Rāy, poem 40), Rāmcandra Bhaṭṭācārya (ibid., poem 43), and Brajmohan Rāy (ibid., poem 44).

67. Anonymous, in ibid., poem 72.

68. Lakṣmīkānta Biśvās, quoted in Īśvarcandra Gupta, *Sambād Prabhākar* 13 Jan. 1855. See *Īśvar Gupter Racanābalī*, ed. Śāntikumār Dāśgupta and Haribandhu Mukhṭi, 2 vols. (Calcutta: Dattacaudhurī and Sons, 1974), 1:207–210.

69. This comes from Dāśarathi's second *pāncālī* on the *āgamanī* and *bijayā* theme; see *Dāśarathi Rāyer Pāncālī*, ed. Haripad Cakrabartī (Calcutta: University of Calcutta, 1962), pp. 590–597.

70. For instance, see a poem by Rājā Mahendralāl Khān (*Śākta Padābalī*, ed. Rāy, poem 59).

71. This text has never been translated into English, and is not considered of very good poetic quality by Bengali commentators—partially because the modeling of Umā on Kṛṣṇa is so apparent. For the Bengali, see Satyanārāyaṇ Bhaṭṭācārya, *Rāmprasād: Jībanī o Racanāsamagra*, 2 parts (Calcutta: Granthamelā, 1975), 1:5–17.

72. For a discussion of these explanations, see McDermott, *Mother of My Heart*, pp. 284–285.

73. Sadhan Kumar Ghosh, in *Statesman Puja Supplement*, 4 Oct. 1953, p. 1.

74. *Amrita Bazar Patrika*, 22 Oct. 1950, pp. 1 and 5; *Ānanda Bājār Patrikā*, 29 Sept. 1949, pp. 9 and 11.

75. *Amrita Bazar Patrika*, 10 Oct. 1948, p. 12.

76. See *Telegraph*, 19 Oct. 2001, p. 23; *Telegraph*, 28 Oct. 2001, p. III of the "Women" section; *Asian Age*, 6 Oct. 2001, pp. 9–10; and *Ājkāl*, 8 Oct. 2001, p. 4.

77. A classic treatment of nostalgia is that by Fred Davis, *Yearning for Yesterday: A Sociology of Nostalgia* (New York: Free Press, 1979). He describes three types of nostalgia: (1) simple, a feeling that things were once better, healthier, happier (pp. 17–21); (2) reflexive, as one begins to wonder whether the past was really as happy as one thought (pp. 21–24); and (3) interpreted, when one puts the nostalgic feeling itself under scrutiny (pp. 24–26).

78. Roberta Rubenstein, *Home Matters: Longing and Belonging, Nostalgia and Mourning in Women's Fiction* (New York: Palgrave, 2000), p. 5.

79. See Davis, *Yearning for Yesterday*, pp. 34–35 and 49.

80. Jean Starobinski, "The Idea of Nostalgia," *Diogenes* 54 (1966): 81–103.

81. Rubenstein, *Home Matters*, pp. 4 and 87.

82. Jane Marie Law, *Puppets of Nostalgia: The Life, Death, and Rebirth of the Japanese Awaji Nongyō Tradition* (Princeton: Princeton University Press, 1997), p. 206.

83. For a similar glorification of rural life, see Chris Waters, "Autobiography, Nostalgia, and the Changing Practices of Working-Class Selfhood," in *Singular Continuities: Tradition, Nostalgia, and Identity in Modern British Culture*, ed. George K. Behler and Fred M. Leventhal (Stanford: Stanford University Press, 2000), pp. 178–195.

84. Rubenstein, *Home Matters*, pp. 6 and 164.

85. Leo Spitzer, in his discussion of Nazi refugees, catalogues various Marxist critiques of nostalgia for being escapism, a betrayal of history, a tool of the heritage industry, and an opiate with dysfunctional consequences; "Back Through the Future: Nostalgic Memory and Critical Memory in a Refuge from Nazism," in *Acts of Memory: Cultural Recall in the Present*, ed. Mieke Bal, Jonathan Crewe, and Leo Spitzer (Hanover: Dartmouth College, 1999), p. 91. See also Stephanie Coontz, *The Way We Never Were: American Families and the Nostalgia Trap*, 2nd ed. (1992; New York, Basic Books, 2000), pp. 12 and 15. People living in those romanticized "periods were seldom as enamored of their family arrangements as modern nostalgia might suggest" (p. 12). David Lowenthal, in *The Past Is a Foreign Country* (Cambridge: Cambridge University Press, 1985), however, champions the elasticity of the past. We do not need a fixed past, he says, but a "heritage with which we continually interact, one which fuses past with present" (p. 410). The danger arises when we do not admit that the feeling of emancipation we derive from the cult of nostalgia rests on our creative transformation, not the recovery of a "true" history.

86. Ibid., p. 4.

87. Law, *Puppets of Nostalgia*, p. 263.

88. Spitzer, "Back Through the Future," p. 92.

89. Benedict Anderson, *Imagined Communities: Reflections on the Origin and Spread of Nationalism*, 2nd rev. ed. (London: Verso, 1991), p. 143.

## 4. The Artistry of Durgā and Jagaddhātrī

1. I am grateful to the members of the Spalding Symposium, Oxford University, 23 March 2002, who gave me valuable feedback on an initial version of this chapter.

2. According to famed Bengali historian Haraprasād Śāstrī, Durgā Pūjā was originally an agricultural *nabapatrikā* festival: "Durgā-devī, all adorned, came later to sit in the midst of that garden"; cited by Suhṛdkumār Bhaumik, "Durgā: Bāṅgālīr Ādibāsī," in *Lok Saṁskṛti Gabeṣaṇā*, ed. Sanatkumār Mitra, vol. 13, no. 2 (July–Aug. 2000): 294–295.

3. The full pot (*ghaṭ* or *pūrṇa-kumbha*) is placed on a *yantra*; decorated with an abstract figure of a human being made of vermillion paste; and covered with a mango branch, on top of which are placed rice, betel nut, and a vermillion-smeared green coconut. See Amita Ray, "The Cult and Ritual of Durgā Pūjā in Bengal," in *Shastric Traditions in Indian Arts*, ed. Anna Libera Dallpicolla (Stuttgart: Steiner Verlag Wiesbaden GMBH, 1989), esp. p. 139.

4. These are *kadalī* (banana), *kacī* (mango), *haridrā* (turmeric), *jayantī* (nutmeg), *bilva* (maremelos), *dāḍimba* (pomegranate), *aśoka* (Saraca asoca), *māna* (arum), and *dhānya* (rice). For a good description of the plants, plus illustrations, see Madhu Khanna, "The Ritual Capsule of Durgā Pūjā: An Ecological Perspective," in *Hinduism and Ecology: The Intersection of Earth, Sky, and Water*, ed. Christopher Key Chapple and Mary Evelyn Tucker (Cambridge: Harvard University Press, 2006), pp. 476–478.

5. The *nabapatrikā* is also called the *kalā bau*, signaling that she is Gaṇeśa's banana plant wife and Durgā's banana-plant daughter-in-law.

6. R. P. Chandra, *The Indo-Aryan Races: A Study of the Origins of Indo-Aryan People and Institutions* (1916; New Delhi: Indological Book Corp., 1976), p. 131, cited in Jitendranāth Bandyopādhyāy, *Pañcopāsanā* (Calcutta: Firma K. L. Mukhopādhyāy, 1960), p. 282. See also p. 283.

7. See Bimalcandra Datta, *Durgā Pūjā: Sekāl theke Ekāl* (Calcutta: Ramakrishna Vivekananda Institute of Research and Culture, 1986), p. 52.

8. To give an example, the goddess Poḍāmā, whose image is presently established at the root of a big banyan tree in Navadvip, is said to have been "discovered" by a Tantrik *sādhaka* who did *pūjā* to her with a *ghaṭ* in a forest. In the fifteenth century the famous Pandit Bāsudeb Sārbabhauma brought the *ghaṭ* to Navadvip. In 1804 a permanent *mūrti* was donated by Kṛṣṇacandra Rāy's son, Girīścandra. See Śibsaṅkar Bhārati, "Kālī-kathā," in *Sāptahik Bartamān* 16, no. 324 (29 Oct. 2000): 10. No one in the entire village of Kshirgram in Burdwan installs a *mūrti*; all ritual actions are done for *nabapatrikās* alone; see Mohit Rāy, *Rūpe Rūpe Durgā* (Calcutta: Adhīr Pāl, 1985), pp. 38–42.

9. See Atanu Ghoṣ, "Mukhārjider Sonār Durgā," in *Ājkāl*, 20 Sept. 1998, p. 14; and Śrīkānta Gauḍ, "Durgā: Kāṭhkodāi-e," in *Lok Saṁskṛti Gabeṣaṇā*, ed. Sanatkumār Mitra, vol. 13, no. 2 (July–Aug. 2000): 256–264.

10. In other words, the artisan and his patron are responsible *together* for the change. Interview, Dr. Sanatkumār Mitra, 6 Dec. 2000.

11. Jyotindra Jain, *Kalighat Painting: Images from a Changing World* (Ahmedabad: Mapin, 1999), p. 35.

12. See Śibśaṅkar Bhārati, "Durgāpujo Jelāy Jelāy," in *Bartamān*, 8 Oct. 2000, p. 11; *Times of India*, 6 Oct. 2000, p. 6; and Roy, *Rūpe Rūpe Durgā*, pp. 25–27.

13. *Pratidin*, 20 Oct. 2000, p. 12; and *Hindustan Times*, Kolkata, 24 Oct. 2001, p. 2. For more details about the customs of the Malla *rājās* of Mallabhum, see Roy, *Rūpe Rūpe Durgā*, pp. 43–50.

14. Datta, *Durgā Pūjā: Sekāl theke Ekāl*, p. 71.

15. See Kṣetra Gupta, "Durgā: Lokabhāskaryer Pahelā Pāṭh," in *Lok Saṁskṛti Gabeṣaṇā*, ed. Sanatkumār Mitra, vol. 13, no. 2 (July–Aug. 2000): 191–197.

16. Pratapchandra Ghosha, *Durga Puja, with Notes and Illustrations* (Calcutta: Hindoo Patriot Press, 1871), p. 5.

17. According to Śrīkṛṣṇa Pāl, secretary, Kumartuli Mṛtśilpī Sangathan, the following are the stages of image construction, as performed in Kolkata: (1) In April, *śāl* wood is shaped by a carpenter to prepare the frame; (2) in autumn hay padding for the deities is made; (3) the hay is joined to the frame; (4) one layer of clay soil, brought from Diamond Harbor or Uluberia, is applied to the hay; (5) a second layer of sandy soil is applied; (6) the fingers and toes of hands and feet are molded, and the whole image is dried (this takes fifteen days in good weather, more in bad); (7) cracks that appeared during drying are fixed; (8) coats of paint are applied (first white clay, then paint, then red lac-dye for the hands and feet); (9) the images are dressed with clothes and jewelry; (10) they are transported to their pandals; and (11) once they are in place, the Goddess's weapons are fitted in her hands. Heard and transcribed by Hena Basu from "Ālāpan (Dialogue)," broadcast on All India Radio, Kolkata, 5 p.m., 21 Sept. 2000.

18. Apūrba Caṭṭopādhyāy, "Kumorṭulir Kathā," in *Bartamān*, 27 Sept. 2000, p. 12.

19. One rare example of a permanent Durgā temple in Kolkata is the eighteenth-century Citteśvarī Sarvamaṅgalā Temple near Ciria Mor. Here the lion has a horse's head. For an overview of the many cases of horse-headed lions on West Bengal's terracotta temple slabs, see Tārāpad Sāntrā, "Durgā: On Terracotta/Clay Temple Slabs, in *Lok Saṁskṛti Gabeṣaṇā*, ed. Sanatkumār Mitra, vol. 13, no. 2 (July–Aug. 2000): 221–227. Families who trace their tradition of Durgā Pūjā back at least into the eighteenth century, who still follow the iconographic conventions of their forebears, and whose Durgās stand upon horse-faced lions include the Hatkhola Dattas, the Khelātcandra Ghoṣes, the Rāmdulāl Sarkār Debs, and the major line of the Shovabazar Rāj family. Note that the rival minor Shovabazar line has changed its horse's head back into a lion's head. The Nadia Rāj at Krishnanagar also has a horse-faced lion.

20. See Adip Datta, "The Three Eyes, the Ten Arms, and the Lie of the Land," in *Telegraph*, 30 Sept. 1995, Section III: Arts and Ideas, p. 1.

21. See "Bāṅgāl Durgāi Jitlen," in *Ānanda Bājār Patrikā*, 4 Oct. 2000, p. 4.

22. Historic families that still commission the rarer second type include: the Sābarṇa Rāy Caudhurīs of Behala, the Singhis of Paddapukur, and the Chātu-Bābu Lātu-Bābu family and Khelātcandra Ghoṣes, both of north Kolkata. There are other minor variations on these old-style backdrops. For example, the *cāl* at the Thanthania Ghoṣ family Pūjā is triangular; Sohini Sarkar, "Keeping the Faith," in *Statesman*, 15 Oct. 1999, "Downtown" section, pp. 1–2. For an exhaustive account of all possible *cāl* types, see Jayanta Dās, "Kumorṭulir Cārśo Bacharer Bibartan," *Deś* 64, no. 24 (19 Sept. 1998): 63–70.

23. Interview, 22 Sept. 2000.

24. Susan S. Bean, "The Art of Exchange: Circulation of Visual Culture in Colonial India," talk given at Columbia University, 28 Oct. 2006.

25. Susan S. Bean, in "Mud and Divinity: Changing Shapes of Patronage in Nineteenth-Century Bengal" (draft paper, 1998), p. 19, cites Christopher Pinney on this point: "Colonial Anthropology in the 'Laboratory of Mankind,'" in *The Raj: India and the British, 1600–1900*, ed. Christopher Bayly (London: National Portrait Gallery, 1990), pp. 252–263.

26. Pāl grew up in the house of his maternal grandfather in Krishnanagar. At around the age of twenty he took employment with the Potter Works of Burn and Co. in Ranigunge. Within a few days he bewildered everyone by creating an image of the Goddess. Resigning after a few years from Burns, he built himself a workshop, where, from about 1919 to 1924, he started making goddess images. Later, with the help of a Marwari industrialist, he set up a studio in Calcutta. Shortly after this he went to London. See Añjali Basu, ed., *Saṁsad Bāṇali Caritabhidhān* (Kolkata: Sāhitya Saṁsad, 1994), p. 141. Although accounts differ as to the means by which Pāl's work came to the notice of the British (Dās, below, has Pāl meeting Lord Carmichael in Krishnanagar in 1915, whereas Siddheśvar Pāl claims that it was Lord Bentley [interview with Hena Basu, on my behalf, 5 March 2002]), it is clear that at a young age Gopeśvar impressed a British civil servant enough to be remembered—and invited to compete for a position at the Wembley exhibition. See Dās, "Kumorṭulir Cārśo

Bacharer Bibartan." For a description of Wembley and all the Indian artists present there, see Partha Mitter, *The Triumph of Modernism: India's Artists and the Avant-Garde, 1922–1947* (London: Reaktion Books, 2007), pp. 191–194.

27. *Daily Telegraph*, London, 7 July 1924, p. 13.

28. Interview with Gopeśvar Pāl's son, Siddheśvar Pāl, 16 Oct. 1998.

29. Susan Bean thinks that the application of naturalism spread from humans to deities around the end of the nineteenth century, probably starting with the figure of Kārtik; "The Art of Exchange."

30. Both quotations are from the *Amrita Bazar Patrika* newspaper from 1932: 2 Oct., p. 5, and 12 Oct., p. 7. Siddheśvar Pāl avers that his father was self-consciously attempting to revert to the spirit of the *dhyānas* (interview with Hena Basu, 5 March 2002).

31. See "Bāṅgāl Durgāi Jitlen." This Muslim bearer was killed in the 1946 Calcutta riots for the sin of carrying a Hindu image.

32. Some artisans still follow this method; *Ānanda Bājār Patrikā*, 11 July 2002, p. 1, features a photo of Jātīn Pāl modeling his demons after real gymnasts.

33. See "New Orientation in Clay-Modelling," in *Amrita Bazar Patrika*, 15 Oct. 1936, p. 10.

34. "From the point of view of the image, the place of honour should go to the Kumartuli celebration where the renowned artist Mr. G. Pal has constructed a most impressive image of Mother Durga which in conception and working out of details marks a departure from the traditional style" (*Amrita Bazar Patrika*, 1 Oct. 1938, p. 7). For encomia about N. C.'s Bagbazar image, which by 1936 was the highest in the city, at 16'6", see *Amrita Bazar Patrika*, 18 Oct. 1936, p. 7.

35. *Amrita Bazar Patrika*, 5 Oct. 1932, p. 3.

36. *Ājkāl*, 22 Sept. 1998, pp. 1 and 5.

37. For these critiques, see "Bāṅgāl Durgāi Jitlen."

38. Jayanta Dās writes that Gopeśvar Pāl's images caught on among immigrant artisans from East Bengal after the 1950s, because the practice of humanizing the Goddess in East Bengal actually predated Pāl's innovation. Rameścandra Pāl, an artisan from East Bengal whom Dās interviews, agrees: the West Bengali artisans did most of the images for home Pūjās, and since the *sarbajanīn* Pūjās were increasing, that left a lot of work for the East Bengali artists. Dās, "Kumorṭulir Cārśo Bacharer Bibartan," 63–70.

39. "Busy Spell for Image Makers," *Statesman*, 27 Sept. 1957, p. 10.

40. One Pūjā committee in Bhowanipur, south Kolkata, dressed their Durgā as Śāradādebī (1853–1920), Rāmakṛṣṇa's famous wife. Absent were Mahiṣamardinī and Durgā's four children.

41. In 2004 this trend was said to be a "new phenomenon"; *Amrita Bazar Patrika*, 10 Oct. 2004, p. 17.

42. *Times of India*, 3 Oct. 2002, p. 2.

43. B. Datta, *Durgā Pūjā: Sekāl theke Ekāl*, p. 141.

44. *Ānanda Bājār Patrikā*, 11 Nov. 2000, p. 4.

45. In 2000 I surveyed 146 Durgā images in *Pratidin* newspaper photo spreads; of these, 68 were completely humanized, 65 were of the hybrid variety, and only

13 had the old bodies and old faces. In 1999 the same paper printed 109 different images: of these, 53 were humanized, 44 had sweet faces, and 12 were of the traditional style.

46. *Amrita Bazar Patrika*, 29 Sept. 1968, p. 1.

47. According to Jagaddhātrī's *dhyāna mantra* in Kṛṣṇānanda Āgambāgīś's sixteenth-century *Tantrasāra*, she is described as follows: "Seated on a lion's back, adorned with various ornaments,/ With four hands, the Great Goddess, a snake for a sacred thread,/ In her two left hands a conch and a bow,/ In her two right hands a discus and five arrows,/ Wearing a red garment, her young body outshining the sun,/ Served by Narada and other sages, the Beauteous wife of Bhava,/ The three folds of her navel shine like a clump of lotuses./ She is seated on a blooming lotus on top of a lion on a gem-encrusted island." See *Bṛhat Tantrasāra*, ed. Rasikmohan Caṭṭopādhyāy and translated into Bengali by Candrakumār Tarkālaṅkar (Calcutta: Nababhārat, 1982), section called "Atha Durgā Mantrāḥ," p. 488. In most modern images the Goddess holds one arrow, not five, and she wears white, not red.

48. Although I can find no explicit equation of Jagaddhātrī's elephant-demon with Durgā's adversary Mahiṣa, who in the "Devī-Māhātmya" temporarily changes from a buffalo into an elephant, it seems fairly clear that the elephant is a variant of the buffalo. Both demons are killed by the Goddess, and in both cases the Goddess's lion is actively engaged in the struggle.

49. Of the 121 freestanding temples to single goddesses (not male gods with their female consorts) described by David McCutchion in his exhaustive survey of Bengali temples, 33 are dedicated to Kālī (the oldest dated is from 1712), 15 to Śītalā (oldest dated from 1811), 14 to Caṇḍī (oldest dated from 1649), 11 to Durgā (oldest dated from 1705), and 10 to Simhavāhinī (oldest dated from 1490). See *Brick Temples of Bengal: From the Archives of David McCutchion*, ed. George Michell (Princeton: Princeton University Press, 1983).

50. The Asutosh Museum at the University of Calcutta has an eighth-century image from Barisal and an eighteenth-century image from Jessore, both in present-day Bangladesh. These scant museum holdings may indicate that Jagaddhātrī was popular earlier and further east than other sources can corroborate at present.

51. Famous old-style Jagaddhātrī images can be seen at Kumartuli Friends Circle and Prabhat Smriti Sangha in Kolkata; Chaulpatti in Chandannagar; Baubazar and Malopara in Krishnanagar; Kagram in Murshidabad; and Shorbhujbazar Sutragar in Shantipur.

52. *Amrita Bazar Patrika*, 16 Oct. 1980, p. 7.

53. *Statesman Puja Supplement*, 4 Oct. 1953, p. 1.

54. *Statesman*, 5 Oct. 1961, p. 1.

55. *Telegraph*, 26 Sept. 2006, p. 1.

56. Interview, 23 Sept. 1998.

57. *Sunday Times of India*, Kolkata, 3 Sept. 2006, p. 2.

58. *Statesman*, 14 Oct. 1983, p. 16.

59. See *Hindustan Times*, Kolkata, 21 Oct. 2004, p. 1, for the before and after photos.

60. Soumitra Das, "Swingback to Tradition," in *Statesman*, 19 Oct. 1988.

61. The Bagbazar Pūjā committee apparently never gets involved in the "rat-race (*idũrdauḍe*) for wowing people with their pujas," but nevertheless they nearly always win prizes for their old-style images; *Pratidin*, 22 Sept. 2000, p. 5.

62. See Meredith Borthwick, *The Changing Role of Women in Bengal, 1849–1905* (Princeton: Princeton University Press, 1984); Partha Chatterjee, "The Nation and Its Women" and "Women and the Nation," in *The Nation and Its Fragments* (Delhi: Oxford University Press, 1995), pp. 116–157; Rajat Kanta Ray, "Man, Woman, and the Novel: The Rise of a New Consciousness in Bengal," in *Exploring Emotional History: Gender, Mentality, and Literature in the Indian Awakening* (Delhi: Oxford University Press, 2001), pp. 67–117; and Judith E. Walsh, "What Women Learned When Men Gave Them Advice: Rewriting Patriarchy in Late-Nineteenth-Century Bengal," *Journal of Asian Studies* 56.3 (August 1997): 641–677, and *Domesticity in Colonial India: What Women Learned When Men Gave Them Advice* (Lanham, Md.: Rowman and Littlefield, 2004).

63. Although this was primarily a male ideal, as Judith Walsh demonstrates in "What Women Learned," it was taken up and championed by women who saw in companionate marriage a way to break free of the constraints of the mother-in-law.

64. From the Introduction by S. N. Mukherjee to *The Poison Tree: Three Novellas by Bankim Chandra Chatterjee* (New Delhi: Penguin, 1996), p. xxxi. For more on the rise of individualism, see Partha Mitter, *Art and Nationalism in Colonial India, 1850–1922: Occidental Orientations* (Cambridge: Cambridge University Press, 1994), pp. 120–136.

65. Bankim's six domestic novels are: *Rajmohan's Wife* (1864, in English), *Biṣabṛkṣa* (1873), *Rajanī* (1877), *Kṛṣṇakānter Uil* (1878), *Rādhārāṇī* (1886), and *Indirā* (1873, 1893). For further discussion, see Tanika Sarkar, *Hindu Wife, Hindu Nation: Community, Religion, and Cultural Nationalism* (Delhi: Permanent Black, 2001), chaps. 4 and 5, pp. 134–190.

66. According to Ray's persuasive study, other indigenous ideas conveyed in the novels are the relationships between men and women, as framed by conceptions of *puruṣa* and *prakṛti*, and the particular type of pouting love known as *māna* or *abhimāna*. See "Man, Woman, and the Novel."

67. For an overview of these early genres, see Mitter, *Art and Nationalism*, pp. 3–25; and Tapati Guha-Thakurta, "Art in Old Calcutta: The Melting Pot of Western Styles," and R. P. Gupta, "Art in Old Calcutta: Indian Style," in *Calcutta: The Living City*, vol. 1: *The Past*, ed. Sukanta Chaudhuri (Calcutta: Oxford University Press, 1990), pp. 137–138 and 146–148, respectively.

68. Mitter, *Art and Nationalism*, p. 271. In an extraordinary statement, Bankim opines, "Our idols are hideous, they say. True, we wait for our sculptors. It is a question of art only. The Hindu pantheon has never been adequately represented in stone or clay, because India has produced no sculptors. . . . The images we worship in Bengal are, as works of art, a disgrace to the nation. Wealthy Hindus should get their Krishnas and Radhas made in Europe"; from one of his letters to Hastie, published in the *Statesman* for 28 Oct. 1882, reproduced in *The English Writings of Bankimchandra*, ed. Sudin Chattopadhyay (Kolkata: Deep Prakashan, 2003), p. 280. I am grateful to Dermot Killingley for alerting me to this passage.

69. The first printing press reached Calcutta in 1777–1778; by the end of the century there were seventeen printing presses, all owned by Europeans. The first Indian-owned press was established in 1807 in Khidirpur; within a few years Bengalis operated presses all over Calcutta. The first illustrated Bengali book was the *Annadāmaṅgal*, from 1816, and the first illustrated Bengali periodical was from 1818.

70. The definitive work on these is Ashit Paul's edited volume, *Woodcut Prints of Nineteenth-Century Calcutta* (Calcutta: Seagull Books, 1983). Although Bat-tala woodcuts begin to appear in the 1820s, their golden age is 1860–1900. By the end of this period, they went from being book illustrations to loose prints, colored by hand. In this, and the themes they covered, they were parallel to the Kalighat *paṭs*, which slightly outlived them.

71. The best, most recent study of the *paṭs* is Jyotindra Jain's *Kalighat Painting*; his bibliography contains a comprehensive list of older works on the subject. The *paṭ* genre lasted from approximately 1830 to 1930.

72. See Purnendu Pattrea, "The Continuity of the Battala Tradition: An Aesthetic Reevaluation," in Paul, *Woodcut Prints*, pp. 70–71.

73. Jain, *Kalighat Painting*, p. 123.

74. Ibid., pp. 26–34.

75. Mitter, *Art and Nationalism*, p. 55. Also see his discussion of the first major academic sculptor, Ganpatrao Mhatre (1876–1947), from Pune, who absorbed the Greco-Roman style and produced several masterpieces—"To the Temple," "Saraswai," and "Parvati"—that are voluptuous and sensual (pp. 103–107).

76. Jain, *Kalighat Painting*, p. 37.

77. B. N. Mukherjee, "Pictures from Woodcut Blocks: An Iconological Analysis," in Paul, *Woodcut Prints*, p. 108.

78. Mitter, *Art and Nationalism*, p. 178.

79. For an example of Greek sculpture entering his paintings, see Tapati Guha-Thakurta, "Clothing the Goddess: The Modern Contest Over Representation of Devi," in *Devi: The Great Goddess: Female Divinity in South Asian Art*, ed. Vidya Dehejia (Washington, D.C.: Arthur M. Sackler Gallery, 1999), p. 171.

80. Sandria Freitag discusses this juxtaposition of the religious and the domestic in calendar art in "Visions of the Nation: Theorizing the Nexus Between Creation, Consumption, and Participation in the Public Sphere," in *Pleasure and the Nation: The History, Politics, and Consumption of Public Cultures in India*, ed. Rachel Dwyer and Christopher Pinney (Delhi: Oxford University Press, 2001), pp. 53–59. See also Erwin Neumayer and Christine Schelberger, *Popular Indian Art: Raja Ravi Varma and the Printed Gods of India* (New York: Oxford University Press, 2003).

81. For overviews of these critiques, see Guha-Thakurta, "Clothing the Goddess," pp. 157–180; Mitter, *Art and Nationalism*, pp. 221–266; and Mitter, *The Triumph of Modernism*, pp. 29–122.

82. See Mitter, *The Triumph of Modernism*, pp. 132–140, and especially the comparison of paintings by C. Raja Raja Varma, Ravi Varma's brother, and Hemendranāth Majumdār on pp. 134–135.

83. Guha-Thakurta, "Clothing the Goddess," p. 173.

84. Guha-Thakurta, "Art in Old Calcutta," p. 155.

85. For more on the nationalistic feminization of women, see Partha Chatterjee, "Colonialism, Nationalism, and Colonialized Women: The Contest in India," *American Ethnologist* 16.4 (Nov. 1989): 622–633, as cited in Annapurna Garimela, "Engendering Indian Art," in *Representing the Body: Gender Issues in Indian Art*, ed. Vidya Dehejia (Delhi: Kali for Women, 1997), p. 33; Sarkar, *Hindu Wife, Hindu Nation*, p. 266; and Patricia Uberoi, "Feminine Identity and National Ethos in Indian Calendar Art," *Economic and Political Weekly* (28 April 1990): 43. For further reading on calendar art and goddesses, see Gerald Larson, Pratapaditya Pal, and H. Daniel Smith, *Changing Myths and Images: Twentieth-Century Popular Art in India* (Bloomington: Indiana University, 1997), especially essay and associated prints by Pal, "The Printed Image: An Iconographic Excursus," pp. 33–35, pls. 27–48.

86. Richard Davis, "Introduction," in idem, ed., *Picturing the Nation: Iconographies of Modern India* (Hyderabad: Orient Longman, 2007), p. 5. The same point is made by Christopher Pinney, in *"Photos of the Gods": The Printed Image and Political Struggle in India* (London: Reaktion Books, 2004), p. 8.

87. Neumayer and Schelberger, *Popular Indian Art*, p. 56, pl. 36. Earlier, in 1898, Ravi Varma had already depicted Durgā as a four-armed, red sari–clad maiden standing in front of two reclining lions, but this did not become as famous as the Tagore piece. See ibid., p. 61, pl. 39.

88. Sumathi Ramaswamy, "Body Politic(s): Maps and Mother Goddesses in Modern India," in *Picturing the Nation: Iconographies of Modern India*, ed. Richard H. Davis (Hyderabad: Orient Longman, 2007), p. 34.

89. The image was stationed at Bijaygarh Colony, Calcutta. *Ānanda Bājār Patrikā*, 29 Sept. 1952, p. 8.

90. *Pratidin*, 24 Oct. 2001, p. 6.

91. See chapter 2, nn. 83, 84.

92. *Ānanda Bājār Patrikā*, 22 Oct. 1950, p. 4.

93. A marvelous collection of such prints is collected in Erwin Neumayer and Christina Schelberger, *Bharat Mata: India's Freedom Movement in Popular Art* (Oxford: Oxford University Press, 2008).

94. R. P. Gupta, "Pujas Then and Now," in *Sunday Statesman Miscellany*, 20 Oct. 1985, pp. 1 and 2.

95. Francesca Orsini, *The Hindi Public Sphere, 1920–1940: Language and Literature in the Age of Nationalism* (New York: Oxford University Press, 2002).

96. *Statesman*, 1 Oct. 1922, p. 10.

97. The Durgā in Bangar at North 24 Parganas is called Biṛālhāṭ Durgā because eight of her ten hands look like caw's paws; see *Bartaman*, 22 Oct. 2001, p. 11. The face of the stone image of Mahāmāyā at Garhraipur in Bankura is like that of a fox (*kokmukhī*). The attribution of a fox's face to the Goddess is as old as the *Mahābhārata* (Bhīṣma Pārva 23). See Debjyoti Chattopadhyay, "Durga in Rarhanchal," in *Statesman*, 26 Sept. 1990, p. 12. The Durgā image at the Kuchbihar zamindars' house is sculpted as Cāmuṇḍā.

98. Thomas B. Coburn, *Encountering the Goddess: A Translation of the Devī-Māhātmya and a Study of Its Interpretation* (Albany: State University of New York Press, 1991), 4.11, p. 49.

## 5. Durgā on the *Titanic*: Politics and Religion in the Pūjā

1. I am grateful to participants in the symposium "Experiencing Devi: Hindu Goddesses in Indian Popular Art," held at the University of Iowa in Feb. 2001; to the members of the Indology Seminar at Oxford University in May 2001; and to C. J. Fuller, Henrike Donner, and Laura Bear, of the London School of Economics, all of whom gave valuable feedback on earlier drafts of this chapter.

2. *Calcutta Journal*, 7 Oct. 1820, p. 367. The article goes on to comment that of any 100 Rs. collected, only 20 are spent on the "idol," and the rest on the entertainments.

3. See Rev. Alexander Duff, *India and Indian Missions: Including Sketches of the Gigantic System of Hinduism Both in Theory and in Practice* (Edinburgh, 1839; Delhi: Swati Publications, 1988), pp. 243–264.

4. Evidence for this claim is overwhelming in the papers of 1926 through the late 1950s, in all news coverage at all Pūjā seasons. One precedent for the present-day illuminations of the public Pūjās derives from zamindari festivals of the mid-nineteenth century: the wealthy landowning houses sometimes entertained their guests by festooning their houses with oil lamps placed to effect the shape of figures; *Englishman and Military Chronicle*, 7 Oct. 1851, p. 3.

5. *Ānanda Bājār Patrikā*, 27 Sept. 1952, p. 1. The Hindu Mahasabha's accompanying exhibition at Girish Park in 1953 was more controversial: its models ridiculed the Hindu Code Bill, death duties, widow remarriage, and the Partition of India; *Amrita Bazar Patrika*, 15 Oct. 1953, pp. 1 and 5.

6. *Amrita Bazar Patrika*, 15 Oct. 1953, pp. 1 and 5.

7. For example, see *Amrita Bazar Patrika*, 18 Oct. 1953, p. 1; and 6 Oct. 1954, p. 1.

8. *Amrita Bazar Patrika*, 8 Oct. 1962, pp. 1 and 7. "Pandal-hopping" is also referred to in the *Statesman*, 10 Oct. 1970, p. 1.

9. *Amrita Bazar Patrika*, 18 Oct. 1969, p. 1.

10. *Amrita Bazar Patrika*, 20 Oct. 1966, pp. 1 and 7.

11. *Amrita Bazar Patrika*, 19 Oct. 1969, p. 7.

12. One finds this first from the early 1980s, and what is mentioned is the sacrifice of animals and the application of oil and vermilion to weaponry, which is then laid down in front of Durgā. See *Statesman*, 6 Oct. 1981, pp. 1 and 3.

13. A photograph of one such pandal can be seen in *Amrita Bazar Patrika*, 3 Nov. 1984, p. 36.

14. These six structures are mentioned in *Bartamān*, 9 Oct. 2001, p. 2; *Ājkāl*, 20 Oct. 2001, p. 6; *Asian Age*, 24 Oct. 2001, p. 10; and *Ājkāl*, 25 Oct. 2001, p. 1.

15. See *Ānanda Bājār Patrikā*, 28 Sept. 2006, Pūjā insert, p. 1.

16. *Pratidin*, 24 Oct. 2001, p. 1.

17. Kalyāṇ Singh, chair of a committee in Halishahar. See *Bartamān*, 22 Sept. 2006, p. 3.

18. This pandal belonged to Baruipur Madarhat Dakshinpara. *Telegraph*, 26 Aug. 2006, p. 23. Another pandal of this ilk was erected at Palta Netaji Sangha, where the pandal was a copy of the Munich football stadium, decorated inside as if for the final match between Italy and France. The Devī was depicted giving a trophy to Italy's captain, Fabio Canabarok. *Bartamān*, 22 Sept. 2006, p. 3.

19. *Times of India*, Kolkata, 11 Oct. 2004, p. 3.

20. *Telegraph*, Kolkata, 19 Oct. 2004, p. 14.

21. This was the theme at Ladies' Park. *Times of India*, Kolkata, 15 Oct. 2007, City section, p. 1.

22. *Hindustan Times Live*, Kolkata, 4 Sept. 2008, p. 4.

23. This was the theme of the Selimpur Palli committee. *Hindustan Times Live*, Kolkata, 19 Sept. 2008, p. 2.

24. 41 Palli, Haridevpur, was the site of this Sundarbans theme. *Hindustan Times Live*, Kolkata, 17 Sept. 2008, p. 2.

25. Absar Sarbojanin, on Townshend Road, and Putiary Club, in the south. *Telegraph*, 17 Sept. 2006, Metro section, p. 1.

26. See, respectively, *Dainik Basumatī*, 26 Oct. 1968, p. 3; *Amrita Bazar Patrika*, 18 Nov. 1977, p. 5; www.giridoot.com/puja2.htm (accessed 3 Nov. 2003); and www.calcuttaweb.com/picture/jagaddhatripuja (accessed 27 Dec. 2008).

27. On the *ghaṭ bisarjan*, see *Pratidin*, 27 Oct. 2000, p. 12.

28. Quoted from the *Englishman*, 15 Feb. 1849, cited in Rajat Sanyal, *Voluntary Associations and the Urban Public Life in Bengal (1815–1876): An Aspect of Social History* (Calcutta: Riddhi-India, 1980), p. 62 n. 9.

29. One reads of this particularly in the early years of CPI(M) power in the state. For instance, in 1967, in Bhatpara, 24 Parganas, there was a clash over which procession should be allowed to cross the road first. Seven people were killed and 50 injured, including 15 policemen. In Bhadreshwar that same year, one group carried swords, lathis, and torches soaked in kerosene. The area through which they traveled objected, so the police disarmed them and had them process through a different route; *Amrita Bazar Patrika*, 15 Oct. 1967, p. 3. In 1969 the newspapers reported stabbings and deaths over the right of passage between two different processions, both in Calcutta and in Tribeni, Hooghly district; *Amrita Bazar Patrika*, 22 Oct. 1969, p. 7.

30. *Amrita Bazar Patrika*, 16 Oct. 1969, p. 14, and 20 Oct. 1969, p. 1.

31. *Amrita Bazar Patrika*, 17 Oct. 1975, p. 7.

32. This attention to priests is recent, and is mostly attributable to the efforts of the Vaidic Pandit o Purohit Mahamilan Kendra and the Paścimbanga Vaidic Academy, local affiliates of the All India Pracchovidya Academy, organizations committed to priestly authenticity and welfare. These institutions provide training camps for priests and issue certifications for graduates. For representative articles, see the Kolkata editions of *Hindustan Times*, 12 Oct. 2002, p. 1; *Times of India*, 12 Sept. 2006, p. 1; *Telegraph*, Sunday Metro, 17 Sept. 2006, p. 1; and *Hindustan Times*, 6 Sept. 2008, p. 2.

33. The organizer is Prayasam, a city NGO working for underprivileged children. *Hindustan Times*, Kolkata edition, 6 Oct. 2002; http://timesofindia.indiatimes.com/articleshow/24303374.cms (accessed 7 July 2009).

34. This prize was sponsored by the Indian UTI Bank. *Times of India*, 20 Oct. 2004, p. 1.

35. *Telegraph*, Kolkata, 28 Sept. 2006, p. 22.

36. The police forbid pandals from encroaching too far into public thoroughfares, artisans from making images higher than ten feet, and committee members

from blaring loud music from microphones, forcibly collecting subscriptions, or stealing electricity.

37. *Hindustan Times*, 8 Oct. 2001, p. 3.

38. In an article called "The Goddess Comes to Harijans," the first Harijan-sponsored Pūjā, from 1946, is described as continuing to flourish, without discrimination; *Statesman*, 14 Oct. 1983, p. 16. But other news items report social ostracism of low-caste fishermen and lepers who wish to organize their own Pūjās. They are not prevented, but no one else visits. *Times of India*, Kolkata, 24 Oct. 2001, p. 5; and *Ānanda Bājār Patrikā*, 9 Oct. 2006, p. 1.

39. For example, fearing that the attraction of the Trinamul in Midnapur would cost them elected seats, in 2000 CPI(M) cadres physically harassed Midnapuri villagers and their property. Reacting to what she termed this "red terror," Mamatā directed her Trinamul workers to aid homeless victims of the Communist backlash by sponsoring Pūjās. In order to give the appearance that all was back to normal, CPI(M) workers apparently "forced" villages under their control to hold Pūjā celebrations. See *Bartamān*, 14 Sept. 2000, p. 3, and *Ānanda Bājār Patrikā*, 7 Oct. 2000, p. 7.

40. Arun Shourie, in his *Eminent Historians: Their Technology, Their Line, Their Fraud* (New Delhi: ASA, 1998), surveys Bengali public school textbooks expressing the Communist opinion of religion as an instrument of the ruling class to perpetuate its hegemony. For example, on p. 73 he cites *Itihās o Bhūgal*, pt. II (West Bengal: Bidyālay Śikṣā Adhikār, 1975), pp. 25–26, meant for class IV students, where Pūjās are criticized for their inception by kings and landlords; and on p. 157 he quotes D. N. Jha, *Ancient India, An Introductory Outline* (1977; New Delhi: Manohar, 1997), p. xviii, who says, "*Bhakti* is just the reflection of the complete dependence of the serfs or tenants on the landowners in the context of Indian feudal society."

41. *Times of India*, Utsav Special, Oct. 2001, p. 38.

42. *Telegraph*, 24 Sept. 2006, Insight section, p. 9.

43. See *Ānanda Bājār Patrikā*, 3 Oct. 1995, pp. 1 and 3; *Statesman*, 30 Sept. 1998, p. 3; and *Ānanda Bājār Patrikā*, 11 Oct. 2001, p. 1, and 23 Oct. 2001, p. 2.

44. *Indian Express*, Newsline section, 28 Sept. 2006, p. 1.

45. For three sarcastic and plaintive laments on the departure of current Communist ideology from its origins, refer to Tārāśankar Bandyopādhyāy in an article for *Ānanda Bājār Patrikā*, 27 Sept. 1952, pp. 1 and 5; Rāghab Bandyopādhyāy, "Bāṅglā Mahiṣamardinī Banām Mārks-bāhinī," in *Deś* 65, no. 24 (19 Sept. 1998): 59–62; and Pārtha Mukhopādhyāy in an article for *Pratidin*, 27 Oct. 2000, p. 3.

46. So says Anil Bhandari, managing director of Travel House. *Times of India*, Kolkata, 31 Aug. 2002, p. 3.

47. Arjun Appadurai, "Consumption, Duration, and History," chap. 4 of his *Modernity at Large: Cultural Dimensions of Globalization* (Minneapolis: University of Minnesota Press, 1996), p. 84.

48. *Amrita Bazar Patrika*, 3 Oct. 1954, Sunday magazine, pp. I and IV.

49. *Bengalee*, 5 Oct. 1924, p. 6.

50. The following newspaper reports contain accounts and photographs of various Titanic models, at both Durgā and Kālī Pūjās, and in areas all over Bengal. "Jelā-

Śaharer Pūjo," in *Sāptahik Bartamān*, 26 Sept. 1998, pp. 16–19; *Statesman*, 30 Sept. 1998, p. 3; *Ājkāl*, 18 Oct. 1998, p. 5; and *Ānanda Bājār Patrikā*, 3 Oct. 2000, p. 12.

51. Such creative borrowing of "other people's" cultural productions can lead to trouble. In 2007 the FD Block Pūjā Committee in Salt Lake was threatened with a lawsuit when the publisher of Harry Potter in India, Penguin India, sued it over its pandal shaped like Hogwarts Castle, complete with Harry inside, next to Durgā. The suit claimed Rs. 20 million, but was thrown out by the Delhi High Court.

52. One lighting display I saw in more than one city during the 2000 Pūjā season depicted a little girl whose father married her to a dog earlier in the year, for fear of the bad luck in her destiny. For additional examples, in 1991, the Ramakrishna Sebak Committee bound its image of Durgā in chains to symbolize the exploitation of women, and the Hari Ghosh Street Pūjā members organized an exhibition on "Take No Dowry, Give No Dowry." See *Statesman*, 17 Oct. 1991, p. 11, for descriptions of both.

53. In 1994, Gaṇeśa's rat was often absent from the divine tableau, because of the association of rats with the recent plague in Surat; Laxmi Parasuram (pers. comm., 11 Oct. 1994).

54. See *India Today*, 12 Oct. 1998, pp. 66–68.

55. As stated in *Ānanda Bājā Patrikā*, 4 Oct. 2000, p. 4.

56. As exceptions, see critiques of the Kamdahari pandal and its demonization of Clinton and Blair (*Ājkāl*, 18 Sept. 2000, pp. 1 and 5; and *Ānanda Bājār Patrikā*, 1 Oct. 2000, p. 1); a Durgā who has doves, not weapons, in her hands (*Yugāntar*, 3 Oct. 1995, p. 3); and a depiction of Durgā in front of a nuclear explosion. The demon she is killing is a politician (*Telegraph*, 15 Oct. 1999, p. 17). There are also other ways of promoting peace. The Calcutta–Dhaka bus, a sign of new friendship, has been shown through colored lights since 1999 (*Bartamān*, 7 Nov. 1999, p. 5).

57. For a perceptive discussion of this issue, see *Sambad Pratidin*, 20 Sept. 2001, p. 2.

58. From an article by Somini Sengupta for the *New York Times* for 22 Oct. 2007. Accessed online 8 Nov. 2007.

59. *Amrita Bazar Patrika*, 7 Oct. 1962, p. 7; *Amrita Bazar Patrika*, 1 Oct. 1984, p. 1; *Amrita Bazar Patrika*, 27 Sept. 1987, p. 2; and *India Today International*, 18 Dec. 2001, p. 24s.

60. See chapter 1, pp. 14 and 24. The holiest, most auspicious part of the festival, which occurs at the conjunction, or *sandhi*, of the eighth and ninth days, is supposed to confer divinity upon the sponsor; this is another reason that the elite, always searching for symbols of their sovereignty, were eager to promulgate the Pūjā. See C. J. Fuller, *The Camphor Flame: Popular Hinduism and Society in India* (Princeton: Princeton University Press, 1992), pp. 106–127.

61. *Calcutta Journal*, 7 Oct. 1820, pp. 366–367.

62. Kālīprasanna Siṃha, "Durgotsab," in his *Hutom Pyāṃcār Nakśā*, with commentary, 2nd ed. (1862; Calcutta: Subarṇarekhā, 1991), p. 247.

63. Dr. Jadunath Sarkar, "Durga Puja in the Villages of Old," *Statesman*, 16 Sept. 1952, Puja Supplement, pp. 1 and 4.

64. See Colin Campbell, *The Romantic Ethic and the Spirit of Modern Consumerism* (Oxford: Blackwell, 1987), pp. 161–172; Grant McCracken, *Culture and Consumption:*

*New Approaches to the Symbolic Character of Consumer Goods and Activities* (Bloomington: Indiana University Press, 1990), pp. 3–30; Neil McKendrick, John Brewer, and J. H. Plumb, *Birth of a Consumer Society: The Commercialism of Eighteenth-Century England* (Bloomington: Indian University Press, 1982), pp. 9–33; Chandra Mukerji, *From Graven Images: Patterns of Modern Materialism* (New York: Columbia University Press, 1983), pp. 2–29; and Rosalind H. Williams, *Dream Worlds: Mass Consumption in Late Nineteenth-Century France* (Berkeley: University of California Press, 1982), pp. 19–51.

65. For an argument to this effect from Stuart England, refer to Leah S. Marcus, *The Politics of Mirth: Jonson, Herrick, Milton, Marvel, and the Defense of Old Holiday Pastimes* (Chicago: University of Chicago Press, 1978).

66. Williams, *Dream Worlds*, p. 56.

67. Campbell, *Romantic Ethic*, pp. 77–95 and 153–154. For an alternative explanation of the same enthusiasm for novelty, see McCracken, *Culture and Consumption*, pp. 40–41.

68. Chris A. Bayly, *Rulers, Townsmen, and Bazaars: North Indian Society in the Age of British Expansion, 1770–1870* (Cambridge: Cambridge University Press, 1983), esp. pp. 57–63 and 369–393.

69. Sandria B. Freitag, *Collective Action and Community: Public Arenas and the Emergence of Communalism in North India* (Berkeley: University of California Press, 1989).

70. Ibid., pp. 42, 35, and 135–136.

71. Lawrence Alan Babb, "Mirrored Warriors: On the Cultural Identity of Rajasthani Traders," *International Journal of Hindu Studies* 3.1 (April 1999): esp. pp. 15–17.

72. Joanne Punzo Waghorne, "The Diaspora of the Gods: Hindu Temples in the New World System, 1640–1800," *Journal of Asian Studies* 58.3 (Aug. 1999): 653. A fuller treatment of this topic may be found in her book, *Diaspora of the Gods: Modern Hindu Temples in an Urban Middle-Class World* (New York: Oxford University Press, 2004).

73. See Walter Benjamin, "The Work of Art in the Age of Mechanical Reproduction," in *Illuminations*, edited with an introduction by Hannah Arendt and translated by Harry Zohn (New York: Harcourt, Brace, and World, 1968), pp. 219–253.

74. Of course, sudden wealth does not always precipitate conspicuous consumption, which depends in large part upon the meaning of consumer goods to the community in which one lives. For an Indian example of an upwardly mobile caste who hid rather than displayed their wealth, see Alfred Gell, "Newcomers to the World of Goods: Consumption Among the Muria Gonds," in *The Social Life of Things: Commodities in Cultural Perspective*, ed. Arjun Appadurai (Cambridge: Cambridge University Press, 1986), pp. 110–138.

75. At the end of the "Māhātmya," the Goddess gives worldly fame and enjoyment to King Suratha and spiritual emancipation to the merchant Samādhi—as each had requested. See Thomas B. Coburn, *Encountering the Goddess: A Translation of the Devī-Māhātmya and a Study of Its Interpretation* (Albany: State University of New York Press, 1991), pp. 82–84.

76. Thomas Blom Hansen, *The Saffron Wave: Democracy and Hindu Nationalism in Modern India* (Princeton: Princeton University Press, 1999), p. 54.

77. Pamela Shurmer-Smith, *India: Globalization and Change* (London: Oxford University Press, 2000), p. 35.

78. There are many examples of this type of *paṭ*. For one, see Pratapaditya Pal, "Kali, Calcutta, and Kalighat Pictures," in his *Changing Visions, Lasting Images: Calcutta Through Three Hundred Years*, ed. Pratapaditya Pal (Bombay: Marg, 1990), p. 121.

79. From "Basantak," edited by Prāṇnāth Datta, reproduced in Partha Mitter, *Art and Nationalism in Colonial India, 1850–1922: Occidental Orientations* (Cambridge: Cambridge University Press, 1994), pl. 104.

80. Summarized by Jayanta Gosvāmī in his *Samājcitre Unaviṁśa Śatābdīr Bāṅglā Prahasan* (Calcutta: Sāhityaśrī, 1974), section called "Pūjā-Pārbaṇ o Anācār," pp. 1167–1181.

81. See Christopher Pinney, *"Photos of the Gods": The Printed Image and Political Struggle in India* (London: Reaktion Books, 2004); Ajay Sinha, "Against Allegory: Binode Bihari Mukherjee's *Medieval Saints* at Shantinitekan," in *Picturing the Nation: Iconographies of Modern India*, ed. Richard H. Davis (Hyderabad: Orient Longman, 2007), pp. 66–91; and Joanne Punzo Waghorne, *Diaspora of the Gods*, esp. chapter 3, "The Gentrification of the Goddess," pp. 129–170.

82. Susan S. Bean, "The Art of Exchange: Circulation of Visual Culture in Colonial India," talk presented at Columbia University, 28 Oct. 2006.

83. Frank J. Korom, *Village of Painters: Narrative Scrolls from West Bengal*, photography by Paul J. Smutko (Santa Fe, N.M.: Museum of New Mexico Press, 2006), pp. 17, 18, 80, 83, 95, 101, and 84, respectively.

84. Hena Basu (pers. comm., 16 Aug. 1995).

85. Hansen, *The Saffron Wave*, p. 12.

86. Cited by Shurmer-Smith, *India: Globalization and Change*, p. 23.

87. I am indebted to Henrike Donner, of the London School of Economics, for this insight (pers. comm., 6 June 2001).

88. *Telegraph*, 16 Sept. 2006, p. 10.

89. Richard Schechner, "A Maharajah's Festival for Body and Soul," *New York Times*, 26 Nov. 2000, pp. 1 and 37. Classic treatments of this multiday outside theater may be found in Linda Hess, "An Open-air Ramayana: Ramlila, the Audience Experience," in *Bhakti in Current Research, 1979–1982*, ed. Monika Thiel-Horstmann (Berlin: Dietrich Reimer, 1983), pp. 171–194; and Anuradha Kapur, *Actors, Pilgrims, Kings, and Gods: The Ramlila of Ramnagar* (London: Seagull, 2006).

90. Stephen P. Huyler, *Meeting God: Elements of Hindu Devotion* (New Haven: Yale University Press, 1999), p. 200.

91. Hansen, *The Saffron Wave*, p. 263 n. 58. Further detail on the Maharashtrian Gaṇapati Utsav may be found in: V. Barnauw, "The Changing Character of a Hindu Festival," *American Anthropologist* 56 (1954): 74–86; R. I. Cashman, *The Myth of the Lokamanya: Tilak and Mass Politics in Maharashtra* (Berkeley: University of California Press, 1975), chap. 4; Paul Courtright, *Ganesha: Lord of Obstacles, Lord of Beginnings* (New York: Oxford University Press, 1985), chap. 8; C. Jaffrelot, "Processions hindoues, stratégies politiques and émeutes entre Hindous et Musulmans," *Purusartha* 16 (1994): 261–287; and Raminder Kaur, "Performative Politics: Artworks, Festival Praxis, and Nationalism with Reference to the Ganapati Utsava in Western India" (Ph.D. diss., University of London, 1998). I am grateful to Chris Fuller for alerting me to many of these sources.

92. The following presentation of Fuller's work derives from his public talk entitled, "The Vinayaka Chaturthi Festival and the Spread of Hindu Nationalism in Tamilnadu," delivered on 10 April 2000 at Columbia University in New York, and from his published article, "The 'Vinayaka Chaturthi' Festival and Hindutva in Tamil Nadu," *Economic and Political Weekly* 36, no. 19 (12–18 May 2001): 1607–1616.

93. Ibid., p. 1608.

94. Pers. comm., 23 May 2001.

95. Raminder Kaur argues that it was not Tilak who was the first to pioneer the public politicized festival, but rather Bhausaheb Lakshman Javale, a Maratha ayurvedic doctor and cloth-dyer, in 1892. See Raminder Kaur, "Fire in the Belly: The Mobilization of the Ganapati Festival in Maharashtra," in *The Politics of Cultural Mobilization in India*, ed. John Zavos, Andrew Wyatt, and Vernon Hewitt (New Delhi: Oxford University Press, 2004), pp. 44–45. See also Raminder Kaur, "Spectacles of Nationalism in the Ganapati *Utsav* of Maharasthra," in *Picturing the Nation: Iconographies of Modern India*, ed. Richard H. Davis (Hyderabad: Orient Longman, 2007), pp. 207–241.

96. Gérard Heuzé, "Cultural Populism: The Appeal of the Shiv Sena," in *Bombay: Metaphor for Modern India*, ed. Sujata Patel and Alice Thorner (New Delhi: Oxford University Press, 1995), p. 241.

97. Ibid., p. 242.

98. Kaur, "Fire in the Belly," p. 55. For a detailed overview of such politicizing, see pp. 58–66.

99. Fuller, "The 'Vinayaka Chaturthi' Festival and Hindutva in Tamil Nadu," pp. 1608, 1614.

100. Kaur, "Spectacles of Nationalism in the Ganapati *Utsav* of Maharasthra," p. 231.

101. Sandria Freitag comments, "Given that competition quickened most public arena activity, the identity or label attached to the 'Other' proved highly significant in conveying legitimacy" (*Collective Action and Community*, p. 284).

102. The Taj Mahal was modeled in 1994 and the Ayodhya temple in 1990.

103. Jyotindra Jain, "Introduction: Image Mobility in India's Popular Cultures" and "India's Republic Day Parade: Restoring Identities, Constructing the Nation," in *India's Popular Culture: Iconic Spaces and Fluid Images*, ed. Jyotindra Jain (Mumbai: Marg Publications, 2007), pp. 16 and 67; see also splendid photographs on pp. 64–66, 68–69.

104. Paul Younger, *Playing Host to Deity: Festival Religion in the South Indian Tradition* (New York: Oxford University Press, 2002).

105. Peter Mason, *Bacchanal! The Carnival Culture of Trinidad* (Philadelphia: Temple University Press, 1999).

106. Ibid., p. 62.

107. Peter Stallybrass and Allon White, *The Politics and Poetics of Transgression* (London: Methuen, 1986), p. 14.

108. Svetlana Boym, *The Future of Nostalgia* (New York: Baasic Books, 2001), pp. xv–xvi.

109. In 2001, the Rashtriya Swayamsevak Sangh decided to open stalls at pandals to try to put its message across. But they admitted that in spite of strenuous

efforts, the organization had units in only 8,000 villages of the 38,000 in the state: they made little headway. *Times of India*, 13 Oct. 2001, Kolkata section, p. 3.

110. The criticism that each year Pūjā patterns become increasingly innovative and hence regrettably depart from an original reverence may be seen in newspaper editorials (*Calcutta Journal*, 7 Oct. 1820, pp. 366–367; and *Statesman and Friend of India*, 9 Oct. 1883, p. 3), as well as in satirical plays (*Kali Hāṭ*, by Atulkṛṣṇa Mitra [1892), as summarized in Jayanta Gosvāmī, *Samājcitre Unaviṁśa Śatābdīr Bāṅglā Prahasan* [Calcutta: Sāhityaśrī, 1974], section called "Pūjā-Pārbaṇ o Anācār," pp. 1167–1181).

111. *Amrita Bazar Patrika*, 13 Oct. 1964, p. 6. The term "Fast Bābus" was coined by Kiśorīcānd Mitra; see Bela Dutt Gupta, "Festivals of the Hindus," in *Sociology in India* (Calcutta, 1972), p. 95, cited by Rajat Sanyal, *Voluntary Associations and the Urban Public Life in Bengal (1815–1876): An Aspect of Social History* (Calcutta: Riddhi-India, 1980), pp. 44 and 64 n.11.

112. Nirmal Brahmachari, "Some Puja Thoughts," *Amrita Bazar Patrika*, 20 Oct. 1974, Sunday magazine, p. 1.

113. The article is called "Bijaya," and was published in *Bande Mataram*, 15 Ashwin, 1313 (1906), p. 4.

114. Richard A. Horsley, "Religion and Other Products of Empire," *Journal of the American Academy of Religion* 71.1 (March 2003), p. 3, citing Kathleen Sands, "Still Dreaming: War, Memory, and Nostalgia in the American Christmas," in *Christmas Unwrapped: Consumerism, Christ, and Culture*, ed. Richard Horsley and James Tracy (Harrisburg, Penn.: Trinity Press International, 2001), pp. 57–58.

## 6. The "Orientalist" Kālī: A Tantric Icon Comes Alive

1. I am indebted to the participants in the South Asia Seminars at Columbia University and the University of Virginia, where I gave versions of this paper in October 1999.

2. The best studies known to me on the history of Dakṣiṇākālī's Bengali iconography are: Nṛsimhaprasād Bhāḍuri, *Śyāmāmāyer Caritkathā Śyāmāmāyer Gān* (Calcutta: Antaraṅga Prakāśanā, 1993); Chintaharan Chakravarti, *The Tantras: Studies on Their Religion and Literature* (Calcutta: Punthi Pustak, 1963), pp. 89–93; Bratīndranāth Mukhopādhāy, *Śaktir Rūp Bhārate o Madhye Eśiyāy* (Calcutta: Ānanda Publications, 1990), pp. 47–57; and Pratapaditya Pal, *Hindu Religion and Iconology According to the Tantrasara* (Los Angeles: Vichitra Press, 1981). None of these, however, compares the details of modern Pūjā images with Tantric textual prescriptions in an attempt to discern evolutionary history.

3. For a readable overview of this literary history, see David R. Kinsley, *The Sword and the Flute: Kālī and Kṛṣṇa, Visions of the Terrible and the Sublime in Hindu Mythology* (Berkeley: University of California Press, 1975), pp. 81–149.

4. Note that I am concentrating on the Dakṣiṇākālī, or south-facing, form of the Goddess. There are other forms—such as Bhadrakālī, Guhyakālī, Mahākālī, Rakṣākālī, and Śmaśānakālī—who hold, stand on, and are ornamented with different things, but they are not nearly as important to current Bengali devotionalism

and are rarely sculpted for Kālī Pūjā. For descriptions of these other Kālīs, see: C. Chakravarti, *The Tantras*, pp. 90–91; and P. Pal, *Hindu Religion and Iconology*, pp. 60–63.

5. *Mahābhāgavata Purāṇa* 23.13–28 and 77.2–25; *Devībhāgavata Purāṇa* 5:26–29 and 10:10–11; and *Bṛhaddharma Purāṇa* 23.6–17. For usable editions, consult: *The Mahābhāgavata Purāṇa (Ancient Treatise on Śakti Cult)*, ed. and intro. Pushpendra Kumar (Delhi: Eastern Book Linkers, 1983); *The Srimad Devi Bhagawatam*, ed. and trans. Swami Vijnanananda, 2 parts., 2nd ed. (New Delhi: Oriental Books Reprint Corporation, 1977); and *Bṛhaddharma Purāṇam*, ed. Haraprasād Śāstrī, 2nd ed. (1897; Varanasi: Chaukhambha Amarabharati Prakashan, 1974). In notes to follow, notations for such Purāṇas refer to these editions.

6. Bratīndranāth Mukhopādhyāy also cites material evidence from as far back as the eighth century. See his *Śaktir Rūp Bhārate o Madhye Eśiyāy*, pp. 49–51.

7. Teun Goudriaan and Sanjukta Gupta, *Hindu Tantric and Śākta Literature*, vol. II, fasc. 2 of *A History of Indian Literature*, ed. Jan Gonda (Wiesbaden: Harrassowitz, 1981), pp. 76–78.

8. Works by these authors most relevant to Kālī *sādhanā* include: Sarvānandanāth's *Sarvollāsa Tantra*; Brahmānanda Giri's *Śāktānandataraṅgiṇī* and *Tārārahasya*; Pūrṇānanda Giri's *Śāktakrama*, *Śrītattvacintāmaṇi*, and *Śyāmārahasya*; Kṛṣṇānanda Āgambāgīś's *Tantrasāra*; Raghunāth Tarkabāgīś Bhaṭṭācārya's *Āgamatattvavilāsa*; and Rāmtoṣaṇ Tarkabāgīś's *Prāṇatoṣiṇī*. Some of these are available in Sanskrit, Hindi, or Bengali: *Sarvvollāsatantram*, ed. Kṛṣṇānanda Sagara (Varanasi: Pratyabhijñā-Prakāśanā, 1987); *Śāktānandataraṅgī*, translated into Hindi by Rāmkumār Rāy (Varanasi: Prācya Prakāśanā, 1993); *Tārārahasya*, translated into Bengali by Tārānanda Giritīrthābadhūt (Calcutta: Nababhārat, 1977); *Śyāmārahasya*, translated into Bengali by Śyāmānanda Tīrthanāth (Calcutta: Nababhārat, 1982); *Bṛhat Tantrasāra*, edited by Rasikmohan Caṭṭopādhyāy and translated into Bengali by Candrakumār Tarkālaṅkar (Calcutta: Nababhārat, 1982); *Āgamatattvavilāsa*, translated into Bengali by Pañcānan Śāstrī (Calcutta: Nababhārat, 1985); and *Prāṇatoṣiṇī* (Varanasi: Chowkhambha Vidyabhawan, 1992). In notes to follow, page references for such Tantras come from these editions.

9. *Hindu Religion and Iconology*, p. 65.

10. The most famous is "*Karālavadanāṃ ghorāṃ muktakeśīṃ caturbhujāṃ*," from the *Kālī Tantra*; it is quoted by Kṛṣṇānanda Āgambāgīś in the *Tantrasāra* (pp. 387–388). Other Tantric *dhyānas* include: "*Añjanādrinibhāṃ Devīṃ Karālavadanāṃ Śivāṃ*," from the *Svatantra Tantra*, also quoted in the *Tantrasāra*, p. 389; "*Dhāyet Kālīṃ karālāsyāṃ daṃṣṭrābhīṃ vilocanāṃ*," from the *Kulacūḍāmaṇi Tantra*, quoted in Pūrṇānanda Giri's *Śyāmārahasya*, pp. 250–251; "*Virūpākṣakṛta-dhyāna*," from the *Āgamatattvavilāsa*, pp. 1020–1021; "*Śavārūḍhāṃ mahābhīmāṃ*," from the *Siddheśvara Tantra*, quoted in *Tantrasāra*, p. 397; and "*Sadyaśchinnaśiraḥ kṛpāṇamabhayaṃ*," from the *Mantramahodadhiḥ* 3.9–29 (see *Mahidhara's Mantra Mahodadhiḥ*, ed. and trans. Ram Kumar Rai [Varanasi: Prachya Prakashan, 1992], pp. 133–145). The Purāṇic descriptions are: "*Ityuktā sā Himasutā Śambhunā munisattama*" and "*Kāmākhyā Kālikā Devī svayamādyā sanātanā*," from the *Mahābhāgavata* 23.16–28 and 77.3–25 (pp. 111–112 and 321–322), and "*Rātrāu niśithavyāptāyāmamāvāsthāmihāiva tu*," from the *Bṛhaddharma* 23.6–17 (pp. 251–252).

11. For further details on this point, consult Sanjukta Gupta, "Tantric Sādhanā: Pūjā," in Sanjukta Gupta, Dirk Jan Hoens, and Teun Goudriaan, *Hindu Tantrism*

(Leiden: Brill, 1979), pp. 121–162; and K. R. van Kooij, *Worship of the Goddess According to the Kālīkā Purāṇa* (Leiden: Brill, 1972), pp. 18–19.

12. The writings of Teun Goudriaan and Sanjukta Gupta are a good example of the former view (see *Hindu Tantric and Śākta Literature*, pp. 82–84, 179–180, 199–201, and 208). Two authors who see antagonism where Goudriaan and Gupta find rapprochement are Dīneścandra Sen, *Baṅgabhāṣā o Sāhitya*, ed. Asit Kumār Bandyopādhyāy, 9th ed., 2 vols. (Calcutta: West Bengal State Book Board, 1986): 2:594–595, and Malcolm McLean, *Devoted to the Goddess: The Life and Work of Ramprasad* (Albany: State University of New York Press, 1998), pp. 43–45.

13. See T. Goudriaan, *Hindu Tantric and Śākta Literature*, pp. 82–85, for a list of such Tantras, with dates and contents.

14. P. Pal, *Hindu Religion and Iconology*, pp. 4–6.

15. S. C. Banerji, *Tantra in Bengal: A Study in Its Origins, Development, and Influence*, 2nd rev. ed. (New Delhi: Manohar, 1992), pp. 255–272.

16. See my *Mother of My Heart, Daughter of My Dreams: Kālī and Umā in the Devotional Poetry of Bengal* (New York: Oxford University Press, 2001), pp. 28–30.

17. See: Edward C. Dimock Jr., "The Goddess of Snakes in Medieval Bengali Literature, Part I," in *The Sound of Silent Guns and Other Essays* (Delhi: Oxford University Press, 1989), pp. 150–151; T. Goudriaan and S. Gupta, *Hindu Tantric and Śākta Literature*, pp. 185–186; and Carol Goldberg Salomon, "Govindadāsa's 'Kālikāmaṅgal' (The Vikramāditya and Vidyāsundara Sections): An Edition and Translation" (Ph.D. diss., University of Pennsylvania, 1983), pp. 31–37.

18. Ibid., pp. 120–128.

19. Ibid., pp. 271–273.

20. The songs of the Bāuls, Nāths, and Sahajiyās are similar in form and imagery to the Śākta *padas*, but since they are not often centered on Kālī, they are not included here.

21. For a summary of his Vidyā-Sundara section, see C. Salomon, "Govindadāsa's 'Kālikāmaṅgal,'" pp. 142–143.

22. For a representative sample of such opinions, refer to Aruṇkumār Basu, *Śaktigīti Padābalī* (Calcutta: Orient Book Co., 1964), pp. 7–21 and 63–66; and Śaśibhūṣaṇ Dāśgupta, *Bhārater Śakti-Sādhanā o Śākta Sāhitya* (Calcutta: Sāhitya Saṁsad, 1960), pp. 206–226.

23. Prabhas Sen, in *Crafts of West Bengal* (Ahmadabad: Mapin Publishing, 1994), p. 164, says that Kṛṣṇacandra brought talented clay modelers to Ghurni, a suburb of his capital, and supplied them with the iconographic details of deities codified by his court scholars. Sen also credits him with instituting the idea of *bisarjan*, immersing the temporary images in water after their use.

24. The best source from which to get a sense for the temple-building fever among Bengali landed families during this period is A. K. Bhattacharyya, *A Corpus of Dedicatory Inscriptions from Temples of West Bengal (c. 1500 a.d. to c. 1800 a.d.)* (Calcutta: Shri K. K. Ray, 1982). David McCutchion cites the 1712 Dakṣiṇākālī Temple at Malanca in Medinipur as the oldest terracotta Kālī temple in Bengal; see his *Late Medieval Temples of Bengal* (Calcutta: Asiatic Society, 1972), pp. 32, 34.

25. Selected references to the voluminous literature on Kālīghāṭ include: Abadhūt, "Kālītīrtha Kālīghāṭ," in *Sādhak Jīban Samagra* (Calcutta: Mitra and Ghoṣ

Publishers, 1982), pp. 355–485; Subhendugopal Bagchi, "Kālīghāṭā," in *Eminent Indian Śākta Centres in Eastern India* (Calcutta: Punthi Pustak, 1980), pp. 14–72; Sūryakumār Caṭṭopādhyāy, *Kālīkṣetra Dīpikā* (1891; Calcutta: Pustak Bipaṇi, 1986); Sanjukta Gupta, "The Domestication of a Goddess: Caraṇa-tīrtha Kālīghāṭ, the Mahāpīṭha of Kālī," in *Encountering Kālī: At the Margins, at the Center, in the West*, ed. Rachel Fell McDermott and Jeffrey J. Kripal (Berkeley: University of California Press, 2003), pp. 60–79; Upendranāth Mukhopādhyāy, *Kālīghāṭ Itibṛtta* (Calcutta: Jagannāth Mukhopādhyāy, 1925); Dīptimay Rāy, "Kālītīrtha Kālīghāṭ o Debī Kālikā," in *Paścimbaṅger Kālī o Kālīkṣetra* (Calcutta: Maṇḍal Book House, 1984), pp. 38–54; P. C. Roy Choudhury, "The Kalighat Temple of Calcutta," chap. 1 of *Temples and Legends of Bengal* (Bombay: Bharatiya Vidya Bhavan, 1967); Surajit Sinha, "Kali Temple at Kalighat and the City of Calcutta," in idem, ed., *Cultural Profile of Calcutta* (Calcutta: Indian Anthropological Society, 1972), pp. 61–72; and Nagendra Nath Vasu and Upendra Chandra Vasu, "Kalighat and Calcutta," *Calcutta Review* 92, no. 184 (April 1891): 305–327.

26. With the exception of the Dakṣiṇeśvar Temple, most of the temples to follow are much less well documented than Kālīghāṭ. However, Kālī Pūjā time in Bengal usually elicits magazine and newspaper articles on the various famous Kālī temples in the city; from these one can gain information about all of the sites to be mentioned here. Dīptimay Rāy's *Paścimbaṅger Kālī o Kālīkṣetra* also has individual chapters on many Bengali Kālī temples.

27. Aside from the voluminous publications by the Rāmakṛṣṇa Mission, see: Praṇabeś Cakrabartī, "Śrī Rāmakṛṣṇer Mahāsādhanpīṭh Dakṣiṇeśvar Mandir," in *Nabakallol*, vol. 30 (Kārtik 1396): 73–78; Elizabeth U. Harding, *Kali: The Black Goddess of Dakshineswar* (York Beach, Maine: Nicholas-Hays, 1993); and Sumit Sarkar, "Calcutta and the 'Bengal Renaissance,'" in *Calcutta, the Living City*, ed. Sukanta Chaudhuri, vol. 1: *The Past* (Calcutta: Oxford University Press, 1990), pp. 95–105. See also note 26 above.

28. Other iconographically similar though less famous images in the Kolkata city limits include: Kumartuli's Ḍomkālī; Brahmamayī Mā at Pramanik Ghat and Siddheśvarīkālī at Kuthighat, both in Baranagar; and Bhavatāriṇī of Syampukur. All of these date from the nineteenth century. Three outstanding images of this fierce type, also nineteenth century but from outside Kolkata, include the Guhyakālī image in Bhadrapur, Birbhum, who sports a row of teeth and enormous eyes and who sits on a high altar among a circle of serpents; Devī Nistāriṇī at the temple in Seoraphuli, Hooghly, who has large eyes, prominent teeth, and jackals on the altar; and Devī Āgameśvarī at the temple in Shantipur, Nadia, whose bared teeth, outstretched tongue, and skeletal frame make her truly awe-inspiring.

29. Rāy, *Paścimbaṅger Kālī o Kālīkṣetra*, p. 72. The Uluberiya temple was constructed only in 1920.

30. Tantric *sādhakas* traditionally meditated on a seat placed over the skulls of five unclean beings (a jackal, a snake, a dog, a bull, and a Śūdra), as conquering their distaste for these gave them special power. See S. C. Banerji, *Tantra in Bengal*, p. 336.

31. Ibid., p. 188.

32. Solvyns was in Calcutta from 1791 to 1804. This painting comes from *Les Hindous* (1808), vol. 1, sec. 9, pl. 1, and is reproduced as fig. 13 in Robert L. Hardgrave Jr., "A Portrait of Black Town: Baltazard Solvyns in Calcutta, 1791–1804," in *Changing Visions,*

*Lasting Images: Calcutta Through Three Hundred Years*, ed. Pratapaditya Pal (Bombay: Marg Publications, 1990), p. 45. For similar figures, see: Charles Coleman, *The Mythology of the Hindus* (London: Parbury, Allen, 1832), fig. 1, reproduced in Hugh Urban, "India's Darkest Heart: Kālī in the British Colonial Imagination," in *Encountering Kālī: Cultural Understanding at the Extremes* (Berkeley: University of California Press, 2003), ed. Jeffrey K. Kripal and Rachel Fell McDermott, p. 176; and fig. 17 of Pratapaditya Pal, "Indian Artists and British Patrons in Calcutta," in *Changing Visions, Lasting Images*, p. 139.

33. This painting is reproduced in Pratapaditya Pal, "Kali, Calcutta, and Kalighat Pictures," in *Changing Visions, Lasting Images*, p. 113.

34. Recall Valentine Chirol, who, in his collection of "subversive" writings from Indian newspapers, *Indian Unrest* (London: Macmillan, 1910), quotes a Bengali author from *Yugāntar* exhorting his countrymen to sacrifice white goats to Kālī (pp. 345–346 n. 10).

35. Partha Mitter, *Art and Nationalism in Colonial India, 1850–1922: Occidental Orientations* (Cambridge: Cambridge University Press, 1994), color pl. XII.

36. This theme has been argued in numerous publications since the mid-1980s. For two seminal early contributions, see Partha Chatterjee, "The Nation and Its Women" and "Women and the Nation," in his *The Nation and Its Fragments: Colonial and Postcolonial Histories* (Delhi: Oxford University Press, 1995), pp. 116–157; and Lata Mani, "Contentious Traditions: The Debate on *Sati* in Colonial India," in *Recasting Women: Essays in Colonial History*, ed. Kumkum Sangari and Sudesh Vaid (New Delhi: Kali for Women, 1989), pp. 88–126.

37. The first *sarbajanīn* Kālī Pūjās were done at Kālī Bābur Maṭh, on the corner of Patuyatola and Harrison Roads, at Baubazar's Daymanda Boarding House, and at the Vivekananda Society. See *Ānanda Bājār Patrikā*, 13 Nov. 1993, advertisement page; and Sunīl Dās, "Kālī Parikrama," in *Ānanda Bājār Patrikā*, 23 Oct. 1995, p. 9, cols. 5–6.

38. The following account derives from an extensive review of contemporary Bengali and English newspapers, and an interview with Pradīp Pāl, the grand-nephew of G. Pāl, on 23 Oct. 1995.

39. Cambridge: Cambridge University Press, 1992.

40. For a photograph of the 1934 *pratimā*, see *Amrita Bazar Patrika*, 8 Nov. 1934, p. 5. The caption reads, "[O]ne of the finest specimens of anthropomorphized art that one has seen of late." Since the microfilm copy is extremely poor, I have reproduced a similar image, from 1937.

41. *Amrita Bazar Patrika*, 6 Nov. 1934, p. 7.

42. *Amrita Bazar Patrika*, 27 Oct. 1935, p. 6.

43. "Shri Dakshina Kalika: The Divine Black Mother," in *Amrita Bazar Patrika*, 3 Nov. 1936, pp. 13 and 15.

44. For examples from the late 1930s, see *Amrita Bazar Patrika*, 2 Nov. 1937, p. 6; 22 Oct. 1938, p. 6; and 10 Nov. 1939, p. 14. Spot-checking into the early 1960s yields the same result: it is the humanized Kālī who continues to be photographed almost exclusively.

45. Both may be seen in *Statesman*, 15 Nov. 1963, p. 1.

46. I am grateful to Dr. Ghosh for undertaking this survey project for me and for accomplishing it so meticulously.

47. *Ānanda Bājār Patrikā*, 13 Nov. 1993, advertisement page.

48. In an article called "Kālī, the Mother Terrible," Haridas Chatterji states: "One noticeable feature of the forms and images of most of these deities is that they are both pleasing to the eye and appealing to the heart, and that in their execution the artist tries to introduce as much as possible the beauty and grace which one discerns in one's own mother's face" (*Amrita Bazar Patrika*, 18 Oct. 1952, pp. 3 and 7).

49. Satish Bahadur, "The Context of Indian Film Culture," in *Film Miscellany* 1 (Dec. 1976): 96.

50. *Yugāntar*, 22 Oct. 1995, p. 5; and *Asian Age*, 23 Oct. 1995, p. 9.

51. Pārtha Pāl told me that an average modern Kālī costs about Rs. 5,000 to buy. The older variety costs more because of her more elaborate crown, clothes, and decorations.

52. Kajri Jain, "The Efficacious Image: Pictures and Power in Indian Mass Culture," in *Picturing the Nation: Iconographies of Modern India*, ed. Richard H. Davis (Hyderabad: Orient Longman, 2007), p. 149. It should be noted that Ravi Varma himself, the father of modern calendar art, depicted a variety of Kālīs, some frightening and some sweet; see Erwin Neumayer and Christine Schelberger, *Popular Indian Art: Raja Ravi Varma and the Printed Gods of India* (New York: Oxford University Press, 2003), pls. 124 and 126.

53. This pandal was erected by the Matalibagan Alley Club. Remarked the newspaper reporter covering the event, "The search for novelty may lead to the ridiculous" (*Telegraph*, Metro section, 12 Nov. 2004, p. 24).

54. See *Statesman*, 29 Oct. 1970, p. 1.

55. See chapter 7, p. 189.

56. Interview, 27 Oct. 1995. I am grateful to Hena Basu for introducing me to him and accompanying me to Professor Bhāḍuri's house.

57. Selected stanzas from the poem "And Let Shyama Dance There," in *Swami Vivekananda's Collected Works*, 8 vols., 7th impression (Mayavati: Advaita Ashrama, 1959) 4:506–510. See also his poem "Kali the Mother," which speaks in a similar vein; ibid. 4:384.

58. "Killing the Feringhee, we say, is no murder"—the slogan quoted by Chirol in his collection of terrorist newspaper writers (see *Indian Unrest*, p. 346, n. 10)—is lifted directly from Kālī's ritual prescriptions: in the *Kālīkā Purāṇa* 57.10–11 (p. 53 of van Kooij's translation), the ritual specialist assures the donor of the goat that because Kālī is thirsty for its blood the sacrificial act is not a crime. "For the sake of the sacrifice the animals have been created by Brahmā himself; I shall put thee to death now; because of this, murder is no-murder in sacrifice."

59. The most popular story about Dakṣiṇākālī's image relates that after slaying a host of demons, Kālī became so inebriated that she ran amok, charging over the battlefield and threatening to destroy the world with her stomping feet. In a panic the gods approached Śiva, who agreed to pacify his wife. He lay down in front of her path, and when she stepped on him she realized the impropriety of her act, stopped her mad frenzy, and stuck out her tongue in obedient, wifely shame. This story is no older than the eighteenth century, and has no Sanskrit textual origin. See Jeffrey J. Kripal, "Kālī's Tongue and Ramakrishna: 'Biting the Tongue' of the Tantric

Tradition," in *History of Religions* 34.2 (Nov. 1994): 152–189; Rachel Fell McDermott, "Kālī's Tongue: Historical Reinterpretations of the Blood-Lusting Goddess," paper delivered at the Mid-Atlantic Regional Conference of the American Academy of Religion, Barnard College, 21 March 1991; and Usha Menon and Richard Shweder, "Kali's Tongue: Cultural Psychology and the Power of Shame in Orissa, India," in *Emotion and Culture: Empirical Studies of Mutual Influence* (Washington, D.C.: American Psychological Association, 1994), pp. 241–284.

## 7. Approaches to Kālī Pūjā in Bengal

1. I am grateful to the participants at the South Asia Seminar, University of Chicago, where I delivered a version of this chapter on 25 May 2006.

2. There are two other public festivals to Kālī—Raṭanti Kālī Pūjā (the fourteenth night of the dark fortnight of the month of Māgh) and Phalaharaṇī Kālī Pūjā (the fourteenth night of the dark fortnight of Jyeṣṭha)—but these are very minor in comparison with the autumnal Pūjā and are rarely marked publicly. They are mentioned by William Ward, in *A View of the History, Literature, and Mythology of the Hindoos*, 3rd ed., 4 vols. (1817; Delhi: Low Price Publications, 1990), 3:154. Raṭanti Caturdaśī is also discussed by Chintaharan Chakravarti, *The Tantras: Studies on Their Religion and Literature* (Calcutta: Punthi Pustak, 1963), p. 92, and by Śaśibhūṣaṇ Dāśgupta, *Bhārater Śakti-Sādhanā o Śākta Sāhitya* (Calcutta: Sāhitya Saṁsad, 1960), pp. 75–76. For one Kolkata temple that celebrates them both, see Apūrba Caṭṭopādhyāy, "Ṭhanṭhane Siddheśvarī Kālī," *Sāptahik Bartamān* (21 Oct. 2000): 17–21.

3. It is hard to know exactly when the first public Kālī Pūjā was established, as there are conflicting claims. For instance, in 1927, the Shyampukur Boy's Barowari announced that it was already in its sixth year of the *sarbajanīn* format (*Amrita Bazar Patrika*, 23 Oct. 1927, p. 3). However, most sources agree that the first *sarbajanīn* Kālī Pūjās were done in 1928; see chapter 6, p. 173 and n. 37. The mania for themes has now affected Kālī Pūjā too, the preparations being referred to as a "total package" even in Bengali. If you do not have a theme-and-lighting "cocktail," say the organizers, your Pūjā will not come off. *Ānanda Bājār Patrikā*, 21 Oct. 2006, Kolkata insert, p. 3. As a single example: the members of Chetla Agtani Club decided to put Kālī in the forests of South India, in the jungle where Veerappan held sway until he was killed on 18 Oct. 2004; next to her "hideout" was a model of the dacoit (*Telegraph*, 11 Nov. 2004, Metro section, p. 22). However, see n. 9 below.

4. Ward, *A View of the History, Literature, and Mythology of theHindoos*, 3:156–157.

5. This lack is true of the *Kulārṇava Tantra* (10.74–79 refers to the *amāvasya* lights of the Kārtik festival, but not to Kālī), Āgambāgīś's *Tantrasāra*, and even Pūrṇānanda Giri's *Śyāmārahasya*.

6. Chakravarti, *The Tantras*, p. 92. The text has been briefly described by Hara Prasad Shāstri, *A Descriptive Catalogue of the Sanskrit Manuscripts in the Collections of the Royal Asiatic Society of Bengal*, revised and edited by Chintaharan Chakravarti, vol. 8, pt. 1: *Tantra Manuscripts* (Calcutta: Asiatic Society, 1939), p. 469. See folios 4a, 4b, 19a, and 24b of the *Śyāmāsaparyāvidhi*. Although the *Śyāmāsaparyāvidhi* itself does

not mention Rājā Kṛṣṇacandra Rāy or any specific historical efforts to popularize Kālī's public festival, Kāśīnāth's purpose seems to be to attest to the benefits of Kālī worship, as though it were fairly new and needed justifying. For further specifics, see my *Mother of My Heart, Daughter of My Dreams: Kālī and Umā in the Devotional Poetry of Bengal* (New York: Oxford University Press, 2001), p. 174.

7. The oldest references to Kālī Pūjā I have been able to find derive from the 1830 September–October twice-weekly editions of the Dharmasabhā-sponsored Bengali *Samācār Candrikā*, which discuss controversies over the holiday's dates. Most newspapers, whether in English or Bengali, however, do not mention Kālī Pūjā as a festival in its own right, aside from its rowdiness or benefit in providing a holiday escape from Calcutta, until 1915, when—oddly enough—it is the pro-British *Englishman* that begins to mention Diwali and Kālī Pūjā in the same article. The first photos of Kālī in the popular *Statesman* paper do not appear until 1 Nov. 1921, p. 9.

8. The three Kālī pictures were published on 3 Nov. 1964, p. 9.

9. In only 77 out of 302 *pandals* in Abhijit Ghoṣ's survey (see chapter 6) did organizers attempt to make creative marks on their *pandal* exteriors. Most structures were open-air displays, with only enough roof and depth to cover the image. If anything was to be done on the outside, it was the opening lintels or gateways that received a little ornamentation. When budgets and imaginations expanded to allow the enclosure to become a full room, the typical choice was a thatched hut or small Bengali house, a generic temple, church, or gurudwara, or some sort of small civic building. Only eighteen committees in the 1998–2000 survey were more ambitious. Noteworthy displays included a small Bengali village scene, complete with paddy and water bodies; a mountainous terrain, featuring caves, tunnels, and even an underground goddess; the Kargil battlefield; replicas of the Somnāth Temple, the Taj Mahal, the Char Minar, the second Hooghly Bridge, and a beached Titanic; a representation of the sun chariot with its four horses; a house of cards; and a fiery volcano spewing out lava (and Kālī, who periodically sprang out of the mouth of the volcano together with smoke and loud exploding noises). These few are highly creative, but when compared to the plethora of much larger and more complex thematic designs evident at Durgā Pūjā, it becomes clear how much smaller and more subdued Kālī's festival still is. Nevertheless, to the extent that Kālī Pūjā committees have the funds or the inclination, they now seek to copy Durgā Pūjā in the use of the "theme" "packages."

10. Interview, 27 Oct. 1995.

11. I have only come across one story, told repeatedly in several variants, about Kālī's identification with a small girl. One Gopīmohan Ṭhākur apparently had a daughter named Brahmamayī, whom he married off at the age of eight. When she was drowned while undergoing the bridal ritual of being bathed in the Ganges, the father collapsed in shock. Several days later he had a dream in which the Goddess appeared and said that she left him because he was marrying her off and sending her away. She told him to find a stone statue of her on the banks of the Ganges, and to install it and worship it; then she would never leave him. The image was found, but the temple could not be finished in Gopīmohan's lifetime. See Amit Sen, "Śyāmnagarer Śyāma," *Sāptahik Bartamān* (21 Oct. 2000): 19.

12. Interview, 9 Oct. 1991.

13. 24 Sept. 1957, pp. 1–2. Adds Hena Basu regarding that same, pre-Naxalite period, "I . . . remember clearly how senior members of my ancestral house would often warn that worship of Kali requires accurate rituals[,] or else beneficiaries of the Puja would have to suffer the wrath of the Goddess" (letter, 16 Aug. 1995).

14. Sudhīr Kumār Cakrabartī, "Kālīmūrti Rahasya," in *Dibyajyotir Pathe: Dharma o Darśan* 8, no. 3 (1405/1998): 24.

15. *Hindustan Times*, Kolkata, 17 July 2003, p. 3.

16. 7 Nov. 1923, p. 2, in an article called "Śrī Śrī Kālī Pūjā."

17. This Goddess tends to be large, without a distended tongue. She has only two hands, in the right of which is a demon's forearm and in the left of which is a bowl of wine. Her eyes are bloodshot. She stands on Śiva lengthwise, with her right foot forward. In front of her, when depicted, are the cremation pits.

18. See *Sāptahik Bartamān*, 13 Nov. 1993, p. 8. Other Kolkata examples include Pūṭe Kālītalā, on Kalikrishna Thakur Street, which was once a forested area known for its dacoits who used to drown their victims down a particular nearby well, and Ḍākātī Kālī Temple on Southern Avenue. The town of Ranaghat is said to derive its name from that of a Kālī-dacoit named Rāṇā (or Rañjit?); Śibsaṅkar Bhārati, "Kalkātār Kālī-kathā," *Sāptahik Bartamān* 12, no. 24 (6 Nov. 1999): 37–39.

19. *Statesman*, 12 Nov. 1993, p. 1.

20. But, retorts Islam, that belief goes both ways: police also say that any criminal they put behind bars on Kālī Pūjā will not bother them for the year to come. *Times of India*, 24 Oct. 2000, p. 2.

21. For an overview of such stories, see *Bartamān*, 22 Oct. 2000, p. 10.

22. Some family members apparently sit on a large *cakra*, and others have special garlands made from the bones of an Untouchable woman. Rādhāramaṇ Rāy, "Tāntrik Grāme Kālī Pujo," *Sāptahik Bartamān* 13, no. 21 (21 Oct. 2000): 20–21.

23. The fact that Kālī did not emerge into the popular mainstream as fast as Durgā is partly because the Tantras consider *naimittika pūjās* (those done on special occasions) to be *rajas*ic (not of the highest purity), and because such *pūjās* tended to attract householders, whereas most Tantric authors wrote their ritual manuals for *sādhakas*, not priests. Pratapaditya Pal suggests that the reason Kṛṣṇānanda Āgambāgīś did not include instructions on Durgā's annual festival, though it was available by his time in *smṛti* texts, is that he did not conceive of his work as having relevance to householders' interests. See Pratapaditya Pal, *Hindu Religion and Iconology According to the Tantrasara* (Los Angeles: Vichitra Press, 1981), pp. 10–11 and 21.

24. Although not featured in this book, it is worth noting that while the Durgās of the locality are being immersed, North Indians resident in Bengal celebrate Rāma's victory over Rāvaṇa by burning the latter's effigy.

25. Abhī Dās, "Sekāle Bāṅgālīr Kālīpūjā," in *Ānanda Bājār Patrikā*, 10 Nov. 1985, p. 7.

26. Śaibāl Biśvās, "Ye ādhār ālor adhik," *Rabibār Pratidin*, 10 Nov. 1996, p. G.

27. *Amrita Bazar Patrika*, 18 Oct. 1971, p. 7; 31 Oct. 1978, pp. 4 and 5; and 23 Oct. 1984, p. 4.

28. The most famous of Kālī's meditational images, from the fifteenth-century *Kālī Tantra*, "*Karālavadanāṃ ghorāṃ muktakeśīṃ caturbhujām*," first introduces the word

*viparītaratā*. This emphasis on the sexualized relationship between Kālī and Śiva is repeated in later Tantric *dhyānas*: "*Añjanādrinibhāṃ Devīṃ Karālavadanāṃ Śivām*," from the *Svatantra Tantra*; "*Virūpākṣakṛta-dhyāna*," from the *Āgamatattvavilāsa*; and "*Sadyaśchinnaśiraḥ kṛpāṇamabhayaṃ*," from the *Mantramahodadhiḥ*. See chapter 6, n. 10. See also *Śrī Śrī Kālīpūjā Paddhati*, by Paṇḍit Śyāmācaraṇ Kabiratna, 7th ed. (Calcutta: Rādhā Pusthakālay, 1393/1986), pp. 54–55; and same title by Paṇḍit Śyāmācaraṇ Sāṃkhyatīrtha (Calcutta: Rājendra Library, n.d.), pp. 46–47.

29. Viewed on 13 Dec. 2000.

30. This was acquired, probably in a set from an exhibition, by the British Museum in 1894. Viewed on 1 Aug. 2000.

31. I am grateful to T. Richard Blurton, curator for South Asian art at the museum, who showed me this piece in the museum's archives on 1 Aug. 2000.

32. This temple was established in 1804. Note that the Goddess is seated cross-legged on Śiva, though at right angles to him, which masks the suggestion of *viparīta rati*.

33. Abadhūt lived in Chinsurah, where Narendra Nath Bhattacharyya took me to see the painting in his house on 9 Oct. 1991. He was a colorful figure, and wrote about his spiritual experiences and travels as a Tantric practitioner. See his *Sādhak Jīban Samagra* (Calcutta: Mitra and Ghoṣ Publishers, 1982), also mentioned in chapter 6, n. 25.

34. This discomfort was related to me by a Bengali woman who grew up in Kolkata; our communication was facilitated through the kindness of Jeffrey J. Kripal, who introduced her husband to me via email, 9 Aug. 2006.

35. *Times of India*, 10 Oct. 2000, Calcutta insert, p. 1.

36. For a discussion of this story as it is found in the *Caṇḍī Purāṇa*, see Usha Menon and Richard Shweder, "Dominating Kālī: Hindu Family Values and Tantric Power," in *Encountering Kālī: In the Margins, at the Center, in the West*, ed. Rachel Fell McDermott and Jeffrey J. Kripal (Berkeley: University of California Press, 2003), pp. 80–99.

37. Interviews, Sujay Ganguli, 17 Sept. 2000; Chameli Mitra, 22 Sept. 2000; Súbhamay Dawn, 5 Oct. 2000; and Amarnāth Dawn, 5 Oct. 2000.

38. Interviews, Śephāli Bose and Ārati Deb, 29 Sept. 2000; and Śiśir Mallik, 30 Sept. 2000.

39. Interview, Milan Datta (of the Thanthania Datta family), 30 Sept. 2000.

40. Binay Ghoṣ, in an article called "Mā: Mātṛpūjā," *Vibhāva* (Monsoon no., 1386/1979): 30.

41. Peter L. Berger and Thomas Luckmann, *The Social Construction of Reality: A Treatise in the Sociology of Knowledge* (New York: Irvington, 1966).

42. See Eric Hobsbawm, "Introduction: Inventing Traditions," in *The Invention of Tradition*, ed. Eric Hobsbawm and Terence Ranger (Cambridge: Cambridge University Press, 1983), pp. 1–14.

43. Milton B. Singer, *When a Great Tradition Modernizes: An Anthropological Approach to Indian Civilization* (Chicago: University of Chicago Press, 1972), pp. 148–196.

44. Gananath Obeyesekere, *The Cult of the Goddess Pattini* (Chicago: University of Chicago Press, 1984), pp. 64–70.

45. See Joanne Punzo Waghorne, "Chariots of the Gods: Riding the Line Between Hindu and Christian," in *Popular Christianity in India: Riting Between the Lines*, ed. Selva J. Raj and Corinne G. Dempsey (Albany: State University of New York Press, 2002), pp. 11–37.

46. Joanne Punzo Waghorne, *Diaspora of the Gods: Modern Hindu Temples in an Urban Middle-Class World* (New York: Oxford University Press, 2004), p. 170.

47. See discussion in the conclusion, pp. 243–245.

48. *Telegraph*, 18 June 2004, Metro section, p. 17.

49. *Bartamān*, 27 Oct. 1995, p. 3.

## 8. Controversies and the Goddess

1. I am grateful to members of the Conference on Religion in South India, held at Mount Holyoke College in June 2001, who gave me excellent feedback on an earlier draft of this essay.

2. *Amrita Bazar Patrika*, 23 Oct. 1966, p. 1.

3. *Sunday Times of India*, 24 Sept. 2006, p. 2.

4. See *Devīpurāṇokta Durgāpūjā Paddhatī*, collected and edited by Jagadīścandra Tarkatīrtha (Calcutta: Saṁskṛt Pustak Bhāṇḍār, 1388), p. 30, and Madhu Khanna, "The Ritual Capsule of Durgā Pūjā: An Ecological Perspective," in *Hinduism and Ecology: The Intersection of Earth, Sky, and Water*, ed. Christopher Key Chapple and Mary Evelyn Tucker (Cambridge: Harvard University Press, 2006), appendix, p. 493. This washing, or *snān*, of the *nabapatrikā* is one of the elements of Durgā Pūjā that makes it a great festival (*mahotsab*) and distinguishes it from lesser Pūjās like those devoted to Jagaddhātrī and Kālī, which do not have ritual bathing.

5. These three points were made, respectively, by Śiśir Mallik, a store-owner in a Marwari neighborhood of Kolkata (interview, 30 Sept. 2000); artist Maṇṭu Caudhurī, in an interview with *Pratidin* (14 Jan. 2001, p. 6); and Minati Kar (interview, 3 Oct. 2000).

6. The situation was certainly different in the early nineteenth century. See Sumanta Banerjee, *Under the Raj: Prostitution in Colonial Bengal* (New York: Monthly Review Press, 1998).

7. I heard this from several scions of old family Pūjās and found it also in the most authoritative English translation of the Pūjā ritual prescriptions: Pratap Chandra Ghosha, *Durga Puja, with Notes and Illustrations* (Calcutta: Hindoo Patriot Press, 1871), n. 40.

8. I am grateful to Jonathan Riceman for suggesting that I look at this scene. Email comm., 10 Aug. 2005.

9. The image was placed at the Muhammad Ali Park pandal. The artist, Aloke Sen, called his creation "Māyer Kānnā," or the Grief of the Mother, and said in an interview that those who destroy the environment (who commit sacrifice of trees and wildlife) are worse than Durgā's traditional demons.

10. The information to follow comes from an interview I was fortunate to have with Mr. Datta on 13 Dec. 2000; it is supplemented by subsequent newspaper coverage.

11. *Times of India*, 17 Oct. 2000, p. 4.

12. *Pratidin*, 24 Oct. 2000, p. 2.

13. See *India Today*, 30 Oct. 2000, p. 75; and *Pratidin*, 30 Sept. 2000, p. 1.

14. *New York Times International*, 3 Sept. 2000, p. 3.

15. Purnima Toolsidass, interview, 22 Dec. 2000. See n. 19 below.

16. The birds in question are egrets and Asian open-billed storks, which are under the Protected Species category. *Times of India*, 26 Sept. 2006, "Calcutta Times" section, p. 1.

17. *Times of India*, 13 Sept. 2008, p. 3.

18. Beauty Without Cruelty was founded in England in 1959 and in India in 1974. Their headquarters is in Pune, and they have had great success in the South, especially in Mysore. Compassionate Crusaders, an activist group lobbying for animal welfare, was started in 1993 by Debāśis Cakrabartī, who joined his organization to the Humane Society and to the Animal Welfare Board of India. People for Animals was founded in 1994 by Menaka Gandhi; the Kolkata chapter is headed by Purnima Toolsidass.

19. In chronological order of legal enactment, see the Animals and Bird Sacrifices Prohibition Acts of Andhra Pradesh (1950), Tamilnadu (1950), Karnataka (1959, amended in 1963 and 1975), Pondicherry (1965), Kerala (1968), Gujarat (1972), and Rajasthan (1975).

20. 1 Oct. 2000.

21. See Kṛṣṇānanda Āgambāgīś, *Tantrasāra*, ed. Rasikmohan Caṭṭopādhyāy and translated into Bengali by Candrakumār Tarkālaṅkar (Calcutta: Nababhārat, 1982), pp. 682–694, and Raghunāth Tarkabāgīś Bhaṭṭācārya, *Āgamatattvavilāsa*, translated into Bengali by Pañcānan Śāstri (Calcutta: Nababhārat, 1985), pp. 238–250.

22. See, for Durgā: *Durgāpūjā Paddhati*, derived from the *Kālikā Purāṇa* and prepared by Jagadīścandra Tarkatīrtha (Calcutta: Saṁskṛta Pustak Bhāṇḍār, 1982), pp. xxxvi–xlii; *Durgāpūjā Paddhati*, derived from the *Devī Purāṇa* and prepared by Jagadīścandra Tarkatīrtha (Calcutta: Saṁskṛta Pustak Bhāṇḍār, 1981), pp. 66–70; and *Śrī Śrī Durgāpūjā Paddhati*, derived from the *Bṛhannandikeśvara Purāṇa* and prepared by Paṇḍit Śyāmācaraṇ Bhaṭṭācārya (Calcutta: Beṇīmādhab Śīl's Library, n.d.), pp. 77–91; and, for Kālī, *Śrī Śrī Kālīpūjā Paddhati*, prepared by Paṇḍit Śyāmācaraṇ Sāṁkhyatīrtha (Calcutta: Rājendra Library, n.d.), pp. 72–84.

23. All of the Kālī ritual manuals available for sale in the bazaars have lengthy sections on the prescriptions for goat and buffalo sacrifice. There are five steps to the rite: the sanctification of the animal; the dedication of the cleaver that will decapitate it; the consecration of the y-shaped stake that will hold the animal's neck in place; the actual beheading; and the offering of the animal's flesh, blood, and head to the Goddess. Though Brahman priests do all the dedicatory parts of the ritual, the decapitation is performed only by members of the blacksmith, or Kāmār, caste. See Sāṁkhyatīrtha, *Śrī Śrī Kālīpūjā Paddhati*, pp. 72–83.

24. See his *History of Dharmaśāstra*, 6 vols., 2nd ed. (Poona: Bhandarkar Oriental Research Institute, 1974), vol. V, pt. 1, pp. 164–168.

25. Bhaṭṭācārya, *Śrī Śrī Durgāpūjā Paddhati*, p. 78.

26. Amarnāth Dawn, interview, 5 Oct. 2000.

27. Tarkatīrtha, *Durgāpūjā Paddhati*, p. 12. For a similar recounting of Rāma's role in the justification for *bali*, see *Mahābhāgavata Purāṇa* 45.31–33 and 46.18–33, as cited in Patricia Dold, "Kālī the Terrific and Her Tests: The Śākta Devotionalism of the *Mahābhāgavata Purāṇa*," in *Encountering Kālī: At the Margins, at the Center, in the West*, ed. Rachel Fell McDermott and Jeffrey J. Kripal (Berkeley: University of California Press, 2003), p. 56 n. 10.

28. For accounts of these and other, similar temples, see Charles Joseph, "Topographical Survey of the River Hooghly from Bandel to Garden Reach," *Calcutta Review* 3, no. 5 (Jan.–June 1848): 428–462; S. C. Mitra, "On the Recent Instance of Human Sacrifice," *Journal of the Anthropological Society of Bombay* 15, no. 5, p. 481, as cited in Aparna Bhattacharya, *Religious Movements of Bengal (1800–1850)* (Patna: Aparna Bhattacharya, 1981), p. 98 n. 42; Śibśaṅkar Bhāratī, "Kalkātār Kālī-kathā," *Ānanda Bājār Patrikā*, 6 Nov. 1999, pp. 37–39; Sukumār Nāth, "Naihatir Ḍākāte Kālī," *Bartamān*, 29 Oct. 2000, p. 10; and Benay Ghoṣ, *Paścim Baṅga Saṁskṛti*, 4 vols. (Calcutta: Prakāś Bhaban, 1978), 2:58–59.

29. As cited in Sudhirkumar Mitra, *Huglī Jelār Itihās o Baṅgasamāj*, 2nd ed., 3 vols. (Calcutta: Mitrāṇi Prakāśan, 1953), 1:248.

30. *Friend of India*, 9 Feb. 1837, p. 41.

31. See, in order of reference, Mitra, *Huglī Jelār Itihās o Baṅgasamāj* 1:249; *Statesman*, 4 Oct. 1927, p. 8; *Times of India*, 21 Dec. 1999, p. 9; *Ājkāl*, 22 Nov. 2000, p. 6; Reuters, 9 Feb. 2001 (accessed through www.abcnews.go.com); and BBC News for 12 April 2006 (accessed through www.news.bbc.co.uk) and for 16 April 2010 (accessed at http://news.bbc.co.uk/2/hi/south_asia/8624269.stm).

32. The "goddess" in question is usually Kālī and less often Durgā. An engraving from 1917 of "Human Sacrifice to the goddess Juguddhatree," included in the *Missionary Papers* of the Church Missionary Society, may indicate that Jagaddhātrī had more of a share in these blood offerings in prior decades than is true today. See Brian K. Pennington, *Was Hinduism Invented? Briton, Indians, and the Colonial Construction of Religion* (New York: Oxford University Press, 2005), p. 97, fig. 3.7.

33. Felix Padel, *The Sacrifice of Human Being: British Rule and the Konds of Orissa* (Delhi: Oxford University Press, 1995).

34. Story by Sumali Moitra, from the *Independent*, 28 July 2001. Accessed at http://news.independent.co.uk/world/asia_china (4 August 2001).

35. On the Kuchbihar family and its customs, see *Ājkāl*, 3 Oct. 1995, p. 3; D. N. Majumdar, "The Custom of Burning Human Effigies," *Man in India* 3 (1923): 97–103; and Mohit Rāy, *Rūpe Rūpe Durgā* (Calcutta: Adhī Pāl, 1985), p. 33.

36. This custom is observed by Howrah's Bhaṭṭācārya family of Kailash Banerjee Lane, and, in Kolkata, the Sen family in Kumartuli, the Datta family of Hatkhola, and the Madan Mohan Datta family in Nimtola. For *śatrubali*, see references in *Devī Purāṇa* 22.16 and *Mahābhāgavata Purāṇa* 45.33, and Rajendra Chanda Hazra, *Studies in the Upapurāṇas*, 2 vols. (Calcutta: Sanskrit College, 1963), 1:80–85, 220, 229, 271, 278.

37. There is evidence for this transition from human to animal sacrifice in regions outside Bengal, as well. For South India, see the older work of the Rev. Henry Whitehead, who recorded in Telegu-speaking villages the practice of burying live pigs and hook-swinging live sheep, instead of humans; he believed that

human sacrifices were discontinued either when the victim escaped or when someone said the wrong thing (*The Village Gods of South India* [London: Oxford University Press, 1916], pp. 58–60 and 90–92). For an overview of this material, see Brenda E. F. Beck, section 7, "Animal Sacrifices and Other Festivals Offerings," in her "The Goddess and the Demon: A Local South Indian Festival and Its Wider Context," *Puruṣārtha* 5 (1981): 112–116. Researchers in Orissa make similar claims: Edgar Thurston writes of Khond tribesmen using buffalo instead of human sacrifice at the turn of the twentieth century (*Ethnographic Notes in Southern India* [Madras: Government Press, 1906], p. 517), and even though he states that the last recorded human sacrifice was in 1852, there have been reports as late as 1981 of the same; see the documentary film, "The Khonds of Baphlai Mali," produced by John Shepherd for the BBC (2000). Even the name of the festival in which buffalos are now offered, Meriah, used to be the generic name for human sacrifice.

38. See Suchitra Samanta, "The Self-Animal and Divine Digestion: Goat Sacrifice to the Goddess Kālī in Bengal," *Journal of Asian Studies* 53.3 (1994): 782.

39. This is the Gobarjana Kālī Temple, in Ratuya Thana, Maldah, said to have been built by Debī Caudhurāṇī, the housewife-turned-dacoit immortalized by Bankim Chandra Chatterjee, who vowed to erect a temple if she was successful in her fight against the British. At Kālī Pūjā time in 1996 5,000 goats and 10,000 pigeons were sacrificed within thirty hours. In 1998, because of the floods in the district, only 3,000 goats and 3,000 pigeons were immolated, but in 2000 the numbers were the same as in 1996. "The blood of the *balis* flows into the river, and the severed heads lie about the village" (*Ājkāl*, 28 Oct. 2000, p. 6).

40. One of the worst stories to surface in the news in 2000 was about the starvation and beating of captive owls at Kālī Pūjā time; it is believed that a suffering owl, Lakṣmī's vehicle, will tell the future in a human voice. *Bartamān*, 27 Oct. 2000, p. 5.

41. *Hindustan Times*, 30 July 2008, p. 5.

42. *Telegraph*, 11 Nov. 2004, p. 22.

43. *Telegraph*, weekend section, 26 Sept. 1998, p. 1.

44. Mr. Priya Gopāl Hājrā, scion of the Rāṇī Rāsmaṇi house in central Calcutta (interview, 16 Sept. 2000).

45. Interview, 17 Sept. 2000.

46. See chapter 6, nn. 34 and 58.

47. The Sābarṇa Rāy Caudhurīs apparently began sacrificing white goats (as a symbol of white skin) during Durgā Pūjā, 1917. After Independence, this practice was discontinued, but black goats are still sacrificed.

48. Quoted in *Ānanda Bājār Patrikā*, 1 Oct. 2000, p. 18.

49. *Ānanda Bājār Patrikā*, 4 Oct. 1922, p. 2.

50. *Ānanda Bājār Patrikā*, 5 Nov. 1945, p. 5.

51. Sumathi Ramaswamy, "Maps, Mother/Goddesses, and Martyrdom in Modern India," *Journal of Asian Studies* 67.3 (Aug. 2008): 843.

52. Aditi Sen (interview, 11 Oct. 1991) and Sanatkumār Mitra (interview, 6 Dec. 2000) reflect what is popularly written about sacrifice in Bengal—namely, that it is patronized mainly by lower-caste people. See Augustus Somerville, *Crime and Religious Beliefs in India*, 2nd ed. (1929; Calcutta: Thacker, Spink, and Co., 1966), pp. 140–141.

53. Interviews: Minati Kar, 2 Oct. 2000; Pradīp Pāl, 27 Oct. 1998; and Rītā Rāy, 1 Dec. 2000.

54. In this connection one thinks of the trouble Gandhi had in garnering support in Bengal, and of the success of the lionized, more militant Subhas Chandra Bose.

55. Interview, 21 Sept. 2000.

56. See Indira Goswami, *The Man from Chinnamasta*, trans. Prashant Goswami (New Delhi: Katha, 2006).

57. Mr. Asit Mukherjee devotes himself particularly to the issue of municipal slaughter houses. In Kolkata there are only four legal slaughter houses, at Tangra, Chitpur, Halsibagan, and Lansdowne. This means that it is not legal to kill animals anywhere else, though every small meat shop (*dokān*) does so. Most of these, he says, are run by Muslims. In November and December 1997, Mr. Mukherjee wrote letters of protest, which bore partial fruit: the courts ruled—in effect admitting that they could not enforce the law—that no meat shop could *openly* slaughter or display their meat. But even this, bemoans Mr. Mukherjee, "no one heeds" (*keu māne nā*). Interview, 19 Nov. 2000. It is noteworthy that for the sake of communal harmony Muslims are forbidden by law to slaughter cows at Bak'r-Id (see Supreme Court Judgment on Cow Slaughter in West Bengal—Civic Appeal no. 6790 of 1983). A second, 1994 civil appeal to overturn this law was rejected by the courts on the grounds that cow killing, in particular, is not essential to religious identity.

58. *Times of India*, 17 Oct. 2006, p. 12.

59. Spoken by a man in eastern Orissa about his local deity Pañcubarāhī (*Statesman*, 7 Oct. 2000, p. 2).

60. This was said to have occurred in Jangipur Mahakumir Gadaipur village; see Śibśaṅkar Bhāratī, "Durgāpūjo Jelāy Jelāy," *Bartamān Rabibār*, 8 Oct. 2000, p. 11; and Roy, *Rūpe Rūpe Durgā*, pp. 15–17.

61. Interviews, 29 Sept. 2000 and 10 Oct. 1991.

62. See *Bengalee*, 5 Oct. 1924, pp. 6–8, and Bipin Chandra Pal, *Memories of My Life and Times* (Calcutta: Bipinchandra Pal Institute, 1973), pp. 100–102.

63. *Telegraph*, 25 Oct. 2000, p. 27.

64. *Indian Express*, 30 July 2008, p. 2.

65. Most of the temples associated with the Rāmakṛṣṇa Mission, for example, have prohibited animal sacrifice. The first Rāmakṛṣṇa Mission Durgā Pūjā was celebrated, with the offering of animal meat, at the newly established Belur Maṭh in 1901. But the killing so upset Śāradādebī and others that it was decided to discontinue the practice thereafter. In addition to evidence provided by the several states that have banned animal sacrifice in temple precincts, and for individual case studies of slowly vegetarianized goddesses, see: Richard L. Brubaker's analysis of the sanitizing of Tamil goddesses in general ("The Ambivalent Mistress: A Study of South Indian Village Goddesses and Their Religious Meaning" [Ph.D. diss., University of Chicago, 1978]); Eveline Meyer's study of Aṅkāḷaparamēcuvari (*Aṅkāḷaparamēc uvari: A Goddess of Tamilnadu, Her Myths and Cult* [Stuttgart: Steiner Verlag Wiesbaden GMBH, 1986]); Kathleen Erndl's work on the Vaiṣṇo Devī cult in the Panjab Hills (*Victory to the Mother: The Hindu Goddess of Northwest India in Myth, Ritual, and Symbol* [New York: Oxford University Press, 1993]); William Sax's book on the Uttarkhand

region (*Mountain Goddess: Gender and Politics in a Himalayan Pilgrimage* [New York: Oxford University Press, 1991]); and David Pocock's older work on central Gujarat (*Mind, Body, and Wealth: A Study of Belief and Ritual in an Indian Village* [Totowa, N.J.: Rowman and Littlefield, 1973]).

66. See chapter 6, n. 58. Jan E. M. Houbens also traces this desire to exculpate the worshiper to Vedic ritual prescriptions: "You do not really die here, you are not hurt; you are going to the gods along paths easy to traverse, where those go who have acted well, not the evildoers" (*Taittirīya Brāhmaṇa* 3.7.7.14). He also cites a similar *mantra* said before killing the horse in the *aśvamedha* ceremony (*Ṛg Veda* 1.162.21). See his "To Kill or Not to Kill the Sacrificial Animal (yajña-paśu)? Arguments and Perspectives in Brahmanical Ethical Philosophy," in *Violence Denied: Violence, Non-Violence, and the Rationalization of Violence in South Asian Cultural History*, ed. Jan E. M. Houbens and Karel R. Van Kooij (Leiden: Brill, 1999), pp. 105–183.

67. Letter to the editor, *Pratidin*, 11 Oct. 1998, p. 4.

68. *Pratidin*, 3 Oct. 2000, p. 4.

69. The front slogan from *Excalibur, the Official Newsletter of People for Animals*. The fact that the Hindu gods have animal mounts, or *vāhanas*, is said to be an example of the divine love for wildlife (ibid., p. 2).

70. As Mr. Asit Mukherjee phrased it on 19 Nov. 2000, "I am not an atheist, but I tell Kālī that I won't go to her or worship her as long as she allows this sort of practice. She is not being a proper mother." Placards held during the protest vigil at Kālīghāṭ on 26 Oct. 2000 read, "Does the compassionate mother want the blood of a child?"

71. For an example of this interpretation, see Sir John Woodroffe's commentary on the nineteenth verse of the "Karpūrādi Stotram," in *Hymns to the Goddess and Hymn to Kālī* (Madras: Ganesh and Co., 1913), p. 329.

72. From "*Man tomār ei bhram gelo nā*," as translated in Rachel Fell McDermott, *Singing to the Goddess: Poems to Kālī and Umā from Bengal* (New York: Oxford University Press, 2001), poem 99.

73. See the Calcutta Municipal Corporation Act, sections 303, 338, 428(b), 490, and 501, as well as the West Bengal Animal Slaughter Control Act 22 (1950 and amended in 1979).

74. Interview, 30 Sept. 2000.

75. See Sanjukta Gupta, "The Domestication of a Goddess: Caraṇa-tīrtha Kālīghāṭ, the Mahāpīṭha of Kālī," in *Encountering Kālī: At the Margins, at the Center, in the West*, ed. Rachel Fell McDermott and Jeffrey J. Kripal (Berkeley: University of California Press, 2003), pp. 60–79; and *Pratidin*, 20 Oct. 2000, p. 12.

76. *Ānanda Bājār Patrikā*, 1 Oct. 2006, p. 14.

77. Interviews, 22 Sept. and 26 Oct. 2000.

78. Interview with Mr. Maṇimohan Rāy Caudhurī, Behala, 13 Sept. 2000.

79. Even in states with tough anti-sacrifice laws, "official" proscriptions are not totally effective against the practice. As early as the late nineteenth century, Gustav Oppert cautioned that the lack of sacrifices in temple contexts says nothing about what goes on at home before the domestic deity (*On the Original Inhabitants of Bharatavarṣa or India* [1893; New York: Arno Press, 1978], p. 477), and both Crad-

dock and Babb report, for the modern period in Tamilnadu and Rajasthan, respectively, that animal, especially buffalo, sacrifice has simply been pushed "into the closet"; Norma Elaine Craddock, "Anthills, Split Mothers, and Sacrifice: Conceptions of Female Power in the Mariyamman Tradition" (Ph.D. diss., University of California at Berkeley, 1994), p. 167, and Lawrence Alan Babb (pers. comm., 17 June 2001). See also Babb, "Mirrored Warriors: On the Cultural Identity of Rajasthani Traders," *International Journal of Hindu Studies* 3.1 (April 1999): esp. pp. 19–20.

80. Much of the material we have on blood sacrifice in the South Indian context indicates that the deities concerned are local gods and goddesses who are largely worshiped by lower castes. See Thurston, *Ethnographic Notes in Southern India*, p. 339, and Whitehead, *The Village Gods of South India*, pp. 18–19, 89, 94–95, 102–103. For more modern sources, consult Brubaker, "The Ambivalent Mistress"; Craddock, "Anthills, Split Mothers, and Sacrifice"; and Isabelle Nabokov, *Religion Against the Self: An Ethnology of Tamil Rituals* (New York: Oxford University Press, 2000).

81. J. C. Heesterman makes the same point even for sacrifice in the Vedic period; see "Vedic Sacrifice and Transcendence," in his *The Inner Conflict of Tradition: Essays in Indian Ritual, Kingship, and Society* (Chicago: University of Chicago Press, 1985), pp. 81–94.

82. Different cartoons on the front page of the newspaper *Pratidin*, for 18 Oct. 1999 and 6 Oct. 2000, show two goats talking to each other. One, being led away to the stake, says to the other, "Jump about as much as you like; tomorrow it's your turn."

83. See both *Statesman*, 7 Dec. 1999, p. 4, and *Pratidin*, 8 Dec. 1999, p. 2.

84. *Pratidin*, 23 April 2000, p. 5.

85. "The witness stand—wood for burning bodies—Oh Death, you are preferable to this./ Shyambazar, black night, a chopping block, a goat given for sacrifice./ Blood is flowing—blood is laughing—a rose despoiled in the mud of blood—/ A flower garden—a blind alley, an escapee—certified by the government stamp." Pūrbā Mukhopādhyāy, "Śāsti" ("Punishment"), published in *Deś* 67, no. 24 (30 Sept. 2000): 19. This poem, dedicated to Candrā, builds upon the characters and situation of a story by Rabindranath Tagore called "Śāsti," or "Punishment," in which an eighteen-year-old girl named Candrā, falsely accused by her husband of committing a murder, is sentenced to hang at the gallows. Too proud to defend herself and preferring death to life with a man who does not value her, she takes the stand at court and admits her guilt, thus sealing her fate. By the mention in the second line of Shyambazar, a densely populated neighborhood in northern Kolkata, Mukhopādhyāy intends to jar her readers into realizing that such injustices are still occurring in the city today: like goats offered at Kālī temples in the dead of night with no hope of escape, innocent, flower-like girls are raped and killed, their perpetrators getting off without punishment, since they have official and even police connections. The escapee can also be interpreted as the condemned girl, who, through death, is released from the injustices of her circumstances. By Kolkata municipal laws all goats must be certified suitable for slaughter; in this case, society has wrongly stamped Candrā and those she symbolizes as fit for abuse and

death. Phulbagan, lit. "a flower garden," is an area of northern Kolkata where a little girl was raped and killed in 1999. See Rabindranath Tagore, "Śāsti," in *Galpaguccha* (Calcutta: Biśvabhāratī Granthanbibhāg, 1969), pp. 182–190. Translated by William Radice as "Punishment," in *Rabindranath Tagore: Selected Short Stories*, rev. ed. (New York: Penguin, 1994), pp. 125–133.

86. Henri Hubert and Marcel Mauss, "Essai sur la nature et la fonction du sacrifice" (1899), translated by W. D. Halls as *Sacrifice: Its Nature and Function* (Chicago: University of Chicago Press, 1964).

87. An overview of sacrificial theories proposed over the past century is too ambitious to be treated in this short chapter. For good summaries, see Christopher J. Fuller, *The Camphor Flame: Popular Hinduism and Society in India* (Princeton: Princeton University Press, 1992), pp. 83–105; Luc de Heusch, *Sacrifice in Africa: A Structuralist Approach*, trans. Linda O'Brien and Alice Morton (Manchester: Manchester University Press, 1985); Nabokov, *Religion Against the Self*; and Valerio Valeri, *Kingship and Sacrifice: Ritual and Society in Ancient Hawaii*, trans. Paula Wissing (Chicago: University of Chicago Press, 1985).

88. This idea of debt fits well with the Vedic concept of debts, "which, in Brahmanism, governs not only men's individual lives, but also the whole organization of the world, and especially sacrifice. From his birth, man is a debt for which death is the creditor" (from Charles Malamoud, "Terminer le sacrifice: Remarques sur les honoraires rituels dans le Brahmanisme," in Madeleine Biardeau and Charles Malamoud, *Le sacrifice dans l'Inde ancienne* [Paris: Presses Universitaires de France, 1976], p. 194, quoted in de Heusch, *Sacrifice in Africa*, p. 193).

89. According to Maurice Bloch, one of the key elements of sacrifice is the equation of the self with the victim, who represents one's problems, one's animality (*Prey Into Hunter: The Politics of Religious Experience* [Henry Lewis Morgan Lectures 1984] [Cambridge: Cambridge University Press, 1992], pp. 35–36). Luc de Heusch agrees: "One constant practice pervades the sacrificial field: the possibility of substituting an animal for a man" (*Sacrifice in Africa*, p. 15).

90. De Heusch, *Sacrifice in Africa*, p. 202.

91. See René Girard, *Violence and the Sacred*, trans. Patrick Gregory (Baltimore: Johns Hopkins University Press, 1977).

92. Bell makes this point succinctly in the excerpt from her work, "Constructing Ritual," in *Readings in Ritual Studies*, ed. Ronald L. Grimes (Upper Saddle River, NJ: Prentice Hall, 1996), pp. 21–33; see her more sustained treatment in *Ritual Theory, Ritual Practice* (New York: Oxford University Press, 1992). Geertz's classic example of a ritual expressive of disquieting destructiveness is his "Deep Play: Notes on the Balinese Cockfight," in his *The Interpretation of Cultures: Selected Essays* (New York: Basic Books, 1973), pp. 412–453.

93. Nabokov, *Religion Against the Self*, pp. 11–12.

94. Ibid., p. 178.

95. The sense of harmony achieved from cooking a feast according to socially acceptable culinary rules, and then from sharing it with the community, resonates with de Heusch's notion of sacrifice as expressing order through food; *Sacrifice in Africa*, pp. 17–23.

96. Walter Burkert too notes the hesitation before a ritualized killing, as well as typical disclaimers of responsibility. Walter Burkert, *Homo Necans: The Anthropology of Ancient Greek Sacrificial Ritual and Myth*, trans. Peter Bing (Berkeley: University of California Press, 1983), pp. 16, 37–41, 81–82.

97. Hugh B. Urban, *The Power of Tantra: Religion, Sexuality, and the Politics of South Asian Studies* (London: I. B. Tauris, 2010). He references Michel Foucault, *Language, Counter-Memory, Practice: Selected Essays and Interviews* (Ithaca: Cornell University Press, 1977), *The History of Sexuality*, vol. 1: *An Introduction* (New York: Vintage, 1978), and *Power/Knowledge: Selected Interviews and Other Writings* (New York: Pantheon, 1980); Gilles Deleuze, "Désir et plaisir," *Magazine littéraire* 325 (Oct. 1994), pp. 59–65; and Gilles Deleuze and Félix Guattari, *Anti-Oedipus: Capitalism and Schizophrenia* (Minneapolis: University of Minnesota Press, 1983).

98. *The Village Gods of South India*, p. 44.

99. Burkert, *Homo Necans*, p. 2. Also from p. 2: "The worshipper experiences the god most powerfully not just in pious conduct or in prayer, songs, and dance, but in the deadly blow of the axe, the gush of blood."

100. *Ānanda Bājār Patrikā*, 22 Oct. 2001, p. 10.

101. *Sunday Statesman*, "Impressions" insert, 31 Oct. 1999, p. 2.

## 9. Devī in the Diaspora

1. I am grateful to members of the Religion Seminar at the University of Pennsylvania on 4 Feb. 2004, who gave valuable feedback on an earlier version of this chapter.

2. *Amrita Bazar Patrika*, 13 Oct. 1985, p. 9.

3. Prema Kurien, "Becoming American by Becoming Hindu: Indian Americans Take Their Place at the Multicultural Table," in *Gatherings in Diaspora: Religious Communities and the New Immigration*, ed. R. Stephen Warner and Judith G. Wittner (Philadelphia: Temple University Press, 1998), pp. 42–43. See also Steven Vertovec, *The Hindu Diaspora: Comparative Patterns* (London: Routledge, 2000). Good overview chapters on the history of South Asian immigration in general include Martin Baumann, "A Diachronic View of Diaspora, the Significance of Religion, and Hindu Trinidadians," in *Diaspora, Identity, and Religion: New Directions in Theory and Research*, ed. Waltrand Kokot, Khachig Tölölyan, and Carolin Alfonso (London: Routledge, 2004), pp. 170–188; Roger Daniels, "The Indian Diaspora in the United States," in *Migration: The Asian Experience*, ed. Judith Brown and Rosemary Foot (Oxford: St. Martin's Press, 1994), pp. 83–103; Karen Isaksen Leonard, "Early South Asian Immigrants, 1900–1947," in *The South Asian Americans* (Westport, Conn.: Greenwood, 1997), pp. 39–65; Johanna Lessinger, "Indian Immigrants in the United States: The Emergence of a Transnational Population," in *Culture and Economy in the Indian Diaspora*, ed. Bhikshu Parekh, Huhapal Singh, and Steven Vertovec (London: Routledge, 2003), pp. 165–182; and Anantanand Rambachan, "Global Hinduism: The Hindu Diaspora," in *Contemporary Hinduism: Ritual, Culture, and Practice*, ed. Robin Rinehart (Santa Barbara: ABC-CLIO, 2004), pp. 390–400.

4. From Prasanta K. Basu, "Trends in the Growth of Bengali Musical Enterprises in Toronto During 1955–1984: An Overview," in *Bengali Immigrants: A Community in Transition*, ed. Joseph T. O'Connell and Ritendra K. Ray (Toronto: Rabindranath Tagore Lectureship Foundation, 1985), pp. 9–10.

5. Pratapaditya Pal comments that when he first came to the United States in the mid-1960s, there were no Durgā Pūjās anywhere. See "Durga Puja in South California," *Statesman*, Festival booklet, 1991, p. 63. The oldest Pūjā association in Germany also dates from this decade: in Berlin, from 1975.

6. See description of artist Amarnath Ghosh, in Somshankar Bandyopadhyay, "Shola Durga Idols Getting Ready for Export," *Times of India*, 25 Sept. 2000, p. 2. Artisans fortunate enough to acquire an overseas following can make a lot of money; one *śolā* Jagaddhātrī image, only 3.5 feet, was sent to New York in October 2000 to the cost of Rs. 50,000 (*Times of India*, 19 Oct. 2000, p. 5). A West Bengali community in Schaumberg, outside Chicago, had a new image designed in Kumartuli but cast in Italy out of plastic so that it would be permanent (Clinton B. Seely, pers. comm., 6 April 2003.)

7. Stated by Dr. Mrs. Anima Bhattacharya in a questionnaire filled out on 5 April 2003.

8. The Bangladeshi Hindu Mandir, in Queens, New York, contains permanent, old-style images of Durgā, Jagaddhātrī, and Kālī from Kolkata. The same is true, for Durgā, of the Jersey City Durga Puja and the New York Puja Association. Sweet bluish Kālīs may be seen at the New York Puja Association and the East Coast Durga Puja Association. Not all organizers want the traditional tableau, however. The Durgā belonging to the Bengali Association of Greater Chicago is large, humanized, with a woman's face and a realistic demon and lion. Says artist Amarnath Ghosh of the export market to which he caters, "Earlier, there were requests for traditional images. But in the past few years, some customers have been asking for a more modern, womanly face of the goddess" (quoted by Bandyopadhyay, "Shola Durga Idols Getting Ready for Export," p. 2).

9. Prior to the 2003 Durgā Pūjā celebrations, the organizers of the Garden State Puja Committee (Jersey City) bought a new *mūrti* from Kolkata for $2,192. In the same year their neighbors, the New Jersey Durga Puja Association, or Kallol (Somerset), paid $7,000 for theirs.

10. Most of the Pūjās that I have attended or noticed advertised have collapsed the five-day festival into two: Ṣaṣṭī, Saptamī, and Aṣṭamī are celebrated on the first day, and Nabamī and Daśamī on the second. Some committee, however, proudly proclaim that they do the Pūjā "properly" by observing the full five-day sequence, and on the correct *tithi*s. See n. 20 below.

11. The most elaborate Pūjā I have yet seen occurs under the auspices of the Garden State Cultural Association, held at the Plainfield High School. Women engage in the traditional farewell rituals of *baraṇ*, when they offer the Goddess sweets, betel leaf, and vermillion, as well as the playful ritual of *sindūr-* or *rang-khelā*, when they smear each other's faces with red powder.

12. Some Pūjā associations or permanent temples, such as the Washington Kālī Bāḍī, fly in priests for important occasions; such opportunities are considered

plums by Indian Brahmans. See Dwaipayan G. Dastidar, "Part-Time Purohits Make a Quick Buck at Ma's Expense," *Times of India*, 29 Sept. 2000, p. 2. However, in general American Pūjās are served by locally available Brahmans, whose number is growing, due to immigration. Mr. Abhas Bhattacharya, the priest of the Jersey City Durga Puja, originally hails from the Kalighat area of Kolkata. Here, he works both as an engineer and as a registered Hindu priest for the Jersey City area.

13. The controversial nature of Kālī's bloodlust is exemplified by the contradictory answers I received from different organizers of the New York Puja Association on the occasion of Kālī Pūjā on 2 Nov. 2002. Two men at the reception area explicitly told me that because Kālī likes blood she must be offered meat, while another man within the auditorium adamantly affirmed that in this Pūjā there was "no meat!"

14. Examples include the State Bank of India, Air India, Bangladesh Biman, the Indian Tourist Promotion Office, Money Dart, Western Union, and Volvo.

15. In 2002 the East Coast Durga Puja Association charged $100 to sit up near the stage in the Gujrati Samaj in Queens, New York, to hear the Bollywood singer Abhijit perform. In 1997 they brought Amrik Singh Arora, who sang Śyāmā-*saṅgīt*, for which he has become very popular in Kolkata.

16. These tend to be local people of eminence; particularly popular are Bangladeshi ambassadors.

17. See Pal, "Durga Puja in South California," p. 64.

18. Interview with Dr. Dwijen Bhattacharjya, 19 Oct. 2002, regarding the formation of what became the Bangladesh Hindu Mandir.

19. The first Pūjā of the fledgling Bangladeshi group was held in the Corpus Christi Church, Queens, New York, in 1990. But by 1991, due to leadership disputes, there were two rival groups, the Bangladesh Puja Samiti and the Bangladesh Puja Samity. It is the former, original group that managed to build the Bangladesh Hindu Mandir, a permanent Durgā Temple in Queens that opened in 1998.

20. Some permanent temples, such as the Kālī Temple in Toronto and the Bangladesh Hindu Mandir in New York, insist on observing the correct *tithi*s. After all, observes Pratapaditya Pal, the scriptures say that a Pūjā not performed on the correct *tithi* is not efficacious. Do the gods like waiting for the weekends? See Pal, "Durga Puja in South California," p. 64.

21. This is not a Bengali example; the practice was initiated by Gujaratis celebrating Navarātrī in New Jersey in 1990. See Diana L. Eck, "Negotiating Hindu Identities in America," in *The South Asian Religious Diaspora in Britain, Canada, and the United States*, ed. Harold Coward, John R. Hinnells, and Raymond Brady Williams (Albany: State University of New York Press, 2000), p. 232.

22. Sometimes the food offered to the deities and then to the devotees is an American-Bengali mix. At the BAPS Swamy Narayan Mandir in Brunswick, Ohio, *ārati* and *bhajan*s are followed by dinner. "Unlike India, here the gods accept anything as offering—chole, rice sabji, pakoras, sweets. Anything that does not have onion or garlic in it," says Narhari Patel, coordinator of the temple. "Don't be surprised if you see a bar of chocolate as prasad, or a Muslim offering Diwali prayers in Swamy Narayan Mandir. The festival is Indian, after all" (Kaumudi Marathe, North American Special, "Celebrating the Diwali Spirit," *India Today* [1 Nov. 1999], p. 4). On

4 Oct. 2008, I noted that the Garden State Cultural Association, which holds its Pūjā at the Plainfield High School, New Jersey, served vegetarian "chicken fingers," "hot dogs," and french fries for the Americanized Bengali children.

23. Ghoṣāl sang at the Garden State Puja Committee, at the Golden Door Charter School, on 4 Oct. 2003, and Gangopādhyāy was featured at the Garden State Cultural Association, in the Plainfield High School, on 5 Oct. 2003.

24. Interview with T. Richard Blurton, 25 Sept. 2006, London.

25. According to the 2001 Census for Bangladesh, Hindus constitute only 9.2 percent of the population.

26. Both statements were written by Praṇabendu Kumār Cakrabartī, the editor. See *Prācī* (2002), p. 3, and *Prācī* (2003), p. 4, respectively.

27. See "Open Letter" to Dr. Debabrata Dutta by Dilip Nath, director for communications and public relations, Bangladesh Hindu Mandir, October 2002.

28. This tendency to revert to the language of the host country is demonstrated in other Western countries as well. Aśok Sengupta, in an article in *Ānandamelā*, 4 Oct. 2000, pp. 13–17, describes a Kālī Pūjā in Brazil, with signs and publications in Portuguese, and a souvenir *patrikā* printed in German for a veteran Pūjā association centered in Hamburg, Germany.

29. The 2002 New York Puja Association booklet, on p, 2, in English, opens by asking Durga "to bless our beloved America and all of us with prosperity and peace," and one of the later essays, by a Bengali-American teenager, is called "Why I love America" (p. 46). The East Coast Durga Puja Association, also West Bengali, prints in its booklet, *Durga Puja and Dushera*, a letter of thanks from the American Red Cross for the $1,000 donation it had made in December 2001. The West Bengali groups, therefore, appear to feel more tied into and proud of their life in the United States.

30. Said Rana Ghosh, of the Bangladesh Hindu Mandir, "West Bengalis are more organized, but we have more *niṣṭhā*" (12 Oct. 2002). And Dwijen Bhattacharjya, a Bangladeshi Hindu present at the cultural show of the New York Puja Association that same evening, said to me in a scandalized fashion, commenting on the fact that one of the songs had included references to women's bras, "these people have no *niṣṭhā*!"

31. Said Abhas Bhattacharya, the priest of the Jersey City Durga Puja, on 13 Oct. 2002, "We do [the Pūjā] with more precision than elsewhere." And on 2 Nov. 2002, a couple attending the Kālī Pūjā celebration at the smaller of the two New York West Bengali groups, the New York Puja Association, commented that while theirs was smaller than the rival organization, the East Coast Durga Puja Association, it is also "more homey."

32. Interview, 1 July 2006.

33. This temple is blessed by but not formally affiliated with the Ādyāpīṭh Kālī Temple in northern Kolkata. It was inaugurated in 2002. I visited the temple for the first time on 14 Nov. 2004.

34. Pal, "Durga Puja in South California," p. 63.

35. Chicago's Sri Ramakrishna Universal Temple, inaugurated in September 2008, includes a full Kālī Pūjā ritual in its festival calendar. By contrast, Swami Tathagatananda of the Westside Vedanta Center, New York City, privately reads

the *Caṇḍī*, performs the *ārati*, and then offers flowers and songs. Then, on the Sunday closest to the proper day, selected close devotees are invited to come upstairs to his private shrine to offer flowers to his image of the Goddess. There is no public Kālī Pūjā.

36. This overseas branch of the Sangha was formed in 1995. In 2006 they erected their own temple, the one in Franklin Township, New Jersey, and have hired a resident priest. At Kālī Pūjā, their main event of the year, they rent a school auditorium in Somerset. Interestingly, they do not do Durgā Pūjā at all, but substitute instead Jagaddhātrī Pūjā, which they host in their temple. For the past several years, monks Subrata Bhāi and Murāl Bhāi from Kolkata's Ādyāpīth Temple have come to New Jersey to conduct both Pūjās, which they do in a clearly heartfelt manner.

37. See www.kalimandir.org. In the summer of 2008 they constructed a new temple room for Mā; further expansion is planned.

38. Some sample comparative costs for Durgā and Kālī Pūjās, for 2002: $21,000 vs. $7,200 (New York Puja Association); and $30,000 vs. $10,000 (East Coast Durga Puja Association). In 2003 the latter organization kept Durgā Pūjā expenses at around $30,000 but increased the lavishness of its Kālī Pūjā by spending $21,500. No matter how humble the celebration, the cultural program is always the most expensive, followed by the hall rental and then the food. The image usually costs nothing, since it is reused from the previous year, and the priest's fees are relatively minimal.

39. The temple priest always does the worship of the Goddess with a picture of Rādhā and Kṛṣṇa right in front, between himself and Durgā; devotees entering the temple routinely ejaculate, "Hare Krishna, Hare Rama!"; Kṛṣṇa *kīrtan* plays in the background at most occasions; and the temple devotees place special emphasis on Vaiṣṇava holidays, even Ratha Yātrā.

40. Of course, as Steven Vertovec reminds us, it is a mistake to view India as "the ideal culture, the fountainhead, the yardstick," as if it were an unchanging archetype; Vertovec, *The Hindu Diaspora*, p. 2. K. K. A. Venkatachari wholeheartedly agrees: Hinduism has always been a tradition of change and adaptation. The authors of the *dharma-śāstras* disagreed on points, the *gṛhyasūtras* allowed for regional differences in the performance of rituals, new rituals have been Vedicized to look older, and texts have always been less rich than the actually practiced rituals they describe. "[Adaptation] is not a new process that should be attacked as dangerous; indeed, it is essential to the vitality of any religion." See his chapter, "Transmission and Transformation of Rituals," in *Modern Transmissions of Hindu Traditions in India and Abroad*, ed. Raymond Brady Williams (Chambersburg, Penn.: Anima, 1992), p. 190.

41. Gurharpal Singh, "Introduction," in *Culture and Economy in the Indian Diaspora*, ed. Bhiskhu Parekh, Guhapal Singh, and Steven Vertovic (London: Routledge, 2003), pp. 3–4. A similar approach is taken by Steven Vertovec in *The Hindu Diaspora*, pp. 146–153.

42. Kurien, "Becoming American by Becoming Hindu," p. 58.

43. See Raymond Brady Williams, "Introduction: A Sacred Thread," in *A Sacred Thread: Modern Transmissions of Hindu Traditions in India and Abroad*, ed. Raymond Brady Williams (Chambersburg, Penn.: Anima, 1992), p. 5.

44. Interview, 14 Nov. 2004.

45. See *Ānanda Bājār Patrikā*, 1 Oct. 2006, p. 13.

46. Subhendu Mukherjee for the *Statesman*, 2 Oct. 1987, p. 13.

47. First stanza of Anon., "*Āmrā yārā prabāse āchi tāder janye* (For those of us who live abroad)," Garden State Puja Association, 2006, p. 22.

48. "Nostalgic Notes from Toronto," *Hindustan Times*, Puja Parikrama section, 8 Oct. 2004, p. 3.

49. It is noteworthy about the perceived place of Bengali Hinduism in the rest of India that one of the oldest such "virtual pūjā" sites on the Web, www.eprarthana.com, features no Bengali temples, cities, or deities of any *sampradāya* whatsoever.

50. As of January 2009, this had not been updated since 2007, and did not appear to be very easy to use. See *Hindustan Times Live*, Kolkata, 1 Sept. 2008, p. 2.

51. Milton Singer, *When a Great Tradition Modernizes: An Anthropological Approach to Indian Civilizations* (Chicago: University of Chicago Press, 1980), p. 71. This idea of the reflexivity of ritual in diasporic settings is also enunciated by Paul Younger, *Playing Host to Deity: Festival Religion in the South Indian Tradition* (New York: Oxford University Press, 2002), p. 163; and Sunita S. Mukhti, *Doing the Desi Thing: Performing Indianness in New York City* (New York: Garland, 2000), pp. 45–51.

52. Milton Gordon (in *Assimilation in American Life: The Role of Race, Religion, and National Origins* [New York: Oxford University Press, 1964], as referred to in Raymond Brady Williams, *Religions of Immigrants from India and Pakistan: New Threads in the American Tapestry* [Cambridge: Cambridge University Press, 1988], pp. 33–34) outlines three functional characteristics of ethnic groups: they serve psychologically as a source of group identity; they provide patterned networks of groups and institutions, which allows an individual to define his relation to the whole through life-cycle rites; and they refract the national cultural patterns of behavior and values through the prism of a narrower cultural heritage.

53. This point is made by Vasudha Narayanan in "Hinduism in America," in *Religion and American Cultures: An Encyclopedia of Traditions, Diversity, and Popular Expressions*, ed. Gary Laderman and Luis Leon, 3 vols. (Santa Barbara, Calif.: ABC-CLIO, 2003), 1:107.

54. Suhas Ghosh, interview, Oct. 5, 2003.

55. Fred Clothey, "Rituals and Reinterpretation: South Indians in Southeast Asia," in *A Sacred Thread*, ed. Williams, pp. 127–135. Steven Vertovec is uncomfortable with this concept if it rests upon an assumption of rational choice: not all compromises are consciously "chosen." He prefers to utilize Pierre Bourdieu's notion of *habitus*, a "non-conscious set of dispositions and classificatory schemes that people gain through experience, providing a repertoire for situationally competent action, improvisation, and the generation of new practices"; see *The Hindu Diaspora*, pp. 156–159.

56. Younger, *Playing Host to Deity*, p. 159.

57. In another example, in a November 2003 New Jersey rendition of Jagaddhātrī Pūjā by the devotees of the Dakshineswar Ramkrishna Sangha Adyapeath, "*Americabāsi ki jay!*" was added to the traditional set of exclamations of victory for deities at the end of the ritual.

58. According to Raymond Brady Williams, more than 90 percent of the Hindu organizations in the United States are founded and led by lay persons who have

little training in and often limited knowledge of Hinduism. Many rely on guidance from teachers in India. See his *Religions of Immigrants from India and Pakistan*, p. 55.

59. See "Sacred Threads of Several Textures: Strategies of Adaptation in the United States," in *A Sacred Thread*, ed. idem, pp. 231–244.

60. Kurien, "Becoming American by Becoming Hindu," p. 64.

61. For a representative statement of this opinion, see Williams, *Religions of Immigrants from India and Pakistan*, pp. 287–288.

62. Jhumpa Lahiri, *The Namesake* (Boston: Houghton Mifflin, 2003), p. 64.

63. See Kurien, "Becoming American by Becoming Hindu," p. 46.

64. For instance, the Bangladesh Hindu Mandir uses its Pūjā souvenir booklet to advertise a Bengali Sunday School, in which participating children and teenagers learn Bengali, Hindu religion, and Bengali songs and dances. Note that most non-temple-based Durgā Pūjā societies exist only to sponsor the Pūjās, and do not hold regular meetings throughout the year.

## Conclusion

1. Durgā Pūjā is asserted to be "the most important festival of West Bengal" by the writer of the "West Bengal" section of *Fairs and Festivals of India*, chief editor M. P. Bezbaruah; compiler Krishna Gopal; photographer Phal S. Girota, 5 vols. (New Delhi: Gyan Publishing House, 2003), V:168.

2. Ralph W. Nicholas, "The Bengali Calendar and the Hindu Religious Year in Bengal," in *Fruits of Worship: Practical Religion in Bengal* (New Delhi: Chronicle Books, 2003), pp. 13–27.

3. Stanley A. Freed and Ruth S. Freed, *Hindu Festivals in a North Indian Village* (Washington, D.C.: American Museum of Natural History, 1998).

4. Hanumān is not a Bengali deity; Hanumān temples in Bengal are built by Bihari migrants; see Philip Lutgendorf, *Hanuman's Tale: The Messages of a Divine Monkey* (New York: Oxford University Press, 2007), p. 250. We have evidence for non-Bengali Rāmlīlā performances, at least in the gardens of the wealthy, from the mid-nineteenth century in Calcutta; see Clinton B. Seely, *The Slaying of Meghanada: A Ramayana from Colonial Bengal* (New York: Oxford University Press, 2004), p. 51. My newspaper survey, however, turns up public enactments of Rāma's victory over Rāvaṇa by North Indians on the Calcutta maidan only from the early 1970s. The *Amrita Bazar Patrika*, 8 Oct. 1973, p. 1, gives a notice of Panjabis celebrating Rāmlīlā in the city for the second year in a row. The effigy for the first year is photographed in *Ānanda Bājār Patrikā*, 18 Oct. 1972, p. 5.

5. The image was at Chetla Park Cultural Club. *Telegraph*, 13 Feb. 2005, Metro section, p. 1.

6. Four Thursdays are especially important: those in the months of Caitra, Bhadra, Pauṣ, and Āśvin. In Caitra, the rainy season, the rice is sown; in Bhadra it is growing; in Pauṣ it is brought inside and tied in a pot; and in Āśvin it is threshed.

7. Said artisan Babu Pal, in 2000, evidently pleased about the increased business, "More and more nuclear families are now performing Lakshmi pujas." He estimated

that eight to ten thousand earthen plate Lakṣmī images were being made in Kumartuli each year. *Times of India*, 12 Oct. 2000, p. 2.

8. "*Ghare ghare Lakṣmīr āsan-pātā*": "Lakṣmī's seats are spread out in every house."

9. "*Mukher madhye beś ekṭā Lakṣmī-Śrī ācche*": "There is something very graceful about her face." "*Lakṣmī-chāḍā lok*" means someone whom fortune has abandoned. "*Lakṣmī chele! Lakṣmī meye!*": "Good boy! Good girl!" I am grateful to Keshab Chandra Sarkar, who taught me these expressions on 12 Oct. 2000.

10. *Times of India*, 18 Nov. 2000, "Calcutta Times" section, p. 1.

11. The yearly cycle of vows to Ṣaṣṭī and of festivals for what he calls the "village goddesses of calamities" (Śītalā and Manasā) may be found in Nicholas, "The Bengali Calendar," diagrams 6 and 7, pp. 24–25.

12. I am grateful to Jayanta Roy, who participated in and photographed the entire festival for me in Shalkia on 14 Feb. 2001 and 27 Feb. 2002.

13. Pratap Chandra Ghosha, *Durga Puja, with Notes and Illustrations* (Calcutta: Hindoo Patriot Press, 1871), p. xxiv of end matter, n. 13.

14. Kunal Chakrabarti, *Religious Process: The Purāṇas and the Making of a Regional Tradition* (New Delhi: Oxford University Press, 2001), p. 208.

15. Ralph W. Nicholas, *Rites of Spring: Gājan in Village Bengal* (New Delhi: Chronicle Books, 2008), especially chap. 1, "Gājan and Bengali Rituals," pp. 1–36.

16. The village in question is Kurmun. See *Sunday Times of India*, 13 April 2008, p. 2.

17. M. N. Roy, "Disintegration of a Priestly Family," in *The Radical Humanist* 18, no. 6–7 (7 Feb. 1954), pp. 73–74.

18. *Statesman*, 5 Oct. 1919, p. 19.

19. This point is made by Hillary Peter Rodrigues, *Ritual Worship of the Great Goddess: The Liturgy of the Durgā Pūjā with Interpretations* (Albany: State University of New York Press, 2003), p. 253.

20. *Bartamān*, 1 Oct. 1995, Pūjā enclosure, p. 9.

21. Quoted by Ghosha, *Durga Puja, with Notes and Illustrations*, p. 15.

22. This was the manner in which the Bengali *bhakta* and saint Rāmakṛṣṇa viewed Durgā; see Swami Saradananda, *Sri Ramakrishna, The Great Master*, trans. Swami Jagadananda, 2 vols., 6th ed. (Mylapore: Sri Ramakrishna Math, 1984), p. 123.

23. Quoted from "Durga Puja in the Villages of Old," *Statesman*, 6 Sept. 1952, Puja Supplement, pp. 1 and 4.

24. Spoken by Sudhir Pāl; see the "Calcutta Times" section of the *Times of India*, 23 Oct. 2001, p. 1.

## Appendix. An Overview of the Press in Bengal up to 1947

1. Good overviews of the Indian press include Smarajit Chakraborti, *The Bengali Press (1818–1868): A Study in the Growth of Public Opinion* (Calcutta: Firma KLM, 1976); Mrinal Kanti Chanda, *History of the English Press in Bengal: 1780 to 1857* (Calcutta: K. P. Bagchi, 1987); and Rangaswami Parthasarathy, *Journalism in India: From the Earliest Times to the Present Day* (Bangalore: Sterling Publishers, 1989).

2. Chanda, *History of the English Press in Bengal*, p. xxi.

# Bibliography

## Newspapers

In English and Bengali, consulted for the Pūjā season (covering Durgā, Jagaddhātrī, and Kālī Pūjās) in each year listed.

*Ājkāl* (Bengali; 1981 to the present): 1995, 1996, 1998–2008

*Amrita Bazar Patrika* (English; 1867 to the present): 1905–1946, 1948–1954, 1962–1990, 1994–2008

*Ānanda Bājār Patrikā* (Bengali; 1922 to the present): 1923–1924, 1926, 1944–1945, 1947–1952, 1962–1977, 1979, 1981–1986, 1989–1990, 1995–1996, 1998–2008

*Asian Age* (English; 1994 to present): 1988–2003

*Bande Mataram* (English; 1906–1908): 1906–1908

*Bartamān* (Bengali; 1984 to the present): 1995, 1996, 1998–2008

*Bengalee* (English; 1858–1932): 1872, 1875, 1879, 1883, 1885–1891, 1893–1896, 1898, 1900–1918, 1920–1932

*The Bengal Hurkaru* (English; 1822–1866): 1822–1866

*The Bengal Herald* (English; 1829–1843): 1829, 1842–1843

*Bhāratabarṣa* (Bengali; 1913–1963): 1913, 1940

*Calcutta Chronicle* (English; 1787–1790): 1788

*Calcutta Gazette / Oriental Advertiser* (English; 1784–1818): 1784, 1785

*Calcutta Journal* (English; 1818–1823): 1818–1823

*Calcutta Morning Post* (English; 1797–1818): 1812

*The Calcutta Review* (English; 1844 to the present): 1844–1902

*Dainik Basumatī* (Bengali; 1913 to the present): 1966, 1968
*The Englishman* (English; 1834–1934): 1834–1872, 1875–1878, 1880–1886, 1889–1891, 1894, 1898, 1902–1934
*Friend of India and Statesman*, monthly (English; 1818–1834): 1820–1826
*The Friend of India / Friend of India and Statesman*, weekly (English; 1835–1914): 1835–1840, 1845, 1848–1850, 1864–1865, 1870, 1875, 1902–1907
*The Hindoo Patriot* (English; 1854–1922): 1853, 1857, 1859–1863, 1885–1886, 1889, 1891, 1894, 1998, 1901–1906
*Hindustan Times* (English; 1998 to the present for the Kolkata edition): 2001–2008
*India Gazette / Calcutta Public Advertiser* (English; 1780 to 1834): 1781, 1782, 1784, 1831
*Indian Mirror* (English; 1861–1889): 1878–1889
*Māsik Basumatī* (Bengali; 1923–1969?*): 1943–1945
*Nabyabhārat* (Bengali; 1883–1923): 1888, 1894–1895, 1897–1901, 1903–1906
*Pratidin* (Bengali; 1992 to the present): 1992, 1995, 1998–2008
*Samācār Candrikā* (1822–1866?): 1830
*Statesman*, daily (English; 1922 to the present): 1922–1970, 1981–1988, 1990, 1991, 1995–1996, 1998–2008
*Statesman and Friend of India*, daily (English; 1875–1922): 1878–1889, 1915–1922
*Tattvabodhinī Patrikā* (Bengali; 1839–1932): 1843–1851, 1909–1939
*Telegraph* (English; 1982 to the present): 1991, 1995, 1996, 1998–2008
*Times of India* (English; 1996 to the present for the Kolkata edition): 1999–2008
*Yugāntar* (Bengali; 1937 to the present): 1995

## Articles and Books

Abadhūt. "Kālītīrtha Kālīghāṭ." In *Sādhak Jīban Samagra*, pp. 355–485. Calcutta: Mitra and Ghoṣ Publishers, 1982.

Āgambāgīś, Kṛṣṇānanda. *Bṛhat Tantrasāra*, ed. Rasikmohan Caṭṭopādhyāy and trans. Candrakumār Tarkālaṅkar. Calcutta: Nababhārat, 1982.

Akhtar, Shirin. *The Role of the Zamindars in Bengal, 1707–1772*. Dacca: Asiatic Society of Bangladesh, 1982.

Anderson, Benedict. *Imagined Communities: Reflections on the Origin and Spread of Nationalism*. 2nd rev. ed. London: Verso, 1991.

Anon. "Article III.—Radhakant Deb." *Calcutta Review* 44, no. 90 (Aug. 1867): 317–326.

Anon. *Durgā Debīr Bṛttānta*. Midnapur: Mission Press, 1867.

Anon. "West Bengal." In *Fairs and Festivals of India*, chief editor M. P. Bezbaruah; compiler Krishna Gopal; photographer Phal S. Girota, 5 vols. 5:165–259. New Delhi: Gyan Publishing House, 2003.

Appadurai, Arjun. "Consumption, Duration, and History." In *Modernity at Large: Cultural Dimensions of Globalization*, pp. 66–85. Minneapolis: University of Minnesota Press, 1996.

Archer, William. *Songs for the Bride: Wedding Rites of Rural India*. Ed. Barbara Stoler Miller and Mildred Archer. New York: Columbia University Press, 1985.

Babb, Lawrence Alan. "Mirrored Warriors: On the Cultural Identity of Rajasthani Traders." *International Journal of Hindu Studies* 3, no. 1 (April 1999): 1–25.

Bagal, Jogesh C. "Women in India's Freedom Movement." *Modern Review* 93.6 (June 1953): 467–473.

Bagchi, Subhendugopal. "Kālīghāṭā." In *Eminent Indian Śākta Centres in Eastern India*, pp. 14–72. Calcutta: Punthi Pustak, 1980.

Bahadur, Satish. "The Context of Indian Film Culture." *Film Miscellany* 1 (Dec. 1976): 90–107.

Bandyopādhyāy, Haricaran. *Durgā Pūjā*. Calcutta: Bānārji and Co., 1877.

Bandyopādhyāy, Indralāl. "Bibarṇa Kyānbhāse Sābarṇa Śāradā." *Sāptahik Bartamān*, 16 Oct. 1999, p. 31.

Bandyopādhyāy, Jitendra Nāth. *Pañcopāsanā*. Calcutta: Firma K. L. Mukhopādhyāy, 1960.

Bandyopadhyay, Somshankar. "Shola Durga Idols Getting Ready for Export." *Times of India*, 25 Sept. 2000, p. 2.

Banerjea, Sir Surendranath. *A Nation in Making: Being the Reminiscences of Fifty Years of Public Life*. Bombay: Oxford University Press, 1925.

Banerjee, Gauri Charan. "Durga Puja in the Aboriginal Tracts." *Amrita Bazar Patrika*, Sunday, 3 Oct. 1926, p. 30.

Banerjee, Sudeshna Banerjee. *Durga Puja: Yesterday, Today, and Tomorrow*. New Delhi: Rupa, 2004.

Banerjee, Sumanta. *The Parlour and the Streets: Elite and Popular Culture in Nineteenth-Century Calcutta*. Calcutta: Seagull Books, 1989.

——. *Under the Raj: Prostitution in Colonial Bengal*. New York: Monthly Review Press, 1998.

Banerjee, Syamalendu. "Rajas to Marxist Overlords." *Amrita Bazar Patrika*, 20 Oct. 1985, Sunday magazine, p. 1.

Banerji, S. C. *Tantra in Bengal: A Study in Its Origins, Development, and Influence*. 2nd rev. ed. New Delhi: Manohar, 1992.

*Bankimchandra Chatterjee: Sociological Essays: Utilitarianism and Positivism in Bengal*, ed. and trans. S. N. Mukherjee and Marian Maddern. Calcutta: Rddhi-India, 1986.

Barnauw, V. "The Changing Character of a Hindu Festival." *American Anthropologist* 56 (1954): 74–86.

Basu, Añjali, ed. *Saṁsad Bāṇali Caritabhidhān*. Kolkata: Sāhitya Saṁsad, 1994.

Basu, Aruṇkumār. *Śaktigīti Padābalī*. Calcutta: Orient Book Co., 1964.

Basu, Prasanta K. "Trends in the Growth of Bengali Musical Enterprises in Toronto During 1955–1984: An Overview." In *Bengali Immigrants: A Community in Transition*, ed. Joseph T. O'Connell and Ritendra K. Ray, pp. 3–16. Toronto: Rabindranath Tagore Lectureship Foundation, 1985.

Basu, S. K. "Santal Festivals." In *To Be with Santals*, ed. Ujjwal Kanti Ray, Amal Kumar Das, and Sunil Kumar Basu, pp. 73–80. Calcutta: Government of West Bengal: Cultural Research Institute, Scheduled Castes and Tribes Welfare Department, 1982.

Baumann, Martin. "A Diachronic View of Diaspora, the Significance of Religion, and Hindu Trinidadians." In *Diaspora, Identity, and Religion: New Directions in Theory and Research*, ed. Waltrand Kokot, Khachig Tölölyan, and Carolin Alfonso, pp. 170–188. London: Routledge, 2004.

Bayly, Chris A. *Rulers, Townsmen, and Bazaars: North Indian Society in the Age of British Expansion, 1770–1870*. Cambridge: Cambridge University Press, 1983.

Bean, Susan S. "The Art of Exchange: Circulation of Visual Culture in Colonial India." Talk presented at Columbia University, 28 Oct. 2006.

Beck, Brenda E. F. "The Goddess and the Demon: A Local South Indian Festival and Its Wider Context." *Puruṣārtha* 5 (1981): 83–136.

Bell, Catherine. "Constructing Ritual." In *Readings in Ritual Studies*, ed. Ronald L. Grimes, pp. 21–33. Upper Saddle River, N.J.: Prentice Hall, 1996.

——. *Ritual Theory, Ritual Practice*. New York: Oxford University Press, 1992.

Benjamin, Walter. "The Work of Art in the Age of Mechanical Reproduction." In *Illuminations*, ed. Hannah Arendt and trans. Harry Zohn, pp. 219–253. New York: Harcourt, Brace, and World, 1968.

Bennett, Lynn. *Dangerous Wives and Sacred Sisters: Social and Symbolic Roles of High-Caste Women in Nepal*. New York: Columbia University Press, 1983.

Berger, Peter L., and Thomas Luckmann. *The Social Construction of Reality: A Treatise in the Sociology of Knowledge*. New York: Irvington Publishers, 1966.

Bhāḍuri, Nṛsimhaprasād. *Śyāmāmāyer Caritkathā Śyāmāmāyer Gān*. Calcutta: Antaraṅga Prakāśanā, 1993.

*Bhāratcandrer Annadāmaṅgal*. Ed. Nirmalendu Mukhopādhyāy. Calcutta: Modern Book Agency, 1986.

Bhāratī, Śibśaṅkar. "Durgāpūjo Jelāy Jelāy." *Bartamān Rabibār*, 8 Oct. 2000, p. 11.

——. "Kalkātār Durgā Pūjā 1586–1951." *Bartamān Rabibār*, 10 Oct. 1999, p. 10.

——. "Kalkātār Kālī-kathā." *Ānanda Bājār Patrikā*, 6 Nov. 1999, pp. 37–39.

Bhaṭṭācārya, Hamsanārāyaṇ. *Hinduder Debadebī: Udbhav o Kramabikāś*. 3 vols. Calcutta: Firma KLM, 1986.

Bhaṭṭācārya, Kamalākānta. *Śyāmā Saṅgīt*. Calcutta: Barddhamān Mahārājādhirāj Māhtāb Bāhādur, 1857.

Bhaṭṭācārya, Raghunāth Tarkabāgīś. *Āgamatattvavilāsa*. Trans. Pañcānan Śāstrī. Calcutta: Nababhārat, 1985.

Bhaṭṭācārya, Satyanārāyaṇ. *Rāmprasād: Jībanī o Racanāsamagra*. 2 parts. Calcutta: Granthamelā, 1975.

Bhattacharya, Aparna. *Religious Movements of Bengal (1800–1850)*. Patna: Aparna Bhattacharya, 1981.

Bhattacharya, Swagata. "Pride and Prejudice." *Statesman*, 25 Sept. 1998, Downtown section, p. 1.

Bhattacharya, Tithi. "Tracking the Goddess: Religion, Community, and Identity in the Durga Puja Ceremonies of Nineteenth-Century Calcutta." *Journal of Asian Studies* 66.4 (Nov. 2007): 919–962.

Bhattacharyya, A. K. *A Corpus of Dedicatory Inscriptions from Temples of West Bengal (c. 1500 A.D. to c. 1800 A.D.)*. Calcutta: Shri K. K. Ray, 1982.

Bhattacharyya, Narendra Nath. *History of Śākta Religion*. New Delhi: Munshiram Manoharlal, 1973.

Bhaumik, Suhṛdkumār. "Durgā: Bāṅgālīr Ādibāsī." In *Lok Saṁskṛti Gabeṣaṇā*, ed. Sanatkumār Mitra, vol. 13, no. 2 (July–Aug. 2000): 293–299.

Biśvās, Śaibāl. "Ye ādhār ālor adhik." *Rabibār Pratidin* (10 Nov. 1996): G.

Bloch, Maurice. *Prey Into Hunter: The Politics of Religious Experience*. Henry Lewis Morgan Lectures 1984. Cambridge: Cambridge University Press, 1992.

Borthwick, Meredith. *The Changing Role of Women in Bengal, 1849–1905*. Princeton: Princeton University Press, 1984.

Bose, S. C. *The Hindoos As They Are (A Description of the Manners, Customs, and Inner Life of Hindoo Society in Bengal)*. Calcutta: Thacker, Spink, and Co., 1883.

Bose, Subhas Chandra. *Netaji: Collected Works*. Ed. Sisir K. Bose. 11 vols. Vol. 3: *Correspondence, May 1923–July 1926*. Vol. 4: *Correspondence, January 1926–January 1932*. Calcutta: Netaji Research Bureau, 1981, 1982.

Boym, Svetlana. *The Future of Nostalgia*. New York: Basic Books, 2001.

Brahmānandagiri. *Śāktānandataraṅginī*. Trans. Rāmkumār Ray. Varanasi: Prācya Prakāśanā, 1993.

*Bṛhaddharma Purāṇam*. Ed. Haraprasād Śāstrī. 2nd ed. 1897; Varanasi: Chaukhambha Amarabharati Prakashan, 1974.

Brubaker, Richard L. "The Ambivalent Mistress: A Study of South Indian Village Goddesses and Their Religious Meaning." Ph.D. diss., University of Chicago, 1978.

Buhnemann, Gudrun. *The Iconography of Hindu Tantric Deities*. Groningen: Forsten, 2000.

Burkert, Walter. *Homo Necans: The Anthropology of Ancient Greek Sacrificial Ritual and Myth*. Trans. Peter Bing. Berkeley: University of California Press, 1983.

Burwick, Frederick. *Mimesis and Its Romantic Reflections*. University Park: Pennsylvania State University Press, 2001.

Cakrabartī, Mukundarām. *Kabikaṅkaṇ Caṇḍī*. Calcutta: Basumatī-Sāhitya-Saṁsad, 1963.

Cakrabartī, Praṇabeś. "Śrī Rāmakṛṣṇer Mahāsādhanpīṭh Dakṣiṇeśvar Mandir." *Nabakallol* 30 (Kārtik 1396): 73–78.

Cakrabartī, Sudhīr Kumār. "Jagaddhātrīpujoy Kāgrāme." In *Deś* 57, no. 1 (Nov. 4, 1989): 52–55.

——. "Kālīmūrti Rahasya." *Dibyajyotir Pathe: Dharma o Darśan* 8, no. 3 (1405/1998): 24.

Cakrabartī, Śyāmalkānti. "Durgā: Anya o Banya." In *Lok Saṁskṛti Gabeṣaṇā*, ed. Sanatkumār Mitra, vol. 13, no. 2 (July–Aug. 2000): 308–313.

"Calcutta Gazette." Monday, 5 Oct. 1829. In *The Days of John Company: Selections from the Calcutta Gazette, 1824–1832*, compiled and edited by Anil Chandra Das Gupta, pp. 418–420. Calcutta: Government Printing, 1959.

*Calcutta in the Eighteenth Century: Impressions of Travelers*. Ed. P. T. Nair. Calcutta: Firma KLM, 1984.

*Calcutta in the Nineteenth Century: Company's Days*. Ed. P. T. Nair. Calcutta: Firma KLM, 1989.

Campbell, Colin. *The Romantic Ethic and the Spirit of Modern Consumerism*. Oxford: Blackwell, 1987.

Carey, William H., ed. *The Good Old Days of Honorable John Company*. 1882; Calcutta: Quins Book Co., 1964.

Cashman, R. I. *The Myth of the Lokamanya: Tilak and Mass Politics in Maharashtra*. Berkeley: University of California Press, 1975.

Caṭṭopādhyāy, Apūrba. "Ālor Banyāy Bhāsbe Jagaddhātrī Candranagar." *Sāptahik Bartamān* (13 Nov. 1999): 11–16.

——. "Ṭhanṭhane Siddheśvarī Kālī." *Sāptahik Bartamān* (21 Oct. 2000): 17–21.

Caṭṭopādhyāy, Sūryakumār. *Kālīkṣetra Dīpikā*. 1891; Calcutta: Pustak Bipaṇi, 1986.

Chakrabarti, Kunal. *Religious Process: The Purāṇas and the Making of a Regional Tradition*. New Delhi: Oxford University Press, 2001.

Chakrabarty, Dipesh. "Communal Riots and Labour: Bengal's Jute Mill-Hands in the 1890s." In *Mirrors of Violence: Communities, Riots, and Survivors in South Asia*, ed. Veena Das, pp. 146–184. Delhi: Oxford University Press, 1992.

—. *Rethinking Working-Class History: Bengal, 1890–1940*. Princeton: Princeton University Press, 1989.

Chakraborti, Manish. "Beadon Ballads." *Times of India*, 6 March 2001, "Calcutta Times" section, p. 4.

Chakraborti, S. "The Dansaey Festival of the Santals." In *To Be with Santals*, ed. Ujjwal Kanti Ray, Amal Kumar Das, and Sunil Kumar Basu, pp. 81–89. Calcutta: Government of West Bengal: Cultural Research Institute, Scheduled Castes and Tribes Welfare Department, 1982.

Chakraborti, Smarajit. *The Bengali Press (1818–1868): A Study in the Growth of Public Opinion*. Calcutta: Firma KLM, 1976.

Chakravarti, Chintaharan. *The Tantras: Studies on Their Religion and Literature*. Calcutta: Punthi Pustak, 1963.

Chanda, Mrinal Kanti. *History of the English Press in Bengal: 1780 to 1857*. Calcutta: K. P. Bagchi, 1987.

Chatterjee, Bankim Chandra. *Ānandamaṭh*. Translated as *The Abbey of Bliss* by Nares Candra Sengupta. Calcutta: Cherry Press, 1902.

—. *Ānandamaṭh; or, The Sacred Brotherhood*. Trans. Julius J. Lipner. Oxford: Oxford University Press, 2005.

—. *Bankim Rachanavali*. Ed. Jogesh Chandra Bagal. Calcutta: Sahitya Samsad, 1969.

—. *The English Writings of Bankimchandra*. Ed. Sudin Chattopadhyay. Kolkata: Deep Prakashan, 2003.

—. "On the Origin of Hindu Festivals." In *Bankim Rachanavali*, ed. Shri Jogesh Chandra Bagal, pp. 91–96. Calcutta: Sahitya Samsad, 1969.

Chatterjee, Partha. "The Nation and Its Women" and "Women and the Nation." In *The Nation and Its Fragments: Colonial and Postcolonial Histories*, pp. 116–157. Delhi: Oxford University Press, 1995.

Chatterji, Jogesh Chandra. *In Search of Freedom*. Calcutta: Firma KLM, 1967.

Chatterji, Joya. *Bengal Divided: Hindu Communalism and Partition, 1932–1947*. Cambridge: Cambridge University Press, 1994.

Chatterji, Shoma A. *The Goddess Kali of Kolkata*. Photographs by Nilanjan Basu. New Delhi: UBSPD, 2006.

Chaudhuri, A. B. *Witch-Killings Amongst Santals*. New Delhi: Ashish Publishing House, 1984.

Chaudhuri, Rosinka. "Hemchandra's Bharata Sangeet (1870) and the Politics of Poetry: A Pre-history of Hindu Nationalism in Bengal?." In *Indian Economic and Social History Review* 42 (2005): 213–247.

Chirol, Valentine. *Indian Unrest*. London: Macmillan, 1910.

Chowdhury, Indira. *The Frail Hero and Virile History: Gender and the Politics of Cultures in Colonial Bengal*. Delhi: Oxford University Press, 1998.

Clothey, Fred. "Rituals and Reinterpretation: South Indians in Southeast Asia." In *A Sacred Thread: Modern Transmissions of Hindu Traditions in India and Abroad*, ed. Raymond Brady Williams, pp. 127–146. Chambersburg, Penn.: Anima, 1992.

Coburn, Thomas B. *The Devī-Māhātmya: Crystallization of the Goddess Tradition.* New Delhi: Motilal Banarsidass, 1985.

——. *Encountering the Goddess: A Translation of the Devī-Māhātmya and a Study of Its Interpretation.* Albany: State University of New York Press, 1991.

Cohn, Bernard S. *Colonialism and Its Forms of Knowledge: The British in India.* Princeton: Princeton University Press, 1996.

Coontz, Stephanie. *The Way We Never Were: American Families and the Nostalgia Trap.* 2nd ed. 1992; New York: Basic Books, 2000.

Courtright, Paul. *Ganesha: Lord of Obstacles, Lord of Beginnings.* New York: Oxford University Press, 1985.

Craddock, Norma Elaine. "Anthills, Split Mothers, and Sacrifice: Conceptions of Female Power in the Mariyamman Tradition." Ph.D. diss., University of California at Berkeley, 1994.

Dalrymple, William. *White Mughals: Love and Betrayal in Eighteenth-Century India.* New York: Penguin, 2004.

Daniels, Roger. "The Indian Diaspora in the United States." In *Migration: The Asian Experience*, ed. Judith Brown and Rosemary Foot, pp. 83–103. Oxford: St. Martin's Press 1994.

Das, Hari Hara. *Subhas Chandra Bose and the Indian National Movement.* Delhi: Sterling Publishers, 1983.

Dās, Jayanta. "Kumorṭulir Cārśo Bacharer Bibartan." *Deś* 64, no. 24 (19 Sept. 1998): 63–70.

Das, Soumitra. "Puja Arcades of Calcutta." *Statesman,* 26 Oct. 1982, p. 3.

——. "Memories of Our Past Splendour." *Statesman,* 15 Oct. 1983, p. 13.

Dās, Sunīl. "Kālī Parikrama." *Ānanda Bājār Patrikā*, 23 Oct. 1995, p. 9.

Dās, Ujjvalkumār. "Kālī Kalkāttāoyālī." *Nabakallol*, vol. 36, no. 7 (Kārtik 1402/1995): 25–30.

Das Gupta, Anil Chandra, ed. *The Days of John Company: Selections from the Calcutta Gazette, 1824–1832.* Calcutta: Government Printing, 1959.

Das Gupta, Hemendranath. *Subhas Chandra.* Calcutta: Jyoti Prokasalaya, 1946.

Dāśgupta, Śaśibhūṣaṇ. *Bhārater Śakti-Sādhanā o Śākta Sāhitya.* Calcutta: Sāhitya Saṁsad, 1960.

Dastidar, Dwaipayan G. "Part-Time Purohits Make a Quick Buck at Ma's Expense." *Times of India*, 29 Sept. 2000, p. 2.

Datta, Bimal Candra. *Durgā Pūjā: Sekāl theke Ekāl.* Calcutta: Ramakrishna Vivekananda Institute of Research and Culture, 1986.

Datta, Mahendranāth. *Kalikātār Purātan Kāhinī o Prarthā.* 2nd ed. 1973; Kalikata: Mahendra Publishing Committee, 1975.

Davis, Fred. *Yearning for Yesterday: A Sociology of Nostalgia.* New York: Free Press, 1979.

Davis, Richard. "Introduction." In *Picturing the Nation: Iconographies of Modern India*, ed. Richard Davis, pp. 1–31. Hyderabad: Orient Longman, 2007.

Deb, Chitra. "The 'Great Houses' of Old Calcutta." In *Calcutta, the Living City*, vol. 1: *The Past*, ed. Sukanta Chaudhuri. Calcutta: Oxford University Press, 1990.

Deb, Kṛṣṇaśarbarī, and Prasūn Ācārya. "Kālī Kalkātāoyālī." *Sāptāhik Bartamān* 1, no. 24 (5 Nov. 1988): 11–13.

de Heusch, Luc. *Sacrifice in Africa: A Structuralist Approach*. Trans. Linda O'Brien and Alice Morton. Manchester: Manchester University Press, 1985.

De Premtoṣ. "Candanagarer Jagaddhātrī Pujo." *Sāptahik Bartamān* 12, no. 25 (3 Nov. 1999): 8–10.

*Devīpurāṇokta Durgāpūjā Paddhatī*. Ed. Jagadīścandra Tarkatīrtha. Calcutta: Saṁskṛt Pustak Bhāṇḍār, 1388.

Dimock, Edward C., Jr. "The Goddess of Snakes in Medieval Bengali Literature, Part I." In *The Sound of Silent Guns and Other Essays*, pp. 150–165. Delhi: Oxford University Press, 1989.

Dold, Patricia. "Kālī the Terrific and Her Tests: The Śākta Devotionalism of the Mahābhāgavata Purāṇa." In *Encountering Kālī: At the Margins, at the Center, in the West*, ed. Rachel Fell McDermott and Jeffrey J. Kripal, pp. 39–59. Berkeley: University of California Press, 2003.

Duff, Rev. Alexander. *India and Indian Missions: Including Sketches of the Gigantic System of Hinduism Both in Theory and in Practice*. Edinburgh, 1839; Delhi: Swati Publications, 1988.

*Durgāpūjā Paddhati*. Derived from the *Devī Purāṇa* and prepared by Prof. Jagadīścandra Tarkatīrtha. Calcutta: Saṁskṛta Pustak Bhāṇḍār, 1981.

*Durgāpūjā Paddhati*. Derived from the *Kālikā Purāṇa* and prepared by Prof. Jagadīścandra Tarkatīrtha. Calcutta: Saṁskṛta Pustak Bhāṇḍār, 1982.

Dutta, Abhijit. *Mother Durga: An Icon of Community and Cultures*. Kolkata: Readers Service, 2003.

Dutta, Kalyani. "Kalighat." In *Calcutta, the Living City*, vol. 1: *The Past*, ed. Sukanta Chaudhuri. Calcutta: Oxford University Press, 1990.

Eaton, Richard. *The Rise of Islam and the Bengal Frontier, 1204–1760*. Berkeley: University of California Press, 1993.

Eck, Diana L. "Negotiating Hindu Identities in America." In *The South Asian Religious Diaspora in Britain, Canada, and the United States*, ed. Harold Coward, John R. Hinnells, and Raymond Brady Williams, pp. 219–237. Albany: State University of New York Press, 2000.

Einoo, Shiṅgo. "The Autumn Goddess Festival: Described in the Purāṇas." In *Living with Śakti: Gender, Sexuality and Religion in South Asia*, ed. Masakazu Tanaka and Musashi Tashikawa, pp. 33–70. Osaka: National Museum of Ethnology, 1999.

Elwin, Verrier. *Myths of Middle India*. Bombay: Oxford University Press, 1949.

——. *Tribal Myths of Orissa*. Bombay: Oxford University Press, 1954.

Engels, Dagmar. *Beyond Purdah? Women in Bengal, 1890–1939*. Delhi: Oxford University Press, 1996.

Erndl, Kathleen. *Victory to the Mother: The Hindu Goddess of Northwest India in Myth, Ritual, and Symbol*. New York: Oxford University Press, 1993.

Falk, Nancy Auer. "Mata, Land, and Line: Female Divinity and the Forging of Community in India." In *Invoking Goddesses: Gender Politics in Indian Religion*, ed. Nilima Chitgopekar, pp. 140–164. Delhi: Shakti Books, 2002.

Freed, Stanley A., and Ruth S. Freed. *Hindu Festivals in a North Indian Village.* Washington, D.C.: American Museum of Natural History, 1998.

Freitag, Sandria B. *Collective Action and Community: Public Arenas and the Emergence of Communalism in North India.* Berkeley: University of California Press, 1989.

——. "Visions of the Nation: Theorizing the Nexus Between Creation, Consumption, and Participation in the Public Sphere." In *Pleasure and the Nation: The History, Politics, and Consumption of Public Cultures in India*, ed. Rachel Dwyer and Christopher Pinney, pp. 35–75. Delhi: Oxford University Press, 2001.

Fuller, C. J. *The Camphour Flame: Popular Hinduism and Society in India.* Princeton: Princeton University Press, 1992.

——. "The 'Vinayaka Chaturthi' Festival and Hindutva in Tamil Nadu." *Economic and Political Weekly* 36, no. 19 (12–18 May 2001): 1607–1616.

——. "The Vinayaka Chaturthi Festival and the Spread of Hindu Nationalism in Tamil Nadu." Talk delivered on 10 April 2000 at Columbia University, New York.

Gandhi, Mohandas. *The Collected Works.* 100 vols. Vol. 24: *May–August 1924.* New Delhi: Ministry of Information and Broadcasting, Government of India, 1967.

Gangoly, Joguth Chunder. *Life and Religion of the Hindoos, with a Sketch of My Life and Experience.* Boston: Crosby, Nichols, Lee, and Co., 1860.

Garimela, Annapurna. "Engendering Indian Art." In *Representing the Body: Gender Issues in Indian Art*, ed. Vidya Dehejia, pp. 22–41. Delhi: Kali for Women, 1997.

Gauḍ, Śrīkānta. "Durgā: Kāṭhkodāi-e." In *Lok Saṁskṛti Gabeṣaṇā*, ed. Sanatkumār Mitra, vol. 13, no. 2 (July–Aug. 2000): 256–264.

Geertz, Clifford. "Deep Play: Notes on the Balinese Cockfight." In *The Interpretation of Cultures: Selected Essays*, pp. 412–453. New York: Basic Books, 1973.

Gell, Alfred. "Newcomers to the World of Goods: Consumption Among the Muria Gonds." In *The Social Life of Things: Commodities in Cultural Perspective*, ed. Arjun Appadurai, pp. 110–138. Cambridge: Cambridge University Press, 1986.

Ghoṣ, Atanu. "Mukhārjider Sonār Durgā." *Ājkāl*, 20 Sept. 1998, p. 14.

Ghoṣ, Binay. "Mā: Mātṛpūjā." *Vibhāva* (Monsoon no., 1979): 17–31.

——. *Paścim Baṅga Saṁskṛti.* 4 vols. Calcutta: Prakāś Bhaban, 1978.

Ghoṣ, Pradīpkumār. "Durgā: Mallabhūmer." In *Lok Saṁskṛti Gabeṣaṇā*, ed. Sanatkumār Mitra, vol. 13, no. 2 (July–Aug. 2000): 347–355.

Ghose, Aurobindo. "Bhawani Mandir." In *Bande Mataram: Early Political Writings*, pp. 61–74. Pondicherry: Sri Aurobindo Ashram, 1973.

Ghose, Benoy. *Selections from English Periodicals of Nineteenth-Century Bengal.* Vol. 1: *1815–1833.* Calcutta: Papyrus, 1978.

——. *Selections from English Periodicals of Nineteenth-Century Bengal.* Vol. 4: *1857.* Calcutta: Papyrus, 1979.

Ghosha, Pratap Chandra. *Durga Puja, with Notes and Illustrations.* Calcutta: Hindoo Patriot Press, 1871.

Girard, René. *Violence and the Sacred*. Trans. Patrick Gregory. Baltimore: Johns Hopkins University Press, 1977.

Gooptu, Nandini. *The Politics of the Urban Poor in Early Twentieth-Century India*. Cambridge: Cambridge University Press, 2001.

Gordon, Leonard. *Bengal: The Nationalist Movement, 1876–1940*. New York: Columbia University Press, 1974.

——. *Brothers Against the Raj: A Biography of Indian Nationalists Sarat and Subhas Chandra Bose*. New York: Columbia University Press, 1990.

Gosvāmī, Jayanta. *Samājcitre Unaviṁśa Śatābdīr Bāṅglā Prahasan*. Calcutta: Sāhityaśrī, 1974.

Goswami, Indira. *The Man from Chinnamasta*. Trans. Prashant Goswami. New Delhi: Katha, 2006.

Goudriaan, Teun, and Sanjukta Gupta. *Hindu Tantric and Śākta Literature*. Vol. II, fasc. 2 of *A History of Indian Literature*, ed. Jan Gonda. Wiesbaden: Harrassowitz, 1981.

Grainge, Paul. *Monochrome Memories: Nostalgia and Style in Retro America*. Westport, Conn.: Praeger, 2002.

Guha-Thakurta, Tapati. "Art in Old Calcutta: The Melting Pot of Western Styles." In *Calcutta: The Living City*, vol. 1: *The Past*, ed. Sukanta Chaudhuri, pp. 146–155. Calcutta: Oxford University Press, 1990.

——. "Clothing the Goddess: The Modern Contest Over Representation of Devi." In *Devi: The Great Goddess: Female Divinity in South Asian Art*, ed. Vidya Dehejia, pp. 157–180. Washington, D.C.: Arthur M. Sackler Gallery, 1999.

——. *The Making of a New "Indian" Art: Artists, Aesthetics, and Nationalism in Bengal, c. 1850–1920*. Cambridge: Cambridge University Press, 1992.

Gupta, Brijen K. *Sirajuddaullah and the East India Company, 1756–1757: Background to the Foundation of British Power in India*. Leiden: Brill, 1966.

Gupta, Īśvarcandra. *Īśvar Gupter Racanābalī*. Ed. Śāntikumār Dāśgupta and Haribandhu Mukhṭi. 2 vols. Calcutta: Dattacaudhurī and Sons, 1974.

Gupta, Kṣetra. "Durgā: Lokabhāskaryer Pahelā Pāṭh." In *Lok Saṁskṛti Gabeṣaṇā*, ed. Sanatkumār Mitra, vol. 13, no. 2 (July–Aug. 2000): 191–197.

Gupta, R. P. "Art in Old Calcutta: Indian Style." In *Calcutta: The Living City*, vol. 1: *The Past*, ed. Sukanta Chaudhuri, pp. 137–145. Calcutta: Oxford University Press, 1990.

——. "Pujas Then and Now." Sunday *Statesman* Miscellany, 20 Oct. 1985, pp. 1–2.

Gupta, Sanjukta. "The Domestication of a Goddess: Caraṇa-tīrtha Kālīghāṭ, the Mahāpīṭha of Kālī." In *Encountering Kālī: At the Margins, at the Center, in the West*, ed. Rachel Fell McDermott and Jeffrey J. Kripal, pp. 60–79. Berkeley: University of California Press, 2003.

——. "Tantric Sādhanā: Pūjā." In Sanjukta Gupta, Dirk Jan Hoens, and Teun Goudriaan, *Hindu Tantrism*, pp. 121–162. Leiden: Brill, 1979.

Gupta, Sanjukta, and Richard Gombrich. "Kings, Power, and the Goddess." *South Asia Research* 6.2 (Nov. 1986): 123–138.

Hansen, Thomas Blom. *The Saffron Wave: Democracy and Hindu Nationalism in Modern India*. Princeton: Princeton University Press, 1999.

Hardgrave, Robert L., Jr. "A Portrait of Black Town: Balthazar Solvyns in Calcutta, 1791–1804." In *Changing Visions, Lasting Images: Calcutta Through Three Hundred Years*, ed. Pratapaditya Pal, pp. 31–46. Bombay: Marg Publications, 1990.

Harding, Elizabeth U. *Kali: The Black Goddess of Dakshineswar*. York Beach, Maine: Nicholas-Hays, 1993.

Hazra, Rajendra Chanda. *Studies in the Upuapurāṇas*. 2 vols. Calcutta: Sanskrit College, 1963.

Heesterman, J. C. "Vedic Sacrifice and Transcendence." In *The Inner Conflict of Tradition: Essays in Indian Ritual, Kingship, and Society*. Chicago: University of Chicago Press, 1985.

Hess, Linda. "An Open-air Ramayana: Ramlila, the Audience Experience." In *Bhakti in Current Research, 1979–1982*, ed. Monika Thiel-Horstmann, pp. 171–194. Berlin: Reimer, 1983.

Heuzé, Gérard. "Cultural Populism: The Appeal of the Shiv Sena." In *Bombay: Metaphor for Modern India*, ed. Sujata Patel and Alice Thorner, pp. 212–247. New Delhi: Oxford University Press, 1995.

Hobsbawm, Eric. "Introduction: Inventing Traditions." In *The Invention of Tradition*, ed. Eric Hobsbawm and Terence Ranger, pp. 1–14. Cambridge: Cambridge University Press, 1983.

Holwell, J. Z. *Événemens historique interéssans, relatifs aux provinces de Bengale, & à l'empire de l'Indostan*. Translated from the English. Amsterdam: Arkstée and Merkus, 1768.

Horsely, Richard A. "Religion and Other Products of Empire." *Journal of the American Academy of Religion* 71.1 (March 2003): 13–44.

Houbens, Jan E. M. "To Kill or Not to Kill the Sacrificial Animal (yajña-paśu)? Arguments and Perspectives in Brahmanical Ethical Philosophy." In *Violence Denied: Violence, Non-Violence, and the Rationalization of Violence in South Asian Cultural History*, ed. Jan E. M. Houbens and Karel R. Van Kooij, pp. 105–183. Leiden: Brill, 1999.

Hubert, Henri, and Marcel Mauss. "Essai sur la nature et la fonction du sacrifice" (1899). Translated by W. D. Halls as *Sacrifice: Its Nature and Function*. Chicago: University of Chicago Press, 1964.

Humphrey, Caroline, and James Laidlaw. *The Archetypal Actions of Ritual: A Theory of Ritual Illustrated by the Jain Rite of Worship*. Oxford: Clarendon Press, 1994.

Husain, Shahanara. *The Social Life of Women in Early Medieval Bengal*. Dhaka: Asiatic Society of Bangladesh, 1985.

Huyler, Stephen P. *Meeting God: Elements of Hindu Devotion*. New Haven: Yale University Press, 1999.

Ingham, Kenneth. *Reformers in India, 1793–1833: An Account of the Work of Christian Missionaries on Behalf of Social Reform*. Cambridge: Cambridge University Press, 1956.

Islam, Sirajul. *Permanent Settlement in Bengal: A Study of Its Operation, 1790–1819*. Dacca: Bangla Academy, 1979.

Jaffrelot, C. "Processions hindoues, stratégies politiques and émeutes entre Hindous et Musulmans." *Purusartha* 16 (1994): 261–287.

Jain, Jyotindra. "Introduction: Image Mobility in India's Popular Cultures" and "India's Republic Day Parade: Restoring Identities, Constructing the Nation." In *India's Popular Culture: Iconic Spaces and Fluid Images*, ed. Jyotindra Jain, pp. 6–17 and 60–75. Mumbai: Marg Publications, 2007.

—. *Kalighat Painting: Images from a Changing World*. Ahmedabad: Mapin, 1999.

Jain, Kajri. "The Efficacious Image: Pictures and Power in Indian Mass Culture." In *Picturing the Nation: Iconographies of Modern India*, ed. Richard H. Davis, pp. 144–170. Hyderabad: Orient Longman, 2007.

Joseph, Charles. "Topographical Survey of the River Hooghly from Bandel to Garden Reach." *Calcutta Review* 3, no. 5 (Jan.–June 1848): 428–462.

Kabirāj, Gangādhar. *Durgotsab Bidhi Bijñānam*. Murshidabad: Nabīncandra Caudhurī, 1875.

*Kālikā Purāṇam*. Ed. and trans. Biswanarayan Shastri. 3 vols. Delhi: Nag Publishers, 1991.

*Kāmākhyā Tantram*. Ed. and trans. Jyotirlāl Dās. Calcutta: Nababhārat, 1978.

Kane, Pandurang Vaman. *History of Dharmasastra*. 6 vols., 2nd ed. Vol. V, pt. 1. Poona: Bhandarkar Research Institute, 1974.

Karlekar, Malavika. *Reflections on Kulin Polygamy: Nistarini Debi's Sekeley Katha*. Occasional Paper no. 23. New Delhi: Centre for Women's Development Studies, 1995.

—. "Woman's Nature and the Access to Education." In *Socialisation, Education, and Women: Explorations in Gender Identity*, ed. Karuna Channa, pp. 129–165. New Delhi: Orient Longman, 1988.

Kaur, Raminder. "Fire in the Belly: The Mobilization of the Ganapati Festival in Maharashtra." In *The Politics of Cultural Mobilization in India*, ed. John Zavos, Andrew Wyatt, and Vernon Hewitt, pp. 37–70. New Delhi: Oxford University Press, 2004.

—. "Performative Politics: Artworks, Festival Praxis, and Nationalism with Reference to the Ganapati Utsava in Western India." Ph.D. diss., University of London, 1998.

—. "Spectacles of Nationalism in the Ganapati *Utsav* of Maharasthra." In *Picturing the Nation: Iconographies of Modern India*, ed. Richard H. Davis, pp. 207–241. Hyderabad: Orient Longman, 2007.

Ker, James Campbell. *Political Trouble in India, 1907–1917*. 1917; Delhi: Oriental Publishers, 1973.

Khān, Rāja Mahendralāl. *Śāradotsab (Gītināṭya)*. Calcutta: Īśvarcandra Basu, 1881.

Khanna, Madhu. "The Ritual Capsule of Durgā Pūjā: An Ecological Perspective." In *Hinduism and Ecology: The Intersection of Earth, Sky, and Water*, ed. Christopher Key Chapple and Mary Evelyn Tucker, pp. 469–498. Cambridge: Harvard University Press, 2006.

"The Khonds of Baphlai Mali." Produced by John Shepherd for the BBC (2000).

King, Richard. *Orientalism and Religion: Postcolonial Theory, India, and "The Mystic East."* London: Routledge, 1999.

Kinsley, David R. *The Sword and the Flute: Kālī and Kṛṣṇa, Visions of the Terrible and the Sublime in Hindu Mythology*. Berkeley: University of California Press, 1975.

Kopf, David. *British Orientalism and the Bengal Renaissance: The Dynamics of Indian Modernization.* Berkeley: University of California Press, 1969.

——. *The Brahmo Samaj and the Shaping of the Modern Indian Mind.* Princeton: Princeton University Press, 1979.

Korom, Frank J. *Village of Painters: Narrative Scrolls from West Bengal.* Photography by Paul J. Smutko. Santa Fe, N.M.: Museum of New Mexico Press, 2006.

Kripal, Jeffrey J. "Kālī's Tongue and Ramakrishna: 'Biting the Tongue' of the Tantric Tradition." *History of Religions* 34.2 (Nov. 1994): 152–189.

*Kubjikā Tantram.* Ed. and trans. Jyotirlāl Dās. Calcutta: Nababhārat, 1978.

Kulke, Herman. "Rathas and Rajas: The Car Festival at Puri." In *Car Festival of Lord Jagannath, Puri,* ed. Sarat Chandra Mahapatra. Puri: Sri Jagannath Research Centre, 1994.

Kumar, Radha. *The History of Doing: An Illustrated Account of Movements for Women's Rights and Feminism in India, 1800–1990.* London: Verso, 1993.

Kurien, Prema. "Becoming American by Becoming Hindu: Indian Americans Take Their Place at the Multicultural Table." In *Gatherings in Diaspora: Religious Communities and the New Immigration,* ed. R. Stephen Warner and Judith G. Wittner, pp. 37–70. Philadelphia: Temple University Press, 1998.

Lahiri, Jhumpa. *The Namesake.* Boston: Houghton Mifflin, 2003.

Larson, Gerald, Pratapaditya Pal, and H. Daniel Smith. *Changing Myths and Images: Twentieth-Century Popular Art in India.* Bloomington: Indiana University, 1997.

Law, Jane Marie. *Puppets of Nostalgia: The Life, Death, and Rebirth of the Japanese Awaji Nongyō Tradition.* Princeton: Princeton University Press, 1997.

Leonard, Karen Isaksen. "Early South Asian Immigrants, 1900–1947." In *The South Asian Americans,* pp. 39–65. Westport, Conn.: Greenwood, 1997.

Lessinger, Johanna. "Indian Immigrants in the United States: The Emergence of a Transnational Population." In *Culture and Economy in the Indian Diaspora,* ed. Bhikshu Parekh, Huhapal Singh, and Steven Vertovec, pp. 165–182. London: Routledge, 2003.

Lorenzen, David N. *Who Invented Hinduism? Essays on Religion in History.* New Delhi: Yoda Press, 2006.

Losty, J. P. *Calcutta, City of Palaces: A Survey of the City in the Days of the East India Company, 1690–1858.* London: Arnold Publishers, 1990.

Lovett, Sir H. Verney. "Social Policy to 1858." In *The Cambridge History of India,* vol. 6: *The Indian Empire, 1858–1918,* ed. H. H. Dodwell, pp. 121–143. Cambridge: Cambridge University Press, 1932.

Lowenthal, David. *The Past Is a Foreign Country.* Cambridge: Cambridge University Press, 1985.

Luchesi, Brigitte. "'It Should Last a Hundred Thousand Years': Rali Worship and Brother–Sister Bond in Kangra." *Manushi* 130 (May–June 2002): 20–25.

Lutgendorf, Philip. *Hanuman's Tale: The Messages of a Divine Monkey.* New York: Oxford University Press, 2007.

*The Mahābhāgavata Purāṇa (Ancient Treatise on Śakti Cult).* Ed. and trans. Pushpendra Kumar. Delhi: Eastern Book Linkers, 1983.

*The Mahārāshṭa Purāṇa: An Eighteenth-Century Historical Text*. Trans. Edward C. Dimock Jr. and Pratul Chandra Gupta. Chicago: University of Chicago Press, 1967.

*Mahīdhara's Mantra Mahodadhiḥ*. Ed. and trans. Ram Kumar Rai. Varanasi: Prachya Prakashan, 1992.

Mahmood, A. B. *The Revenue Administration of Northern Bengal, 1765–1793*. Dacca: National Institute of Public Administration, 1970.

Mandair, Arvind-Pal S. *Religion and the Spectre of the West: Sikhism, India, Postcoloniality, and the Politics of Translation*. New York: Columbia University Press, 2009.

Majumdar, D. N. "The Custom of Burning Human Effigies." *Man in India* 3 (1923): 97–103.

Majumdar, R. C. *History of Modern Bengal*. Calcutta: G. K. Roy Mukherjee, 1978.

Malchow, Howard L. "Nostalgia, 'Heritage,' and the London Antiques Trade: Selling the Past in Thatcher's Britain." In *Singular Continuities: Tradition, Nostalgia, and Identity in Modern British Culture*, ed. George K. Behler and Fred M. Leventhal, pp. 196–216. Stanford: Stanford University Press, 2000.

Mani, Lata. "Contentious Traditions: The Debate on *Sati* in Colonial India." In *Recasting Women: Essays in Colonial History*, ed. Kumkum Sangari and Sudesh Vaid, pp. 88–126. New Delhi: Kali for Women, 1989.

Marathe, Kaumudi. "Celebrating the Diwali Spirit." *India Today* (1 Nov. 1999), North American Special, pp. 1–4.

Marcus, Leah S. *The Politics of Mirth: Jonson, Herrick, Milton, Marvel, and the Defense of Old Holiday Pastimes*. Chicago: University of Chicago Press, 1978.

Mason, Peter. *Bacchanal! The Carnival Culture of Trinidad*. Philadelphia: Temple University Press, 1999.

McCracken, Grant. *Culture and Consumption: New Approaches to the Symbolic Character of Consumer Goods and Activities*. Bloomington: Indiana University Press, 1990.

McCutchion, David. *Brick Temples of Bengal: From the Archives of David McCutchion*. Ed. George Michell. Princeton: Princeton University Press, 1983.

——. *Late Medieval Temples of Bengal*. Calcutta: Asiatic Society, 1972.

McDaniel, June. *Making Virtuous Daughters and Wives: An Introduction to Women's Brata Rituals in Bengali Folk Religion*. Albany: State University of New York Press, 2003.

McDermott, Rachel Fell. "A Festival for Jagaddhātrī and the Power of Localized Religion in West Bengal." In *Breaking Boundaries with the Goddess: New Directions in the Study of Śāktism. Essays in Honor of Narendra Nath Bhatacharyya*, ed. Cynthia Ann Humes and Rachel Fell McDermott, pp. 201–222. New Delhi: Manohar, 2009.

——. "Kālī's Tongue: Historical Reinterpretations of the Blood-lusting Goddess." Paper delivered at the Mid-Atlantic Regional Conference of the American Academy of Religion. Barnard College, 21 March 1991.

——. *Mother of My Heart, Daughter of My Dreams: Kālī and Umā in the Devotional Poetry of Bengal*. New York: Oxford University Press, 2001.

——. "Playing with Durgā: Ritual Levity in Bengal." In *Sacred Play: Ritual Levity and Humor in South Asian Religions*, ed. Selva J. Raj and Corinne G. Dempsey, pp. 143–159. Albany: State University of New York Press, 2009.

——. *Singing to the Goddess: Poems to Kālī and Umā from Bengal*. New York: Oxford University Press, 2001.

McKendrick, Neil, John Brewer, and J. H. Plumb. *Birth of a Consumer Society: The Commercialism of Eighteenth-Century England.* Bloomington: Indian University Press, 1982.

McLane, John R. *Land and Local Kingship in Eighteenth-Century Bengal.* Cambridge: Cambridge University Press, 1993.

—. "Partition of Bengal, 1905: A Political Analysis." In *The History of Bangladesh, 1704-1971*, vol. 1: *Political History*, ed. Sirajul Islam, pp. 161–201. 2nd ed. Dhaka: Asiatic Society of Bangladesh, 1997.

—. "Revenue Farming and the Zamindari System in Eighteenth-Century Bengal." In *Land Tenure and Peasant in South Asia*, ed. R. E. Frykenberg. New Delhi: Orient Longman, 1979.

McLean, Malcolm. *Devoted to the Goddess: The Life and Work of Ramprasad.* Albany: State University of New York Press, 1998.

*The Memoirs of Dr. Haimabati Sen: From Child Widow to Lady Doctor.* Trans. Tapan Raychaudhuri. Ed. Geraldine Forbes and Tapan Raychaudhuri. New Delhi: Lotus Collection, 2000.

Menon, Usha, and Richard Shweder. "Dominating Kālī: Hindu Family Values and Tantric Power." In *Encountering Kālī: In the Margins, at the Center, in the West*, ed. Rachel Fell McDermott and Jeffrey J. Kripal, pp. 80–99. Berkeley: University of California Press, 2003.

—. "Kali's Tongue: Cultural Psychology and the Power of Shame in Orissa, India." In *Emotion and Culture: Empirical Studies of Mutual Influence*, pp. 241–284. Washington, D.C. : American Psychological Association, 1994.

Metcalf, Thomas R. *Ideologies of the Raj.* The New Cambridge History of India III, 4. Cambridge: Cambridge University Press, 1997.

Meyer, Eveline. *Aṅkāḷaparamēcuvari: A Goddess of Tamilnadu, Her Myths and Cult.* Stuttgart: Steiner Verlag Wiesbaden GMBH, 1986.

Midyā, Bikāśkānti. "Durgā: Bāṅglā Lokasāhitye." In *Lok Saṁskṛti Gabeṣaṇā*, ed. Sanatkumār Mitra, vol. 13, no. 2 (July–Aug. 2000): 335–346.

Mitra, Sudhīrkumār. *Huglī Jelār Debideul.* Kalikata: Aparna Book Distributers, 1991.

—. *Huglī Jelār Itihās o Baṅgasamāj.* 2nd ed., 3 vols. Calcutta: Mitrāṇi Prakāśan, 1953.

Mitter, Partha. *Art and Nationalism in Colonial India, 1850-1922: Occidental Orientations.* Cambridge: Cambridge University Press, 1994.

—. *The Triumph of Modernism: India's Artists and the Avant-Garde, 1922-1947.* London: Reaktion Books, 2007.

Mookerjee, Ajit. *Kali: The Feminine Force.* London: Thames and Hudson, 1988.

Mukerji, Chandra. *From Graven Images: Patterns of Modern Materialism.* New York: Columbia University Press, 1983.

Mukherjee, B. N. "Foreign Elements in Iconography of Mahishāsuramardinī—The War Goddess of India." In *Zeitschrift der Deutschen Morgenländischen Gesellschaft.* Supplement VI, pp. 402–414. Stuttgart: Steiner, 1985.

—. "Pictures from Woodcut Blocks: An Iconological Analysis." In *Woodcut Prints of Nineteenth-Century Calcutta*, ed. Ashit Paul, pp. 108–121. Calcutta: Seagull Books, 1983.

Mukherjee, S. N. "Introduction." In Bankimchandra Chatterjee, *Sociological Essays: Utilitarianism and Positivism in Bengal.* Trans. and ed. S. N. Mukherjee and Marian Maddern. Calcutta: Rddhi-India, 1986.

———. "Introduction." *The Poison Tree: Three Novellas by Bankim Chandra Chatterjee*, pp. xix–liii. Delhi: Penguin, 1996.

Mukherjee, Sumita, and Robin D. Tribhuwan. "Influences of Kali Puja Festival on Tribals of West Bengal." In *Fairs and Festivals of Indian Tribes*, ed. Robin David Tribhuwan, pp. 116–120. New Delhi: Discovery Publishing House, 2003.

Mukherjee, Trina. "Eating Religiously." *Telegraph*, Saturday, 28 Sept. 1998, section 3, p. 1.

Mukhopadhay, Ajit Kumar, and Kalyan Chakrabortty. *Discover Chandernagore*. Chandannagar, Hooghly: Kumar Printers, 1999.

Mukhopādhāy, Bratīndranāth. *Śaktir Rūp Bhārate o Madhye Eśiyāy*. Calcutta: Ānanda Publications, 1990.

Mukhopādhyāy, Pūrbā. "Śāsti." In *Deś* 67, no. 24 (30 Sept. 2000): 19.

Mukhopādhyāy, Upendranāth. *Kālīghāṭ Itibṛtta*. Calcutta: Jagannāth Mukhopādhyāy, 1925.

Mukhti, Sunita S. *Doing the Desi Thing: Performing Indianness in New York City*. New York: Garland, 2000.

Nabokov, Isabelle. *Religion Against the Self: An Ethnology of Tamil Rituals*. New York: Oxford University Press, 2000.

Nair, P. T., ed. *Calcutta in the Eighteenthth Century: Impressions of Travelers*. Calcutta: Firma KLM, 1984.

———, ed. *Calcutta in the Nineteenth Century: Company's Days*. Calcutta: Firma KLM, 1989.

Narayanan, Vasudha. "Hinduism in America." In *Religion and American Cultures: An Encyclopedia of Traditions, Diversity, and Popular Expressions*, ed. Gary Laderman and Luis Leon,1:99–109. 3 vols. Santa Barbara: ABC-CLIO, 2003.

Nāth, Sukumār. "Naihatir Ḍākāte Kālī." *Bartamān*, 29 Oct. 2000, p. 10.

Neumayer, Erwin. *Popular Indian Art: Raja Ravi Varma and the Printed Gods of India*. New York: Oxford University Press, 2003.

Neumayer, Erwin, and Christina Schelberger. *Bharat Mata: India's Freedom Movement in Popular Art*. Oxford: Oxford University Press, 2008.

———. *Popular Indian Art: Raja Ravi Varma and the Printed Gods of India*. New York: Oxford University Press, 2003.

Nevile, Pran. "Echoes of a Lost Tradition." *India Today* (15 Aug. 1996): 106–111.

Nicholas, Ralph W. *Rites of Spring: Gājan in Village Bengal*. New Delhi: Chronicle Books, 2008.

———. "The Bengali Calendar and the Hindu Religious Year in Bengal." In *Fruits of Worship: Practical Religion in Bengal*, pp. 13–27. New Delhi: Chronicle Books, 2003.

Novetzke, Christian Lee. *Religion and Public Memory: A Cultural History of Saint Namdev in India*. New York: Columbia University Press, 2008.

Obeyesekere, Gananath. *The Cult of the Goddess Pattini*. Chicago: University of Chicago Press, 1984.

O'Flaherty, Wendy Doniger. *Śiva, the Erotic Ascetic*. Oxford: Oxford University Press, 1973.

Oppert, Gustav. *On the Original Inhabitants of Bharatavarṣa or India*. 1893; New York: Arno Press, 1978.

Orsini, Francesca. *The Hindi Public Sphere, 1920–1940: Language and Literature in the Age of Nationalism*. New York: Oxford University Press, 2002.

Padel, Felix. *The Sacrifice of Human Being: British Rule and the Konds of Orissa.* Delhi: Oxford University Press, 1995.

Pakhirāj, Airābat Candra. *Durgā Pūjā.* Calcutta: n.p., 1876.

Pal, Bipin Chandra. *Memories of My Life and Times.* Calcutta: Bipinchandra Pal Institute, 1973.

Pāl, Kṛṣṇacandra. *Durgā Pujā Mahādhūm.* Calcutta: K. C. Pāl, 1882.

Pal, Pratapaditya. *Durga: Avenging Goddess.* Pasadena, Calif.: Norton Simon Museum, 2005.

——. "Durga Puja in South California." *Statesman.* Festival booklet, 1991, pp. 63–65.

——. *Hindu Religion and Iconology According to the Tantrasara.* Los Angeles: Vichitra Press, 1981.

——. "Indian Artists and British Patrons in Calcutta." In *Changing Visions, Lasting Images: Calcutta Through Three Hundred Years*, ed. Pratapaditya Pal, pp. 125–142. Bombay: Marg Publications, 1990.

——. "Kali, Calcutta, and Kalighat Pictures." In *Changing Visions, Lasting Images: Calcutta Through Three Hundred Years*, ed. Pratapaditya Pal, pp. 109–124. Bombay: Marg Publications, 1990.

Pandey, Gyanendra. *Remembering Partition: Violence, Nationalism, and the History of India.* Cambridge: Cambridge University Press, 2001.

Parthasarathy, Rangaswami. *Journalism in India: From the Earliest Times to the Present Day.* Bangalore: Sterling Publishers, 1989.

Pāṭhak, Rāmratna. *Durgotsab.* Calcutta: Nūtan Bhārata Yantre, 1281/1874.

Pattrea, Purnendu. "The Continuity of the Battala Tradition: An Aesthetic Revaluation." In *Woodcut Prints of Nineteenth-Century Calcutta*, ed. Ashit Paul, pp. 50–79. Calcutta: Seagull Books, 1983.

Paul, Ashit, ed. *Woodcut Prints of Nineteenth-Century Calcutta.* Calcutta: Seagull Books, 1983.

Pennington, Brian K. *Was Hinduism Invented? Briton, Indians, and the Colonial Construction of Religion.* New York: Oxford University Press, 2005.

Pinney, Christopher. *"Photos of the Gods": The Printed Image and Political Struggle in India.* London: Reaktion Books, 2004.

Pocock, David. *Mind, Body, and Wealth: A Study of Belief and Ritual in an Indian Village.* Totowa, N.J.: Rowman and Littlefield, 1973.

Raha, M. K. "Religious Beliefs and Practices Among the Santals." In *To Be with Santals*, ed. Ujjwal Kanti Ray, Amal Kumar Das, and Sunil Kumar Basu, pp. 49–58. Calcutta: Government of West Bengal: Cultural Research Institute, Scheduled Castes and Tribes Welfare Department, 1982.

Rahejia, Gloria Goodwin. "'Crying When She's Born, and Crying When She Goes Away': Marriage and the Idiom of the Gift in Pahansu Song Performance." In *From the Margins of Hindu Marriage: Essays on Gender, Religion, and Culture*, ed. Lindsey Harlan and Paul B. Courtright, pp. 19–59. New York: Oxford University Press, 1995.

*Rāmacaritam of Sandhyākaranandin.* Ed. Haraprasad Sastri. Rev. Radhagovinda Basak. Calcutta: Asiatic Society, 1969.

Ramaswamy, Sumathi. "Body Politic(s): Maps and Mother Goddesses in Modern India." In *Picturing the Nation: Iconographies of Modern India*, ed. Richard H. Davis, pp. 32–50. Hyderabad: Orient Longman, 2007.

—. "Maps, Mother/Goddesses, and Martyrdom in Modern India." *Journal of Asian Studies* 67.3 (August 2008): 818–853.

*Rāmāyaṇ Kṛttibās Biracita*. Ed. Harakṛṣṇa Mukhopādhyāy. Calcutta: Sāhitya Saṁsad, 1957.

Rambachan, Anantanand. "Global Hinduism: The Hindu Diaspora." In *Contemporary Hinduism: Ritual, Culture, and Practice*, ed. Robin Rinehart, pp. 381–413. Santa Barbara: ABC-CLIO, 2004.

Rauph, Ābdur. "Durgā: Bāṅgāli Musulmān." In *Lok Saṁskṛti Gabeṣaṇā*, ed. Sanatkumār Mitra, vol. 13, no. 2 (July–Aug. 2000): 270–292.

Ray, Amita. "The Cult and Ritual of Durgā Pūjā in Bengal." In *Shastric Traditions in Indian Arts*, ed. Anna Libera Dallapicolla, pp. 131–143. Stuttgart: Steiner Verlag Wiesbaden GMBH, 1989.

Rāy, Bhāratcandra. *Bhāratcandrer Annadāmaṅgal*. Ed. Nirmalendu Mukhopādhyāy. Calcutta: Modern Book Agency, 1986.

Rāy, Binaybhūṣaṇ. "Durgā in Lakṣmīsarāis." In *Lok Saṁskṛti Gabeṣaṇā*, ed. Sanatkumār Mitra, vol. 13, no. 2 (July–Aug. 2000): 228–237.

Rāy, Dāśarathi. *Dāśarathi Rāyer Pāncālī*. Ed. Haripad Cakrabartī. Calcutta: Calcutta University, 1962.

Rāy, Dīptimay. "Kālītīrtha Kālīghāṭ o Debī Kālikā." In *Paścimbaṅger Kālī o Kālīkṣetra*, pp. 38–54. Calcutta: Maṇḍal Book House, 1984.

Rāy, Mohit. *Rūpe Rūpe Durgā*. Calcutta: Adhīr Pāl, 1985.

Rāy, Rādhāramaṇ. "Tāntrik Grāme Kālī Pujo." *Sāptahik Bartamān* 13, no. 21 (21 Oct. 2000): 20–21.

Ray, Rajat Kanta. "Man, Woman, and the Novel: The Rise of a New Consciousness in Bengal." In *Exploring Emotional History: Gender, Mentality, and Literature in the Indian Awakening*, pp. 67–117. Delhi: Oxford University Press, 2001.

"Religious and Charitable Endowments of Bengal Zemindars." *Calcutta Review*, vol. 111, nos. 221 and 222 (July and Oct. 1900): 79–100, 223–249, and vol. 112, no. 223 (January 1901): 50–77.

Rodrigues, Hillary Peter. *Ritual Worship of the Great Goddess: The Liturgy of the Durgā Pūjā with Interpretations*. Albany: State University of New York Press, 2003.

Rosselli, John. *Lord William Bentinck: The Making of a Liberal Imperialist, 1774–1839*. Berkeley: University of California Press, 1974.

Roy, Bharati. *Early Feminists of Colonial India: Sarala Devi Chaudharani and Rokeya Sakhawat Hossain*. New Delhi: Oxford University Press, 2002.

Roy, M. N. "Disintegration of a Priestly Family." *Radical Humanist* 18, nos. 6–7 (7 Feb. 1954): 66–68, 72–74.

Roy, Nirmal Kumar. *The West Bengal Estates Acquisition Act, 1953 (West Bengal Act 1 of 1954)*. 2nd rev. ed. Calcutta: Eastern Law House, 1965.

Roy, Ratnalekha. *Change in Bengal Agrarian Society, c. 1760–1850*. Delhi: Manohar, 1979.

Roy Choudhury, P. C. "The Kalighat Temple of Calcutta." In *Temples and Legends of Bengal*, pp. 1–10. Bombay: Bharatiya Vidya Bhavan, 1967.

Rubenstein, Roberta. *Home Matters: Longing and Belonging, Nostalgia and Mourning in Women's Fiction*. New York: Palgrave, 2000.

Saha, A. N. *The West Bengal Land Reforms Act (West Bengal Act 10 of 1956)*. Calcutta: S. C. Sarkar and Sons, 1966.

*Śākta Padābalī*. Ed. Amarendranāth Rāy. Calcutta: University of Calcutta, 1942.

Salomon, Carol Goldberg. "Govindadāsa's *'Kālikāmaṅgal'* (The Vikramāditya and Vidyāsundara Sections): An Edition and Translation." Ph.D. diss., University of Pennsylvania, 1983.

Samanta, Suchitra. "The Self-Animal and Divine Digestion: Goat Sacrifice to the Goddess Kālī in Bengal." *Journal of Asian Studies* 53.3 (Aug. 1994): 779–803.

*Sambādpatre Sekāler Kathā*. Vol. 1:1818–1830. Ed. Brajendranāth Bandyopādhyāy. 2nd ed., 2 vols. 1932; Calcutta: Baṅgīya Sāhitya Pariṣad, 1937.

Sands, Kathleen. "Still Dreaming: War, Memory, and Nostalgia in the American Christmas." In *Christmas Unwrapped: Consumerism, Christ, and Culture*, ed. Richard Horsley and James Tracy, pp. 55–83. Harrisburg, Penn.: Trinity Press International, 2001.

*Saṅgī-Sār-Saṅgraha*. Ed. Harimohan Mukhopādhyāy. 2 vols. Calcutta: Aruṇoday Rāy, 1899.

Sāntrā, Tārāpad. "Durgā: On Terracotta/Clay Temple Slabs." In *Lok Saṁskṛti Gabeṣaṇā*, ed. Sanatkumār Mitra, vol. 13, no. 2 (July–Aug. 2000): 221–227.

Sanyal, Rajat. *Voluntary Associations and the Urban Public Life in Bengal (1815–1876): An Aspect of Social History*. Calcutta: Riddhi-India, 1980.

Saradananda, Swami. *Sri Ramakrishna: The Great Master*. Trans. Swami Jagadananda. 2 vols. 6th ed. Mylapore: Sri Ramakrishna Math, 1984.

Sarkar, Kalyan Kumar. "Terra-cotta Art of Some Temples of Birbhum: Iconographic Observations." In *Calcutta, Bangladesh, and Bengal Studies*, ed. Clinton B. Seely, pp. 259–262. South Asia Series Occasional Paper no. 40, 1990. Bengal Studies Conference Proceedings. East Lansing: Michigan State University Press, 1991.

Sarkar, Sumit. "Calcutta and the "Bengal Renaissance." In *Calcutta, the Living City*, vol. 1: *The Past*, ed. Sukanta Chaudhuri. pp. 95–105. Calcutta: Oxford University Press, 1990.

——.*The Swadeshi Movement in Bengal, 1903–1908*. Delhi: People's Publishing House, 1973.

Sarkar, Tanika. *Hindu Wife, Hindu Nation: Community, Religion, and Cultural Nationalism*. Delhi: Permanent Black, 2001.

Sarma, Jyoritmoyee. "Pūjā Associations in West Bengal." *Journal of Asian Studies* 28.3 (May 1969): 579–594.

*Sarvvollāsatantram*. Ed. Kṛṣṇānanda Sagara. Varanasi: Pratyabhijñā-Prakāśanā, 1987.

Sastri, Sivanath. *History of the Brahmo Samaj*. 1911–1912; Calcutta: Sadharan Brahmo Samaj, 1974.

Sax, William. *Mountain Goddess: Gender and Politics in a Himalayan Pilgrimage*. New York: Oxford University Press, 1991.

Scrafton, Luke. *Reflections on the Government of Indostan, with a Short Sketch of the History of Bengal, from 1739 to 1756, and an Account of the English Affairs to 1758*. London, 1763; repr. London: W. Strahan Ivb., 1770.

Seely, Clinton B. "Raja Pratapaditya: Problematic Hero." In *Barisal and Beyond: Essays on Bangla Literature*, pp. 208–230. New Delhi: Chronicle Books, 2008.

——. *The Slaying of Meghanada: A Ramayana from Colonial Bengal*. New York: Oxford University Press, 2004.

Sen, Amit. "Śyāmnagarer Śyāma." *Sāptahik Bartamān* (21 Oct. 2000): 19.

Sen, Dīneścandra. *Bangabhāṣā o Sāhitya*. Ed. Asit Kumār Bandyopādhyāy. 2 vols. Calcutta: West Bengal State Book Board, 1986.

Sen, Dineshchandra. *Eastern Bengal Ballads, Mymensing*. 4 vols. Calcutta: University of Calcutta, 1923–1932.

Sen, Keshub Chunder. *Jeevan Veda: Being Sixteen Discourses in Bengali on Life—Its Divine Dispensation*. Trans. Jamini Kanta Koar. 3rd ed. Calcutta: Nababidhan Trust, 1969.

Sen, Prabhas. *Crafts of West Bengal*. Ahmadabad: Mapin Publishing, 1994.

Śāstrī, Hara Prasad. *A Descriptive Catalogue of the Sanskrit Manuscripts in the Collections of the Royal Asiatic Society of Bengal*. Rev. and ed. Chintaharan Chakravarti. Vol. 8, pt. 1: *Tantra Manuscripts*. Calcutta: Asiatic Society, 1939.

Shourie, Arun. *Eminent Historians: Their Technology, Their Line, Their Fraud*. New Delhi: ASA, 1998.

Shurmer-Smith, Pamela. *India: Globalization and Change*. London: Oxford University Press, 2000.

Singer, Milton B. *When a Great Tradition Modernizes: An Anthropological Approach to Indian Civilization*. Chicago: University of Chicago Press, 1972.

Singh, Gurharpal. "Introduction." In *Culture and Economy in the Indian Diaspora*, ed. Bhiskhu Parekh, Guhapal Singh, and Steven Vertovic, pp. 1–12. London: Routledge, 2003.

Sinha, Ajay. "Against Allegory: Binode Bihari Mukherjee's *Medieval Saints* at Shantinitekan." In *Picturing the Nation: Iconographies of Modern India*, ed. Richard H. Davis, pp. 66–91. Hyderabad: Orient Longman, 2007.

Sinha, Kāliprasanna. *Hutom Pyāncār Nakśa*. 2nd ed. 1868; Calcutta: Subarṇarekhā, 1991.

Sinha, Mrinilanini. *Colonial Masculinity: The "Manly Englishman" and the "Effeminate Bengali" in the Late Nineteenth Century*. Manchester: Manchester University Press, 1995.

Sinha, N. K. Sinha. "Administrative, Economic, and Social History, 1757–1793." In idem, ed., *History of Bengal (1757-1905)*. Calcutta: Calcutta University, 1967.

——. *Economic History of Bengal*. 2 vols. Calcutta: Firma K. L. Mukhopadhyay, 1962.

Sinha, Surajit. "Kali Temple at Kalighat and the City of Calcutta." In *Cultural Profile of Calcutta*, ed. Surajit Sinha, pp. 61–72. Calcutta: Indian Anthropological Society, 1972.

Smith, William L. "Śiva, Lord of the Plough." In *Essays on Middle Bengali Literature: Studies by David L. Curley, Rahul Peter Das, Mazharul Isam, Amzad Hossain Mian, Asim Roy, and William L. Smith*, ed. Rahul Peter Das, pp. 208–228. Calcutta: Firma KLM, 1999.

Somerville, Augustus. *Crime and Religious Beliefs in India*. 2nd ed. 1929; Calcutta: Thacker, Spink, and Co., 1966.

Southard, Barbara. "The Political Strategy of Aurobindo Ghosh: The Utilization of Hindu Religious Symbolism and the Problem of Political Mobilization in Bengal." *Modern Asian Studies* 14.3 (1980): 353–376.

Spitzer, Leo. "Back Through the Future: Nostalgic Memory and Critical Memory in a Refuge from Nazism." In *Acts of Memory: Cultural Recall in the Present*, ed. by Mieke Bal, Jonathan Crewe, and Leo Spitzer, pp. 87–104. Hanover: Dartmouth College, 1999.

*The Srimad Devi Bhagawatam*. Ed. and trans. Swami Vijnanananda. 2 pts. 2nd ed. New Delhi: Oriental Books Reprint Corporation, 1977.

*Śrī Śrī Durgāpūjā Paddhati*. Derived from the *Bṛhannandikeśvara Purāṇa* and prepared by Paṇḍit Śyāmācaraṇ Bhaṭṭācārya. Calcutta: Beṇīmādhab Śīl's Library, n.d.

*Śrī Śrī Kālī Pūjā Paddhati*. Prepared by Paṇḍit Śyāmācaraṇ Sāṃkhyatīrtha. Calcutta: Rājendra Library, n.d.

Stallybrass, Peter, and Allon White. *The Politics and Poetics of Transgression*. London: Methuen, 1986.

Starobinski, Jean. "The Idea of Nostalgia." *Diogenes* 54 (1966): 81–103.

Sugirtharajah, Sharada. "Colonialism." In *Studying Hinduism: Key Concepts and Methods*, ed. Sushil Mittal and Gene Thursby, pp. 75–83. London: Routledge, 2008.

Sur, Atul. "Bāroiyāri Pūjār Sekāl Ekāl." *Sāptahik Bartamān*, 30 Sept. 1999, p. 10.

Śyāmācaraṇ Kabiratna. *Śrī Śrī Kālīpūjā Paddhati*. 7th ed. Calcutta: Rādhā Pusthakālay, 1393/1986.

*Śyāmārahasya*. Trans. Śyāmānanda Tīrthanāth. Calcutta: Nababhārat, 1982.

Tagore, Rabindranath. "Śāsti." Translated by William Radice as "Punishment." In *Rabindranath Tagore: Selected Short Stories*, rev. ed., pp. 125–133. New York: Penguin, 1994.

*Tārārahasya*. Trans. Tārānanda Giritīrthābadhūt. Calcutta: Nababhārat, 1977.

Tarkabāgīś, Rāmtoṣaṇ. *Prāṇatoṣiṇī*. Varanasi: Chowkhambha Vidyabhawan, 1992.

"The Territorial Aristocracy of Bengal—The Nadiya Raj." *Calcutta Review* 55, no. 109 (1872): 85–118.

Thomas, P. *Epics, Myths, and Legends of India*. Bombay: D. B. Taraporevala Sons, 1942.

Thurston, Edgar. *Ethnographic Notes in Southern India*. Madras: Government Press, 1906.

Troisi, J. *Tribal Religion: Religious Beliefs and Practices Among the Santals*. New Delhi: Manohar, 1978.

Uberoi, Patricia. "Feminine Identity and National Ethos in Indian Calendar Art." *Economic and Political Weekly* (28 April 1990): 41–47.

Urban, Hugh B. *The Economics of Ecstasy: Tantra, Secrecy, and Power in Colonial Bengal*. New York: Oxford University Press, 2001.

—. "India's Darkest Heart: Kālī in the British Colonial Imagination." In *Encountering Kālī: Cultural Understanding at the Extremes*, ed. Jeffrey K. Kripal and Rachel Fell McDermott, pp. 169–195. Berkeley: University of California Press, 2003.

—. *The Power of Tantra: Religion, Sexuality, and the Politics of South Asian Studies*. London: I. B. Tauris, 2010.

Urquhart, Margaret M. *Women of Bengal*. 1925; Delhi: Gian Publishing House, 1987.

Valeri, Valerio. *Kingship and Sacrifice: Ritual and Society in Ancient Hawaii*. Trans. Paula Wissing. Chicago: University of Chicago Press, 1985.

Van der Veer, Peter. *Imperial Encounters: Religion and Modernity in India and Britain.* Princeton: Princeton University Press, 2001.

Van Kooij, K. R. *Worship of the Goddess According to the Kālīkā Purāṇa.* Leiden: Brill, 1972.

Vasu, Nagendra Nath, and Upendra Chandra Vasu. "Kalighat and Calcutta." *Calcutta Review* 92, no. 184 (April 1891): 305–327.

Venkatachari, K. K. A. "Transmission and Transformation of Rituals." In *A Sacred Thread: Modern Transmissions of Hindu Traditions in India and Abroad*, ed. Raymond Brady Williams, pp. 177–190. Chambersburg, Penn.: Anima, 1992.

Vertovec, Steven. *The Hindu Diaspora: Comparative Patterns.* London: Routledge, 2000.

Vivekananda, Swami. "And Let Shyama Dance There." In *Swami Vivekananda's Collected Works*, 4:506–510. 8 vols., 7th impression. Mayavati: Advaita Ashrama, 1959.

—. "Kali the Mother." In *Swami Vivekananda's Collected Works*, 4:384. 8 vols., 7th impression. Mayavati: Advaita Ashrama, 1959.

Vṛndāvanadāsa. *Śrīśrīcaitanyabhāgavata.* 3 vols. Vṛndāvana: Śrīcaitanya Gauḍīya Maṭha, 1997–2003.

Waghorne, Joanne Punzo. "Chariots of the Gods: Riding the Line Between Hindu and Christian." In *Popular Christianity in India: Riting Between the Lines*, ed. Selva J. Raj and Corinne G. Dempsey, pp. 11–37. Albany: State University of New York Press, 2002.

—. "The Diaspora of the Gods: Hindu Temples in the New World System, 1640–1800." *Journal of Asian Studies* 58.3 (Aug.1999): 648–486.

—. *Diaspora of the Gods: Modern Hindu Temples in an Urban Middle-Class World.* New York: Oxford University Press, 2004.

—. "Seeing the Goddess in an Urban World: Temple Iconography for a New Age." Talk delivered at a conference on the Goddess at the University of Iowa, 24 Feb. 2001.

Walsh, Judith E. *Domesticity in Colonial India: What Women Learned When Men Gave Them Advice.* Lanham, Md.: Rowman and Littlefield, 2004.

—. "What Women Learned When Men Gave Them Advice: Rewriting Patriarchy in Late-Nineteenth-Century Bengal." *Journal of Asian Studies* 56.3 (Aug. 1997): 641–677.

Ward, William. *A View of the History, Literature, and Mythology of the Hindoos.* 3rd ed. 4 vols. 1811; Delhi: Low Price Publications, 1990.

Waters, Chris. "Autobiography, Nostalgia, and the Changing Practices of Working-Class Selfhood." In *Singular Continuities: Tradition, Nostalgia, and Identity in Modern British Culture*, ed. George K. Behler and Fred M. Leventhal, pp. 178–195. Stanford: Stanford University Press, 2000.

"West Bengal." In *Fairs and Festivals of India*, ed. M. P. Bezbaruah, compiled by Krishna Gopal, with photography by Phal S. Girota, V:165–251. 5 vols. New Delhi: Gyan Publishing House, 2003.

Westmacott, E. V. "The Territorial Aristocracy of Bengal—The Dinagepoor Raj." *Calcutta Review* 55, no. 109 (1872): 205–224.

Whitehead, Rev. Henry. *The Village Gods of South India.* London: Oxford University Press, 1916.

Wilkins, W. J. *Hindu Mythology, Vedic and Puranic*. Calcutta: Thacker, Spink, 1882.

Williams, Raymond Brady. *Religions of Immigrants from India and Pakistan: New Threads in the American Tapestry*. Cambridge: Cambridge University Press, 1988.

—. "A Sacred Thread: Introduction." In *A Sacred Thread: Modern Transmissions of Hindu Traditions in India and Abroad*, ed. Raymond Brady Williams, pp. 3–6. Chambersburg, Penn.: Anima, 1992.

—. "Sacred Threads of Several Textures: Strategies of Adaptation in the United States." In *A Sacred Thread: Modern Transmissions of Hindu Traditions in India and Abroad*, ed. Raymond Brady Williams, pp. 228–257. Chambersburg, Penn.: Anima, 1992.

Williams, Rosalind H. *Dream Worlds: Mass Consumption in Late Nineteenth-Century France*. Berkeley: University of California Press, 1982.

Woodroffe, Sir John. *Hymns to the Goddess and Hymn to Kālī*. Madras: Ganesh and Co., 1913.

Younger, Paul. *Playing Host to Deity: Festival Religion in the South Indian Tradition*. New York: Oxford University Press, 2002.

## Web Sites

www.banglalive.com
www.calcuttaweb.com
www.eprarthana.com
www.giridoot.com/puja2.htm
www.kumartuli.com
www.westbengaltourism.com

# Index

Abadhūt, 189, 310n33
Ādī Brāhmo Samāj, 53, 54
Advani, L. K., 72
Ādyāpīṭh Kālī Temple (Kolkata), 171, 322n33, 323n36
*āgamanī* songs. *See* Umā-*saṅgīt*
*Āgamatattvavilāsa* (Raghunāth Tarkabāgīś Bhaṭṭācārya), 165, 204
Āgambāgīś, Kṛṣṇānanda, 91, 163, 164, 166–167, 204, 282n44, 290n47, 309n23
agricultural traditions, 103–105, 286nn2–4, 287n8
Ajeya Sanghati, 119
ʿAlīvardī Khān, 16
Allahabad, Treaty of (1765), 259n25
All India Pracchovidya Academy, 295n32
All India Radio, 4
*Amar Chitra Katha,* 126
Ambubācī, 242
*Amrita Bazar Patrika,* 55, 58, 64, 253, 254
*Ānanda Bājār Patrika,* 65, 67, 185, 186, 210–211, 254
*Ānandamaṭh* (Bankim Chandra Chatterjee), 54, 55, 59, 61, 126, 273n66
Ānandamayīkāli Temple (Kolkata), 187
Ānandamayī Kālī Temple (Krishnanagar), 189, *190,* 310n32
Anderson, Benedict, 102
animal sacrifice. *See* blood sacrifice
*Annadāmaṇgal* (Bhāratcandra Rāy), 22, 78
Anuśīlan Samiti, 58, 61
Appadurai, Arjun, 141
architecture, 20–21, *21,* 262n44
art. *See* Durgā iconography; goddess images; iconography; Kālī iconography
artisans, 1, 2, *2;* and *banedi bāḍīr* Pūjās, 106; and contemporary innovations, 118–119; and diaspora Pūjās, 225,

artisans (*continued*)
236, 320nn6,8, 324n50; and Durgā *mūrti* origins, 105, 287n10; East Bengali, 114, 289n38; and Lakṣmī worship, 243, 325–326n7; and 1920s innovations, 109–114, *111*, *112*, 288–289nn26,29–32,34,38; and Umā-daughter tradition, 95, 284n62; and zamindars, 35
*Asiatic Mirror*, 252
Asim-us-Shāh, 15–16
Assam Rifles, 71, 133, 294n12
Assmann, Jan, 37
*Aṣṭāviṁśatitattva* (Raghunandana), 13, 22
Ayodhya, proposed Rām temple, 133, 156, 231, 300n102

Babb, Lawrence, 149, 317n79
Bābus, 14, 25, 56, 151, 259n21, 273n71
Bagbazar Pūjā, 291n61
Bahadur, Satish, 176–177
*bali*. *See* blood sacrifice
*Bande Mataram*, 58, 254
Bandyopādhyāy, Kirancandra, 56
Bandyopādhyāy, Tārāśankar, 277n131
*banedi bāḍīr* (traditional family) Pūjās, 32–38; and blood sacrifice, 33, 209–210, 217–218; decrease in, 35, 267n115; and Durgā iconography, 104–105, *104*, 106–109, *108*, 287n17, 288nn19,22; as *ekak* Pūjās, 266n102; and Jagaddhātrī Pūjā, 32, 266n101; and nostalgia, 35–38, 268n126; public access to, 267n118; and ritual practice, 33–34, 267nn104,107,108; and rivalry, 34, 136–137; and Umā-daughter tradition, 86–87, *108*, 109, 280–281nn28,29,31. *See also* wealth displays; zamindars
Banerjea, Surendranath, 55–56, 58, 248, 253
Banerjee, Bāmapada, 173
Banerjee, Mamatā, 139, 140, 296n39
Banerjee, Sumanta, 40
Banerjee, Syamalendu, 241
Banerji, S. C., 167
*Baṅgabāsī*, 58
Bāngāliyānā, 141
Bangladesh, 71–72, 225, 230–232, 324n25
Bangladeshi Hindu Mandir (New York), 231–232, 233, 320n8, 321nn19,20, 322nn26,30, 325n64
Bangladesh Puja Samiti (New York), 227, 229, 322n19
Bangladesh Puja Samity (New York), 227, 321n19
Bank of Bengal, 50
*bāroiyāri* Pūjās: Jagaddhātrī Pūjā, 21; origins of, 131–132, 294n2; and rivalry, 136–137, 147; and wealth displays, 30, 31, 265n96; and zamindar poverty under British, 19, 20, 261n39
Bāsantī Pūjā, 256n4
Basu, Hena, 266n99, 309n13
Basu, Jyoti, 140, 159, 276n131
Basu, Manmohan, 272n58
Basu, Rajnarain, 272n58
Basu, Rām, 278n5
Basumallik, Rādhānāth, 23–24
Bat-tala publications, 123, 292n70
Bayly, C. A., 148
Bean, Susan S., 152, 289n29
Beauty Without Cruelty, 204, 312n18
Becker, Richard, 18
Bell, Catherine, 220
Belur Maṭh, 267n108
Bengal District Board Act (1885), 53
*Bengalee*, 55, 57–58, 253, 254, 274n85
Bengal famine (1943), 67, 70
*Bengal Gazette*, 252
*Bengal Gazette/Calcutta General Advertiser*, 251
*Bengal Herald*, 252
*Bengal Hircarrah*, 252
*Bengal Hurkaru*, 44, 48, 52, 252, 253
Bengali Association of Greater Chicago, 320n8
Bengali Association of Southern California, 225

Bengali religious calendar, 241–249; categorization in, 241–242; Kārtik Pūjā, 244; Lakṣmī worship, 243–244, 325–326nn6–9; and Manasā worship, 244, 326n11; Rāmlīlās, 325n4; and Śaivism, 247, 326n16; Sarasvatī Pūjā, 243; Ṣaṣṭī worship, 244; Śītalā worship, 244–245, *245*, 326n11; Vaiṣṇava festivals, 242, 245–247; Viśvakarmā Pūjā, 244
Bengal Municipal Act (1884), 53
Bengal Pact (1923), 65
Bengal Tenancy Act (1885), 53
Benjamin, Walter, 149–150
Bentinck, Lord William, 27, 45, 73
Berger, Peter, 192
Bhāḍuri, Nṛsimhaprasād, 180
*Bhāgavata Purāṇa*, 245
Bhāi, Murāl, 323n36
Bhāi, Subrata, 323n36
Bhāi-phõṭā, 242
*bhakti*: and blood sacrifice, 215, 216, 218, 222; and Kālī, 168, 191, 192, 193, 196
Bhandari, Anil, 296n46
Bharatiya Janata Party (BJP), 139, 155, 200
Bhārat Mātā, 56, 102, 126–128, 211
*Bhārat Mātā* (Kirancandra Bandyopādhyāy), 56
Bhaṭṭācārya, Ahibhūṣaṇ, 151
Bhaṭṭācārya, Buddhadeb, 139, 159
Bhaṭṭācārya, Kamalākānta, 78–84, 222
Bhaṭṭācārya, Raghunāth Tarkabāgīś, 164, 204
Bhaṭṭācārya, Rāmeśvara, 78
Bhaṭṭācārya, Śantipada, 214
Bhattacharya, Abhas, 321n12
Bhattacharya, Aparna, 16
Bhattacharya, Dwijen, 322n30
Bhattacharyya, Narendra Nath, xi, 185, 310n33
Bhattbati village temple (Murshidabad), 282n46
*Bhaviṣya Purāṇa*, 12, 23, 248
"Bhawani Mandir" (Aurobindo Ghosh), 59
Bhūtbāḍīr Pūjā, 280–281n28
Bijayā Daśamī, 4, 188, 309n24
*bijayā* songs. *See* Umā-*saṅgīt*
Bīrāṣṭamī Utsab, 58
bird release ritual (*nīlkaṇṭha pākhī*), 28–29, 33, 35, 87
BJP (Bharatiya Janata Party), 139, 155, 200
Bloch, Maurice, 318n89
blood sacrifice, 4, 5, 202–222; and *banedi bāḍīr* Pūjās, 33, 209–210, 217–218; and caste, 211, 218, 314n52, 317n80; and diaspora Pūjās, 227, 321n13; and Durgā iconography, 88–89, 281n36; and Durgā Pūjā, 204, 209–210; and economic interests, 211–213; and Kālī iconography, 206, 306n58; and Kālī Pūjā, 187, 202–203, *203*, 204, 314nn39,40; and Kālī temple worship, 206–209, 313–314nn32,36,37,39,40; as metaphor, 218–219, 317–318nn82,85; and nationalism, 210–211, 314n47, 315n54; opposition to, 204, 212, *212*, 214–218, 312nn18,19, 315n65, 316nn69,70; and religious belief, 213–214, 315nn59,60; scriptural support for, 204–206, 312n23; theories of, 219–222, 318nn88,89,95, 319nn97,99; and Umā-daughter tradition, 88–89, 281n36; and Vaiṣṇavas, 215, 216–217, 246; and Vedas, 316n66; and wealth displays, 28
*Bodhan Bisarjan* (Ahibhūṣaṇ Bhaṭṭācārya), 151
Bonerpukur Danga Pūjā, 281n38
Borthwick, Meredith, 121
Bose, Debashish, 268n126
Bose, Kailās, 24
Bose, Nandalal, 113, 174
Bose, Sarat, 74

Bose, Śephāli, 216, 266n99
Bose, Subhas Chandra, 66, 74, 127, 315n54
Bourdieu, Pierre, 24–25, 324n55
Boym, Svetlana, 37–38, 158–159
Brahmanization, 13, 14, 257n13, 258n17
Brahman participation: *banedi bāḍīr* Pūjās, 33, 267n104; and blood sacrifice, 208, 211, 312n23; and diaspora Pūjās, 320–321n12; and wealth displays, 28
*Brahmavaivarta Purāṇa*, 12
Brāhmo Samāj, 48, 56–57, 121, 265n89, 272n61; Ādī Brāhmo Samāj, 53, 54; New Dispensation, 54, 272n61; Sādharan Brāhmo Samāj, 54, 272n61
*Bṛhaddharma Purāṇa*, 12, 164, 180
*Bṛhannandikeśvara Purāṇa*, 12, 33, 257n7
British attitudes toward Durgā Pūjā: continued participation, 48–49; and Cornwallis Code, 44–45, 49–50, 269n14, 271n42; and Durgā Pūjā as time for relaxation, 52; early liberalism, 26–27, 40–45, *42*, *43*, 73; holiday controversies, 49–51, 271–272nn47,55; and missionaries, 45–48, 51, 73; official disapproval, 26; and travel, 52; twentieth century, 68–69; variations in, 39–40, 73–74
British Indian Association, 53, 63, 253
British-Indian relations: and blood sacrifice, 207–208, 214; and charity, 29, 265n87; complexity of, 30; and Dharma Sabhā, 265n89; Indian catering to British guests, 26–27, 44, 75, 105–106, 277n139; Indian imitation of British, 28, 259n21; missionaries, 45–48, 51, 73, 252, 270n15; and zamindar impoverishment, 49; zamindar resentment, 29. *See also* East India Company rule
British Museum, 230
Bṛndāvandās, 13
Brother's Second, 63
Burdwan rājās, 16, 17, 18, 29, 261n38
Burkert, Walter, 222, 319n979
Byām Rāy Temple (Bishnupur), 283n48

Caḍak Pūjā, 247
Caillois, Roger, 8
Cakrabartī, Debāśis, 211, 312n18
Cakrabartī, Mukundarām, 13, 91, 282n44
Cakrabartī, Praṇabendu Kumār, 322n26
Cakrabartī, Sudhīr Kumār, 185
Cakrabarty, Nirmal, 238
*Calcutta Chronicle*, 251
*Calcutta Gazette or Oriental Advertiser*, 252
*Calcutta Journal*, 25, 131, 251, 253
*Calcutta Monthly Journal*, 252
*Calcutta Morning Post*, 252
Calcutta Municipal Bill (1899), 57
*Calcutta Review*, 265n87
calendar art, 125, 127–128, 177, 211, 306n52
*cāls*, 107–108, 114, 124, 288n22
Campbell, Colin, 148
Cāmuṇḍā, 5, 97, 187, 196, 264n81, 293n97
*Caṇḍī*. *See* "Devī-Māhātmya"
*Caṇḍīmaṇgal* (Mukundarām Cakrabartī), 13, 91, 282n44
Candracūḍacintāmaṇi, 22
*cāpāno* Pūjās, 265n97
Carey, William, 45
carnival, 157–158
caste, 10; and blood sacrifice, 211, 218, 314n52, 317n80; irrelevance to Durgā Pūjā sponsorship, 23, 33; and lower-class exclusion from Pūjās, 296n38. *See also* socioeconomic class
Caṭṭopādhyāy, Rāmkumār, 100
Caudhurāṇi, Debī, 314n39
Caudhurāṇi, Śaralādebī, 58–59, 274n78
Caudhurī, Indranārāyaṇ, 22, 23
Chakrabarti, Kunal, 247, 257n13
Chakrabarty, Dipesh, 62
Chakravarti, Chintaharan, 184
challenge. *See* rivalry

Chanda, Mrinal Kanti, 252
charity: and British-Indian relations, 29, 265n87; and rivalry, 138; and wealth displays, 23, 27
Charnock, Job, 268n119
Chatterjee, Bankim Chandra: on Bābus, 273n71; and blood sacrifice, 314n39; on Durgā iconography, 122, 291n68; on Durgā Pūjā origins, 56; and mother images, 59, 60–61; and nationalism, 54–55, 60–61, 126, 273nn66,70; and women's roles, 121–122, 291n65
Chatterjee, Joya, 66–67
Chatterjee, Partha, 121, 172–173
Chatterji, Jogesh Chandra, 59, 275n109
Chatterji, Tapanmohan, 185
Chātu-Bābu Lātu-Bābu family, 108–109, 288n22
Chaudhuri, Nirad C., 38, 118
Chetla Agtani Club, 307n3
children's activities, 90, 102
Chingree, Ramchunder, 48
Chinmoy, Sri, 239
Chittaranjan Park Kali Mandir (Delhi), 235
Christmas, 131, 160
Chunder, Bhaskar, 36, 266n99
Chunder, Gaṇeścandra, 86–87
Citizen's Democratic Association (Gaṇatāntrik Nāgarik Samiti), 200
Citteśvarī Sarvamaṇgalā Temple (Kolkata), 288n19
Clive, Lord Robert, 26–27, 36
Clothey, Fred, 238
Club Bangla, 240
Cohn, Bernard, 46, 73
colonialism, 73, 277n136. *See also* colonial period
colonial period, 51–70, 72–75; communal tensions, 61–63, 66–67, 74–75, 274–276nn93,113; and cultural/religious revivalism, 53–55, 272nn58,61,62, 273n66; Durgā Pūjā as time for relaxation, 52, 55–56, 68–70, *69*, 276n123; early noninterference policies, 51–53, 73; Hindu critiques of Durgā Pūjā, 56–57, 63, 272n61, 273n71; and masculinity, 57–58, 273n76; partition of Bengal, 58–63, *60*, 74, 75, 125, 126, 254, 274nn78,81,85,87,89, 277n139; public-sphere activity, 67–68; twentieth century, 64–70; World War I, 63–64. *See also* nationalism
Communal Award (1932), 66
communal tensions: in Bangladesh, 231; and blood sacrifice, 212, 315n57; colonial period, 61–63, 66–67, 74–75, 274–276nn93,113; CPI(M) efforts to prevent, 70, 72, 75, 239; and Pūjās as sociopolitical barometer, 155; and September 11, 2001 terrorist attacks, 145
Communist Party of India (Marxist) (CPI[M]): attitudes toward religion, 71, 140, 276–277n31, 296n40; and communal tensions, 70, 72, 75, 239; and environmental concerns, 201; and Pūjās as sociopolitical barometer, 156, 159; and rivalry, 138–140, 295n29, 296n39; and September 11, 2001 terrorist attacks, 145; and zamindar impoverishment, 35
companionate marriage, 121, 291n63
Compassionate Crusaders, 204, 211, 214, 312n18
Congress Pūjā, 66
consumerism, 147–150, 152–153, 298n74
controversies, 222–223; environmental concerns, 199–202, 311n9, 312n16; prostitute earth, 197–199, 311n6. *See also* blood sacrifice
Coontz, Stephanie, 286n85
Cornwallis, Lord Charles, 44
Cornwallis Code (1793), 44–45, 49–50, 269n14, 271n42
CPI(M). *See* Communist Party of India (Marxist)

Craddock, Norma Elaine, 317n79
Cremation-Ground Kālī (Śmaśānakālī), 186, 309n17
criminality, 186, 206, 309nn18,20
Cuḍāmaṇi, Śrīnātha Ācārya, 22
*cupḍicāl,* 107, 288n22
Curzon, Lord George, 57

Ḍākāt Kālīs, 186, 309n18
Dakshineswar Ramkrishna Sangha Adyapeath, 281, 323n36, 324n57
Dakshinpara, Baruipur Madarhat, 294n18
Dakṣiṇākālī, 301–302n4
Dakṣiṇākālī Temple (Midnapur), 283n48
Dakṣiṇeśvar Kālī Temple (Kolkata), 171, 233
Dalrymple, William, 263–264n68
Dāmodar Temple (Howrah), 283n46
*daṇḍīkāṭā, 246*
Dās, Abhī, 188–189
Das, C. R., 65, 74
Dās, Jayanta, 289n38
Das, Shimarani, 244
Dasae Festival, 258n15
Daśamī, 28–29, 87, 277n2. *See also* immersion rituals
Dasgupta, R. K., 89
Datta, Akrūr, 23
Datta, Bimalcandra, 259n23, 282n44
Datta, Dvāraknāth, 281n29
Datta, family of (Hatkhola), 30, 32, 265n89, 266n99, 288n19, 313n36
Datta, Gītā, 266n99
Datta, Milan, 216, 266n99
Datta, Subhās, 200, 201
Davis, Fred, 285n77
Davis, Richard, 126
Dawn, Amarnāth, 266nn99,101
Dawn, Rāmnārāyaṇ, 87
Dawn, Śubhamay, 266nn99,101
De, Āśutoṣ, 41
De, Rāmdulāl, 23, 262n45, 265n89, 266n99
Deb, Alok Kṛṣṇa, 34, 36, 213, 266n99
Deb, Ārati, 216
Deb, Gopimohan, 41, 47. *See also* Shovabazar Rāj
Deb, Kālīkṛṣṇa, 21, 29, 41, 265n89. *See also* Shovabazar Rāj
Deb, Kalyāṇkumār, 36, 108–109, 266nn99,101
Deb, Nabakṛṣṇa, 14, 36, 41, 107, 264n69. *See also* Shovabazar Rāj
Deb, Rādhākānta, 30, 41, 56, 252
Deb, Rājkṛṣṇa, 41, 44. *See also* Shovabazar Rāj
Deb, Rāmdulāl Sarkār, 109, 288n19
Deb, Shovabazar (family). *See* Shovabazar Rāj
De Grandpre, L., 25, 44
de Heusch, Luc, 220, 318nn89,95
Deleuze, Gilles, 221
Delhi Pūjās, 234–235
Depressed Classes Status Bill (1934), 66
Derozians, 48
*Deś,* 232
"Devdas" (film), 199
*Devībhāgavata Purāṇa,* 12, 164, 262n47
"Devī-Māhātmya" (*Mārkaṇḍeya Purāṇa*): and blood sacrifice, 204, 206; and Durgā iconography, 111, 114, 290n48; and Durgā Pūjā duration, 256n4; and Durgā Pūjā importance, 248; and Durgā Pūjā origins, 12, 13; Jagaddhātrī in, 262n47; and nationalism, 65; and Pūjās as sociopolitical barometer, 150, 298n75; and ritual practice, 4, 28, 29, 33; and Umā-daughter tradition, 99
*Devī Purāṇa,* 12, 24
Ḍhākeśvarī Durgā Mandir (Dhaka), 231
Dhar, Kāśīnāth, 281n36
Dharma Sabhā, 30, 252, 265n89, 308n7
*dhuno/dhunā* pūja, 28, 33
Dhurandhar, M. V., 173
*dhyānas,* 111, 164–165, 179, 180, 289n30
diaspora Pūjās, 224–240, *228;* and Bangladesh vs. West Bengal, 225, 230–232, 322nn25,28–31,33; and

blood sacrifice, 227, 321n13; costs of, 323n38; duration of, 229, 320n10, 321nn20,21; entertainment, 227, 229, 321n15, 322n23; and ethnic identity, 237–240, 324–325nn52,55,57,58,64; food, 321–322n22; growth of, 225, 320n5; iconography, 225, *226*, 227, 320n8; Jagaddhātrī Pūjā, 323n36; Kālī Pūjā, 233, 322–323nn35–38; and nostalgia, 102, 225, 227, 234–236, 320n8, 323n40, 324nn49,50; and prestige, 227, 321nn14–16; and ritual practice, 227, 229–230, 238, 320nn6,8–14, 324–325nn57,58; and rivalry, 227, 228–229, 321n19; and social networking, 236–237

*Digdarśan*, 252

Dinajpur Rāj, 18, 261–262nn37,42

Direct Action Day (Great Calcutta Killings) (1946), 70

Diwali, 184–185, 188–189, 243

Doniger, Wendy, 279n14

Driver, Tom, 8

Duff, Alexander, 45, 131, 270n15

Durgā: and blood sacrifice, 206; springtime worship of, 256n4; as symbol of pretension, 31–32; temples to, 93, 283n56, 288n19, 290n49; transport modes, 1, 255n1. *See also* Durgā iconography; Durgā Pūjā; Umā-daughter tradition

Durgābāḍī (Kolkata), 281n28

*Durgābhaktitaraṅginī* (Vidyāpati), 12, 91, 282n44

Durgā iconography, 1–2, 103–129; and agricultural traditions, 103–105, 286nn3,4; and artisans, 105, 287n10; and *banedi bāḍīr* Pūjās, 104–105, *104*, 106–109, *108*, 287n17, 288nn19,22; Bat-tala publications, 123, 292n70; and blood sacrifice, 88–89, 281n36; contemporary innovations, 114–116, 120–121, 289–290nn40,41,45; and diaspora Pūjās, 225, *226*, 227, 320n8; and Indian catering to British guests, 105–106; *kāṭhkodāis*, 105; and lithography, 124–126; local variations, 129, 293n97; and nationalism, 125–129, 293nn87,89; 1920s innovations, 109–114, *111*, *112*, 288–289nn26,29–32,34,38; and nostalgia, 119–120, 225, 227, 291n61, 320n8; *paṭs*, 92, 93, 105, 123, 124; and street art, 123–124, 292n70; and Umā-daughter tradition, 88–89, 91–93, *94*, 281nn35,36,38, 282–283n45–48, 284n58; and Western influences, 109–110, 122–123, 291n68, 292n75; and women's roles, 121–122

Durgā Pūjā: and blood sacrifice, 204, 209–210; caste irrelevance to sponsorship of, 23, 33; colonial period defenses of, 56; colonial period Hindu critiques of, 56–57, 63, 272n61, 273n71; duration of, 3, 229, 256n3, 320n10, 321nn20,21; importance of, 241, 247, 248–249, 325n1; and Kālī Pūjā, 193–194; and Lakṣmī worship, 243; and nationalism, 65–66, 275n109; and partition of Bengal, 59–60, *60*, 274n85; post-Independence period, 70–72; prostitute controversy, 197–199, 311n6; rejections of, 248; ritual practice overview, 4–5; as self-authenticating measure, 19, 261n40; and Tantra, 256n6; Theme Pūjās, 134–135, 140, 294n18; as time for relaxation, 52, 55–56, 68–70, *69*, 86, 276n123; and World War I, 64. *See also* British attitudes toward Durgā Pūjā; diaspora Pūjās; Durgā Pūjā origins

Durgā Pūjā digests, 12–13

Durgā Pūjā origins, 259n23; ballads on, 13, 257n11; and Brahmanization, 13, 14, 257n13, 258n17; individual figure attributions, 14, 259n22; and *nawāb* oppression/British tolerance,

Durgā Pūjā origins (*continued*) 15–17, 20, 259–260nn26,27,32, 261–262n42; and Pūjās as sociopolitical barometer, 150–151; and rivalry, 146, 150–151; and royalty, 12, 24, 146, 297n60; scriptural evidence, 12–13, 257n7; and symbolic capital, 24–25; and tribal culture, 13–14, 257–258nn13–15,17; and wealth displays, 11, 20–21, 23–24; and zamindar opportunity under *nawābs*/poverty under British, 15, 19–20, 259n25, 261nn37–39
*Durgāpūjātattva* (Raghunandana), 12, 91
*Durgotsava Prayoga* (Śūlapāṇi), 12
*Durgotsavatattva* (Raghunandana), 12
*Durgotsavaviveka* (Śūlapāṇi), 12, 13

East Coast Durga Puja Association, 225, 320n8, 321n15, 322nn28,30, 323n38
Eastern Orthodox icons, 182
East India Company rule: and *bāroiyāri* Pūjās, 261n39; as constraint on zamindars, 17–20, 261nn37–39; Cornwallis Code, 44–45, 49–50, 269n14, 271n42; and Durgā Pūjā as self-authenticating measure, 19, 261n40; and media, 251; and *nawābs*, 15, 259n25; and nostalgia, 36; as opportunity for zamindars, 15–17, 20
Eaton, Richard M., 283n50
Eck, Diana L., 229
*ekak* Pūjās, *104*, 266n102
*ekcāl*, 107
elites. *See nawābs*; wealth displays; zamindars
Engels, Dagmar, 279n19
*Englishman*, 48, 52, 70, 252, 253, 254, 277n139
entertainment: diaspora Pūjās, 227, 229, 321n15, 322n23; and wealth displays, 26, 263–264nn68,69,71
environmental concerns, 199–202, 311n9, 312n16
epic poetry. *See* Maṅgalakāvyas
ethnic identity, 237–240, 324–325nn52,55,57,58,64

Fast Bābus, 159, 301n111
FD Block Pūjā, 297n51
fire sacrifice, 4, 5
folk culture, 91–92, 283n50. *See also* tribal culture
food, 26–27, 32–33, 321–322n22
Foucault, Michel, 221
Freed, Ruth S., 242
Freed, Stanley A., 242
Freitag, Sandria, 148–149, 152, 300n101
*Friend of India*, 45, 47, 52, 253, 308n7. *See also Statesman and Friend of India*
Fuller, Christopher (C.J.), 24, 154, 155

Gaganeśvar Temple (Gopalpur), 283n48
Gājan, 247, 326n16
Gaṇapati Utsav (Gaṇeśa Pūjā/Cāturthi), 58, 71, 154–156, 201
Gaṇatāntrik Nāgarik Samiti (Citizen's Democratic Association), 200
Gandhi, Indira, 128, 133
Gandhi, Menaka, 204, 209, 312n18
Gandhi, Mohandas, 63, 64–65, 67, 74, 254, 315n54
Gandhi, Rajiv, 152
Gaṇeśa, 1; and Diwali, 188; and Durgā as symbol of pretension, 31; and early Durgā iconography, 107; and *kalā bau*, 104, 228, 286n5; and nationalism, 71; and 1920s iconographic innovations, 114; and public art traditions, 151; and Pūjās as sociopolitical barometer, 143, 297n53; and Theme Pūjās, 135; and Umā-daughter tradition, 88, 91, 93, 281n36, 283n47, 284n58; and Western influences, 92; worship of, 5, 58, 71, 154–156, 201
Gangāsāgar bathing ritual, 242
Gangopādhyāy, Sunil, 229, 322n23
Ganguli, Sujay, 210, 266n99, 267n104

Garden State Cultural Association (New Jersey), *226*, *228*, 235, 237, 322nn22,23
Garden State Puja Committee (New Jersey), 229, 230, 320n9, 322n23
Gaurī. *See* Umā-*saṅgīt*
Geertz, Clifford, 220
*ghaṭ*, 104–105, 286n3, 287n8
*ghaṭe-paṭe pūjās*, 105
Ghoṣ, Āśis, 100
Ghoṣ, Khelātcandra, 216, 288n19, 288n22
Ghoṣāl, Anup, 229, 322n23
Ghoṣāl, Bāhādur Jaynārāyaṇ, 264n77
Ghosh, Amarnath, 320n8
Ghosh, Aurobindo, 58, 59, 63, 127, 254
Ghosh, Girish Chandra, 198, 253
Ghosh, Rana, 322n30
Ghosha, Pratapchandra, 106
Girard, René, 220
Giri, Brahmānanda, 164
Giri, Pūrṇānanda, 164
Gobarjana Kālī Temple (Maldah), 314n39
goddess images, 1, *2*, 27, 44, 264n77, 287n17. *See also* Durgā iconography; Kālī iconography; ritual practice
Gombrich, Richard, 24
Gooptu, Nandini, 62, 67, 68
Gordon, Milton, 324n52
Goswami, Indira, 211
Goudriaan, Teun, 164
Graham, Mary, 44
Grant, Charles, 45
Guha-Thakurta, Tapati, 174
Gupta, Brijen, 20
Gupta, R. P., 128
Gupta, Sanjukta, 24, 217
Gurkha Rifles, 71, 133, 294n12
Gyanendra (king of Nepal), 191–192

Hājrā, Priya Gopāl, 36, 266nn99,101
Hāldār, Prāṇkṛṣṇa, 29, 41, 269n9
Hansen, Thomas Blom, 154
Hanumān, 325n4
Hara-Gaurī, 88, 281nn29,35
Hardgrove, Anne, 68
Harding, Usha, 233
Harijans, 296n38
Hastie, W., 55
Hastings, Warren, 29, 40
Hatibagan Sarbajanīn Pūjā, 281n36
Hazra, R. C., 13
Heuzé, Gérard, 154–155
Hicky, James Augustus, 251
*Hindoo Patriot*, 55, 63, 253, 254
Hindu College, 29
Hindu Mahāsabhā, 65, 294n5
Hindu Munnani, 155, 156
Hindu Sabhā, 53
Hindu Theophilanthropic Society, 48
Hobsbawm, Eric, 192
Holwell, J. Z., 41, 259n23
Houbens, Jan E. M., 316n66
Houston Tagore Society, 233
Hubert, Henri, 219
Huizinga, Johan, 8
human sacrifice (*narabali*), 171, 206–208, 313–314nn32,36,37
Huyler, Stephen, 154

iconography: diaspora Pūjās, 225, *226*, 227, 320n8; Jagaddhātrī, 2, 116–118, *117*, 290nn47,48,50,51. *See also* Durgā iconography; Kālī iconography
Ilbert Bill (1883), 53
immersion rituals, 4, 5; and contemporary innovations, 115; and diaspora Pūjās, 229–230; and environmental concerns, 199; and *nawāb* rule, 16; and Umā-daughter tradition, 87; and wealth displays, 28–29, 264n81
*India Gazette/Calcutta Public Advertiser*, 252
*Indian Mirror*, 56–57, 254
Indian National Congress, 54, 74, 253
Islam, Nazrul, 186, 309n20
Islam. *See* Muslims

Jagaddhātrī: iconography, 2, 116–118, *117*, 290nn47,48,50,51; temples to,

Jagaddhātrī (*continued*)
118, 290n49. *See also* Jagaddhātrī Pūjā
Jagaddhātrī Pūjā, 5, 269n6; and *banedi bāḍīr* Pūjās, 32, 266n101; and *cāpāno* Pūjās, 265n97; diaspora, 323n36; growth of, 136; origins of, 21–23, 262n47; ritual practice, 29; and rivalry, 138; as time for relaxation, 276n124
Jagannath Hall (Dhaka University), 231
Jain, Jyotindra, 123, 124, 156
Jallianwala Bagh massacre (1919), 64
Javale, Bhausaheb Lakshman, 300n95
Jaykāli Temple (Kolkata), 187
Jersey City Durga Puja, 320n8, 321n12
Jhaḍeśvarnāth Temple (Midnapur), 283n46
Jīmūtavāhana, 12, 13
Jing, Jun, 25
*Jñānānveṣan*, 48
Joḍbāṅglā Kṛṣṇarāy Temple (Bishnupur), 282n46

*kabigān*, 92
*kabioyālās*, 278n5
*kalā bau* (*nabapatrikā*), 27–28, 33, *34*, 104–105, *104*, 198–199, 286n5, 311n4
*Kālaviveka* (Jīmūtavāhana), 12, 13
*Kālaviveka* (Śūlapāṇi), 22
Kālī: and nationalism, 70; and partition of Bengal, 58, 60–61; and Umā-daughter tradition, 95–98, 284n63. *See also* Kālī iconography; Kālī Pūjā
Kālidāsa, 77, 279n17
Kālīghāṭ Temple (Kolkata), *169*, 170, 187, 191–192, 212, 215, 217
Kālī iconography, 2, 161–182; and blood sacrifice, 206, 306n58; child images, 185, 308n11; contemporary styles, 176–180, *178*, 182, 306nn51–53; Cremation-Ground form, 186, 309n17; Dakṣiṇākālī form, 301–302n4; and diaspora Pūjās, 320n8; dual types, 161–162, *162*; and Kālī Pūjā, 172–173; late medieval context, 165–166; and nationalism, 172–173, 181–182, 306n58; 1920s innovations, 173–176, *175*, 305n44; and nostalgia, 193; and sexuality, 165, 179, 180, 182, *190*, 306n59, 310n32; and Tantra, 163–165, 166–168, 171, 178–180, 181, 187, 304n30; and temple worship, 168–172, *169*, *170*, 177–178, 304nn28,30
*Kālīkāmaṇgalakāvyas*, 167–168
*Kālikā Purāṇa*, 12, 22, 204, 205, 306n58
*Kālīkīrtan* (Rāmprasād Sen), 99, 285n71
Kali Mandir (Laguna Beach, California), 233
Kālī Pūjā, 5, 183–196; and blood sacrifice, 187, 202–203, *203*, 204, 314nn39,40; diaspora, 233, 322–323nn35–38; and Durgā Pūjā, 193–194; and fear, 185–189, *195*, 196, 203, 309nn13,17; and holiday controversies, 50; and iconography, 172–173; lack of textual evidence, 184, 307–308nn5,6; meager popularity of, 184–185, 308nn7,9; and nationalism, 186, 191; and nostalgia, 192–193; origins of, 22, 184; pandals, 185, 308n9; and partition of Bengal, 61; and rivalry, 138; and Śāktism, 191–192; *sarbajanīn* Pūjās, 183, 185, *193*, 307n3; and sexuality, 189–191, 309–310nn28,33–34; and Tantra, 187–189, *188*, 194–195, 309nn22,23; Theme Pūjās, 183, 307n3
*Kālī Tantra*, 164, 165, 179, 309–310n28
Kālī Temple (Toronto), 321n20
Kālī Temple (Washington, D.C.), 232, 234, 322n33
Kālī temple worship: and blood sacrifice, 206–209, 313–314nn32,36,37,39,40; and criminality, 186–187; diaspora, 232–233, 322n33, 323n37; and iconography, 168–172, *169*, *170*, 177–178, 304nn28,30; and nationalism, 59; and pandals, 185
Kāma, 84, 279n17

*Kāmākhya Tantra*, 22
Kāmākhya Temple (Assam), 208, 211, 242
Kaṃsanārāyaṇ (zamindar of Taherpur), 14, 259n22
Kane, P. V., 205
Karlekar, Malavika, 93
Kārtik, 1; and early Durgā iconography, 107; and nationalism, 71; and 1920s iconographic innovations, 114, 115, 289n29; and public art traditions, 151; and Umā-daughter tradition, 88, 91, 93; worship of, 50, 244, 307n5
Kārtik Pūjā, 50, 244, 307n5
Kasba Kheyali Sangha, 153
Kāśīnāth, 184, 307–308n6
*kāṭhāmo*, 27
*kāṭhkodāis*, 105
Kaur, Raminder, 300n95
Kāyasthas, 23. *See also* caste
Khān, Mahendralāl, 284n59
Khilafat movement, 64
Khorda temple (Midnapur), 283n46
King, Richard, 46
Knight, Robert, 253
Kopf, David, 40
Korom, Frank, 152
Kripal, Jeffrey, 161
*Krityatattvārṇava* (Śrīnātha Ācārya Cuḍāmaṇi), 22
Kṛṣṇa, *108*, 216, 285n71. *See also* Kṛṣṇa and Rādhā; Vaiṣṇavism
Kṛṣṇa and Rādhā: and novels, 122; and Umā-daughter tradition, 98, 99, 285n71
*Kubjikā Tantra*, 22
Kuchbihar Rāj, 281n29, 293n97
*Kulacūḍāmaṇi Tantra*, 164
*Kulārṇava Tantra*, 307n5
Kulīnism, 84, 86, 279n19, 280n21
*Kumārasambhava* (Kālidāsa), 77, 279n17
*kumārī pūjā*, 4, 5, *88*, 265n84; and *banedi bāḍīr* Pūjās, 33, 267n108; and Umā-daughter tradition, 87; and wealth displays, 28
Kumartuli district (Kolkata), 1, 106. *See also* artisans
Kurien, Prema, 239
Lāhā family, 264n77
Lahiri, Jhumpa, 240
Lake Kālī Temple (Kolkata), 187
Lakṣmī, 1; and blood sacrifice, 314n40; and Diwali, 188, 189; and early Durgā iconography, 107; and nationalism, 127; and 1920s iconographic innovations, 114; and street art, 123; and Umā-daughter tradition, 88, 91, 92–93; worship of, 194, 243–244, 271n47, 325–326nn6–9
*lakṣmīsarāis*, 92
Law, Jane Marie, 101
Left Front Party, 139
Long, James, 207, 252
longing. *See* nostalgia
Lorenzen, David, 46
Lowenthal, David, 37, 101–102, 286n85
Luckmann, Thomas, 192
Lytton, Lord Edward, 254

Macaulay, Thomas, 45
*Mahābhāgavata Purāṇa*, 12, 164
*Mahābhārata*, 12, 13, 277n1, 279n17
Mahālāya, 4, 87, 242
*Mahānirvāṇa Tantra*, 204, 205
Mahiṣa iconography, 1; and contemporary innovations, 116–117, 136; early images, 106, 107; and Jagaddhātrī, 290n48; and 1920s innovations, 111, 112–113; and Pūjās as sociopolitical barometer, 144, 145, *145*, 146; and Theme Pūjās, 135; and Umā-daughter tradition, 91, 281n36
Mahiṣamardinī, 1, 24, 91, 282–283nn45,46
Majumdār, Rameścandra, 71
Mallik, Baiṣṇabdās, 41
Mallik, Nīlmaṇi, 41
Mallik, Nimāicānd, 41
Mallik, Rūplāl, 41
Mallik, Sābarṇabānik, 265n89

Mallik, Śiśir, 266n99
Manakar, 279n16
Manasā, 244, 326n11
*Manasāmaṅgalakāvya* (Manakar), 279n16
Maṅgalakāvyas, 13, 78, 92, 151, 167–168
Mani, Lata, 172–173
*Mantramahodadhiḥ*, 165
Mārāṭhas, 19, 261n40
*Mārkaṇḍeya Purāṇa*. *See* "Devī-Māhātmya"
marriage customs: companionate marriage, 121, 291n63; and Umā-daughter tradition, 84–86, 99, 279n19, 280nn21,25. *See also* women's roles
Marshman, John, 45
Marwaris, 68, 276n121
masculinity, 57–58, 273n76
*Māsik Basumatī*, 70
Mason, Peter, 158
Matalibagan Alley Club, 306n53
*māthā khelā*, 247
Mauss, Marcel, 219
McCutchion, David, 290n49
McLane, John R., 17–18, 62
media: Bengali press overview, 251–254; and diaspora Pūjās, 235–236; and Durgā Pūjā as time for relaxation, 55, *69*, 276n123; and Kālī iconography, 176, 176–177, 305n44; and Kālī Pūjā, 184–185, 308n7; and Lakṣmī worship, 243; and Mahālāya, 4; and nationalism, 253–254, 276n122; and nostalgia, 36; and *sarbajanīn* Pūjās, 132–133; and wealth displays, 26; and World War I, 64
*melās*, 53–54, 272n58
Metcalf, Thomas, 46
Metcalfe, Sir Charles, 253
Mhatre, Ganpatrao, 292n75
Midyā, Bikāśkānti, 31
*Mirāt-ul-Ākhbar*, 253
Mīr Jaʿfar, 22, 262n42
Mīr Qāsim, 16, 260n32
missionaries, 45–48, 51, 73, 252, 270n15
Mitchell, James, 259n23
Mitra, Bāsantī, 32
Mitra, Chāmeli, 217, 266nn99,101
Mitra, Gobindarām, 14, 23, 41, 107, 264n77
Mitra, Nabagopāl, 272n58
Mitra, Surajit, 229
Mitter, Partha, 122, 124
Montagu-Chelmsford Reforms (1919), 64
Moore, Arthur, 253
Morley-Minto Reforms (1909), 63
mother images: and blood sacrifice, 215, 316n70; and Kālī iconography, 173, 176, 182, 193, 306n48; and nationalism, 53, 54–55, 56, 58, 59, 60–61. *See also* Umā-daughter tradition
Mughal dynasty, 17, 92. *See also nawābs*
Muhammad Ali Park Pūjā, 311n9
Mukherjee, Asit, 315n57, 316n70
Mukherjee, Dakṣiṇrañjan, 48
Mukherjee, S. N., 55
Mukhopādhyāy, Pūrbā, 219
Mukhopādhyāy, Rāmcandra, 280n21
Mukhopādhyāy, Subrata, 214
Mukhopādhyāy, Tapan, 217
*Muṇḍamālā Tantra*, 204
Murshid Qūlī Khān, 16, 17, 20
music, 26, 264n69
Muslim League, 61
Muslims, 10; and blood sacrifice, 212, 315n57; and diaspora Pūjās, 237–238; and Durgā iconography, 128–129; public-sphere activity, 68. *See also* communal tensions; Mughal dynasty
Mymensingh Suhrid Samiti, 59

*nabapatrikā* (*kalā bau*), 27–28, 33, *34*, 104–105, *104*, 198–199, 286n5, 311n4
*Nabaśakti*, 254
Nabokov, Isabelle, 220–221
Nadia Rāj, 136, 288n19
*nagarkīrtan*, 67–68
Nair, P. T., 268n119

*narabali* (human sacrifice), 171, 206–208, 313–314nn32,36,37
Nārada, 279n16
Narasiṁha Temple (Murishidabad), 282n46
nationalism: and blood sacrifice, 210–211, 314n47, 315n54; and Durgā iconography, 125–129, 293nn87,89; and Durgā Pūjā, 65–66, 275n109; and Kālī, 59, 70; and Kālī iconography, 172–173, 181–182, 306n58; and Kālī Pūjā, 186, 191; and media, 253–254, 276n122; post-Independence, 70–72; and Pūjās as sociopolitical barometer, 144, 154–155, 297n56; and Śāktism, 53, 68, 70, 71, 276n122; and Umā-daughter tradition, 89–90
naturalism, 109–114, *111*, *112*, 289n29; and contemporary innovations, 115–116; critiques of, 113–114, 118–119, 125; and East Bengali artisans, 289n38; and Kālī iconography, 173–176; and lithography, 124–125; and models, 112–113, 289nn31,32; popularity of, 113, 289n34; and scriptural tradition, 111, 289n30; and Western influences, 109–110
nautch girls, 26, 85, 263–262n68, 280n23
Navarātrī, 24, 229, 237, 321n21. *See also* Durgā Pūjā
*nawābs*: changing leadership styles of, 261–262n42; defined, 259n24; and East India Company, 15, 259n25; and Jagaddhātrī Pūjā origins, 23; zamindar constraint under, 15–16, 19, 259–260nn26,27,32; zamindar imitation of, 17, 20
Naxalites, 152, 191, 277n31
Nehru, Jawaharlal, 152
New Dispensation, 54, 272n61
New Jersey Durga Puja Association, 320n9
newspapers. *See* media
New York Puja Association, 233, 320n8, 321n13, 322nn29,30, 323n38
Nicholas, Ralph, 241, 247
*nīlkaṇṭha pākhī* (bird release ritual), 28–29, 33, 35, 87
Nimtala Burning Ghat, 171
Non-Cooperation movement, 64–65, 210–211
nostalgia, 9; and *banedi bāḍīr* Pūjās, 35–38, 268n126; critiques of, 286n85; and diaspora Pūjās, 102, 225, 227, 234–236, 320n8, 323n40, 324nn49,50; and Durgā iconography, 119–120, 225, 227, 291n61, 320n8; and Kālī Pūjā, 192–193; and Pūjās as sociopolitical barometer, 158–159, 301n110; and rivalry, 141–142; types of, 285n77; and Umā-daughter tradition, 100–102
novels, 121–122, 291nn65,66
novelty, 114–115, 149–150, 151, 158, 306n53
Novetzke, Christian, 37
Nugent, Maria, 263n68

Obeyesekere, Gananath, 193
old elite family Pūjās. *See banedi bāḍīr* (traditional family) Pūjās
Oppert, Gustav, 316n79
*Oriental Star*, 252
Orme, Robert, 15
Orsini, Francesca, 128

*padas*, 168
Padel, Felix, 207–208
Pāl, Amar, 100
Pal, Babu, 325–326n7
Pal, Bipin Chandra, 30–31, 58, 60–61, 63, 214, 254, 272n61
Pāl, Chinā, 198
Pāl, Gopeśvar, 110–114, *111*, 122, 288–289nn26,30,31,34,38
Pāl, Mohanbāśi Rudra, 119
Pāl, N. C., 113–114, 173–176, 178, 181, 193
Pāl, Pārtha, 177, 180, 306n51
Pāl, Pradīp, 119, 177, 180

Pāl, Pradyut, 236
Pal, Pratapaditya, 164, 166–167, 282n44, 309n23, 320n5, 321n20
Pāl, Rameścandra, 113, 289n38
Pāl, Sanātan Rudra, 119
Pāl, Siddheśvar, 110, 288n26, 289n30
Pāl, Śrīkṛṣṇa, 287n17
pandals, 3–4; contemporary styles, 132–136, *134*, 294nn12,18, 295nn21,23–25; and environmental concerns, 199, 311n9; Kālī Pūjā, 185, 308n9; and Muslims, 129; and nostalgia, 37, 141; origins of, 66. *See also* Pūjās as social/political barometer; *sarbajanīn* (public) Pūjās
Pandey, Gyanendra, 75
Paṇḍit Bidāy, 33
partition of Bengal, 58–63, *60*, 74, 75, 125, 126, 254, 274nn78,81,85,87,89, 277n139
Pārvatī, 77, 88, 277n1. *See also* Umā-daughter tradition
Paścimbanga Vaidic Academy, 295n32
Patel, Narhari, 321n22
*paṭs*, 92, 93, 105, 123, 124, 151, 172
*paṭuās*, 152
Pennington, Brian, 46
People for Animals, 201, 204, 212, 214, 216, 312n18
Permanent Settlement Act (1793), 16, 19, 49, 53, 261n38
Phalaharaṇī Kālī Pūjā, 307n2
Phiringi Kālī Temple (Kolkata), 170
Pinney, Christopher, 126, 152
Plassey, Battle of (1757), 14, 22
political parties: and Pūjās as sociopolitical barometer, 159, 300–301n109; and rivalry, 138–140, *139*, 296nn59–60. *See also specific parties*
Prāmāṇik, Gurucaraṇ, 24
*Prāṇatoṣiṇī* (Rāmtoṣaṇ Tarkabāgīś), 12, 171
Pratāpāditya, Rājā, 58, 274n78
Prayasam, 295n33
press. *See* media
prestige: and blood sacrifice, 209–210, 218; and diaspora Pūjās, 227, 321nn14–16; and Durgā Pūjā as self-authenticating measure, 19, 261n40; and Durgā Pūjā origins, 11, 20–21; and East India Company rule, 16–17; and pandals, 3–4; and prizes, 137–138; and symbolic capital, 24–25. *See also banedi bāḍīr* (traditional family) Pūjās; rivalry; wealth displays
Prevention of Cruelty to Animals Act (1960), 216
priests, 3, 295n32; and *banedi bāḍīr* Pūjās, 33; and blood sacrifice, 204, 312n23; and diaspora Pūjās, 227, 320–321n12; and Durgā iconography, 113–114; and environmental concerns, 201; and prizes, 138. *See also* ritual practice
Prinsep, William, 42
printing press, 121, 123, 292n69
prizes, 137–138, 295nn32–4
prostitute controversy, 197–199, 311n6
public Pūjās. *See sarbajanīn* (public) Pūjās
Pūjās as sociopolitical barometer, 142–146, 150–159; and carnival, 157–158; and cultural productions, 115–116, 142–143, *143*, 297n51; diaspora Pūjās, 229; and disasters/social problems, 133, 143, 297nn52,53; early examples, 132; and festival origins, 150–151; Indian parallels, 153–157, *157*; and nationalism, 144, 154–155, 297n56; 1950s, 132, 294n5; 1980s innovations, 133; and nostalgia, 158–159, 301n110; and political parties, 159, 300–301n109; and public art traditions, 151–152; real building copies, 133, 142, 156, 300n102; and recent liberalization policies, 152–153; and rivalry, *139*, 151; and September 11, 2001 terrorist attacks, *144*, 145, *145*, 152; U.S. parallel example, 130–131; and women's oppression, 143, 297n52

Purāṇas: on blood sacrifice, 204, 205, 306n58; Durgā in, 12, 23, 248, 257n7; Jagaddhātrī in, 22, 262n47; Kālī in, 163, 164, 180; and royalty, 24; and tribal culture, 257n13; and Umā-daughter tradition, 77, 91, 278n12, 279n14; and Vaiṣṇava traditions, 245. *See also* "Devī-Māhātmya"

Rādhā, and Kālī, 168
Rādhāgovinda Temple (Midnapur), 282–283n46
Raghunandana, 12, 13, 22, 91, 257n7
Raghunāth Temple (Birbhum), 282n46
*rājās*, 255n2. *See also* zamindars
*rākhi-bandhan*, 63
Rākhīpūrṇimā, 242
*Rāmacarita* (Sandhyākaranandin), 12
Rāmakṛṣṇa, 54, 171, 218, 326n22
Rāmakṛṣṇa Mission, 215, 231, 233, 237, 239, 315n65
Ramaswamy, Sumathi, 127, 211
*Rāmāyaṇa*, 12, 33, 277n1
Rāmlīlās, 153–154, 325n4
Rāmnā Kālī Mandir (Dhaka), 231
Rao, Narasimha, 152
Rashtriya Swayamsevak Sangh (RSS), 65, 300–301n109
Raṭanti Kālī Pūjā, 307n2
Rath Din, 27, 33
Rāy, Bhāratcandra, 22, 78, 259n22
Rāy, Bṛhaspati, 22
Rāy, Dāśarathi, 98
Rāy, Dīptimay, 171
Rāy, Īśvarcandra, 184, 259n22
Rāy, Kṛṣṇacandra (zamindar of Nadia): and Durgā iconography, 105; and Durgā Pūjā origins, 14, 15, 18, 259n22; and Jagaddhātrī Pūjā origins, 22–23; and Kālī iconography, 169, 303n23; and Kālī Pūjā, 22, 184, 192
Rāy, Mohit, 87
Rāy, Nandakumār, 29
Rāy, Naranārāyaṇ, 208
Ray, Rajat Kanta, 121, 122, 291n66
Rāy, Rāmakṛṣṇa, 15–16, 184
Rāy, Rāmcandra, 41
Ray, Sarasibala, 86
Ray, Subhas, 185
Rāy, Sukhamay, 41
Rāy Caudhuri, Maṇimohan, 265n97, 266n99
Rāy Caudhuri, Sābarṇa (family), 268n119; and blood sacrifice, 210, 218, 314n47; and British-Indian relations, 41; and Durgā iconography, 288n22; and Durgā Pūjā origins, 14; poverty of, 3, 36; and ritual practice, 267n104
Rāy Caudhuri, Subhās, 210
realism. *See* naturalism
refugees, 71–72, 102
Republic Day Parades, 156–157
revelry, 8, 9; and Bengali religious calendar, 248–249; and British-Indian relations, 26–27, 41, 44; and diaspora Pūjās, 227, 229; and Durgā Pūjā as time for relaxation, 52, 55–56, 68–70, *69*, 86, 276n123; and Kālī Pūjā, 195, 196; and rivalry, 141–142; and *sarbajanīn* Pūjās, 3, 4. *See also* entertainment
*Ṛg Veda*, 279n17
ritual practice: and agricultural traditions, 104–105, 286nn3,4; and *banedi bāḍīr* Pūjās, 33–34, 267nn104,107,108; "Devī-Māhātmya" recitation, 4, 28, 29, 33; and diaspora Pūjās, 227, 229–230, 238, 320nn6,8–14, 324–325nn57,58; Durgā Pūjā overview, 4–5; and Umā-daughter tradition, 87, *88*, *89*, 281n33; and wealth displays, 27–29, 264n81, 265n84; and women's roles, 198. *See also* blood sacrifice
rivalry, 8–9, 136–142, 146–150; and *banedi bāḍīr* Pūjās, 34, 136–137; and carnival, 158; and charity, 138; and consumerism, 147–150, 298n74; and diaspora Pūjās, 227, 228–229, 321n19; and Durgā iconography,

rivalry (*continued*)
107; and Durgā Pūjā origins, 146, 150–151; and nostalgia, 141–142; and novelty, 149–150, 151, 158; and pandals, 4; and political parties, 138–140, *139*, 296nn59–60; and Pūjās as sociopolitical barometer, *139*, 151; and *sarbajanīn* Pūjās, 137–138, 147, 295nn29,32–34; and tourism, 141, 296n46; and violence, 72, 137, 295n29. *See also* prestige; wealth displays
Rowlatt Bills (1919), 64
Roy, Jamini, 113, 125
Roy, M. N., 248
Roy, Mohit, 202. *See also* Rāy, Mohit
Roy, Ram Mohan, 48, 252, 272n61
royalty: and blood sacrifice, 209; and Durgā Pūjā origins, 12, 24, 146, 297n60; and Kālī, 191–192; and Pūjās as sociopolitical barometer, 153–154; and wealth displays, 27–28
Rubenstein, Roberta, 100, 101
Russian icons, 182

Śabarotsab, 13
Sādharan Brāhmo Samāj, 54, 272n61
Sahgal, Bittu, 201
Śaivism, 242, 247, 326n16
Śākta poetry, 168
Śākta Purānas, 12
Śāktism: and Bengali religious calendar, 242; and blood sacrifice, 209, 215, 217; and Jagaddhātrī Pūjā origins, 22–23; and Kālī, 164, 166–167, 191–192; and nationalism, 53, 68, 70, 71, 276n122; and partition of Bengal, 59, 63, 74, 274n81; and Pūjās as social/political barometer, 150; and Vaiṣṇavism, 246–247
*śālgrāmśila*, 246–247
Salomon, Carol, 167
*Samācār Candrikā*, 252, 253, 308n7
*Samācār Darpaṇ*, 17, 45, 252
Samajwadi Party, 209, 215
*Sambād Kaumudī*, 252, 253
*sampradāya*, 242
Samrite, Kishore, 209, 215
*sandhi pūjā*, 5, 28, 33, 264n81, 267n107, 297n60
*Sandhyā*, 254
Santals (Sāotāls), 257n14, 258n15
Sānyāl, Baikuṇṭanāth, 281n33
Sar, Atul, 248
Sarasvatī, 1; and diaspora Pūjās, 125; and early Durgā iconography, 107; and nationalism, 127; and 1920s iconographic innovations, 114, 118; and public art traditions, 151; and street art, 123; and Umā-daughter tradition, 88, 91, 93; worship of, 225, 243
Sarasvatī Pūjā, 225, 243
Sārbabhauma, Bāsudeb, 287n8
*sarbajanīn* (public) Pūjās, 3–4, 30; vs. *banedi bāḍīr* Pūjās, 32, 33, 34; and Durgā iconography, 110, 289n38; environmental concerns, 199–202, 311n9, 312n16; illuminations, 132, 133, 294n4; Kālī Pūjā, 183, 185, *193*, 307n3; and media, 132–133; and nostalgia, 37; origins of, 19, 65–66, 68, 110, 131–132; regulation of, 138, 185, 199–200, 295–296n36; and rivalry, 137–138, 147, 295nn29,32–34. *See also* pandals; Pūjās as social/political barometer
Sarkar, Jadunath, 94, 147, 248–249
Sarkar, Keshab Chandra, 244
Sarkar, Sumit, 58
Ṣaṣṭī, 244, 326n11
"Śāsti" (Rabindranath Tagore), 317n85
Śāstrī, Haraprasād, 286n2
Śāstrī, Rameś, 259n23
Sastri, Sivanath, 54, 272n61
Satī, 278n12
*satyāgraha*, 64–65, 201
Savarkar, V. D., 65
Sax, William, 90
Schechner, Richard, 153
Scrafton, Luke, 260n27

Sen, Aditi, 161
Sen, Alok, 119
Sen, Aloke, 311n9
Sen, Dineshchandra, 13, 184
Sen, Haimabatī, 31
Sen, Keshab Chandra, 54, 254, 272n62
Sen, Paritosh, 119
Sen, Prabhas, 303n23
Sen, Rām Komal, 50
Sen, Rāmprasād, 78, 99, 167, 168, 216, 222, 285n71
Sengupta, Aśok, 322n28
September 11, 2001 terrorist attacks, *144*, 145, *145*, 152, 229
sexuality: and Kālī iconography, 165, 179, 180, 182, *190*, 306n59, 310n32; and Kālī Pūjā, 189–191, 309–310nn28,33–34; and tribal culture, 14
Shastri, Ashokanath, 175, 178
Sher-Gil, Amrita, 125
Shivaji Utsav, 273n76
Shiv Sena, 155, 156
Shourie, Arun, 296n40
Shovabazar Rāj, *21*; and blood sacrifice, 210, 216; and British-Indian relations, 29, 41, 44, 47, 52, 55, 56, 277n139; and Dharma Sabhā, 265n89; and Durgā iconography, 107, 288n19; and Durgā Pūjā origins, 14; and media, 252; and nostalgia, 36; and ritual practice, 218, 267n104; and Umā-daughter tradition, 284n61; and wealth displays, 28, 264n69
Shujāʿ-ud-dīn Khān, 20
Shyampukur Boy's Barowari, 307n3
Siddheśvarīkālī Mandir (Dhaka), 231
Siddheśvarīkālī Temple (Kolkata), *170*, 171, 187
Simla Byayam Samiti, 132
*sindūr khelā,* 87, *89*
Singer, Milton, 193, 236
Singh, Manmohan, 209
Singhi family, 288n22
Sinha, Ajay, 152
Śītalā, 244–245, *245*, 326n11
Śītalā Temple (Midnapur), 283n46
Śiva, 77, 78, 84, 278n12; and Kālī, 165, 189–190, *190*, 306n59, 309–310n28. *See also* Umā-daughter tradition
Śivarātrī, 247
Śiva Temple (Jotmudi), 283n48
Śiva Temple (Surul), 283n48
*Śivayanas,* 78
Śmaśānakālī (Cremation-Ground Kālī), 186, 309n17
*Smṛtiratnahāra* (Bṛhaspati Rāy), 22
*śobhāyātrās,* 29
socioeconomic class: lower-class exclusion from Pūjās, 30–32, 138, 199, 265n97, 296n38; and Pūjā origins, 11. *See also* caste; wealth displays
Solvyns, Balthazar, 30, 172
Southard, Barbara, 59
Spitzer, Leo, 286n85
Sri Ramakrishna Universal Temple (Chicago), 322n35
Srivastava, Ravi, 153
Stallybrass, Peter, 158
*Statesman and Friend of India,* 52, 74, 90, 128, 252, 253, 254, 273n66
status. *See* prestige
Stephens, Ian, 253
street art, 123–124, 292n70
Strobinski, Jean, 101
Subrahmanyam, Sanjay, 25
Sugirtharajah, Sharada, 46
Śūlapāṇi, 12, 13, 22, 257n7
Sureś, Jayrāmān, 217
*Svatantra Tantra,* 165
Swamy Narayan Mandir (Ohio), 321n22
Swaraj Party, 65
*Śyāmāsaparyāvidhi* (Kāśīnāth), 184, 307–308n6
symbolic capital, 24–25

Tagore, Abanindranath, 126, 174
Tagore, Bābu Benoylāl, 41

Tagore, Balendranath, 125
Tagore, Debendranath, 48, 54, 272n61
Tagore, Dwaraknath, 48, 264n71
Tagore, Rabindranath, 63, 74, 214, 222, 248, 273n76, 274n78, 317n85
Tagore, Satyendranath, 54
Tagore family, 29, 272n58
Tantra: and agricultural traditions, 105, 287n8; and blood sacrifice, 208; and Durgā iconography, 111; and Durgā Pūjā, 256n6; and Kālī iconography, 163–165, 166–168, 171, 178–180, 181, 187, 304n30; and Kālī Pūjā, 187–189, *188*, 194–195, 309nn22,23; and naturalism, 175; text proliferation, 166–167; and Umā-daughter tradition, 91
*Tantrasāra* (Kṛṣṇānanda Āgambāgīś), 91, 163, 166–167, 204, 282n44, 290n47
Tarkabāgīś, Rāmtoṣaṇ, 12, 164, 171
Tata Motors, 139, *139*
Tathagatananda, Swami, 322–323n35
*Tattvabodhinī Patrikā,* 48, 64, 252
Tejascānd (Burdwan zamindar), 261n38
*Telegraph,* 138, 243
temples: Durgā, 93, 283n56, 288n19, 290n49; Jagaddhātrī, 118, 290n49. *See also* Kālī temple worship
temple slabs, and Umā-daughter tradition, 92–93
Ṭhākur, Annadā, 233
Ṭhākur, Darpanārāyaṇ, 41
Ṭhākur, Haru, 278n5
*ṭhākurdālāns,* 2–3, *21*; and *banedi bāḍīr* Pūjās, 32, 36; and nostalgia, 268n126; and wealth displays, 21, 26
Ṭhanṭanīya Kālī Temple (Kolkata), 170–171, 187
Thanthania Kālī Pūjā, 174–176, 177
Theme Pūjās, 134–135, 140, 183, 294n18, 307n3
Thurston, Edgar, 314n37
Tilak, B. G., 58, 154, 273n76
Tilakcānd (Burdwan zamindar), 18
Toolsidass, Purnima, 312n18
tourism, 8, 36, 37, 101–102, 137, 141, 210, 296n46
tradition. *See banedi bāḍīr* (traditional family) Pūjās; nostalgia
tribal culture: and Durgā Pūjā origins, 13–14, 257–258nn13–15,17; and Umā-daughter tradition, 282n41
Trinamul Congress, 139–140, 201–202, 296n39
Trinidad, 158
Tripura Rāj, 88–89
Tuṣu, 282n41

Ulṭo Rath Din, 27, 33
Uluberiya Temple (Howrah), 171
Umā-daughter tradition, 1, 76–102; and *banedi bāḍīr* Pūjās, 86–87, *108*, 109, 280–281nn28,29,31; and children's activities, 90; and Durgā iconography, 88–89, 91–93, *94*, 281nn35,36,38, 282–283n45–48, 284n58; and folk culture, 91–92, 283n50; and Kālī, 95–98, 284n63; in Maṅgalakāvyas, 78; and marriage customs, 84–86, 99, 279n19, 280nn21,25; and nationalism, 89–90; and nostalgia, 100–102; origins of, 90–95, 282–283nn44–46; and Purānas, 77, 91, 278n12, 279n14; recent disappearance of, 99–100; and ritual practice, 87, *88*, *89*, 281n33; and tenderness, 95, 284nn61,62; and tribal culture, 282n41; and Vaiṣṇava, 88, 98–99, 109; and zamindars, 93–94, *94*, 284nn58,59. *See also* Umā-*saṅgīt*
Umā-*saṅgīt,* 77–86; *āgamanī* and *bijayā* meanings, 277n2; and Bengali marriage customs, 84–86, 279n19, 280nn21,25; Bengali regionalization in, 13, 78, 79, 83, 278nn6; composers of, 78, 278n5; and Kālī, 95–98; Kāma in, 84, 279n17; and Maṅgalakāvyas, 78; plot in, 79–83, 278nn7,9; and Purānas, 77, 278n12, 279nn14,16;

recent disappearance of, 99–100; siblings in, 279n15; and Umā-daughter tradition origins, 92, 94
United Progressive Alliance (UPA), 209
Universities Act (1904), 57
Untouchability Abolition Bill (1933), 66
Upādhyāya, Brahmobandhab, 254
UPA (United Progressive Alliance), 209
Urban, Hugh B., 25, 221
Urquhart, Margaret, 84–85

Vaidic Pandit o Purohit Mahamilan Kendra, 201, 295n32
Vaiṣṇavism, 28, 50; and Bengali religious calendar, 242, 245–247, *246*; and blood sacrifice, 215, 216–217, 246; and diaspora Pūjās, 233, 323n39; and Kālī, 168, 181; and Tantric texts, 166–167; and Umā-daughter tradition, 88, 98–99, 109
Varma, Ravi, 113, 124–125, 173, 293n87, 306n52
*Vāsantaviveka* (Śūlapāṇi), 12
Vedāntins, 48
Vedas, 33, 316n66, 318n88
Venkatachari, K. K. A., 323n40
Vertovec, Steven, 323n40, 324n55
Victoria (Queen of England), 29
Vidyāpati, 12, 91, 257n7, 282n44
Vināyaka Caturthī (Gaṇeśa Pūjā), 154–156
virtual pūjā Web sites, 236, 324n49
Vishwa Hindu Parishad, 239
*Viṣṇuyamalā,* 13
Viśvakarmā Pūjā, 244
Vivekananda, Swami, 181, 210

Waghorne, Joanne, 149, 152, 155, 193–194
Walsh, Judith, 121, 291n63
Ward, William, 184, 259n23, 269n6
wealth. *See* socioeconomic class; wealth displays
wealth displays, 25–29; and architecture, 20–21, 262n44; "Bābus," 14, 259n21; and *banedi bāḍīr* Pūjās, 32–33; and *bāroiyāri* Pūjās, 30, 31, 265n96; and blood sacrifice, 28; and charity, 23, 27; and Durgā as symbol of pretension, 31–32; and Durgā Pūjā origins, 11, 20–21, 23–24; and entertainment, 26, 263–264nn68,69,71; and exclusion of lower classes, 30–32, 265n97; and food, 26–27, 32–33; and foreign trading contacts, 21, 262n45; and *nawāb* rule, 15–16, 19, 259–260n26; and ritual practice, 27–29, 264n81, 265n84; and *ṭhākurdālāns,* 21, 26. *See also* prestige; rivalry
Web sites, 236, 324n49
Wellesley, Marquess Richard, 40
West Bengal State Congress Party, 139
Westmacott, E. V., 261–262n42
Westside Vedanta Center (New York City), 322–323n35
White, Allon, 158
Whitehead, Henry, 222, 313–314n37
Williams, Raymond Brady, 238–239, 324–325n58
Williams, Rosalind, 148
women's oppression: blood sacrifice as metaphor for, 219, 317–318n85; and Pūjās as sociopolitical barometer, 143, 297n52
women's roles, 121–122, 197–199, 291n63. *See also* marriage customs; women's oppression
World Cup Soccer, 153
World War I, 63–64

Younger, Paul, 157, 238
*Yugāntar,* 58, 61, 254

zamindars, 3; decline of, 35; defined, 255n2; East India Company rule as constraint on, 17–20, 261nn37–39; East India Company rule as

zamindars (*continued*)
opportunity for, 15–17, 20; individual figures and Durgā Pūjā origins, 14, 259n22; and Kālī temple worship, 169; and Mughal dynasty, 17; *nawāb* rule as constraint on, 15–16, 19, 259–60nn26,27,32; and Permanent Settlement Act, 53, 149; and rivalry, 150–151; and royalty, 24; and symbolic capital, 24–25; and Umā-daughter tradition, 93–94, *94*, 284nn58,59. *See also banedi bāḍīr* (traditional family) Pūjās; wealth displays

GPSR Authorized Representative: Easy Access System Europe, Mustamäe tee 50, 10621 Tallinn, Estonia, gpsr.requests@easproject.com

www.ingramcontent.com/pod-product-compliance
Lightning Source LLC
Chambersburg PA
CBHW032148010526
44111CB00035B/1245
*9780231129190*